Travaux
du Grand Siècle

N° XVIII

www.droz.org

ALISON SAUNDERS

THE SEVENTEENTH-CENTURY FRENCH EMBLEM

A STUDY IN DIVERSITY

LIBRAIRIE DROZ S.A.
11, rue Massot
GENÈVE
2000

T

ISBN: 2-600-00452-1
ISSN: 1420-7699

.1002398427

IN MEMORY OF

DUDLEY WILSON

WHO FIRST FIRED MY ENTHUSIASM FOR
EARLY FRENCH ILLUSTRATED BOOKS

TABLE OF CONTENTS

Preface XI

Chapter I   Introduction and overview: Tradition and innovation from
                 the sixteenth into the seventeenth century 1

Chapter II   Emblems and emblematic fables: The continuation of the
                 generalist tradition 21

Chapter III   Devices and their continuation of the generalist tradition. 65

Chapter IV   The use of emblems and devices for educational purposes 109

Chapter V   The Dutch contribution to French and international
                 emblem culture 161

Chapter VI   The religious uses of emblems in France 201

Chapter VII   Royal glorification and celebrations through the medium
                 of emblems and devices.. 247

Chapter VIII   Theory and practice of emblems and devices 305

Conclusion   357

Bibliography   361

List of illustrations 415

General index   417

Index of subjects and themes of emblems and devices 427

Index of titles and mottoes of emblems and devices 431

PREFACE

The emblem phenomenon becomes ever more important as a socio-cultural force as the sixteenth century moves into the seventeenth, making its influence felt in a wide range of areas extending well beyond the purely literary. Already in its early days in the sixteenth century the practical utility of emblems as iconographic models for craftsmen was stressed, but as the century progresses, and gives way to the seventeenth century, so the range of practical applications extends. Emblems and devices are used for educational purposes in Jesuit schools; for devotional purposes; for royal propaganda (playing a major role, for example, in the propaganda campaign of Louis XIV); for ephemeral architecture designed for festival and other celebrations; for general moral edification of the young and not so young; to name only some of their fields of influence.

At the same time national frontiers become blurred, as cross-European influences become more dominant. Georgette de Montenay's *Emblemes, ou devises chrestiennes* is an early example of the truly international emblem book. Published originally in French in the late sixteenth century, it subsequently appeared in a bilingual French/Latin version and then in a polyglot version, with the text available in English, German, Italian, Spanish and Dutch as well as Latin and French. Already from the 1550s the Lyon publishing partnership of Guillaume Roville and Macé Bonhomme had made their editions of emblem books available to a multilingual readership by publishing them in a range of different languages, but with the development of the Plantin Press in Antwerp the internationalisation of the emblem book via the publication of polyglot editions or editions in different languages is given further impulse. Similarly with the development of the copper engraving, cross references, imitations and borrowings become ever more common.

We see, therefore two quite distinct trends developing: on the one hand the emblem in France plays an ever more important part in the manifestation of national identity, in the context of court entertainment, royal propaganda and ephemeral festival architecture, while on the other hand in other contexts such as education, moral edification and devotional works it tends, in many cases, to lose its national identity, and become instead a contributory part of a much broader cross fertilisation process taking place across Europe.

In view of the increasingly cosmopolitan aspect of so much emblem literature in the seventeenth century, and of the increasing blurring of frontiers between emblem, device and other associated illustrated forms, it would not be sensible to elaborate tight and exclusive definitions and limitations for this study, other than those dictated by the period under consideration. Even here it would be foolish to attempt to discuss the seventeenth-century emblem as if it suddenly sprang into being in 1600, without taking some cognisance of the sixteenth-century emblem from which it naturally evolved. At the other end of the century, while recognising that interest in emblems does not simply stop in 1700, I have imposed a general terminus at that date, though here also I have on occasion intentionally strayed into the early eighteenth century when there has seemed good reason to do so. To restrict this study to works entitled emblems, to the exclusion of all other associated forms which do not happen to be given that title would certainly have resulted in a much smaller Bibliography, but it would have resulted also in a very distorted picture which would not take account of the important wider context in which emblems were created in the seventeenth century. Similarly on the linguistic front, to exclude works that are of interest simply because they are not wholly in French, or because they were not published in France would also result in a very partial and distorted picture. Conversely to include systematically everything which includes some French text would result in a cumbersome and overloaded study. Consequently I have opted here for freedom and flexibility in the selection of works discussed.

The research on which this book is based could not have been accomplished without access to the resources of many great libraries both in Europe and North America, and without the cooperation and help of many of the staff in their Special Collections departments, to all of whom my warmest thanks are extended. Particular gratitude is owed to Jeanne Veyrin-Forrer, former *Conservateur en chef* of the *Réserve des Imprimés* in the then Bibliothèque Nationale, who has for many years been a constant source of support and encouragement as well as of unequalled expertise. I am very grateful also to Geneviève Guilleminot and Ursula Baurmeister of the *Réserve des Imprimés*. Within the United Kingdom, I am particularly grateful to David Weston, Keeper of Special Collections in Glasgow University Library in which is housed the immensely rich Stirling Maxwell Collection of emblem books. In such a cross-disciplinary and multi-national discipline as emblematics it is essential to be able to call upon the support and wisdom of specialists in other aspects of the genre, and in this respect I have been particularly fortunate in having for many years worked collaboratively, under the aegis of ERASMUS, with a number of colleagues from universities in Belgium, France, Germany and Holland as well as the United Kingdom, and to all these - many of whose works are cited in the Bibliography - I should like to extend my thanks for the stimulating exchange of ideas and wisdom which resulted from this. Among the many university colleagues in Britain from whom I have received help, support and encouragement, I should like to thank above all Judi Loach in Cardiff and Jennifer Carter in Aberdeen, and of course my two colleagues in Glasgow, Alison Adams and Stephen Rawles, with whom I have been working for so many years on the *Bibliography of French Emblem Books*. Much of the research which I did for the *Bibliography* and for this book was done at the same time, and each fed into the other, but this book has also profited enormously from the bibliographical research of my two co-authors, and for this I am extremely grateful.

Finally I should like also to express my gratitude to the British Academy, the Arts and Humanities Research Board, the Carnegie Trust for the Universities of Scotland, and the University of Aberdeen for financial support in carrying out the research for this study.

Aberdeen, 2000   AMS

CHAPTER I

INTRODUCTION AND OVERVIEW:
TRADITION AND INNOVATION FROM
THE SIXTEENTH INTO THE SEVENTEENTH CENTURY

The seventeenth-century French emblem did not spring into life suddenly. It is rather the product of a lengthy evolution of the genre as it developed in the course of the sixteenth century, and thus must be seen in the context of that development, which I have treated in my earlier book on the sixteenth-century French emblem book, as have also others.[1] Although it develops from the sixteenth-century emblem, and in many cases retains characteristics of its earlier ancestor, it would be a mistake to see the seventeenth-century emblem as no more than a servile continuation of that form. Instead it must be seen as an evolving form which takes on its own distinct shape (or shapes, since diversity is one of its characteristic attributes), reflecting the very different social, religious and political context in which it is produced in the course of the seventeenth century, and indeed changing as the century progresses, in keeping with developing social, religious and political trends. The genre did not, of course, come to a sudden end at the end of the seventeenth century. Emblem books continued to appear into the eighteenth century, and indeed beyond, serving a variety of purposes and readerships.[2] It can be argued, however, that the form finds its widest usefulness

---

[1]   Alison Saunders, *The Sixteenth-Century French Emblem Book: a Decorative and Useful Genre*, Geneva, 1988 (hereafter cited as 'Saunders, *Sixteenth-Century French Emblem Book*'. See also Daniel Russell, *The Emblem and Device in France*, Lexington, Kentucky, 1985, and *Emblematic Structures in Renaissance French Culture*, Toronto, 1995; Jean-Marc Chatelain, *Livres d'emblèmes et de devises, une anthologie (1531-1735)*, Paris, 1993 (hereafter cited as 'Chatelain'); Paulette Choné, *Emblèmes et pensée symbolique en Lorraine (1525-1633)*, Paris, 1991; Anne-Elisabeth Spica, *Symbolique humaniste et emblématique. L'évolution et les genres (1580-1700)*, Paris, 1996.

[2]   In particular in England the emblem enjoyed considerable popularity under the Victorians. For discussion of this see K.-J. Höltgen, 'The Victorian emblematic revival' in *Aspects of the Emblem. Studies in the English Emblem Tradition and the European Context*, Kassel, 1986,

and reaches its largest audience in the seventeenth century.

Religious and civil conflict had increasingly dominated France in the latter decades of the sixteenth century, and much of the earlier part of the seventeenth century was preoccupied with the rebuilding of France both internally as a harmonious and united nation, and externally as a European force to be reckoned with. A key element in that process was the glorification of the ruling monarch and the establishment in the minds both of the people of France and of the outside world of the absolute authority and dominance of that ruling monarch. In this process emblems and devices had a vital role to play. On the religious front also, as the Counter-Reformation gathered strength, devotional literature played an increasingly significant role, with the Jesuits in particular using the emblem book form as a ready made model for meditational works in accordance with the methodology elaborated in St Ignatius Loyola's *Spiritual Exercises*. At the same time the increasingly frequent crossing of European frontiers led to a more pan-European mode of publishing. Already in the mid-sixteenth century, Lyon had supplied books for an international market, but this was a relatively small-scale operation compared with the practice established by Plantin in the Netherlands in the later sixteenth century, and in the course of the seventeenth century innumerable books of international appeal, published in a range of languages, poured from the presses in the Netherlands. Not only did this lead to an internationalisation of book production, but it also led to an internationalisation of actual books, with works originating in one country, but being translated into other languages, or being produced in polyglot versions. It also led to a great internationalisation of styles, particularly in the field of erotic and devotional emblem books. With the development of more sophisticated printing methods - particularly the introduction of copperplate engraving - common illustrations could be easily used by one publisher after another, popping up in different parts of Europe in different guises. We see this already in the late sixteenth and early seventeenth centuries with Georgette de Montenay.[3] We see it more markedly with the engravings of the Wierix

---

pp.141-96.

[3]   Until very recently it has always been assumed that her emblem book was first published in Lyon in 1571 (*Emblemes, ou devises chrestiennes, composées par Damoiselle Georgette de Montenay*, Lyon, J. Marcorelle, 1571, 4°). However, an important discovery by Alison Adams of a copy of a hitherto unknown edition published four years earlier by Marcorelle in 1567, in which it is stated that the text was completed some years even before that casts new light on the dating of this work. (For a full description of this newly discovered edition see Alison Adams, 'Les *Emblemes ou devises chrestiennes de Georgette de Montenay*: édition de 1567' in *Bibliothèque d'Humanisme et Renaissance*, 62, 3, 2000, forthcoming.) Seventeen years after this first edition in French it was republished in Zurich in a bilingual French-Latin version (*Georgiae Montaneae nobilis gallae emblematum christianorum centuria. Cum eorundem latina interpretatione. Cent emblemes chrestiens de Damoiselle Georgette de Montenay*, Zurich, C. Froschover, 1584, 4°). Eighteen years later, in 1602, this bilingual version was again published, in Heidelburg by J. Lancelot and A. Cambieri; seventeen years after that it was again published in Frankfurt, in a new polyglot version in seven different languages, with a different title page for each language (*Livre d'armoiries en signe de fraternité, contenant cent comparaisons de vertus et emblemes chrestiens*, Frankfurt, J.C. Unckels, 1619, 4°). In 1620 in La Rochelle a reissue of the original French version of 1571 was published by Jean Dinet. In

brothers which were disseminated across Europe and even into Latin America,[4] or with the delightful figures of Vaenius's erotic emblems and likewise his equally delightful emblems of divine love which inspired the immensely influential *Pia desideria* of Herman Hugo.[5]

France in the seventeenth century thus cannot be seen in isolation. It must be seen in its broader European context, and this is very true of its emblem literature which inherits and borrows from many cultures other than purely French, and which for this reason as well as by virtue of the more complex social, political and religious patterns developing in France in the seventeenth century, takes on itself a much more varied guise than that - already varied - which it enjoyed in the sixteenth century. Decorative it remains, useful it remains, but in more complex manners.

In geographical terms we see a distinct change in pattern in the publication of emblem books from the sixteenth into the seventeenth century. In the earlier sixteenth century this was the virtually exclusive domain of the two main publishing centres, Paris and Lyon. In the earliest period of the 1530s and 1540s Paris dominated in the publication of emblem literature, but in the later 1540s to mid 1560s, Lyon took over

---

all these editions published variously in France, Switzerland and Germany, the same copper plates were used.

[4] For details see M. Funck, *Le livre belge à gravures*, Paris and Brussels, 1925; M. Mauquoy-Hendrickz, *Les estampes des Wierix conservées au Cabinet des Estampes de la Bibliothèque Royale Albert 1er. Catalogue raisonné enrichi de notes prises dans diverses autres collections*, Brussels, 1978-83, 4 vols. For discussion of the 'heart' engravings of the *Cor Iesu amanti sacrum* see Anne Sauvy, *Le miroir du coeur. Quatre siècles d'images savantes et populaires*, Paris, 1989, p.55 *et seq.*, and E. Dubois, 'Some interpretations of the notion of *coeur* in seventeenth-century France', *Seventeenth-Century French Studies*, 9, 1987, pp.4-25. See also J.B. Knipping, *Iconography of the Counter-Reformation in the Netherlands. Heaven on Earth*, Nieuwkoop and Leiden, 1974, 2 vols.

[5] Vaenius's *Amorum emblemata* was first published in Antwerp in 1608 (*Amorum emblemata, figuris aeneis incisa Studio Othonis Vaeni Batavo-Lugdunensis*, Antwerp, 'Venalia apud auctorem', 1608, 4° obl., but we find the engravings being used as late as 1683 in Philip Ayres's London published *Emblemata amatoria* (see below, footnote 34). His *Amoris divini emblemata* was published seven years later (*Amoris divini emblemata studio et aere Othonis Vaeni concinnata*, Antwerp, M. Nutius and J. Meursius, 1615, 4°). The Jesuit Herman Hugo's *Pia desideria* was likewise originally published in Antwerp, with engravings by Boëtius à Bolswert (*Pia desideria emblematis elegiis & affectibus SS. patrum illustrata. Authore Hermanno Hugone Societatis Iesu...Vulgavit Boetius a Bolswert*, Antwerp, H. Aertssens, 1624, 8°), but subsequently French, Spanish, English, Flemish, German, Polish and Italian versions of the work were published in the course of the seventeenth century. For an overall bibliography of emblem books see M. Praz, *Studies in Seventeenth-Century Imagery*, 2nd ed., Rome, 1964 (henceforth cited as 'Praz'). See also J. Landwehr, *Emblem Books in the Low Countries 1554-1949. A Bibliography*, Utrecht, 1970, and J. Landwehr, *French, Italian, Spanish, and Portuguese Books of Devices and Emblems 1534-1827. A Bibliography*, Utrecht, 1976 (hereafter cited as 'Landwehr, *Dutch Emblem Books*' and 'Landwehr, *Romanic Emblem Books*') . See also A. Adams, S. Rawles, and A. Saunders, *A Bibliography of French Emblem Books of the Sixteenth and Seventeenth Centuries*, vol.1, Geneva, 1999 (hereafter cited as 'BFEB'.

the dominant role from Paris, where very little was published.[6] From the mid 1560s until the end of the century no more than a trickle of emblematic works emanated from either Paris or Lyon, and this situation continued into the seventeenth century. Only in the mid 1630s did Paris once again become a serious centre for the publication of emblem literature, while Lyon did

not emerge again until the 1660s. However, even as Paris and Lyon ceased to be such active publishing centres for emblem literature, so correspondingly other provincial centres entered the market from the 1550s, and even more so in the seventeenth century - notably Metz and Strasbourg in the 1580s and Douai, Lille, Rouen, Auxerre, La Rochelle, Grenoble, Avignon and Chartres in the seventeenth century. On a broader European front, as a result primarily of the efforts of Christopher Plantin, from the 1560s Antwerp establised itself as a centre for publishing books intended for the French market, but other publishers also followed Plantin's lead in Antwerp, while Brussels, Leiden and Amsterdam also joined the movement. Less well know, but important also, the publisher Lucas Jennis in Frankfurt likewise tapped into the French market in the early seventeenth century, producing polyglot versions, including, French, of Daniel Cramer's *Emblemata sacra* in 1622   and *Emblemata moralia nova* of 1630, and a wholly French version of Andreas Friedrich's *Emblemes nouveaux* in 1617.[7]

---

[6]   For discussion of the swing in the publication of emblems between Paris and Lyon, see Alison Saunders, 'Paris to Lyon and back again: trends in emblem publishing in the mid sixteenth century in France', in P. Ford and G. Jondorf, eds, *Intellectual Life in Renaissance Lyon*, Cambridge, 1993, pp.63-80.

[7]   Daniel Cramer, *Emblemata sacra, Hoc est decades quinque emblematum ex Sacra Scriptura de dulcissimo nomine & cruce Iesu Christi, figuris aeneis incisa. Primò opera ac studio, Rever. DN. Danielis Crameri SS. Theologiae Doctoris. Nunc vero in hac secundo editione non solum una decade ab ipso aucta, sed etiam rhythmis sive versibus Latinis, Germanicis, Gallicis & Italicis ab aliis ornata, & ad Philothecam Christianam seu album amicorum utilia*, Frankfurt, L. Jennis, 1622, 8°; *Emblemata moralia nova, Das ist: Achtzig sinnreiche nachdenckliche figuren auss heyliger Schrifft in Kupfferstücken fürgestellet, worinnen schöne Anweisungen zu wahrer Gottesforcht begrieffen*, Frankfurt, L. Jennis, 1630, 8°; Andreas Friedrich, *Emblemes nouveaux: esquels le cours de ce monde est depeint et represente par certaines figures, desquelles le sens est explique par rimes: dressés pour plus grande incitation au* (sic) *gens de bien & honorables, d'ensuivre la pieté & vertu, & pour sincere instruction & advertissement aux meschans & dissolus de fuïr le vice. Premierement en Allemand par André Frideric, & maintenant en François, pour le bien de la jeunesse, & du simple peuple. Mis en lumiere par Jaques de Zettre*, Frankfurt, L. Jennis, 1617, 4°. That these works were intended for the French market is clear from copies of both in the Bibliothèque nationale de France and the Library of Congress. A copy of Cramer's *Emblemata sacra* is found in the Library of Congress with a customised title page in French: *Emblemes sacrez, c'est à dire recueil de cinquante figures en taille doulce, tirez de l'Escriture saincte, traictans du doulx et amiable nom et croix de Jesu Christ*, while copies of Friedrich's work exist in the Bibliothèque nationale de France in which Jennis's imprint on the title page is covered by a patch indicating the French booksellers in Paris and Lyon who distributed it: 'Imprimé à Francfort. Et se vendent à Paris chez Abraham Pacard rue Sainct Jaques à l'Estoille d'Or Anno 1617' ; 'Se vendent chez B.Vincent. A Lyon 1608'. (The work was reissued as late as 1644,

The first emblem book, that of Alciato,[8] established a model which significantly influenced the earliest French writers of emblems. Alciato's *Emblemata* covered a diversity of topics and expressed via these a diversity of reflections on human life and of moral lessons to be derived from these. Diversity was a key element. Although Alciato's immediate imitators in France, Guillaume de la Perrière with his *Theatre des bons engins*, and Gilles Corrozet with his *Hecatomgraphie* and *Emblemes*,[9] adopted different structural patterns in their own emblem books, as far as diversity of theme was concerned, they here followed Alciato's model absolutely, as indeed did the next wave of French emblem writers, all publishing in the 1550s, Guillaume Guéroult with his *Premier livre des emblemes*, Pierre Coustau with his *Pegme*, La Perrière with his *Morosophie*, and Barthélemy Aneau with his *Imagination poetique*.[10] Again the structural form of their emblem books varies, but their range of subject matter and moral lesson was as all-embracing as ever. However, from as early as 1548 a significant modification was made to this norm, with the arrangement by Barthélemy Aneau of Alciato's hitherto deliberately disordered collection of emblems into a logical order according to topics such as the vices, the virtues, love, fortune, marriage, etcetera. The earliest edition of this new version of the text was published in Latin by

---

with another patch bearing the further imprint 'Francofurti apud Jacobum de Zetter. Anno 1644'.) For a bibliography of German emblem books see J. Landwehr, *German Emblem Books, 1531-1888. A Bibliography*, Utrecht, 1972 (hereafter cited as Landwehr, *German Emblem Books*).

[8] Originally published in Latin in 1531 in Augsburg (*Viri clarissimi D. Andree Alciati...emblematum liber*, Augsburg, H. Steyner, 1531, 8°) it was then published in Paris first in Latin in 1534, and then in a French translation in 1536 (*Andreae Alciati emblematum libellus*, Paris, C. Wechel, 1534, 8°; *Livret des emblemes de maistre Andre Alciat, mis en rime francoyse, et presente a mon seigneur ladmiral de France* , Paris, C. Wechel, 1536, 8°). For an overall bibliography of Alciato see H. Green, *Alciati and his Books of Emblems. A Biographical and Bibliographical Study*, London, 1872. For a detailed description of the editions of Alciato in French, or published in France see *BFEB*, vol.1, nos 1-72.

[9] *Le theatre des bons engins, auquel sont contenuz cent emblemes*, Paris, D. Janot, n.d. (1540), 8°; *Hecatomgraphie. C'est à dire les descriptions de cent figures et hystoires contenantes plusieurs appophtegmes, proverbes, sentences et dictz tant des anciens que des modernes*, Paris, D. Janot, 1540, 8°; *Emblemes* in *Le tableau de Cebes de Thebes, ancien philosophe, et disciple de Socrates: auquel est paincte de ses couleurs, la vraye image de la vie humaine, et quelle voye l'homme doit elire, pour pervenir à vertu et perfaicte science. Premierement escript en Grec, et maintenant exposé en ryme francoyse*, Paris, G. Corrozet, 1543, 8°.

[10] Guillaume Guéroult, *Le premier livre des emblemes*, Lyon, B. Arnoullet, 1550, 8° ; Pierre Coustau, *Le pegme de Pierre Coustau, mis en Francoys par Lanteaume de Romieu gentilhomme d'Arles*, Lyon, M. Bonhomme, 1555, 8° (originally composed in Latin and published the same year, likewise by Bonhomme: *Petri Costalii pegma, cum narrationibus philosophicis*); Guillaume de la Perrière, *La morosophie de Guillaume de la Perriere tolosain, contenant cent emblemes moraux illustrez de cent tetrastiques latins, reduitz en autant de quatrains françoys*, Lyon, M. Bonhomme, 1553, 8°; Barthélemy Aneau, *Imagination poetique, traduicte en vers François, des Latins, & Grecz, par l'auteur mesme d'iceux. Horace en l'art. La poesie est comme la pincture*, Lyon, M. Bonhomme, 1552, 8° (originally composed in Latin and published the same year, likewise by Bonhomme: *Picta poesis. Ut pictura poesis erit*).

Macé Bonhomme in 1548, and the following year an equivalent French version was published in a new translation by Aneau, with the further addition of short prose commentaries to each emblem.[11] Thereafter, this logically ordered arrangement of the emblems became the norm for nearly all editions published both by the Roville/Bonhomme partnership and by other publishers. The effect of this change was to create a much more clearly focused emblem book, enabling the reader to select specific topics of interest to himself, and to ignore those topics which were of less interest, in a way which had not been possible with the work in its earlier non-ordered state. The addition of a detailed index (previously wholly lacking) made the process of selection by the reader even easier. With Georgette de Montenay's *Emblemes, ou devises chrestiennes* we see a further significant step in the direction of more focused collections of emblems. Here we find for the first time an emblem book which is quite specifically Christian in its moral message, and Christian likewise in many, though not all of its individual emblems. This later sixteenth-century innovation is further developed in a trend which we find continuing to evolve in the course of the seventeenth century - that of the specifically devotional emblem book.

Influential in this respect, Montenay's emblem book is also influential in another important respect in the seventeenth century - though it is possible that she herself was not responsible for this initiative. In 1584 Montenay's emblem book was transformed from a French vernacular emblem book (albeit with Latin mottoes) into a bilingual French/Latin emblem book, and thirty-five years later, in 1619, it was further transformed into a massive polyglot text with verses in German, Spanish, English, Italian, Dutch and Latin as well as the original French.[12] Bilingual emblem books were not, of course, unknown prior to Montenay: when Alciato's emblem book was first published in a French translation, the original Latin text was retained to accompany the vernacular version on each facing page. La Perrière's *Morosophie* was published from the outset in a bilingual version, while Aneau's *Picta poesis/Imagination poetique* and Coustau's *Pegma/Pegme* were both available in either a Latin or a vernacular version, as was also, rather later, Bèze's *Icones/Vrais pourtraits* with its little collection of emblems.[13] What is more unusual, though, is the

---

[11] *Emblemata Andreae Alciati iurisconsulti clarissimi*, Lyon, M. Bonhomme and G. Roville, 1548, 8°; *Emblemes d'Alciat, de nouveau translatez en François vers pour vers jouxte les Latins. Ordonnez en lieux communs, avec briefves expositions, et figures nouvelles appropriées aux derniers emblemes*, Lyon, M. Bonhomme and G. Roville, 1549, 8°.
[12] In this latter 1619 edition, as well as the new vernacular versions of the text, a second set of Latin verses was added, in addition to that first added to the collection in 1584. This edition was published in versions with a range of different title pages reflecting the different vernaculars: *Livre d'armoiries en signe de fraternité contenant cent comparaisons de vertus et emblemes chrestiens; Stamm Buch darinnen Christlicher Tugende Beyspiel einhundert auszerlesener Emblemata; Cien emblemas christianos; Cento emblemi christiani; Monumenta emblematum christianorum virtutum; A Booke of Armes or Remembrance, wherein are one hunderd godly emblemes*, Frankfurt, J.C. Unckels, 1619, 8°.
[13] *Icones, id est verae imagines virorum doctrina simul et pietate illustrium, quorum praecipuè ministerio partim bonarum literarum studia sunt restituta, partim vera religio in variis orbis Christiani regionibus, nostra patrúmque memoria fuit instaurata: additis eorundem vitae & operae descriptionibus, quibus adiectae sunt nonnullae picturae quas*

fact that Montenay's emblem book was translated from the vernacular into Latin rather than the other way round.[14] And certainly in its full polyglot guise, it is a notable forerunner of the phenomenon which characterised many emblem books in the seventeenth century, which became increasingly 'European' in nature rather than specifically identified to one particular country rather than another.[15] Significantly this polyglot edition of Montenay was published not in France, but in Germany, where - as we have already noted - another Frankfurt publisher, Lucas Jennis, was also at this date about to tap into the international market with polyglot editions. In the seventeenth century, however, the most dominant country in the production of polyglot emblem books catering for the vernacular reader in a range of different countries, including of course France, is the Low Countries, and in particular Antwerp.

All three of these sixteenth-century trends - generalist, Christian and polyglot - continue to develop in the seventeenth century. The generalist emblem book - descendant of Alciato, La Perrière and Corrozet - continued to be produced throughout the century. Dating from the beginning of the century we find Andreas Friedrich's *Emblemes nouveaux* of 1617, published in Germany for the French market,[16] while Martinet's *Emblemes royales à Louis le Grand*, published towards the end of the century in 1673, which despite its title is also a generalist emblem book, reflects the continuing popularity of the form.[17] But the enduring popularity of the generalist emblem book is most clearly demonstrated by Jean Baudoin's two-volume French *Recueil d'emblemes divers*, which was first published quite early in the century, in 1638/39, but which continued to be republished thereafter in a number of editions at approximately ten-year intervals throughout the century until 1698.[18] The Christian

---

emblemata vocant. Theodoro Beza auctore, Geneva, J. de Laon, 1580, 4° ; *Les vrais pourtraits des hommes illustres en pieté et doctrine, du travail desquels Dieu s'est servi en ces derniers temps, pour remettre sus la vraye religion en divers pays de la Chrestienté, avec les descriptions de leur vie & de leurs faits plus memorables. Plus, quarante quatre emblemes chrestiens. Traduicts du Latin de Theodore de Besze*, Geneva, J. de Laon, 1581, 4°.

[14] More commonly we find works composed originally in Latin being thereafter translated into one or other vernacular. Another case of an emblem book originally composed in French being thereafter translated into Latin is Etienne Luzvic's *Coeur devot* of 1627, which was subsequently translated into Latin by Charles Musart and published the following year under the title *Cor Deo devotum*. (For details see below, footnote 21.)

[15] For discussion of this phenomenon, see Alison Saunders, 'French emblem books or European emblem books: transnational publishing in the sixteenth and seventeenth centuries', *Bibliothèque d'Humanisme et Renaissance*, 61, 1999, pp. 415-27.

[16] See above, footnote 7.

[17] *Emblesmes royales à Louis le Grand, par le Sr Martinet, Aide des ceremonies de France*, Paris, C. Barbin, 1673, 12°.

[18] *Recueil d'emblemes divers. Avec des discours moraux, philosophiques, et politiques, tirez de divers autheurs, anciens & modernes. Par J. Baudoin*, Paris, J.Villery, 1638/39, 2 vols, 8°; *ibid.*, 1646/47; *ibid.*, Paris, J.B. Loyson, 1659/60; *ibid.*, Paris, J. Cochart, 1685, 3 vols; *ibid.*, 1698. A selection of 33 emblems from the *Recueil* was also published in 1679 under the title *Tableaux des sciences et des vertus morales. Contenant tout ce qu'il y a de plus beau & de plus curieux, à sçavoir de la peinture, de l'histoire, de l'embleme, de la fable, de la morale, & de la*

emblem book, as pioneered in the sixteenth century by Montenay and Bèze, becomes a major force in the early years of the seventeenth century, and one which continues throughout the century, but developing in two quite distinct directions. On the one hand we find it being exploited specifically as a devotional and meditational tool, notably by the Jesuits, as for example in Jan David's *Veridicus christianus* of 1601 and *Paradisus sponsi et sponsae* of 1607,[19] or Antoine Sucquet's *Via vitae aeternae iconibus illustrata* of 1620,[20] or Etienne Luzvic's *Coeur devot* of 1627,[21] while on the other hand it also develops in a pattern more reminiscent of earlier sixteenth-century biblical picture books such as Gilles Corrozet's *Historiarum veteris testamenti icones* and *Tapisserie de l'eglise chrestienne*.[22] This was a popular form which continued to be produced throughout the sixteenth century, as for example in Claude Paradin's *Quadrins historiques* and Charles Fontaine's *Figures du Nouveau Testament* in the 1550s, Guillaume Guéroult's *Figures de la Bible* in the 1560s, and Claude de Pontoux's *Figures du Nouveau Testament* in the 1570s.[23] As late as 1594 Paul Perrot de la Sale produced a collection of *Tableaus sacrez* derived from the Old Testament,[24] and we see the tradition continuing into the seventeenth century with, for example, another collection of similarly named *Tableaux sacrez* dating from 1601 - those of the

---

politique. Enrichies de figures. Par M.B. de l'Academie Françoise (Paris, J.B. Loyson, 1679, 12°). For details of the various editions see *BFEB*, vol.1, nos 95-9.

[19] *Veridicus christianus: auctore P. Ioanne David, sacerdote Societatis Iesu*, Antwerp, J. Moretus (Officina Plantiniana), 1601, 4°; *Paradisus sponsi et sponsae: in quo messis myrrhae et aromatum, ex instrumentis ac mysteriis passionis Christi colligenda, ut ei commoriamur. Et Pancarpium Marianum, septemplici titulorum serie distinctum: ut in B. Virginis odorem curramus, et Christus formetur in nobis. Auctore P. Ioanne David, Societatis Iesu sacerdote*, Antwerp, J. Moretus (Officina Plantiniana), 1607, 8°.

[20] *Antoni Sucquet è Societate Iesu via vitae eternae iconibus illustrata per Boëtium a Bolswert*, Antwerp, M. Nutius, 1620, 4°.

[21] *Le coeur devot throsne royal de Jesus pacifique Salomon. Par le P. Estienne Luzvic, de la Compagnie de Jesus*, Antwerp, H. Aertssens, 1627, 12°; also published in a Latin translation by Charles Musart: *Cor Deo devotum Iesu pacifici Salomonis thronus regius è gallico P Stephani Luzvic, cui adiunctae ex P. Binet imaginum expositiunculae Latinitati dedit, & ad calcem auxit P. Carolus Musart eiusdem cum prioribus Societatis Iesu*, Douai, B. Bellere, 1627, 12°; *ibid*., Antwerp, H. Aertssens, 1628, 12°.

[22] *Historiarum veteris testamenti icones ad vivum expressae. Unà cum brevi, sed quoad fieri potuit, dilucida earundem et Latina et Gallica expositione*, Lyon, M. and G. Trechsel, 1539, 4°; *Tapisserie de l'eglise chrestienne et catholique: en laquelle sont depainctes la nativité, vie, passion, mort, et resurrection de nostre Sauveur et Redempteur Jesus Christ. Avec un huictain soubz chacune hystoire, pour l'intelligence d'icelle*, Paris, E. Groulleau, n.d., 16°.

[23] Claude Paradin, *Quadrins historiques de la Bible*. Lyon, J. de Tournes, 1553, 8°; Guillaume Guéroult, *Figures de la Bible illustrées de huictains francoys pour l'interpretation et intelligence d'icelles*, Lyon, G. Roville, 1564, 8°; Charles Fontaine, *Figures du Nouveau Testament*, Lyon, J. de Tournes, 1554, 8°; Claude de Pontoux, *Figures du Nouveau Testament illustrées de huictains francoys pour l'interpretation et intelligence d'icelles*, Lyon, G. Roville, 1570, 8°.

[24] *Tableaus sacrez de Paul Perrot Sieur de La Sale. P. Qui sont toutes les histoires du Viel Testament representees & exposees selon leur sens en poesie francoise*, Frankfurt, J. Feyrabendt, 'aux despends de Theodore de Bry', 1594, 8°.

Jesuit Louis Richeome,[25] or Bernard Sellius's *Emblemata sacra* of 1613,[26] while Jacques Callot's bilingual *Vita beatae Mariae virginis, matris Dei emblematibus delineata* of 1646[27] follows a not dissimilar pattern despite its rather different subject matter. Lastly the polyglot development, instigated with Georgette de Montenay's Christian emblem book, evolves in the seventeenth century not just within the field of devotional literature, but also within the flourishing field of love emblems which flooded from the Dutch printing presses above all, for dissemination across Europe.

Devotional emblem books tended to be published in a range of different languages, including Latin and the main European vernaculars, but most commonly separate versions were produced for each vernacular, as, for example, in the case of Sucquet's *Via vitae aeternae* which was made available in the 1620s in either French, or German, or English or Spanish versions,[28] while Benedict van Haeften's originally Latin *Schola cordis*[29] was similarly also published in separate versions in English, or Spanish or German (though curiously not in a French version),[30] and in addition to the original Latin version, his *Regia via crucis*[31] was also made available in either French, Spanish, or Dutch versions.[32] Although this was the most common pattern,

---

[25] *Tableaux sacrez des figures mystiques du tres-auguste sacrifice et sacrement de l'Eucharistie. Dediez à la tres chrestienne Royne de France et de Navarre Marie de Medicis par Louis Richeome, Provençal de la Compagnie de Jesus*, Paris, L. Sonnius, 1601, 8°.

[26] *Emblemata sacra, è praecipuis utriusque testamenti historiis concinnata a Bernardo Sellio Noviomago & a Petro van der Burgio figuris aeneis elegantissimis illustrata*, Amsterdam, M. Colinius, 1613, folio obl. (In the Bibliothèque nationale de France Estampes copy of this edition a French translation of the printed Latin text has been added in manuscript). Daniel Russell refers to an earlier edition published in Antwerp by F. Raphelengius in 1593, of which no known copy exists (*The Emblem and Device in France*, p.203, footnote 75).

[27] *Vita beatae Mariae virginis, matris Dei emblematibus delineata. Vie de la bien-heureuse vierge Marie mere de Dieu. Representée par figures emblematiques, dessignées & gravées par Jacques Callot*, Paris, F. Langlois, dit Chartres, 1646, 4°.

[28] *Le chemin de la vie eternele composé en Latin par le R.P. Antoine Sucquet de la Compagnie de Jesus. Translaté par le R.P. Pierre Morin, Parisien, de la mesme Compagnie. Declaré par images de Boëte a Bolswert*, Antwerp, H. Aertssens, 1623, 4° ; *Den Wech des eeuwich levens beschreven int Latijn door p. Antonius Sucquet, over-geset door p. Gerardus Zoes, beyde priesters der Societeyt Iesu...*, Antwerp, H. Aertssens, 1622, 4°; *Weg zum Ewigen Leben, durch R.P.F. Carolum Stengelium verteutscht*, Augsburg, M. Langenwalder, 1627, 4°. For details of English and Spanish versions see Praz, p.507.

[29] *Schola cordis sive aversi à Deo cordis ad eundem reductio, et instructio. Auctore D. Benedicto Haefteno Ultraiectino, reformati monast. Affligeniensis, ordinis S. Benedicti praeposito*, Antwerp, J. Verdussen, 1629, 8°.

[30] For details of vernacular versions see below, chapter 5, footnotes 67 and 68.

[31] *Regia via crucis auctore D. Benedicto Haefteno Ultraiectino reformati monasterii Affligeniensis ordinis S. Benedicti praeposito*, Antwerp, B. Moretus (Officina Plantiniana), 1635, 8°.

[32] The first edition of the very popular French version was published in Paris in 1651 under the title *Le chemin royal de la croix, composé par Dom Benoist Haeften d'Utrecht, Prieur du monastére réformé d'Afflighen, de l'Ordre de S. Benoist. Traduict de Latin en François, & dedié à Madame la Duchesse d'Orleans, par le R.P. Didac religieux de l'Observance de S. François son confesseur. Enrichy de quarante figures en taille-douce* (Paris, N. Jacquart for J.

there were, however, exceptions, such as Daniel Cramer's Frankfurt published *Emblemata sacra* of 1624 and *Octoginta emblemata moralia nova* of 1630 which were both, as we have seen, published from the outset in true polyglot fashion in the manner of the 1619 edition of Montenay's emblem book. Within the area of love emblems, however, true polyglot editions abound. Heinsius's Leiden published *Emblemata amatoria nova* of 1613 had verses in French and Dutch as well as Latin,[33] while Vaenius's *Amorum emblemata* of 1608 was published in a range of different language combinations: Dutch, French and Latin; French, Italian and Latin; Italian, Spanish and Latin; Italian, English and Latin, and Philip Ayres' 1683 London published *Emblemata amatoria*, inspired by these Dutch love emblems, was likewise available in a polyglot version whose title reflects the range of languages provided.[34]

Interest in hieroglyphics and in the association between these and emblems is another sixteenth-century phenomenon which we find continuing into the seventeenth century. From as early as 1505 Greek and Latin versions of the *Hieroglyphica* of Horapollo had been available, and from 1543 the parallel between hieroglyphs and emblems was demonstrated the more evidently with the publication in Paris of a French version of the text in which for the first time each hieroglyph was accompanied by a woodcut illustration.[35] The earliest French emblem writers commonly drew attention in their prefaces to the association which they perceived to exist between emblem and hieroglyph,[36] and later writers in the sixteenth century, and

---

Henault, 1651, 8°). For details of subsequent editions in French, and of editions in Spanish and Dutch, see below, chapter 5, footnotes 64 and 65.

[33] Leiden, J. Marcusz, 1613, 4°.

[34] *Emblemata amatoria. Emblems of love. Embleme d'amore. Emblemes d'amour. In four languages. Dedicated to the Ladies. By Philip Ayres Esq.*, London, R. Bently and S. Tidmarch, J. Osborn, H. Overton, J. Wren, 1683, 8°. See also the undated derivative *Emblemata amatoria*, published 'A Londe chez l'Amoureux'.

[35] *Habentur hoc volumine haec, videlicet: vita et fabellae Aesopi...Ori Apollinis Niliaci hieroglyphica*, Venice, Aldus, 1505, folio; *Ori Apollinis hierogliphica*, Paris, P. Vidoue, 1521, 8°; *Orus Apollo de Aegypte de la signification des notes hieroglyphiques des Aegyptiens, c'est à dire des figures par les quelles ilz escripvoient leurs mysteres secretz & les choses sainctes & divines. Nouvellement traduict de grec en francoys & imprimé avec les figures à chascun chapitre*, Paris, J. Kerver, 1543, 8°.

[36] See, for example, Guillaume de la Perrière in the dedication of his *Theatre des bons engins* to Marguerite de Navarre: 'Au surplus (Madame) ce n'est pas seulement de nostre temps, que les Emblemes sont en bruict, pris & singuliere veneration, ains c'est de toute ancienneté & presque des le commencement du monde: Car les Egiptiens qui se reputent estre les premiers hommes du monde, avant l'usage des lettres, escripvoient par figures & ymages tant d'hommes, bestes & oyseaulx, poissons, que serpentz, par icelles exprimant leurs intentions, comme recitent tresanciens autheurs Chaeremon, Orus Apollo, & leurs semblables qui ont diligemment & curieusement travaillé à exposer & donner l'intelligence desdictes figures hierogliphicques...' (A4v) or Gilles Corrozet in the dedicatory *épître* 'aux bons espritz & amateurs des lettres' in his *Hecatomgraphie*:
Chascune hystoire est d'ymage illustrée
Affin que soit plus clairement monstrée
L'invention, & la rendre autenticque
Qu'on peult nommer lettre hierogliphicque

likewise in the seventeenth century continued to stress this association. Forty years after the publication of Kerver's illustrated French edition, Pierre L'Anglois spelt it out in the title of his *Discours des hieroglyphes aegyptiens, emblemes, devises et armoiries* of 1583, accompanying his theoretical treatise with a collection of 54 hieroglyphs presented in emblematic form, albeit without illustration.[37] The title of Gabriel Chappuys's French translation of Valeriano's Latin treatise on hieroglyphics, first published in Lyon in 1576, similarly associates hieroglyphs with devices among a range of other cognate forms which he also cites,[38] and here - unlike L'Anglois's unillustrated work - each hieroglyph is illustrated by a woodcut figure in the manner established in the much earlier Kerver edition of Horapollo. Reflecting the continuing seventeenth-century interest in editions of hieroglyphics (both illustrated and non-illustrated) is the fact that yet a further Latin version of Valeriano by Louis de Caseneuve was published in Lyon in 1626, following the pattern of Chappuys's earlier French version, while the Jesuit Nicolas Caussin's non-illustrated Latin treatise on hieroglyphics also ran through a series of editions in France from 1618 until 1647.[39] As well as these works, Ripa's immensely influential *Iconologia* also continues in the seventeenth century to point to the association between hieroglyphs on the one hand

Comme jadis faisoient les anciens
Et entre tous les vieulx Egyptiens
Qui denotoient vice ou vertu honneste
Par ung oyseau, ung poison, une beste. (A3v)

[37] Paris, pour A. l'Angelier, 1583, 4°.

[38] Valeriano Bolzani, *Commentaires hieroglyphiques ou images des choses de Jan Pierius Valerian, esquels comme en un vif tableau est ingenieusement depeinct & representé l'estat de plusieurs choses antiques: comme de monnoyes, medales, armes, inscriptions & devises, obelisques, pyramides & autres monumens: outre une infinité de diverses & profitables histoires, proverbes & lieux communs: avec la parfaicte interpretation des mysteres d'Aegypte, & de plusieurs passages de l'escriture saincte conformes à iceux...mis en François par Gabriel Chappuys Tourangeau*, Lyon, B. Honorat, 1576, folio. A further French translation was published in 1615: *Les hieroglyphiques de Jan-Pierre Valerian vulgairement nommé Pierius. Autrement commentaires des lettres et figures sacrées des Aegyptiens & autres nations...nouvellement donnez aux François par J de Montlyart*, Lyon, P. Frellon, 1615, folio. In its original Latin form, Valeriano's *Hieroglyphica* was first published in Basle in 1556 (*Hieroglyphica sive de sacris Aegyptiorum aliarumque gentium literis, commentarii Ioannis Valeriani Bolzani Bellunensis*, Basle, M. Isengrin, 1556, folio) and thereafter in Lyon in 1579 and 1586 (B. Honorat); in 1595 (T. Soubron), and again in 1602 and 1610 (P. Frellon).

[39] Louis de Caseneuve, *Ioannis Pierii Valeriani Bellunensis hieroglyphica, seu de sacris Aegyptiorum, aliarùmque gentium literis commentarii, libri quinquaginta octo digesti: quibus additi sunt duo hieroglyphicorum libri, Caelii Augustini Curionis: Eiusdem Pierii pro sacerdotum barbis declamatio, & poëmata varia, cum diversis hieroglyphicis collectaneis, in sex libros ordine alphabetico dispositis, & nunc diligenter expurgatis. Accesserunt in hac postrema editione Hori Apollonis hieroglyphicorum libri duo...Authore Ludovico a Casanova*, Lyon, P. Frellon, 1626, folio; Nicolas Caussin, *Electorum symbolorum et parabolarum historicarum syntagmata. Ex Horo, Clemente, Epiphanio & aliis cum notis & observationibus. Auctore P. Nicolao Caussino Trecensi, Societate Iesu*, Paris, R. de Beauvais, 1618, 4°; *Symbolica Aegyptiorum sapientia. Authore P. Nicolao Caussino Trecensi, è Societate Iesu*, Paris, J. Jost and A. Taupinart, 1633 and 1634, 8°; *ibid.*, Paris, S. Piget, 1647, 4°.

and emblems and devices on the other. Originally published as a non-illustrated Italian text in Rome in 1593 (followed by an illustrated version in 1603)[40] Ripa's work enjoyed considerable popularity in France, where a French version by Jean Baudoin was repeatedly published in Paris between 1636 and 1681, with a final edition appearing in Amsterdam in 1698. Once again the title of Baudoin's French translation (*Iconologie ou explication nouvelle de plusieurs images emblemes et autres figures hieroglyphiques*) reflects the way in which seventeenth-century emblematic writers continued to emphasise the parallels between emblems, devices and hieroglyphs which had been much earlier identified by their sixteenth-century predecessors.[41]

Interest in emblems and interest in devices had from the earliest days of the genre run hand in hand, and this pattern also continues in the seventeenth century. The pioneering collections of devices compiled by Simeoni, Giovio and Paradin were all extremely popular in France in the first half of the sixteenth century, but somewhat surprisingly no French versions of Giovio were published after the 1560s,[42] although interest in the work of the native French Paradin was more enduring, with editions of his devices continuing to be published in France into the first two decades of the seventeenth century. To some of these editions Simeoni's collection of devices was also attached.[43] But not content with simply perpetuating earlier collections dating

[40] Cesare Ripa, *Iconologia overo descrittione dell'imagini universali cavate dall'antichità et da altri luoghi da Cesare Ripa Perugino*, Rome, Heirs of G. Gigliotti, 1593, 4°; *Iconologia...di nuovo revista & dal medesimo ampliata di 400 & piu imagini et di figure ad intaglio adornata*, Rome, L. Faci, 1603, 4°.

[41] *Iconologie, ou, explication nouvelle de plusieurs images, emblemes, et autres figures hyeroglyphiques des vertus, des vices, des arts, des sciences, des causes naturelles, des humeurs differentes, & des passions humaines. Oeuvre necessaire a toute sorte d'esprits, et particulierement à ceux qui aspirent à estre, ou qui sont orateurs, poetes, sculpteurs, peintres, ingenieurs, autheurs de medailles, de devises, de ballets, & de poëmes dramatiques. Tirée des recherches & des figures de Cesar Ripa, desseignées & gravées par Jacques de Brie, et moralisées par J. Baudoin*, Paris, 'chez l'autheur', 1636, folio; *ibid.*, Paris, J. Villery, 1637, folio; Paris, M. Guillemot, 1644, folio; Paris, L. Billaine, 1677, 4°; Paris, L. d'Houry, 1681, 4° ; *Iconologie ou la science des emblemes*, Amsterdam, A. Braakman, 1698, 12°.

[42] Originally composed in Italian, the *Dialogo dell'imprese militari et amorose* and *Imprese heroiche et morali* were first published in a French translation in 1561, under the title *Dialogue des devises d'armes et d'amours du S. Paulo Jovio, avec un discours de M. Loys Dominique sur le mesme subjet. Traduit d'Italien par le S. Vasquin Philieul. Auquel avons adjousté les Devises heroiques et morales du Seigneur Gabriel Symeon* (Lyon, G.Roville, 1561, 4°). The devices were also published by Roville in a variant form in both Italian and French with the prose text replaced by emblematic verses: *Le sententiose imprese di Monsignor Paulo Giovio, et del Signor Gabriel Symeoni ridotte in rima per il detto Symeoni al sereniss. Duca di Savoia*, Lyon, G. Roville, 1561, 4°; *Tetrastiques faictz sur les devises du Seigneur Paulo Jovio, et de Messire Gabriel Simeon, pour servir en verrieres, chassis, galeries et tableaux, ainsi qu'il plaira au lecteur de les accommoder*, Lyon, G.Roville, 1560, 4°. The only edition of the work published after the 1560s was an edition of the Italian text (*Dialogo dell'imprese militari et amorose*) published by Roville in 1574.

[43] Originally published in a simple version without text in 1551 under the title *Devises*

from the preceding century, seventeenth-century writers also produced their own new collections of devices in great numbers, some following the generalist pattern of Giovio and Simeoni, while other collections were addressed more specifically to individuals. Of the generalist kind is the Jesuit Pierre Le Moyne's *Devises heroiques et morales* of 1649 or Florent Chovayne's *Divertissements* of 1645 or - rather later in the century - Daniel de la Feuille's anthology of *Devises et emblemes anciennes et modernes, tirées des plus celebres autheurs*, published in Amsterdam in 1691.[44] Typical of the more specific kind are - at one end of the scale - Adrian d'Amboise's *Devises royales* of 1621, dedicated to Louis XIII and addressed to the king himself and to members of his family and - more modestly at the other end of the scale - the Jesuit Gabriel Charonier's little collection of *Devises sur les armes de Monsieur Le Tellier* of 1668, or his similar collection of *Devises sur le nom, les armes et la charge de Messire François du Gué* of 1667.[45]

---

heroiques par M. Claude Paradin, Chanoyne de Beaujeu (Lyon, J. de Tournes and G. Gazeau, 1551, 8°), a fuller version with prose commentary accompanying each device was published under the same title by J. de Tournes and G. Gazeau in 1557. An edition of Paradin including also devices of Simeoni was published in Antwerp in 1561 (*Les devises heroiques de M. Claude Paradin, Chanoine de Beaujeu, du Seigneur Symeon et autres aucteurs*, Antwerp, C. Plantin, 1561, 8°), after which further editions of this French version of the combined work of the two writers were published in Antwerp by Plantin in 1562 and 1567, and by the Veuve Jean Stelsius in 1563. Plantin likewise published a Latin version of the combined work of Paradin and Simeoni in 1562 (*Heroica M. Claudii Paradini Belliiocensis Canonici, & D. Gabrielis Symeonis, symbola: Iam recens ex idiomate Gallico in Lat...a Iohan. Gubernatore*, Antwerp, C. Plantin, 1562, 16°), and again in 1567 and 1583, while the Veuve Jean Stelsius also published an edition in 1563, and F. Raphelengius a further edition in Leiden in 1600. An expanded French edition of the work of Paradin only was published in Paris in 1614 (*Devises heroiques et emblemes. De M. Claude Paradin. Reveues et augmentées de moytié*, Paris, J. Millot, 1614, 8°) and a further edition of this in Paris by Rolet Boutonne in 1621 and 1622 (*Devises heroiques et emblemes de M. Claude Paradin. Reveuës & augmentées de moitié par Messire François d'Amboise. Et dedié à Monseigneur le premier Président*, Paris, R. Boutonne, 1621/22, 8°). For details of editions published in The Netherlands see Landwehr, *Dutch Emblem Books*, nos 465-73; and for details of editions published in France see Landwehr, *Romanic Emblem Books*, nos 563-73. For details of the publishing history of the Plantin editions see L.Voet, *The Golden Compasses. A History and Evaluation of the Printing and Publishing Activities of the Officina Plantiniana*, Amsterdam, 1967-72, 2 vols, vol.1, pp.33-4. For discussion of Paradin's devices see Claude Paradin, *Devises heroïques*, facsim.ed., Alison Saunders, Aldershot, 1989.

[44] *Devises heroiques et morales du P. Pierre Le Moine de la Compagnie de Jesus*, Paris, A. Courbé, 1649, 4°; *Les divertissements de Florent Chovayne Chartrain. Contenans un recueil de diverses devises & emblemes, la plus grande partie de son invention, divisé en vingt-cinq centuries*, Chartres, M. Georges, 1645, 8°; *Devises et emblemes anciennes et modernes, tirées des plus celebres auteurs. Avec plusieurs autres nouvellement inventées et mises en Latin, en François, en Espagnol, en Italien, en Anglais, en Flamand et en Allemand par les soins de Daniel de La Feuille*, Amsterdam, D. de La Feuille, 1691, 4°.

[45] *Devises royales par Adrian d'Amboise. Au Roy*, Paris, R. Boutonne, 1621, 8°; *Devises sur les armes de Monseigneur Le Tellier, secretaire d'estat. Presentées à Monsieur l'Abbé Le Tellier, revenant d'Italie*, Lyon, A. Jullieron, 1668, 4°; *Devises sur le nom, les armes, et la*

Devices could be put to many purposes, and this versatility is well reflected in the various collections produced in the seventeenth century, as it had also been in those produced in the preceding century. As well as being produced as straightforward flattery of the great, they could also be published with a view to fulfilling a more narrowly educational purpose, as in Le Vasseur's *Devises des roys de France latines et françoises...à Monseigneur le Dauphin*, published in 1610 and designed specifically for the edification of its dedicatee, the 8-year old future Louis XIII, or - rather later - Ménestrier's better known *Histoire du Roy Louis le Grand* of 1689, likewise designed for the edification of royal children - in this case Louis's three young grandchildren, all aged under seven at this date.[46] Likewise for educational purposes, but in a very different domain, devices were also exploited as a pedagogic exercise for schoolboys who - particularly in Jesuit colleges - were set the task of composing, as a whole class, a collection of devices all focusing on one particular topic. Such devices would then often be put on public display on the walls of the college, and thereafter commemorative manuscript anthologies produced, often, though not always, by professional artists commissioned to do the job. A particularly rich collection of such manuscripts was produced over the years at the Jesuit college in Brussels. The exercise was an annual event at the Brussels college, and an almost complete run of manuscript anthologies produced between 1630 and 1685 by the boys of the two senior classes, Humanity and Rhetoric, still survive. Two particularly decorative manuscripts dating from 1642 and 1649 which found their way to France are now housed in the Bibliothèque nationale de France, but the bulk of the series (almost all of which have survived) are now housed in the Royal Library of Belgium.[47] Such professionally produced commemorative manuscripts as these are particularly decorative, but many less grandiose examples of emblematic work by schoolboys in Jesuit colleges also exist.[48]

Traditionally devices had long been used as an important part of the iconography of triumphal entries and festivities. Throughout the sixteenth century we find them

---

charge de Messire François du Gué, chevalier, conseiller du Roy en ses conseils d'estat, & privé...Intendant de la police & des finances dans les provinces du Lyonnois, Forests, Beaujollais & Dauphiné. Recitées au mesme Seigneur par les rhetoriciens du Collège de la tres-sainte Trinité, de la Compagnie de Jesus, le huitiesme Janvier 1667, jour auquel il leur fit l'honneur d'assister à une de leurs Déclamations, Lyon, P. Guillemin, 1667, 4°.

[46] *Devises des roys de France latines et françoises...à Monseigneur le Dauphin*, Paris, F. Bourriquant, 1609,8°; *Histoire du Roy Louis le Grand par les medailles, emblemes, devises, jettons, inscriptions, armoiries, et autres monumens publics, recueillis, et expliquez par le Pere Claude-François Menestrier de la Compagnie de Jesus*, Paris, J.B. Nolin, 1689, folio.

[47] BnF Ms. lat. 10170 and Ms. lat. 10171. For a very detailed, and lavishly illustrated discussion of these manuscripts, and of the structure of the education offered in the Jesuit college in Brussels generally, see K. Porteman, ed., *Emblematic Exhibitions (affixiones) at the Brussels Jesuit College (1630-1685). A Study of the Commemorative Manuscripts (Royal Library, Brussels)*, Brussels, 1996.

[48] For discussion of these see Alison Saunders, 'Make the pupils do it themselves: emblems, plays and public performances in French Jesuit colleges in the seventeenth century' in Marc van Vaeck and John Manning, eds, *The Jesuits and the Emblem Tradition*, Turnhout, 1999, pp.187-206.

being used in ever more ambitious and lavish displays, notable among which are the entries of Henri II and Catherine de Medici into Lyon in 1548 and Paris in 1549, or the celebrations which took place at Bayonne in 1565 to mark the meeting of the youthful Charles IX with his elder sister Elisabeth, Queen of Spain, or the entry into Paris a few years later, in 1571 of Charles IX and his new wife, Elisabeth of Austria, or yet again the celebrations held on the occasion of the wedding of the Duc de Joyeuse in 1581.[49] This pattern takes on even greater import in the seventeenth century, as a country torn for decades by civil and religious wars and other forms of internal strife, seeks to reestablish a pattern of order and national identity focusing around the figurehead of the monarch. The triumphal entries of the Valois monarchs of the sixteenth century used devices to convey appropriate political iconographic messages, but even more so does this become the case under the Bourbon dynasty. With Henri IV and Louis XIII, but above all with Louis XIV, we see in its most fully developed form the full panoply of extravagant court festivities, spreading their instant iconographic message to all onlookers and participants, but also - and perhaps more influentially - spreading that same message subsequently to a wider audience in the form of the lavishly documented and illustrated published accounts which were

---

[49]   For contemporary accounts of these see *La magnificence de la superbe et triumphante entrée de la noble et antique cité de Lyon faicte au treschrestien Roy de France Henry deuxiesme de ce nom, et à la Royne Catherine son espouse le XXIII. de Septembre M.D.XLVIII*, Lyon, G. Roville, 1549, 4°; *C'est l'ordre qui a esté tenu à la nouvelle et joyeuse entrée, que treshault, tresexcellent, trespuissant prince, le Roy treschrestien Henry deuxiesme de ce nom a faicte en sa bonne ville et cité de Paris, capitale de son royaume, le sezieme jour de Juin M.D.XLIX* and *C'est l'ordre et forme qui a esté tenu au sacre et couronnement de treshaulte et tresillustre dame Madame Catherine de Medicis, Royne de France, faicte en l'eglise Monseigneur sainct Denys en France, le X. jour de Juin. M.D.XLIX*, Paris, J. Dallier, 1549, 8°; *Recueil des choses notables, qui ont esté faites à Bayonne, à l'entreveuë du Roy treschrestien Charles neufieme de ce nom et la Royne sa treshonorée mere avec la Royne catholique sa soeur*, Paris, M. de Vascosan, 1566, 4°; Simon Bouquet, *Bref et sommaire recueil de ce qui a esté faict et de l'ordre tenuë à la joyeuse et triumphante entrée de tres-puissant tres-magnanime et tres-chrestien Prince Charles IX...avec le couronnement de tres-haute, tresillustre et tres-excellente Princesse Madame Marguerite Elizabet d'Austriche son espouse...et entrée de la dicte dame en icelle ville le jeudi xxix dudict mois de mars M.D.LXXI*, Paris, D. du Pré for O. Codoré, 1572, 4°; Balthasar de Beaujoyeulx, *Balet comique de la Royne, faict aux nopces de monsieur le Duc de Joyeuse et madamoyselle de Vaudemont sa soeur, par Baltasar de Beaujoyeulx, valet de chambre du Roy, et de la Royne sa mere*, Paris, A. le Roy, R. Ballard and M. Patisson, 1582, 4°. See also Richard Cooper (ed.), *The Entry of Henri II into Lyon, September 1548*, Tempe, Arizona, 1997; I.D. McFarlane (ed.), *The Entry of Henri II into Paris, 16 June 1549*, New York, 1982; V. Graham and W. McAllister-Johnson, *The Royal Tour of France 1564-66*, Toronto, 1979; V. Graham and W. McAllister-Johnson, *The Paris Entries of Charles IX and Elisabeth of Austria 1571, with an Analysis of Simon Bouquet's Bref et sommaire recueil*, Toronto, 1974; F.Yates (ed), Simon Bouquet, *La joyeuse entrée de Charles IX roy de France en Paris 1572*, Amsterdam, 1974; M. McGowan (ed.), Balthasar de Beaujoyeulx, *Le Balet comique de la royne*, New York, 1982; F. Yates, *The Valois Tapestries*, London, 1959; M. McGowan, *L'art du ballet de cour en France 1581-1643*, Paris, 1978. For discussion of these and other sixteenth-century festivities using emblems and devices see Saunders, *Sixteenth-Century French Emblem Book*, pp.279-92.

regularly produced after the event for wider dissemination, as part of the propaganda campaign establishing the persona of a great king of a great nation.

The seventeenth century opens appropriately with a magnificent celebration of the greatness of the first of the new dynasty of French monarchs, Henri IV, as displayed on the occasion of the entry of his queen into Avignon in 1601. The emblems and devices which formed an important part of the iconography adorning the labyrinthine route through the streets of Avignon, all of which focused on different aspects of the overarching theme of Henri's kingly and military prowess, are described and also in many cases reproduced visually in Valladier's account of the occasion, the lengthy title of which makes clear the relationship between the iconography of Hercules and the glory of the French king: *Labyrinthe royal de l'Hercule gaulois triomphant sur le suject des fortunes, batailles, victoires, trophées, triomphes, mariage, & autres faicts heroiques, & memorables de tres-auguste & tres-chrestien prince Henri IIII. Roy de France, & de Navarre. Représenté à l'entrée triomphante de la royne en la cité d'Avignon. Le 19 novembre. l'an M.DC. Ou sont contenuës les magnificences et triomphes dressez à cet effect par ladicte ville.*[50] No less grandiose in conception were the decorations planned a quarter of a century later for the entry into Aix of Henri's son, Louis XIII in 1624, and lavishly produced also is Galaup de Chasteuil's subsequently published account of the entry. In this particular event not only were emblems and devices used generally to adorn the various key sites across the city with meaningful decoration, but a purpose-built gallery was erected specifically to house a series of devices whose function was to represent allegorically the particular virtues of the king.[51] As for Louis XIV, 1660, the year of the peace celebrations between France and Spain and the marriage between Louis and Maria Theresa, marked a high spot for festivities, of which perhaps the most familiar account is that by the prolific Ménestrier of the ceremonies which took place in Lyon to mark the occasion.[52] In his detailed account Ménestrier describes the event itself, and provides illustrations of the main allegorical decorations, explaining characteristically also why particular themes were chosen and how particular erections were constructed. This account is just one of many such accounts by Ménestrier of celebrations on a greater or lesser scale, in the case of several of which he was responsible not just for the subsequent printed account, but also for the original design and orchestration of the event. The Bibliothèque nationale de France catalogue lists under Ménestrier's name more than fifty such accounts of ceremonial occasions. Some, at least, of these (in which neither the title page nor the text gives any indication of authorship) are probably falsely attributed to Ménestrier, but even if these are discounted, Ménestrier emerges as the dominant figure in this domain. Among the many works attributed to him, for example, is a lavishly illustrated account, produced in folio, of the funeral ceremonial

---

[50] Avignon, J. Bramereau, 1601, 4°.
[51] Galaup de Chasteuil, *Discours sur les arcs triumphaux dressés en la ville d'Aix à l'heureuse arrivée de tres-chrestien tres-grand & tres-juste monarque Louis XIII Roy de France & de Navarre*, Aix, J.Tholosan, 1624, folio.
[52] *Les resjoüissances de la paix, avec un recueil de diverses pieces sur ce sujet: dedié à messieurs les prevost des marchands & eschevins de la ville de Lyon. Par le P.C.F.M. de la Compagnie de Jesus*, Lyon, B. Coral, 1660, 8°.

for the Vicomte de Turenne in 1675, in which 34 devices associated with the life of Henri de Turenne are reproduced;[53] at the other end of the scale we find a much more modest, short account of the celebrations on the birth of the first grandson of Louis XIV, the Duc de Bourgogne, published without illustration in 1682,[54] but simply giving a description of all the devices employed in the celebration, together with their inscriptions, and noting any verses which were also included. Likewise attributed to Ménestrier is another account of a parallel celebration of the same event, also exploiting emblematic material, but via a different medium, in the form of a firework display held outside the Hôtel de Ville in which the device of the *Dauphin* figured prominently in the temporary theatre erected in front of the Hôtel de Ville.[55] What was done for one grandchild had to be done for another, and four years later we find another account of a similar firework display held to celebrate the birth of the third royal grandson, the Duc de Berry, in 1686, in which curiously no mention is made of the actual fireworks themselves, but great emphasis is given to describing the four meaningful devices which adorned the facade of the arena.[56]

It is particularly in the domain of court festivities that devices develop a significantly greater role in the course of the seventeenth century, as the festivities became ever more extravagant and lavish during the reign of Louis XIV. Jousting was already established as an important gentlemanly pursuit in the sixteenth century (as shown so clearly in the Valois Tapestries, and indeed as witnessed by the untimely death of Henri II in a jousting accident, after which less dangerous versions of the sport were practised),[57] but it became much more of a public display of magnificence in the seventeenth century. In 1648 Marc de Vulson dedicated to Mazarin his lavishly illustrated account of the 3-day *carrousel* that took place in the Place Royale in April 1612 to celebrate the double marriage contract of the 11-year old Louis XIII to the Spanish Infanta, Anne of Austria, and of his sister Elisabeth to the Infante, later to become Philip IV of Spain, an account which formed part of his longer treatise on chivalric exercises in general.[58] Not only does Vulson here describe the costume of

---

[53] *Les vertus chrestiennes et les vertus militaires en deüil. Dessein de l'appareil funebre dressé par ordre du roy dans l'eglise de Nostre Dame de Paris le neuviéme septembre 1675 pour la ceremonie des obseques de...Monseigneur Henry de la Tour d'Auvergne, vicomte de Turenne,* Paris, E. Michallet, 1675, 4°.

[54] *Illuminations de la galerie du Louvre pour les rejouissances de la naissance de Monseigneur le Duc de Bourgogne,* Paris, R.J.B. de la Caille, 1682, folio.

[55] *Explication du feu d'artifice dressé devant l'hostel de ville par les ordres de messieurs les Prevost des Marchands & Echevins, pour la naissance du prince que nous vient de donner Madame la Dauphine,* Paris, Veuve G. Adam, 1682, 4°.

[56] *Explication du feu d'artifice dressé devant l'hostel de ville...à la naissance de Monseigneur le Duc de Berry,* Paris, T. Guillain, n.d. (1686), 4°.

[57] The title of Charles Perrault's account of a tournament held in 1662 (*Courses de testes et de bague, faites par le Roy et par les princes et seigneurs de sa cour, en l'année M.DC.LXII,* Paris, S. Mabre-Cramoisy for the *Imprimerie royale,* 1670, folio) reflects this change in style. Henceforth gentlemen tilted at obstacles rather than at each other.

[58] M. de Vulson, *Le magnifique et admirable Carrosel qui fut fait à Paris dans la Place Royalle, le cinq, le six & le septiesme jour d'Avril, l'an mil six cens & douze, pour les resjouissances de la publication de la double alliance, par les mariages du Roy Louis XIII, &*

each of the participating gentlemen, but also the devices which they all wore. Henri de Gissey likewise produced an account, albeit a much more modest one, of the emblems and devices similarly worn by the king and his courtiers at a cavalcade held in the Palais Cardinal in 1656 in which he reproduces and explains 25 individual devices worn by the various participants.[59]   Much the most lavish, however, is Charles Perrault's *Courses de testes et de bague, faites par le Roy et par les princes et seigneurs de sa cour en l'année M.DC.LXII*, in which all aspects of the spectacle are reproduced in full page and double opening engravings, as well as the individual devices which were such a key element in the iconography of the event. Associated with these spectacular celebratory events in Paris are the even more lavish festivities which took place at Versailles in the 1660s and 1670s, immortalised by the printed accounts which were published subsequently by the *Imprimerie royale*, the *Plaisirs de l'Isle enchantée*; the *Relation de la feste de Versailles*; and the *Divertissemens de Versailles*, marking the triumphant return of the French army from its successful conquest of the Franche Comté, all once again published in grandiose illustrated versions for wide dissemination as part of the royal propaganda campaign.[60]

A final area of emblematic interest which becomes much more dominant in the seventeenth century than had been the case in the sixteenth century is that of theory. In the sixteenth century, by and large, the writers of emblems were more interested in creating them than in theorising about them. At most brief reference was made in

---

de Madame sa soeur avec l'Infante et le Prince d'Espagne; & la description des machines, des habits, des armes, des livrées, des cartels & des devises des chevaliers qui y parurent. Ensemble les courses qui s'y firent à la quintaine & à la bague &c, in *Le vray theatre d'honneur et de chevalerie ou le miroir heroique de la noblesse, contenant les combats ou jeux sacrez des Grecs & des Romains, les triomphes, les tournois, les joustes, les pas, les emprises ou entreprises, les armes, les combats à la barriere, les carrosels, les courses de bague & de la quintaine, les machines, les chariots de triomphe, les cartels, les devises, les prix, les voeux, les sermons, les ceremonies, les statuts, les ordres, & autres magnificences & exercices des anciens nobles devant la paix. Avec le formulaire d'un tournoy tel qu'on le pourroit faire à present avec les armes dont les gentils-hommes se servent à la guerre. Le tout enrichy de figures en taille-douce sur les principales matieres. Dedié à Monseigneur le Cardinal Mazarin. Par Marc de Vulson, Sieur de la Colombiere*, Paris, A. Courbé, 1648, folio, 2 vols.

[59] H. de Gissey, *Les emblesmes et devises du Roy, des princes et seigneurs qui l'accompagnerent en la Calvacate Royale, et course de bague que Sa Majesté fit au Palais Cardinal 1656. Recueillies & dediees à son Altesse de Guise, par Gissey*, Paris, A. de Sommaville, 1657, 4°.

[60] *Les plaisirs de l'Isle enchantée. Course de bague; collation ornée de machines; comedie, meslée de danse et de musique; ballet du Palais d'Alcine; feu d'artifice; et autres festes galantes et magnifiques, faites par le Roy à Versailles le VII may M.DC.LXIV. et continuées plusieurs autres jours*, Paris, S. Mabre-Cramoisy for the *Imprimerie royale*, 1673, folio; *Relation de la feste de Versailles. Du 18 Juillet mil six cens soixante-huit*, Paris, S. Mabre-Cramoisy for the *Imprimerie royale*, 1679, folio; *Les divertissemens de Versailles donnez par le Roy à toute sa cour au retour de la conqueste de la Franche Comté en l'année M.DC.LXXIV*, Paris, S. Mabre-Cramoisy for the *Imprimerie royale*, 1676, folio. (Both these latter two works are reprinted in A. Félibien, *Les fêtes de Versailles. Chroniques de 1668 et 1674*, ed. Martin Meade, Paris, 1994.)

their prefaces to the antiquity of the genre, to its associations with hieroglyphics and
to the efficacy of the form as a morally edifying, or otherwise didactic tool. Emblems
and devices co-existed as two basically distinct forms (Paradin's non-moralising
collection of person-specific *devises heroiques*, in which each - verseless - device
reflects the character and aspirations of its owner, for example, contrasting with
Corrozet's clearly moralising collection of emblems, addressed to society as a whole,
and pointing out - in clearly expressed verse form - universal truths for mankind)
which could however on occasion be fused together, as in Montenay's *Emblemes ou
devises chrestiennes*. But in the seventeenth century much greater interest is focused
on theory, and on the elaboration of definitions of the nature of the device and the
emblem, and of distinctions between the two, and - in the case of devices in particular
- considerable pains are taken to draw up elaborate rules and conventions for their use,
which are curiously reminiscent, in their apparent inflexibility, of those of heraldry,
but paradoxically such apparently strict rules and conventions are in reality all too
often ignored by the actual practitioners of the genre, even by those who lay down the
theories, when they are themselves composing devices as opposed to theorising about
them. Just as the major seventeenth-century playwrights were subject to criticism for
failure to conform to the rules, so also writers of devices could face similar criticism
for breaking the rules - notably by that great theorist and watch-dog on emblems,
devices and allied matters, the redoubtable Jesuit Claude-François Ménestrier.

A number of different strands are thus identified, linking seventeenth-century
emblems with their sixteenth-century predecessors, but these are not, of course, totally
discreet strands. Inevitably there are overlaps between one and another. Ménestrier,
for example, is not just a theorist, but also a writer of innumerable devices.[61] He also
played a major role in organising numerous festivities, for which many of his own
devices were originally designed. Devices which have at one level an educational
function may also serve, at a further level, an additional purpose of flattering a royal
or otherwise notable personage. Nevertheless, we shall structure this study according
to the various strands here identified, looking first at generalist collections of emblems
and devices following on from the earlier tradition established by Alciato back in the
1530s, and focusing thereafter on the exploitation of emblems and devices for
educational purposes. From here we shall move onto a wider European stage with an
examination of the important influence in France of the Dutch input, in the
contrasting forms of erotic and sacred emblems emanating from such influential
writers as Cats, Vaenius, Heinsius, Hugo and Haeften. Thereafter we shall look at the
exploitation of the emblematic form first for religious purposes, and then in the very
different domain of glorification and flattery of the great, focusing in particular on
royal glorification. Finally, having seen the diversity of ways in which emblems and

---

[61]   Witness his *tour de force* of ingenuity in creating one hundred devices from the first 80
lines of Horace's *Ars poetica* as he explains in *La science et l'art des devises dressez sur de
nouvelles regles, avec six cens devises sur les principaux evenemens de la vie du Roy. Et quatre
cens devises sacrées, dont tous les mots sont tirés de l'Ecriture Sainte. Composées par le P.
Menestrier de la Compagnie de Jesus*, Paris, R.J.B. de la Caille, 1686, 8°, ẽ 6v. In the
preliminaries to this work he modestly remarks that he has produced 2000 devices:'Voila ce
qui a fait naître les deux mille devises que je donne.' (ã2v)

devices were exploited in reality we shall look, in our final chapter at the writings of
the theorists to see the extent to which these are or are not borne out by the evidence of
actual practice.

CHAPTER II

EMBLEMS AND EMBLEMATIC FABLES:
THE CONTINUATION OF THE GENERALIST TRADITION

While recognising that in the latter decades of the sixteenth century and in the seventeenth century the distinction between emblem and device, always somewhat ambiguous, becomes even more blurred, we shall nevertheless for organisational purposes, focus on 'emblems' in this chapter and 'devices' in the next. Devices were often sub-classified as either *héroiques* (relating to a particular person) or *morales* (more universal in their application)[1] and it is this latter category of *devises morales* which increasingly overlap with emblems, whose function had traditionally been a moralising or otherwise didactic one. While the heroic devices which were produced in the seventeenth century continued to remain in appearance like the familiar heroic devices of Giovio and Simeoni, *devises morales* in contrast become in many cases indistinguishable from emblems, as they find themselves increasingly accompanied by explanatory moral glosses in prose or in verse, or on occasion in both. It is perhaps in recognition of this blurring of frontiers between moral device and emblem - which even the great theorist Ménestrier acknowledges in his 1684 *Art des emblemes ou s'enseigne la morale*[2] - that we find an increasing number of later sixteenth-century and seventeenth-century writers hedging their bets and including both words in the titles or preliminaries to their collections, in the manner already pioneered by

---

[1] Pierre Le Moyne, for example, defines heroic devices as 'des éloges d'un mot & d'une figure; & ont esté faites pour des personnnes de condition & de vertu eminentes' and moral devices as 'des leçons abregées; & comme je l'ay oüy dire, des dogmes par extrait, & une philosophie en essences', indicating here clearly their similarity of intent with emblems (*Devises heroiques et morales*, 1649, A2v).

[2] *L'art des emblemes ou s'enseigne la morale par les figures de la fable, de l'histoire, & de la nature. Ouvrage rempli de pres de cinq cent figures. Par le P.C.F. Menestrier de la Compagnie de Jesus*, Paris, R.J.B. de la Caille, 1684, 8°. As he remarks in his introduction to the work: 'On a tellement confondu jusqu'icy les Emblêmes, les Devises, les Symboles, les Hieroglifiques, & les autres Images sçavantes, qui sont de differentes especes, qu'il n'est aucune d'elles à qui on ne donne encore tous les jours le nom d'Emblêmes.' (p.3)

Georgette de Montenay with her *Emblemes, ou devises chrestiennes*. Thus in the opening remarks of his 1621 *Devises royales* Adrian d'Amboise describes the work as 'Cet ouvrage de devises & emblemes',[3] while nearly thirty years later both Albert Flamen and Claude-François Ménestrier include both words in their titles of two very different works, Flamen's popular *Devises et emblesmes d'amour moralisez*, which went through several editions from 1648 onwards,[4] and Ménestrier's *Genereux exercices de la Majesté, ou la montre paisible de la valeur representée en devises & en emblesmes* of 1659, designed to keep Louis XIV amused when the weather was not appropriate for making war.[5] It is interesting to note that - in keeping with this trend - Claude Paradin's collection of devices which had originally been entitled simply *Devises heroiques* in the sixteenth-century editions, became renamed *Devises heroiques et emblemes* in the seventeenth-century editions, reflecting their increased potential for didacticism once each individual device became later accompanied by a substantial prose gloss.[6]

Despite the fact that the distinction between the two forms is thus in many cases no more than a difference of nomenclature, we shall nevertheless follow this distinction, examining in this chapter the extent to which the generalist tradition is preserved among those works which continue to be called emblems (including with these the cognate form of vernacular emblematic fables which enjoyed renewed popularity in the seventeenth century, and which were often, as had also been the case in the sixteenth century, produced by the same writers who produced collections of emblems[7]). In the following chapter we shall look at the equivalent continuing

---

[3]   *Devises royales par Adrian d'Amboise. Au Roy*, 1621, A1r.

[4]   *Devises et emblesmes d'amour moralisez. Gravez par Albert Flamen, peintre demeurant au Faux bourg S. Germain, rüe des Fossoyeurs*, Paris, Veuve Jean Rémy, 1648, 8°. After this first edition it was republished in Paris in 1650 by Samuel Margat; in 1653 and 1658 by Olivier de Varennes; in 1666 by Gervais Clouzier and in 1672 by Etienne Loyson. For details see *BFEB*, vol.1, nos 258-61.

[5]   Lyon, G. Barbier, 1659, 4°. Ménestrier explains the reason for writing this work in his dedication to Louis XIV: 'Sire, Pendant que les rigueurs d'une saison incommode ostent à vostre Majesté le moyen de cueillir des Palmes & des Lauriers sur les terres ennemies, elle n'a point de plus agreable repos, que la montre paisible des combats, & l'exercice de la valeur. L'ardeur qu'elle inspire à cette genereuse Compagnie dont elle est le Chef, est un spectacle digne d'arrester les yeux de tous les braves des premiers siecles, & l'addresse qu'elle fait paroistre dans le plus nobles des exercices est le charme secret qui attache la victoire à son parti, qui arreste la fortune à ses drappeaux.' (A3r)

[6]   For details see above, chapter 1, footnote 43.

[7]   See, for example, Jean Baudoin, who in addition to his popular *Recueil d'emblemes divers* which ran through several editions from 1638 onwards, also produced in 1649 a French version of Aesop (*Les fables d'Esope Phrygien. Illustrées de discours moraux, philosophiques & politiques. Nouvelle edition. Augmentée de beaucoup en divers endroits. Où sont adjoutées les fables de Philelphe. Avecque des reflexions morales, par J. Baudoin*, Paris, A. Courbé, 1649, 8°, 2 vols). This work was also popular enough to run through several editions, published in Paris by Courbé in 1659, in Rouen by Jean and David Berthelin in 1660 and 1670, and in Brussels by F. Foppens in 1669 and again without date (1680). A further Paris edition was published by C. Osmont in 1683. This same phenomenon was also seen in the sixteenth century when Corrozet, author of two emblem books, also produced a French version of

generalist tradition within the domain of devices, including in this latter chapter various ambiguously named works such as Flamen's *Devises et emblesmes d'amour moralisez*. The first part of this chapter on emblems will be devoted to an examination of the continuing interest in the seventeenth century in earlier generalist emblem books dating from the sixteenth century, beginning inevitably with Alciato's most influential work, after which the latter part of the chapter will be devoted to a consideration of the various generalist collections of emblems (and emblematic fables) which were produced *de novo* in the course of the seventeenth century.

The popularity of Alciato continued unabated in France well into the seventeenth century. Editions of his emblem book in both Latin and French (though strikingly more in Latin than in French) continued to flow from the printing presses in both Paris and Lyon, throughout the sixteenth century and into the seventeenth. The last French published edition (published in Lyon by the heirs of Guillaume Roville) dates from 1626,[8] but the de Tournes dynasty (by then operating in Geneva, however, rather than Lyon) continued to publish the work until 1639,[9] while elsewhere the work was also published across Europe in Antwerp, Leiden, Cologne and Padua, with editions of the Latin text being produced in Madrid well into the late eighteenth century.[10] (One of the unexplained mysteries of the history of emblem books is the absence of any edition published either in England or in English.[11]). Alciato's work

---

Aesop's fables in emblematic form: *Les fables du tresancien Esope phrigien premierement escriptes en Graec, et depuis mises en rithme Françoise*, Paris, D. Janot, 1542, 8°.

[8]   *And. Alciati emblemata, ad quae singula, praeter concinnas inscriptiones, imagines, ac caetera, quae ad ornatum & correctionem adhibita continebantur. Nunc recens adiecta sunt epimythia, quibus emblematum amplitudo & qua in iis dubia sunt, aut obscura, illustrantur*, Lyon, Heirs of G. Roville, 1626, 16°. A copy of this rare edition is to be found in the Folger Shakespeare Library, Washington. (For details see *BFEB*, vol.1, no.71.)

[9]   *Clariss. viri Dn. Andreae Alciati emblematum libri duo. Aucti & restituti, & perelegantibus figuris illustrati, cum succinctis commentariolis. Additus est index locupletissimus*, Geneva, Jean III de Tournes, 1639, 16°. (For details see *BFEB*, vol.1, no.72.)

[10]   *Emblemata v.c. Andreae Alciati Mediolanensis Iurisconsulti. Cum facili & compendiosa explicatione, qua obscura illustrantur, dubiaque omnia solvuntur, per Claudium Minoem Divionensem. Eiusdem Alciati vita. Editio novissima a mendis expurgata, priorique integritati restituta*, Madrid, O. de Mercede, 1749, 8°; *ibid.*, Madrid, P. Aznar, 1781, 8°. For details see Landwehr, *Romanic Emblem Books*, nos 104-5.

[11]   Geffrey Whitney's *Choice of Emblemes and Other Devises, for the most parte gathered out of sundrie writers, Englished and Moralized and divers newly devised by Geffrey Whitney* (Leiden, F. Raphelengius for C. Plantin, 1586, 4°) includes over 80 free adaptations of Alciato's emblems, while Thomas Palmer's manuscript *Two hundred poosees devysed by Thomas Palmer* (BL Sloane Ms. 3794) includes English verses added to woodcuts from Alciato and others. (For details see John Manning, 'Continental emblem books in sixteenth-century England: the evidence of Sloane Ms. 3749', *Emblematica*, 1,1, 1986, pp.1-11); likewise BL Add. Ms. 61822 (Philip Sidney, *Astrophel and Stella*, 1586-96) contains 4 leaves of *Pithie sentences and wise sayings* translated by William Briton. (For details see John Manning, 'An unedited and unpublished sixteenth-century English translation of some Alciato emblems...' *Emblematica*, 7,1, 1993, pp.181-8.) A seventeenth-century manuscript English translation of 91 of Alciato's emblems, earlier in the possession of Joseph Brooks Yates of Liverpool, is now

was thus readily available to the seventeenth-century reader. However the form (or rather forms) in which the work would have been available to him would have been very different from that which an early sixteenth-century reader of Alciato would have seen.

There is a striking contrast between the little 88-page sedecimo volume produced by Steyner in Augsburg in 1531 and the vast 1000-page quarto volume produced 90 years later in Padua by Paulo Tozzi in 1621 - and again in 1661 by Paulo Frambotti - in which Alciato's short emblems (more than doubled in number from the original 104 in the early Steyner edition) are totally submerged by the three weighty commentaries by Mignault, Sanchez and Pignorius which are all included in this version.[12] But reflecting the diversity of form in which Alciato's work rapidly came to be produced, after the earliest editions published by Steyner, it is interesting to note that at much the same time that Tozzi was producing such a massive, commentary-packed scholarly edition, the de Tournes dynasty, who had been responsible for publishing so many editions of the work in Lyon from 1547 onwards, were continuing to produce from their new base in Geneva, very different - much shorter, and much less scholarly - versions of the work in both French and Latin in sedecimo format right up until 1628 and 1639 respectively.[13] Even more strikingly the Roville dynasty -

---

housed in a private collection. (For details see K.-J. Höltgen, review of Andreas Alciatus, vol. 1, *The Latin Emblems* and vol.2, *Emblems in Translation*, in *Emblematica*, 1,2, 1986, pp.361-7, in which Höltgen describes briefly this manuscript whose whereabouts he does not reveal.) The lack of any published English version of Alciato until the 20th century must suggest that English readers were satisfied by the Latin and continental vernacular versions available to them. Only in 1985 did a full English translation by Virginia Callahan become available in Andreas Alciatus, vol.1, *The Latin Emblems. Indexes and Lists*, ed. P. Daly with V. Callahan, Toronto, 1985, followed by a further translation by Betty Knott in A. Alciato, *Emblemata D.A. Alciati, denuo ab ipso autore recognita, ac quae desiderabantur, imaginibus locupletata. Accesserunt nova aliquot ab autore emblemata, suis quoque eiconibus insignita*, Lyon, M. Bonhomme and G. Roville, 1550, 8°. (facsim. ed., J. Manning, Aldershot, 1996).

[12] *Andreae Alciati emblemata cum commentariis Claudii Minois I.C. Francisci Sanctii Brocensis, et notis Laurentii Pignorii Patavini novissima. Hac editione in continuam unius commentarii seriem congestis, in certas quasdam quasi classes dispositis, et plusquam dimidia parte auctis. Opera et vigiliis Ioannis Thuilii Mariaemontani Tirol. Phil. et Med. D. atque olim in Archiduc Friburg. Brisgoiae Universitate human. liter. professoris ordinarii. Opus copiosa sententiarum, apophthegmatum, adagiorum, fabularum, mythologiarum, hieroglyphicorum, nummorum picturarum et linguarum varietate instructum et exornatum: proinde omnibus antiquitatis et bonarum litterarum studiosis cum primis viris. Accesserunt in fine Federici Morelli professoris regii corollaria et monita, ad eadem emblemata. Cum indice triplici*, Padua, P. Tozzi, 1621, 4°; *ibid.*, Padua, P. Frambotti, 1661, 4°.

[13] *Les emblemes de M. Andre Alciat. Traduits en rime Françoise, enrichis de belles figures, & esclaircis par petits commentaires, lesquels expliquent les fables & histoires qui y sont contenues*, Geneva, Jean III de Tournes, 1628, 16°. (For details of the 1639 Latin edition see above, footnote 9.) In the de Tournes Latin editions from 1556 Alciato's emblems were accompanied only by the much shorter Stockhamer commentary to Book 1, while the French editions included no commentary at all. From 1614 Jean II de Tournes' own commentary on Book 2 was added to their Latin editions, and from 1615 a French version of that commentary (and of Stockhamer's commentary for Book 1) was also added to their French editions. For a

continuing the pattern which they had already established in the sixteenth century -
also provided in the early seventeenth century for very different types of reading public
by publishing variant versions of the work. In the sixteenth century, as well as
publishing the work in a range of different vernaculars, they had also from a very
early date produced editions of both the Latin and the French text with the short
Aneau commentary in either octavo or sedecimo editions, the former including
decorative borders around the emblems, and the latter not.[14] But when in 1600 (and
again in 1614) the heirs of Guillaume Roville embarked on a new venture by
publishing for a scholarly readership a much more substantial octavo edition of the
Latin text, running to almost 900 pages, in which the emblems were accompanied by
the much lengthier erudite Mignault commentary in place of the short Aneau
commentary,[15] they prudently also continued to cater at the same time for their other -
less erudite - reading public by producing in 1616 (and again in 1626) further short
sedecimo editions, running to less than 300 pages, of the old version with the brief
Aneau commentary.[16]

Alciato's emblem book indeed went through a large number of transformations
from the original very crude and simple form in which it was published in Augsburg

---

full analysis of the various de Tournes editions see *BFEB*, vol.1, pp.4-5.

[14] The earliest Roville/Bonhomme 16° Latin edition (*Emblemata Andreae Alciati
iurisconsulti clarissimi. Locorum communium ordine, ac indice, novisque posteriorum
eiconibus aucta*, Lyon, M. Bonhomme and G. Roville, 1548, 16°) did not include the Aneau
commentary, but this was incorporated into their 16° Latin editions from 1557 (*Omnia D. And.
Alciati emblemata ad quae singula, praeter concinnas acutasque inscriptiones, lepidas &
expressas imagines, ac caetera omnia quae prioribus nostris editionibus cum ad eorum
distinctionem, tum ad ornatum & correctionem adhibita continebantur. Nunc primùm
perelegantia persubtiliaque adiecta sunt epimythia, quibus emblematum amplitudo, &
quaecunque in iis dubia sunt aut obscura tanquam perspicuis illustrantur*, Lyon, M.
Bonhomme and G. Roville, 1557, 16°). Their earliest 16° French edition incorporating the
Aneau commentary was produced in 1558: *Toutes les emblemes de M. Andre Alciat, de
nouveau translatez en Françoys vers pour vers, jouxte la diction Latine. Et ordonnez en lieux
communs, avec sommaires inscriptions, schemes, & briefves expositions epimythiques, selon
l'allegorie naturelle, moralle, et historialle. Avec figures nouvelles appropriées aux derniers
emblemes envoyées par l'autheur, peu avant son decez, cy devant non imprimées*, Lyon, M.
Bonhomme and G. Roville, 1558, 16°. (For details see *BFEB*, vol.1, nos 21, 38 and 39.)

[15] *Andreae Alciati. v.c. emblemata. Cum Claudii Minois ad eadem commentariis & notis
posterioribus. Quibus emblematum omnium aperta origine, mens auctoris explicatur, &
obscura omnia dubiaque illustrantur*, Lyon, Heirs of G. Roville, 1600, 8°; *Andreae Alciati I.
v.c. emblemata. Elucidata doctissimis Claudii Minois commentariis: Quibus additae sunt
eiusdem auctoris notae posteriores... Postrema hac editione à mendis quamplurimis, quibus
superiores scatebant, omnia repurgata, atque in nitidiorem sensum reducta*, Lyon, Heirs of G.
Roville, 1614, 8°. (For details see *BFEB*, vol.1, nos 63 and 67.)

[16] *And. Alciati emblemata, ad quae singula, praeter concinnas inscriptiones, imagines, ac
caetera, quae ad ornatum & correctionem adhibita continebantur. Nunc recens adiecta sunt
epimythia, quibus emblematum amplitudo, & qua in iis dubia sunt, aut obscura, illustrantur*,
Lyon, Heirs of G. Roville, 1616, 16°; *ibid.*, Lyon, Heirs of G. Roville, 1626, 16°. (For details
see *BFEB*, vol.1, nos 69 and 71, and for an analysis of the various editions produced by the
Roville dynasty see pp.5-6.)

by Steyner in 1531. Its early transformation by the Paris publisher, Chrestien Wechel, into a work which was both aesthetically more pleasing and visually more accurate, as likewise the further significant textual change it underwent a few years later when the originally 'disordered' text of Alciato was arranged into a logical thematic order by Barthélemy Aneau and published by the Roville/Bonhomme partnership in Lyon, and the very different treatment of the original Latin text by its three sixteenth-century French translators, Jean Le Fevre in 1536, Barthélemy Aneau in 1549 and Claude Mignault in 1584,[17] are fully discussed in my earlier study of the sixteenth-century French emblem book.[18] But some of the many other modifications undergone by Alciato's work are less well known, including the evolution of the various commentaries which were added to the emblems at different stages and by different publishers in both the sixteenth and the seventeenth centuries.

The pattern of adding a commentary was begun by Aneau who, as well as translating and ordering Alciato's Latin verses, also supplied a very brief French commentary to accompany the editions of the work in French published in Lyon from 1549 by the Roville/Bonhomme partnership,[19] while - not to be outdone - Jean de Tournes, also in Lyon, introduced a rival, scholarly Latin commentary by Sebastian Stockhamer into his Latin editions published from 1556.[20] In his French editions, however, published from 1548,[21] for which he continued to use the old Le Fevre translation dating from 1536, he did not include any form of commentary. When the second wave of Latin emblems by Alciato was published in Venice in 1546,[22] de Tournes incorporated these in his Latin editions as 'Book 2', with Stockhamer's commentary covering both books. But since Le Fevre's 1536 translation predated the 1546 emblems, all the de Tournes editions of the text in French published in the sixteenth century continued to include only Book 1 (without any form of commentary), although his Latin editions included both books. In the seventeenth century, however, a significant, and little known change occurred: in 1614/15 (and again in 1628, and ultimately in 1639) new Latin and French editions were published under the de Tournes imprint, but no longer in Lyon, and no longer by the same Jean de Tournes.

---

[17] *Emblemata Andreae Alciati / C.clariss. Latinogallica, unà cum succinctis argumentis quibus emblematis cuiusque sententia explicatur. Ad calcem Alciati vita. Les emblemes Latin-François du Seigneur Andre Alciat excellent jurisconsulte. Avec argumens succincts pour entendre le sens de chaque embleme. En fin est la vie d'Alciat. La version Françoise non encore veuë cy devant,* Paris, J.Richer, 1584, 12°; *ibid.,* 1587, 12°.

[18] Saunders, *Sixteenth-Century French Emblem Book,* chapter 4.

[19] Their earliest Latin editions of the newly ordered text did not include any commentary. Only from 1557 onwards was a Latin version of Aneau's commentary included in the series of 16° editions which they published (1557, 1564, 1566, 1574, 1580 and 1588) and in the 8° editions of 1564 and 1566. (For details see *BFEB,* vol.1, nos 38, 44, 52, 56, 60, 43, 47.)

[20] *Clarissimi viri D. And. Alciati emblematum lib. II. Nuper adiectis Seb. Stockhameri Germ. in primum librum succinctis commentariolis,* Lyon, J. de Tournes and G.Gazeau, 1556, 16°. (De Tournes had been publishing Latin editions of the emblems, but without Stockhamer's commentary, since 1547.)

[21] *Les emblemes de M. Andre Alciat, traduits en ryme Françoise par Jean le Fevre,* Lyon, J. de Tournes, 1548, 16°.

[22] *Andreae Alciati emblematum libellus, nuper in lucem editus,* Venice, Aldus, 1546, 8°.

They were published in Cologny/Geneva by Jean de Tournes' son and grandson, Jean II and Jean III,[23] and for the first time a de Tournes edition of the French text included both Book 1 and Book 2, using the old Le Fevre translation for Book 1 but a new translation provided by the publisher himself for Book 2. Stockhamer's commentary on Book 1 (hitherto available only in Latin) was also here published for the first time in a French translation, while a new French commentary, again by Jean II himself, was included for Book 2 (translated from the original Latin commentary he had provided for Book 2 in a Latin edition which he had published in 1614, and again in 1628. This late 'new' translation and commentary, discussed by Alison Adams,[24] has until now largely escaped the notice of scholars.

Aneau's early commentary is very brief. Stockhamer's commentary and that of Jean II de Tournes are significantly longer than that of Aneau, but not to the extent that they overpower the actual emblems. Mignault also produced a Latin commentary which in its original form as published in an unillustrated version of the *Emblemata* in Paris by Denis du Pré in 1571[25] was similarly quite short. However when the Plantin Press began from 1573 to publish a series of Latin editions of Alciato with Mignault's commentary replacing that of Stockhamer, Mignault's originally modest commentary was expanded, reaching its ultimate full length in the 1581 edition.[26] In its shorter form it was available also in a French version to accompany the two editions of his French translation of the emblems published by Jean Richer in Paris in 1584 and again in 1587. In 1589 Richer together with François Gueffier and Etienne Vallet shared an edition of the Latin text accompanied by further *Notae posteriores* by Mignault, added on after the main text.[27] These were incorporated into the main commentary in their subsequent editions of 1602 and 1608, but in the Richer/Gueffier

[23] *Clariss. viri Dn. Andreae Alciati emblematum libri duo. Aucti & restituti & perelegantibus figuris illustrati. Cum succinctis commentariolis. Additus est index locupletissimus*, Cologny/Geneva, Jean II de Tournes, 1614, 16°; *ibid.*, Jean III de Tournes, 1628; *ibid.*, Jean III de Tournes, 1639; *Les emblemes de M. André Alciat, traduits en rime Françoise, enrichis de belles figures, & esclarcis par petits commentaires, lesquels expliquent les fables & histoires qui y sont contenues*, Cologny, Jean II de Tournes, 1615, 16°; *ibid.*, Geneva, Jean III de Tournes, 1628, 16°. (For details see *BFEB*, vol.1, nos 66, 72, 68.)
[24] 'The woodcuts of Alciato's Death emblems', *Emblematica*, 6,2, 1992 (1994), pp.391-7.
[25] *Omnia And. Alciati v.c. emblemata cum luculenta et facili ennaratione qua cuiusque emblematis origo, mensque autoris explicatur, et obscura vel dubia illustrantur. Per Claudium Minoem Divionensem. Excerpta omnia ex integris eiusdem in eadem emblemata commentariis*, Paris, D. du Pré, 1571, 4°.
[26] *Omnia Andreae Alciati v.c. emblemata. Adiectis commentariis et scholiis, in quibus emblematum fermè omnium aperta origine, mens auctoris explicatur, et obscura omnia, dubiaque illustrantur. Per Claudium Minoem Divionensem*, Antwerp, C. Plantin, 1573, 16°; *Omnia Andreae Alciati v.c .emblemata: cum commentariis quibus emblematum omnium aperta origine, mens auctoris explicatur, et obscura omnia dubiaque illustrantur. Per Claudium Minoem Divionensem. Editio tertia aliis multo locupletior*, Antwerp, C. Plantin, 1581, 8°.
[27] *Omnia Andreae Alciati v.c. emblemata, cum commentariis, quibus emblematum aperta origine mens auctoris explicatur, & obscura omnia dubiaque illustrantur. Adiectae ad calcem notae posteriores. Per Claud. Minoem, Iurisc.*, Paris, J. Richer, F. Gueffier and E.Vallet, 1589, 8°.

edition of 1618 yet more new commentary (this time provided by Fédéric Morel) was added.[28] Interestingly the Roville heirs in Lyon - like the successors of Jean de Tournes at much the same time, though these were no longer in Lyon but rather in Geneva and Cologny - undertook new Latin editions of Alciato in the early seventeenth century, abandoning the Aneau commentary that had been used in earlier Roville/Bonhomme editions since 1549 (French editions) and 1550 (Latin editions), and replacing this with the full Mignault commentary as derived from the Plantin editions in 1600, but adding to it in 1614 the further supplement of *Notae posteriores* in imitation of the 1589 Richer/Gueffier/Vallet edition.[29] In all these various editions containing the full-length Mignault commentary - whether in French or Latin - each emblem is accompanied by several pages of detailed commentary tracing sources, analysing implications and interpretations, and with marginal notes in addition, with the result that the emblem book - although still a small-format book - is a very solid 800-page octavo volume, almost unrecognisable as being the same work as the modest little 44-page small-octavo edition produced by Steyner half a century earlier. Even more striking, however, is its subsequent transformation in the seventeenth century at the hands of an Italian publisher, Paulo Tozzi in Padua, into a massive 1000-page quarto critical edition in which Alciato's short verses are accompanied not by just one weighty commentary, but by three (by Mignault, Sanchez and Pignorius). In this extreme form it resembles more an encyclopedia than anything which we would normally recognise as an emblem book.

The 1626 edition published in Lyon by the Roville heirs marks the last edition of Alciato to be produced in France. Jean III de Tournes published the last edition of the work to emanate from his family presses (in Latin) in 1639, but this, like his earlier seventeenth-century editions was in Geneva rather than France. Elsewhere in Europe, however (with the notable exception of Germany where the last edition was published as early as 1583),[30] editions of Alciato continued to be published beyond 1639, but fairly sporadically: in Padua Tozzi published his last edition in 1626, but a further edition was produced in Padua in 1661 by P. Frambotti, based on Tozzi's 1621 edition.[31] In the Low Countries the Plantin tradition continued into the seventeenth century with Latin editions being published in Leiden by F. Raphelengius in 1591, 1599, 1608, 1610 and in Antwerp by B. Moretus in 1622 and again in 1648. Even at the very end of the seventeenth century and running into the eighteenth century we find editions (again of the Latin text) being published by H. and C. Verdussen in

---

[28] *Omnia Andreae Alciati v.c. emblemata, cum commentariis, quibus emblematum detecta origine dubia omnia, et obscura illustrantur. Per Claud. Minoem I.C. Accesserunt huic editioni Fed. Morelli Profess. Reg. decani corollaria et monita*, Paris, J. Richer for F. Gueffier, 1618, 8°.
[29] See above, footnote 15.
[30] *Emblemata Andreae Alciati I.C. clariss. Postremo ab autore recognita, vivisque imaginibus artificiosissime illustrata. Adiuncta sunt epimythia quibus, quae obscuriora videbantur sunt declarata*, Frankfurt, N. Bassee, 1583, 8°. For details of editions published in Germany see Landwehr, *German Emblem Books*.
[31] For details of 17th-century Italian editions see Landwehr, *Romanic Emblem Books*, nos 98-100, 103.

Antwerp in 1692 and again in 1715.[32] In Spain the tradition continued even longer: editions of Alciato's Latin text with commentary in Spanish by Diego Lopez were published in Najera in 1615, and in Valencia by G.Vilagrasa in 1655 and 1670, and by Francisco Duarte in 1684, while well into the eighteenth century two editions of the Latin text accompanied by Mignault's Latin commentary were published in Madrid, the first by O. de Mercede in 1749, and the second by P. Aznar in 1781.[33]

Alciato's pioneering emblem book thus clearly enjoyed enduring popularity across Europe long after the death of its author, although it is significant that the last date of its publication in France (and in Geneva) is markedly earlier than in the Netherlands, Italy and Spain. It is also significant that in the case of all these late editions published in the Netherlands, Italy and Spain it is the Latin version which is reproduced rather than a vernacular text. In France also we find the same pattern, with Latin editions being markedly more favoured. After the publication by Jean Richer in Paris in 1584 and 1587 of a bilingual Latin/French version of the text accompanied by a French translation of the shorter version of Mignault's commentary, all other editions published thereafter in France (or Geneva) in the latter part of the sixteenth century, and the seventeenth century, with the sole exception of the two little sedecimo editions of Le Fevre's original translation produced by Jean II de Tournes in 1615, and Jean III de Tournes in 1628, were likewise in Latin. What is particularly interesting about the evolution of Alciato's emblem book over the century following its initial publication, however, is the extent to which in the various Latin editions (and to a slightly lesser extent in the French editions also) it is progressively transformed from a small-format collection of little epigrams accompanied by crude woodcut illustrations into a larger-format, and much more weighty compilation, in which the original short epigrams, now adorned by highly detailed and ornate copper engravings, and also arranged in encyclopedic form according to theme, are furthermore also dominated by ever more substantial passages of erudite commentary, reaching its height of prolixity in Sozzi's lengthy version with its triple commentary. Having said which, however, it is interesting to note that this ultimate version was published in Italy rather than in France, where - as we have seen - an alternative - reverse - trend was also developing alongside the main trend for editions accompanied by learned commentaries, as manifested in the little sedecimo editions published in the seventeenth century in both Latin and French by the later members of the de Tournes dynasty, and similarly (though in Latin only) by the later members of the Roville dynasty, all contrasting dramatically with the massive Tozzi quarto edition.

Just as no native French emblem book enjoyed anything like the popularity of that of Alciato in the sixteenth century, so also none of them enjoyed the same continuing popularity into the seventeenth century. The very earliest French emblem book, La Perrière's *Theatre*, which attracted enough European interest to justify three editions in a Dutch translation published in Antwerp in 1554, 1556, and 1564 and - rather later - two editions in an English translation published in London in 1593 (?) and

---

[32] For details of editions published in the Low Countries see Landwehr, *Dutch Emblem Books*, nos 8-25.

[33] For details of editions published in Spain see Landwehr, *Romanic Emblem Books*, nos 104-5, 487-90.

1614,[34] is interestingly also the one which enjoyed the most enduring popularity in France, running through a number of editions up to nearly the end of the sixteenth century, but not - in that form, at least - extending into the seventeenth century. As well as the four produced by its first publisher, Denis Janot, other editions were also published in Paris by Janot's successor, Etienne Groulleau in 1548 and 1551, while Jean de Tournes in Lyon published a first edition of the work in 1545, followed by further editions in 1546, 1549 and 1553, and his successor, Jean II de Tournes, published a final edition as late as 1583.[35] This was the last published edition of the *Theatre* as such, but some emblems from the work did, however, continue to be published well into the seventeenth century, even later than the last edition of Alciato, but not under their own name. In 1641 Gilles Corrozet's descendant, Jean Corrozet, published in Paris a small and very old-fashioned looking volume of *Emblemes ou preceptes moraux* - dedicated, interestingly, to the three-year old future Louis XIV - which he describes as being the work of his famous ancestor.[36] This attribution is not strictly accurate in fact, since the work - which is an anthology of moralising verses such as his ancestor did indeed love to produce - also includes (among other things) a selection of emblems from La Perrière's *Theatre*. In this very late version there are no woodcut figures accompanying the verses, but conversely they do have moralising titles such as were not included in the earlier Paris editions published by Janot and Groulleau.[37]

Curiously Jean Corrozet does not include in this seventeenth-century anthology any emblems from Corrozet's best known emblem book, the *Hecatomgraphie*, although he does include together with the *Theatre* emblems (but again without

---

[34] *Tpalays der gheleerder ingienen oft der constiger gheesten; inhoudende hondert morale figueren*, Antwerp, Widow J. van Liesfeldt, 1554, 8°; *ibid.*, 1556 and *ibid.*, H van Liesfeldt, 1564. *The theater of fine devices, containing an hundred morall emblemes: first penned in French by Guillaume de la Perriere, and translated into English by Thomas Combe*, London, R. Field, 1593, 16°; *ibid.*, 1614, 16°.

[35] The text in all the de Tournes editions is significantly different from the Janot/Groulleau version in that all the emblems are here accompanied by a moral title whereas in La Perrière's original version of the work the emblems comprised simply woodcut figure and verse. It is the de Tournes version with titles which is used as the basis for the Dutch and English versions. In addition to all these editions, Denis de Harsy in Lyon also published an undated and unillustrated edition of the *Theatre*, as he did also of Alciato's emblems in the Le Fevre French translation, and of Corrozet's *Hecatomgraphie*.

[36] *Emblemes ou preceptes moraulx. Tirez des escrits de feu Gilles Corrozet, non encore imprimez. A Monseigneur le Dauphin*, Paris, J. Corrozet, 1641, 8°.

[37] Titles were added to the emblems in the later editions by de Tournes, but interestingly the titles introduced here, by Jean Corrozet, although similar, are not the same as those of the de Tournes editions. For example in the 1545 de Tournes edition emblem 56, depicting the crow risking death by swallowing an excessively large worm, is accompanied by the title *Par trop manger, plus meurent, que par glaive*, whereas in this 1641 Corrozet edition the title is *Le trop manger conduit l'homme à la* mort (C2r); in the 1545 de Tournes edition emblem 82, depicting the tree being strangled by the ivy which it supports, is accompanied by the title *Ingratitude on doibt fuyr grandement*, whereas in this 1641 Corrozet edition the title is *Qui est ingrat sans raison* (C4r).

illustration) emblems from his much less well-known, second collection (entitled simply *Emblemes*, and appended to his 1544 translation of the *Tableau de Cebes de Thebes*). Paradoxically a similar compilation of such moralising verses from a variety of sources, which had been published by Etienne Groulleau at a much earlier date in the mid sixteenth century under the archaic title, *Le jardin d'honneur*, and which was popular enough to run through several editions,[38] did include a selection from the *Hecatomgraphie*, together with a selection from the *Theatre*, but none in this case from the *Emblemes*. Although the full version of the *Hecatomgraphie* itself (which was the second French emblem book to be written) was popular enough to run through several editions in the mid sixteenth century, it clearly did not enjoy the same enduring success within France as the *Theatre*, nor yet did it attract the attention of publishers elsewhere in Europe in the way that the *Theatre* did. Although it was published in Lyon and Valence as well as Paris, it was never published outside France or in any language other than French, and after the 1550s no further edition at all was published even in France.[39]

   Although a further wave of emblem books were published in France in the course of the 1550s, none of these was as popular, even in the sixteenth century, as the *Theatre* and *Hecatomgraphie*, and none continued to be published into the seventeenth century. In striking contrast to his earlier, vernacular *Theatre*, La Perrière's second emblem book, the *Morosophie*, which was bilingual, clearly did not appeal to the market to the same extent. Although two editions of the work were

---

[38] *Le jardin d'honneur, contenant plusieurs apologies, proverbes, & ditz moraux, avec les histoires & figures. Aussi y sont ajoustez plusieurs ballades, rondeaux, dixains, huitains & trioletz fort joyeux. Reveu & corrigé outre les precedantes impressions*, Paris, E. Groulleau, 1550, 16°; *ibid.*, 1555 and 1559. Lachèvre also cites editions dating from 1548 and 1549 of which no copy has been located, and similarly an edition published in Rouen 1545 by Jean Petit for Robert and Jean Dugort of which no copy has been located. (F. Lachèvre, *Bibliographie des recueils collectifs de poésies du XVIe siècle*, Paris, 1922, pp.77-8). For details see *BFEB*, vol.1, nos 345-50.

[39] Its original Paris publisher, Denis Janot, produced editions in 1540, 1541, 1543 and 1543 (1544?), and his successor Etienne Groulleau published a further edition in 1548. It was also published under a new title in Lyon in 1548 by Claude de la Ville, and a year later in 1549 in Valence by Philibert Rollet and Barthélemy Frain for Claude de la Ville. A further edition was published in Lyon two years later by Balthazar Arnoullet, in 1551, under a slight variant of the Claude de la Ville title, but this was to be the last edition of the work. After this date, unlike the *Theatre*, no more editions of the *Hecatomgraphie* appeared in any form. Although the full work was never translated into any other language, it is interesting to note that in both the 1548 and 1549 Claude de la Ville editions, as also in the Arnoullet edition which follows their pattern, a token Italian element is introduced, in that although the main text remains in French, the titles to each emblem are given not just in French but also in Italian - a fact noted proudly in the title: *La fleur des sentences certaines, apophthegmes, et stratagemes, tant des anciens, que des modernes, enrichy de figures, & sommaires Françoys & Italiens, propres à chascune sentence* (Lyon, C. de la Ville, 1548, 16°; *ibid.*, Valence, P. Rollet and B. Frain for C. de la Ville, 1549, 16° ; *La fleur des sentences moralles, extraictes tant des anciens que des modernes*, Lyon, B. Arnoullet, 1551, 16°).

published, both bearing the date 1553, no other edition was produced thereafter.[40]
Neither Guéroult's 1550 *Premier livre des emblemes* nor Coustau's Latin *Pegma* of
1555 were subsequently republished, although the French version of the *Pegma* (also
first published in 1555) did run to one further edition in 1560, but none thereafter.
Aneau's *Picta poesis/Imagination poetique* of 1552 aroused more enduring interest,
with both versions running to a second edition in 1556, and a further edition of the
Latin version (but not the French) being produced in the 1560s.[41]   After this date,
however, no further edition was produced, although evidence from two separate copies
of the 1563/64 Latin edition, in which the date on the title page has been changed by
hand from 1564 to a date in the early seventeenth century, does suggest that copies of
this mid sixteenth-century work were still available on the market at that much later
date.[42] Overall, however, it cannot be argued, on the basis of their publishing history,
that the native French emblem books produced in the 1550s continued to arouse
interest into the seventeenth century in the way in which Alciato's emblem book did,
or to a much lesser extent, La Perrière's *Theatre* also.

Among the native French produced emblem books, those of Montenay and Bèze
alone are the exceptions which did indeed continue to be popular enough to be
republished into the seventeenth century, but it must be remembered first that both
their emblem books are significantly later in date than the other French emblem books
mentioned here, and second that it was not basically in France that they were mainly
published. Although Montenay's emblem book did indeed continue to be published in
several editions well into the seventeenth century, after its first publication in Lyon in
the late sixteenth century, only one of the subsequent editions was published in France
(in La Rochelle). The others were all published elsewhere in Europe - in Zurich,
Heidelberg and Frankfurt.[43] Similarly in the case of Bèze, whose short collection of
emblems was published first in Latin in 1580 and then in French the following year,
as an addendum to his *Icones* and *Vrais pourtraits*, and thereafter in a number of
Latin editions of his *Poëmata varia*, none of these were published in France, but
rather in Geneva, by Jean de Laon in the case of the *Icones* and *Vrais pourtraits* and
by Jacob Stoer in the case of the *Poëmata varia*.[44]

Of the few French emblem books which were published in France in the last
decades of the sixteenth century, none was popular enough to survive into
seventeenth-century editions. Among his many collections of illustrated epigrammatic

---

[40]   The decorative borders around the emblems appear in a different order in the two editions,
but - unlike the *Theatre* which underwent significant textual modification in later editions -
textual differences in the two editions of the *Morosophie* are very minor.

[41]   Both the French and the Latin versions were republished in 1556 by their original
publisher, Macé Bonhomme, but additionally the Latin version ran through two issues of a
further edition published in 1563/1564 by Bonhomme for Charles and Louis Pesnot.

[42]   The two copies are in the Bodleian and John Rylands Library, Manchester. I am grateful to
Stephen Rawles for drawing this fact to my attention.

[43]   For details see above, chapter 1, footnote 3.

[44]   *Theodori Bezae Vezelii poëmata varia. Sylvae. Elegiae. Epitaphia. Epigrammata. Icones.
Emblemata. Cato Censorius. Omnia ab ipso auctore in unum nunc corpus collecta &
recognita*, Geneva, J. Stoer, 1597/8, 4°; *ibid.*, 1599; *ibid.*, 1614.

works, Jean-Jacques Boissard published in the last two decades of the sixteenth century two quite separate collections of Latin emblems, both of which were also published in versions with a French text, but although some of Boissard's other works continued to be published into the seventeenth century, this was not the case with either of his two emblem books. Boissard's first collection of 4-line Latin emblems, each accompanied by a French sonnet by Pierre Joly, was first published in Metz in 1584, and again four years later in 1588.[45] His second emblem book of 1593 was not originally published in France, but rather in Frankfurt, with a title which is confusingly similar to that of the first collection, *Iani Iacobi Boissardi Vesuntini emblematum liber. Ipsa emblemata ab auctore delineata: a Theorodo de Bry sculpta, & nunc recens in lucem edita*,[46] but two years later, in 1595, a new version of the text was published not in Frankfurt but in his home town of Metz,[47] with commentaries in French and with 8-line French verses replacing the original 4-line Latin verses. But although both volumes of his emblems were popular enough to warrant a second edition, in neither case did demand for them extend into the seventeenth century. Even more so is this true in the case of another provincial emblem writer, Jean Mercier, who published a little collection of 50 Latin emblems in Bourges in 1592.[48] Mercier's emblem book - like that of Guillaume Guéroult forty years earlier - did not extend even to one further edition in its own century, far less in the seventeenth

---

[45]   *Iani Iacobi Boissardi Vesuntini emblemata cum tetrastichis latinis*, Metz, J. Aubry, n.d. (1584), 4° obl.; *Iani Iacobi Boissardi Vesuntini emblematum liber. Emblemes Latins de I.I. Boissard, avec l'interpretation Françoise du I. Pierre Joly Messin*, Metz, J. Aubry and A. Faber, 1588, 4°.

[46]   The similarity between the titles of Boissard's two emblem books (the first published in Metz in 1584 and 1588, and the second published in Frankfurt in 1593 and Metz in 1595) has led scholars to confuse the two works and sometimes to describe them as one single work, although they are quite different. John Landwehr does this. in his bibliography of German emblem books (no.133) and more recently Anne-Elisabeth Spica in the bibliography of her *Symbolique humaniste et emblématique. L'évolution et les genres (1580-1700)*, p.545.

[47]   Frankfurt, Th. de Bry, 1593, 4°; *Emblemes de I.I. Boissard nouvellement mis de Latin en françois par Pierre Joly Cons. du Roy, & son proc. general aux gouvernemens Messin & Verdunois. Le tout taillé en cuivre & mis en lumiere par Theodore de Bry*, Metz, A. Faber, 1595, 4°. It is interesting that the 51 Latin verses at least of the second collection of emblems, which did not see the light of day in published emblematic form until 1593, were already published in unillustrated form, together with the 41 Latin verses of the first emblem book as early as 1587, together with a further 64 'naked' emblems under the title *Tetrasticha in emblemata Iani Iacobi Boissardi Vesuntini* (Metz, A. Faber, 1587, 8°). These same 156 plain Latin *tetrasticha* are also found in a new form, transformed into complete emblems, accompanied by illustrations, and by a French prose commentary in an undated manuscript in the Bibliothèque de l'Institut in Paris. It has been suggested that this manuscript may indeed be the work of Boissard himself. See H. Wischermann, 'Ein Emblembuchmanuskript von Jean-Jacques Boissard', *Archiv für Geschichte des Buchwesens*, 14, 1974, pp.433-64; see also Chatelain, no. 92. Chatelain notes that some of the emblems in the manuscript are to be found in the two printed collections of emblems, but he does not explain that the remainder of the manuscript emblems, which indeed he suggests are 'inédits', are actually published (together with all the others in the manuscript) in the 1587 edition of the *Tetrasticha*.

[48]   *Io. Mercerii I.C. emblemata*, Bourges, no publisher, 1592, 4°.

century.

There is, therefore, an almost total lack of direct continuity between the sixteenth and the seventeenth century in France in the publication of emblem books. Those that do continue to be published into the seventeenth century tend largely to be published elsewhere in Europe, rather than in France itself. The Roville heirs continued to publish Alciato in Lyon until 1626, and the Richer/Gueffier/Vallet consortium likewise continued to publish him in Paris until 1618, but the later de Tournes editions (the last of which dates from 1639) were all published in Geneva. Bèze was published throughout in Geneva and of the various later editions of Montenay, one alone was published in France, the remainder being published in Germany or Switzerland. Of the earlier native French emblem books none continued to be published in France under its own name into the seventeenth century. Only La Perrière's *Theatre* was published in England, but under the name of its translator, Thomas Combe, while some *Theatre* emblems together with the Corrozet *Emblemes* did appear in print as late as 1641, but only anonymously, and mixed in among other verses in an anthology of generally moralising verses, and certainly not obviously recognisable for what they actually were.

Yet although we do not find much emblematic continuity from the sixteenth century into the seventeenth century in the sense of actual sixteenth-century works continuing to be published in the seventeenth century, there is nevertheless a significant degree of continuity of style. Certainly the old familiar authors from the sixteenth century do not by and large continue to appear in print in the seventeenth century, but many of the old familiar patterns which they established in their emblem books do continue to feature in seventeenth-century emblem books in France: stylistically there is no total or immediate change of direction. Generalist emblem books continued to be produced within France in the seventeenth century, both in Latin and in French. Typical examples of this continuing tradition might be Antoine La Faye's non-illustrated collection of Latin *Emblemata et epigrammata miscellanea* of 1610,[49] or Jean Baudoin's lengthy, and extremely popular, vernacular collection of emblems, the *Recueil d'emblemes divers*, which was first published as a two-volume work in 1638/39, and thereafter in a number of further editions until 1698, expanding from two to three volumes from 1685 onwards. Both these two collections of emblems follow the generalist tradition, established early in the sixteenth century by La Perrière and Corrozet, in imitation of Alciato, perpetuated in the 1550s by writers such as Aneau, Guéroult and Coustau, and still later, at the end of the sixteenth century, by Boissard and Mercier. The full title to Baudoin's work, in which it is specifically described as 'tirez de divers autheurs, anciens et modernes', reflects clearly the extent to which it represents a continuation of an already existing emblematic pattern, and this is further confirmed by Baudoin's acknowledgement in his preface of his debt to earlier emblem writers, a debt which - interestingly - is not exclusively to Alciato and the earlier French emblem writers, but reflects also the growing influence on French emblems of other European writers. Certainly Baudoin singles Alciato out for

---

[49]   *Emblemata et epigrammata miscellanea selecta ex stromatis peripateticis Antonii Fayi*, Geneva, P. and J. Chouet, 1610, 8°.

particular emphasis, but he also cites the German Bruck-Angermundt and the Spanish Covarrubias, indicating thereby the increasingly international character of emblem books:

> J'advoüe neantmoins, qu'en tout cét ouvrage je me suis particulierement servy d'Alciat, qui a excellé sur tous les autres en ce genre d'escrire; & des commentaires Latins du docte Minos. J'en ay usé de mesme des Observations morales & politiques de Jacques Bruck, & de Covarruvias, l'un Aleman, & l'autre Espagnol; si bien que de tous leurs emblemes ensemble, j'ay composé ce volume; auquel j'en adjousteray possible un second, si je voy que celuy-cy vous soit agreable.   (Baudoin, *Recueil d'emblemes*, 1638, ẽ 7v-8r)

Other seventeenth-century emblem writers also continuing the generalist tradition do not spell out so explicitly as Baudoin the extent of their debt to earlier emblem writers, but this debt is nevertheless very apparent both in the themes of their emblems, and in the moralities which they derive from them, even though they do not directly acknowledge the fact.

Likewise indicative of the growing trend towards European cross-fertilisation in the domain of emblem literature are the number of other generalist emblem books which were published abroad (particularly in Germany) but in the French language, and designed to cater specifically for the French reading market, in much the same way that the same process had happened in reverse in the previous century, with emblem books being produced within France in a variety of other vernaculars, in addition to French and Latin, in order to cater for the needs of readers in other European countries. Of such a kind is Andreas Friedrich's collection of emblems. This work which was originally composed in German, was, however, published in Frankfurt, by Jennis, in a French version in 1617, the same year that the original German text was published. That copies of this edition in French were intended for distribution in France is evident from the fact that in some copies a patch is placed over the original German imprint on the title page, substituting for it, or adding to it, either a Paris or a Lyon address.[50] In much the same way as Friedrich's collection of emblems, and at much the same date, Gabriel Rollenhagen's originally Latin *Nucleus emblematum* and *Centuria secunda* were also published in a French version designed for the French market: editions of the work were published in Germany and in the Low Countries in 1611 and 1613 with the original, wholly engraved, Latin emblems accompanied by a supplementary letterpress French text in order to make them accessible to the French reading public.[51] Yet again, when Jacob à Bruck-

---

[50]   *Emblemes nouveaux: esquels le cours de ce monde est depeint et representé par certaines figures, desquelles le sens est expliqué par rimes...Premierement en Allemand par André Frideric, & maintenant en François ...Mis en lumiere par Jaques de Zettre.* See above, chapter 1, footnote 7. Curiously, although the title of the French version is given in the vernacular (for the obvious reason of making it apparent that the text is in French) the title of the original German version is, in the first part at least, in Latin: *Emblemata nova, das ist New Bilderbuch...durch Andreas Friedrichen*, Frankfurt, J. de Zetter, 1617, 4°.

[51]   *Nucleus emblematum selectissimorum, quae Itali vulgo impresas vocant privata industria*

Angermundt's wholly engraved collection of Latin *Emblemata moralia & bellica* was published in Strasbourg by Jacob van Heyden in 1615 and 1616, some copies of the work were also produced which included - for the same reason - a supplementary letterpress text of the emblems in French.[52] It is variant versions such as these, which were produced elsewhere in Europe but tailored to the needs of a French reading public, which are of particular relevance here, though French readers were not, of course, exclusively privileged in this respect. Copies of Bruck-Angermundt's work were also similarly produced with an equivalent supplementary letterpress text in German (and some copies indeed contain both the French and the German supplement), and the publisher responsible for the French version of Rollenhagen also made available, a few years later, an equivalent vernacular version of the *Nucleus emblematum* and *Centuria secunda* to cater for the needs of a Dutch reading public.[53]

The late sixteenth-century emblem books of Jean-Jacques Boissard and Jean Mercier are particularly interesting works in the extent to which they can be seen as a representing a transitional stage, poised between the earlier sixteenth-century French emblem books which preceded them, and the seventeenth-century emblem books which followed them. In their visual appearance, with their decorative copperplate engravings, both Boissard's two emblem books look forward to the seventeenth century by which time copperplate engraving had taken over from the woodcut illustrations which characterised the earlier sixteenth-century French emblem book. Mercier's 1592 emblem book published in Bourges also points forward in this respect. Yet in their content and in the moral lessons they express, both have strong affinities with the earlier traditions. Although Boissard's second collection of emblems is intended to serve as a sequel to the first, as he explains in his dedication of it to Catherine de Heu,[54] and both basically follow the tripartite pattern of the early editions

---

studio singulari, undique conquisitus, non paucis venustis inventionibus auctus, additis carminibus illustratus. A Gabriele Rollenhagio Magdeburgense/Les emblemes de maistre Gabriel Rollenhague, mis en vers francois par un professeur de la langue françoise a Colongne, Cologne, S. Erffens, and Arnhem, J. Jansson, 1611, 4°; *Gabrielis Rollenhagii selectorum emblematum centuria secunda* (*La seconde centurie des emblemes du Sr Gabriel Rollenhague Magdeburgois, paraphrastiquement mise en ryme francoyse. Par T.D.L.S.D.O.*), Utrecht, C. de Passe, and Arnhem, J. Jansson, 1613, 4°. In several cases the first and the second century are found bound together in a single volume. In not all cases do both centuries include the French translation.

[52] *Iacobi à Bruck Angermundt cogn. sil. emblemata moralia & bellica. Nunc recens in lucem edita / Les emblemes moraulx et militaires du sieur Jacob de Bruck Angermundt. Nouvellement mis en lumiere,* Strasbourg, J. van der Heyden, 1615, 4°.

[53] For details of the French and German versions of the *Emblemata moralia et bellica* see *BFEB,* vol.1, no.130. For details of the Dutch version of Rollenhagen's *Nucleus emblematum* and *Centuria secunda* (*Emblemata vollsinnighe uytbeelsels by Gabrielem Rollenhagius uyt andere versamelt en vermeerdert met syn eygene sinrijcke vindingen gestelt in Nederduytsche rijme door Zacharias Heyns,* Arnhem, J. Jansson, 1615/17, 4°) see Landwehr, *Dutch Emblem Books,* no.574.

[54] 'Madame, d'autant que je me suis apperceu par plusieurs fois, que, comme estes addonnee à la speculation des choses qui appartiennent à l'instruction de l'ame, avez prins pleisir à la lecture d'un petit livret d'Emblemes que je mis en lumiere il y a environ quatre ans. J'ay

of Alciato's emblem book, there are some structural differences between the first
collection and the second, reflecting the ever increasing diversity of acceptable
practice within the form, and indeed reflecting the diverse forms in which Alciato's
emblem book itself came to be published. While Boissard's first collection includes no
commentary to accompany the emblems in the manner of the earliest editions of
Alciato, the second includes for each emblem a short prose commentary in the manner
of the later Alciato editions. Similarly whereas the emblems in the first collection
follow no thematic order, as in the early editions of Alciato, those in the second
collection are loosely grouped according to theme, again in the manner of the later
editions, although in Boissard's work this thematic arrangement is achieved more
informally than had been the case with the thematic structure imposed on Alciato's
emblems from 1548. Emblems on cognate themes such as *virtus*, *amicitia*, *invidia*,
voluptas etcetera are in Boissard's collection simply all grouped together, but without
any formal division of the text into separate named sections according to topic as was
the case with the thematically arranged editions of Alciato.

Not only do Boissard's emblems follow a traditional form in terms of structure,
but also in theme. In both his collections familiar emblematic figures recur, such as
Fortune who appears in both collections. In the earlier collection with her attributes of
bald head and long forelock she is accompanied by one man bearing a whip and
another pulling her by the forelock, with the title *A tergo calva est* and
complementary verse:

> Arripe, se quoties offert occasio: calva est
>   A tergo: & volucri labitur illa pede.
> Pone sequens torto sequitur Metanoea flagello:
>   Et tantum ignavis poena dolenda venit.
>   (Boissard, *Emblematum liber/Emblemes latins*, 1588, H3r)

while in the later collection she figures again in *Nulli prestat velox Fortuna fidem*, in
which the engraving depicting her with her other traditional attributes of wheel, ball
and floating veil, offering a crown and a bag of gold to two men is accompanied by the
verse:

> Dum nobis fortuna favet, blanditur, & offert
>   Subsidium, nobis est metuenda magis.
> Illiusque bonis, dum arridet laeta, fruamur:
>   Hanc reperire quidem, non retinere licet.
>   (Boissard, *Emblematum liber*, 1593, O3r)

She appears once again in this same collection, once more in familiar guise, naked
and holding the sail of the ship in which she stands, together with symbols of wisdom,

---

estimé estre de mon devoir...d'en recuillir un autre volume, les pourtrais desquels j'ay
interpreté par diverses sentences, appropriees à la matiere de laquelle traictent lesdits
Emblemes, extraictes de divers autheurs Philosophes & Poëtes.' (1593 ed., A2r) Here again, as
with Baudoin, we find Boissard indicating his debt to earlier writers.

in *Expers fortunae est sapientia* with the explanatory verse:

> Fortuna dubia haud vehitur sapientia cymba;
>   Nec vanis fulta est indiga divitiis.
> Sed cura vigili & studio solerte parata,
>   In varia rerum cognitione sedet. (Boissard, *Emblematum liber*, 1593, P4r)

Many other equally familiar emblematic figures recur in both Boissard's emblem
books. In the 1588 collection appear, for example, the phoenix in *Vivit post funera
virtus* (F4r), the dolphin and anchor in *Nec temere nec segniter* (H4r) and the vine
coiled around a dead elm in *Amicitiae immortali* (I1r), while in the 1593 collection we
find a reworking of the Pythagorean dictum about not stirring a fire with a sword,
familiar from the very first French emblem book, La Perrière's *Theatre des bons
engins*. In *Invitum qui servat idem facit occidenti* not only is the engraved figure
depicting a man stirring a fire with a sword very similar to that of La Perrière's earlier
emblem, but also the verse:

> Ignem ne gladio fodito: furor haud habet aures.
>   Servare invitum maxima stultitia est.
> Sic refragantem è scopulo detrudit asellum
>   Rusticus: ingratum nil benefacta iuvant.
>   (Boissard, *Emblematum liber*, 1593, I4r)

has similarly clear echoes of La Perrière's earlier French text:

> Feu ne se doibt de cousteaux attiser
> Disoit ce beau propos pithagorique:
> Duquel le sens est, pour nous adviser,
> Que celuy la commet folle pratique,
> Qui le cheval felon au ventre picque.
> Pareillement ne debvons irriter
> Gens courroucez, mais plustost inviter
> A bonne amour, par joyeuse parolle:
> Cheval qui court vouloir trop inciter,
> Ne vint jamais que d'entreprinse folle. (La Perrière, *Theatre*, B4v-5r)[55]

Like Boissard's collections, Mercier's slightly later emblem book also follows a
generalist pattern, and contains a range of familiar emblematic figures derived from
traditional classical, mythological or bestiary sources. The structure and typographic
layout adopted by Mercier are also clearly designed to give particular weight to the

---

[55] Unlike La Perrière, Boissard does not refer to the Pythagorean source in his actual verse,
but he does so in the opening lines of the accompanying prose commentary: 'Gladio ignem ne
fodito, inquit Pythagoras...' (1593 ed., I3v) The same image was also used by Corrozet, shortly
after La Perrière, as the basis for his *Hecatomgraphie* emblem *Accroissement d'yre est à
eschever* (G1v-2r), although in this case Corrozet does not identify Pythagoras as his source.

moral lesson which he intends to convey, in a manner reminiscent of the way in
which earlier sixteenth-century emblem writers used similar strategies for the same
purpose.[56] Each emblem occupies a double opening: the engraved figure together with
a double moralising title or motto, one part above the engraving and the other below,
appear on the verso, and a short Latin verse plus moralising couplet on the facing
recto. The moralising couplet is given further visual emphasis by being separated from
the main verse text by a space on the printed page. Thus, for example, in emblem 27
the traditional figure of the viper with its lamentable family relationships, which
featured so commonly in earlier emblem books, and derived possibly from
hieroglyphic sources,[57] is used to point out the moral: *Quod fecit, patitur/Quod tibi
non optes fieri, ne feceris ulli*. The engraving depicts both the cruel behaviour of the
female viper biting off the head of the male after it has impregnated her, and the
equally cruel subsequent behaviour of the young vipers, splitting open their mother's
body in order to emerge into the world, and in familiar emblematic manner Mercier's
accompanying verse on the facing page describes both scenes in order to lead up to his
final moral lesson that such is the law of nature:

> Cum ruit in venerem, tumidum caput inserit ori
>   Uxoris, coitu turpis Echidna novo.
> Sed foecunda maris satiata libidine coniunx,
>   Insertum rabido conterit ore caput.
> Parturit haec eadem corroso viscere foetus
>   Insidiis: proli cedit uterque parens.
>
> Naturae ius est ut quod quis fecerit ultrò,
>   Posthac invitus perpetiatur idem.   (Mercier, *Emblemata*, H4r)

Pierre Coustau had earlier used the theme of the female viper biting off the male's
head in his 1555 *Pegme* (*Sur la vipere selon les hieroglyfiques des Aegyptiens*, G7v)
and La Perrière had similarly used that of the thankless young vipers killing their
mother in his 1553 *Morosophie* (emblem 65), but in Guillaume Guéroult's 1550
Premier livre des emblemes we find both themes brought together as cause and effect,
in the same manner as Mercier in one single emblem, entitled *Le malfaiteur retourne
à son maistre. De la vipere et du serpent*, and using them some forty years earlier to
make the same moral point as Mercier. Interestingly, though, although Mercier
follows the same structural pattern as Guéroult, of physically separating the moral
lesson from the rest of the narrative and descriptive verse he does this in reverse order
from that of Guéroult. Mercier puts the narrative and descriptive verse first and the

---

[56]   In the Roville/Bonhomme editions of Aneau's translation of Alciato, for example, the
moral lesson is highlighted in many cases by being printed in italic to contrast with the roman
type which is used for the rest of the verse, while in Guéroult's *Premier livre des emblemes* the
moral lesson is emphasised by being expressed in a preliminary quatrain between the woodcut
figure and the longer explanatory verse.

[57]   See, for example, its representation in Kerver's 1543 edition of *Orus Apollo de Aegypte de
la signification des notes hieroglyphiques des Aegyptiens*, i5v.

moral last, whereas in Guéroult's earlier emblematic treatment of the theme, in common with the structural pattern adopted throughout the work, the emblem began with a clear statement of the moral message to be derived in the form of a short quatrain, and only thereafter was this theme further expanded and clarified in the following narrative verse:

> Le mal qu'on pourchasse
> A tort à aultruy
> Souvent sur celuy
> Revient qui le brasse
>
>   La vipere (cruelle beste)
> Quand desir ha de concevoir
> Vient du serpent, lascif, la teste:
> Dedens sa gueule recevoir,
>   Mais le mal est à la ravoir,
> Pource qu'estant d'ayse ravie,
> De la ronger fait tel devoir:
> Qu'elle luy ravist teste, & vie.
>   Ceste beste conçoit à l'heure,
> Puis fait ses petits en temps deu,
> Et lors il convient qu'elle meure:
> O plaisir cherement vendu.
>   Or luy est son malfait rendu,
> Car de ceux à qui el' done estre
> Son ventre est crevé, & fendu:
> A l'heure qu'ilz viennent à naistre.
>   Le prouffit qui vient de malfaire
> Se peut voir icy par effect,
> Et pource au prochain on doit faire:
> Ce qu'à soy on veut estre fait.
>   Dieu est juge seur, & parfait,
> Et le mal que le fol machine,
> Sur luy mesme tomber il fait:
> Affin de le mettre en ruine.   (Guéroult, *Premier livre des emblemes*, B6v-7r)

Similarly familiar from earlier works is emblem 24, on the subject of the swine with a ring in its nose. Here the engraved figure of the swine is accompanied on one page by the double title *Nil addit honoris/Praestat sapientia formae*, with the facing recto containing the complementary verse and moral lesson which Mercier wishes to convey:

> Setigeri ex rostro pendet suis annulus, auro,
>   Et gemma, & doctae nobilis arte manus.
> Absimilis non est mulier quae pulchra, sed amens:

Quae male morata est virgo, timenda viro est.

Qui nubis, mores non formam uxoris amato;
   Nil expers animi forma venusta iuvat.   (Mercier, *Emblemata*, H1r)

The engraved figure is very similar in style to that used by Paradin in his *Devises heroiques* of 1551 and also to that used even earlier by La Perrière in his *Theatre*. In the *Devises heroiques* Paradin accompanied the figure with the motto *Prostibuli elegantia*, adding to it in 1557 the further prose gloss, which finds a very clear echo in Mercier's treatment of the theme:

Le Sage en ses Proverbes fit comparaison de la beauté & ordure de la femme
prostituee, à une Truie, qui ha un anneau d'or au groin.
                    (Paradin, *Devises heroiques*, 1557, f3r)

Indicative yet again of the diversity of interpretation to which common emblematic material could be subjected, while La Perrière's much earlier woodcut figure is very similar to Mercier's engraved figure of the swine, his verbal exploitation of the theme in emblem 24 of the *Theatre* is quite different, taking it as a basis for a discourse on the rather different theme of appropriateness:

Pensez si c'est chose tresbien seante
A ung porceau, de porter une bague:
Pensez si c'est chose bien convenante
A ung enfant, de porter une dague:
A ung coquin, de mener grosse brague:
A ung lourdault, contrefaire le saige:
A ung asnier, traicter subtil ouvraige:
A ung gros beuf, presenter des chapeaulx.
Propre doibt estre à chascun son paraige,
La bague à l'homme, & le gland aux porceaulx.   (La Perrière, *Theatre*, D6r)

   Just as we find traditional, generalist, themes familiar from earlier emblem books being treated by both Boissard and Mercier at the end of the sixteenth century, so also we find them continuing to be used in the seventeenth century in the lengthy, and clearly very popular, emblem book of Jean Baudoin which first appeared in 1638/39. In both the subject matter treated, and the strong didactic and moralising preoccupation which permeates the work (immediately apparent from the titles of the first few emblems in the collection: *Qu'il n'y a point de prosperité perdurable*; *Que les choses douces deviennent souvent ameres*; *Que l'honneste Amour, l'Honneur & Verité sont inseparables*; *Qu'il ne faut point publier le secret des Princes*; *Que par la Valeur & par la Prudence on vient à bout de la fourberie & des efforts les plus violents*), Baudoin's debt to his sixteenth-century predecessors is clearly evident, even if the structure he adopts is rather different. As we saw earlier, Baudoin includes in his introduction an acknowledgement of his particular debt to Alciato, and rightly so, since many of his emblems are clearly derived from this source. Emblem 1,7, for example, entitled *Des fruits de la paix*, depicting the halcyon, is a reworking of Alciato's *Ex pace ubertas* (*Emblemata*, 1550, M8v), and 1,31 entitled *Que la Curiosité est toujours nuisible*, depicting Acteon being devoured by his own hounds is similarly derived from Alciato's *In receptatores sicariorum* (*Emblemata*, 1550, D6v), while the grotesque figure of a man with an elongated neck and an enormous stomach

Figure 1: Baudoin, *Contre la gourmandise, Recueil d'emblemes*, Paris, 1638, M6v.

depicted in 1,15, under the title *Contre la gourmandise* (see fig.1), is equally clearly inspired from Alciato's *Gula*. Alciato's accompanying epigram:

> Curculione gruis tumida vir pingitur alvo,
>   Qui Laron, aut manibus gestat Onocrotalum.
> Talis forma fuit Dionysi, & talis Apici,
>   Et gula quos celebres deliciosa facit. (Alciato, *Emblemata*, 1550, G1v)

finds a clear echo in Baudoin's prose commentary to his emblem:

> A voir cét homme qui n'est que ventre, on juge aussitost qu'il represente la Gourmandise. Il a le col d'une grüe, tel que le souhaittoit avoir autrefois le dissolu Philoxene, affin de gouster mieux les viandes, & de les savourer plus long temps. Avecque cela il tient d'une main un Loir & de l'autre un Butor, pource qu'à l'imitation de ces oiseaux insatiables, il ne se peut jamais saouler; & tant plus il mange, tant plus il s'imagine d'en avoir besoin.
> (Baudoin, *Recueil d'emblemes*, 1638, vol.1, M7r)

Unlike these emblems which are clearly inspired from Alciato, the engraved figure of Baudoin's *Contre les temeraires* (1,59) does not so obviously imitate either of Alciato's two emblems on the subject, *Temeritas* and *In Temerarios* (*Emblemata*, 1550, D8r and E1r). In *Temeritas* Alciato's woodcut figure depicts an unspecified charioteer striving vainly to control his horses, while in *In Temerarios* it is Phaeton who is depicted, crashing to earth as he loses his struggle to control the fiery horses pulling his father's sun chariot. In contrast to these, Baudoin's engraved figure which depicts a rider rather than a charioteer is much more reminiscent of the woodcut used by La Perrière in emblem 22 of the *Morosophie* emblems, depicting foolish youth striving vainly to control a bridleless horse:

> Sur ce cheval, qui fol vouloir se nomme,
> Jeunesse court sans bride, mordz ne frain:
> Ce cheval fait perir maint un jeune homme,
> Si de bonne heure il ne change de train. (La Perrière, *Morosophie*, E3r)

Interestingly, however, although the rider in La Perrière's emblem is female (representing *Jeunesse*), Baudoin's rider is masculine in conformity with Alciato's charioteers, and this masculine gender is further confirmed in his prose commentary, in which he also alludes to Plato's image in the *Phaedrus* of a chariot pulled by two warring horses, thereby textually aligning his emblem with those of Alciato, even though the engraved figure he uses does not bear out this association:

> Par ce temeraire jeune homme, qui sans avoir ny art ny adresse, s'imagine follement de pouvoir dompter ce cheval fougueux, il nous est enseigné, Qu'il fait mauvais se fier à la conduitte d'une personne qui n'en a point, & qui se laisse emporter à ses Passions desreglées.

A ce propos aussi le divin Platon compare judicieusement nostre Ame a un
Cocher; & les brutales affections de nostre Corps, à des chevaux indomptez.
(Baudoin, *Recueil d'emblemes*, 1638, vol.1, Nn7r-7v)

Emblem 1,17, entitled *Contre l'Amour de soy-mesme*, and depicting Narcissus is
once again more closely derived from Alciato's equivalent emblem *Philautia*, and
indeed in his commentary, as well as explaining the significance of the tale, Baudoin
concludes by explicitly citing Alciato as his source (his use of the word *fable* to
describe this particular emblem reflecting the considerable parity between the two
forms at this period):

Cette Fable represente le succez & le naturel de ceux qui de la beauté du
corps, ou de telle autre qualité, dont la seule Nature les a doüez, & non leur
propre industrie, en tirent un sujet de s'aymer eux-mesmes, avec une passion
excessive...Ce docte Discours touchant l'Amour propre est du mesme
Autheur que j'ay nommé cy devant, & se peut conclure par cét Epigrame tiré
d'Alciat... (Baudoin, *Recueil d'emblemes*, 1638, vol.1, O4v-6r)

The French verse which Baudoin then reproduces :

Narcisse pour avoir esté
Trop amoureux de sa beauté,
Se mirant dans une fonteine;
Par un insensible mal-heur,
Se perdit dans son humeur vaine,
Et prit la forme d'une Fleur;

Ainsi, quand les jeunes Esprits
Ont les vieux Autheurs à mespriss (sic)
Et blasment les grands Personnages;
Dans cét amoureux sentiment
Qu'ils ont de leurs propres Ouvrages,
Ils se perdent honteusement.
(Baudoin, *Recueil d'emblemes*, 1638, vol.1, O6r)

is indeed a loose translation of the text of Alciato's emblem:

Quòd nimium tua forma tibi Narcisse placebat,
In florem, & noti est vera stuporis olus.
Ingenii est marcor, cladésque Philautia: doctos
Quae pessum plures dátque dedítque viros.
Qui veterum abiecta methodo, nova dogmata quaerunt,
Nilque suas praeter tradere phantasias. (Alciato, *Emblemata*, 1550, E7r)

This translated epigram from Alciato is one of the very rare pieces of verse in

Baudoin's emblem book. For the most part the work is entirely in prose. Thus, whereas its strong didactic and moralising preoccupation and its use of many traditional themes, place it firmly in a familiar long generalist tradition stretching back to Alciato, in terms of form - with its almost total absence of epigrams to accompany each engraved figure - it represents a significant departure from the emblematic structures which we have seen hitherto in the sixteenth century. The structural pattern which it adopts is to begin each emblem with a highly ornate and detailed full-page engraving, which is much more complete and pictorial than those of earlier emblem books, with a full background sketched in to complement the meaningful scene in the foreground. This engraving, however, is accompanied by neither motto, nor title, nor verse, nor even by a number. It stands entirely alone on the verso. On the facing recto is the moralising title, followed by the word *Discours* and its number (which is the number of the emblem), after which is printed the very discursive prose commentary (or *discours*) which can run variously from five to fifteen pages in length.

In structure then, albeit not in theme and intent, Baudoin's emblem book marks a significant departure from hitherto accepted emblematic patterns, and in this respect it has to be seen against a background of other developing trends in the seventeenth century which had hardly impinged in the earlier century. In particular we see strong affinities here with works such as Blaise de Vigenère's *Images ou tableaux de platte peinture des deux Philostrates* which, with its preoccupation with ekphrastic description of meaningful pictures, became increasingly popular and influential in France in the first half of the seventeenth century, after the publication in 1614 of a lavishly illustrated edition of the work by the Veuve Abel L'Angelier, which was followed by a series of subsequent editions. [58] As Chatelain has rightly suggested, the primacy given in Baudoin's *Recueil d'emblemes* to the engraved pictures, and to the lengthy descriptions of these and the corresponding absence of conventional accompanying motto or verse, must reflect the impact on the emblem writer of Vigenère's influential work.

> Le recueil de Jean Baudoin manifeste fortement l'influence exercée par les *Tableaux ou images de platte peinture* (sic) de Philostrate...Le recueil de Baudoin est fait d'une suite de discours qui tirent leur argument de figures dépourvues de tout *motto* et *subscriptio*, d'un caractère beaucoup plus pictural que de traditionnelles figures emblématiques même si bon nombre

---

[58] *Les images ou tableaux de platte peinture des deux Philostrates sophistes grecs et les statues de Callistrate. Mis en Francois par Blaise de Vigenere Bourbonnois. Enrichis d'arguments et annotations. Reveus et corrigez sur l'original par un docte personnage de ce temps en la langue Grecque. Et representez en taille douce en cette nouvelle edition. Avec des epigrammes sur chacun d'iceux par Artus Thomas Sieur d'Embry*, Paris, Veuve A. l'Angelier, 1614, folio; further editions were published in 1615; 1629; 1630 and 1637. An earlier edition of the work had been published in 1578, but being unillustrated, this did not attract the same degree of interest as the later illustrated editions (*Les images ou tableaux de platte-peinture de Philostrate Lemnien sophiste Grec. Mis en François par Blaise de Vigenere. Avec des argumens & annotations sur chacun d'iceux*, Paris, N. Chesneau, 1578, 4°).

d'entre elles procèdent des *Emblèmes* d'Alciat: les gravures sur cuivre manifestent un souci plus poussé du détail, des arrière-plans et du mouvement... C'est... dans ce retrait de l'emblème dans la peinture au mépris du *motto*, un nouveau rapport qui s'instaure entre le texte et l'image, qui n'est plus celui du recueil d'emblèmes à strictement parler mais plutôt celui du recueil de descriptions de tableaux, dans la tradition rhétorique de l'*ekphrasis* dont l'oeuvre de Philostrate constituait l'un des modèles les plus accomplis et, à l'âge classique, l'un des plus prégnants.[59]

Baudoin himself tends to confirm this association in the lengthy preface to his work in which - as well as stressing the important didactic function of emblems, and acknowledging his own debt to Alciato and earlier emblem writers - he also discusses in great detail what he understands to be the nature of emblems and devices. Throughout this discussion it is notable how frequently he uses the words *tableau* or *peinture*, clearly indicating the close allegiance he perceives between his own work and such works as the *Images ou tableaux de platte peinture*:

Comme tout le Monde est un Tableau, où les choses qui s'y voyent dépeintes nous font admirer l'Ouvrier qui les a faites; Ainsi les diverses Copies qui se tirent sur ce grand Original, nous plaisent quelque-fois autant que le naturel mesme, quand elles sont bien imitées. Il s'ensuit de là, que pour plusieurs advantages qu'a la peinture par dessus les autres Arts, elle merite à bon droit d'estre universellement dans l'aprobation, & dans l'estime des hommes. Aussi l'a-t-elle tousjours esté, pour diverses raisons; La principale desquelles est, ce me semble, pour avoir contribué de tout temps à la conservation de l'Histoire: car les Tableaux qu'elle fait, se peuvent nommer autant de Letres mystiques, qui sont connuës generalement de tous les Peuples du monde. Il ne faut donc pas s'estonner si telles Figures servoient autrefois de Caractheres aux Egyptiens, comme elles en servent encore aujourd'huy, à la pluspart des Nations du nouveau Monde. Et d'autant que les actions vertueuses estoient ordinairement signifiées par ces Caractheres Hyerogliphiques, c'estoit la coustume aussi, de les appeller mysterieux & sacrez. A leur imitation ont esté inventés les Emblemes, qui sont tousjours tels, tant que le principal but qu'on s'y propose, est d'instruire le public...Que si l'on recherche la vraye definition de *l'Embleme*, on trouvera que *c'est une Peinture servant à instruire*, & qui sous une Figure ou sous plusieurs, comprend des advis utiles à toute sorte de personnes...Quoy qu'il en soit, cette sorte de besoigne est maintenant fort en usage en Europe; Et n'est pas

---

[59] Chatelain, p.141. It should, however, be noted that although the bulk of the text in Vigenère's version of Philostratus is indeed made up of detailed description and commentary on the perceived or actual illustrations in the manner of Baudoin's prose *discours*, each engraved picture in the illustrated versions published from 1614 onwards is actually also accompanied on the same page by a short verse epigram, as well as by a lengthy prose commentary on following pages, whereas with only rare exceptions verse passages are wholly absent from Baudoin's emblems.

jusques à nos Relieurs, qui n'en fassent la principale parure des livres. J'obmets que dans les Palais des Grands, se voyent des Cabinets de Menuiserie, & des Tableaux mesme faits à pieces de rapport...

(Baudoin, *Recueil d'emblemes*, 1638, vol.1, ẽ 1r-2v)

Another work of similar type, also using the word *tableaux* in the title, but not one which could have directly influenced Baudoin, however, since it was published after the first edition of his emblem book had appeared, is Marolles' *Tableaux du temple des Muses* of 1655.[60]

With Baudoin we see, therefore, a continuation of the traditional generalist emblem book in terms of its content and didactic or moralistic preoccupation, borrowing frequently from Alciato in particular, and freely acknowledging this debt to the very earliest of all the sixteenth-century emblem writers. At the same time, however, the structure which he adopts is very different from that of his predecessors, and one which marks him clearly as a man of his own time, with aesthetic interests matching those of his contemporaries, rather than as a man looking back to the sixteenth century. Indeed, although when analysing the distinctions between emblem and device, he notes that while no explanatory text is allowed in a device, such text is permissible in an emblem,[61] it is nevertheless tempting to suggest that in his own particular collection he understands the word 'emblem' to denote no more than the engraving, since the number and moralising title which appear on the facing page relate to the *Discours* rather than to the engraved figure on the facing page. The lengthy accompanying *discours*, with its affinities to the similar passages of discourse in the *Images ou tableaux de platte peinture*, would then be seen as a novel structural departure from hitherto accepted emblematic patterns elaborated and developed in the course of the sixteenth century.

With La Faye's early seventeenth-century Latin emblem book, published nearly twenty years before that of Baudoin, in 1610, we find a similarly generalist moralising approach. Although some of the emblems are specifically Christian, rather in the manner of Montenay's late sixteenth-century emblem book, most are more generally applicable. Once again we find familiar emblematic topics recurring, but in marked contrast to Baudoin's emblem book which on the structural front breaks with tradition, La Faye's work is not at all discursive, but rather reiterates the succinct pattern of the earliest emblems. Notably lacking, however, is any illustrative woodcut or engraved figure. Thus each emblem comprises only two elements: a title and a short four- to

---

[60] *Tableaux du temple des Muses; tirez du cabinet de feu M Favereau, conseiller du Roy en sa Cour des aydes, & gravez en tailles-douces par les meilleurs maistres de son temps, pour representer les vertus & les vices, sur les plus illustres fables de l'antiquité. Avec les descriptions, remarques & annotations. Composées par Mre Michel de Marolles, Abbé de Villeloin*, Paris, A. de Sommaville, 1655, folio.

[61] 'Qu'on peut faire entrer des parolles dans les Emblemes, pour en expliquer les Figures; ce qui n'est aucunement permis en matiere de Devises; où la Figure demonstre une partie de l'intention que l'on a, & le Mot declare l'autre. Il est vray qu'il est permis encore d'en donner à connoistre le sujet par une Inscription, ou par un tiltre; comme qui diroit: *Contre l'Ingratitude*; *Contre les mauvais Juges*, & ainsi du reste.' (ẽ 3v-4r)

ten-line Latin verse. In the manner of the ordered version of Alciato's emblem book produced by Barthélemy Aneau, which introduced an index of topics at the end, La Faye's emblem book also includes not just an index of topics at the end, but also an index of sources at the beginning. His titles are normally double ones, in the manner of Pierre Coustau's earlier emblem book, with the first part referring to the image forming the basis for the emblem (and which should ideally be represented visually) and the second indicating the sense to be derived from it. Thus in La Faye's emblem using the symbol of an anchor to denote friendship, the double title, *Anchora/Amicitia fida*, signals both of these two key elements. The four-line verse directly apostrophises the reader in the manner developed by Alciato many decades earlier, urging him to visualise the image of the anchor holding firm the tossing ship, and derive from it its meaningful message:

> Aspicis ut cymbas luctantes anchora firmat?
>   Haec verae robur monstrat amicitiae.
> Iactatam navim vetat anchora sacra perire:
>   Adversis mersum servat amicitia.
>   (La Faye, *Emblemata et epigrammata*, C4r)

Similarly reminiscent of the style of Alciato with its repeated questions addressed to the reader is La Faye's emblem on men and worms, *Homo vermis. In contemptores aliorum:*

> Quid stolidè reliquos elatus despicis? Ohe,
>   Si vermis vermem despicit, ecquid erit?
> Spectatum admissis risus nascetur: erítque,
>   Longior aut brevior, vermis uterque tamen.
> Quot spectas homines, tot dic te cernere vermes.
>   Vermem vermis? Homo despicies hominem?
>   (La Faye, *Emblemata et epigrammata*, A7r)

Many of La Faye's emblems are derived from the animal world, as, for example, *Raptores esurient* dealing with birds:

> Nonne vides mites nutriri farre columbas,
>   Innocuum quarum cernitur esse genus?
> Unguibus ast aquilas uncis rostróque minaces,
>   Importuna solet saepe necare fames.
>   (La Faye, *Emblemata et epigrammata*, F5r)

or *Anguillae. Hospes non ingratus. Ex Plinio* on the behaviour of eels, in which La Faye (again in the manner occasionally used by Coustau) actually includes a note of his source in the title, as well as citing the moral lesson to be derived:

> Limoso lentè quae defluit amne, putatur,

Si fovet anguillas, esse salubris aqua.
Hospitibus venit haec anguillis gratia: limo
Quas vitii quod adest, tollere posse putant.
Si sic est, pendunt non parvo munere munus:
Hospitibúsque velis gratus ut esse, monent.

(La Faye, *Emblemata et epigrammata*, C2r)

Equally moralising in intent, and equally generalist in the range of subject matter covered, is the German Andreas Friedrich's *Emblemes nouveaux*, published in 1617, seven years after La Faye's Latin emblem book. Its heavily didactic character is made clear in the full title to the work:

> *Emblemes nouveaux; esquels le cours de ce monde est depeint et representé par certaines figures, desquelles le sens est expliqué par rimes: dressés pour plus grande incitation au (sic) gens de bien & honorables, d'ensuivre la pieté & vertu, & pour sincere instruction & advertissement aux meschans & dissolus de fuïr le vice. Premierement en Allemand par André Frideric, & maintenant en François, pour le bien de la jeunesse, & du simple peuple. Mis en lumiere par Jaques de Zettre.*

and this strong moral dimension is further emphasised by Friedrich in his preface to the work:

> Et ay pris le subject de ces meditations pour la plus part de l'estat & cours du monde, loüé la vertu & ce qui est bon, & exhorté à l'ensuivre; & reprins le vice, & fidelement dissuadé d'icelui.   (Friedrich, *Emblemes nouveaux*, A3v)

But an important difference between Friedrich's collection and that of La Faye is that Friedrich's emblems, as he explains in his preface, are composed in the vernacular with the specific aim of targeting a different audience, to whom existing collections of emblems written in Latin are not accessible:

> Je n'ignore pas que d'autres excellents & doctes personnages, tant ecclesiastiques que seculiers ont par ci-devant mis en lumiere des Emblemes en Latin avec un singulier artifice...Mais d'autant qu'un chascun ne les entend pas, n'ayant la cognoissance de la langue; J'ay bien voulu faire un essay pour ce fait en nostre language Allemand, esperant que ce ne sera sans fruict.   (Friedrich, *Emblemes nouveaux*, A4r)

By producing in the same year as the original German version a further version of the work in French for distribution in France, the publishers were able to spread the moralising lesson to a much wider audience (and also, more mundanely, to recoup some of the financial outlay in getting the engravings made, by tapping into the French market), as Jacques de Zetter (who was responsible for the original German edition) explains in his introduction to the French version:

J'estime que l'Autheur de ce livret, se souvenant de ces choses, n'a pas mal
colloqué les heures qu'il y a employées & partant aussi, que les despens que
j'ay fait (sic) pour l'impression d'icelui en Allemand & graveure des figures,
ne sont perdus. Ce qui m'a poussé encore plus outre, en sorte que voyant
qu'il a esté bien receu en sa langue je l'ay fait vestir d'une autre robbe, que je
me persuade ne lui estre mal seante, & ne doute point qu'il ne puisse
atteindre son but, qui est de representer aux simples & moins doctes, tant le
mal que le bien; cestui-ci, pour l'ensuivre, & cestui-là pour le fuïr.
(Friedrich, Emblemes nouveaux, A2r)

However where Friedrich's collection differs most significantly from that of La Faye is
in the fact that unlike La Faye's generalist collection of moralising emblems, only
some of which have a specifically Christian dimension, Friedrich's morality is - like
that of Montenay before him - a specifically Christian one, as he again explains in his
preface:

Je n'ay cerché en tout ceci en façon quelconque ma gloire, mais par un zele
Chrestien, seulement le profit de mon prochain qui est Chrestien avec moy, &
devant toutes choses l'honeur du Dieu tout-puissant.
(Friedrich, Emblemes nouveaux, A4r)

Again, however, like Montenay's earlier Christian emblem book (which in many ways
it resembles) in Friedrich's collection, also, it is only the moral lesson to be derived
from the image which is specifically Christian, whereas the image itself may be
derived from a wide range of material.

In structure the work follows the familiar pattern established nearly eighty years
earlier by Gilles Corrozet in his similarly didactic *Hecatomgraphie*, in order to make
sure that the full implications of the emblem are conveyed to the reader. Each of the
88 emblems comprises an engraved figure, a moralising title and a short four-line
verse on the verso, while the facing recto is devoted to a 16 to 20-line explanatory
verse gloss. Not only is the structure familiar from that of much earlier emblem books,
but so also is the material used by Friedrich. In, for example, emblem 33, *Faire
sedition ce n'est pas grand science*, the complex engraved figure below this title
comprises (as is often the case in this emblem book) more than one layer. In the
foreground is an owl with an ink pot and quill pen, while in the background we see a
large crowd of people (see fig.2). The quatrain accompanying this scene draws a
rather elliptical parallel between the alarming cry of the owl in the middle of the night
and the noise made by seditious people:

Le Chathuant mausade est fuyant la lumiere,
De nuit jette ses cris espouvantablement,
A maint fait belle peur: Ainsi semblablement

Font les seditieux sortans de leur tasniere.
(Friedrich, *Emblemes nouveaux*, I1v)

66   EMBLEMES NOUVEAUX.

Faire sedition ce n'est pas grand science.

L E Chathuant mausade est fuyant la lumiere,
   De nuit jette ses cris espouvantablement,
   A maint fait belle peur : Ainsi semblablement
Font les seditieux sortans de leur tasniere.

                                   Declara

Figure 2: Friedrich, *Emblemes nouveaux*, Frankfurt, 1617, I1v

but the point is more fully explained in the *Declaration de la XXXIII Figure* on the facing page:

La chanson du Hibou n'est pas guere plaisante,
Par laquelle de nuict maint il en espouvante,
Le bruit est que ses cris & leur son vehement

Guerre & sedition denotent proprement:
Ainsi maint garnement aujourd'huy ne demande,
Qu'a chanter la chanson de l'apostate bande,
Par haine & par rancune, par dit, & par escrit
Il esmeut bien souvent ce que coeurs enaigrit,
Et maint homme de bien à mal faire il incite,
Au corps, honeur & biens grand malheur lui suscite.
Las! qu'à maint ennuyeuse est alors la saison,
Qui souffre en son esprit angoisse en sa maison!
Mais en fin toutesfois se remet la balance,
L'honeur & verité apportent abondance,
L'alme justice fait revivre gens de bien,
Au Diable le Hibou, car son cri ne vaut rien.
                            (Friedrich, *Emblemes nouveaux*, I2r)

Nearly seventy years earlier La Perrière had used the owl to make a similar point, although he did so much more succinctly, and without, of course, any reference to the 'apostate bande'. In a similarly complex but reversed woodcut figure he depicted in the foreground an anxious sleepless couple in bed, with the owl in the background disturbing their repose with its noise, accompanying the figure with the quatrain:

Comme la nuyt le chant de la chouëte
Garde les gens de dormir en repos,
Tout detracteur aux gens de bien souhaite
Nuyre tousjours par ses méchants propos.
                            (La Perrière, *Morosophie*, I3v-4r, emblem 55)

All these works date from the early decades of the seventeenth century, but the continuation of the generalist pattern is not limited to this early period. Late in the century, in 1673, the Sieur Martinet's little collection of sixty emblems which he dedicated to Louis XIV and which he describes in the title as 'royal' emblems, in fact treat a wide range of familiar emblematic themes, including the dolphin and anchor (emblem 22) or the halcyon (emblem 35), the actions of various gods such as Mars (emblem 4) or Neptune (emblem 5), and narrative fables such as *Le Soleil & les grenoüilles* (emblem 20). Martinet's *Emblesmes royales à Louis le Grand* is a very loosely constructed emblem book, in which not all the items can be considered strictly emblematic. Some are simply poems in praise of Louis XIV or of a member of his entourage.

Among the emblems proper Martinet does not impose one single structural pattern. Some are long and others short, while particularly in the case of the fable-based emblems there is a tendency to prolix narrative, in a manner reminiscent of Guillaume Guéroult's much earlier and similarly rather discursive *Premier livre des emblemes*, in which a number of the emblems were also inspired from fables. In many of Martinet's emblems the moral interpretation is indeed oriented specifically towards the king, as suggested in the title, as in emblem 14, entitled *Le Chesne,* in which

Martinet makes the obvious flattering parallel between the strength and solidity of the
tree and that of the French monarch:

> Par une inévitable & funeste avanture,
> Que l'ordre soit troublé dans toute la Nature
> Que l'air soit ébranlé, que le Maistre des Flots
> Exerce sa fureur contre les Matelots.
> Qu'on voye les humains & sur mer & sur terre,
> Acharnez à se faire une mortelle guerre;
> Que le tonnerre en gronde, & que chaque élement
> Tâche à se revolter contre le Firmament
> Renfermé dans l'éclat de ta grandeur suprême;
> Tu sçauras, ô grand Prince, estre toûjours le mesme,
> Et ton Trône un écüeil où viendra se briser
> A tes justes desseins qui voudroit s'opposer.
> Il est trop glorieux à tout ce qui respire,
> De vivre sous les Loix de ton auguste Empire.
> Tant de Trônes bastis sur des sables mouvans,
> Dépendent du caprice, & du sort, & des vents;
> Mais ton Trône est semblable à ces plantes divines,
> Dont les vents n'oseroient ébranler les racines
> A ces Chesnes sacrez qui sont voisins des Cieux,
> Que protege la main du plus puissant des Dieux.
>   (Martinet, *Emblesmes royales*, C8r-D1r)

Similarly in emblem 7, which is again one of the shorter emblems, the message is
clearly related to Louis XIV, using as it does the familiar sun image. This emblem is
particularly interesting in that Martinet here gives a new twist to the relationship
between the brilliance of the sun and that of Louis. Instead of seeing Louis's brilliance
as reflecting that of the sun, Martinet actually goes so far as to represent the sun's
brilliance as inferior to that of his monarch. The engraved figure depicts a sun shining
across the earth, but in the centre of the sun is the head of Louis, and the superiority of
Louis to the sun is clearly spelled out in the verse:

> J'ay beau recommencer & finir ma carriere,
> J'ay beau répandre mes clartez,
> D'une course si reguliere,
> Dans les lieux les plus écartez.
> J'ay beau porter le jour de Province en Province,
> Mes plus vives clartez, mes plus perçans rayons,
> Ne sont que de foibles crayons
> Des grandes qualitez qu'on adore en ce Prince,
> Et pour faire voir en effet
> Que ses vertus sont sans secondes,

Il porte pour devise un Astre si parfait,
Qu'il peut suffire à mille mondes.   (Martinet, *Emblesmes royales*, C2r-2v)

70   E M B L E S M E S

X X I V.

Les Iumeaux de la Trape.

Ous nâquimes Jumeaux
Avec cét avantage
De ne souffrir aucun partage
Dans l'amitié **,** dans les biens **,** dans
maux.

Figure 3: Martinet, *Emblesmes royales*, Paris, 1673, G5v.

Not all the emblems in Martinet's collection, however, are related to the king, as
suggested in the title. Emblem 49 on the theme of Echo and Narcissus, in which the
engraving depicting Narcissus pursuing Echo is accompanied by the verse:

Fascheux Dedale qui m'enfermes,
Et par mille importuns détours
Charmes mes pas, & trompes mes amours,
Tes plaisantes erreurs auront bientost leurs termes,
Et mes cruels ennuis auront toûjours leurs cours,
Quoy! courir nuit & jour, & courir sans espoir

Apres ce qui me fuit, & que je ne puis voir.
Rochers plus tendres que Silvie,
Quand je vous entretiens icy
Et de mon amoureux soucy,
Et du triste estat de ma vie,
A mes profonds soûpirs, à mes plaintifs accens,
Répond vostre Echo favorable;
Mais, helas! cette inexorable
Se rit des peines que je sens.

Agreable trompeur à de si douces peines,
Egale donc les miennes,
Et fais que mes mal-heurs
Qui font naistre mes plaintes,
N'ayent pas plus de cours qu'en auront tes erreurs.
(Martinet, *Emblesmes royales*, R2r-3r)

No parallel is drawn between the theme of this emblem and Louis XIV. Similarly in emblem 24 the unusual theme of Siamese twins, is used to denote perfect harmony between two individuals, and again no association is drawn with the king. Inspired by the tomb of the Siamese twins of La Trappe, and entitled quite simply *Les Jumeaux de la Trape*, it is very reminiscent in style of the sepulchral Greek Anthology epigrams which inspired several tombal emblems in Alciato original collection,[62] as the verse (which is accompanied by a realistic engraving depicting the Siamese twins (see fig.3)) harangues the passer-by to contemplate the tomb and reflect upon the total harmony of the twins, inseparable both physically and spiritually:

Nous nâquimes Jumeaux
Avec cét avantage
De ne souffrir aucun partage
Dans l'amitié, dans les biens, dans les maux.
Par les ordres du Ciel sur chaque creature
Conceus dedans un mesme sein,
La Grace nous forma pour un mesme dessein.
Nous prismes mesme nourriture,
Et la Nature
Qui sembloit avoir mis un seul ouvrage en deux;
Mais n'en voulant jamais consentir la rupture,
Ne nous donna qu'un coeur, qu'un esprit de Closture,
Qu'un objet, qu'un desir, nous fismes mesmes voeux,

---

[62] See, for example, *Abstinentia* (1550 ed., C3v); *Signa fortium* (1550 ed., C4v); *In victoriam dolo partam* (1550 ed., D4v); *Maledicentia* (1550 ed., D6r); *Tumulus meretricis* (1550 ed., F1v); *Tumulus Ioannis Galeacii Vicecomitis, primi Ducis Mediol.* (1550 ed., K1r); *Strenuorum immortale nomen* (1550 ed., K2r); *In mortem praeproperam*, (1550 ed., L5r).

Aucun ne disputa la primogeniture,
Et Freres doublement nous vescumes heureux.
Nostre sort fut commun, & nostre sepulture,
Penetré du recit d'une telle avanture.
Passant tu peux bien si tu veux
T'imaginer en cette conjoncture,
Que deux corps differens n'eurent qu'une ame entre-eux.
                        (Martinet, *Emblesmes royales*, G5v-6v)

Already in the mid sixteenth century the close affinity between fable and emblem was accepted. Individual fable-based emblems occur frequently from the earliest collections onwards, while Guillaume Guéroult's *Premier livre des emblemes* owes a significant debt to Aesop for the particularly high proportion of fable-based emblems it contains. But the association between the two forms goes beyond simple emblematic borrowing of fabulous material. In more than one case in the sixteenth century we find whole collections of fables published in such a way that they are indistinguishable in form and structure from actual emblem books. Within two years of publishing France's first two emblem books, the *Theatre des bons engins* and the *Hecatomgraphie*, the specialist printer in illustrated vernacular books, Denis Janot, also published in 1542 an illustrated edition of Aesop's fables translated into French verse by Corrozet (author of the *Hecatomgraphie*), and using exactly the same layout as in the *Hecatomgraphie*. Each fable comprises a moralising title, a woodcut figure depicting the key feature of the fable, and a quatrain explaining the overall moral lesson to be derived. All three elements are encased in a decorative framework in the same way that the equivalent three elements in the *Hecatomgraphie* emblems were also encased and unified by an equivalent decorative framework, while on the facing page is a longer passage of verse, again as in the *Hecatomgraphie*, in which the actual fable is narrated. Visually the two works are indistinguishable in layout, and even some of the woodcuts used in the *Hecatomgraphie* are reutilised two years later in the *Fables du tresancien Esope*.[63] But this is not a unique case. A few years later Jean de Tournes, who to a large extent took over the mantle of emblematic publishing on the death of Janot in 1544, also published an emblematically arranged version of Aesop's fables in 1547, and thereafter in several subsequent editions again using Corrozet's text.[64] With the wide dissemination of Aesop's Fables in such obviously emblematic

---

[63]   Indeed two *Hecatomgraphie* woodcuts are used in the *Fables du tresancien Esope* (that of a man feeding a dog, from *Insuffisance* (B2v), and that of a shipwreck from *Peril incongneu* (M6v). These are used respectively in fable 19 (*Du larron et du chien*, D2v) and fable 84 (*Les deux ennemys*, M3v). Furthermore four of the *Fables du tresancien Esope* are used the following year in Corrozet's second emblem book, the *Emblemes*. For details see Alison Saunders, 'Emblem books for a popular audience? Gilles Corrozet's *Hecatomgraphie* and *Emblemes*', *Australian Journal of French Studies*, 17, 1980, pp.5-29. See also Stephen Rawles, 'Corrozet's *Hecatomgraphie*: where did the woodcuts come from and where did they go?', *Emblematica*, 3,1, 1988, pp.31-64.
[64]   *Les fables d'Esope phrygien, mises en ryme francoise, avec la vie dudit Esope extraite de plusieurs autheurs par M. Antoine du Moulin Masconnois*, Lyon, J. de Tournes and G. Gazeau,

form, the association between the two forms was inescapable, and even as late as 1684, the great emblematic theorist, Ménestrier, specifically designates Aesop's Fables as emblems, giving further authority to the association:

> Les Apologues d'Esope sont aussi d'eux-mêmes des Emblêmes, parce que ces Apologues ou les Autheurs font parler les plantes, les animaux, & les autres choses naturelles ou artificielles ont toûjours leur instruction morale jointe aux discours & aux actions de ces animaux. [65]

Interest in fables continued unabated through the latter part of the sixteenth century and into the seventeenth century. The de Tournes emblematic edition of Aesop was republished as late as 1583, while in 1578 the first edition of the lavishly produced, but similarly emblematically arranged *XXV. fables des animaux. Vray miroir exemplaire, par lequel toute personne raisonnable pourra voir & comprendre, avec plaisir & contentement d'esprit, la conformité & vraye similitude de la personne ignorante (vivante selon les sensualitez charnelles) aux animaux & bestes brutes: composé et mis en lumiere par Estienne Perret, citoyen d'Anvers* was published in Antwerp by the Plantin Press.[66] Although in its forceful visual impact this large-scale folio volume is very different from the earlier emblematic collections of fables published by Janot or de Tournes in more modest octavo or sedecimo format, in actual structure it is hardly different, though much more space proportionately is accorded to the engraved figures. Each emblematic fable again occupies two facing leaves, the first of which is given over entirely to a magnificent engraving of the key scene of the fable, while the facing verso contains the text, comprising a moralising title in the form of a couplet, a sixteen-line poem narrating the fable, followed by a further eight-line explanatory *Allusion* and lastly a short biblical quotation. The moralising intent behind this work is no different from that of Corrozet's earlier emblematic version of Aesop, but the audience for which it was intended is rather different. This beautifully produced volume was clearly intended for the top end of the market, and this is confirmed by the fact that the Bibliothèque nationale de France copy of the 1618 Delft edition (Rés Ye 96) belonged to the royal library.

Less popular in that it did not go through several editions in the way that Perret's collection of emblematic fables did is another similar, but much larger, though less

---

1547, 16°. Corrozet's translation of the text is accompanied here by a life of Aesop by Antoine du Moulin. The de Tournes presses produced further editions of the work in 1549, 1551 and as late as 1583. For discussion of the de Tournes editions, all of which are very rare, see A. Cartier, *Bibliographie des éditions des De Tournes imprimeurs lyonnais*, Paris, 1937, 2 vols, vol.1, pp.214-6; 269-70; 305-6; vol.2, p.610. See also Ruth Mortimer, *Harvard College Library Department of Printing and Graphic Arts. Catalogue of Books and Manuscripts. Part 1. French Sixteenth-Century Books*, Cambridge Mass., 1964, 2 vols, vol.1, item 5.

[65] *L'art des emblemes où s'enseigne la morale par les figures de la fable, de l'histoire, & de la nature*, p.27. Ménestrier goes on to discuss other contemporary collections of fables, such as those of La Fontaine, in the same context of their association with emblems.

[66] Antwerp, C. Plantin, 1578, folio. Further editions were published in Delft by Adrien Gerards in 1618 and again in 1621.

lavishly produced anonymous collection of 125 strongly moralising fables likewise published in Antwerp in 1578 under the title *Esbatement moral des animaux*. In this case we have a translation into French (and adaptation) of an originally Dutch work, whereas Perret's *XXV. fables* were originally composed in French and only thereafter published in a Dutch version.[67] As in Perret's collection, once again here a full opening is devoted to each 'emblem' with the engraving on the recto and the fable narrated in the form of a French sonnet on the facing verso, and once again the strongly moralising character of the work is given a specifically Christian emphasis by the inclusion of a biblical text in French to accompany each engraving. The Christian nature of the moral message is further emphasised on the title page where the engraved figure of a lion and other animals on a stage watched by an audience of human onlookers is accompanied by the Biblical quotation: 'Louez le Seigneur vous qui estes de la terre, dragons, & tous abysmes. Bestes, & tous troupeaux, serpens, & oyseaux qui ont ailes. Psal.148.7.10'. In an article on 'Les fables emblématiques de Paul Perret (1578)' Paul Smith points to the strong influence exercised not just on Perret's collection but also on these various other collections of emblematic fables by Corrozet's sixteenth-century emblematic adaptation of Aesop, in the Jean de Tournes version published in Lyon in several editions from 1547.[68]

The tradition continues unbroken into the seventeenth century. In 1620, we find a collection of fables by Philippe Desprez published in Paris, again arranged in the manner of Corrozet's *Fables du tresancien Esope* but here with the verses composed in sonnet form as in the *Esbatement moral des animaux*. In Desprez's *Theatre des animaux, auquel sous plusieurs diverses fables & histoires est représenté la pluspart des actions de la vie humaine. Enrichy de belles sentences tirées de l'Escriture saincte, et orné de figures pour ceux qui ayment la peinture*[69] each fable once again comprises a moral title, an engraved illustration and a quotation from the Bible, together with a descriptive title and a sonnet, in which the final tercet is devoted to the moral lesson. Typical of the collection is the fable, *Le Herisson et le Serpent*:

> Il vaut mieux estre seul, qu'à mauvaise compagnie.
> [figure]

---

[67]   Antwerp, G. Smits for P. Galle, n.d. (1578), 4°. The French text is based on Edewaerd de Dene's *De warachtighe fabulen der dieren* (Bruges, P. de Clerck, 1567, 4°). Landwehr ascribes the French work to Pierre Heyns (*Romanic Emblem Books*, no.380) but although the liminary verses are signed by Pierre Heyns, there is no indication that the rest of the text is by him. Indeed in the latter part of the work (from T2v onwards), the sonnets are signed E.W.

[68]   *Emblematica*, 8,2, 1994, pp.221-42. Smith establishes a *stemma* with *De warachtige fabulen der dieren* at the top, from which all the others descend, and notes that 'La plupart des fables de ce recueil ront inspirées des *Fables* de Corrozet. La mise en pages de toutes les fables du recueil suit l'exemple de Corrozet, avec cependant quelques changements, dont le plus important est la citation biblique rimée qui remplace la *subscriptio* de Corrozet' (p.223). For further discussion of these emblematic fable books see Marc van Vaeck, 'Sixteenth- and seventeenth-century Dutch "emblematic" fable books from the Gheeraerts filiation', *Emblematica*, 7,1, 1993, pp.25-38.

[69]   Paris, J. Le Clerc, 1620, 4°.

N'introduits point tout homme en ta maison: car les trahisons du cauteleux
sont diverses. Eccles. II.31.

        Le Herisson, et le Serpent.
Un Herisson s'adresse au Serpent, & luy prie,
Qu'il le laisse avec luy (l'Hyver) en paix loger,
L'accord faict, il y va: mais par trop se bouger,
En virant & roulant, au Serpent il ennuye.
Tu ne devrois (dit-il) me faire fascherie,
En me piquant ainsi, c'est par trop m'outrager:
Ce lieu est fort estroit, vueilles donc desloger;
J'ayme mieux estre seul, qu'à telle compagnie.
Mais puis que tu ne peux ma presence endurer,
Dit l'Herisson, va-t'en, sans icy demeurer:
Le Serpent, pour son bien, va chercher autre place.
Tel pense estre seigneur, qui n'est que serviteur:
Ainsi advient à ceux qui font à maints faveur,
Pour les voir gens de bien seulement à la face.
        (Desprez, *Theatre des animaux*, F2r)

Even in the late seventeenth century, over one hundred years after Corrozet
produced his arrangement of Aesop's Fables, we find the tradition established in his
collection still being continued by La Fontaine and also by Benserade. The aim of La
Fontaine's collection (which was first published in 1668)[70] is undoubtedly to promote
virtue and to teach a moral lesson, but above all to do so agreeably and painlessly, as
he explains in his dedication of the work to the seven-year old *dauphin*, echoing many
similar earlier justifications by writers of emblems of the efficacity of their works in
this respect. He stresses that despite their apparent air of simplicity, fables are a means
by which important messages can be conveyed:

> L'apparence en est puerile, je le confesse; mais ces puerilitez servent
> d'envelope à des veritez importantes...La lecture de son ouvrage (Aesop)
> répand insensiblement dans une ame les semences de la vertu, & luy apprend
> à se connoistre, sans qu'elle s'aperçoive de cette étude.
>   (La Fontaine, *Fables choisies*, 1668, ã2v-3r)

A simple and symmetrical structure is adopted, echoing that of many emblem books.
Each fable begins a new page: at the top is the engraving, preceded by the number and
title of the fable, and followed by the verse narrative, with in some cases a quickly
sketched in moral lesson at the beginning or end, and in some cases with no explicit
explanation of the moral lesson being given at all. Similarly arranged in symmetrical
emblematic pattern, and with even shorter verses, is Benserade's collection of *Fables
d'Esope en quatrains, dont il y en a une partie au labyrinthe de Versailles*, published

---

[70] *Fables choisies mises en vers par M. de la Fontaine*, Paris, C. Barbin, 1668, 4°.

ten years later in 1678.[71] But what is particularly interesting here is the way in which
the combination of figure and verse in fable form is exploited for applied decorative
purposes in architecture in exactly the same way that the same combination in emblem
form was also so often exploited, thus further underlining the close affinity between
the two forms. Many examples could be cited of emblematic material being used in
this way, from painted ceilings, to carved fireplaces to embroidered wall hangings. In
the case of Benserade's work we find emblematic fables being used as decorative
motifs for garden architecture. The labyrinth in the gardens of Versailles had been
constructed two years earlier, in 1676, and - reflecting the current fashion for fables -
a fountain was placed at each turning of the labyrinth, the design of which was
inspired from one of Aesop's Fables, and which included an inscription bearing a
four-line French verse summarising the fable. It is these verses, supplied by
Benserade, which were thereafter put together and published in 1678, thus
perpetuating them in book form, although the original labyrinth and the fountains for
which they were designed have long disappeared. It is because of the particular
applied purpose for which they were originally designed that Benserade's version of
Aesop's Fables takes the particular form it does. While Corrozet similarly used
quatrains over a century earlier, he could also allow himself the luxury on the printed
page of an accompanying longer verse gloss in order to make sure that both the fable
itself and its moral lesson were clearly conveyed. Such luxury of space was not
available to Benserade, and thus, as in the very earliest editions of Alciato, where the
text is kept to a minimum and there is little room within it for description of the
central image, the visual figure illustrating the scene becomes the more important in
his collection as conveyer of part, at least, of the message. In, for example, the second
fable in the collection, the oval figure depicting a wolf and a lamb standing opposite
each other on either side of a stream is a necessary complement to the verse, which
cannot in the space of a mere four lines convey both the full image and its moral
lesson:

> Un Loup querelloit un Agneau
> Qui ne sçavoit pas troubler l'eau:
> A tous coups l'injuste puissance
> Opprime la foible innocence.
>
> (Benserade, *Fables d'Esope en quatrains*, A2r)

In this fable a clear moral lesson is explained in the second couplet of the quatrain
only after the first couplet has glossed the scene depicted in the figure. Interestingly,
in 1677, the year before Benserade's collection of fables was published, Charles
Perrault had also published an illustrated description of the fountains in the labyrinth
at Versailles, including not just Benserade's verses but also engravings of them by Le
Clerc.[72] In this edition also the verse fables are arranged to look like emblems, with
the quatrain and its title on the verso and on the facing recto an engraving of the

---

[71] Paris, S. Mabre-Cramoisy, 1678, 12°.
[72] *Le labyrinthe de Versailles,* Paris, S. Mabre-Cramoisy for the *Imprimerie royale*, 1677, 8°.

fountain in which the scene is represented. Thus for the opening fable of the cockerel
and the diamond Benserade's verse is accompanied by an engraving of the fountain in
which the water spouts upwards from the mouth of the cockerel, which is represented
standing on a stylised dung heap on top of which the diamond is clearly visible.
However here Perrault is not constrained by considerations of space, and thus in
addition to Benserade's brief quatrain:

> Le Coc sur un fumier grattoit, lors qu'à ses yeux
> Parut un Diamant: helas, dit-il, qu'en faire?
> Moy qui ne suis point Lapidaire,
> Un grain d'orge me convient mieux.

a prose synopsis of the fable is also included, as well as a brief description of the
fountain:

> Au milieu d'un bassin, le Coq qui tient sous sa patte un gros morceau de
> cristal taillé en Diamant, jettant un long trait d'eau en l'air, semble se
> plaindre au Ciel de n'avoir pas plûtost trouvé un grain d'orge.
> (Perrault, *Labyrinthe de Versailles*, pp.8-9)

We see here, therefore, an example of the phenomenon which was to become
particularly common in the seventeenth century, under Louis XIV, whereby the art
object (be it fountain, tapestry or painting) was created first, and only thereafter was it
reproduced for wider dissemination in illustrated printed book form, whereas more
commonly the pattern in the sixteenth century was rather the reverse, with artists and
craftsmen in a variety of different domains taking printed collections of emblematic
material and using the designs provided in these as the basis for their for own artistic
creations. Further indicative of the close affinities between fables and emblems is the
fact that this work by Perrault, describing the use of fables for decorative architectural
purposes at Versailles is one of several such accounts that he produced, describing
similar applied use of emblematic or cognate material. In, for example, his *Cabinet
des Beaux Arts ou recueil d'estampes gravés d'apres les tableaux d'un plafond ou les
beaux arts sont representés. Avec l'explication de ces mêmes tableaux,*[73] the various
elements represented in a painted ceiling are each reproduced in an engraving,
accompanied by a six-line verse commenting on the significance of the allegorical
painting, and by a further passage of prose commentary. Thus an engraving (by Le
Paultre) of the section of the ceiling representing poetry is accompanied by an
explanatory verse, defining the versatile nature of poetry :

> Je chante des heros les glorieux dangers
> Je chante les amours des fideles bergers
> Icy d'un ton naif; là d'un air magnifique,
> Si je charme en chantant l'heroique valeur,

---

[73]   Paris, G. Edelinck and A.C. Boulle, 1690, 4° obl.

Je ne plais pas moins quand j'explique
Ce qui se passe au fond du coeur.

and a prose gloss:

Ne pensez pas que ce soit la peine de trouver une rime ou la mesure d'un vers
qui lui fasse ronger ses ongles, c'est à quoi la veritable Poësie s'arrete le
moins, quoi qu'elle ne le neglige pas. Cette action est l'effet de son
application profonde à inventer et à creer de nouvelles choses. Ses yeux
elevés au ciel et le petit souris qu'on void sur son visage montrent la joie que
lui donne une idée agreable qu'elle entrevoit, qu'elle poursuit et dont elle est
sur le point de se saisir.   (Perrault, *Cabinet des Beaux Arts*, pp.15-16)[74]

In all these various late sixteenth- and seventeenth-century collections of fables
following the emblematic pattern established by Corrozet in the first half of the
sixteenth century, the textual message is - as might be expected - expressed in verse
form. But we also find developing in the mid seventeenth century and continuing right
through the century, a variant pattern whereby the overall arrangement still follows a
structure similar to that of emblem books, but the textual message is expressed in
prose rather than in verse. Of such a kind is Raphael du Fresne's *Figures diverses
tirées des fables d'Esope et d'autres et expliquées par R.D.F.* of 1659, in which each
fable follows a tripartite structure, comprising narrative, engraving and morality. The
work is symmetrically arranged, with each fable occupying a double opening in which
the prose narrative occupies the verso, while facing it on the recto is an ornate
engraving, followed by a short prose morality (printed in italic to contrast with the
roman of the facing passage of narrative).[75] In Audin's similar collection of fables
inspired from Aesop we see a further development of this same form. The full title of
Audin's collection of fables in the 1669 edition stresses their universal moralising
force: *Fables heroiques, imitées de celles d'Esope, avec des moralitez historiques,
pour l'explication de chaque fable. Comprenans les veritables maximes de la
politique, & de la morale. Enrichies de figures en taille-douce,*[76] and this is borne out

---

[74] See also an anonymous work, the *Explication en vers des tableaux de la galerie de
Versailles. Dediée à Monseigneur le Duc de Bourgogne* (Paris, M. Guerout and T. Girard,
1691, 4°) in which are similarly described and interpreted for the edification of the 9-year old
boy the series of eleven allegorical paintings at Versailles depicting the magnificent exploits of
his grandfather, Louis XIV. Here, however, there is no actual reproduction of the paintings, but
simply a brief prose description of what is to be seen, and a verse interpretation of its
significance.

[75] Paris, C. Cramoisy for F. Léonard, 1659, 4°. Even at the end of the seventeenth century we
find the tradition of prose fables such as these still continuing with, for example, Veneroni's
collection of 95 bilingual Italian/French fables which were published in Amsterdam in 1700
(*Fables choisies traduites en Italien, avec le François à côté. Par le Sieur de Veneroni, maître
des langues Italienne & Françoyse, à Paris. Le tout enrichi de figures en taille douce à chaque
fable*, Amsterdam, G. Gallet, 1700, 8°).

[76] Paris, R. Guignard and E. Loyson, 1669, 12°. Earlier editions were published in 1648, 1660
and 1664.

in the structure of the work itself. Once again the text is wholly in prose, with half a
page devoted to the engraved figure, and a further half page to a short gloss on its
significance. Thereafter approximately one and a half pages are devoted to a prose
narration of the fable. However the significant new development in this collection lies
in the all important *moralité historique* which is here developed at much greater
length than we have seen hitherto, explaining in a prose discourse extending to eight
or nine pages of text the essential moral lessons to be derived. In this increasing
tendency to prolixity as more and more emphasis is given to backing up the basic fable
with lengthy moralising commentary, we see clear similarities with the parallel
development taking place at the same period on the emblem front, a parallel which is
borne out also in the similar collection of fables by Jean Baudoin. As we saw earlier,
Baudoin produced a very popular emblem book which ran through several editions in
the course of the century after its first appearance in 1638/39. Hardly less popular,
judging by the number of editions it went through, was the French version of Aesop's
fables which he produced ten years later.[77] Both in structure and intent the two works
have close affinities. The title to the 1649 collection of fables, in which they are
described as '*illustrées de discours moraux, philosophiques & politiques*', echoes that
of the earlier collection of emblems in which they are similarly described as being
accompanied by '*des discours moraulx, philosophiques, et politiques*'. Like Audin
Baudoin stresses in his preliminaries the morally edifying nature of such fables:

> C'est une école où les creatures capables de raison, apprennent de celles qui
> n'en ont point ce qu'elles doivent eviter ou suivre, pour la conduitte &
> l'instruction de leur vie...je m'asseure que vous ferez quelque cas de celles de
> ce Philosophe, non pas pour le plaisir qu'elles peuvent donner; mais à cause
> des belles leçons qu'elles font aux hommes. Aussi est-il vray que des divers
> personnages que cet Autheur leur fait joüer si plaisamment sur ce theatre,
> j'ay tiré de riches secrets de la Nature, de la Morale, & de la Politique;
> comme vous verrez dans les Discours que j'ay formez là dessus selon
> l'occurrence des matieres.
>   (Baudoin, *Fables d'Esope phrygien*, 1670, ã4v-5r)[78]

echoing once again the firmly moralising intentions earlier expressed in the
preliminaries to his emblem book in which - as we saw earlier - he used such phrases
as ' le principal but qu'on s'y propose, est d'instruire le public' and 'si l'on recherche
la vraye définition de l'*Embleme*, on trouvera que *c'est une Peinture servant à
instruire*, & qui sous une Figure, ou sous plusieurs, comprend des advis utiles à toute

---

[77]   For details of editions see above, footnote 7.
[78]   In his *Apologie en faveur des Fables* Audin argues that they should not be dismissed as
inferior, since they have since the earliest times been used to convey major truths, citing
notably Demosthenes and Plato: 'Demosthene ne trouva pas de meilleur moyen, pour vaincre
l'opiniastreté des Atheniens, que de les entretenir de la gayeté d'une Fable. Platon en a
parsemé ses Lois comme de riches fleurs; et les Poëtes de l'Antiquité s'en sont adroitement
servis, pour faire recevoir plus doucement à des Peuples Barbares les Mysteres sacrez de leur
Theologie.' (ã3r)

sorte de personne' (*Recueil d'emblemes divers*, 1638, vol.1, ẽ 2r). Not only are there
significant similarities between his emblem book and his collection of fables, but there
is also overlap of terminology in the two works, as, for example, as we noted earlier,
when Baudoin uses the word *fable* to describe his narrative of the Narcissus myth in
the emblem *Contre l'Amour de soy-mesme* (*Recueil d'emblemes divers*, 1638/39, O4r-
O6r). Slightly less prolix than Audin, Baudoin nevertheless follows essentially the
same pattern in his collection of fables, accompanying each full-page engraving with a
half-page prose narration of the fable, followed by some two or more pages of
commentary under the title *Discours*, following thus very much the structural pattern
he had established ten years earlier in his collection of emblems, and in both using the
vehicle of prose rather than verse, to complement the decorative engraved figure, in
order to convey thereby the important didactic message embedded in the
fable/emblem.

We see from all this how enduring throughout the seventeenth century are certain
emblematic traditions which have their roots in the sixteenth century. While the actual
emblem books themselves which were composed by writers in the sixteenth century -
with the notable exception of Alciato, and to a lesser extent of Georgette de Montenay
- did not on the whole continue to be published into the seventeenth century, many of
the structures and concepts which they developed did undoubtedly continue to
flourish. Many of the common emblematic themes treated by the sixteenth-century
writers likewise continued to form the basis for the emblems composed by the
seventeenth-century writers. Similarly the strong moral and didactic purpose to which
these themes were exploited remains constant in the seventeenth century, in some
cases being generally humanist in inspiration, as in the earlier sixteenth-century
emblem books, and in others taking on a more specifically Christian application as
indeed it did also in some cases in the later sixteenth century. Certainly there are
differences: copperplate engravings take over from woodcuts, and emblems tend to
become more discursive, with a greater incidence of prose commentaries, and in some
cases with passages of prose entirely replacing the more traditional verse element of
the emblem. Yet despite these differences, the extent to which so many of the various
key features of the generalist moralising emblem book as originally created in the
early sixteenth century by Alciato, and rapidly adopted and adapted by his various
French emulators survived, and continued to flourish in the following century is a
remarkable tribute to the enduring worth of the product as originally created. In the
following chapter we shall look at the sister form of the device, to see the extent to
which the same pattern prevails there also.

CHAPTER III

DEVICES AND THEIR CONTINUATION OF
THE GENERALIST TRADITION

From a relatively early stage in their development in the sixteenth century devices were often put to specialist uses, but nevertheless there also persisted well into the seventeenth century a continuation of the generalist collection of devices, just as there continued also a generalist tradition of emblems. The generalist collections of devices of Paradin and Simeoni, for example, which were first published in the 1550s, enjoyed enduring popularity throughout the second half of the sixteenth century, and this lasted well into the seventeenth century also, with augmented editions of the French version of Paradin's devices (minus those of Simeoni) being republished in Paris in 1614 and again in 1621 and 1622. This lasting popularity was not reserved just to France. As well as these seventeenth-century editions of Paradin in French published in Paris, the Plantin Press also published a series of editions of a Latin version of the work of the two authors in Antwerp and Leiden between 1562 and 1600.[1] A first edition of a Dutch version was published in Antwerp in 1563, and as late as 1615 Raphelengius published another Dutch version in Leiden.[2] The popularity of the work extended to England also, where an English version (based on the Latin translation, rather than on the original French) was published in London in 1591.[3] Interestingly - unlike the later publishers of Alciato's collection of emblems, who showed no sign of embarrasment at the age of the work they were continuing to publish one hundred years after it had originally been composed - Jean Millot, who was responsible for the edition of Paradin's devices which was published in Paris in 1614, clearly was

---

[1] For details see Landwehr, *Dutch Emblem Books*, nos 468-71.

[2] *Princelijcke devijsen ofte wapenen van M. Claude Paradyn Canonick van Beaujeu. Ende van den Heere Gabriel Simeon, ende meer ander Auteurs*, Antwerp, Willem Silvius, 1563, 16° ; *Princeliicke deviisen van Claude Paradin, Gabriel Simeon, ende meer ander*, Leiden, F. Raphelengius (Officina Plantiniana), 1615, 12°.

[3] *The Heroicall Devises of M. Claudius Paradin Canon of Beaujeu.Whereunto are added the Lord Gabriel Symeon's and others. Translated out of Latin into English by P.S.*, London, W. Kierney, 1591, 12°.

sensitive to the age of this collection, and took steps to modernise it. As he remarks somewhat patronisingly in his dedication of the work to the Comte de Beaumont he took the precaution of giving the text to a learned gentleman to correct and polish for the needs of a modern audience, since the original was 'dressé en forme un peu rude...du temps du grand Roy François' (ã2r). Yet despite his claim that he has made the text 'plus polly & en meilleur estat' (ã2v), his version is in reality considerably less elegant than the sixteenth-century versions. The text is certainly fuller, but aesthetically the book is less pleasing than in earlier editions. Symmetry of layout is abandoned, and the devices tend to be overcrowded on the page, to the extent that in some cases the engravings which replace the earlier woodcut illustrations are too big for the space allowed, with the result that figure and text are actually printed on top of each other.[4]

Paradin's pioneering collection of devices is no more than that; it does not include an additional treatise on devices. However, his seventeenth-century successors vary in this respect, with some including a theoretical treatise with their collections, and others not. Florent Chovayne, for example, follows Paradin's pattern in his three-part *Divertissements* of 1645-47, and includes no more than a short discussion of theory in his preliminaries, whereas in contrast Boissière's collection of devices, dating from ten years later, is accompanied by a full treatise on theory and practice.[5] The Jesuit Pierre Le Moyne produced a collection of *Devises heroiques et morales* in 1649 (published, like Boissière's collection, by Augustin Courbé in Paris), which was not accompanied by any theoretical treatise, but followed this a few years later in 1666 by a further work in which theoretical treatise on devices and actual devices themselves are brought together, and indeed primacy is given to the theory side of things rather than to the actual practice in the title of the work, *De l'Art des devises...Avec divers recueils de devises du mesme autheur.*[6] That most prolific of writers, Claude-François Ménestrier, produced both free-standing collections of devices and theoretical treatises accompanied by collections of devices, though his free-standing collections tend more

---

[4]   See, for example N5r; P7r; Q1r; Q3v; Q4v. Typical of the more developed text is the device of François 1er, *Nutrisco et extinguo*. Not only is a French version of the Latin device added *(Je nourry & étein)*, but also the Latin distich with which the original prose commentary ended is also translated into French:
    Ursus atrox, Aquillaeque leves, & tortilis Anguis:
    Cesserunt flammae iam Salamandra tuae.

    L'ours fier, l'aigle legere, & le serpent tortu,
    Salamandre ont cedé à ton feu & vertu.
and a further prose gloss of the significance of these three symbols is added:
    Par ces trois s'entendent les victoires que ce Roy avait euës sur les Suisses, les Bermains (sic) & les Milanois. (pp.14-15)
[5]   *Les devises de Monsieur de Boissiere. Avec un traitté des reigles de la devise, par le mesme autheur*, Paris, A. Courbé, 1654-57, 8°. The work is divided into two books, of which the second is dated 1657. Only one known copy of this work exists, in the Bibliothèque Sainte Geneviève in Paris.
[6]   *De l'art des devises. Par le P. Le Moyne de la Compagnie de Jesus. Avec divers recueils de devises du mesme autheur*, Paris, S. Cramoisy and S. Mabre-Cramoisy, 1666, 4°.

commonly to be subject-specific, rather than generalist, being in many cases composed for particular persons or particular occasions.[7] It is more commonly in accompaniment to his various theoretical treatises that we find his generalist collections of devices.[8]

In structure, also, the various generalist collections of devices follow a number of different patterns. While some follow in the traditional pattern established by Paradin in the sixteenth century, and continued throughout all his editions, of including a woodcut or (subsequently) an engraved figure, economic considerations lead many to abandon the visual element and rely simply on a description of what should be depicted. In consequence these works become aesthetically much less pleasing to the eye than their more decorative counterparts. Neither Boissière nor Chovayne, for example, includes illustrations. Chovayne's text in particular is very basic, comprising no more than a brief description in French of what should be depicted in the figure plus a note of its (usually) Latin motto. There are no verses, and no explanatory gloss is given, nor yet any indication of suitable or actual owners for the various devices. Although the subtitle to the work describes it as a 'recueil de diverses devises & emblesmes', it is difficult to see any obvious justification for the reference to emblems, since the devices in the collection are quite unambiguously that, and indeed - other than in one incidental reference in his *Au lecteur* to his friends having shown him several books of emblems and devices[9] - Chovayne himself uses only the word *devise* throughout the work when referring to his own collection. Although overall the devices cover a range of different material, they are grouped according to subject matter, as for example three consecutive ones (nos 57-59) which all relate to the

---

[7]   He produced many collections of emblems and devices for specific people, such as the *Devises, emblemes, et anagrammes, à Monseigneur le Chancelier*, dedicated to Seguier, and *Estreines de la cour en devises et madrigaux*, or the *Genereux exercices de la Majesté, ou la montre paisible de la valeur, representée en devises & en emblesmes*, all of which were published in Lyon in the same year, 1659, by Guillaume Barbier; or for specific festivities such as *L'autel de Lyon consacré à Louys Auguste, & placé dans le temple de la gloire. Ballet dedié à Sa Majesté en son entrée à Lyon* (Lyon, J. Molin, 1658, 4°) including at the end as well as the emblematic ballet, a little collection of *Devises sur les principaux evenements de la vie de S.M.*; or *Les resjoüissances de la paix, avec un recueil de diverses pieces sur ce sujet* of 1660.

[8]   Among his theoretical treatises including collections of devices are his *Philosophie des images. Composée d'un ample recueil de devises, & du jugement de tous les ouvrages qui ont été faits sur cette matiere. Par le P.C.F. Menestrier, de la Compagnie de Jesus*, Paris, R.J.B. de la Caille, 1682, 8° and his *La science et l'art des devises dressez sur de nouvelles regles, avec six cens devises sur les principaux evenemens de la vie du Roy. Et quatre cens devises sacrées, dont tous les mots sont tirés de l'Ecriture Sainte. Composées par le P. Menestrier, de la Compagnie de Jesus*, Paris, R.J.B. de la Caille, 1686, 8°. For details of the numerous publications by Ménestrier see J. Renard, *Catalogue des oeuvres imprimées de Claude-François Ménestrier de la Compagnie de Jesus*, ed. C.Sommervogel, Lyon, 1883. See also P. Allut, *Recherches sur la vie et sur les oeuvres du P. Claude-François Ménestrier*, Lyon, 1856. For discussion of Ménestrier's theory see J. Loach, 'Ménestrier's emblem theory', *Emblematica*, 2, 2, 1987, pp.317-36.

[9]   'aucuns de mes amis m'ayant fait voir quantité de livres de Devises, & d'Emblemes, les unes peintes, les autres seulement décrittes.' (*Divertissements*, ã4v)

heavens:

> Un ciprés, qui porte sa cime jusques dans le Ciel. *Coelo tenus altum.*
> Une Colomne qui s'éleve proche du Ciel. *Coelum ferit ardua fama.*
> Des trompettes qui sonnent sur une haute montagne. *It clamor Coelo.*

In his discussion of the criteria for a good device Chovayne stresses the importance of the combination of the verbal and the visual trigger, and draws the parallel between devices and enigmas, pointing to ingenuity and wit as important elements in a collection of devices, providing the reader with intellectual stimulus and pleasure,:

> Pour vous exposer proprement ce que c'est que Devise, l'on la peut definir. Une signification de nostre esprit, & de nostre pensée soubz un noeud de parolles & de choses. Son but est d'exprimer, par une peinture de choses visibles, & par une brefve sentence, quelque gentille conception, que l'on veut tenir partie ouverte, partie cachée. Les Devises ne doivent pas estre si obscures, & si dificiles, qu'elles ayent besoin d'un ample commentaire; ny si claires aussi que chacun les puisse entendre du premier coup. On les accompagne de parolles, & d'écrits, qui aident a ouvrir le sens, servent de clef aux ressorts de la peinture, & qui delectent l'oreille & l'esprit. Ce n'est pas chose facile à un chacun d'inventer une devise parfaictement bonne. Il arive souvent en la Devise qu'un sens en a plusieurs, ou que plusieurs ayent mesme mot, avec diverses peintures. Elles doivent estre de choses intelligibles; & la gentillesse se doit tirer de l'acouplement de la chose & des parolles. Car les Devises, soit en la peinture, soit en la diction, doivent donner quelque peu à songer. On les peut dire estre participantes en quelque chose des Enigmes & des chifres; au moins pour ceux qui ne comprennent pas du premier aspect. Surtout elles ont de grandes aliances avec la peinture & la poisie (sic), desquelles Horace a tres-bien dit, *Ut pictura poesis erit.*
> (Chovayne, *Divertissements*, ã 4v- ẽ 1r)

but these three typical examples of his own somewhat pedestrian devices reflect the rather laborious efforts of an undistinguished provincial writer who finds difficulty in fulfilling his stated criteria. The mediocrity of this lengthy, but very basic anthology published in Chartres, in which there are no engraved figures to enliven the text probably explains why the work was never subsequently reprinted.

Although Boissière's devices, like those of Chovayne, also provide only a summary prose description of what should be represented, rather than an actual engraving depicting the scene, unlike Chovayne's collection they also include, in addition, an explanation of the sense to be derived from the device and its underlying implications. In this respect Boissière follows in the tradition established by Paradin, whose collection included a prose gloss for each device in all editions from 1557 onwards. (Only the original 1551 edition of Paradin's devices included no such commentary.) Unlike those of both Paradin and Chovayne, however, Boissière's collection of devices is altogether much more discursive in structure, with one device and its commentary following straight on from another in continuous prose, with no attempt at achieving any form of symmetry of layout on the printed page. The consequence is that even the main section of the work - the actual collection of devices, which is preceded by a short theoretical treatise - itself looks more like another prose treatise on devices, rather than an actual collection of devices. Only very occasionally does Boissière's collection include any passages of verse. This occurs in the rare cases where he is describing a particular festivity in which visually represented devices also included a passage of verse. In such cases Boissière's account faithfully reproduces the verse as well as a description of the figure.

Like those of Chovayne, Boissière's devices are also grouped according to topic, but more formally so with each category defined by a separate sub-heading, such as *Devises chrestiennes*, *Devises pour divers desseins amoureux* or *Devises burlesques*.[10] In such categories as these, the grouping is according to theme, but in other cases Boissière also groups devices on the basis of the type of recipient for whom they are designed , as in *Devises pour des veufves illustres*, *Devises pour des grands hommes de nostre temps* or *Devises pour l'Academie Françoise*.[11] Other sub-headings refer to the occasion on which groups of devices were first used, as in *Devises recueillies du Carrosel de Monsieur le Duc de Montmorency, de l'an 1619* or *Devises de l'entree du Roy à Tolose en l'an 1621*.[12] In this category we find two separate groups of devices originally designed for ballet performances: *Devises pour des balets. Au Balet de la Nuict, dansé en l'an 1624*, and *Au Balet de l'Amour & du contr'amour, dansé en l'an 1618*.[13] Boissière's collection is thus much more of a compilation of devices originally designed for specific purposes than is the case with Chovayne's collection, and in this respect it is more reminiscent of some of Ménestrier's rather later collections. Again like Ménestrier, Boissière also includes in his commentary on his devices not just a description and explanation of the individual devices, but also information on the particular circumstances in which they were used, and the reasons why they were chosen, as in his account of devices which he designed for the entry of Louis XIII into Toulouse in 1621:

> Le sujet de la guerre que le Roy faisoit alors contre ceux de la Religion pretenduë Reformée, ayant pour sujet la querelle du Ciel: je jugeay qu'il n'y avoit point de dessein plus convenable pour le Triomphe de son entrée, que de faire que le Ciel mesme en fit la pompe, & se trouvât comme present à cette action.
>
> Voicy quelques-unes des Devises que j'ay choisies de toutes celles que je fournis pour cette entrée Royale.
>
> A la premiere face de l'Arc de Saturne, dedié à la Prudence, il y avoit pour devise au Piedestal de la main droicte, un Horloge avec sa monstre, dont les heures estoient marquées par une main, le mot Espagnol

---

[10]   Book 1, C2r; Book 1, F5r; Book 2, D5v.
[11]   Book 2, C3v; Book 2, A8v; Book 2, C1r. Boissière's collection of devices actually opens with a dedicatory *épître*, *A Messieurs de l'Academie Francoise*, signed F.B (Book 1, ã2r).
[12]   Book 1, G7v; Book 1, C5v.
[13]   Book 1, G2v; Book 1, H3r.

estoit,

> *Assi mi mano como mi sonido.*

Et le mot Latin estoit,

> *Quae sonat haec agit.*

Pour monstrer que nostre Roy tres-prudent, ayant meurement deliberé, & resolu un dessein, l'executoit promptement, & que ses actions suivoient de point en point ses conseils.

> (*Les devises de Monsieur de Boissiere*, Book 1, C6v-7r)

Similarly in Book 2, a collection of *Devises Heroïques pour des grands hommes de nostre temps* opens with a description of a rather later device designed for Mazarin:

> Pour Monseigneur le Cardinal Mazarin premier Ministre d'Estat, pour témoigner que l'estat où il estoit parvenu, estoit aussi bien un ouvrage de sa vertu, que celuy de sa fortune.
>
> La Navire Dargos voguant en pleine mer à voiles & à rames, dont les voiles pour marquer sa bonne fortune estoient enflées par un vent favorable, & dans laquelle ramoient ces illustres Heros de l'Antiquité, qui entreprirent la conqueste de la Toison, representans les vertus de ce grand Ministre, & pour mot,
>
> > *Virtutis remis, velisque fortunae.*
>
> Ce mot est pris de cette maniere de parler des Latins, *velis remisque*, pour dire *omniconatu*, ou de toute nostre force.
>
> (*Les devises de Monsieur de Boissiere*, Book 2, A8v-B1r)

The long time lapse between the date when many of Boissière's devices were actually created and when they were published is striking. Although the bulk of the devices in Book 2 date from the reign of Louis XIV, many of those in Book 1 go back well into the reign of Louis XIII, with those dating from the 1620s and earlier being already over thirty years old when the collection was put together for publication. Book 1 was published in 1654 and Book 2 three years later. The fact that the Paris publisher Augustin Courbé should have considered them to be still of sufficient interest to be published in the 1650s must reflect on the enduring nature of the genre.[14]

Strikingly different in form is another little collection of devices which was published at much the same time as that of Chovayne and a few years before that of Boissière. Albert Flamen's *Devises et emblemes d'amour moralisez* was first published in 1648, but unlike Chovayne's and Boissière's collections, which were never republished after their first edition, Flamen's work was extremely popular, running through a number of editions over the next twenty-five years.[15] Like those of Chovayne and Boissière, Flamen's devices include no verse at all, but in other respects the collection is very different. Aesthetically the work is far more pleasing to the eye,

---

[14]   Courbé clearly had a particular interest in devices. It is he who was also responsible for publishing Le Moyne's *Devises heroiques et morales*.

[15]   See above, chapter 2, footnote 4.

since not only is illustration included, but also a symmetrical layout is adopted, with each device occupying one opening, with a full-page engraving on the recto, together with the motto in both Latin and French incorporated into it, while the facing verso contains the French prose commentary. However the particularly interesting innovation in Flamen's collection lies in the fact that for each device there are two quite distinct prose commentaries, the first offering a conventional profane gloss on the device, while the second offers, in contrast, a spiritual interpretation.[16]

Figure 4: Flamen, *Devises et emblemes d'amour moralisez*, Paris, 1648, F1r.

Unlike Boissière's collection in which many of the devices were originally designed for the particular needs of a specific occasion, and only subsequently put together in an anthology, Flamen's collection is truly generalist in its source material. The title of the work is misleading, suggesting as it does a restricted range of subject matter centred on the theme of love. In fact a full range of themes familiar from sixteenth-century emblems and devices are exploited by Flamen, including both

---

[16] It is interesting that in the 1672 edition the distinctive approach of the two commentaries is further highlighted by being entitled *Explication* and *Moralité* respectively.

allegorical and realistic subjects. Among the familiar allegorical ones we find the two palms bending their heads together with the bilingual motto *Iungit amor/L'Amour les joint*, inspired from Jacob Cats' emblem on the same theme but with the motto *Vivite concordes*,[17] or the monkey hugging its young to death with the motto *Amari nocet/Caresses nuisibles* (see fig.4), which figures in many emblem books from La Perrière's *Theatre* onwards.[18] Among the realistically depicted devices we find a man pouring water on a fire with the motto *Aqua vehementius ardet/Il le rend plus ardent*, or a man standing against a wild countryside landscape with the motto *Loca sola caveto/Fuis la solitude*.[19]

Among the familiar emblematic figures we find the phoenix, the cameleon and the sunflower all depicted in the engravings in their traditional guises, and with their traditional significance signalled in their mottoes, but in each case Flamen offers a dual interpretation by means of his two contrasting commentaries accompanying the engravings. In the case of both the phoenix and the sunflower the second commentary is a specifically Christian one, in common with the normal pattern of the collection, but in the case of the chameleon, more uncommonly, Flamen simply gives the usual moral interpretation of the chameleon's changing colours without any Christian gloss. In all three cases the first interpretation relates to the overall theme of human love. Thus in *Usque sequar/Je le suyvray jusques là* the faithful flower following the sun is first glossed as denoting a faithful human lover, and secondly as the the faithful soul following Christ:

> Heureux celuy qui rencontre un amy du naturel de cette fleur. *Tu mihi, si qua fides cura perennis erit*: Je me souviendray eternellement de vous, ou me croiés homme sans foy, dit Ovide au premier de ses Amours, & apres luy generalement tous les Amoureux: cependant combien en voyons-nous qui accompagnent ce qu'ils ayment jusques au tombeau? combien peu qui suivent leurs maistresses jusques'en leur couchant?

> Ce tourne-sol, apres avoir suivy le Soleil pendant sa course, ne l'abandonne

---

[17] *Devises et emblemes d'amour moralisez*, p.57. See J. Cats, *Proteus ofte minne-beelden verandert in sinne-beelden*, Rotterdam, P. van Waesberge, 1627, 4°, Part 2, *Emblemata moralia et aeconomica*, emblem 1.

[18] *Devises et emblemes d'amour moralisez*, p.65. See *Theatre*, emblem 47. See also *Caecus amor prolis* in Paradin's *Devises heroiques* (1557, p1v); it also figures in Nicolas Reusner's emblem book under the same motto (*Emblemata Nicolai Reusneri IC partim ethica, et physica: partim verò historica & hieroglyphica, sed ad virtutis, morumque doctrinam omnia ingeniosè traducta: & in quatuor libros digesta, cum symbolis & inscriptionibus illustrium & clarorum virorum*, Frankfurt, S. Feyerabendt, 1581, 4°, Book 2, emblem 12); and under a variant motto, *Caecus amor sobolis* in Camerarius' *Symbolorum et emblematum ex animalibus quadrupedibus desumtorum centuria altera collecta* (Nuremberg, P. Kaufmann, 1595, 4°, emblem 77). See also Sebastian de Covarrubias Orozco, *Emblemas morales* (Madrid, L. Sanchez, 1610, 4°, Book 2, emblem 87). Other examples of this very common emblematic figure could also be cited.

[19] *Devises et emblemes d'amour moralisez*, p.3 and p.95.

point qu'il ne le voye coucher. Que devons-nous faire pour le Soleil de nos
ames? JESUS CHRIST est sur le Calvaire, où toutes ses lumieres se cachent à
nos yeux; il est sur la Croix, où les rayons de sa Divinité esclattent le moins:
en un mot, il se couche, ne soyons pas si lasches que de l'abandonner.

(Flamen, *Devises et emblemes d'amour moralisez*, pp.16-17)

and even the phoenix is given an interpretation relating to human love, as well as a
more conventional Christian one in *Invito funere vivet/Il vivra malgré la mort*:

Le Phoenix, disent les Naturalistes, revit de sa cendre, il se brusle, & dans
l'esperance qu'il a de se voir renaistre, il entretient un Amour qui n'est pas
infructueux: *Uritur, nec sterilem sperando nutrit amorem.* Quand cette
imagination ne seroit pas veritable, elle vient trop bien à nostre sujet pour la
rejetter; & comme elle s'explique d'elle-mesme, je reserve le reste de cette
page pour la moralité.

Voicy une bien naïfve representation du Chrestien, qui ne peut vivre à la
grace que par la mort qu'il reçoit dans le Baptesme: Il faut qu'il soit ensevely
dans le sepulchre que l'Amour de Jesus-Christ luy a basty, s'il veut vivre sous
la Loy que Dieu luy a prescripte; il faut qu'il s'aneantisse, s'il veut estre
quelque chose aux yeux de l'Eternel, & qu'il face mourir en luy la vieille
creature, pour y establir la nouvelle.

(Flamen, *Devises et emblesmes d'amour moralisez*, 1648, pp.44-5)

In the case of the chameleon, however, in *Mutabile semper/Rien de constant* while the
first commentary uses the chameleon's ability to change colour to reflect on the
fickleness of women, the second simply draws the conventional moral lesson from the
chameleon as representing hypocrisy, rather than giving it a spiritual gloss:

La peau du Cameleon est si susceptible des couleurs, qu'elle prend tousjours
celle du sujet qui luy est le plus proche: Et l'esprit de la femme est si
changeant, qu'il se laisse aller à toutes sortes d'impressions; Il change à tant
de vents, qu'on peut dire, que ce sexe n'a rien de si constant que son
inconstance, rien de si ferme que sa legereté, *Varium & mutabile semper
foemina*, dit Virg.

Nous pourrions en dire autant des Hypocrites, dont la vie est semblable à ces
visions fantastiques, qui ne manquent point de faire voir tout ce qui n'est pas
en effect: Ils changent à tous propos, ils se transforment selon les places
qu'ils ont à occuper; mais cela n'a point de suitte, ils reviennent tousjours à
leur premiere nature, parce que, comme disoit autresfois Seneque à Neron:
*Nemo potest naturam fictam diu ferre, ficta in naturam suam redeunt, quibus
autem veritas subest ex solido evanescunt.*

(Flamen, *Devises et emblesmes d'amour moralisez*, 1648, pp.20-21)

    With Le Moyne's *Devises heroiques et morales* of 1649 we find yet another
variant pattern. As with Flamen's collection dating from the previous year, Le
Moyne's also observes symmetry of layout, with each complete device occupying a
double opening, with a prose commentary facing the engraved device proper.
However, the new variant in Le Moyne's collection is the inclusion of a short passage
of French verse accompanying the engraving and motto.[20] As the title suggests, the
devices are grouped together as either 'heroic' or 'moral'. Interestingly it is the
publisher, Augustin Courbé, rather than Le Moyne himself, who defines the
distinction to be drawn between the two types in his preliminary address to the reader,
explaining that the heroic devices are 'des eloges d'un mot & d'une figure; & ont esté
faites pour des Personnes de condition & de vertu eminentes' whereas 'les secondes
qui sont les Morales, sont des leçons abregées; & comme je l'ay oüy dire, des dogmes
par extraict, & une philosophie en essence' (A2v). In reality, however, the distinction
between the two categories is blurred, since many of the supposedly heroic devices are
not in fact attributed to a particular person, and in many cases they are no less
moralising than those which are specifically defined as 'morales'. Courbé's ingenious
explanation of the function of the passage of French verse, for which he lays claim to
originality, suggests that here again, as in Flamen's collection, each device is
susceptible of two quite separate readings, the one provided by the prose gloss, and the
other by the verse:

> Au reste, parce que la Devise, qui est une Similitude suspenduë & sans
> attache, peut souffrir autant de sens differens, qu'elle souffre de convenances;
> on a trouvé à propos de t'interpreter celles cy; & d'arrester par une courte
> explication la similitude qui est vague & comme imparfaite dans la
> Devise...Encore te faut-il dire un mot de l'artifice des vers adjoustez à ces
> Devises. Ce n'en sont pas de simples interpretations; ce sont plustost d'autres
> Devises mieux marquées & plus estenduës, plus distinctes & plus achevées
> que les premieres. Ce sont des images à deux faces, & des portraits qui ont
> deux visées: & comme ils regardent de front le symbole qu'ils expliquent; ils
> regardent aussi de front & sans détour, ou la personne ou le sujet à qui
> s'aplique le symbole. Jusques icy on ne s'estoit point avisé, ny d'expliquer
> ainsi les Devises, ny de les parer de la sorte.
>   (Le Moyne, *Devises heroiques et morales*, A2v-3r)

In fact, however, just as the distinction between heroic and moral is blurred, so also
the distinction between the sense of the prose gloss and that of the verse is less
marked than Courbé suggests, as is seen in Le Moyne's treatment of the familiar topos
of the ivy twined around a tree. The engraving depicting this scene includes within it
the Latin motto *Mihi non senuit* and below the engraving appears the French version
of this in letterpress, *Il n'est point vieux pour moy*, followed by the French verse:

---

[20]   The motto appears in both Latin and French. The Latin version is incorporated into the
engraving, while the French version is printed below the engraving, together with the short
French verse.

> Lié des bras, lié du coeur.
> Au cher appuy de mon bonheur,
> Je dépite la mort, & brave la tempeste:
> Le temps qui détruit tout luy garantit ma foy;
> Et quoy que la vieillesse ait depoüillé sa teste,
> Il est encore jeune pour moy.
>
> (Le Moyne, *Devises heroiques et morales*, L3v)

thus making a self-contained unit. However the prose passage on the facing page does not offer an alternative reading, as was the case with Flamen's devices, by providing a new gloss relating purely to the engraved figure and motto, but rather simply serves as a complementary gloss, expanding and clarifying the message already contained in the combination of figure, motto and verse on the facing page:

> Le Lierre ne quitte jamais un arbre à qui il s'est une fois attachée; il l'embrasse vieil & dépoüillé, comme il l'a embrassé jeune & verdoyant: il n'y a point de vent ny de gresle, il n'y a point de tempeste ny de foudre, qui l'en puisse separer: & encor apres que la mort l'a abattu & qu'il est pourry, il luy est aussi uny que s'il estoit debout & en vie. Le symbole est noble & bien marqué pour nous enseigner que l'amitié n'est pas seulement une societé pour le printemps, & pour les beaux jours: qu'elle doit estre de toutes les saisons & de tous les âges: que ses liens doivent estre plus forts que le fer que l'on donne au Temps, & que celuy-là mesme que l'on donne à la Fortune: & qu'il faut estimer jusqu'à l'écorce & à la cendre d'une personne qu'on a aimée; qu'il faut garder fidelité à son ombre mesme & à sa memoire.[21]

Thus despite Courbé's suggestion that the prose gloss and the verse passage should be seen as each acting independently together with the engraving to form two distinct devices, this is not actually the case. In fact the individual elements of Le Moyne's devices all complement each other, and collectively form one single (albeit complexly developed) whole.

This device on the ivy-entwined tree comes from the latter section of the collection containing *devises morales*, but even among the *devises heroiques* in the first part of the collection, relatively few are person-specific. Among the devices relating to specific individuals is *Vincula restant sola mihi/Il ne me reste que les liens* for the Duke of Alva. The figure depicts a chained and hooded falcon and the significance of the combination of figure and motto is developed in the accompanying

---

[21] *Devises heroiques et morales*, L4v. More commonly it is a vine coiled round a tree, rather than ivy, which is used as the symbol of enduring friendship, as in Alciato's *Amicitia etiam post mortem durans* (1550 ed., L6v). Far from representing lasting friendship and fidelity, ivy coiled round a tree, as depicted in this device, normally denotes ingratitude, as the ever stronger ivy gradually strangles to death the tree which supported it in its youth. See, for example, among many other instances, Corrozet's *Hecatomgraphie* emblem, *Ingratitude* (B5v) or Aneau's *Nuysible copulation* in the *Imagination poetique* (E5r).

verse:

> Tout aujourd'huy j'ay fait la guerre:
> Soit dans la nuë ou sur la terre,
> Il n'est point d'Ennemy que ma main n'ait détruit;
> Et cependant recompense funeste,
> Pour tant de peine il ne me reste,
> Que d'injustes liens, & qu'une obscure nuit.
> (Le Moyne, *Devises heroiques et morales*, D2v)

and then further glossed in the prose commentary which explains the specific relevance of this to the Duke of Alva, and his military disgrace:

> Le Duc d'Alve disgracié allant reduire le Portugal, se plaignoit d'estre envoyé les chaines aux mains à la conqueste d'une Couronne. Le Faucon pourroit faire une semblable plainte, quand on le porte à la chasse avecque le chaperon & la longe. Des Capitaines d'aussi grande reputation que le Duc d'Alve ont encore esté plus mal traittez de la Fortune; & nous en avons veûs de disgraciez & de prisonniers, apres des batailles gagnées & des Provinces reduites. C'est le sens de cette Devise, où un faucon attaché, se plaint de ce qu'apres avoir chassé si long temps & avec tant de courage, pour recompense de son courage & de sa chasse, il ne luy reste que le chaperon & la perche.[22]

More commonly, however, among the *devises heroiques* such attributions as there are, are more vaguely expressed: several refer at most to a 'king' or a 'princess' without further identification. *Non radium excutient/Ils ne m'osteront pas un seul rayon*, in which the figure depicts a shining sun and the accompanying verse points to the vanity of the attempts of the envious to diminish its brilliance:

> Ma lumiere m'a fait naistre ces Envieux,
> Qui de leur souffle injurieux,
> Poussent contre moy la tempeste.
> Mais ils ont beau tempeste & nuages pousser,
> Ils pourroient le Ciel renverser,
> Avant qu'il me tombe un rayon de la teste.
> (Le Moyne, *Devises heroiques et morales,* G2v)

is not associated explicitly with any particular individual, but despite the absence of any specific reference to Louis XIV, it is clearly intended to relate to the eleven-year-old monarch for whom the sun had been chosen as his device virtually from the

---

[22] *Devises heroiques et morales*, D3r. Here again, as with the device of the ivy-entwined tree, the prose commentary serves as an additional gloss on the sense already conveyed by the combination of figure, motto and verse, rather than as a different reading of the combination of figure and motto.

moment of his birth,[23] as is indicated, albeit indirectly in the prose commentary:

> Les vents qui soufflent contre le Soleil, & qui semblent le vouloir abattre, sont des envieux indiscrets & turbulents, qu'il s'est fait luy mesme par sa lumiere. Mais quelques nuages qu'ils amassent, & quelques tempestes qu'ils excitent, le Soleil ne pert rien de sa hauteur ny de sa clarté; il marche toujours d'un pas égal: il ne manque ny à sa route ny à son Intelligence. Et l'Esprit à qui ce symbole est appliqué, quelque bruit que l'Envie & la Médisance fassent au dessous de luy, se conservera tousjours dans une égale élevation, & répandra tousjours également sa lumiere & sa renommée.
>
> (Le Moyne, *Devises heroiques et morales*, G3r)

Similarly, but rather more specifically dedicated to Louis XIV is another device in which the familiar image of the phoenix is associated with that of the sun, in order to reinforce the association with the monarch. The engraving of the phoenix is accompanied by the motto *Quoque post patrem/Et moy encore apres mon Pere* and the verse describing the youthful Louis following in the footsteps of his illustrious father:

> Que le Feu de cét Astre est pur & glorieus!
> Que le jour est puissant qu'il porte dans les yeux!
> Et que son ascendant est fort sur l'Hemisphere!
> Mon coeur est à peine formé,
> Et sur les cendres de mon Pere,
> Desja de ses rayons mon coeur est allumé.

while the prose gloss explains more fully the relationship between the symbol of the phoenix and that of the sun and the new young king following the model of his father before him:

> Le Phenix naist de la cendre de son pere bruslé au Soleil: & de cette cendre encore chaude luy vient cette inclination solaire, qui luy fait aimer le Soleil, & se tourner à sa lumiere dés qu'il a les yeux ouvers & les aisles libres. Ce symbole est noble & royal, & represente assez naturellement l'inclination que le Roy encore enfant a euë apres le feu Roy son Pere pour une personne illustre dont la vertu eminente a long temps fait l'honneur de la Cour.
>
> (Le Moyne, *Devises heroiques et morales*, B4v-C1r)

Such specifically royal devices as these are, however, in a minority in this collection of heroic and moral devices. The majority are more general in their

---

[23] As we are told by Ménestrier: 'Le Soleil est tellement l'image du Roy, que ce fut sous ce symbole que l'on celebra sa naissance en un temps où l'on avoit presque desesperé de voir aucun fruit du mariage du feu Roy.' (*La devise du Roy justifiée. Par le P. Menestrier de la Compagnie de Jesus. Avec un recueil de cinq cens devises faites pour S.M. & toute la maison royale*, Paris, E. Michalet, 1679, 4°, G2v-3r).

application, and traditional also in the familiar emblematic figures which they use, and in this they conform to the pattern of other generalist collections already discussed. Where Le Moyne's collection differs significantly from these is in the extent to which his devices are much more fully elaborated than those we have seen earlier. Not only does the engraved image add to the visual appeal of the devices, but it also contributes to greater clarity of meaning, in comparison to those earlier non-illustrated collections. But a more important difference lies in the introduction of a passage of verse to accompany that engraving (together with its Latin and French mottoes) on the same page, thereby relegating the prose passage to the facing page. The result is a structure which is remarkably similar to that adopted over one hundred years earlier by one of the earliest French writers of emblems, Gilles Corrozet in his mid-sixteenth-century *Hecatomgraphie*. In this work each individual emblem comprised woodcut figure, motto and short verse all printed on one page, together with an accompanying longer passage of verse commentary on the facing page. In Corrozet's emblems the function of this commentary was to develop in greater detail the background to the figure, and to clarify the significance of the overall message to be read into the combination of figure motto and short verse. In Le Moyne's devices, despite Courbé's claim that each device should properly be seen as two devices, the structure functions in precisely the same way, so that the combination of figure, motto and verse, together with accompanying prose gloss all work together to form one single unit. So strong are the similarities that although Le Moyne uses the word device, it would be tempting to substitute the word 'emblem', in view of the particular structure adopted, which is so akin to that of Corrozet's emblem book, and of the heavy moralising intent of the collection overall.

When Le Moyne published his theoretical treatise on devices, seventeen years later, in 1666, under the title *De l'art des devises* he included with it not only an expanded version of the *Devises heroiques et morales*, under the new title *Cabinet de devises*, but also a collection of devices on the subject of flowers entitled *Jardin de devises*, and a collection of *Devises royales* taken from his own work, *De l'art de regner*, which had been published the previous year by the same publishers as *De l'art des devises*.[24] (In addition to his own devices, Le Moyne also included with *De l'art des devises* a further collection of *Devises adoptées* by Monsieur de Montmor.[25]) As reproduced in this later edition, Le Moyne's original *Devises heroiques et morales* are somewhat modified. Although the same basic structure is retained, the prose gloss is more fully developed, and more explicit references are often made to the owner of the devices. In the case of devices addressed to members of the royal family, their particular identity is further underpinned by the addition of their own shield beneath each device.[26] In keeping with this new emphasis on the royal character of many of

[24] *De l'art de regner. Au Roy. Par le Pere Le Moyne de la Compagnie de Jesus*, Paris, S. Cramoisy and S. Mabre-Cramoisy, 1665, folio.
[25] They are included here, we are told, because Monsieur de Montmor would not himself get them published. (*De l'art des devises*, Mmm1r).
[26] A further minor difference is that whereas the Latin mottoes incorporated into the engraved figures were also reproduced in a French letterpress version in the original edition of *Devises heroiques et morales*, here no equivalent French version of the Latin mottoes is given.

the devices, is the inclusion of a specifically named collection of *Devises royales*, all of which take as their theme the inevitable sun. Typical of this collection is its opening device on the theme of the king's piety:

> La piete royale.
> *L'image du Soleil dans une nuë.*
> Respicio ut perficiar
>
> A la lumiere, à la figure,
> On me prendroit, sinon pour le Soleil,
> Au moins pour son pareil;
> S'il en estoit plus d'un dans la Nature.
> J'en ay les traits, j'en ay le tour,
> Je n'éclate que de son jour,
> Et ne luis que du feu, que sa face me jette;
> J'en suis ceint, j'en suis couronné;
> Mais son Image veut, pour estre en moy parfaite,
> Qu'à son regard mon regard soit tourné.
> (Le Moyne, *De l'art des devises*, p.429)

with the accompanying prose gloss:

> Le Soleil qui est le Peintre de toutes choses, ne peint jamais mieux, que quand il se peint luy-mesme sur le fond d'une nuë, qui le regardant de front & en droite ligne, reçoit sans dissipation tous les traits de sa lumiere. De cette nuë ainsi preparée, il se fait un second Soleil, qui à le tour, la lueur, & la figure du premier, & ce Soleil peint ressemble si parfaitement au Soleil peintre, que les meilleurs yeux ont de la peine à distinguer l'un d'aveque l'autre.
>
> Que le Prince apprenne delà, qu'estant lumineux, comme il est, de la ressemblance de Dieu, & couronné de la participation de son Diademe, son premier soin doit estre de se tourner continuellement vers luy, par les actes d'une sincere pieté, s'il veut regner glorieusement dans le Temps, & plus glorieusement dans l'Eternité. (Le Moyne, *De l'art des devises*, p.428)

What is lacking in this particular collection of *Devises royales*, however, as also in the flower devices in the *Jardin des devises* is any illustration for the individual devices (although curiously the *Devises adoptées* by Monsieur de Montmor *do* include engraved illustrations into which their Latin motto is incorporated). In these two collections by Le Moyne we find, therefore, a further variant structural pattern. In the case of the flowers each device once again occupies a double opening with a prose description and gloss on one page, and on the facing page the name of the flower, its motto and accompanying verse. The structure is in effect the same as that of his illustrated devices, but with a description of the flower rather than an actual illustration. Le Moyne justifies the absence of engraved figures here on the grounds that since everyone knows what flowers look like, there is no need to include illustrations of them. The actual reason is more probably economic. Once again, as in his *Devises heroiques et morales*, the claim is made (this time by Le Moyne himself rather than by the publisher) suggests that each device offers a double reading,[27] although once again it is not clear how this is so, since again here, as in the *Devises heroiques et morales*, the prose gloss complements the combination of title, motto and verse, rather than standing independent of the verse. Typical of Le Moyne's flower devices is that on the rose. On the verso is the prose gloss:

> Il ne reste plus de bon mot à dire de la Rose, Sapho l'a declarée Reyne des Fleurs; & a dit qu'elle estoit l'oeil du Printemps & la Pourpre de la Terre: Un autre eust pû dire, qu'elle est un Escarboucle vivant, une Estoile vegetable, un feu parfumé. Elle peut estre tout cela en Poësie. En cette Devise, elle est la figure de ce bien fragile & dangereux, qui est tout composé de feux & de traits. Ceux qui se permettent d'y jetter la veuë, en doivent demeurer là: Encore ne le doivent-ils faire que de loin & en passant; de peur de s'embrasser dans ses épines.   (Le Moyne, *De l'art des devises*, p.394)

and on the facing recto is the title, motto and verse:

LA ROSE
Aspice & abstine

Est-ce pourpre, est-ce feu, dont je suis couronnée?
Soit pourpre ou feu, l'éclat en plaist également:
Jamais d'un plus pompeux, d'un plus rare ornement,
L'Aurore en ses beaux jours, ne fut environnée.
Non seulement les yeux en sont surpris;
L'effet en va jusques dans les Esprits;
Et rien ne peut resister à mes charmes:
Mais aussi, l'on ne doit que des yeux m'approcher:
La Pudeur est ma Garde, elle m'a fait des armes,
Qui ne permettent pas aux mains de me toucher.
(Le Moyne, De l'art des devises, p.395)

With Monsieur de Montmor's collection of *Devises adoptées* we see a return to the much earlier pattern established by Paradin in the mid sixteenth century and continued in the seventeenth-century editions of his devices. Symmetry is here maintained in that each device occupies a single page, and each device comprises three elements: engraved figure, Latin motto incorporated into the engraving, and short prose gloss describing and explaining it, and in some cases identifying the owner of the device, very much in the style of the devices of Paradin. Typical of the

---

[27] 'En chaque Devise la Fleur parle; toutes ses paroles ont double sens; & ne luy appartiennent pas plus qu'à la Personne pour qui elle parle.' (p.[380])

collection is Montmor's device on the subject of the bird of paradise in which the engraved figure depicting the bird, and incorporating the motto *Non sum terra tuus* is accompanied by the following gloss:

> Ce mot d'Ovide attribué à l'Oyseau de Paradis, luy est propre. Il ne descend jamais à terre; la haute Region du Monde est son élement; il se nourrit là de la pureté de l'Air & de la lumiere: & par là il est le Symbole d'un Homme qui est detaché du Monde, & qui a tous ses desirs & toutes ses pretensions dans le Ciel. (Le Moyne, *De l'art des devises*, p.480)

We see well demonstrated in these various sub-collections of devices included in Le Moyne's *De l'art des devises* the considerable diversity of structure which can be adopted even within one single volume. With a writer like Claude-François Ménestrier - likewise a member of the Jesuit order - we see the even greater diversity of structure that can be adopted by one single author.

Ménestrier was undoubtedly the most prolific seventeenth-century writer of emblems, devices and theoretical treatises on both. In the course of a publishing career extending from the 1650s to the late 1680s as well as innumerable collections of emblems and devices, he also produced accounts of celebrations at which they had been displayed, and manuals on the art of organising such celebrations. In the preliminaries to his late work, *La science et l'art des devises* dating from 1686, he gives a brief résumé of his career over the last thirty years, explaining that having begun to write royal devices as early as 1658, the peace celebrations and royal marriage following two years later in 1660 offered him great scope, and that thereafter he never looked back. He lists the numerous ceremonial occasions for which he had designed the decor since that early date, concluding with the striking statistic: 'Voila ce qui a fait naître les deux mille Devises que je donne'(ã2v), and explaining that this present collection is a compilation of those devices which he has created over the last thirty years for divers festivities, which he has now felt necessary to publish under his own name since others have been plagiarising them:

> Plusieurs raisons m'obligent de publier un assez bon nombre de Devises, que j'ay faites depuis trente ans. La plûpart de ces Images ont paru en des Decorations, sur des Medailles, autour de quelques portraits, & à l'entrée de quelques livres, ou n'ayant pas affecté de faire connoistre de qui elles estoient, quelques uns ont crû qu'ils pouvoient les adopter, & s'en declarer les autheurs. (Ménestrier, *La science et l'art des devises*, ã1r)

The composition of emblems and devices was embedded into the Jesuit educational system, and to demonstrate how easy it is to create devices to order, once one is into the swing of it, Ménestrier goes on to reproduce a string of one hundred devices which he has created on the basis of the first eighty lines of Horace's *Ars poetica* (ẽ 6v-õ2r).[28]

---

[28]   See, for example, the fourth device in this series, which is a doubly ingenious device for a

The three principal treatises in which he includes significant generalist collections of devices are *La science et l'art des devises* and two slightly earlier works, the two-volume *Philosophie des images* of 1682 and *La devise du Roy justifiée* of 1679. In *La science et l'art des devises,* which is a compilation of a number of discrete collections composed earlier in his career, Ménestrier respects the order of these collections, reproducing each of them, one after another, and identifying them by allusion to the occasion for which they were designed. But in the other two works, in which there is wide diversity of material, Ménestrier imposes a logical order upon them by grouping them according to general theme, in much the same way that Aneau did for Alciato's collection of emblems over 150 years earlier. Thus in a collection of devices subtitled *Le monde entier consacré à la gloire du Roy, recueil de devises faites pour le Roy, dont tous les corps sont rangez selon l'ordre naturel des choses* (P2r-Dd1v) in *La devise du Roy justifiée,* the devices are arranged in such categories as *Les astres*; *La lune*; *Les etoiles*; *Les elemens*; *L'histoire sainte*; *Les arts*; *La fable,* while we find similar divisions in *La philosophie des images,* such as: *Le ciel*; *Les astres*; *Le soleil*; *L'aurore et la lumiere*; *Les planetes*; *Les oyseaux.* In such works as these Ménestrier is essentially intent on conveying information, rather than on producing a volume which is in itself an aesthetically pleasing work. Hence the devices in such treatises as these are usually simply described rather than actually depicted visually by means of engraved figures. Presumably for reasons of economy of space, the devices are furthermore described as succinctly as possible, with no unnecessary elaboration, as, for example, in the opening device of *Le monde entier consacré à la gloire du Roy* in *La devise du Roy justifiée,* in which we are given the explanation for Louis's enduring symbol of the sun:

> Le Soleil naissant qui dore les nuës, & qui éclaire les campagnes,
> QUALIS APEX ORTUS TANTI?
> Quel sera le midi d'un si bel Orient?
> Pour la naissance du Roy au milieu des Victoires du Roy son pere, & aprés avoir été desiré & attendu vingt-ans entiers.
>   (Ménestrier, *La devise du Roy justifiée*, P2r)

or as in a series of devices for the *Dauphin* which appear later in the same collection, representing him as a young eagle flying skywards, following in the track of his illustrious father:

> Un Aiglon volant vers le Soleil,
> FATIS CONFISUS AVORUM.
> C'est parce qu'il se sert de ses ayeuls.

---

collection of devices:
   Pour un recueil de Devises ramassées de divers endroits, & tirées de divers ouvrages.
   L'Ocean, où toutes les eaux sont ramassées
   UNDIQUE COLLATIS
   De mille endroits elles sont ramassées. ($\tilde{e}$ 7r)

Le même,
PATRIOS SEQUITUR AUSUS.
Il marche sur les traces de son Pere.

L'une & l'autre est pour Monseigneur le Dauphin.

Un jeune Aiglon,
CRESCENS IN FULMINA.
Il croît pour porter les foudres.

Pour le même,
Un grand Aigle qui conduit un Aiglon vers le Soleil,
LAETATUR GENUISSE PAREM
Il se réjoüit d'avoir fait son semblable.
Pour le Roy & Monseigneur le Dauphin.
                    (Ménestrier, *La devise du Roy justifiée*, Y1r-v)

Since, as Ménestrier explains in *La science et l'art des devises*, the volume contains two thousand devices, it would not be practical for these to be more fully developed. Thus the general pattern followed in all three collections is that of simply providing a brief description of the figure, together with its motto (usually in Latin) and a French version of this. Only occasionally is the ownership of a particular device identified, and only very occasionally is an illustration included (as, for example, at the beginning of individual sections in *La philosophie des images*). There are no verses, and no passages of prose commentary, other than the very occasional very brief explanation of the circumstance in which a particular device was created, as in a series of devices identified as having been created on the occasion of the death of the Queen Mother in 1666, included in *La science et l'art des devises*, of which the first is:

Pour la mort de la Reine mere, l'an 1666.
I. Une Peone, qui se défüeille.
NEC PARCITUR OSTRO
Le pourpre ne met pas à couvert de la mort.
                    (Ménestrier, *La science et l'art des devises*, N2r)

Such works as these by Ménestrier do not set out to be attractive works of art. Their function is rather to be business-like treatises on the science of device-writing, in which the collections of actual devices serve as demonstration of the points made by the author in the theoretical treatise. A brief description of what is to be shown in the figure is enough. It is not necessary for it to be reproduced also in visual form. In certain other works by Ménestrier where he is using his emblems or devices rather differently, in order to teach, or to persuade or to demonstrate as we shall see later in this study, the presence of actual visual illustration is more important. Thus, for example, in the *Histoire du Roy Louis le Grand par les medailles*, dating from late in his career, and dedicated to Louis XIV's three then very youthful grandsons, Louis,

Duc de Bourgogne, aged seven, Philippe, Duc d'Anjou, aged six, and Charles, Duc de Berry, aged three, the various meaningful medals and *jetons* are carefully reproduced in engraved form, while in his much earlier *Resjouissances de la paix* of 1660, the various triumphal arches which were erected in Lyon to celebrate this occasion are not just described but also illustrated by engravings. But in theoretical treatises like *La science et l'art des devises* in which collections of devices are also included, actual illustration is largely omitted as being less essential, and thus unnecessarily extravagant of space.

Right at the very end of the seventeenth century we find the generalist tradition still being perpetuated in collections of devices similarly produced in as succinct a form as possible in order to condense as much material into as small a space as possible, but designed for a very different purpose, from that of Ménestrier, and thus taking a very different form. In the very earliest days of the sixteenth-century French emblem, writers and publishers had stressed the utility of books of emblems and devices for artists and craftsmen, and it is interesting to see that at the very end of the seventeenth century and even into the eighteenth century this claim is still amply vindicated. We saw it expressed first in Gilles Corrozet's liminary *épître* in his *Hecatomgraphie*:

> Aussy pourront ymagers & tailleurs,
> Painctres, brodeurs, orfevres, esmailleurs
> Prendre en ce livre aulcune fantasie
> Comme ilz feroient d'une tapisserie. (Corrozet, *Hecatomgraphie*, A3v)

and then again on the title page of Guillaume Roville's French edition of the devices of Giovio and Simeoni: *Tetrastiques faictz sur les devises du Seigneur Paulo Jovio, et de Messire Gabriel Simeon, pour servir en verrieres, chassis, galeries et tableaux, ainsi qu'il plaira au lecteur de les accommoder.* At the end of the seventeenth century we find a number of editions of works being produced for precisely this function, but interestingly put together not by writers or publishers, but by practising engravers. In 1685 the Paris engraver Nicolas Verrien put together a manual specifically designed to cater for the needs of craftsmen, including decorative engraved monograms for different combinations of letters, heraldic supporters, hieroglyphic figures and many other decorative designs, among which a large number of engraved figures of emblems and devices. The full title to the work gives clear indication to craftsmen of the range of designs that are to be found in the volume:

> *Livre curieux et utile pour les sçavans, et artistes. Composé de trois alphabets de chiffres simples, doubles & triples, fleuronnez et au premier trait. Accompagné d'un tres grand nombre de devises, emblêmes, médailles et autres figures hieroglyfiques. Ensemble de plusieurs supports et cimiers pour les ornemens des armes. Avec une table tres ample par le moyen de*

> *laquelle on trouvera facilement tous les noms imaginables. Le tout inventé,*
> *dessiné et gravé par Nicolas Verien maistre graveur*[29]

A very business-like approach is adopted in this working manual, with little concession being made to aesthetic considerations. Since the work is designed as a pattern book for craftsmen the illustration is obviously much more important than had been the case with Ménestrier's collections of devices, but there is no unnecessary waste of space. Fifteen small circular engraved figures are grouped together all on one single page and on the facing recto are listed, as concisely as possible, the appropriate accompanying texts. Originality is certainly not an issue here. On the contrary, Verrien's aim is to provide a work of compilation and the figures he includes in the volume cover a range of topoi familiar from earlier collections of emblems and devices, and his collection subtitled *Emblemes et devises latines, espagnoles, et italiennes. Avec leurs explications françoises,* [30] is characterised by a great diversity of subject matter, as is clear from the opening devices in the collection. Equally a glance at the first few of them is sufficient to show the extent to which they are indeed derived from earlier emblematic sources. Of the first fifteen, for example, seven are certainly taken from Alciato:

1. Un Vaisseau en Mer, qui arrive à pleines voiles dans le Port. *Spes proxima.* Son desir est sur le point d'estre accomply.

2. Un Homme qui se fait traîner dans un Chariot attelé de deux Lions. *Etiam ferocissimos domari.* L'Homme sage peut dompter & venir à bout des plus emportez & des plus furieux.

4. Un Homme armé, & un habillé en Homme de Justice. *Unum nihil, duos plurimum posse.* Un des deux ne peut rien faire seul, mais estans ensemble, ils peuvent tout.

8. Un Vieillard couché & considerant les Astres. *Desidia.* C'est la paresse.

10. Une Femme maigre coëffée avec des Serpens, & ayant un bâton d'épine. *Invidia.* C'est l'Envie.

11. Une Chévre qui est taitée par un jeune Loup. *Sibi damna parat.* Elle travaille pour sa rüine.

12. Un jeune Homme qui se mire & s'admire dans une Fontaine. *Philautia.* Amour propre.

---

[29]   Paris, N. Verrien, 1685, 8°.
[30]   Although this subtitle suggests that this is a trilingual work, in fact the basic text is all in French. The majority of the mottos are in Latin, but some are in Spanish or Italian, and it is these which justify the reference to 'devises Latines, Espagnoles et Italiennes'.

while number 6 'Un Hercule assis avec ses Armes ordinaires, & un Enfant armé qui l'attaque. *Temeritas*. C'est une temerité que cette insulte' is also probably inspired from Alciato's *In eos qui supra vires quicquam audent*, depicting Hercules being attacked by pygmies (see fig. 5).[31]

That Verrien's work *Livre curieux et utile* did indeed fulfil a need is evident from the fact that it was republished eleven years later, in 1696, under the revised title *Recueil d'emblêmes, devises, medailles et figures hieroglyphiques, au nombre de plus de douze cent, avec leurs explications*, and even 28 years later - well into the eighteenth century - it was popular enough to justify yet another edition.[32] Even more popular, however, judging by the number of editions they ran through, were a series of very similar works published slightly later in Amsterdam by another engraver, Daniel de La Feuille, who seems to have been something of a specialist in this particular field. In some of his works the debt to Verrien's earlier model is very evident. The full title of La Feuille's *Livre nouveau et utile* of 1690, for example, in which he stresses very clearly its function as a manual for craftsmen, is an obvious imitation of Verrien's *Livre curieux et utile*:

> *Livre nouveau et utile pour toutes sortes d'artistes. Et particulierement pour les orfevres, les orlogeurs, les peintres, les graveurs, les brodeurs &. Contenant quatre alphabets de chiffres fleuronnez au premier trait avec quantité de devises, d'emblemes et de noeuds d'amour. Avec une table exacte pour trouver en général tous les noms et surnoms entrelassez. Le tout exactement recherché, dessiné et gravé. Par Daniel de La Feuille.*[33]

La Feuille clearly perceived a market at the end of the seventeenth century for collections of engraved emblems and devices, and other such useful designs, catering for the needs of craftsmen, and set about satisfying this market by producing various such works, with the engravings provided by himself and the text by local academics.[34] In his first such collection, *Devises et emblemes anciennes et modernes*, for which the text was provided by Henri Offelen, who is described modestly as 'professeur en toutes ces langues à Amsterdam' (N1v), he follows closely the model of Verrien's collection. Once again the engraved figures are packed together, with either twelve or fifteen per page, and with the mottoes and descriptions on the facing page,

---

[31] See Alciato, *Emblemata*, 1550, D1v; C2v; C8v; F4v; E8r; E4v; E7r; E1v. These Alciato-derived devices are not exceptional. Many others throughout the collection are also taken from Alciato, as, for example, 'Un Satire assis au bord d'un Bois. *Luxuria*. Luxure' (*Livre curieux et utile*, A2r) is taken from Alciato's *Luxuria* (*Emblemata*, 1550, E8v).

[32] Paris, J. Jombert, 1696, 8°; Paris, J. Jombert, 1724, 8°. See Praz, p.528.

[33] Amsterdam, D. de La Feuille, 1690, 8° obl.; *ibid.*, 1691.

[34] As well as his more obvious published collections of devices, see also La Feuille's illustrated manual on heraldry and naval flags published five years later: *Methode nouvelle pour apprendre l'art du blason, ou la science des nobles par dialogues. Avec un discours sur les devises, supports, cimiers, lambrequins, & tombeaux. Enrichis des pavillons & des enseignes que chaque nation porte en mer, & des figures necessaires pour leurs explications, en François & en Flamand*, Amsterdam, D. de La Feuille, 1695, 4°.

Figure 5: Verrien, *Livre curieux et utile*, Paris, 1685, A1v-2r.

but the significant difference between the Amsterdam published work and the earlier French published work is that where in Verrien's earlier version only a Latin motto was given, Offelen here provides a polyglot text with the motto supplied in seven languages, as in the opening two devices of the collection:

1. Un Vaisseau en Mer, *Non dormit qui custodit*, Qui le gouverne, ne dort pas, *Chi là custodisce non dorme, Quien lo govierna no duerme*, Die t'

bewaart, en slaapt niet, He that governs it, does not sleep, *Der es bewahrt schläfft nicht.*

2. Un Soleil sur une Chauve-Souris, *Potiùs mori quam abstinere,* Plûtôt mourir, que s'abstenir, *Più presto morire, che astenersi,* Mas presto morir que abstener, *Liever sterven, als onthouden,* Rather dye than hold up, *Lieber sterben als aufhören.*
   (La Feuille/Offelen, *Devises et emblemes anciennes et modernes,* A1v)

The title makes clear that although some devices are original, the material is - as we have seen already in many other works in this chapter - essentially taken from earlier writers:

Devises et emblemes anciennes et modernes.Tirées des plus celebres auteurs. Avec plusieurs autres nouvellement inventées et mises en Latin, en Francois, en Espagnol, en Italien, en Anglois, en Flamand et en Allemand, par les soins de Daniel de la Feuille.[35]

and this is indeed the case. Offelen's device of a sword entwined in an olive branch, for example:

3. Une Epée environnée d'une branche d'Olivier, *Utroque clarescere pulcrum,* Bonne pour la guerre & pour la paix, *Son per la pace, e per la guerra,* Soy por la guerra y la paz, *Voor vrede, en oorlog,* I am for war and peace, *ich bin fûr fried und krieg.*
   (La Feuille/Offelen, *Devises et emblemes anciennes et modernes,* A1v)

is inspired from Zincgref's emblem on the same theme, *Idem pacis mediusque belli.*[36] But in fact, whatever the original source may have been, the immediate source for the *Devises et emblemes anciennes et modernes,* published in Amsterdam in 1691 is undoubtedly Verrien's *Livre curieux et utile,* published in Paris six years earlier in 1685. The eight devices quoted earlier from the beginning of Verrien's sub-collection of *Emblemes et devises latines, espagnoles, et italiennes. Avec leurs explications françoises* in the *Livre curieux et utile* appear also - in a slightly different order - in Offelen's collection of *Devises et emblemes anciennes et modernes* put together for Daniel de La Feuille, as do a large proportion of the other emblems in Verrien's collection. The engravings in the Amsterdam edition are clearly modelled on the earlier Paris engravings, and Offelen's sole originality lies in his expansion of the number of languages in which the mottoes are expressed, so that Verrien's opening emblem, for example ('Un Vaisseau en Mer, qui arrive à pleines voiles dans le port. *Spes proxima.* Son desir est sur le point d'estre accomply') becomes expanded in

---

[35]   Although the work is referred to on the title page as a collection of *devises et emblemes* the running title more appropriately uses the phrase *Devises choisies* throughout.
[36]   *Emblematum ethico-politicorum centuria Iulii Guilielmi Zincgrefi,* n.p. (Heidelburg), M. Merian, 1619, 4°, emblem 66.

Offelen's later version published in Amsterdam to read:

> 3. Un Vaisseau en Mer qui arrive à pleines voiles dans le Port, *Spes proxima*, Son désir est sur le point d'étre accompli. *La sua speranza stà per essere compita*, Zyn wensch staat vervult te worden, His wishes are to be accomplished, Seine wünsche werden erfüllet werden.
> (La Feuille/Offelen, *Devises et emblemes anciennes et modernes*, A2v)

while his emblem of Envy ('Une Femme coëffée avec des Serpens, & ayant un bâton d'épine. *Invidia*. C'est l'Envie') similarly becomes:

> 12. Une Femme maigre coiffée avec des Serpens, & ayant un Bâton d'Espine, *Invidia*, C'est l'Envie, *Quest'è l'Invidia*, Aquesta es embidia, *T'is de Nijd*, T'is Envy, *Es ist der neid*.
> (La Feuille/Offelen, *Devises et emblemes anciennes et modernes*, A2v)

This work, which was originally published in 1691, enjoyed quite striking popularity, being republished in a number of subsequent editions not just in Amsterdam, but elsewhere in Europe also, continuing into the eighteenth century.[37] The polyglot text advertised on the title page clearly reflects La Feuille's intention that the work should be accessible to a wide readership across Europe, and the fact that the work was indeed published in several editions in Augsburg, as well as in Amsterdam, with a variant German title page for its German readers reflects its international appeal. The much larger number of editions which this work went through compared with Verrien's earlier version published in Paris with the text only in French, with Latin mottoes, reflects the greater popularity of such polyglot editions.

In this first collection La Feuille includes at the end an *avertissement* in which he promises that he will produce another such volume every year,[38] but in fact, although he continued to reissue the original collection at two-yearly intervals for several years, he only produced one further new volume, five years later in 1696, with a confusingly similar title to that of the earlier work:

> *Devises & emblemes d'amour, anciens & modernes moralisez & expliquez en*

---

[37] Amsterdam, D. de La Feuille, 1691, 4°. The collection was reissued at intervals, with the date on the title page changed by hand to read 1693, 1697 and 1712. It was also published in several editions in Augsburg, by L.Kroniger and G.Göbels in 1693, 1695, 1697, 1699, 1702 and 1703 with a variant German title page, *Emblematische Gemüths-Vergnügung bey Betrachtung der curieusten und ergözlichsten Sinnbildern mit ihren zuständigen Deutsch-Lateinisch-Frantzösisch und Italienischen Beyschrifften.*

[38] 'Ces 51. planches d'Emblêmes & Devises, mises en Latin, en François, en Italien, en Espagnol, en Flaman, en Anglois, & en Alleman, par le Sieur *Henry Offelen*, Professeur en toutes ces Langues à Amsterdam, & données au Public par *Daniel de La Feuille*, pour l'Année 1692; seront suivies d'un pareil nombre tous les ans, des plus belles qui se trouveront.' (N3v)

sept sortes de langues par M. Pallavicini, professeur des langues etrangeres.[39]

Capitalising on the popularity of the earlier work, this second collection of engraved devices by La Feuille also included a polyglot text, provided this time by Offelen's successor, Pallavicini, described on the title page as 'Mr Pallavicini, professeur des langues etrangeres'. In this latter volume, however, the debt to Verrien is less obvious than in La Feuille's first collection. Here the range of subject matter is less diverse than in the earlier collection. As suggested in the title there is here an overall unifying theme, in that the devices or emblems are all loosely related to the subject of love, whereas in the earlier volume with the text supplied by Offelen they were much more generalist in subject. (They are in fact just as derivative as the earlier collection, but in this latter work they are more commonly imitated from a range of Dutch love emblems, notably those of Vaenius, Heinsius and Cats and the *Thronus Cupidinis.*[40]) In structure also they follow a rather different format from those of the earlier collection with text by Offelen. Here there are fewer engraved figures packed onto one single page. Where the earlier work included variously twelve or fifteen, here each recto contains only six small circular engravings, while on the facing verso are printed their description and appropriate mottoes, once again in seven different languages, as in the earlier volume. However the significant difference here is that Pallavicini introduces a short passage of French verse in addition to the description and mottoes. See for example his emblem on the familiar topos of Cupid the honey-thief. The little engraved figure depicts in the foreground Cupid being comforted by Venus, while in the background we see him earlier engaged in stealing honey from beehives, around which angry bees are flying (A2r). On the facing verso are printed the accompanying mottoes in seven languages, followed by a quatrain in French:

> Par pari. *Al pari.* A la pareille. *A la pareja.* Elk zijn maal. Like with like.
> Gleich mit gleichem.
> Cupidon fut piqué d'une Abeille traitresse,
> D'où vient qu'un animal si petit fort blesse,
> Dit-il? Venus repond: Et toi, mon petit Nain,
> Tu blesses bien chacun, & le tiens sous ta main.
> > (La Feuille/Pallavicini, *Devises & emblemes d'amour, anciens &*
> > *modernes*, A1v)

While this device on Cupid and the honey bee clearly fits into the overall theme of love, not all of the devices in the collection do so. More tenuously associated with the

---

[39]   Amsterdam, D. de La Feuille, 1696, 4°. This work was also reissued the following year, 1697.

[40]   Jacob Cats, *Silenus Alcibiadis sive Proteus, vitae humanae ideam, emblemate trifariàm variato, oculis subiiciens. Deus nobis haec otia fecit*, Middelburg, J. van der Hellen, 1618, 4°. (For details of other editions, see Landwehr, *Romanic Emblem Books*, p.67.) ; P.T.L. *Thronus cupidinis. Editio altera; priori emendatior, & multo auctior*, Amsterdam, W. Janszon, 1618, 16° obl.

theme of love, for example, is a little series of devices on birds. While the familiar pelican feeding her young with the mottoes and verse:

> Pro grege. *Per la greggia.* Pour les miens. *Para la manada.* Voor de meine.
> For mine own. Vor die meine.
> Le Pelican pour ses Petits
> Donne son sang, donne sa vie:
> C'est l'Emblême parfait de ces hommes cheris,
> Qui s'epuisent pour leur Patrie.
>> (La Feuille/Pallavicini, *Devises & emblemes d'amour, anciens & modernes*, C2v)

just fits into this category, with parental love and sacrifice representing love and sacrifice for one's country, the bird of paradise pointing skywards, with its mottoes and verse:

> Nil terrestre. *Niente de terrestre.* Point de commerce avec la terre. *Nada de terrestre.* Niets aardisch. Nothing terrestial. Nichts irdisch.
> C'est pour la Vertu que je vis,
> La terre n'est point ma Patrie;
> Comme l'Oiseau de Paradis,
> Je vole dans les Cieux, & j'y passe ma vie.
>> (La Feuille/Pallavicini, *Devises & emblemes d'amour, anciens & modernes*, C2v)

hardly does so. However, love is the underlying theme of the majority of devices in this collection, but as so often despite the single overall unifying theme, the range of actual images exploited to relate to this overall theme is extremely wide.

Yet another, rather later, work by La Feuille, the *Essay d'un dictionnaire contenant la connoissance du monde, des sciences universelles, et particulierement celle des medailles, des passions, des moeurs, des vertus et des vices &c. Representé par des figures hyerogliphiques, expliquées en prose & en vers*, which was first published in Amsterdam in 1700,[41] again follows the same structure as that of Verrien published several years earlier in Paris. But La Feuille, the professional engraver/publisher, makes his manual further helpful to the artists and craftsmen for whom it is designed by arranging the material in alphabetical order (at least as far as the letter T, after which it is arranged more loosely according to topic), thus making it even more of a work of handy reference than Alciato's emblem book as adopted by Barthélemy Aneau a century and a half earlier. The reference to *médailles* in the title is appropriate, since once again, as in the earlier works we find the same pattern of fifteen little engravings in circular frames, very much in the style of *revers de médailles*, all crammed into one single verso, in the manner of Verrien's *Livre*

---

[41] The work appeared with several variant imprints: Amsterdam, D. de La Feuille and N. Chevallier, 1700, 4°; Amsterdam, D. de La Feuille, 1700, 4°; Wesel, J. van Wesel, 1700, 4°.

curieux et utile, each including a one- or two-word motto, while on the facing recto
and thereafter is the accompanying text for each of the fifteen engravings. But unlike
Verrien's work, and unlike the earlier volumes produced by La Feuille, we find a
further innovation here in that a short passage of prose explanation is also included.
Interestingly La Feuille does not here offer a polyglot set of mottoes, as he had done in
the earlier volumes, although he does include a French quatrain in the manner of
those included in the *Devises & emblemes d'amour* published four years earlier. Thus,
for example, the opening emblem of the collection, *Amour domté* comprises an
engraving of Cupid together with a little bird and an hour-glass, followed by the verse:

> Lors que je suis dans mon Printemps,
> Je domte le Berger, le Roi, l'homme de Lettres:
> Mais je suis domté par le temps,
> Le plus puissant de tous les Maitres.

and the prose gloss:

> *Amour domté*. Vous voyez ce petit Dieu assis sur une Montagne, fouler au
> pied son Arc & ses flêches, aiant perdu son flambeau, tenant une horloge de
> sable en sa main droite, & de la gauche un petit oiseau maigre & décharné
> que l'on nomme plongeon, qui represente la misere.
>   Le flambeau que l'Amour a perdu montre sa pauvreté qui le conduit
> au desespoir jusqu'à fouler aux pieds ses propres armes, l'horloge qu'il tient
> est le symbole du Tems, qui modere toutes les passions de l'ame, &
> particulierement celle de l'amour.
>   (La Feuille, *Essay d'un dictionnaire*, A1r)

As we have seen in his other works, many of the devices in the *Essay d'un
dictionnaire* (or emblems, as they might well be termed) also reiterate familiar topoi,
as for example, *Bonne Fortune* in which we first see depicted the familiar figure of
Fortune with her wheel, and also a cornucopia, and are then given a general moral
lesson to be derived in the quatrain:

> Defie toy toûjours de la foule importune,
> De ses hableurs impertinents,
> Qui se vantent a tous momens,
> D'être gens à bonne fortune.   (La Feuille, *Essay d'un dictionnaire*, H2r)

and finally a verbal reiteration of the correct iconography of Fortune (already
represented visually in the engraving), together with an explanation of the correct
allegorical interpretation of her various attributes:

> Elle nous est representée par une belle Femme assise, & s'apuye du Bras droit
> sur une Roüe, tenant de la main gauche une corne d'Abondance, dont elle
> prodigue souvent sans s'arrêter au merite. Elle a des aisles pour marquer sa

legereté, comme la Roüe abaisse tantost l'un & tantost prend plaisir à élever l'autre.   (La Feuille, *Essay d'un dictionnaire*, H2r)

As in the earlier works, several of La Feuille's figures in the *Essay d'un dictionnaire* can be traced to identifiable earlier emblematic sources, as for example *Luxure*, in which the couplet:

Sans Ceres & sans Bacchus,
Il fait froid auprès de Venus.   (La Feuille, *Essay d'un dictionnaire*, L3v)

is a virtual paraphrase of Aneau's *Imagination poetique* emblem, *Sans Ceres et Bacchus Venus est froide* (K7r), or *Necessité, Mere d'invention* depicting in the engraving and describing in the text the ingenious strategy of the thirsty crow, dropping pebbles into a vase in order to raise the water level so that he can drink from it, which is equally clearly derived from Paradin's device on the subject, *Ingenii largitor*. Unusually this emblem does not include a verse, but as in the previous example, the prose gloss in La Feuille's work:

La necessité nous fournit des moyens a quoy l'on ne songerois (sic) pas autrement, le Corbeau, dont Pline nous parle, nous en fournit un exemple, comme vous voyé (sic) par ce Corbeau qui étant pressé de la soif, & voyant de l'eau dans une vase où il ne pouvoit entrer, y porta tant de pierres, qu'il fit venir l'eau à sa porté (sic).   (La Feuille, *Essay d'un dictionnaire*, P1r)

is clearly a slightly shortened paraphrase of Paradin's commentary added to his device in 1557:

Il n'est que la necessité, pour faire inventer les habilitez, & subtils moyens. Comme naturellement demonstre le Corbeau, duquel Pline fait mencion: qui estant pressé de soif (& neanmoins ne pouvant avenir à boire sus un monument, dens un seau, auquel residoit eau de pluie) porta, & getta tant de pierres dens icelui, qu'en fin croissant le monceau, fit remonter de l'eau pour boire.   (Paradin, *Devises heroiques*, 1557, i6r)

The overall title *Essay d'un dictionnaire* gives no indication that this work by La Feuille actually contains two further, quite distinct items, an *Abregé de l'Histoire de France par les devises expliquees en vers & en prose* (S1r) and an account of the life of Mary II of England, wife of William III, entitled *Abregé historique de la naissance, de la vie, & de la mort de Marie II. du nom, reine d'Angleterre, de glorieuse memoire* (Q1r) accompanied at the end by a series of 36 wholly engraved emblems and devices all relating to Mary with their own title page, *Devises, emblemes, et hyerogliphes faits sur la naissance, la vie et la mort de Marie II. du nom, reine d'Angleterre.* (Mary had died of smallpox in 1694, six years prior to the publication of this work.) Although there is no letterpress text in this latter section, an appropriate verse and prose gloss for each engraved emblem is included in the preceding *Abrege historique*. They do, therefore, follow the same structural pattern as that of the *Essay d'un dictionnaire*, although the text is here more physically separated from the engraving it is intended to accompany than in the *Essay d'un dictionnaire*. The engravings are also aesthetically far superior to those of the *Essay d'un dictionnaire*, being more fully depicted and more decorative, and also more spaciously laid out, with only four per page, in contrast to the fifteen per page layout of the *Essay d'un dictionnaire*. Although there is an overall unifying theme in that all the emblems are angled to relate to Queen Mary, the individual emblems cover a wide spectrum of symbols, many of which are once again familiar from earlier sixteenth-century emblem books. We find, for example, the phoenix with the motto *Hanc unam secula plura vident*, and note 'Sur la perfection de toutes ses illustres qualitez', and the accompanying verse and prose gloss:

> Mon sort est glorieux comme il est sans pareil,
> Et j'ose en mon effort m'approcher du Soleil,
> Sans craindre que son feu me blesse;
> En tout admirable & parfait
> Je ne pouvois être en effet,
> Que rare ou seul en mon espece.

> L'Oiseau Phoenix qui surpasse de beaucoup tous les oiseaux en Bauté (sic). *Aussi excellent en ma nature que rare en mon espece*; pour donner une Idée de l'excellence de toutes les augustes qualitez rassemblées dans la personne de Sa Majesté. (La Feuille, *Essay d'un dictionnaire*, R1v)

We also find the rose and thorn with the motto *Nemo me impunè lacessit* (the word *lacessit* which is present in the engraving is mistakenly omitted in the text:)

> *Nemo me impunè*
> Pour sa Beauté

> Si mon vif incarnat & ma tendre jeunesse
> Ravissent un Mortel qui voudroit les flétrir,
> Le Ciel de peur qu'il ne me blesse,
> M'a donné de quoi l'en punir,
> Ma vertu ne nuit point, je prens plaisir à plaire,
> Mais je puis me vanger d'une main temeraire.

> Une Rose avec des Epines, avec ces paroles: *J'inspire un amour respectueux*. Sa Majesté étoit d'une ravissante beauté que sa Vertu étoit accomplie.
> (La Feuille, *Essay d'un dictionnaire*, Q2r)

and similarly an oyster with its pearl with the motto *Regno nata* (Q1r) and a brightly shining moon eclipsing the sun with the motto *Micat inter omnes* which, apart from the change from sun to moon, is very reminiscent of devices similarly glorifying the royal greatness of Louis XIV. The motto (which is given in a slight variant form in the engraving, as *Illic plus micat*) is subtitled 'Pour la Majesté de sa Personne & l'éclat de ses Chrestiennes & Royales Vertus' and the verse stressing the brilliance of the moon is followed by the prose gloss clearly spelling out the connection between the brilliance of the moon and that of the queen:

> Que sont auprès de moi ces beaux corps lumineux
> Qui fort loin jettent de gros feux.
> Et plusieurs étoiles ternissent?
> Mes rayons les leurs obscurcissent,
> Toute seule je vaux plus que mille d'entre eux.

> La Lune avec ces paroles: *Mon éclat fait ombre à mille autres.* Pour marquer que sa Majesté a de beaucoup surpassé toutes les personnes de son rang; & été un exemple inimitable à un trés-grand nombre d'illustres & de vertueuses personnes qui faisoient la gloire de sa Cour.
> (La Feuille, *Essay d'un dictionnaire,* Q2r)

These latter two historical works incorporated into the *Essay d'un dictionnaire* are clearly somewhat different from the main collection, however, as also from the other collections of more generalist engraved devices published by La Feuille in Amsterdam. Although it was Nicolas Verrien in Paris who pioneered the production of such style books, with their densely packed pages of engraved devices and emblems, designed for use by craftsmen, it was La Feuille who clearly recognised their wider European market potential and thus greatly extended the audience for whom they could be useful by the introduction of polyglot accompanying text, in very much the way in which at a much earlier date Montenay's collection of *Emblemes et devises chrestiennes* were also made available to a much wider European audience in a polyglot version, when the publication of that work moved from France to Zurich and thence to Frankfurt. Certainly La Feuille derived the initial idea from Verrien, as is evident from the very close parallels between Verrien's works and those produced by La Feuille, but La Feuille clearly exploited the market much more systematically than did Verrien, not only by supplying a polyglot text to allow for wider dissemination, but also by producing several collections, whereas Verrien produced only the *Livre curieux et utile.* La Feuille also ensured, by means of systematic advertisement, that his potential audience was always aware of other works of cognate interest that he had produced or was about to produce. Thus, for example, the 1691 edition of *Devises et emblemes anciennes et modernes* with the text by Offelen includes an *avertissement* at the end promising further such collections in future,[42] and also mentioning a further work likewise produced to cater for the needs of craftsmen, which he attributes to Offelen:

> Il donne aussi une Seconde Partie d'un Livre de Chiffres qu'il a mis au jour

---

[42]   See above, footnote 39.

> l'année passée, outre tous les Noms & Surnoms que l'on y trouve entrelassez, il est augmenté de Palmes, Feuillages, Cartouches, Supports, & Couronnes, qui conviennent aux Armes & Chiffres, avec trois Alphabets, un à trois lettres par reprise & simple traits, un à quatre, & l'autre à cinq à double traits Fleuronnez.

This is the *Livre nouveau et utile* which he had published just the previous year. Similarly the sequel which La Feuille published in 1696 under the title *Devises & emblemes d'amour, anciennes & modernes* with the text by Pallavicini also contains an advertisement on the last leaf, referring back to the popularity of the earlier volume:

> Le livre que j'imprimay il y a quelques années contenant plus de 700 Dévises & Emblemes d'Amour, de Politique & de Guerre, expliquées en sept langues, ayant été fort bien receu du Public; il y a lieu d'esperer que celuy-cy n'aura pas un Sort different'
>   (La Feuille/Pallavicini, *Devises & emblemes d'amour, anciens & modernes*, F5v).

The purely commercial potential of collected volumes of engraved emblems and devices at the end of the seventeenth century, in France and - even more so - elsewhere is very evident in such works as these.

In the domain of manuscripts clearly the pattern is very different. As in the domain of printed books so also in manuscripts we find a number of generalist collections of devices, but these are produced for more individual consumption, rather than for such commercial purposes, but rather for more individual consumption. However, just as we find a great variety of practice in printed generalist collections of devices, so also we find possibly even greater diversity in manuscript collections. Some are illustrated while others are not; some include verses while others do not; and some include passages of prose gloss while others follow the more minimalist format of brief description followed by (usually) Latin motto, with or without a French translation. Some are accompanied by (or accompany) prose treatises on the art of devices, while others simply contain devices - in some cases a single collection and in other cases a series of small collections put together. In some cases they comprise a full manuscript, while in others a small collection of devices is simply incorporated into a larger manuscript anthology containing many other different things. Some are beautifully produced luxury items, often designed for presentation, while at the other end of the scale others are much more humble productions.

We find in the Bibliothèque nationale de France, and in the Bibliothèque de l'Arsenal two very finely produced manuscript collections of devices designed for presentation. BnF Ms. lat. 13064 is an extremely elegantly produced collection of devices designed for presentation to the influential Chancelier Seguier (who occupied the post of *chancelier* from 1635). The manuscript is in vellum, and is bound with the arms of Seguier, and these same arms are reproduced as the figure on all the versos of the little collection, together with one of three mottoes, *Surge per te ius*; *Superius reget*; and *Se purius reget*, under which is a further Latin couplet further elaborating on the theme of the motto, as for example

> *Superius reget*
> Beatus orde; morem ut inferius gerat,
> Regat superius, luceque insigni reget.   (BnF Ms. lat. 13064, f.5v)

On the facing rectos are complete devices with their own individual pen-and-ink figures, but similarly playing on the three key mottoes, as in the fourth device in which the figure depicts an angel flying over the universe, with the same motto *Superius reget*, followed by the couplet:

> Ut aequa versent fata concordes poli
>   Coelestis animus SUPERIUS coelum reget.   (BnF Ms. lat. 13064, f.6r)

Dating from much the same period,[43] and equally elegantly produced, is another presentation manuscript, also bound in the arms of its owner, Marie de la Tour, Duchesse de la Tremoille. Arsenal Ms. 5217 (rés) is a folio volume which is even more lavishly illustrated than the Seguier manuscript, containing a collection of forty beautifully painted full-page devices, each identifying the owner of the device at the top, together with a representation of that person's arms, and each encased in a decorative border. The motto of the device is either inscribed below the figure or alternatively enlaced in the decorative border. The collection is clearly designed essentially as an object of beauty rather than as an informative manual, and thus all the emphasis is placed on the decorative figure encased in its equally decorative border of flowers and fruits, while the text itself is kept to a minimum, giving no more than the name of the owner of the device and the motto. Thus, for example, a highly decorative visual representation of a beehive and bee is accompanied by the barest text, simply giving the name 'Marie Claire de Baufremont Comtesse du Freix' and the motto *Prudens et sedula*.

Similarly elegant, though less lavish in its illustration, is another early seventeenth-century manuscript in the Bibliothèque nationale de France which is not, however, a presentation manuscript. BnF Ms. fr. 15257 is in fact designed to look more like a printed collection of devices, with a formal title page on which it is entitled *Devises royalles et heroiques* and dated 1626. It comprises a unified collection of 176 devices symmetrically arranged so that each device occupies one page, and in each case a pen-and-ink illustration is preceded by an explanatory prose gloss in French. The devices are in many cases very familiar ones, and indeed a librarian's note suggests that they are taken from Paradin. Many of them are taken from Paradin, but not all, and even those which are taken from Paradin are not simple reproductions of the printed original.[44] Some are taken from Alciato, but interestingly

---

[43] No date is given for the collection, but one of the devices is that of Anne d'Autriche, in which she is referred to as regent, thus dating the collection within the period 1643-61.
[44] In, for example, *Non inferiora sequutus* depicting the marigold, the prose commentary is a shorter paraphrase, rather than an accurate reproduction of Paradin's text in the 1557 ed.

the mottoes in two consecutive devices taken from Alciato are, as the author acknowledges in his gloss, changed from the original motto used by Alciato. Although devices 172 and 173 in this collection depicting the boy with the palm tree and the eagle and beetle are borrowed from Alciato's emblems *Obdurandum adversus urgentia* and *Iusta ultio*[45] but the mottoes are here changed to *Nititur in pondus* and *Perit qui fata parabat* respectively. In the gloss to *Nititur in pondus* the author alludes to Alciato's motto and explains the sense of the device:

> Ceste devise est tirée d'un embleme d'Alciat qui a pour son inscription ces mots OBDURANDUM ADVERSUS URGENTIA. appropriez à la nature de la palme laquelle plus est chargee plus s'esleve vray symbole d'un homme qui aime le travail ouquel la palme est consacree selon ce dire PALMA LABORI. Les muses antiennement en estoient coronneez: la Palme est aussy le signe de la victoire d'où vient ce mot PALMAM FERRE. S. Hilaire l'attribue a l'Eglise victorieuse & triumphante de tant d'heresies, sectes, & superstitions, voicy les mots.
>
>   Habet hoc proprium Ecclesia dum exercetur floret dum opprimitur, crescit: dum contemnitur proficit; dum caeditur vincit &c.

with the marginal note 'Lib 4 de Trinit'. One of the particularly charming devices in this collection is no.50 with the motto *Nocet empta dolore voluptas* accompanying a figure depicting a fishing scene. On the bank is a man fishing, but the fish in the stream is biting the bait on a line held by a hand stretching down from heaven. The gloss explains:

> Ce poisson s'enferant d'un hameçon cachè soubs une amorce, menace les voluptueux de pareil escheq, si en leurs plaisirs apparans, le traict est de Caton.

Interestingly this same motto was originally used by Reusner to accompany an emblem on a quite different theme derived from Aesop's fable of the ant and the grasshopper (and logically depicting a grasshopper in the woodcut figure),[46] showing once again, as with the devices derived from Alciato emblems how flexible in interpretation is the emblematic form.

In marked contrast to such elegantly produced collections of devices which represent the top end of the scale of elegance, we find at the other end of the scale other manuscripts such as BnF Ms. lat. 10361 which is a seventeenth-century collection of rather crudely drawn devices, some of which include mottoes below them while others do not. In this very basic anthology no indication is given of the owners

---

(p.41): 'Margueritte de France Roine de Navare portoit pour devise estant vefve, la fleur de soucy, fleur qui a grande affinitè avec le Soleil, soit en couleur, soit en ses rayons, soit en luy tenant compagnie par tout ou il se trouve.' (BnF Ms. fr. 15257, no.17)

[45]   Alciato, *Emblemata*, 1550, C6r and M5v.

[46]   *Nicolai Reusneri Leorini Aureolorum emblematum liber singularis. Thobiae Stimmeri iconibus affabre effictis exornatus*, Strasbourg, B. Iobin, 1591, 8°, G8r.

of the devices, nor yet any further text. Even more basic and lacking in aesthetic quality is BnF Ms. fr. nouv. acq. 11253, in which no illustrations at all are included. Marginal notes indicate what is intended to be denoted, as, for example, 'la vertu et force militaire','l'homme constant et immuable', or 'l'amour coeleste',[47] and a brief French prose description is given of the image which should be depicted in order to represent this, together with a Latin motto in some cases, but not in others. The text is very crammed and the work has a look of a student notebook.

However, whether elegantly produced presentation copies, or less elegantly produced anthologies, these are all purpose-built manuscript collections of devices, containing nothing but that. Commonly, however, short collections of devices are found incorporated into *recueils factices*, together with a variety of other totally unconnected texts, and in such collections they can take a number of different forms. Perhaps an extreme case of a manuscript containing an assortment of devices - variously in Latin and French, prose and verse - among a rich hotch potch of other material (including signed instructions by Catherine de Medici for the ordering of portraits and jewellery, among which a letter addresse to a goldsmith dated November 1571) is a late sixteenth-century manuscript in the Bibliothèque nationale de France (BnF Ms. fr. 894). Several of the earlier devices in this manuscript (which was put together by Jean Passerat) include alterations and translations into French added underneath the original Latin, and some include little sketches to accompany the device. Among the assorted works is a little collection of three *Devises d'amour* following the minimalist pattern of short description plus Latin motto, but in this case a French couplet is added, and the source is noted in the margin, as in:

> Un gean de grandeur desmesurée estendu tout de son long, et qui à la poitrine outrepercée d'une flesche. Un grand vaultour luy becquete le foye incessamment. C'est Tityus qui nous represente un amoureux que le souci mange et ronge tousjours.
> > *Curae lacerant in amore iacentem.*
> > Ainsi le soing et les soucis mordens
> > D'un amoureux percent l'ame au dedans.   (BnF Ms. fr. 894, f.19r)

This device is accompanied by the marginal note 'Lucain au 3. Livre'. The same pattern is followed in a further little series of devices on *Paix, Concorde* and *Abondance* in which a device on Neptune and Pallas is identified in the margin as being derived from 'Ovide au V de la Met':

> Neptunus avec son trident frappe un rocher, d'où il faict sortir un cheval. Pallas darde sa lance en terre, et en faict sortir un olivier. Les dieux jugent que Pallas a mieux faict que Neptune et luy donnent le prix: pour signifier non seulement que la paix vault mieux que la guerre, mais aussi que la paix qui vient apres une longue et aspre guerre en est plus agreable.
> > *Gratior est post bella quies*

---

[47]   BnF Ms. fr. nouv. acq. 11253, ff. 9v; 10v; 12v.

> Apres tant de travaux d'une guerre aspre et forte
> Plus doulx est le repos que la paix nous apporte.
>   (BnF Ms. fr. 894, f.103r)

Quite different from these two conventional devices, however, is a much more complex and unusual creation which extends over two pages of the manuscript (f.39r-v):

> Devise d'un clavier composé de trois cercles entrelassez dont le plus hault sera ataché aux cordons pendans à la ceinture, les deux autres pendront à ce premier, qui auront par bas les petits neuds et ataches des clefs.
> Au premier front des trois cercles y aura trois devises, à chacune une, qui seront en Latin, et sont escrites cy dessous avec leur explication en françoys, fors que l'elegance de la langue Latine ny peut estre representée, ny bien souvent l'ambiguite de la devise qui faict portion de sa grace.

> au premier cercle, qui est le plus hault,
>   SERVET IUS DOMINAE CUSTODES SERVET ET IPSOS.
>   De Madame les droicts fidelement il garde,
>   Et des gardes il soit la seure contregarde.

> Les droicts de la femme en une famille sont les clefs, les gardes sont aussy les clefs, la contregarde, ce clavier.

> au premier des deux cercles de dessoubs,
>   HIC SESE ATQUE ARCAS ARCANAQUE CONTINET ARCUS.
>   Les coffrets des papiers et des bagues il serre,
>   Et luymesme soymesme de soymesmes enserre.

> Le rond qui est figure parfaicte, se soustient et apuie soymesme, ce qui est propre aussy à la sagesse et continance.

> à l'autre cercle, qui est le dernier des trois,
>   QUAE MUNDUM CLAUDUNT TENUEM CLAUDUNTUR IN
> ORBEM.
>   Ainsi se trouve enceint en sa vousture ronde
>   Ce qui enceint en soy et enclost nostre monde.

> C'est une allusion sur nostre monde qui est la terre, et le ciel qui l'environe, mais en effect c'est tousjours le mésme subject, car ORBIS c'est ce rond ou cercle qui tient les clefs et le munde sont en Latin les bagues et afiquets des femmes.

> à lautre costé des cercles lequel se presentera aussy quelquefois de front y aura semblablement trois autres devises qui modestement diront les

perfections et bonnes graces de leur maistresse.
> UT INCEPIT SIC DESINET IN SE
> Ceste celeste semance
> En soy finit et commance.

C'est à dire se trouve tousjours en soy mesme, n'est jamais alieurs, et a tousjours esté à soy, se maintenant ferme en sa propre vertu.

> ET CHARITES NECTUNTUR IN ORBEM
> Aussy les trois graces sont
> Enlassees en un rond.

> MULTA LATENT, PROPIORA DEO
> Le plus caché à nostre humanité
> A plus de part en la divinité.

This is the finished version of the device, but amusingly the manuscript also contains before this finished version several pages of drafts with additions and corrections and also working sketches. Other manuscript compilations containing collections of devices are usually less eccentric than this one, however. In, for example, BnF Ms. fr. 24447, which is a late seventeenth-century manuscript made up of a mixture of printed and manuscript pieces, we find a short collection of assorted devices (ff.323-7) each comprising a brief prose description and motto. No illustrations are included, and only in the earlier ones in the collection is the name of the owner of the device indicated. In some but not all cases the description also includes an explanation of significance of the device, as in that of Henri de Navarre's phoenix:

> Henry de Bourbon Prince de Navarre pour denoter que de luy estoit né un autre semblable sçavoir Henry le Grand fit faire un phoenix couronné sur un buscher battant des ailes avec ce mot *idem exodem.*
> (BnF Ms. fr. 24447, f.86r)

while in others no such explanation is given, as in Diane de Valois's device of an arrow entwined with laurel above a tomb:

> Diane duchesse de Vallois. Un tombeau sur le milieu duquel est une fleche poinctue vers le ciel & entrelacée de deux branches de lauriers. L'ame *Sola vivit in illo.* (BnF Ms. fr. 24447, f.86r)

or likewise in one of the unattributed devices on the subject of the bird of paradise:

> Un oyseau nommé communement l'oiseau de paradis ou cameleon de l'air portant trois de ses petis sur son dos & les eslevant jusque à la plus haute region de l'air avec ce mot *Meos ad sydera tollo.*
> (BnF Ms. fr. 24447, f.326r)

As is often the case in such manuscript collections, no indication is given of the authorship of this work, which is is simply arranged in the form of a list, with each device reproduced one after the other with no preoccupation with symmetrical layout or indeed of calligraphy. BnF Ms.fr. 20159 similarly contains a variety of different materials dating from the fifteenth to the seventeenth century, much of it armorial, but included among this is a little collection of *Devises des princes et autres* (ff.594-602), covering not just France but other parts of Europe also, but restricting the entries to contemporary figures only. Here again no illustrations are provided, and once again the devices are simply listed one after another, with for the most part no explanation of why a particular device was adopted by its owner. Symmetry of layout is once again not observed, as is likewise the case in another similar, but much larger, seventeenth-century manuscript collection of *Symboles et devises* of popes, emperors, cardinals and kings, arranged according to country, in which again there is no illustration and no additional prose explanation.[48]

In a very different aesthetic league from these very basic lists of devices incorporated into longer manuscripts is a series of collections of devices which are found in a much more elegantly laid out manuscript in the Bibliothèque de l'Arsenal (Ms. 3184). In the second collection in this manuscript, which is attributed in its title to Richelieu (*Ces dissept devises furent composees par Monsr de Richellieu Grand Prevost de France, et les mots par Monsr Dauzat poette francoys*) we find a much greater aesthetic preoccupation with symmetry of layout, with each painted device being arranged one per page, together with motto and figure, but with no further text, as for example in the device depicting moths around a lighted candle with the motto *Accenditur. Extinguend* (Arsenal Ms. 3184, Part 2, f.7r). The structure in the next collection in this manuscript is quite different, however, in that here the basic devices are accompanied by French quatrains. This collection is described: *Ces quatorze premieres devizes ont esté faites au temps du feu Roy Charles, par le feu sieur Belleau comme aussi les vers, qui sont au dessoubz. Pour Madamoiselle d'Astige qui depuis a esté Contesse de Chasteauvillain de la Fossette.* The verses accompanying the devices are not of the highest literary order, as for example in *Mole tutus Amor* in which the figure of Cupid riding on a crab is accompanied by the quatrain:

> Ce que je tenois de plus seur
> Au monde est ce qui moins masseure
> Ainsy le Rebours de mon heur
> Me va guidant à l'aventure.   (Arsenal Ms. 3184, Part 2, f.85r)

Different in structure yet again are a series of illustrated devices in BnF Ms. Smith Lesouëf 98, entitled *Devises sur differans sujets*. Here again the individual devices include verses, but addition they also include a further passage of prose gloss, in the manner of some of the printed collections discussed earlier. The majority of the

---

[48]   BnF Ms. fr. 13426. See also BnF Ms. fr. 20244 which contains a series of documents relating to the La Tremoille family, but which also includes a short four-page collection of devices of the kings of France from Pharamond to Louis XIII (f. 91 *et seq.*).

devices in this manuscript relate directly to Louis XIV, to the *Dauphin* or to Colbert, and even the remainder are indirectly associated with the king. The first four are described as having been specifically designed for architectural purposes,[49] and the allegorical significance of their component elements are clearly explained, both in the overall gloss to the four of them:

> Les quatre premieres Devises ont este faites pour mettre aux quatre faces d'un Monument que l'on avoit proposé d'eriger à la gloire du Roy. Elles ont rapport à la devise de S.M. ayant chacune un soleil et un animal solaire. Chaque animal represente une des quatre parties du Monde. L'aigle pour l'Europe, le Phenix pour l'Asie, l'Elephant pour l'Afrique et le Dragon pour l'Amerique. (BnF Ms. Smith Lesouëf 98, f.[1])

and in the separate gloss accompanying each individual device. Elegance and symmetry are once again important here, since each device occupies a double opening: with the prose gloss on the verso, and the pen-and-ink drawing plus motto and quatrain on the facing recto, as in the first of the four, representing the eagle looking up to the sun above him. The figure is accompanied by the verse:

> S'elever contre moy par un vol temeraire
> C'est un peu trop se hazarder:
> Le plus fier de l'Europe ose à peine le faire,
> Et nul autre que luy n'ose me regarder

and the whole thing is glossed on the facing page:

> Dans la I Devise il y [a] un Aigle regardant fixement le Soleil, avec ces mots NON SUSTINET ALTER. Aucun autre que luy ne m'ose regarder: pour donner à entendre que l'Empereur representé par l'Aigle est le seul de l'Europe qui puisse estre en quelque consideration estant comparé au Roy signifié par le Soleil.

The last device of the collection contains Colbert's familiar snake (inspired by the play on his name by the Latin *coluber*), but nevertheless ties this in neatly with Louis XIV himself, by drawing an association between the snake and the sun:

> Dans la XXII Devise il y a un Serpent qui s'eleve comme pour rendre

---

[49] See also a similar little series of devices likewise designed for architectural purposes, and dating from 1668 in BnF Ms. fr. 24713, ff.143-51, The manuscript includes a detailed description of an obelisk together with a note of its various Latin inscriptions, together with a French translation, and also a drawing of the actual obelisk (ff.149-51). Preceding this are a series of nine roundels, in which five are filled in to make complete devices with mottoes, while the remaining four are not illustrated. All the mottoes are related: *Nulla mihi terris requies*; *Terris nulla mihi requies*; *Una mihi coelo requies*; *Coelo sola mihi requies*; *Sola per alta quiescam*; *Post requiem requies*; *Le ciel sera mon seul repos*; *La mort sera mon seul repos*.

hommage au Soleil avec ces mots MIHI VIGOR OMNIS AB ILLO: sans luy
je serois sans vigueur, pour signifier que Monsieur Colbert qui a un Serpent
dans ses armes reconnoist qu'il tient toute sa force et toute sa vigueur du Roy
qui a pris le Soleil pour sa Devise. Chacun sçait que le Serpent est sans
vigueur en hyver lors que le Soleil est éloigné.

The verse similarly points to the dependence of Colbert on the king:

> Je suis de la Prudence une parfaite Image:
> On voit en moy du vif, on y voit du brillant:
> Mais tout ce que j'ay d'excellent
> Je le tiens du bel Astre à qui je rends hommage.

In another Bibliothèque de l'Arsenal manuscript containing material from the
seventeenth and eighteenth centuries, from the collection of the Marquis de Paulmy
(Arsenal Ms. 3328), a substantial *Discours sur l'art des devises* (ff.1-46) includes
within it a series of little autonomous collections of devices, including a non-
illustrated text of the *Devises qui ont été employées dans les tapisseries du Roi où les
quatre elemens sont representés* (f.13v), and other devices which are also
accompanied by passages of verse, as, for example a device of an eagle leading
another young eagle with the motto *Patre viam monstrante* which is reminiscent of
Ménestrier's similar device in the *Devise du Roy justifiée*:

> Un grand Aigle qui conduit un Aiglon vers le Soleil,
> LAETATUR GENUISSE PAREM.
> Il se réjoüit d'avoir fait son semblable.
> (Ménestrier, *La devise du Roy justifiée*, Y1v)

or of that of Le Moyne in his *Devises heroiques et morales* (B4v) using the symbol of
the phoenix with the associated motto *Quoque post patrem*. In the manuscript the
device is not explicitly associated with Louis XIV, but the tenor of the verse which
acts as a gloss makes the indirect association fairly clear:

> Dans cette région ou règne la tempête
> Je menace de l'oeil, j'affronte de la tête
> Le nuage qui gronde, et la foudre qui luit,
> Et gagnant le dessus, à la gloire j'appelle
> Du feu de mon regard, et du bruit de mon aile.

The verse is very similar in tone and style to those created to accompany the
manuscript and printed versions of the allegorical devices around the borders of the
tapestries for the Four Seasons and the Four Elements. These tapestries glorifying
Louis XIV were created by the Gobelins manufacture in the 1660s and the allegorical
devices around their borders - with verses added to them - were reproduced in
manuscript form for inclusion in the royal library, but also in a number of published

editions, both in France and elsewhere for wider dissemination of the royal propaganda.[50] This particular verse echoes closely the equivalent verse which was added to the device of an eagle in the borders of the Air tapestry, denoting the king's valour:

> Pour la valeur dans la piece de l'Element de l'Air. Un Aigle tenant un Foudre dans ses serres, avec ce mot MERUITQUE TIMERI NIL METUENS. Les Poètes ont feint que cet oiseau portoit le foudre de Jupiter, parce qu'il est le seul de tous les animaux qui ne craint point le tonnerre & sur lequel il ne tombe jamais. Ainsi sa Majesté fait trembler toutes les puissances de la terre, parce qu'elle n'a aucun foudre à redouter.
>
> > Du Foudre menaçant qui forme les tempestes
> > Au dessus de nos testes,
> > Il voit loin sous ses pieds la fureur éclatter,
> > Il le porte, & son feu jusqu'à luy n'ose attendre,
> > Ainsi ne voyant rien qu'il doive redouter,
> > Il ne voit rien aussi qui ne le doive craindre.
> > (Bailly ms., ed. Grivel and Fumaroli, p.43)[51]

---

[50] See, for example, André Félibien's *Tapisseries du Roi où sont representez les quatre elemens et les quatre saisons*, Paris, *Imprimerie royale*, 1670, folio. Editions of the work with a German version of the text in addition to the original French text were also published in Augsburg in 1687 and 1690 by Jacob Koppmayer for Ulrich Krauss. For a facsimile edition of the manuscript produiced for the royal library, see M.Grivel and M. Fumaroli, eds, Jacques Bailly, *Devises pour les tapisseries du Roi*, Paris, 1988. For full discussion of these devices see Alison Saunders, 'Emblems to tapestries and tapestries to emblems: contrasting practice in England and France', *Seventeenth-Century French Studies*, 21, 1999, pp.243-55. See also below, chapter 7.

[51] See also a very similar printed series of engraved devices in honour of Louis XIV (BnF Estampes Te 120) each accompanied by a madrigal, which is here actually incorporated into the engraving. Although these devices are not the same as those of the Tapestries, they are virtually indistinguishable in style and tone. See, for example, a device representing a seated lion, with above it the royal arms and the motto *Et dum tenet otia terret*, and below it the subheading 'Pour le Roy pendant la paix'. Included in the engraving is the unsigned madrigal:

> Il n'est rien de si fier qui ne me soit soumis,
> Et je ne vois point d'Ennemis
> Qui m'osent disputer le tiltre d'invincible:
> Qui ne redouteroit ma force et ma fureur
> Si même quand je suis paisible
> D'un seul de mes regards j'Imprime la Terreur.

which compares closely with Charpentier's madrigal accompanying the Falcon device in the Autumn tapestry:

> Lorsque le combat m'est permis,
> Et qu'à perdre mes ennemis
> Leur mauvais sort m'a fait resoudre;
> Je fonds sur eux d'un mouvement
> Aussi terrible que la foudre,
> Et plus rapide que le vent.   (Bailly ms., ed. Grivel and Fumaroli, p.95)

These are just some examples of manuscript collections of devices culled from the Bibliothèque nationale de France and the Bibliothèque de l'Arsenal, but many others exist, both in these libraries and elsewhere. These have been selected to demonstrate that in manuscripts as in printed books there is a great range of diversity. At the end of this discussion of both generalist emblems and generalist devices in the seventeenth century it is evident that there is enormous diversity of both intent and practice in the domain of devices as in that of emblems, and that there is furthermore a considerable grey area of overlap, where devices may be called emblems and emblems called devices (ands here also there is considerable diversity of practice in how these ambiguous creations are structured). Quite apart from the various particular purposes for which emblems and devices came to be created, which we shall be considering in subsequent chapters, it is clear that even the ostensibly generalist collections discussed in these two chapters were intended for a range of different purposes. Some are highly ornate luxury volumes (whether manuscript or printed book) designed to adorn a library and give aesthetic pleasure as well as moral edification to the reader, while others are designed to serve a more utilitarian purpose as style books for craftsmen (as their titles make clear) and yet others have a strong educational bias. Some collections are recreated in literary form, having originally been designed for the purposes of ephemeral architecture, while others are clearly designed for propaganda purposes even if this is not overtly stated. Yet again others are put together in order to serve as exemplars of good and bad practice in support of their author's theoretical treatise to which they form an adjunct. Where in the mid sixteenth century there was - broadly speaking - relatively little differentiation in intended readership between one emblem book and another, this is apparently less the case in the seventeenth century where a much greater hierarchy of readership becomes apparent, with some works clearly designed for an exclusively aristocratic readership, in a way that was not the case in the preceding century.

In structure as in intent they are infinitely variable. Meaningless is now the old formula of the tripartite emblem (or device). Figures (now in the form of engraving rather than woodcut) may be included, but equally they may not. Verses (in the sixteenth century considered a *sine qua non* for emblems may or may not be included. Increasingly we find - even in these generalist works - the inclusion of (sometimes lengthy) prose glosses, such as are very important features of many of the more didactic Jesuit emblem books designed specifically to lead to religious edification. Yet at the same time we find collections of emblems or devices where the text is minimal, and which comprise little more than a tightly packed anthology of small engravings. Even more basic are the collections of devices which comprise no more than a long list of summary descriptions plus motto. Although the theorists grow ever more authoritarian in their explanations of the nature of emblems and devices, and of what is and is not permissible in the two forms, in reality there is often little correlation between what the rules say and what is actually done. In short the generalist emblem and device in the seventeenth century constitute a rich and varied field. Generalist they are in theme, but in application of that theme, while some may indeed remain generalist, many others take on one of many, very diverse, specialist mantles.

CHAPTER IV

THE USE OF EMBLEMS AND DEVICES
FOR EDUCATIONAL PURPOSES

'Educational' is a broad term, embracing a range of different types of education. To an extent all emblems can be deemed to be educational in one way or another but for the purposes of this chapter we shall ignore the generally moral education that emblems and devices could offer, already discussed earlier in chapters 2 and 3, and the religious education that they could likewise offer, to be discussed in chapter 6, and concentrate rather on two central educational functions exercised by emblems and devices in the seventeenth century. Firstly, emblems and devices were exploited as a means of conveying factual information; the combination of visual and verbal offered in the seventeenth century, as it had earlier done in the sixteenth century, an effective means of conveying information in a manner which was both palatable and easily understood. Secondly emblems and devices were exploited more indirectly for educational purposes in a quite different manner in schools where they were frequently employed as a teaching device, designed to cultivate mental agility and rhetorical skills. Not only were pupils often set the task of composing their own emblems and devices for public display within the school, but they also participated in the public performance of plays and ballets in which emblems and devices often had a significant part.

It is particularly in the context of the history of France and of the exploits and achievements of her monarchs that we find emblems, but more especially devices, being exploited for educational purposes. In some cases such 'education' is directed to the reading public in general, but in others it is directed more specifically at a particular person or persons, to whom the collection is dedicated. Thus Vulson's *Portraits des hommes illustres françois qui sont peints dans la gallerie du Palais Cardinal de Richelieu* of 1650[1] provides an illustrated sequence of notable French

---

[1]   *Les portraits des hommes illustres françois qui sont peints dans la gallerie du Palais Cardinal de Richelieu: avec leurs principales actions, armes, devises, & eloges latins; desseignez & gravez par les Sieurs Heince & Bignon, peintres & graveurs ordinaires du Roy. Dediez a Monseigneur Seguier Chancelier de France, Comte de Gyen, &c. Ensemble les*

men from Suger, *abbé* of St Denis, to Louis XIII, compiled for the edification of the general reading public, rather than being tailored to the particular needs of a particular dedicatee. Only a small number of privileged people could actually see and learn from the painted portraits themselves, but Vulson's printed account enabled a much wider audience to do so. Similarly, although Nicolas Chevalier's rather later metallic history of William III of England dating from 1692,[2] is dedicated to the king himself, Chevalier makes it clear in this dedication that the object of his work is to make more widely known to the general populace the exploits of the Prince of Orange, by then king of England for three years:

> Sire, Voyant qu'on celebre Vos Vertus & Vos Actions Heroiques en plusieurs manieres, comme j'ay quelque connoissance des Medailles, j'ay crû que je ne pouvois mieux employer mon étude qu'à recueillir celles que l'on a fait fraper à votre honneur, les ranger selon l'ordre des temps, & y ajoûter des reflexions pour les rendre intelligibles à tout le monde. Ainsi j'en ay fait un Corps d'Histoire Metallique que j'ay crû donner au Public.
>
> (Chevalier, *Histoire de Guillaume III*, *2r-v)

In contrast Claude-François Ménestrier's equivalent metallic history of Lous XIV, the *Histoire du Roy Louis le Grand par les medailles, emblémes, devises, jettons, inscriptions, armoiries, et autres monumens publics. Recueillis, et expliquez par le Pere Claude François Menestrier de la Compagnie de Jesus* which dates from three years earlier, and which possibly served as a model for Chevalier, is dedicated to Louis's three grandsons, Louis, Duc de Bourgogne, Philippe, Duc d'Anjou and Charles, Duc de Berry, who were all under the age of eight at that time, and perhaps reflecting the extreme youth of these dedicatees, the work offers an extremely simplified pictorial account of the achievements of the monarch up to that date, in which the text is kept to a minimum, to appeal to such juvenile readers.[3] Similarly an anonymous *Explication en vers des tableaux de la galerie de Versailles. Dediée à Monseigneur le Duc de Bourgogne*, dating from 1691, two years after the first edition of Ménestrier's metallic history, also describes and explains the meaning of a set of eleven allegorical paintings representing the exploits of his illustrious ancestor, in terms appropriate to the by then nine-year-old eldest grandson of Louis XIV to whom the work is dedicated.

The compilation of simplified illustrated histories of France woven around a

---

abregez historiques de leurs vies, composez par M. de Vulson, Sieur de la Colombiere, gentil-homme ordinaire de la chambre du Roy, &c, Paris, J. Paslé and C. de Sercy, 1650, folio.

[2]   *Histoire de Guillaume III, Roy d'Angleterre, d'Ecosse, de France, et d'Irlande, Prince d'Orange &c. Contenant ses actions les plus memorables, depuis sa naissance jusques à son elevation sur le trône, & ce qui s'est passé depuis jusques à l'entiere reduction du royaume d'Irlande. Par medailles, inscriptions, arcs de triomphe, & autres monumens publics. Recueillis par N. Chevalier*, Amsterdam, no publ., 1692, folio.

[3]   In the first edition the work was wholly engraved, and there was no letterpress text at all. In subsequent editions fuller letterpress text was added, but nevertheless, the work remains primarily a visual history of the achievements of Louis's reign, rather than a verbal one.

series of portraits and/or devices of French monarchs from the earliest days to the present seems to have been a popular exercise throughout the seventeenth century, with the informative text acting as a gloss to complement the engraved figures. At the very beginning of the century, in 1609, Jacques Le Vasseur produced a collection of devices of the kings of France from Pharamond to Henri IV, dedicated to Henri's son, the future Louis XIII, then aged eight years, *Les devises des roys de France, latines et françoises. Tirées de divers autheurs, anciens & modernes. Avec une briefve exposition d'icelles, en vers françois. Par I.L.V.R.D.L.D.P. Et la paraphrase en vers latins, par Michel Grenet de Chartres. Le tout enrichy des figures de tous les rois de France, jusques à Henry IIII. à present regnant. A Monseigneur le Dauphin.*[4] Dating from the middle of the century is Audin's *Histoire de France representée par tableaux, commencant au regne de Hugues Capet, chef des roys de la troisiéme branche. Avec des discours & reflexions politiques. Par le Sieur Audin, prieur de Termes & de la Fage* of 1647,[5] which includes a series of devices of the various kings discussed, although this is not advertised in the title. At the turning point from the seventeenth to the eighteenth century, ninety years after Le Vasseur's work, Daniel de La Feuille still continues the tradition with the *Abregé de l'histoire de France par les devises expliquées en vers & en prose* which forms the last part of his encyclopedically entitled *Essay d'un dictionnaire contenant la connoissance du monde, des sciences universelles, et particulierement celle des medailles, des passions, des moeurs, des vertus, et des vices &c. Representé par des figures hyerogliphiques, expliquées en prose & en vers* of 1700.

Not only were such works produced in published form, but we also find manuscript collections, although here, as so often, the devices are commonly described rather than actually reproduced visually. In BnF Ms. fr. 20244, for example, among a series of documents relating to the La Tremoille family is a short four-page collection of 64 *Devises de tous les roys de France* (f.91r) running like Le Vasseur's collection from Pharamond to Louis XIII. In the interests of brevity only the motto is given here, rather than a description of the device itself also, as in 'Charles 6 Etcunque', although in the case of François 1er both elements are noted: 'Francois 1 Une Salamandre dans les flammes avec Nutrisco et extinguo'. BnF Ms. fr. 23045 includes a wider ranging, but similarly non-illustrated little collection entitled *Divers emblesmes & devises d'empereurs, roys, reynes, princes &c tirés du livre intitulé Jacobi Tipotii symbola pontificum imperatorum regum* (f.22)[6] in which the pattern adopted is that of the

---

[4]   The previous year Le Vasseur had published a similarly structured compilation on the emperors of Rome, Italy, Greece and Germany, also dedicated to then even younger *dauphin* (*Les devises des empereurs romains, tant italiens que grecs & allemans, depuis Jules Caesar jusques à Rodolphe II à present regnant. Avecques les expositions d'icelles par quatrains. Par Jaques Le Vasseur Archidiac. de Noyon. A Monseigneur le Daulphin*, Paris, F. Bourriquant, 1608, 8°).

[5]   Paris, T. Quinet, 1647, 4°, 2 vols.

[6]   This printed collection of devices by Jacobus Typotius was first published in three volumes in 1601-1603: *Symbola divina & humana pontificum imperatorum regum. Accessit brevis & facilis Isagoge Iac. Typotii. Tomus primus. Ex musaeo Octavii de Strada civis Romani. S.C.M. sculptor Egidius Sadeler excu.* (Prague, 1601, folio); *Symbola varia diversorum principum*

François 1er device of BnF Ms. fr. 20244, as in 'Adulphe de Nassau Empereur Un Ancre entortillé d'un Dauphin. Festina lente'.[7] Much more elegantly produced, however, is the collection of painted devices entitled Ces soixantes (sic) et douze devises sont des roys, princes et seigneurs dames et roynes de France which is the first of a series of asssorted collections of devices in Arsenal Ms. 3184. Here the 72 devices beginning with François II and ending once again with Louis XIII, are generously arranged one per page, with each device taking the form of a motto, followed by a painted representation of the figure encased in a roundel, followed by a note of its owner, as, for example *Nec me movent fulmina terrae* accompanied by a figure of an armed man standing firm against arrows and cannons, with the attribution 'Monsr le Baron de Nonant filz' (f.4v).

In Le Vasseur's collection of devices of the kings of France, he does not simply list these chronologically, but subdivides them into their different dynasties, beginning with the 'Race premiere, dicte des Merovingiens' (A4r) followed by the 'Race seconde, des Carolovingiens' (D3v) and so on, thereby further enhancing their educational value.The text is bilingual, with Le Vasseur's original French verse accompanied by a Latin rendering of it by Michel Grenet. Each of the early kings is allotted one illustrated device, but from François 1er onwards two devices are given for each king, one illustrated and one non-illustrated, though in fact the 'illustration' is actually a medallion of the bust of the king rather than a representation of the visual element of the device. Further historical information is also carefully worked into the individual devices, as, for example the fact that Henri III was king of Poland before becoming King of France. In the illustration accompanying the first of his two devices, the bust of Henri III is surrounded by the legend 'HENRI.III. D.G. FRANC ET POLON REX'. The motto *Amor omnia vincit*, is followed by Latin and French verses drawing attention to this fact:

> L'amour est triomphant, il dompte & gaigne tout,
> Il convertit en feu les glaçons de Russie,
> Il amorce les Ours; & par ma courtoisie
> La France je flechis de l'un à l'autre bout.

> VERSION
> Sauromatis mandata dabam legesque ferebam,

---

sacrosanc. ecclesiae & sacri imperii Romani. Cum uberrima Isagoge Iac. Typotii familiaris aulae & historiographi sacrae Caes. Rom. Tomus secundus. Ex musaeo Octavii...simbola desumpta sunt. S.C.Mtis. sculptor Aegidius Sadeler excudit (Prague, 1602, folio); *Symbola varia diversorum principum cum facili isagoge D. Anselmi de Boodt Brugensis sac. Caes. Mai. aulae medici. Tomus tertius. S.C.Mtis. sculptor Aegidius Sadeler excudit* (Prague, 1603, folio). Its popularity is reflected in the fact that it was thereafter published (in whole or in part) in a number of editions throughout the seventeenth century (Frankfurt, 1613, 1642 and 1652; Arnhem 1666, 1679 and 1686; Amsterdam, 1686 and 1690). For details see Praz, p.518.

[7]   See also a similar collection of devices of popes, emperors and kings in BnF Ms. fr. 13426, f.379 *et seq.* See also a collection of *Devises des princes et autres* in BnF Ms. fr. 20159, f.594 *et seq.*

Me patriae pietas revocabit amorque meorum.

and then by a second device further emphasising the same point:

> AUTRE DEVISE DUDIT HENRY III
> *Manet ultima coelo,*
> *La troisiesme m'attend au Ciel.*
>
> La terre m'a chargé d'une double Couronne,
> Attendant que le Ciel la troisiesme me donne.
>
> VERSION
> Sauromatae primam, Galli tribuere secundam,
> Utaque hac potior, spero, manet ultima Coelo.
> (Le Vasseur, *Devises des roys de France*, K2v-3r)

Reflecting the enduring influence of Paradin's collection of devices compiled in the mid sixteenth century, the first of the two devices for François 1er specifically acknowledges Paradin as its source:

> Salamandre ton feu fait tourner en arriere,
> L'Ours cruel, le Serpent, avec l'Aigle legere.
>
> DU LATIN DE PARADIN.
> Ursus atrox aquilaeque leves, & tortilis anguis.
> Cesserunt flammae iam salamandra tuae. (Le Vasseur, *Devises des roys de France*, I3v)[8]

Le Vasseur's slightly earlier *Devises des empereurs romains* follows the same basic pattern as his *Devises des roys de France*, but without illustrations, and - perhaps in deference to the extreme youth of the dedicatee (the *dauphin* was only seven years old when this work was dedicated to him in 1608, as opposed to eight when the *Devises des roys de France* was also dedicated to him the following year) - apart from the original Latin motto itself (which is also translated into French), the rest of the text is wholly in the vernacular. As well as its purely educational function, Le Vasseur manages to include also a moralising dimension, as in the device of the Emperor Charles V with its bilingual motto *Plus ultra/Plus oultre*. The accompanying French quatrain alludes to the motto certainly, but uses it to develop a generally applicable moral lesson about the desirability of following the path of virtue, rather than commenting on its more specific political implications as used by Charles V:

> CHARLES QUINT
> Plus ultra

---

[8] See Paradin, *Devises heroïques*, 1557, b1r.

Plus oultre

Qui la vertu suit à la trace,
Tousjours plus outre il a les yeux,
Et jamais ne s'arreste en place,
Tousjours plus outre on trouve mieux.
                         (Le Vasseur, *Devises des empereurs romains*, p.78)

    Published almost a century after Le Vasseur's two collections of historic devices, La Feuille's short *Abregé de l'histoire de France par les devises expliquées en vers & en prose* included at the end of his *Essay d'un dictionnaire* likewise begins with Pharamond, but brings the collection up to date by the inclusion of Louis XIV, thus increasing the number of kings from 64 to 65. Like Le Vasseur's works it conveys its essential information as succinctly as possible: small engraved busts of all the kings are reproduced, each with their own name (see fig.6), on two unfolding leaves, and the text (which, as in Le Vasseur's *Devises des empereurs*, is all in French other than the Latin mottoes) includes no more than a note of the king's name, the length of his reign, his device in Latin followed by a short French verse translation,

Figure 6: La Feuille, *Abregé de l'histoire de France par les devises*, in *Essay d'un dictionnaire*, Amsterdam, 1700, between pp.136 and 137.

and a brief prose resumé of the essential details of his reign, as in the opening entry on Pharamond:

> PHARAMOND.
> regna 10 ans.
> Sa Devise
> *Imperium sine fine dedi*
>
> J'ay fondé cét Estat sur de si fermes Loys,
> Qu'on ne peut voir la fin de l'Empire François.
>
> Selon la commune opinion il est le Premier Roy des François. Il commença à regner aprés avoir été élevé sur le Pavois l'an 418, & mourut l'an 428. De son Regne, quatre Anciens Seigneurs redigerent pendant quatre Assises la Loy Salique.
>
> (La Feuille, *Abregé de l'histoire de France par les devises*, S1r)

Unlike Le Vasseur, however, La Feuille does not generally cite the most obvious device for the various kings whom he lists. Where Le Vasseur cited for François 1er the habitual salamander device (as did likewise the unknown author of the *Devises de tous les roys de France* in BnF Ms.fr. 20244), La Feuille instead offers a quite different device for François, relating the greatness of the French king to that of Achilles:

> *In Hectora solus Achilles*
> Que ne vis-je en mes jours naistre un second Hector,
> J'estois pour le combattre un autre Achille encor.
> (La Feuille, *Abregé de l'histoire de France par les devises*, T3v)[9]

while Henri II's commonly used *Donec totum impleat orbem* is similarly passed over in favour of a quite different device reflecting his role as a figure of authority:

> *Ora impia lege repressi*
> Par mes frequens Edits pleins de severité,
> J'ay triomphé du vice & de l'impieté.
> (La Feuille, *Abregé de l'histoire de France par les devises*, T3v)

That of the short-lived François II reads like a rather wistful epitaph:

---

[9]   The prose summary of the main facts of François 1er's reign given in La Feuille's *Abregé de l'histoire de France par les devises* is a masterpiece of brevity: 'Il commença à regner en 1515, & mourut en 1547, âgé de 52 ans. Il gagna la Bataille de Marignan, la première année de son Regne. Il passa la nuit d'entre les deux jours que dura la Bataille sur l'afust d'un canon, où un Soldat luy porta un peu d'eau dans un morion mêlée de sang & de bourbe, que sa soif luy fit trouver excellente. En 1525 il fut pris prisonnier à Pavie, par Charles V, à qui il donna ses Enfans en ostage l'année 1526, & l'échange s'en fit sur la Riviere de Bidassoa.' (T3v)

Aetas brevis aptáque Regno
Si la mort ne m'eust pris du printemps de mon âge,
J'estois digne après tous de regner davantage.
            (La Feuille, *Abregé de l'histoire de France par les devises*, T4r)

while the device for the still living Louis XIV makes no allusion to the image of the sun, but simply refers, without the aid of any image at all, to his unsurpassed power and authority in the world:

Armisque potens
Ses Armes, son Conseil, sa Valeur sans seconde,
Le rendent plus puissant que tous les Roys du Monde.
            (La Feuille, *Abregé de l'histoire de France par les devises*, T4v)

with the accompanying brief prose commentary: 'Louis XIV, dit Dieu donné, ou Auguste, regne aujourd'huy glorieusement sur les François'.

    Despite the gap of almost a hundred years between La Feuille's history of the kings of France published at the very end of the seventeenth century and that of Le Vasseur, published at the very beginning of the century there are strong similarities, which reflect the enduring nature of the genre as an effective means of conveying factual details of the history of France in a palatable and visually stimulating manner. In both cases the Latin devices of the kings of France are translated into easily understandable French verses, accompanied by engraved illustrations of their busts, and backed up by a minimum of prose gloss in order to provide a succinct and easily assimilable educational text book. In contrast to these two Audin's *Histoire de France representée par tableaux* of 1647 is a much more discursive work, more akin both in structural pattern and in preoccupation to his own collection of fables, published some twenty years later (discussed above in chapter 2) than to either of these other illustrated histories of France. The historical and political dimensions of Audin's fables, which are clearly indicated in the 1669 title of the work (*Fables heroiques...Avec des moralitez historiques pour l'explication de chaque fable. Comprenans les veritables maximes de la politique, & de la morale*) are similarly highlighted in the descriptive phrase at the end of the title to his history book:

    Histoire de France representée par tableaux, commencant au regne de Hugues Capet, chef des roys de la troisiéme branche. Avec des discours & reflexions politiques.

but - as with Le Vasseur's *Devises des empereurs* - Audin's preoccupation in his history of France, as also in his fables, is not just to be factually informative, but also to include a generally moralising dimension. The structure of his *Histoire de France representée par tableaux* is indeed very similar to that of the fables although the *Histoire de France representée par tableaux* is altogether a much more substantial work than the fables. In it greater primacy is accorded to the illustration which introduces each section than in the fables: whereas in the fables the engraved figure occupies only half of the duodecimo page, in the *Histoire de France representée par tableaux* each very stylised classical '*Tableau du regne de ...*' occupies a full quarto page. Likewise the textual component of the *Histoire de France representée par tableaux* is much more subsantial than that of the fables. Whereas the gloss on the significance of the figure in the fables accounts for only half a page, and the prose narration only a further one and a half pages, in the *Histoire de France representée par tableaux* the '*Explication du tableau du regne de...*' which follows the engraving runs to a full ten pages of prose analysis of the key features of the reign, the key virtues demonstrated by the monarch and the key devices associated with him, backed up, in addition, by marginal notes giving further factual information or moral lessons. As with Le Vasseur's *Devises des empereurs* the text is also wholly in French, with the exception of the Latin mottoes of the devices, and these are likewise translated into French, as for example one of the devices of Philippe 1er:

> *Nec numen, nec nomen erit*
> Je raseray le Temple de la Gloire,
> Perdant du lieu le nom & la memoire.
>> (Audin, *Histoire de France representée par tableaux*, D1r)

Even longer, however, is the final element in each section of the work, entitled *Discours...* in which the particular monarch is identified together with his key attributes and qualities, as, for example, that for Philippe, which is subtitled '*discours touchant ce prince voluptueux & conquerant*'. These *discours* are significantly longer than anything we have seen hitherto, running in the case of the Philippe to over forty pages, but the content is rendered less dense by virtue of being arranged in the form of a dialogue between a number of named interlocutors,[10] who move from *tableau* to *tableau* discussing the contents of each in a manner which is strikingly reminiscent of the strategy adopted by Gilles Corrozet's over a century earlier in his emblematic French rendering of the *Tabula* of Cebes. In Corrozet's *Tableau de Cebes* a group of pilgrims are also given a guided tour of a series of *tableaux*, each of which is reproduced in a full-page woodcut, followed by a short prose description, and lastly by a much lengthier verse discourse, in which - again by means of dialogue between the guide and the pilgrims - the significance of what is represented in each *tableau* is analysed and explained. Here yet again the remarkable continuity of form between sixteenth and seventeenth century is strikingly demonstrated. There are significant affinities between the 'reading' of pictures in Audin's *Histoire de France prepresentée par tableaux* and that of such other seventeenth-century works as Vigenère's *Images ou tableaux de platte peinture des deux Philostrates sophistes grecs* of 1614 or Marolles' rather later *Tableaux du Temple des Muses...pour representer les vertus & les vices, sur les plus illustres fables de l'antiquité*, published in 1655, only a few years after Audin's *Histoire de France*.

---

[10] As, for example, Polindor, Philarque, Eraste, Philadelphe, Alcype, Theotime, Philirandre, Lysandre, Lygdamis, Pymandre.

In all these collections cited thus far the author has set out to exploit the medium of devices to constitute a palatable and easily assimilable history of France, but as we saw earlier in the case of Ménestrier's metallic history of Louis XIV, the *Histoire du Roy Louis le Grand par les medailles, emblémes, devises, jettons, inscriptions, armoiries, et autres monumens publics* of 1689 and Nicolas Chevalier's slightly later, and similarly entitled *Histoire de Guillaume III...Par medailles, inscriptions, arcs de triomphe, & autres monumens publics*,[11] the same approach could also be used to pursue a more restricted goal, limiting the subject to the history of one single reign. Well before either of these two works, the royal engraver, Jean Valdor, had already done this in 1649, with his ambitious emblematic history of the exploits of Louis XIII. This grandiose folio volume, published by the *Imprimerie royale*, has, however, a clear dual function: while it offers a factual history of the reign of Louis XIII, it also is clearly intended to make a statement about the glory of France. The work stands as a splendid testimony of pride in nationhood, expressed indirectly by means of praise of the monarch, and it is not coincidental that it was actually commissioned by Louis XIII, as we are told in the title. As the lengthy title also explains, the text is contributed by several different authors, and it includes as well as an account of the life and exploits of Louis XIII himself, a series of portraits of his allies and military leaders, together with reproduction and explanation of their devices, and also a series of highly detailed maps and plans of scenes of battle:

> *Les triomphes de Louis le Juste XIII. du nom, Roy de France et de Navarre. Contenans les plus grandes actions où Sa Majesté s'est trouvée en personne, representées en figures aenigmatiques exposées par un poëme heroïque de Charles Beys, & accompagnées de vers François sous chaque figure, composez par P. de Corneille. Avec les portraits des rois, princes et generaux d'armees, qui ont assisté ou servy ce belliqueux Louis le Juste combattant; et leurs devises & expositions en forme d'eloges, par Henry Estienne escuyer, Sieur des Fossez, poëte et interprete du Roy és langues Grecque & Latine. Ensemble le plan des villes, sieges et batailles, avec un abregé de la vie de ce grand Monarque, par René Barry, Conseiller du Roy & historiographe de Sa Majesté. Le tout traduit en Latin par le R.P.Nicolai, Docteur en Sorbonne de la Faculté de Paris, & premier Regent du grand Convent des Jacobins. Ouvrage entrepris & fini par Jean Valdor, Liegeois, Calcographe du Roy. Le tout par commandement de leurs Majestez.*[12]

---

[11]   So similar is the phraseology of the two titles that it is tempting to wonder if Chevalier did not indeed take his inspiration for his title, if not indeed for his whole work from the slightly earlier work by Ménestrier. There would be a certain irony if this were the case, since although both works are written in French by Frenchmen, Ménestrier's work is a highly establishment one in praise of the Catholic king of France, whereas that of Chevalier is written in praise of the protestant king of England, a country with which France was at war. Since Chevalier's work was published in Amsterdam, its author may well have been a Huguenot refugee from Catholic France.

[12]   Paris, A. Estienne for the *Imprimerie royale*, 1649, folio.

In the interest of maximum accessibility, the work is wholly bilingual, composed in French and thereafter translated into Latin, with each item printed first in its original vernacular version and then again in Latin. Once again reflecting the tenacity of the emblematic form, we see in the first section of the work, the *Triomphes* proper, the same sort of emblematic pattern of figure accompanied by short verse plus long verse as was used a century earlier in one of the earliest French emblem books, Gilles Corrozet's *Hecatomgraphie*, although here on a much vaster scale. As in the *Hecatomgraphie* each 'emblem' of the *Triomphes* occupies a double opening: on the verso is a substantial French verse describing the *Prise de...* or *Reddition de...*, accompanied by a full-page engraving of the scene on the facing recto, in which is incorporated a six-line French verse. A Latin translation of that verse is included below the engraving, while the translation into Latin of the longer French verse occupies the following two pages. Although the phrase 'representées en figures aenigmatiques' is used in the title, the figures are hardly enigmatic in any real sense of the word, but certainly emblematic with their accompanying allegorical interpretations, as for example in *La Prise de Nancy*, where the engraving of the surrender of the town is accompanied by a six-line verse associating the siege of Nancy with the Siege of Troy:

> Troye, aupres de ses murs l'espace de dix ans
> Vit contr'elle les Dieux et les Grecs combattans
> Et s'arma sans trembler contre la Destinée:
>
> Grand Roy l'on avoüera que l'eclat de tes yeux
> Ta fait plus remporter d'honneur cette journée
> Que la fable, en dix ans n'en fit avoir aux Dieux.
> > (Valdor, *Triomphes de Louis le Juste*, Q2r)

The factual account of the siege of Nancy is then conveyed in a 32-line French poem on the facing verso, rendered in a Latin version on the following double opening, while a Latin version of the shorter verse is reproduced below the engraving:

> Troia Deos bis quinque annis, nec territa, vidit
> In sua Grajugenas impellere tecta phalanges;
> Cedere vix viso Nanceii moenia Regi
>
> Vel sola augusti compellit nominis umbra,
> Macte, Heros invicte, die plus perficis unâ
> Quàm referat gemino de Divis fabula lustro.
> > (Valdor, *Triomphes de Louis le Juste*, Q2r)

'Aenigmatique' must be understood here as more or less a synonym for 'emblématique' as sometimes occurs in the seventeenth century, when enigmas, devices and emblems become increasingly run together as kindred forms.[13]

The second part of the *Triomphes de Louis le Juste*, with its text by Henry Estienne, Sieur des Fossez, author of his own autonomous general treatise on devices,[14] is quite differently structured from the first part, and indeed it has its own separate title page, *Devises des roys, princes et generaux d'armées qui ont assisté ou servi Louis le Juste combattant, avec leur exposition. Par Henry Estienne, Sieur des Fossez, poëte et interprete du Roy és langues Grecque et Latine.* Although it is no less instructional in intent than the first part, the means by which it sets about it are quite different. At one level this is just one more example of teaching history via the medium of devices, but Henry Estienne in fact goes one stage further, offering a broader lesson than this. Much fuller description and analysis of the devices and their implications is given here, together with a note of their source material, so that both literary and cultural instruction are given, in addition to historical information. Furthermore, since the text - like that of the first part - is rendered fully in both French and Latin, the work also has the potential to be used as a manual (albeit an expensive one) for teaching Latin.

The work is indeed lavishly produced. In this section three engraved devices are reproduced on one verso (see fig. 7), together with a full-page engraved portrait on the facing recto, for Louis XIII himself, and then for each of his allies and leaders. Thereafter follows a prose discourse on the devices depicted. The first two devices of Louis XIII, *Timui nec infans* and *Nullas recipit victoria metas* serve to demonstrate the much greater than usual textual detail offered by Henry Estienne:

> Le corps de cette premiere Devise est un Bras royal armé, tenant dans la main une massuë, avec laquelle il s'oppose aux monstres:
>
> La lettre ou sentence qui est comme l'ame de la Devise, pour en exprimer le sens, c'est ce demy-vers pris de Seneque en ses Tragedies,
>
> TIMUI NEC INFANS;
>
> Qui veut dire,
>
> *Je ne les ay pas crains dés mon enfance mesme;*

---

[13]   See, for example, the anonymous *Colloque des trois suppots du Seigneur de la Coquille: où le char triomfant de Monseigneur le Daufin est representé par plusieurs personnages, figures, emblemes & enigmes. A Monseigneur d'Halincourt*, Lyon, 'Par les Suppots de l'Imprimerie', 1610, 8° (Arsenal); or the similarly anonymous *Receuil des plusieurs enigmes, airs, devises et medailles. Enrichis des figures*, Amsterdam, J. de Waesberge, 1680, 12° (republished in 1684). One of Ménestrier's later treatises on emblematics and allied material is entitled *La philosophie des images enigmatiques, où il est traité des enigmes, hieroglyphiques, oracles, propheties, sorts, divinations, loteries, talismans, songes, centuries de Nostradamus, de la braguette. Par le P. Cl. Menestrier de la Compagnie de Jesus*, Lyon, H. Baritel, 1694, 8°.
[14]   *L'Art de faire les devises, où il est traicté des hieroglyphiques, symboles, emblemes, aenygmes, sentences, parabolles, revers de medailles, armes, blasons, cimiers, chiffres & rebus. Avec un traicté des rencontres ou mots plaisans*, Lyon, J. Paslé, 1645, 8°. (This work was popular enough to be published within a year in London, in an English translation by Thomas Blount: *The Art of Making Devises*, London, W.E. and J.G., 1646. Curiously the work was more popular in England than in France, with this version being republished in London in 1648, 1650 and 1655, whereas the French text went through only the one edition.)

2   Lovis le Iuſte combattant.

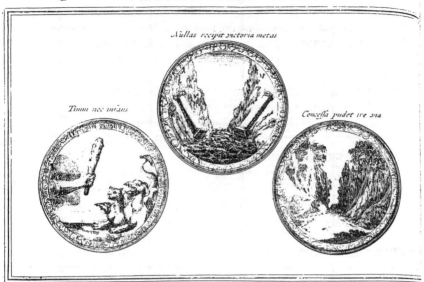

E CORPS de cette premiere Deuiſe eſt vn Bras royal armé, tenant dans la main vne maſſuë, auec laquelle il ſ'oppoſe aux monſtres:

La lettre ou ſentence qui eſt comme l'ame de la De-uiſe, pour en exprimer le ſens, c'eſt ce demy-vers pris de Seneque en ſes Tragedies,

TIMVI NEC INFANS;

Qui veut dire,

Ie ne les ay pas crains dés mon enfance meſme;

Se rapportant à Hercule qui eſtouffa deux Serpens lors qu'il eſtoit encor au ber-ceau, & fut dés cét âge dompteur des monſtres, pour vn fauorable augure de ce qu'il feroit vn iour. Le Roy donc dit ces paroles, pour ſignifier qu'il ne faut pas ſ'eſtonner ſi dans la pleine vigueur de ſon âge il a renuerſé toutes les forces de ſes ennemis, puis que dés le temps de ſes premieres années, il a rompu les deſ-ſeins & les efforts de tous les rebelles, en domptant & abattant l'hereſie.

La ſeconde Figure nous repreſente des colomnes renuerſées en vn deſtroit de mer, d'vne part, & nous fait voir d'vn autre coſté des montagnes entr'ouuertes, auec ces mots empruntez de Claudian,

NVLLAS RECIPIT VICTORIA METAS;

Qui veulent dire,

Ses triomphans exploits ne ſouffrent point de bornes;

ou

Sa victoire n'a point de bornes qui l'arreſtent:

Par contrepointe de L o v i s le Iuſte auec Hercule, pour faire voir combien cét

Figure 7: Valdor, *Les triomphes de Louis le Juste*, Paris, 1649, [2]A1v.

Se rapportant à Hercule qui estouffa deux Serpens lors qu'il estoit encor au
berceau, & fut dés cét âge dompteur des monstres, pour un favorable augure
de ce qu'il feroit un jour. Le Roy donc dit ces paroles, pour signifier qu'il ne
faut pas s'estonner si dans la pleine vigueur de son âge il a renversé toutes les
forces de ses ennemis, puis que dés le temps de ses premieres années, il a
rompu les desseins & les efforts de tous les rebelles, en domptant & abattant
l'heresie.

La seconde Figure nous represente des colomnes renversées en un destroit de
mer, d'une part, & nous fait voir d'un autre costé des montagnes
entr'ouvertes, avec ces mots empruntez de Claudian,

           NULLAS RECIPIT VICTORIA METAS;

Qui veulent dire,

               Ses triomphans exploits ne souffrent point de bornes;

                              ou

             Sa victoire n'a point de bornes qui l'arrestent.
             (Valdor, *Triomphes de Louis le Juste*, [2]A1v)

Ménestrier's *Histoire du Roy Louis le Grand par les medailles, emblemes,
devises, jettons, inscriptions, armoiries, et autres monumens publics* exploits Henry
Estienne's basic pattern, but in a much more ambitious way. Where Estienne simply
provided a commentary (albeit a lengthy and detailed one) on the various devices of
Louis XIII and his allies and military leaders, Ménestrier with his habitual ingenuity
constructs, some forty years later, a coherent chronological account of the life of Louis
XIII's successor, and of the principal achievements of his reign, on the basis of
reproduction of selected medals struck to commemorate particular events, beginning
with his birth in 1638, and continuing up to 1687. Text is minimal, as is appropriate
to the extreme youth of Louis's three grandsons to whom the work is dedicated, and
indeed what little text there is is triggered by each of the individual medals which are
selected to illuminate each key event. There is no overall narrative text to link the
medals which are themselves solely responsible for taking the chronological account
forward. Indeed the extent to which primacy is here given by Ménestrier to a largely
visual representation of history, is reflected in the fact that in the first edition, in 1689,
the entire work is engraved, including even the short passages of textual gloss
accompanying individual medals.[15]

---

[15] This first edition, published in Paris by Nolin alone in 1689, was followed by a further
edition in 1693, published by Nolin in company with Robert Pepié and Jacques Le Fevre under
the title *Histoire du Roy Louis le Grand par les medailles, emblêmes, devises, jettons,
inscriptions, armoiries, et autres monumens publics, recuëillis, et expliquéz par le Pere Claude
François Menestrier de la Compagnie de Jesus. Seconde edition. Augmentée de plusieurs
figures et corrigée*, with a fuller text than that of the earlier purely engraved first edition. A
variant version was also published in 1693 by Pepié and Nolin under the title, *Histoire du
regne de Louis le Grand par les medailles, emblemes, devises, jettons, inscriptions, armoiries,
& autres monumens publics. Recueillis & expliquez par le Pere Claude François Menestrier de
la Compagnie de Jesus. Edition nouvelle. Corrigée & augmentée d'un Discours sur la vie du
Roy, & de plusieurs médailles & figures*, (Princeton University Library), and the work was

In the first part of the folio volume the medals are reproduced six per page, with beneath each a brief description and explanation of what it alludes to, with a note of the date, and (normally) a French translation of the Latin motto. The achievements which are highlighted are mainly military, as for example in the tenth series of six, which marks the events of 1661, under the overall title 'Le Roy gouverne par luy mesme',[16] in which the third medal depicts the capture of Dunkirk:

> Troisiéme medaille
> DUNKERCA RECUPERATA, PROVIDENTIA PRINCIPIS MDCLXII
> Dunkerque recouvrée par la Providence du Prince, en 1661
> Le Roy retire des mains des Anglais la Vile de Dunkerque, & par cette sage
> Prevoyance, S.M. pourvoit à la seureté de la France.
> (Ménestrier, *Histoire du Roy Louis le Grand*, 1691, B3v)

but they also include Louis's role in developing the wellbeing of his country, as in the fourth medal of the same series, depicting his beneficence towards his people in the form of the distribution of food in time of famine:

> Quatriéme Medaille.
> Représentation de deux Femmes.
> FAMES PIETATE PRINCIPIS SUBLEVATA. MDCLXI.
> La Faim soulagée par la Pieté du Roy, en 1661.

---

further reissued under this variant title in 1699 (Vienna, Österreichische Nationalbibliothek) and 1700 (Paris, Mazarine). A counterfeit edition, bearing Nolin's name on the title page, was published in Amsterdam in 1691 (*Histoire du Roy Louis le Grand par les medailles, emblêmes, devises, jettons, inscriptions, armoiries, et autres monumens publics recuëillis, et expliquéz par le Pere Claude-François Menestrier de la Compagnie de Jesus. N.E. augmentée de 5. planches*, Paris, I.B. Nolin, 1691, 4°.) According to Landwehr (*Romanic Emblem Books*, no.519) this edition was published by Mortier in Amsterdam. All quotations are taken from this edition.

[16] *Histoire du Roy Louis le Grand*, 1691, B3v-4r. The first medal of the series focuses on the important event of Louis taking over the reins of government, as cited in the title to this group of six. The medal depicts the figure of the king surrounded by rays of the sun with the accompanying explanation:
> Premiére Medaille.
> LE ROY GOUVERNE PAR LUY-MESME.
> La Teste du Roy.
> LUDOVICUS XIV REX CHRISTIANISSIMUS.
> Louis XIV. Roy Tres-Chrêtien.
>
> Revers.
> L'Image du Soleil.
> ORDO ET FELICITAS, CURAS IMPERII CAPESSENTE MDCLXI.
> L'Ordre & la Felicité, en gouvernant par luy même, en 1661.
>
> Le Roy prend en main le Timon du Gouvernement de l'Etat sous l'Image du Soleil assis sur le Globe du Monde, où il met l'Ordre & la Felicité.

Dans un temps de necessité publique, le Roy soulagea le Peuple par des distributions de blé & de pain cuit aux Tuilleries. 1661.
        (Ménestrier, *Histoire du Roy Louis le Grand*, 1691, B3v)

and in cultivating the sciences, as in the thirteenth series where the fifth medal commemorates his role in establishing the Académie des Sciences and constructing the Observatoire:

Cinquiéme Medaille.
L'Observatoire.
SIC ITUR AD ASTRA. TURRIS SIDERUM SPECULATORIA. MDCLXVII.
C'est ainsi qu'on va Jusqu'aux Cieux. L'Observatoire.
S.M. aprés avoir établi une Academie des Sciences, fait bâtir un Palais magnifique pour observer les Astres, en 1667. On le nomme couramment l'Observatoire. (Ménestrier, *Histoire du Roy Louis le Grand*, 1691, C2v)

His role in the suppression of calvinism, is likewise celebrated, as in the twenty-third series, in which the fifth medal celebrates the Revocation of the Edict of Nantes (unusually, noting the name of the designer of the medal):

Cinquiéme Medaille.
HAERESIS EXTINCTA. EDICTUM OCTOBRIS MDCLXXXV.
L'Heresie éteinte. L'Edit d'Octobre 1685.
Cét Edit pour la Revocation de celuy de Nantes, fut l'entiére Extinction de la Religion P.R. en France, & le Triomphe de la Religion Romaine. Le Sr. Roussel est l'Auteur de cette Medaille.
        (Ménestrier, *Histoire du Roy Louis le Grand*, 1691, E4v)

Also included in this treatise by Ménestrier, among other things, is a similar, but shorter, two-leaf *Histoire du Roy par les jettons*, in which thirty-five *jetons* are reproduced on each page, together with a two- or three-word gloss explaining the particular event to which each *jeton* refers (1691 ed., I1v-3r), and also a further two-page sequence of emblems and devices focusing specifically on Louis's achievements in the domain of religion, entitled *Emblémes et dévises sur ce que le Roy a fait pour la religion* (1691, M3v-4r), stressing in particular his energetic anti-calvinist policies, described here, as elsewhere by Ménestrier, as the extirpation of heresy, as in number seven of the collection:

Un Bâtiment renversé par la Foudre. DEDIT CONVULSA RUINAM. *Le Renversement a causé la ruine.* Pour les Temples des Herétiques détruits.

or number eleven:

L'Hydre, VULNERE UNO CECIDIT. *D'un seul coup abbatuë*. **Pour l'Edit d'Octobre 1685.**

The various devices and emblems are described on one page, and reproduced in the form of engraved figures on the unfolding second page (see fig. 8).

Figure 8: Ménestrier, *Emblémes et dévises sur ce que le Roy a fait pour la religion*, in *Histoire du Roy Louis le Grand*, Paris (Amsterdam), 1691, M4r.

As with Valdor's earlier emblematic history of Louis XIII, commissioned by the king himself, and published by the *Imprimerie royale*, here also there is a very significant element of royal propaganda involved, in addition to straightforward 'history', reflected in the fact that this particular work (unlike any other of Ménestrier's innumerable works) was published in Paris by the royal engraver, I.B.Nolin.[17] Ménestrier's dedication of the work to the three grandchildren of Louis XIV reflects this also. Where in the opening lines of such dedications laudatory comments about the dedicatee would normally be expected, in this particular work the three dedicatees are summarily addressed as 'Augustes enfans de France', after which the full force of the laudatory comments is directed at the more important figure of Louis himself:

> Aux Augustes Enfans de France Louis Duc de Bourgogne, Philippe Duc d'Anjou, Charles Duc de Berry; Fils de Louis Dauphin de France, Petits Fils de Louis le Grand, l'Invincible, le Sage, le Conquerant, la Merveille de son Siecle, la Terreur de ses Ennemis, l'Amour de des Peuples, l'Arbitre de la Paix, & de la Guerre, l'Admiration de l'Univers, & digne d'en estre le Maître: Claude-François Menestrier de la Compagnie de Jesus Offre avec un Profond Respect le Modéle d'un Héros Achevé en leur Presentant les Images de l'Histoire d'un Régne Digne de l'Immortalité & de la Veneration de tous les Siécles.   (Ménestrier, *Histoire du Roy Louis le Grand*, 1691, f. [2]r)

But unlike Valdor's work which did not run to more than a single edition, Ménestrier's was clearly more popular within France, since Nolin himself produced further editions in 1693, 1699 and 1700. Reflecting its broader European interest, however, is the fact that a counterfeit edition with Nolin's name on the title page, was also published in Amsterdam in 1691 with an inserted sequence of five satirical engraved plates.[18] Also reflecting - though in a very different way - the wider European interest of this work (and also perhaps reflecting the way in which one dynasty kept an eye on the doings of another dynasty, even well after the event) is the existence of a copy of the 1691 edition in the British Library bearing the royal binding of George III, King of England from 1760 to 1820.

Although Nicolas Chevalier's metallic history of the life and times of William III follows the same basic pattern as that of Ménestrier's metallic history of the life and times of Louis XIV, there is a slight difference in structural emphasis in that less primacy is given to the engraved figures than in Ménestrier's work. Where Ménestrier's 1689 edition was wholly engraved - medals and brief text alike -

---

[17]   Several of Ménestrier's works were published in Lyon, by a variety of printers, but of those which were published in Paris, the great majority were printed by R.J.B. de la Caille.
[18]   The inclusion of these five additional plates is indicated in the title (*Histoire du Roy Louis le Grand...N.E., augmentée de 5. planches*), but not their satirical character. In the text the five plates have their own title-page (I4r): *Les cinq planches des medailles qui suivent, ne sont pas moins curieuses à l'histoire de Louis le Grand, que les precedentes: mais le Pére Menestrier a eu ses veuës pour ne les avoir pas inserées dans cét ouvrage.*

Chevalier's much fuller passages of explanatory prose accompanying each medallion are more conventionally printed in letterpress, so that the text plays a more dominant narrative and informational role than in Ménestrier's earlier work, leading the reader from device to device, illustrating event after event in the life of William than had been the case in Ménestrier's work. Some of the medals reproduced and described reflect conventionally the general virtues of William III, such as an early one dating from 1657, when William was only seven years old, representing the allegorical figure of *Patientia* accompanied by a yoke:

> La suivante a esté frapée sur les grandes esperances que nôtre grand Prince donnoit comme on le pourra fort bien voir par le revers; il est en buste avec une petite toque de plumes; autour on lit cette inscription.
> WILHELMUS III. D.G. PRINCEPS AURAICAE
> Guillaume III. par la Grace de Dieu Prince d'Orange

[figure]   [figure]

> *REVERS*
> La patience chargée d'un joug nous fait entendre que la grandissime vertu qui éclatoit en nôtre Prince faisoit esperer de grandes choses de son Auguste Personne, comme il n'a point manqué de faire éclater, ainsi que l'on verra dans la suite de cét ouvrage: il n'y a jamais eu de Prince qui ait esté doüé d'autant de belles qualitez que nôtre grand Conquerant; autour on lit ces mots:
> Patientia & virtute
> *Patience & vertu.* (Chevalier, *Histoire de Guillaume III*, B1v)

but more commonly they are more politically oriented, selected as marking particularly significant events in the developing career of the future king of England, as for example a medal struck by the city of Amsterdam in 1674 in honour of William to commemorate his role in bringing to an end the war with England, with the Treaty of Westminster. As usual both sides of the medal are reproduced, the one depicting William on horseback as military leader, and the other an allegorical dove with an olive branch and a palm frond, denoting peace:

> La Ville d'Amsterdam fit frapper cette Medaille à l'honneur du Prince d'Orange au sujet de la paix avec l'Angleterre. Le Prince paroît à cheval & en action avec un baston de Commandement à la main; sur sa Teste est une grande branche d'Oranger, entrelassée d'un Cordon sur lequel on lit.
> VIRES ULTRA SORTEMQUE IUVENTAE
> Au dessus de ses forces & de son âge.[19]

[figure]   [figure]

---

[19]   William was at this date 24 years old.

REVERS

Une Colombe passe la Mer portant en son bec un rameau d'Olivier, & un de Palme, qui sont des symboles ordinaires de la Paix & de la Victoire: autour il y a ces mots.

A DOMINO VENIT PAX ET VICTORIA LAETA.

La Paix vient du Seigneur, & la Victoire agreable.

(Chevalier, *Histoire de Guillaume III*, E2v-3r)

Similarly the noteworthy event of his arrival in London in 1688 is described via the medal struck to mark this occasion:

On fit frapper cette medaille pour conserver la memoire de cet évenement singulier.

Nôtre grand Prince d'Orange en Buste avec ces Paroles autour.

GUILLELMUS   III.   D.G.   PRINCEPS   ARAUSIENSIS, RELIGIONIS, LIBERTATISQUE RESTITUTOR.

Guillaume III. par la Grace de Dieu Prince d'Orange, Restaurateur de la Religion, & de la Liberté.

[figure]   [figure]

REVERS

On void la Ville de Londres; au dessus paroît un Aigle portant en son bec une Branche d'Olivier d'un côté, & de l'autre un Rameau d'Oranger, avec leurs fruits; pour faire connoître que nôtre grand Prince, qui s'avance avec la Victoire, vient rétablir le calme, & redonner la Paix dans les trois Royaumes; dans le tour de la Medaille est cette Inscription.

ALIS NON ARMIS VENIT LIBERATOR

Celuy qui vient & qui nous delivre, n'est point un ennemy qui vient répandre nôtre sang, mais un ami genereux qui vole au secours de ceux qui l'appellent.

Dans l'Exergue

PRINCEPS AURIACUS INGREDITUR LONDINUM XXVIII. DECEMB. M.DC.LXXXVIII.

Le Prince d'Orange entre à Londres le 28. Decembre 1688.

(Chevalier, *Histoire de Guillaume III*, L2r-3v)

while a medal struck the following year, 1689, reflects the religious situation of the time, depicting on one side William and Mary as Defenders of the Faith,

R E V E R S

Un grand Bucher allumé, fur lequel on apporte le bois, & les ornemens de la
Chapelle des Jefuïtes ; une grande foule de Peuple qui court avec rapidité la jet-
ter en bas, & qui en emporte de grandes pieces au feu. Au côté on voit le Châ-
teau de Withal en Perfpective, & autour on lit.

NEC LEX EST JUSTIOR ULLA.

Il n'y eut jamais de Loy plus jufte.

Ce qui s'entend apparemment de l'indignation du Peuple contre les Jefuïtes ;
qui parut trés grande en cette occafion.

Il y a encore une Medaille ; mais ce font deux Revers des Medailles precedentes,
cependant on a trouvé à propos de la joindre encore icy fans l'expliquer, puifque
ces deux Revers ont efté déja expliquez ; comme on pourra l'avoir remarqué : nous
mettrons feulement les Devifes. D'un côté vous trouvez.

CÆLO DELABITUR ALTO.

Cette Benediction defcend du Ciel.

Dans le Pied'eftal l'on trouve ces autres paroles.

ÆRE PERENNIUS.

Plus durable que le Bronze.

Figure 9: Chevalier, *Histoire de Guillaume III*, Amsterdam, 1692, P4r.

and on the other side the looting and burning of a Jesuit chapel by a London mob with the approving motto *Nec lex est iustior ulla* (see fig. 9):

> Voicy Enfin une troisiéme Medaille, qui doit estre jointe icy, puisqu'elle est le fruit d'une joye publique après le Couronnement de leurs Majestez, & l'expression d'un petit accident qui suivit cette joye, sçavoir le brûlement de la Chapelle des Jesuïtes, à laquelle le Peuple de Londres mit le feu. C'est cette Medaille que j'ay dit ci-devant que je ferois voir.
> On voit le Roy & la Reine en Buste, avec une Couronne de Laurier & ces paroles autour.
> GUILLELMUS ET MARIA DEI GRATIA ANGLIAE, FRANCIAE, ET HIBERNIAE REX ET REGINA, FIDEI DEFENSORES
> *Guillaume & Marie par la Grace de Dieu Roy & Reine d'Angleterre, de France & d'Irlande, Défenseurs de la Foy.*
>
> [figure]   [figure]
>
> *REVERS*
>
> Un grand Bucher allumé, sur lequel on apporte le bois, & les ornemens de la Chapelle des Jesuïtes; une grande foule de Peuple qui court avec rapidité la jetter en bas, & qui en emporte de grandes pieces au feu. Au côté on voit le Château de Withal [20] en Perspective, & autour on lit.
> NEC LEX EST IUSTIOR ULLA.
> *Il n'y eut jamais de Loy plus juste.*
> Ce qui s'entend apparemment de l'indignation du Peuple contre les Jesuïtes qui parut trés grande en cette occasion.
> (Chevalier, *Histoire de Guillaume III*, P3v-4r)

Chevalier's work is thus a highly committed and partisan emblematic history of the life of William of Orange. Although he uses the same basic technique as that of Ménestrier, however, he gives greater primacy to the verbal text than did Ménestrier for whom the engravings alone effectively served to convey the message of the magnificence of the reign of Louis XIV, and of the important exploits achieved by that monarch. But for Chevalier (for whom historical detail and information are apparently more important than they were for Ménestrier) while the medals can serve to illustrate admirably the history he wishes to put across, as purely visual triggers they cannot themselves alone convey that history. Hence despite his evident debt to Ménestrier we find in Chevalier's work a much greater dependence on the textual element which provides a gloss to complement the engravings. Chevalier's work thus conforms much more than does that of Ménestrier to the more traditional emblematic combination of visual and verbal communication acting in tandem.

Where Ménestrier and Chevalier use existing medals as a basis for constructing

---

[20]   Whitehall.

emblematic histories in published form, other writers exploit other art forms in a not dissimilar way, either reproducing in engraved form, or on occasion simply describing, paintings or tapestries in royal palaces together with explanation of their allegorical meanings, thereby extending the range of the audience which the message of these paintings or tapestries can reach. As tapestries or paintings hung on walls, they are accessible only to those who can actually see them, but in printed form, accompanied by appropriate explanatory gloss, their meaning becomes accessible to a greater number of people. Often, although there is an element of factual 'history' involved in such works, their main aim is in reality royal propaganda rather than purely informative education, but in many respects these two elements are not easily separable, since factual description of the achievements of a monarch, and eulogy of that monarch for those same achievements mesh so closely together. The full title of Pierre Dan's *Tresor des merveilles de la maison royale de Fontainebleau* - one of the earlier examples of works of this kind - makes clear that as well as providing a splendid tourist guide to the palace, it also has an historical dimension, noting the political events and royal births deaths and marriages happening at Fontainebleau:

> *Le tresor des merveilles de la maison royale de Fontainebleau, contenant la description de son antiquité, de sa fondation, de ses bastimens, de ses rares peintures, tableaux, emblemes, et devises; de ses jardins, de ses fontaines, et autres singularitez qui s'y voyent. Ensemble les traictez de paix, les assemblées, les conferences, les entrées royales, les naissances, et ceremonies de baptesme de quelques enfans de France; les mariages, les tournoys, et autres magnificences, qui s'y sont faictes jusques à present. Par le R.P.F. Pierre Dan.*[21]

At the same time, since it is François 1er who was responsible for building the palace, much of the iconography contained therein relates to François, and Dan's description of this offers a combination of the historical and informative on the one hand, and the eulogistic on the other. He describes in great detail all aspects of the palace, but of particular interest are his descriptions of the paintings contained within it since it is in these that we see the emblematic pattern most strongly. In the section on the ballroom he describes a series of allegorical paintings, itemising the key elements depicted, and explaining the meaning that the onlooker might derive from them:

> Entre autres Tableaux plus remarquables, il y en a huit grands, quatre de part & d'autre.
> Le premier à commencer du costé de la Cour du Donjon vers le Balcon, represente Bacchus assisté de Faunes & de Satyres, avec la Deesse de Jeunesse Hebé, & quelques Lions & Leopards, qui tous ensemble figurent les effets du vin. Quelques uns prennent cette Peinture pour une representation de l'Automne...
> Au sixiéme est representé le cours du Soleil en son zodiaque, assisté du

---

[21]   Paris, S. Cramoisy, 1642, folio.

> Printemps, & des autres saisons, avec les heures sous figures de femmes; &
> Phaëton au pied du Soleil qui le supplie de luy donner la conduite de son
> Char afin de se faire reconnoistre pour son fils. Il y en a qui croyent que ce
> Tableau figure le Printemps.
> Se void au septiéme Vulcan, à qui Venus commande de forger des traits &
> des armes pour son fils Amour. Ce qui est pris par quelques-uns pour
> signifier l'Hyver.
> Au huitiéme & dernier est Cerés avec quelques moissonneurs; où par cette
> Peinture peut bien estre representé l'Esté.
>   (Dan, *Tresor des merveilles*, N3r-v)

In this section Dan suggests no historical or political dimension, and no royal
propaganda, but simply takes the imagery at face value, and explains the conventional
iconographic imagery associated with the seasons as represented in these paintings.
But the pattern is rather different in the section devoted to the *Galerie François 1er*
where the iconography is not simply described and interpreted in general terms, but
instead is related quite specifically to the achievements of François 1er as King of
France,[22] and here historical information and eulogy are not easily distinguishable, as
in the description of the king's role in developing the arts and sciences, and in
banishing ignorance from the land as depicted allegorically in one of a series of
fourteen paintings lining the walls:

> En celuy-cy, qui est un Embleme, sont plusieurs hommes & femmes qui ont
> les yeux bandez, & dont quelques-uns se conduisent avec un baston comme
> des aveugles, & semblent aller vers un Temple, à l'entrée duquel est le grand
> Roy François, ayant une couronne de laurier sur la teste, un livre sous un
> bras, & une épée en main, témoignant vouloir ouvrir la porte de ce Temple
> pour y conduire, & faire entrer ces aveugles. Où par cét Embleme l'on peut
> voir le soin qu'a pris cét illustre Monarque à chasser l'aveuglement de
> l'ignorance qui estoit de son temps, & donner entrée au Temple des Muses
> pour cultiver les Sciences & les Arts.
>   (Dan, *Tresor des merveilles*, L4v)

and also in the following painting focusing on his role as authoritative leader of his
country in both civil and military affairs:

> Au second Tableau est encore representé le mesme Roy armé, & tout de
> bout au milieu d'une Salle, tenant une grenade en main que luy presente un
> enfant à genoux à ses pieds, & est ce Prince accompagné de quantité de
> personnes, les uns vieillards, comme des Senateurs, les autres representans
> des Capitaines & Soldats. Ce qui est pareillement un Embleme en suite du

[22] The iconographic programme of the Galerie François 1er is discussed in A.Chastel,
W.McAllister-Johnson and S.Béguin, *Le programme*, in a special issue of the *Revue de l'art*
devoted to the Galerie François 1er at Fontainebleau (*Revue de l'Art*, 16-17, 1972, pp.143-72)

> precedent, par lequel l'on peut entendre que si tost que ce Roy fut élevé à la
> Couronne, & eut pris le maniement des affaires de cét Estat, son dessein ne
> fut pas seulement de chasser l'aveuglement de l'ignorance de son Royaume,
> mais encore y establir un bon ordre & police, soit aux choses civiles, ou soit
> au gouvernement de la guerre: voulant signifier de plus par cette grenade,
> que tandis que tous ses sujets demeureroient bien unis ensemble, & avec sa
> Majesté, comme les grains de ce fruit, tout ce Royaume iroit fleurissant.
> (Dan, *Tresor des merveilles*, M1r)

Dan's use of the word 'embleme' in this passage to denote a meaningful allegorical
painted picture reflects the breadth of meaning which the term had by this date come
to enjoy, and the extent to which it could be applied to other cognate art forms. Later
in the work he also includes a little section entitled *De quelques devises royales qui se
voyent en ce Chateau* (Aa3v-4v), beginning with François 1er himself and ending
with Louis XIII, the then ruling monarch. Here, however, his use of the word is more
conventional: this little collection follows the pattern of many other such examples. As
usual, each Latin device is given, together with an explanation, and a French
translation. For François 1er we are given the familiar salamander with the motto
Nutrisco et extinguo ('Je nourris & esteins') and for Henri II the equally familiar
crown and three crescents with the motto *Donec totum impleat orbem* ('Jusques à ce
que tout le monde soit remply'), while Henri IV has a sword and two sceptres with the
motto *Duo protegit unus* ('Un en defend deux') and Louis XIII a club with the motto
Erit haec quoque cognita monstris ('Elle sera pareillement connue aux monstres').

   Given the richness and diversity of its content, it is surprising that Dan's work did
not prove popular enough to run to a second edition. In striking contrast, Marc de
Vulson's slightly later account of the portraits of illustrious Frenchmen housed in the
Palais Cardinal (now the *Palais-Royal*) proved remarkably popular, running through
several editions from 1650 to 1669.[23] As the lengthy title of the 1650 edition explains,
the work includes not just their portraits, but also their arms and devices, and an
abregé historique of their life thus providing an effective illustrated history text book:

> *Les portraits des hommes illustres françois, qui sont peints dans la gallerie
> du Palais Cardinal de Richelieu: avec leurs principales actions, armes,
> devises, & eloges latins... Ensemble les abregez historiques de leurs vies....*

The portraits of the individuals are reproduced in full-page engravings, each
accompanied by a substantial two-page textual commentary, constituting the *abregé*

---

[23]   Initially published in 1650 as a large broadsheet edition by Jean Paslé and Charles de
Sercy in Paris, it was republished in this same format in 1655, by De Sercy, Edmé Pepingué
and Guillaume de Luynes, and again in 1664 by De Sercy, Guillaume de Luynes, Jean-
Baptiste Loyson, Jean Guignard, Etienne Loyson and Claude Barbin. Thereafter it was
published in further editions, again in Paris, but in duodecimo format, in 1667 by Michel
Bobin and Nicolas le Gras, and in 1668 by François Mauger and Jacques Cottin, and finally in
1669 by Jacques Cottin. In this smaller format it is, of course, not nearly so impressive a
volume as the earlier broadsheet versions with their large engraved plates.

historique,[24] while a separate section at the end of the work contains the mottoes of their devices and commentary on these under the title *Les devises heroyques peintes dans la galerie du Palais Cardinal* (1650 ed., CC1+1r). But an interesting feature of this particular work is the care with which the three separate elements of the work - portrait, device and *abregé historique* - are given a structural unity: each individual engraved portrait is related to it associated *abregé historique* and device by the borders which surround it. These borders depict, in a series of little compartments, scenes from the life of the individual as described in the *abregé historique*, and also his device as noted in the text. Twenty-five French notables appear in the collection, including, of course, Richelieu himself, but unusually no French king before Henri IV figures in it, despite the long chronological period extending from the twelfth century with Suger, *abbé* of Saint Denis to the reign of Louis XIII. Although the prose sections devoted to Louis XIII, Anne d'Autriche and Richelieu are significantly longer than those for other individuals, reflecting the eminence of these most recent figures, they are not primarily eulogistic, and this is in keeping with the overall emphasis of the work, which is essentially informative and educational, attempting as it does to teach history via the medium of pictures.[25]

Dating from much later in the century is another work which similarly describes a series of paintings in a great palace, and which might be expected to adopt a similar approach to that of Vulson's work. However the anonymous *Explication en vers des tableaux de la galerie de Versailles. Dediée à Monseigneur le Duc de Bourgogne* follows a very different pattern. Published in 1691 and dedicated to Louis XIV's oldest grandchild, it focuses not only on history, but also on royal propaganda in a way that was not the case with Vulson's description of the *Palais Cardinal* paintings. Where the portraits described in Vulson's work covered a long period of history from the twelfth to the mid-seventeenth century, the eleven paintings described here cover a much shorter timescale, and are much more circumscribed in their field of reference. Rather than portraits these are allegorical paintings by Le Brun on the ceiling of the *Grande Galerie* whose object was to represent key events from the reign of Louis XIV, and in his explanation of each of them the anonymous author of this treatise runs

---

[24]   In the case of the three currently most eminent figures, Louis XIII, Anne d'Autriche and Richelieu, the *abregés historiques* extend to four rather than two pages, reflecting their importance.
[25]   Vulson's liking for imparting information in this way (as well as his considerable interest in the theory and practice of heraldry as well as devices) is also reflected in another of his similarly lavishly illustrated works, published by the royal printer Sébastien Cramoisy, whose title indicates its wide-ranging and informative approach to the subject: *La science heroique, traitant de la noblesse, de l'origine des armes, de leurs blasons, & symboles, des tymbres, bourlets, couronnes, cimiers, lambrequins, supports, & tenans, & autres ornemens de l'escu, de la devise, & du cry de guerre, de l'escu pendant & des pas & emprises des anciens chevaliers, des formes differentes de leurs tombeaux, et des marques exterieures de l'escu de nos roys, des reynes, & enfans de France, & des officiers de la couronne, & de la maison du Roy. Avec la genealogie succincte de la maison de Rosmadec en Bretagne. Le tout embelly d'un grand nombre de figures en taille douce, sur toutes les matieres. Par Marc de Vulson, Sieur de la Colombiere, Chevalier de l'Ordre de S. Michel, & gentilhomme ordinaire de la maison du Roy*, Paris, S. Cramoisy and G. Cramoisy, 1644, folio.

factual history and royal propaganda together as he describes and interprets (in terms which are understandable to their nine-year-old dedicatee) the particular exploit of the great monarch depicted in each of the paintings in the gallery. For each painting a clear historical contextualisation is given, including a specific date, in a manner reminiscent of Ménestrier's *Histoire du Roy Louis le Grand par les medailles* or Chevalier's equivalent metallic history of William III, but since these large paintings contain far more detail than could be incorporated into a medal, the anonymous author has much more material to comment on. The author is clearly not constrained by the desirability of brevity, since each individual verse entry runs to between forty and sixty lines of verse. In these he creates ekphrastic pictures, which must be seen as verbal equivalents of the original paintings themselves, and the significance of the various elements contained in them is then interpreted in historical terms but also - and more emphatically - in terms of praise of Louis XIV. Hence, although the text is not actually illustrated, the vividly descriptive verses nevertheless offer an effective substitute for visual depiction.

The heading for the description of the first of the eleven paintings explains that it represents the young king (now grown to maturity) taking full control of his kingdom: 'Le Roy prend luy-mesme la conduite de ses Etats, & se donne tout entier aux Affaires, 1661', and the verse describes how this scene is depicted allegorically in the actual painting, with Louis eschewing youthful pleasures in favour of mature wisdom and valour under the aegis of Minerva and Mars:

> Dans le bas du Tableau, la foule des Plaisirs,
> De sa superbe Cour amuse les desirs.
> Une troupe d'enfans agreable & riante,
> Aux pieds du Souverain voltige, & represente
> Les Festes, les Tournois, & la Chasse & le Bal,
> En vain, dans ses desseins il est tousjours égal,
> Il ne prend point de part aux jeux de la Jeunesse,
> Ce qu'elle a d'attrayant en rien ne l'interesse,
> Et ses yeux, & son geste, & sa mine & son port
> Tout pour la gloire en luy marque un brûlant transport.
> Dans les Cieux la Déesse au dessus d'une nuë,
> Doucement luy sourit, en s'offrant à sa veüe
> Un cercle d'or en main d'etoiles couronné,
> Est par elle un present au Prince destiné,
> Mais afin que son front soit ceint de Diadême,
> Minerve vient à luy se vouër elle-même
> Elle est à ses côtez, preste à suivre ses pas,
> Et par elle suivi que ne fera-t-il pas?
> Si ce n'est point assez que d'agir de la teste
> Pour meriter le don que la Déesse apreste.
> S'il fait dans les combats signaler un grand coeur,
> LOUIS sera servi du Dieu de la Valeur.
> Le voilà qui paroist au dessus de Minerve:

Donc, si Minerve & Mars sont à luy sans reserve,
Des plus fameux Heros il ternira le nom.
Le Temps dont la main leve au coin du pavillon,
Le regarde, & veut estre un témoin oculaire
Des miracles divers que ce Prince va faire
    (*Explication en vers des tableaux de la galerie de Versailles*, A3v-4r)

The second portrait depicts another key point in Louis's career as ruler of France, the decision, ten years later, to invade the Netherlands, under the heading 'Resolution prise de châtier les Hollandois 1671'. In the opening lines to this verse there is the further refinement of a description of a picture within a picture (or more accurately of a tapestry within a picture), and it is interesting to see here the terminology used by the anonymous poet to stress the vividness of the message conveyed by the tapestry. A complex process which is the reverse of ekphrastic is used, whereby the tapestry is described as 'speaking' its message as clearly as if by the use of real words. Instead of words replacing pictures, we find in this poem words describing pictures replacing words:

De son Manteau royal le Prince revestu,
Mais encor plus paré de sa rare vertu,
Dans son Trône s'assied, & de ce qu'il doit faire
Avec Minerve & Mars, & Themis delibere.
Mars luy presente un Char tiré par deux Coursiers,
Il l'invite d'entrer disant que les lauriers
Y tomberont sur luy des mains de la Victoire,
Il montre pour garand de ce qu'il en faut croire,
Des armes en trophée, & des noms de Citez
Mis sur des Boucliers épars de tous côtez,
Citez, que par ses droits LOUIS a pû pretendre,
Et qu'aussi son pouvoir luy sourit dans la Flandre;
Déja depuis leur cheute on voyoit dans les champs
Quatre fois de retour & Flore & le Printemps,
Pres du char de Louis la victoire s'apreste
A le suivre, & poser ces lauriers sur sa teste,
Non loin du Char encor, la Déesse à cent voix
Veut, la trompette en main, publier ses exploits:
D'autre côté Pallas montre un morceau d'ouvrage,
Où de la guerre on voit une vivante image;
Les couleurs & la soye y paroissent parler,
L'aiguille industrieuse y prit soin d'etaler
De cette verité la maxime certaine:
La moisson des lauriers ne se fait qu'avec peine.
    (*Explication en vers des tableaux de la galerie de Versailles*, B1v-2r)

Thus although the titles of this work and of Vulson's *Portraits des hommes illustres françois, qui sont peints dans la gallerie du Palais Cardinal de Richelieu* might suggest that they would be similar in structure, this is not the case. Vulson's work includes engraved portraits depicting visually the paintings to be found in the Palais Cardinal, and it accompanies these engravings with prose commentaries on the life and the devices of the various individuals represented, whereas in the *Explication en vers des tableaux de la galerie de Versailles* there are no visual representations of the paintings in the form of engraved plates; instead a much more vivid verbal representation in verse is offered with, on occasion, the further refinement of 'talking pictures' within pictures. But just as they are different in structure, so also are they different in intent, since Vulson's text is largely informative, and educational, with only a relatively small tendency to propaganda, whereas in contrast, although the anonymous *Explication en vers des tableaux de la galerie de Versailles* certainly does have some educational elements its more fundamental purpose is eulogy of the reigning monarch, Louis XIV, rather than straight history. In many cases, particularly during the reign of Louis XIV, the frontier between education and propaganda is a very blurred one, and several of the works discussed here, (such as this one or Ménestrier's almost contemporaneous *Histoire du Roy Louis le Grand*), in which both objectives are manifest, could equally have been saved for discussion in chapter 7 which deals specifically with the use of emblems and devices for royal glorification. However it has seemed more sensible to keep such hybrid works combining education and propaganda to this chapter, and restrict chapter 7 to emblematic material which is more exclusively designed for the purpose of propaganda.

In the various works discussed so far in this chapter the educational emphasis has been primarily on conveying above all historical information via the medium of analysis and explanation of the significance of royal devices, royal medals and paintings displayed in royal palaces, sometimes aimed at a general reading public, and sometimes directed more specifically towards the particular interests of the work's dedicatee, often a royal child. In three further works we find emblems and devices again being used for educational purposes, but in a very different way. Interestingly, in two of the three the dedicatee is yet again a royal personage. Reflecting the international character of the genre, the first of these three works was written in Spanish, by a Spaniard, and first published in Munich, thereafter in Milan, and only thereafter in his native Spain, but also in many other parts of Europe and in many different languages, including French.[26]

---

[26] *Idea de un principe politico christiano representada en cien empresas Dedicada al Principe de las Españas nuestro Señor por D. Diego Saavedra Fajardo del Consejo de su Magestad en el Supremo de las Indias, i su embajador extraordinario en Mantua i Esguizaros i residente en Alemania*, Munich, N. Heinrich, 1640, 4°. The work was subsequently published in Milan in 1642, and thereafter in numerous editions in Valencia and Madrid throughout the seventeenth and eighteenth centuries. It was also published in several editions in Antwerp, Amsterdam and Paris. A Latin translation was published in Brussels in 1649 (*Idea principis christiano-politico, centum symbolis expressa A Didaco Saavedra Faxardo, Equite &c*, Brussels, J. Mommartius and F. Vivien, 1649, folio) which also ran through several editions in Cologne, Amsterdam, Paris and elsewhere. The work was also translated into Italian, German, Dutch, English and French. Indicative also of its popularity is the fact that within two years of

Diego de Saavedra Fajardo produced in 1640 a first edition in Spanish of his immensely influential collection of devices, the purpose of which was to serve specifically as a manual of political science for the edification of a christian prince, to one of whom - Philip IV of Spain - it was dedicated. This first edition (in Spanish) was published in Munich, but thereafter it appeared in a number of editions published across Europe, translated into Latin as well as into a number of different vernacular languages. Appropriate education for the young prince is sketched out via the medium of devices, and advice given on appropriate behaviour taking the prince from early youth to the grave, together with reflection on all aspects of statecraft relevant to a ruling monarch.[27] As an educational tool, the work could hardly have been expected to exercise any direct influence on its original dedicatee, Philip IV of Spain, since the 35-year-old king had already been ruling Spain for nineteen years when the work first appeared in 1640. However the French translation of the work which was published in Paris 28 years later in 1668, was dedicated to a much younger christian prince, the seven-year-old *Dauphin*, Louis, son of Louis XIV.[28]

Saavedra explains in his preface to the reader that in keeping with the educational aim of the work he has striven to adopt a style which is elevated, using appropriate 'sentences & maximes d'éstat', but which is nevertheless clear in its meaning, and that furthermore he has opted to use a mixture of ancient and modern materials, because - as he interestingly remarks - while the former carry authority, the latter are more persuasive since they carry more immediate relevance.[29] Unusually for a writer of emblems and devices, Saavedra also comments in this remarkably frank preface on his frustration at striving for originality in his devices, and then finding that what he

---

its first appearance, it had inspired an imitation by Andrés Mendo, the *Principe perfecto, y ministros ajustados. Documentos politicos y morales en emblemas*, composed, like Saavedra's original, in Spanish, but published in Lyon in 1642. (See Praz, p.420. No copy of this edition has been identified.) Further editions were published in Lyon by H. Boissat, G. Remeus, C. Bourgeat and M. Lietard in 1661 and 1662: *Principe perfecto y ministros ajustados, documentos politicos, y morales. En emblemas. Por el R.P. Andrés Mendo, de la Compañia de Jesus, Calificador del Consejo de la Inquisicion Suprema, Lector de Theologia, y de Sagrada Escritura en Salamanca*, Lyon, H. Boissat and G. Remeus, 1662, 4° (Glasgow University Library). Although this work was published in France and was popular enough to run through more than one edition, unlike Saavedra's much more popular work, it was never actually translated into French. For details of editions of Saavedra and of other Spanish emblem books see Pedro Campa, *Emblemata Hispanica. An Annotated Bibliography of Spanish Emblem Literature to the Year 1700*, Durham, North Carolina, 1990.

[27] As he says in the commentary to the first device: ' Comme dans la disposition de ces Devises mon dessein a esté de conduire le Prince depuis le berceau jusqu'au cercüeil.' (*Le prince chrestien et politique*, 1668, A6r).

[28] *Le prince chrestien et politique.Traduit de l'Espagnol de Dom Diegue Savedra Faxardo, et dedié à Mr le Dauphin, par I. Rou, Avocat au Parlement*, Paris, Compagnie des marchands libraires du Palais, 1668, 2 vols, 12°. (Re-ed. Amsterdam, J. Schipper, 1670, 12°).

[29] 'J'ay particulierement tâché que le style fust élevé sans affection, & succint sans obscurité...Je me suis servy d'exemples anciens & modernes, de ceux-là à cause de l'authorité, & de ceux-cy parce qu'ils persuadent mieux: & que de plus, estant encore frais, l'estat des choses est moins alteré.' (*Le prince chrestien et politique*, 1668, ã6v-7r)

thought to have been a new idea had already been used by an earlier writer.

> J'ay tâché que l'invention en fust nouvelle, je ne sçay si j'y auray reüssi, y
> ayant tant de beaux Esprits qui ont travaillé sur ce Sujet; & estant si aisé de
> tomber en de mesmes pensées, ainsi qu'il m'est arrivé, lors qu'apres avoir
> inventé quelques Devises, j'ay reconnu en suite que d'autres les avoyent
> trouvées avant moy; ce qui me les a fait laisser, non sans le prejudice de mon
> dessein, puisque nos Predecesseurs s'estant servis des plus nobles corps, &
> des plus riches ames, nous sommes contraints en les voulant eviter d'en
> prendre d'autres beaucoup moins propres.
>   (Saavedra, *Le prince chrestien et politique*, 1668, ã5v)

For good pedagogic reasons the material in the collection is arranged in a logical order, so that the prince can learn the lessons of appropriate kingship progressively, by working through the volume from beginning to end. This is not a work designed so that the reader may feel free to dip at will, but rather one in which - like the meditational emblem book - each individual item should be read and digested in its correct position in the progression. Each individual section of the work relates to a different aspect of kingship, with the fifty devices of Book 1 organised under three headings: 'Comment le Prince se doit comporter en ses actions'; 'Comment le Prince se doit comporter envers ses sujets & envers les Estrangers'; and 'Comment le Prince se doit comporter à l'endroit de ses Ministres', and the equivalent fifty of Book 2 under four headings: 'Comment le Prince se doit comporter dans le Gouvernement de ses Estats'; 'Comment le Prince se doit comporter dans les maux internes & externes de ses Estats'; Comment le Prince se doit comporter dans ses Victoires & dans ses traittez de Paix'; and 'Comment il faut que le Prince se comporte en sa vieillesse'.

Although this systematic presentation of the devices in a progressive order is unusual, the actual pattern of construction of the individual devices adopted by Saavedra is more conventional: each engraved device contains within the engraving its Latin motto, accompanied by a French paraphrase of the motto in typography, followed by a lengthy prose discourse running from ten to fifteen pages, elaborating in great detail on the lesson to be learned, backing this up with anecdotes and supporting quotations from the ancients and also marginal references. The collection opens with a device depicting the youthful Hercules already strangling snakes while still in his cot, in order to denote allegorically the way in which the young prince must from the very outset combine hard work with virtue. The motto is HINC LABOR ET VIRTUS/*Dés icy le Travail & la Vertu*, and the discourse begins by explaining the key point, relevant to any prince by divine right, that virtue is innate, before going on to elaborate upon the theme of the combination of virtue and action:

> La Valeur naist, elle ne s'acquiert point; c'est une qualité interieure de l'ame
> qui se produit en mesme temps qu'elle, & qui opere en mesme temps qu'elle
> se produit.   (Saavedra, *Le prince chrestien et politique*, 1668, A1r)

Hercules, depicted in the engraving, is cited first for his youthful strength in killing the snakes, after which follow other notable examples of youthful strength and virtue:

> Hercules couronna son berceau par la victoire de deux serpens qui le
> vouloyent attaquer: Depuis ce jour-là on eust dit que l'envie l'épargnoit, &
> que la fortune favorisoit sa vertu. Un courage élevé, dés ses premiéres actions
> donne des témoignages de son prix; Dom Fernand Infant d'Espagne vit la
> Bataille de Norlingh presqu'avant le Camp, & sceut en mesme temps
> commander avec prudence & agir avec valeur.
> > Sans âge il devança l'âge & l'experience
> > Et dans sa verdeur meure à peine l'esperance
> > Donnoit-elle ses fleurs, qu'on en goûta les fruits.
> Cyrus estant encore fort jeune, & ayant esté éleu Roy par quelques autres
> enfans de son âge, fit en cét estat de superiorité des actions si heroïques, que
> dés-lors il donna des conjectures de sa naissance Royale qui jusques-là avoit
> esté cachée... (Saavedra, *Le prince chrestien et politique*, 1668, A1v)

This particular device is unusual in this collection, in that the first part of the textual element focuses directly on Hercules, as represented in the engraved figure. More commonly Saavedra's discourse refers only fleetingly, or on occasion not at all, to the image in the engraved figure, concentrating instead on elaborating the particular lesson to be derived from that figure which serves only as the initial trigger. The reader's interest is thus more strongly directed to the significance of the discourse itself, rather than to further reflection on the connection between the discourse and the engraved figure and motto which originally gave rise to it, as is apparent in the examples quoted below.

Although Saavedra's collection of devices focuses on one single overall theme - that of the behaviour fitting to a christian king - and the lengthy prose discourses all relate to that theme, the individual engravings cover a wide range of different subjects, several of which are familiar from earlier emblem literature. Derived from the animal world, for example, we find the chameleon, the vigilant lion, the beehive and the unicorn in numbers 48, 45, 62 and 8, while among other familiar figures are a clock (57) and a pair of compasses (56). In view of his stated desire for originality it is interesting to see how Saavedra treats such familiar figures. In the case of both the lion and the chameleon his interpretation is the traditional one. In his discourse accompanying the device of the lion sleeping with its eyes open, NON MAIESTATE SECURUS/*La majesté ne luy suffit pas*, Saavedra first refers to the hieroglyphic representation of the lion sleeping with its eyes open, denoting vigilance, and thereafter proceeds to discuss the particular kinds of vigilance required by an effective ruler. Similarly in SUB LUCE LUES/*Sous le miel le fiel*, the figure of the chameleon is interpreted conventionally as denoting flattery, but within the specific context of the particular danger that such flatterers represent to the king:

> Que les Princes sont munis contre les Ennemis Estrangers! Qu'ils sont
> desarmez contre les domestiques! Ils en sont investis jusques au milieu de
> leurs propres Gardes, & cependant ils n'y font point de reflection; ces

> Ennemis sont les Courtisans & les Flatteurs; leurs caresses ne sont pas moins dangereuses, que les Armes des Ennemis; la flatterie a plus détruit de Princes que la force. (Saavedra, *Le prince chrestien et politique*, 1668, X11v)

However in his treatment of the unicorn and the beehive Saavedra offers ingenious interpretations which owe nothing to conventional earlier interpretations. In number 8, the unicorn's single forward thrusting horn is interpreted as the symbol of uncontrolled anger in PRAE OCULIS IRA/*La colere au devant des yeux*. In all cases such anger is bad, but - as Saavedra points out - it is particularly damaging in a prince:

> La nature a usé d'une merveilleuse prevoyance envers la Licorne; elle luy a placé les armes de la colere entre les deux yeux...Dans la colere un homme n'est plus le même qu'auparavant, parce que par elle il sort hors de luy...Ce n'est pas avec la legereté de cette boüillante passion que les victoires se remportent & qu'on triomphe des ennemis: On ne peut pas non plus appeller force une chose qui s'émeut contre la raison; En un mot je ne sçache aucun vice plus messeant à un Prince que celuy là.
> (Saavedra, *Le prince chrestien et politique*, 1668, D4r)

Where an illustration of bees flying around a beehive is more commonly interpreted as denoting industry, Saavedra uses this figure as the starting point for a quite different lesson for the prince in NULLI PATET/*Nul n'y peut voir*, in which the bees' preoccupation with keeping activity in the beehive hidden from public view is held up as the model for a well run republic in which domestic matters are kept hidden from the outside world:

> L'ingenieuse Abeille couvre l'artifice de ses rayons avec une finesse admirable; l'ouvrage s'échauffe & personne n'en peut penetrer l'oeconomie; & si parfois la curiosité pense l'épier par le moyen d'une ruche de verre, elle en dément la transparence par un voile de cire pour ne point avoir de tesmoin de ses actions domestiques. O prudente Republique! Maistresse de toutes celles du monde; muette Ecole des Princes.
> (Saavedra, *Le prince chrestien et politique*, 1668, Book 2, G8v)

Equally ingenious are the interpretations given to the familiar figures of the clock and the pair of compasses. In UNI REDATUR/*Tous à un* rather than referring conventionally to some aspect of time, Saavedra instead focuses on the internal mechanism of the clock and the relationship between the multitude of hidden cogwheels and the single visible pointers, reflecting thereby the relationship betweeen king and people:

> Les Roües de l'Horloge font leur devoir dans un silence si caché que ny on ne les voit, ny on ne les entend, & bien que tout l'artifice dépende d'elles, elles ne se l'attribuent pas neantmoins; mais accommodent leur mouvement à

l'aiguille, qui est la seule dispensatrice des heures & que chacun reconnoist pour la regle du temps mesuré.

(Saavedra, *Le prince chrestien et politique*, 1668, Book 2, D2v)

while in QUI A SECRETIS AB OMNIBUS/*Celuy qui a le secret, a tout*, the pair of compasses in the figure is interpreted as denoting the important role played in the affairs of a monarch by his secretary, responsible for the efficient execution of ideas put forward by his Council:

Que sert-il qu'on fasse de bonnes deliberations dans le Conseil si celuy qui les doit dresser y fait des fautes?...Le Conseil forme l'idée de la fabrique; le Secretaire dresse le plan; & si ce plan est irregulier l'edifice basty dessus ne pourra reüssir. Pour mieux signifier cecy vous voyez qu'en la presente Devise sa plume est tout ensemble un compas, parce qu'il a non seulement à escrire mais aussi à mesurer les resolutions, & compasser le temps de peur que l'execution ne se fasse mal à propos.

(Saavedra, *Le prince chrestien et politique*, 1668, Book 2, C12r)

Saavedra uses the word *empresas* in the full title of the original Spanish version of his work, and this is faithfully rendered as *imprese* in the Italian translation and as *symbola* in the Latin translation.[30] For this reason the word 'device' is used here. However the French translation avoids the issue by using a shortened version of the title in which the key word is not included, but in the course of the text it is nevertheless the word *devise* which is used throughout. Interestingly, though, the English translation opts for the word 'emblem' rather than the word 'device'.[31] Which of the two words is the more appropriate in the case of Saavedra's collection is an interesting question. Certainly the engraved figures with their incorporated mottoes have all the look of conventional devices, yet at the same time Saavedra has a clearly didactic and instructional aim and the lengthy passages of prose discourse accompanying the engraved figures each offer a sustained lesson in kingship for which the figure is no more than a starting point. The very length of the prose discourses indicates the importance that Saavedra attaches to the information contained therein, and from this point of view it is difficult to see these as devices containing an element of intellectually challenging puzzle.[32] They are, as he explains, intended for educational purposes, and as a sound educator Saavedra realises that lessons must be conveyed pleasurably if they are to have any impact on the young learner, whether prince or not. One of the early devices in the collection indeed

---

[30] 'representada en cien Empresas'; 'con bellissime imprese'; 'centum symbolis expressa'.
[31] *The Royal Politician represented in One Hundred Emblems Written in Spanish by Don Diego Saavedra Faxardo, Knight...*, London, for M. Gilliflower and L. Meredith, 1700, 8°.
[32] It is interesting that in Andrés Mendo's *Principe perfecto*, which in theme is very akin to Saavedra's *Prince chrestien et politique*, and which follows the same structure, the word 'emblem' is actually used in the title (*Principe perfecto, y ministros ajustados, documentos politicos, y morales. En emblemas. Por el R.P. Andrés Mendo, de la Compaña de Jesus...*, Lyon, H. Boissat and G. Remeus; C. Bourgeat and M. Lietard, 1661, 4°).

focuses on the question of pleasurable education. In DELEITANDO ENSENA/*Il enseigne en divertissant* the figure depicts a well laid out   garden, and the discourse expands on the importance of presenting potentially unpalatable material in a pleasing manner so that the learner does not become disaffected in the early stages of study:

> Les racines des Sciences sont ameres, bien que les fruits en soyent doux: nostre Nature pour cét effet les a en aversion, & ne connoist point de plus grand travail que l'étude de leurs premiers Rudimens; quels chagrins, quelles sueurs ne coûtent-ils point à la jeunesse? aussi, tant pour cela, que parce que l'étude requiert un continuel attachement, chose fort contraire à la santé, & qui ne se peut gueres trouver parmi les occupations, les divertissemens & les ceremonies de la Cour; Je trouve absolument necessaire, l'adresse & l'industrie d'un Maistre qui sçache bien déguiser l'amertume des enseignemens sous la douceur des yeux pueriles, que le Prince les boive insensiblement sans aucun dégoust.[33]

Ostensibly directed towards the education of a christian prince specifically, Saavedra's work clearly had educational interest for a much more diverse readership than this. Although many of the lessons are intended to relate to the particular preoccupations of the prince, many, like the last example on educational strategy, are also susceptible of more general application. That the lessons contained in Saavedra's work did indeed have wide appeal is apparent from the success which the work achieved across Europe. Similarly designed for educational purposes, but much less international in its sphere of influence, and indeed involving a quite different kind of education is the *Adolescens academicus sub institutione Salomonis* by the Jesuit Charles Musart, published in Douai in 1633.[34] This is not a work designed specifically for the education of a prince, nor yet is the emphasis on the communication of information. Instead Musart focuses in this Latin emblem book on the moral education of the studious youth towards the path of virtue, and away from the temptations of vice. Divided into four sections (*Procuranda primùm adventanti in Academiam; Exercitationes Academicae; Vitia cavenda Adolescenti Academico; and Virtutes Academici Adolescentis*), the work resembles a kind of *Pilgrim's Progress* in which the youth is depicted as a *leitmotiv* in each delightful engraved figure, together with the particular image on which the lesson is based. Each engraved figure is accompanied by a substantial passage of prose. In the familiar manner of other, more generally devotional Jesuit emblem books the reader is carefully guided through the

---

[33] Saavedra goes on to describe an alphabet game that he would devise in order to make the process of learning to read into a pleasurable activity: 'je voudrois pour luy apprendre à lire, former un jeu de vingt-deux dez, sur chacun desquels chaque lettre de l'Alphabet fust gravée, afin que joüant avec ses camarades, celuy-là fust vainqueur, qui poussant les dez sur le tapis, ameneroit une ou plusieurs syllabes, ou formeroit un mot entier.' (*Le prince chrestien et politique*, 1668, C1r-v).

[34] *Adolescens academicus sub institutione Salomonis. Authore R.P. Carolo Musart Belga, e Soc. Iesu Doct. Theol. et in Viennensi Austriae Academia Sacr. literarum interprete*, Douai, B. Bellere, 1633, 8°.

lesson in a series of distinct stages: the engraving with its motto is first followed by about two pages of prose explanation (the *Symboli explicatio*) and a further two pages of *Monitum*. Thereafter follow a much fuller *Interpretatio*, analysing all possible ramifications of the scene depicted, and running to some twelve pages, and finally an *Oratio*. In the interests of putting the full message across with total clarity each emblem can run to as much as forty pages - a far cry from the brevity which had once been considered a desirable quality in the emblem, and very different from the infinitely more succinct approach adopted by Saavedra. In emblem 26 (Z3v) which opens Book 4 on the virtues appropriate to the academic youth, Musart exploits a symbol which we have already seen in the work of Saavedra, but he does so very differently. Here Musart uses the symbol of a pair of compasses, familiar also from the Plantin Press printer's mark with its motto *Labore et constantia*, to extol the twin virtues of hard work and constancy. An engraving of a youth sitting peacefully under a tree, with a pair of compasses and a beehive full of industrious bees is accompanied by the double motto *Industria, et constantia*; *Hic labor et fructusque laboris*, and the full implications and ramifications of the scene are analysed in a series of chapters in the *Interpretatio*, variously entitled 'Ingenium & labor ingenium pariunt, idque ex agricultura docemur' (Z6r); 'Laborem industrium docent formicae' (Z8v); 'Apes paria formicis docent' (Aa3r), while the *Oratio* takes the theme 'Pro industrio & constanti labore in excolendae mentis studio' (Bb4v).

Musart's earlier section on the vices to be avoided by the academic youth is similarly constructed, but as so often the vices lend themselves to more picturesque representation than the virtues. In emblem 14 (S4v), for example, expatiating on the dangers of alcohol, the engraving depicts vividly the same youth astride a barrel pulled by Bacchus's leopards. In his hand is a goblet containing a snake, while behind him on the barrel looms the menacing figure of Death, armed with a scythe (see fig.10). Above the engraving is the heading *Ebrietatis vesania* and below it *Vesani calices quid non fecere*, and the *Interpretatio* spells out a series of damning lessons, 'Quid sit Ebrietas, & quàm turpe vitium?' (S7r); 'Ebrietas maximè inimica Sapientiae' (T2v); 'Ebrietas luxuriae parens' (T5v); 'Ebrietas opes ingentes perdit' (T6v); and finally 'Ebrietas rixas, vulnera, caedes parat' (T8v). The overall lesson is summed up very simply in the all-embracing title to the *Oratio*: 'Contra Ebrietatem' (V7r).

The overall pattern of Musart's emblem book is a familiar one, common to other Jesuit devotional emblem books, but the difference between it and other emblem books lies in the fact that Musart focuses his work - as the title suggests - specifically towards the moral education of the young student, rather than towards mankind as a whole. It is perhaps because of the rather more restricted audience to which it was directed, that despite the charm and wit of its engraved figures this particular emblem book enjoyed less popularity than might have been expected. A further contributory factor may have been the fact that it was a provincial work, published in Douai rather than in one of the more important printing centres, although this is not borne out by the printing history of another work by Musart, similarly published in Douai, and by the same publisher, Balthasar Bellere, only a few years prior to the *Adolescens academicus*. Musart's translation into Latin of Etienne Luzvic's *Coeur devot* under the title *Cor Deo devotum*, which was first published by Bellere in Douai in 1627, was republished within a year by Aertssens in Antwerp, and then furthermore formed the basis for the English version of the work under the title *The Devout Hart*, produced by the recusant Henry Hawkins and published in Rouen by John Cousturier in 1634.[35]

Figure 10: Musart, *Adolescens academicus*, Douai, 1633, S4v.

The different degree of success enjoyed by Musart's own *Adolescens academicus* and by his translation of Luzvic's *Coeur devot* is most probably explained, however, by the fact that with his translation of Luzvic's work he was tapping into an already established corpus of material, the immensely popular heart engravings of the Wierix brothers, whereas in his own original work he was breaking new ground.

Exploiting emblems and devices for educational purposes, but in a quite different and much less serious way than Charles Musart, is a curious work by the Sieur Jaugeon which was published published much later in the century, in 1684 and which

---

[35] Henry Hawkins, *The Devout Hart or Royal Throne of the Pacifical Salomon. Composed by F. St. Luzvic S.I. Translated out of Latin into English. Enlarged with Incentives by F. St. Binet of the same S. and now enriched with Hymns by a new hand*, Rouen, J. Cousturier, 1634, 12°.

was once again dedicated to a member of the royal family, Louis XIV. Although it was dedicated to the king himself, his son, the *Grand Dauphin*, must also have possessed the work, since a copy in his royal binding exists in the Bibliothèque nationale de France. *Le jeu du monde ou l'intelligence des plus curieuses choses qui se trouvent dans tous les estats, les terres, & les mers du monde. Ouvrage enrichy des devises des plus grands princes de l'Europe. Dedié au Roy. Par le Sieur Jaugeon*[36] is a prose account by its inventor, Jaugeon, of an ingenious encyclopedic game by means of which the players can - by wholly pleasurable means, as he emphasises - acquire the general knowledge about the world which Jaugeon deems to be necessary if they are to hold their own in gentlemanly conversation:

> Cet ouvrage, dont le Titre semble d'abord ne promettre qu'un amusement, r'enferme...le seul necessaire d'un Gentil-homme, qui est obligé par sa naissance de vivre à la Cour ou dans les Villes, avec des personnes illustres & qualifiées, que leurs emplois y retiennent pour l'interest du public, & la gloire du Souverain...Ce livre estant composé des plus singuliers evenemens de ces trois grands mobiles de la vie humaine; Il ne peut, qu'il ne fournisse dequoy plaire, & qui ne rende ceux qui le possederont, assés habiles, pour former & soustenir quelque conversation que ce soit.
>
> (Jaugeon, *Le jeu du monde*, ã4r-4v)

Throughout Jaugeon stresses the educational nature of the game,[37] in which ships travel across the globe revealing snippets of information at each point, as in his description of the Dardanelles:

> En effet, qu'y a-t'il de plus agreable quand on se trouve au Destroit des Dardanelles, anciennement appellée l'Ellespont, que d'apprendre qu'en cét endroit Xerxes qui veut dire victorieux, fit bastir un pont qui joignoit l'Europe à l'Asie pour se faciliter le passage de la Grece.
>
> (Jaugeon, *Le jeu du monde*, C4r-4v)

In Part 3, entitled *Du jeu des consultes* (I1v), Jaugeon uses a series of devices representing the different countries of Europe in order to convey to the players an awareness of the different characters and motivations of these countries. Each engraved device is followed by a prose description of the device and an analysis of its implications. Some are more evident than others: Sweden, for example, is represented by a ship, Turkey by a crescent moon, and England by a rose, but less meaningful until further explanation is given are the hatchet denoting Poland, or the fistful of arrows denoting the Netherlands. France is represented by three devices all within one single engraving, two of which pay homage to the king, with their theme of the sun, while the third relates to the older French symbol of the *fleur de lis*.[38] Jaugeon clearly

---

[36] Paris, A. Auroy, 1684, 12°.

[37] 'C'est de plus un divertissement qui enseigne...' (A5r); 'C'est le secret de nostre Jeu du Monde qui joint si admirablement le divertissement à l'estude...' (C3v).

[38] *Nec pluribus impar* (the sun shining on the world) and *Non pulchrior ullo* (the sun shining

had great hopes that this game would be a success, promising that this initial version dealing with Europe alone would be followed thereafter by Asia, Africa and America. These follow-up versions seem never to have materialised, which might be taken to suggest that Jaugeon's confidence about the success of his ingenious educational game was perhaps unduly optimistic. The fact that even the first volume came into being does, however, serve as yet another reflection of the extraordinary versatility of the emblematic form, capable of being exploited for educational, as for other purposes in such a range of different ways.

In all the works discussed so far we have seen emblems and devices being exploited as educational tools in a number of different ways, but with the overall unifying feature that in all cases their educational function was essentially the dissemination of information of one sort or another. In all these works we see the conventional pattern whereby it is the writer of the work who is the conveyer of the information, and thus the educator, while the reader or recipient of that information is the learner. But emblems and devices could also be exploited for educational purposes in a quite different way, with these conventional roles being reversed, so that the learner is no longer the passive recipient, but is actually the writer of emblems. In the seventeenth century and still in the eighteenth century we find emblems being exploited in the schoolroom, not, however, as something to be read by the pupils, but rather as something which they were actually required to compose themselves. Particularly in Jesuit colleges, but in other institutions also, classes of senior pupils were often set the exercise of composing a collection of appropriate emblems and devices on particular set subjects, as a means of cultivating both their intellectual ingenuity and their rhetorical skills, and a remarkable number of these collections have survived in manuscript form, and occasionally even in printed form.

The first three years of the cycle in a Jesuit college were the grammar classes (*Figurae*, *Grammatica* and *Syntaxis*) after which pupils progressed to the two senior classes, *Humanitas* (also called *Poesis*) and thereafter *Rhetorica*. It is above all in these two senior classes in which pupils were encouraged to do their own creative writing, part of which included the composition of emblems and devices, having spent the earlier years studying the grammatical mechanics of the classical languages in order to prepare them for this next step.[39] The educational function of the Jesuit

---

on a diamond); *Neque suunt neque nent* (lilies), (16v).

[39] For a detailed discussion of education in Jesuit colleges, see F. de Dainville, *L'éducation des Jésuites XVIe-XVIIIe siècles*, Paris, 1978 and A.D.Scaglione, *The Liberal Arts and the Jesuit College System*, Amsterdam, 1986. See also G. Huppert, *Public Schools in Renaissance France*, Urbana, 1984; T. Hughes, *Loyola and the Educational System of the Jesuits*, New York, 1892; C. Chevalier, 'La pédagogie des collèges jésuites', *Littérature*, 7, 1972, pp.120-28; J. Lacotte, 'La notion de 'jeu' dans la pédagogie des Jésuites au XVIIe siècle', in M. Fumaroli ed., *Aspects de l'humanisme jésuite au début du XVIIe siècle*, Paris, *Revue des Sciences Humaines*, 40, 1975, pp.245-93; For discussion of Jesuit education in Paris see M. Fumaroli, *L'âge de l'éloquence. Rhétorique et 'res literaria' de la Renaissance au seuil de l'époque classique*, Paris, 1994. For discussion of the role of emblematics in Jesuit education see J. Loach, 'The teaching of emblematics and other symbolic imagery by Jesuits within town colleges in seventeenth- and eighteenth-century France', in Marc van Vaeck and John

colleges which sprang up in such large numbers in France and elsewhere in the sixteenth and seventeenth seventeenth centuries[40] should not be confused with that of a seminary whose role was to prepare its inmates for the church. Such preparation came only later. At college level the object of Jesuit education was to provide a good, humanist schooling for the youth (primarily the sons of the aristocracy and professional middle classes, but also to an extent the sons of the merchant classes) in the towns in which they were situated, and to this end the teachers in such schools sought to develop in their pupils not just a good grounding in the classical languages and their literature, but the ability also to put this to good effect. Having studied the writings of others they should be able to imitate these in the cultivation of their own rhetorical skills, and the composition of emblems and devices was one of the intellectual exercises by means of which the pupils could develop their wit and ingenuity, and overall eloquence of expression.[41]

A remarkably rich series of manuscript collections of emblems and devices produced annually by the senior pupils of the Jesuit College in Brussels over a period of more than fifty years, between 1630 and 1685, still survives with only a few gaps, and is now housed in the Royal Library in Brussels. Some volumes in the series were inevitably lost or destroyed over the centuries, while two - those produced in 1642 and 1649 - are now housed in the Bibliothèque nationale de France.[42] These manuscripts were commemorative volumes put together after the event, as Porteman explains,to give permanence to what would otherwise have been a purely ephemeral

Manning, eds, *The Jesuits and the Emblem Tradition*, Turnhout, 1999, pp.161-86.

[40] The earliest Jesuit college (in Messina) dates from 1548; by 1625 it is estimated that there were approximately 550 Jesuit colleges across the world. (Scaglione, p.61). The first Jesuit college in France was founded at Billom in 1556, followed by Tournon (1561); Rodez (1562); Mauriac and Paris - the Collège de Clermont, later to become the Collège de Louis le Grand (1563) and Lyon (where the already existent Collège de la Trinité was taken over by the Jesuits) (1565). For details of these see Huppert, pp.105-7. The Jesuit order quickly established itself as an educational force to be reckoned with in France: by 1627 it is estimated that they were responsible for the education of 40,000 boys in one or other of their colleges. Individual colleges varied considerably in size: large schools such as Rouen or Rennes had 2000 and 1900 pupils in 1609 while small schools like Dijon or Bourges had only 643 and 500 respectively. (For details see Dainville, p.119).

[41] The philosophy underlying the Jesuit educational system, its aims and objectives and the various means by which these should be achieved were very early spelt out in the *Ratio studiorum*, which constituted a set of guidelines for teachers in Jesuit schools, first drafted at the end of the sixteenth century. (See below, chapter 8, p.347.)

[42] In 1794 many manuscripts were taken to France after the French invasion of the Netherlands, and not all of these were returned to Belgium in 1815, once the hostilities were over. Among those that remained in France were the two manuscript emblem books, BnF Ms.lat.10170 and Ms.lat.10171. The manuscripts were exhibited in the Royal Library in Brussels in 1996, and are discussed in detail, with many reproductions in K.Porteman, *Emblematic Exhibitions (affixiones) at the Brussels Jesuit College (1630-1685). A Study of the Commemorative Manuscripts (Royal Library, Brussels)*, Brussels, 1996. For analysis of the earliest collection in the series, dating from 1631, see John Manning, '"Tres potentiae animae": the aims and methodology of Royal Library, Brussels MS 4040', in Marc van Vaeck and John Manning, eds, *The Jesuits and the Emblem Tradition*, Turnhout, 1999, pp.323-40.

demonstration of their of wit, ingenuity and erudition put on public display by the boys of the Jesuit College in Brussels. Such collective productions would not originally have been produced in book form like this, but rather the emblems would have been put on public display in the form of posters, or *affixiones*, on particular open days at the college, so that the world at large could see and admire the fruits of the education provided by the Jesuit College.[43] Only thereafter would the individual emblems be put together in the form of a collected anthology. The Brussels commemorative manuscripts were normally illustrated, probably at considerable expense, by professional artists, as is apparent from the fact that in some of them the name of the artist is actually noted. All the manuscripts in this series are beautifully produced, but the two which never found their way back to Brussels after they were taken to France at the end of the eighteenth century, are among the most elegant of the series, and both bear the name of the distinguished Brussels artist Antoon Sallaerts, indicating that considerable financial investment must have been put into the production of these manuscript collections of schoolboy work.

The two manuscripts each contain two distinct collections of emblems all focusing on one single theme, one devised by the senior class, *Rhetorica*, and the other by the class below, *Humanitas*. In 1642 the Rhetoricians were set the theme of *Amicitia* for their emblems, while the more junior pupils in *Humanitas* were set the possibly slightly easier topic of *Adolescentia*. Seven years later in 1649 the Rhetoricians were required to exercise their ingenuity on the subject of *Labor* while the *Humanitas* class were set the associated theme of *Otium*. The 1642 album is unusual in that there is no connection between the theme set for the Humanists and that set for the Rhetoricians. More commonly in the series the themes set for the two classes each year are in some way connected, as is the case in the 1649 album. In many cases also, the individual emblems within a collection are further unified by the fact that not only do they all cover different aspects of one single theme, but the boys were further required to derive their image from a common field. Thus, in 1655, for example, when the Humanists treated the theme of the praise of old age, they were required to do it via imagery related to trees, while the Rhetoricians were required to treat the theme of the upbringing of children via imagery relating to agriculture and horticulture.[44] The two folio volumes for 1642 and 1649 in which the emblems are painted and handwritten were both clearly prepared in advance for this purpose, with decorative circular borders ready printed on the versos into which the individual emblems could be painted subsequently, and with the facing rectos left blank for the accompanying text to be inserted in calligraphy. Each emblem thus takes the form of a painted miniature depicting the scene, inserted in its ready-printed decorative border, with its accompanying Latin motto and likewise with appropriate classical references, while on the facing page is a four-line Latin verse, accompanied by the name of the boy responsible for the creation of that particular emblem. Thus, in 1642, the Rhetorician Martin Claerbots used the image of a hand extending from heaven, holding a pair of equally balanced scales, to make the point that friendship should be between equals.

---

[43] For detailed discussion of this see Porteman, *Emblematic Exhibitions*, pp.10-46.

[44] See Porteman, *Emblematic Exhibitions*, pp.43, 128-9.

The motto *Conveniunt si quando pares* relating to the image of the scales is incorporated into the figure on the verso, while a further motto relating to the theme of friendship, *Amicitia sit inter aequales*, appears on the facing recto, together with the verse and a note of the author's identity:

> Conveniunt si quando pares sunt pondere lances
>   Conveniunt homines conditione pares.
> Inter inaequales rarus consensus, amicum
>   Si tibi vis aptum sumere, sume parem.
>   Martinus Claerbots. Rhetor Brux: in Gymn: Soc. Iesu. M.DC.XLII.
>   (BnF Ms. lat. 10170, ff.93v-94r)

Rather more picturesquely and imaginatively, the more junior Pierre Cabo from the *Humanitas* class devised a less usual image of centaurs wildly shooting arrows into the air with the motto *Est aliquid quo dirigis arcum* to reflect on the unfocused nature of youth, as expressed in the second motto, *Adolescentia vaga*, accompanying his explanatory verse:

> Quo vaga turba ruis, temere in quo dirigis arcum!
>   Nulla adeò incertâ praeda petenda via est.
> O utinam! hoc vestrâ iuvenes sit mente repostum
>   Quos tot in incertum noxius error agit.
>   Petrus Cabo. Poëta Brux: in Gymn. Soc. Iesu. M.DC.XLII
>   (BnF Ms. lat. 10170, ff.78v-79r)

Seven years later in the 1649 collection structured around the theme of *Labor* the Rhetorician Philippe Cools demonstrated his ingenuity by managing to work in the opposite theme of repose (*requies*), as well as the official theme of *labor*, by his use of the image of a man drawing water from a well, using two buckets in sequence, the full one coming up laboriously, while the empty one goes down effortlessly. The figure is accompanied by the motto *Labor alternus facilis* relating to the image of the two buckets, while the second motto on the facing page, *Iuvat requies alterna laborem* relates to the more general moral interpretation contained in the verse:

> Quos requies alterna fovet labor allicit ipse
>   Nec gravat alternis, si modo fertur onus.
> Aspice pendentes puteis undantibus urnas,
>   Altera dum vacua est altera tollit aquas.   (BnF Ms. lat. 10171, ff.33v-34r)

By the time he came to compose this particular emblem for the 1649 collection, as a Rhetorician, Cools was well experienced in the art, having already, as a member of the *Humanitas* class, contributed an emblem on discord to the previous year's similarly very decorative collection on the twin themes of *Concordia* and *Discordia*.[45] In the

---

[45]   The 'List of pupils' in Appendix 1 in Porteman, *Emblematic Exhibitions* (p.178 *et seq.*)

other half of the same 1649 volume his younger schoolmate Sebastian van den Pangaerden makes public display of his knowledge of classical sources, by including the source of his emblem on the subject of *Otium*. The figure depicts men with whips and tops with the motto *Otium adversis expellitur*, while the verse on the facing recto is accompanied by a further motto citing Virgil as the source (*Dant animos plagae Virg: L: vii*):

> Dant animos pigris plagae, nimine divûm
> Orta fames, pestis, praelia, torpor abit.
> Sic puero flagris agitante volubile buxum.
> Qui iacuit, celeri vertitur orbe trochus.
>   Sebastianus van den Pangaerden Brux.
>   (BnF Ms. lat. 10171, ff.136v-137r)

Rather less lavishly produced than the collections of emblems produced by the pupils of the Brussels college, but nevertheless again reflecting the same practice of making public display of the achievements of their pupils, are similar commemorative manuscripts of *affixiones* produced by the boys of the Jesuit college at Courtrai in the second half of the seventeenth century. Here, however, the lower quality of the illustrations in the Courtrai manuscripts (which are also preserved in the Royal Library in Brussels) suggests that these commemorative manuscripts were perhaps produced by the boys themselves, rather than being the work of professional artists employed to do the job.[46]

Much earlier in the seventeenth century, we find in the *Typus mundi* of 1627 a collection of emblems produced by the class of Rhetoric at the Jesuit college in Antwerp which was actually published.[47] Unusually, unlike the Brussels and Courtrai manuscripts in which the emblems are wholly in Latin, the text of the *Typus mundi* is not wholly in Latin, but rather in a combination of Latin, French and Dutch. Once again this is a professional production, published in Antwerp to give publicity to the academic and intellectual achievement of the boys of the Jesuit college in Antwerp. The thirty-two emblems of the collection are accompanied by engravings signed with the name of the artist and engraver,[48] indicative again of the importance attributed to such public display of intellectual achievement.[49]

---

shows clearly that a number of pupils produced emblems in two consecutive years, once as a member of the *Humanitas* class, and again the following year as a member of the *Rhetorica* class.

[46] For details of the Courtrai *affixiones* see Porteman, *Emblematic Exhibitions*, pp.171-7. For discussion of a similar collection of emblems produced by the pupils of the Jesuit college at Verdun in 1585 see Paulette Choné, 'Domus optima. Un manuscrit emblématique au collège des jésuites de Verdun' in Marc van Vaeck and John Manning, eds, *The Jesuits and the Emblem Tradition*, Turnhout, 1999, pp.35-68.

[47] *Typus mundi in quo eius calamitates et pericula nec non divini humanique amoris antipathia, emblematice proponuntur a R.R..C.S.I.A.*, Antwerp, J. Cnobbart, 1627, 12°·

[48] 'Joan Cnobbaert excud'; Phls de Mallery fecit.'

[49] The use of emblematics as a pedagogic tool was not exclusive to Jesuit colleges. A notable

While such collections of emblems produced by schoolboys provide clear indication that emblems formed an important element of Jesuit teaching in their schools, cultivating in the pupils the mental agility to exploit creatively material derived from their knowledge of the best authors, and the articulacy with which to express their creations ingeniously in a public forum, they are by no means the only demonstration of this preoccupation. Further evidence is found in a number of different domains. Gabriel-François Le Jay's *Triomphe de la religion sous Louis le Grand représenté par des inscriptions & des devises, avec une explication en vers Latins & François*[50] offers an account of the celebration of the opening of the new school year at the Collège de Louis le Grand in Paris in 1686, in which the theme of the oration delivered by the Père Quartier was the successful extirpation of heresy by Louis XIV.[51] Echoing this theme was the iconography of the decoration of the hall in which the ceremony took place. The focal point was a splendid allegorical *appareil* representing Religion crushing Heresy (reproduced as an engraved frontispiece to Le Jay's printed account), but in addition to this the walls were adorned with a series of devices created specifically for this event, and all relating to Louis XIV's role in achieving the triumph of the catholic faith within his kingdom, and these likewise are reproduced in engraved form in Le Jay's account. They praise Louis, for example, for his positive actions in advancing education, and in spreading religion across the world, as well as in conducting a campaign against heresy. The devices as displayed originally on the walls comprised simply figure and Latin motto, but in Le Jay's printed account they are further developed by a French prose gloss describing and explaining each figure and its motto, and by a Latin verse (by Le Jay himself), together with a French translation of this by Fontenelle, thereby ensuring that their allegorical significance would be clear to all levels of readership. Typical of the collection is a pair of devices relating to an inscription 'Ludovico Magno, quod pulsis è regni finibus letiferae doctrinae magistris, suum haeresi praesidium ac spem omnem eripuit' translated as 'A la gloire de Louis le Grand, pour avoir osté a l'heresie son appuy et ses esperances en chassant du royaume les ministres qui fomentoient l'erreur' (C2v-3r). The first device depicts a defeated hydra, chopped into pieces (see fig.11),

---

example of a protestant establishment using emblematics in the teaching of rhetoric is the Altdorf Academy in Nuremberg, which was founded at the end of the sixteenth century, and achieved university status in 1623. Here prize medals were awarded each academic year, and pupils were required to deliver Latin orations based on the emblematic themes of these medals, and these were then published subsequently, together with illustrations of the medals on which they were based. The best known of these are those published in 1597 and 1617 (*Emblemata anniversaria Academiae Altorfinae studiorum iuventutis exercitandorum causa proposita et variorum orationibus exposita*, Nuremberg, C Lochner, 1597, 4°; *Emblemata anniversaria Academiae Noribergensis, quae est Altorfii: studiorum iuventutis exercitandorum caussa inde ab ann. Christi 1577 usque ad annum 1616 proposita...*, Nuremberg, A. Wagenman, 1617, 4°). For discussion of these see F.J. Stopp, *The Emblems of the Altdorf Academy. Medals and Medal Orations 1577-1626*, London, 1974.
[50]   Paris, G. Martin, 1687, 12°.
[51]   The autumn of the previous year, 1685, had seen the Revocation of the Edict of Nantes, with its momentous effect on the Huguenot population of France.

de la Religion.   55

HYDRA RECISIS CAPITIBUS.

Figure 11: Le Jay, *Le triomphe de la religion*, Paris, 1687, C4r.

with the engraved motto *Nequeunt abscissa nocere* and typographic title *Hydra recisis capitibus* (C4r) described and glossed on the facing page:

> La premiére Devise est une Hydre, dont toutes les testes sont abbatuës.
> NEQUEUNT ABSCISSA NOCERE.
> Separez-les du corps, leur venin ne peut nuire.

This is followed by Le Jay's Latin verse and Fontenelle's French version:

> NEQUEUNT ABSCISSA NOCERE
> Tristia quae quondam centeno immanis hiatu
>   Bellua, per populos funera mille dabat:

Ipsa etiam insolitum media inter vulnera robur
  Sensit, & Herculeâ concidit icta manu.
Frustra illa expirans horrentia sibila mittit,
  Et tumidas iactat caesa per ora minas.
Ne terrere minis, *nequeunt abscissa nocere,*
  Inque leves auras murmur inane cadet.

SEPAREZ-LES DU CORPS, LEUR VENIN NE PEUT NUIRE
Un Héros vient de terrasser
Ce Monstre renommé par un cruel ravage.
Formé dans les Enfers, nourri dans le carnage,
Par les vains sifflemens qu'il ose encore pousser,
Il cherche à ranimer une impuissante rage,
Et de nouveaux malheurs semble nous menacer.
  De nôtre sang ses Tetes altérées
Ont assez de chaleur encor pour s'agiter.
Mais non; du corps de l'Hydre elles sont séparées,
  Nous n'avons rien à redouter.   (Le Jay, *Le triomphe de la religion,* C4v-5r)

The second of the pair of devices is described by Le Jay:

La seconde Devise est l'Aurore qui dissipe par sa présence ces petits Feux qu'on voit luire quelquefois pendant la nuit, & qui conduisent insensiblement dans les riviéres & dans les précipices. Ces mots servent d'ame à la Devise: FUNESTOS DISSIPAT IGNES.
Leur faux brillant trompoit,
Son éclat les dissipe.   (Le Jay, *Le triomphe de la religion,* C5v)

The engraving depicts this scene, with the typographic title *Ignes fatui. Aurorae adventu dissipati* and engraved motto *Funestos dissipat ignes.* Again this is followed by Le Jay's Latin verse and Fontenelle's French version:

FUNESTOS DISSIPAT IGNES
Quò ruis imprudens? quò te malus abripit error?
  Quid dubium caeco lumine carpis iter?
Siste gradum, species te lucis fallit euntem,
  Illuditque oculis insidiosa tuis.
Ah! cave, praecipitem scopulo te mittet ab alto,
  Incautum aut mediis perfida merget aquis.
En tibi, *funestos* melior quae *dissipat ignes,*
  Lux micat; optatae dux erit illa viae.

LEUR FAUX BRILLANT TROMPOIT, SON ECLAT LES DISSIPE
Ou vas-tu? Quelle erreur t'entraîne?
Tu suis des guides dangereux,

Tes yeux sont ébloüis d'une apparence vaine.
  Cette fausse lueur te méne
  Dans des précipices affreux
Mais l'Aurore paroist, sa lumiére plus pure
Chasse ces feux trompeurs, que produit l'ombre obscure,
  Et qui ne la quittent jamais.
Ne crains plus, sui l'Aurore, & marche desormais
  Sous une conduite si sûre.   (Le Jay, *Le triomphe de la religion*, C6v-7r)

These devices created at the Collège de Louis le Grand in Paris fulfil a dual function. Not only do they have an educational role in the same way as the Brussels and Courtrai *affixiones* in providing the intellectual challenge of devising a series of devices all on a single theme, but in addition they also have a further role in paying gracious homage to Louis XIV who had at that date only recently bestowed his name on the school.[52]

On a lesser scale we find the same procedure being carried out at the Jesuit College de la Trinité in Lyon in 1667, where the visit to the school of François du Gué, 'Intendant de la Police et des Finances' coinciding with one of their regular public-speaking open days, provided the occasion for the class of *Rhetorica* to declaim before him a series of devices specifically created to relate to this distinguished visitor. Once again the devices were published, including engraved figures, thus ensuring that this academic exercise in literary creativity and public speaking should enjoy more than just ephemeral publicity.[53] Considerable ingenuity was exercised here in inventing devices which would not just be complimentary to Du Gué in general terms, but which would rather be particularly appropriate to him as an individual. Several are based on aspects of his own armorial bearings, while another depicting a boat, is inspired by association with his name. The final device in the collection which relates not to Du Gué himself, but rather to his son, who accompanied him on this particular visit to the school, reflects a further level of ingenuity in that it manages to pay gracious compliment not just to the younger Du Gué, but also at the same time to the king, as is triumphantly noted in the gloss. The figure depicts the Du Gué armorial bearings with two griffon supporters, and above it a large eagle in lofty flight towards the sun, followed by a small eagle, with the motto *Quo videt ire patrem*, with the Latin verse:

  Ut Patrem assequitur minor hic Iovis Armiger Ales!

---

[52] Founded in 1563, it was originally called the College de Clermont, until Louis XIV honoured it with his name in 1684. For further discussion of this event see J. Loach, 'Jesuit emblematics and the opening of the school year at the Collège Louis le Grand', *Emblematica*, 9,1, 1995 (1997), pp.133-76.

[53] As usual with such printed accounts of celebrations in Jesuit colleges, this compilation by Gabriel-Joseph Charonier was published locally: *Devises sur le nom, les armes, et la charge de Messire François du Gué...Recitées au mesme Seigneur, par les rhetoriciens du College de la tres-sainte Trinité, de la Compagnie de Jesus, le huitiesme Janvier 1667, jour auquel il leur fit l'honneur d'assister à une de leurs declamations*, Lyon, P. Guillimin, 1667, 4°.

Ut toto solis combibit ore iubar!
Lumen habet nempe, haud tantis fulgoribus impar,
    Fertque vigor Patrius, QUO VIDET IRE PATREM.

and the dual significance of this, reflecting not just the young man following in the virtuous steps of his father, but in so doing also demonstrating his zeal for the glory of Louis XIV is further explained in the accompanying prose gloss:

> Monsieur du Gué ayant honoré nostre Classe de sa presence, avec Monsieur son Pere; nous luy offrimes cette Devise, qui est le veritable portrait de ses vertus, & luy sert de plus bel eloge que l'on puisse luy donner, puisque on ne sçauroit rien souhaitter de plus grand & de plus avantageus à un tel Fils, que de marcher sur les traces que Monsieur son Pere lui marque, c'est à dire, de luy souhaitter qu'il continue comme il a commencé; car il aura par ce moyen le zele qu'il doit pour la gloire du Roy, dont personne n'ignore que le Soleil est le symbole. En un mot, suivant un si bon guide, il ne s'ecartera jamais du chemin de l'honneur, & de la vertu. Et nous donnera une preuve illustre de ce que l'on dit communement, que les forts & les sages engendrent des forts & des sages comme eux; & pour ne pas m'éloigner du Corps de ma Devise, que les Aigles ne font que des Aiglons, qui dés leur naissance témoignent par leur vigueur celle de leurs peres.
> (Charonier, *Devises sur le nom...de Messire François du Gué*, B3v-4r)

In this collection the names of the individual schoolboys responsible for these devices are not given, but in another similar little collection of devices also created by Jesuit schoolboys five years earlier for presentation to Monseigneur de Macon as part of the New Year celebrations, the names of the individual boys responsible for each device are indicated, as in the Brussels College manuscripts.[54] Here unusually, although the mottoes of the devices are in Latin (or Italian) the short accompanying verse are in French. The collection is much more crudely produced than that produced for François du Gué, but nevertheless each device is accompanied by a purpose-designed engraving, again indicative of the care with which such publicly accessible memorial volumes, marking the academic achievements of the pupils, were produced. Typical of the collection is Jean-Baptiste Desprez de Thulon's device of the mother hen protecting her chicks against a threatening bird of prey, perhaps inspired from Georgette de Montenay's earlier emblem on the same theme, although with a different motto.[55] The motto *Frustra inhiant praedae* is accompanied by the French verse:

> En vain volent autour ces oiseaux ravissans
> Pour attenter sur vous une injuste conquéte
> Vous rendrez, mes petis, leurs efforts impuissans

---

[54] *Devises presentees à Monseigneur de Mascon par les escoliers du college de la Compagnie de Jesus. Le premier jour de l'annee 1682*, n.p.n.d., 8°.
[55] *Emblemes ou devises chrestiennes*, no.84 (*Ibi licet esse securus*).

> Si vous sçavez vers moy chercher une retraite
> Sous mon aile & pres de mon coeur
> Vous avez un azile seur.
>
> *(Devises presentees à Monseigneur de Mascon,* f.[5]r)

Major national events as well could also be used as a trigger for the creation of emblems and devices by pupils in Jesuit schools, as is seen in Ménestrier's account of the celebrations which took place in Lyon to mark the 1659 peace treaty with Spain. His *Resjoüissances de la paix, avec un recueil de diverses pieces sur ce sujet* includes a section devoted specifically to the role played in the celebration by the pupils of the Collège de la Trinité,[56] in which he tells us that not only did the pupils in the two senior classes compose collections of emblems to commemorate this momentous event, but that - unusually - the class below them was also set the task of composing commemorative emblems. All three classes were required to work on the overall theme of peace, but each class had to focus on a different beneficial aspect of the peace treaty, with the most junior class dealing with 'les vertus tributaires de la paix' while the Humanists dealt with 'l'utilité des arts dans la paix' and the most senior class of Rhetoricians with the perhaps most difficult topic of the restoration of Science by Peace.[57] Twenty years later in 1680 it was the turn of the Paris Jesuit schoolboys to compose a set of Latin emblems as part of their celebrations to commemorate the wedding of the *Dauphin* with Marie-Anne Christine of Bavaria. Again the emblems were published as one small part of a longer work describing for posterity the full extent of the celebrations, under the title *Collegii Parisiensis Societatis Iesu festi plausus ad nuptias Ludovici Galliarum Delphini et Mariae Annae Christianae Victoriae Bavarae.*[58] As with many other such collections, however, not only did this particular collection have an educational function, exercising the intellectual capacities and mental agility of the youthful writers, but it also had at the same time an obvious propaganda function since the printed version of the emblems would serve as an advertisement to the general public of the excellent education to be obtained in a Jesuit establishment. In addition it served a further purpose of bringing the Jesuit college in Paris to the attention of those members of the royal family whose marriage it was celebrating. That this was indeed the case is indicated by the fact that two copies of the work housed in the Bibliothèque nationale de France bear the *Dauphin*'s royal binding, and may well, therefore, both have been presentation copies, one

---

[56] *Les resjoüissances de la paix faites dans les colleges de la Compagnie de Jesus.*

[57] For further discussion of this and other such works produced in Jesuit schools see Alison Saunders, 'What happened to the native French tradition? The decline of the vernacular emblem in the seventeenth century', *Seventeenth-Century French Studies,* 17, 1995, pp.69-86. See also Laurence Grove, 'Jesuit emblematics at La Flèche (Sarthe) and their influence upon René Descartes' (in Marc van Vaeck and John Manning, eds, *The Jesuits and the Emblem Tradition,* Turnhout, 1999, pp.87-114) for discussion of emblematic ceremonial at the Jesuit college of La Flèche marking the occasion of the transfer to La Flèche of the heart of Henri IV in 1610, and continued annually thereafter.

[58] Paris, S. Benard, 1680, folio. This individual section is entitled *In iisdem nuptiis symbola heroica.*

perhaps for the *Dauphin* himself and the other for his new wife.

As well as formal collections of emblems and devices such as these (whether in manuscript or printed form) we also find emblems and devices being used less directly for teaching purposes in other aspects of the Jesuit educational process. Not only were Jesuit pupils expected to gain a good classical education, and to develop their intellectual powers and mental agility to enable them to compose persuasive discourse based on sound classical models, but they were also required to develop articulacy, grace and self confidence in public speaking as well as the ability to write. Thus public speaking and public performance (whether in the form of plays, ballets or recitation) formed an important part of the school experience. Regular 'open days' at which the school would put on a display for the outside world provided the opportunity for pupils to practise their skills in this domain, while at the same time serving an additional purpose of providing free publicity for the school. This was formally written into the contract of the Collège de Compiègne in 1653:

> Seront lesdictz Jesuites obligez de faire les declarations qui ont accoustumé d'estre faittes chacun an le second jour de may et une action publique auparavant le temps des vacations, pour former leurs escoliers, leur donner de la grace et de l'amour, et faire cognoistre au public le proffict qu'ils auront faict de leurs estudes.[59]

As well as these regular open days, public performances were also organised as part of specific celebrations of particular events, and here again emblems had a role to play. In Ménestrier's account of the peace celebrations in Lyon in 1660, as well as the collections of emblems on the subject put together by the different classes at the Collège de la Trinité, allegorical plays and ballets on the subject were mounted, and there were public debates, and a recitation of Latin, Greek and French epigrams on the subject by junior pupils. The hall in which the celebrations took place was decorated throughout with emblems and devices.[60] Drama and ballet played a major part in the Jesuit educational system, cultivating as they did self-confidence and grace, as well as important rhetorical skills. The Bibliothèque nationale de France possesses a large number of programmes of plays which were put on for public performance in Jesuit schools in the seventeenth and eighteenth centuries, often printed in alternative forms in Latin and French, giving a summary of the plot, the time, date and place of the performance, and a list of *dramatis personae*.[61] Often these plays and ballets included

---

[59]   Arch. rom. S.J.Franc.43, fol.380. Cited by Dainville, *L'éducation des Jésuites*, p.481.

[60]   See *Les resjoüissances de la paix*, A6r-A7r.

[61]   Several of these bear the signature of the original owner, whose name often figures also in the list of actors in the play. For discussion of the use of drama and ballet in the Jesuit educational system see R. Lowe, 'Les représentations en musique au Collège Louis-le-Grand 1650-88', *Revue de la Société d'Histoire du Théâtre*, 10, 1958, pp.21-34; R.Lowe, 'Les représentations en musique au Collège Louis-le-Grand 1689-1762', *Revue de la Société d'Histoire du Théâtre*, 11, 1959, pp.205-12; R. Lowe, 'Les représentations en musique dans les collèges de Paris et de province 1632-1757', *Revue de la Société d'Histoire du Théâtre*, 15, 1963, pp.119-26; C. Ledré, 'Théâtre et 'exercices' publics dans les collèges lyonnais du XVIIe

interludes in which emblems or devices could be recited, containing some particular allegorical relevance to the celebration. In, for example, a performance of *Timandre*, put on by the Rhetoricians of the Collège de Louis le Grand in 1700 to mark the accession to the Spanish throne of Louis's second grandchild, Philippe, Duc d'Anjou,[62] the third interlude is entitled 'La paix etablie' and is made up of a series of 'speaking emblems' on the subject, as for example:

> *La Paix*
> Le trouble enfin cede à la Paix.
> Cessez Peuples cessez desormais de vous plaindre:
> Des rigueurs du destin vous n'avez rien à craindre,
> 　Vos maux sont finis pour jamais.
> 　La Discorde en vain dans sa rage,
> Contre moy, contre vous a mis tout son usage:
> 　La cruelle jusqu'aux Enfers,
> 　S'est ouvert un passage:
> Mais le calme bien-tost fera cesser l'orage;
> Pour le repos de l'univers,
> J'ay contraint la Discorde à rester dans les fers.　(*Timandre*, B2v)

while at the end of a performance of *Egapathe martyr de Lyon* composed by Charonier, and acted by the Rhetoricians at the Collège de la Trinité in Lyon before a gathering of town dignitaries in 1668 a number of pupils presented orally a series of devices to the assembled gathering as a gracious offering of thanks. The names of the individual pupils and the recipients of their individual devices are noted in the programme:

> La solemnité de ce jour estant principalement établie pour remercier ceulx à qui nos Muses sont redevables du doux repos dont elles jouissent en cette Ville, dans l'assiduité de leurs travaux. Nos Acteurs à la fin de la Tragedie viendront à ceux qui sont les Autheurs de tous nos avantages.
> Reciteront les Epigrammes qui sont au dessous des Devises.
> Au Roy, Sabot
> A la Reyne, De Moly
> A Monseigneur le Dauphin Vial
> A Monseigneur le Maréchal Gentil
> A Monseigneur l'Archevéque Brunet

---

et du XVIIIe siècles', *Bulletin de la Société Littéraire de Lyon*, 16, 1947, pp.1-29 and 17, 1950, pp.4-19. For discussion of ballet in Jesuit schools see M. McGowan, *L'art du ballet de cour en France 1581-1643*, Paris, 1978. See also N. Griffin, *Jesuit School Drama: a Checklist of Critical Literature*, London, 1976.

[62] *Timandre. Poesie pastorale à l'honneur de Philippe de France Duc d'Anjou, pour son heureux avenement à la couronne d'Espagne. Elle sera representée par les Rhetoriciens du College de Louis le Grand chez les Peres de la Compagnie de Jesus. Mercredy 22. Decembre de l'annee 1700 à 2. heures aprés midy*, Paris, Veuve A. Lambin, 1700, 4°.

A Monieur le Marquis, Marquin
A Monseigneur l'Intendant, Des Alymes
A Monsieur le Prevost des Marchands, De Pauly...
(Charonier, *Egapathe martyr de Lyon*, 1668, C1r)[63]

Innumerable other examples could be cited of the use of emblems and devices in this way in Jesuit school drama,[64] but these suffice to demonstrate the centrality of their role in this aspect of the Jesuit educational experience, a role which was equally important, albeit in a quite different way, as that which they played in the Jesuit devotional experience which will be discussed in the next chapter.

In this chapter we have sought to demonstrate the way in which this extraordinarily versatile form could be successfully exploited in so many different branches of education ranging from the basic conveying of information, at one extreme, to the development of sophisticated rhetorical and intellectual skills at the other, and including even the cultivation of physical grace of movement within the context of the public performance of ballets and opera. Yet as so often in the seventeenth century royal propaganda is never far away, and even as they set about their instructional business we see frequently a further underlying dimension of the genre, contributing as it does either directly or indirectly to the glorification of the monarch who for much of the seventeenth century dominated so much of the intellectual, cultural and artistic world of France as well as the purely political world. This very important dimension will be taken up and discussed much more fully in chapter 7.

---

[63] *Egapathe martyr de Lyon, tragedie. Representée le 27 de May 1668, jour de la Tres-sainte Trinité par les Rhetoriciens du College de la Trinité de la Compagnie de Jesus, en la reception solenelle de Messieurs les prevost des marchands & eschevins en qualité de fondateurs*, Lyon, J. Canier, 1668, 4°. Certain plays were particularly popular and were put on repeatedly in schools. For this reason it is important to note the date on the programme to identify which particular performance is being described.

[64] A. and A. de Backer and C. Sommervogel list for France the titles of some 1000 such plays in their 11-volume *Bibliothèque de la Compagnie de Jesus*, Brussels and Paris, 1890-1972. See also L. Desgraves, *Répertoire des programmes des pièces de théâtre jouées dans les collèges en France (1601-1700)*, Geneva, 1986 and M.-M. Compère and D. Julia, *Les collèges français, 16e-18e siècles*, Paris, 1988. The BnF is currently creating a *Répertoire du théâtre des Jésuites en France avant 1762 dans les collections de la BnF*. For more detailed discussion of emblems in public performance in Jesuit schools see Alison Saunders, 'Make the pupils do it themselves: emblems, plays and public performances in French Jesuit colleges in the seventeenth century'.

CHAPTER V

THE DUTCH CONTRIBUTION TO FRENCH AND INTERNATIONAL EMBLEM CULTURE

Already in the latter half of the sixteenth century the Netherlands had begun to play a significant role in the development of the emblem genre in France, as also elsewhere in Europe. It was in the 1560s that the Plantin Press in Antwerp began to establish itself as an international centre for the publication of emblem books designed to cater for a wide European market. With the death of Jean de Tournes in 1564, and the increasing civil unrest which affected the whole of France from the 1560s onwards, but which was particularly serious in Lyon, the impetus for the publication of emblem books in Lyon waned significantly at this period, and the Plantin Press quickly stepped in to corner this particular market, publishing new editions of works which had already been published in France, and also editions of new emblematic works. These were published either in Latin or in one or other European vernacular to provide for the needs of all categories of European reader, including, of course, the French reading public. In the Netherlands it is the Plantin Press which first dominated the field of emblem publishing for the international market in the latter half of the sixteenth century, but the tradition begun by the Plantin Press continued even more strongly in the seventeenth century as other publishers in both the southern and the northern Netherlands followed Plantin's example. In doing so they also themselves opened up new and important lines of development which likewise had considerable impact upon several aspects of the emblematic culture of seventeenth-century France. Many publishers in the Netherlands were active in this field in the course of the seventeenth century, but in particular Jansz Blaeu, Aertssens, Cnobbart and Foppens might be singled out for particular mention. Early in the century Jansz Blaeu in Amsterdam produced editions of various influential collections of love emblems, while slightly later in the 1620s Aertssens and Cnobbart in Antwerp produced editions of very different but equally influential devotional emblem books, and later still in the latter half of the century Foppens in Brussels continued the tradition of producing editions of important Dutch emblem books for the European market.

In 1561 the Plantin Press published a French text of Paradin's *Devises heroiques* (originally published in Lyon by Jean de Tournes and Guillaume Gazeau in 1551), to which were added the devices of Simeoni; this was followed, the next year, by the first of a series of editions of a Latin version of the same work, under the title *Heroica symbola*.[1] In 1565 they published the first of their various editions of Alciato, a Latin version with Stockhamer's commentary[2] (which, as with Paradin's work, had originally been published in Lyon by Jean de Tournes and Guillaume Gazeau, in 1556), and followed this in 1573 (and again in 1577 and 1581) by editions of the Latin version with Mignault's commentary, a shorter (and unillustrated) version of which had originally been published in Paris by Denis du Pré in 1571. Among their own original emblematic publications were notably the works of Sambucus and Junius, both of which they published in a range of different languages. In 1564 they produced the first of a series of editions of the original Latin version of Sambucus's emblem book, following this with a Dutch version in 1566 and a French version in 1567.[3] Similarly in 1565 they produced the first of a series of editions of the original Latin version of Junius's emblem book, following this with a French version (by Jacques Grévin) and a Dutch version both in 1567.[4]

While the emblem books of the sixteenth-century Sambucus and Junius were undoubtedly popular in Europe generally, as well as in the Netherlands, they did not break significant new ground, but rather should be seen as a prolongation of the familiar model established earlier by Alciato. It is, however, in the early seventeenth century that Dutch emblem literature takes on its own distinct identity, and becomes very quickly a major force in the emblematic world, exercising a great impact in Europe generally, and in France in particular. Indeed it takes on not just one identity, but several. A number of new and quite distinct developments in the emblem genre occur in the Netherlands, all of which impact far beyond their country of origin. The first innovation that we find coming from the Netherlands is in the production of emblem books focusing, in the manner of Montenay's earlier emblem book, on one

---

[1]   Further editions were published in 1567 and 1583. For details of the various editions of Paradin's influential work see above, chapter 1, footnote 43.

[2]   *Emblematum clarissimi viri D. Andreae Alciati libri II. In eadem succincta commentariola, nunc multo, quàm antea, castigatiora et longe locupletiora, Sebastiano Stockhamero Germano, auctore*, Antwerp, C. Plantin, 1565, 16°.

[3]   *Emblemata, cum aliquot nummis antiqui operis, Ioannis Sambuci Tirnaviensis Pannonii*, Antwerp, C. Plantin, 1564, 8°. (Further Latin editions were published by the Plantin Press in 1566, 1569, 1576, 1584 and 1599.) *Emblemata I. Sambuci. In Nederlantsche tale ghetrouwelick overgheset*, Antwerp, C. Plantin, 1566, 8°; *Les emblemes du Signeur Jehan Sambucus, traduits de Latin en François*, Antwerp, C. Plantin, 1567, 8°.

[4]   *Hadriani Iunii medici emblemata, ad D. Arnoldum Cobelium. Eiusdem aenigmatum libellus, ad D. Arnoldum Rosenbergum*, Antwerp, C. Plantin, 1565, 8°. (Further Latin editions were published by the Press in 1566, 1569, 1575, 1585, 1595 and 1596); *Les emblesmes du S. Hadrian le Jeune medecin et historien des Estats de Hollande. Au S. Arnold Cobel*, Antwerp, C. Plantin, 1567, 8°. (Further French editions were published by the Press in 1570 and 1575); *Emblemata Adriani Iunii medici, overgheset in Nederlantsche tale deur M.A.G.*, Antwerp, C. Plantin, 1567, 8°. (A further Dutch edition was published by the Press in 1575). For a detailed study of works published in the later sixteenth century by the Plantin Press see L.Voet, *The Plantin Press*. See also Landwehr, *Romanic Emblem Books*; Landwehr, *Dutch Emblem Books*; and Praz.

single theme, but for the first time taking as that single unifying theme the subject of
erotic love. The earliest such collection of twenty-four emblems was published in
1601. This was Heinsius's *Quaeris quid sit amor* (later entitled *Emblemata amatoria*)
which was published in editions from 1613 onwards with the further addition of a
second collection of twenty-four emblems, entitled the *Ambacht van Cupido*).[5] This
important innovative work was quickly followed in 1608 by Vaenius's equally
influential *Amorum emblemata*, and again in 1611 by Hooft's *Emblemata amatoria*.[6]

Within seven years of the publication of his collection of erotic love emblems,
Otto Vaenius introduced a further major innovation with the publication in 1615 of a
new work, the *Amoris divini emblemata*. This collection of emblems, in which the
engravings of the activities of Cupid, formerly seen in the *Emblemata amatoria*, are
replaced by equally charming engravings of the joint activities of *Amor divinus* and
Anima, began the great vogue for emblems of divine love which continued over the
next several decades not just in the Netherlands themselves, but elsewhere in Europe
also. Inspired by Vaenius's collection, a number of other sacred emblem books were
produced in the Netherlands, all likewise focusing around the figures of *Amor divinus*
and *Anima*, of which the Jesuit Herman Hugo's *Pia desideria* was undoubtedly the
most popular and influential across Europe.

Although the figures of *Amor divinus* and *Anima* who appear in the *Pia desideria*
are inspired by those of Vaenius's *Amoris divini emblemata*, the use to which they are
put by Hugo is quite different from that of Vaenius. Hugo's *Pia desideria* is the first in
a series of Jesuit emblem books designed specifically for meditational purposes in
accordance with the principles laid down by Ignatius Loyola in his *Spiritual
Exercises*,[7] and this fact immediately distinguishes them from Vaenius's earlier work.
Whereas in Vaenius's sacred emblems, as also in his erotic love emblems, the textual
element was short, and there was an even balance between figure and text, in Hugo's
Pia desideria the relationship of figure to text is quite different, since the illustrations
are intended to serve as the starting point for a series of prolonged meditations
through which the reader of the emblem book is systematically led by the author.

---

[5]   *Quaeris quid sit amor*, n.p.n.d. (Amsterdam, H. de Buck for J. Matthijsz, 1601), 4° obl.;
Emblemata amatoria; iam demum emendata, Amsterdam, D. Pietersz, 1608, 4° obl.;
*Emblemata amatoria nova; in quibus vis & natura Amoris graphicè depingitur; auctore
Theocrito à Ganda*, Leiden, J. Marcusz, 1613, 4° obl. Several editions of the original shorter
work were published between 1601 and 1612, and likewise of the longer version with the
addition of the *Ambacht van Cupido*, between 1613 and 1619. This longer version was also
incorporated into Heinsius's *Nederduytsche poemata*, several editions of which were published
between 1616 and 1650. Although the mottoes were variously in Latin, French or Italian from
the earliest editions onwards, the verses were initially only in Dutch, despite the Latin title to
the work. Only in the 1613 edition were French verses included for the first time, together with
the original Dutch verses. For details of editions of Heinsius's emblems see *BFEB*, vol.1, nos
296-317. See also R. Breugelmans, '*Quaeris quid sit amor*? Ascription, date of publication and
printer', *Quaerendo*, 3, 1973, pp.281-90.
[6]   *Emblemata amatoria. Afbeeldinghen van minne. Emblemes d'amour*, Amsterdam, W. Jansz
Blaeu, 1611, 4° obl.
[7]   The *Exercitia spiritualia* were first published in Rome in 1548, and thereafter in many
subsequent editions.

Meditational emblem books such as this or the Benedictine van Haeften's *Schola cordis* and *Regia via crucis*, similarly using the familar figures of *Amor divinus* and *Anima*, but focusing all the emblems around the single unifying themes of the heart and the cross respectively, were not designed with the sole aim of giving pleasure to the reader but rather with the intention that they should play their important role in the Counter-Reformation battle for souls.

Yet another innovation coming from the Netherlands at the beginning of the seventeenth century is found in an early collection of emblems, again by Vaenius dating from 1607, the year before the first edition of his *Emblemata amatoria* appeared. In this work, although there is no single overall theme, as is the case in his erotic emblems and emblems of divine love, the originality lies in the fact that all the emblems are derived from one single source, as is indicated in the title to the work, naming the source as the Latin poet Horace: *Q. Horatii Flacci emblemata. Imaginibus in aes incisis notisque illustrata, studio Othonis Vaeni Batavolugdunensis.*[8]

Although the titles of all these 'Dutch' emblem books are in Latin, this should not be taken as indication of the actual language or languages contained in them, since in many cases these works were produced in a polyglot version from the outset, in order to cater for a range of different European readerships. Thus, even if one of these works was not actually published subsequently in France in a French translation (as frequently happened with such popular emblem books), the French text included in the original edition published in the Netherlands made it as accessible to a French readership as if it had been published in a French edition specifically for the French market. Jacob Cats's immensely popular *Silenus Alcibiadis sive Proteus* is a case in point. Originally published in Middelburg in 1618, and thereafter in Amsterdam also, it was never published outside the Netherlands, but was nevertheless perfectly accessible to vernacular readers in France as well as in the Netherlands.[9] Behind the purely Latin title page, it actually offers a trilingual text, in which each emblem includes verses in Dutch and in French as well as in Latin to accompany the engraved figures.

Inspired in large degree from proverbial sources, Cats's *Silenus Alcibiadis sive Proteus* covers a wide range of subject matter in the traditional manner, but the author's originality and sophistication lies in the treatment which he accords to this familiar material. For not only is each engraving accompanied by verses in three different languages, but it is also glossed in three different ways. The work is divided into three books, and in each book a different interpretation is given of the scene depicted in the engraved figure. In Book 1 the engravings are accompanied by verses

---

[8]   Antwerp, J. Verdussen, 1607, 4°. As with Vaenius's subsequent works, this one also was very popular, and was produced in further editions both in Latin and in other European vernaculars throughout the seventeenth century. For details see Landwehr, *Dutch Emblem Books*, and Praz.

[9]   Several further editions were published subsequently in Middelburg after 1618, and also in Amsterdam by Willem Jansz Blaeu. For details see *BFEB*, vol.1, p.261 *et seq.* See also J. Bos and J.A.Gruys, *Cats Catalogus: de werken van Jacob Cats in de Short-Title Catalogue, Netherlands*, The Hague, 1996, and J. Cats, *Sinne- en minnebeelden; Studie-uitgave met inleidung en commentaar*, ed. Hans Luijten, The Hague, 1996.

which interpret the scene in terms of human love, while in Book 2 a further set of verses interpret the same scene in moral terms and finally in Book 3 a third interpretation of the scene is given, this time in religious terms.[10] Among the traditional emblematic figures we find the familiar monkey hugging her young in the third emblem, but in this collection Cats gives the figure three successive interpretations, all of which are quite different from the usual interpretation of the scene. Normally the monkey is described as hugging its young to death, and interpreted as a warning to parents of the dangers of being excessively indulgent to their offspring. The engraving is accompanied by the motto *Amor, formae condimentum*, and the French verse which accompanies the engraving in Book 1 and interprets it in terms of human love, focuses on the way in which love blinds us to faults in others of whom we are fond, under the heading *Jamais laides amours, ny belle prison*:

> Que tu es doux, Amour! par ta plaisante rage
> Estime son petit le plus beau du bocage
> Le Singe craque-noix: nul vice ne luy chaut,
> Car du manteau d'Amour il couvre le defaut.
> > (Cats, *Silenus Alcibiadis sive Proteus*, 1618, Book 1, A3v)

In Book 2 the same image is quite differently interpreted in a second French quatrain, reflecting mysogynistically on the way in which a daughter characteristically inherits the faults of her mother, rather than taking after her father, under the heading *Tel grain, tel pain. De mere piteuse, fille teigneuse*:

> La mere, & ses defaults, quand je te fais paroistre,
> La fille, & ses humeurs de là tu peus cognoistre:
> Il n'est pas vray tousjours, mais ordinairement
> Les meurs & les humeurs, du pere suit l'enfant.
> > (Cats, *Silenus Alcibiadis sive Proteus*, 1618, Book 2, A4v)

while the last of the three French quatrains glosses this same scene in Book 3 in religious terms, under the heading *Qui cele le mesfaict, cerche amitié*, with a reference to its source in Proverbs 17, 9:

> Le Singe son Petit, combien que laid, ne laisse,
> Mais, sans s'en offenser, l'embrasse & le caresse.
> Si de Chrestien le nom ne veus porter en vain,
> Couvrir tousjours te faut les fautes du Prochain.
> > (Cats, *Silenus Alcibiadis sive Proteus*, 1618, Book 3, A4v)

An unexplained curiosity concerning Cats's trilingual text in the *Silenus Alcibiadis*

---

[10] In the interests of economy the engravings are reproduced only once, in Book 1. Thereafter Books 2 and 3 include only the text, without the illustration.

lies in the relative length of the verses in the various languages. Where the Latin and Dutch verses all contain eight lines, the French verses are only half the length. It might have been expected that the Latin version would be shorter than the two vernacular versions in which more words are normally needed to convey the same message.

Like the *Silenus Alcibiadis sive Proteus*, Daniel Heinsius's *Emblemata amatoria*, which went through several editions in Amsterdam and Leiden, was also never published outside the Netherlands. But again like Cats's emblem book, editions of the expanded version of the *Emblemata amatoria* published in 1613 and thereafter included a set of French verses as well as Dutch verses, accompanying the engraved figures with their Latin, French or Italian mottoes and Latin distiches, thus making it similarly easily accessible to a French reading public.[11]   Interestingly we find in Heinsius's *Emblemata amatoria* a circular progression, in that much of the material used in this work actually originated in France, as Mario Praz has pointed out.[12] Nearly a century after its original appearance in France it was repackaged by Heinsius in a different form in the *Emblemata amatoria* and made available once again in this new guise to its original French audience. Although Heinsius exploits a number of sources for this emblem book, among those emblems which have French or Latin mottoes several are derived from earlier native French emblems and devices dating from the sixteenth century. All of them, however, are modified to make them conform to the overall pattern of the collection, by the addition to the illustrations of a little figure of Cupid, such as was not present in the original French version.

Three of Heinsius's emblems are derived from Maurice Scève's *Délie*, which was first published in 1544.[13]   The motto of emblem 2, *Au dedans je me consume*, is almost identical to Scève's *Dedens je me consume* of *dixain* CCCXXXI, and the only difference between the two figures is that the where the figure in the *Délie* simply depicts a boiling pot, Heinsius's engraving of a boiling pot also includes the figure of Cupid. Again the motto of Heinsius's emblem 7, *Je ne le puis celer*, echoes Scève's *Celer ne le puis* of *dixain* XLII, and once more the only difference between the two figures is that while both depict a lantern, that of the Heinsius emblem is accompanied by the figure of Cupid, whereas Scève's is not. In the case of Heinsius's third emblem based on Scève (emblem 3 in the *Emblemata amatoria*), the motto is identical to that of Scève's *dixain* CCXIIII, *Mes pleurs mon feu decelent*. Again in both cases the figure depicts an alembic, with the sole difference that Heinsius's also has the figure of Cupid.

From Paradin's representation of the Cardinal of Lorraine's device of an ivy-covered pyramid with the motto *Te stante virebo* comes Heinsius's emblem 14, representing the same thing, and with the same motto, but again with the addition of a figure of Cupid in the engraving,[14] while emblem 19, depicting an dead elm

---

[11]   In the earlier, shorter, versions published between 1601 and 1613, despite the polyglot mottoes, only a Dutch version of the verses was included. For details of all editions see *BFEB*, vol.1, p.564 *et seq.*

[12]   Praz, pp. 89-98.

[13]   *Delie. Object de plus haulte vertu*, Lyon, S. Sabon for A. Constantin, 1544, 8°.

[14]   Paradin, *Devises heroiques*, 1557, e4v.

supporting a living vine (plus the inevitable Cupid) with the motto *Ni mesme la mort*, is taken from Alciato's *Amicitia etiam post mortem durans* depicting the same scene, but without Cupid.[15] Certainly the overall theme of Scève's *Délie* was love, but neither Paradin's explanation of the image of the ivy-covered pyramid nor Alciato's explanation of that of the dead elm supporting a living vine had any connection with the theme of love, and in both of the two emblems which he derives from these sources Heinsius's verses give a new interpretation, in order to make them conform to the overall theme of love which unifies his collection, as is explicitly stated in his title and symbolised by the introduction of the figure of Cupid into all his engravings.

Where Paradin accompanied his figure of the ivy-covered pyramid with a commentary analysing its appropriateness as device for the Cardinal, and reflecting on the relationship between the Cardinal and his king (and including unusually a passage of verse):

> Entrant dernierement Monsieur le R. Cardinal de Lorreine en son Abbaye de Cluny, estoit eslevee au portal d'icelle sa Devise, qui est une Pyramide, avec le Croissant au dessus: environnee du bas jusques en haut, d'un beau Lierre verdoyant. Et le tout acompagné, de l'inscripcion qui sensuit:

> > Quel Memphien miracle se haussant
> > Porte du ciel l'argentine lumiere,
> > Laquelle va (tant qu'elle soit entiere
> > En sa rondeur) tousjours tousjours croissant?

> > Quel sacre saint Liërre gravissant
> > Jusqu'au plus haut de cette sime fiere,
> > De son apui (ô nouvelle maniere)
> > Se fait l'apui, plus en plus verdissant?

> > Soit notre Roy la grande Pyramide:
> > Dont la hauteur en sa force solide
> > Le terme au ciel plante de sa victoire:
> > Prince Prelat tu sois le saint Liërre,
> > Qui saintement abandonnant la terre
> > De son soutien vas soutenant la gloire.
> > > (Paradin, *Devises heroiques*, 1557, e5r)

Heinsius's treatment of the image is quite different. Facing the engraving is a Latin couplet:

> Ut virides ederae, durat dum Pyramis, errant,
>   Sic mihi te stabit stante virente, viror.

---

[15] Alciato, *Emblemata*, 1550, L6v.

followed by an eight-line Dutch verse and a French quatrain in which the scene is
interpreted as denoting fidelity in love:

> Tant qu'on voirra suspié, cest antique Pyramide,
> Ce lierre verdissant, l'embrassera tousjours.
> Tant que tu deffieras, le faux Acherontide,
> On voirra reverdir, mes fidelles amours.
> (Heinsius, *Emblemata amatoria nova*, e2v)

Similarly, whereas the verse in Alciato's emblem on the dead elm supporting the
living vine developed further the general moral reflection on enduring friendship
expressed already in the motto, *Amicitia etiam post mortem durans*:

> Arentem senio, nudam quoque frondibus ulmum,
>   Complexa est viridi vitis opaca coma.
> Agnoscitque vices naturae: & grata parenti
>   Officii reddit mutua iura suo.
> Exemploque monet, tales nos quaerere amicos,
>   Quos neque disiungat foedere summa dies.
> (Alciato, *Emblemata*, 1550, L6v)

Heinsius interprets it in terms of eternal love rather than of friendship, with his Latin
couplet:

> Nec platani lethum vitem, nec follet amorem
>   Nostrum, quae tollit caetera, summa dies.

and French quatrain:

> Comme à la plane on voit la vigne survivante,
> Mon amour, survivera à l'injure du sort.
> Mesme forçant l'arrest du fatal Radamanthe,
> Je taimeray là bas, en despit de la mort.
> (Heinsius, *Emblemata amatoria nova*, f3v)[16]

   Pieter Corneliszoon Hooft similarly produced an internationally accessible
polyglot collection of love emblems. These were published in Amsterdam in 1611, but
although they ran to further Amsterdam editions in 1618 and 1634, like the works of
Cats and Heinsius they also were never published outside the Netherlands. In this
particular collection, however, Hooft makes it quite clear on the title page that this is a
trilingual work. Where it was not immediately evident from the Latin title pages of
Cats's and Heinsius's emblem books that the actual text was printed in more than one

---

[16]   As in Cats's trilingual emblem book, Heinsius's French verses here are also only four lines
long, in contrast to the original Dutch verses which are twice the length.

language, even Hooft's title page is trilingual in Latin, Dutch and French, mirroring the three languages of the text: *Emblemata amatoria. Afbeeldinghen van minne. Emblemes d'amour*. In this work, furthermore, there is not even any particular weighting in favour of one language rather than another. In each language the verse length is the same. Each emblem occupies a double opening with the engraving plus Latin, Dutch and French mottoes on the recto, and corresponding Latin, Dutch and French couplets on the facing verso, each accompanied once again by its motto in the same language. Only the Dutch preliminaries to the work make clear its Dutch origins, but apart from these, the French or non-Dutch Latin reader would have felt as familiar with this emblem book as the native Dutch reader.

Hooft's emblem book is, as its title suggests, a collection of love emblems. Each of the engraved figures of the thirty emblems depicts Cupid in the foreground, engaged in whatever activity forms the basis for the allegory of the emblem, while in the background are represented the human beings to whom the allegorical interpretation of the emblem applies. But whereas Cupid is depicted as a conventionally stylised figure, in contrast to this the human characters in the background are in almost every emblem depicted as realistic figures clad in contemporary attire. Thus, for example, in emblem 2 with its trilingual motto, *'Touwde deuntjen; Eadem cantilena; Mon mal est sans fin*, we see in the foreground Cupid playing with a squirrel which is rotating the bars of its cage like a treadwheel, while in the background a realistically depicted gentleman hopelessly pursues a lady, set against an equally realistic contemporary backdrop of houses, trees and swans on a lake. The accompanying Dutch, Latin and French couplets on the facing verso spell out the already evident significance of the relationship between these two separate elements of the engraving:

> Altijt hoop nemmer heijl ben ick t'ontfaen ghewent,
> En wat ick loop of jaech, mijn slooven heeft gheen endt.
>
> More rotam inclusi volvo atque revolvo sciuri.
>   Fine carens captum circulus urget: amo.
>
> Ainsi que l'Escurieul j'ay beau tourner sans cesse,
> L'Amour tourne avec moy & jamais ne me laisse.
>   (Hooft, *Emblemata amatoria*, G2v-3r)

As with Heinsius, we find familiar emblematic themes exploited by Hooft, but always interpreted in conformity with his chosen topic of love. Thus, for example, the image of the caged bird is used as the basis for two consecutive emblems. In emblem 27, the caged bird in the foreground, refusing to escape despite the open door of the cage, finds an echo in the background scene in which the lover, as willing prisoner, happily allows himself to be led by the hand by his lady, and this point is noted in the accompanying mottoes, *Willighe vanckenis; Carcer voluntarius; Ma prison est volontaire*, and again further emphasised in the trilingual verses.[17] In the following

---

[17]   As, for example, the French couplet:

emblem the same theme of the caged bird is used quite differently. Here the bird is represented in the figure as being safe in its cage, despite being threatened from outside by a predatory hawk and lion. This foreground scene is, as ever, closely observed by Cupid, while in the background the equivalent human figures are depicted, with the lover lying safe in his lady's arms (see fig.12). Once again the trilingual mottoes spell out the obvious interpretation: *Voor vryheit vailicheit*, *Serva sed secura*; *Plus seur que libre*, backed up by the verses.[18] This is certainly not an emblem book which exposes the reader to any form of intellectual challenge. On the contrary it is one of the simplest emblem books, in which the combination of figure and motto alone are quite suffficient to convey the allegorical message. The acompanying verses which provide verbal interpretation are not in fact necessary, since the relationship between the two elements of the bifocal engraved figures, with allegory in the foreground and its human application in the background, is already clear without further explanation.

Voor vryheit vailicheit.   SERVA SED SECURA

Plus ſeur que libre.

Figure 12: Hooft, *Emblemata amatoria*, Amsterdam, 1611, I2r.

In these various emblem books, despite the fact that they were all published

---

       Le Perroquet ne sort, bien qu'ouverte sa cage,

       Aussi ma liberté c'est l'Amoureux servage. (H4v-I1r)

[18]   As, for example, the French couplet:

       Libre n'est l'Amant, mais bien seur en servage,

       Comme l'Oiseau tenu prisonnier en sa cage. (i1v-2r)

exclusively in the Netherlands, their polyglot character made them accessible to a reading public extending well beyond the confines of the Netherlands. Since French was almost invariably one of the languages included in such polyglot editions, they were particularly easily accessible to a French readership. However, in many cases the popularity of the emblem books produced by Dutch writers in the early seventeenth century was so great that many were actually published in a specifically French version, and/or published in France, thereby making for even easier access and greater benefit to a French readership. The two earliest emblem books of Vaenius, the *Q. Horatii Flacci emblemata* of 1607 and the *Amorum emblemata* of 1608, are particularly interesting in this respect. Both were published in the Netherlands in polyglot editions which included a French text, and both were also subsequently published in France, in an exclusively French version, but the pattern of the evolution of the two works and the way in which they were each progressively modified both for the European market and for the specifically French market is rather different (although equally complex) in each case.

From the outset, as published in Antwerp in 1607, Vaenius's Horatian inspired emblem book targeted a specifically French market as well as a Dutch market: as well as producing a purely Latin version, its first publisher, Hieronymus Verdussen, also produced that same year another version (under the same Latin title) in which although the mottoes were once again in Latin, the verses were in Dutch and French.[19] But the potential appeal of the work to a wider European audience must have been quickly recognised, since within five years another - polyglot - edition was produced in Antwerp in 1612, in which the original bilingual text catering for Dutch and French readers was further expanded by the introduction of sets of verses in Spanish and Italian.[20] Further indicative of its enduring European appeal is the fact that as late as 1684 another polyglot edition was published in Amsterdam, in which yet another language - German - was introduced.[21] But although such polyglot versions published in the Netherlands undoubtedly did provide the French readership (as other European readerships) with a comprehensible text, French readers soon found their needs even better supplied, when in 1646 a version of Vaenius's Horatian emblems was published in France itself, in a new, and wholly French version. So great is the interest in

---

See also emblem 21, depicting Cupid fishing, with the motto *Daer schuijlt; Latet error; Il y a de quoy craindre*, further explained in the couplet:

    Ainsi que le Poisson se prend à cette amorce,

    De mesme Amour nous trompe & nous force sa force. (I2v-3r)

[19] Copies of both the purely Latin version and the version with Dutch and French verses are available in Glasgow University Library. Copies of the purely Latin version are available in the Bibliothèque nationale de France, the Herzog August Bibliothek, Wolfenbüttel; the Folger Shakespeare Library, Washington; and the University of Virginia, Charlottesville. Copies of the version with Dutch and French verses are available in the British Library; the Huntington Library, San Marino; the Royal Library, Brussels; and the Österreichischer Nationalbibliothek, Vienna.

[20] *Quinti Horatii Flacci emblemata. Imaginibus in aes incisis, notisque illustrata. Studio Othonis Vaeni Batavolugdunensis*, Antwerp, P. Lisaert, 1612, 4°.

[21] *Othonis Vaeni emblemata horatiana, imaginibus in aes incisis atque Latino Germanico Gallico et Belgico carmine illustrata*, Amsterdam, H. Wetstein, 1684, 8°.

making this new version appear to be a wholly French production that the names of
both Vaenius and Horace are suppressed, the title is completely changed, and under its
new title, *La doctrine des moeurs*, the work is dedicated by its author, Marin Le Roy,
Sieur de Gomberville, to the young Louis XIV.[22] Although Pierre Daret, the Paris
publisher of this new edition, did not himself follow this up with further editions, this
should not be taken to indicate any lack of success on the part of this version, since
forty years later two other Paris publishers, André Soubron and Jacques Le Gras, took
over the work and between them published a series of editions between 1681 and
1688.[23] This renewal of interest after a forty year gap may perhaps have been
triggered by the fact that in the interim the Netherlands had taken the Gomberville
version of Vaenius's original work back into its own territory, when in 1672 the
Brussels publisher, François Foppens, published the first of three editions of this
purely French version. But curiously - and presumably in order to distance his edition
of the Gomberville text from the earlier editions published in Paris - Foppens once
again gave the work a new title which was quite different both from that of the Paris
editions and from that of Vaenius's original version. The new title adopted by
Foppens, *Le theatre moral de la vie humaine*, offers a clear echo of that of the very
earliest French emblem book, La Perrière's *Theatre des bons engins*, dating from over
a century earlier.[24] The enduring popularity of Vaenius's Horatian emblems across
Europe is quite remarkable. As well as his French version of the *Theatre moral*,
Foppens also published two editions of a Spanish version under the equivalent title,
Theatro moral de la vida humana in 1669 and 1672, while an English translation of
the work was also published in London in the early eighteenth century, under the title
The Doctrine of Morality, based on the title of the Paris editions of the French text, *La
doctrine des moeurs*, and once again suppressing the name of Vaenius.[25]

---

[22] *La doctrine des moeurs. Tiree de la philosophie des Stoiques: representee en cent tableaux.
Et expliquee en cent discours pour l'instruction de la jeunesse. Au Roy*, Paris, L. Sevestre for
P. Daret, 1646, folio.
[23] Paris, A. Soubron, 1681, 1682, 1683, 1684; Paris, A. Soubron and J. Le Gras, 1685; Paris,
J. Le Gras, 1682; 1688. (In these editions by Soubron and Le Gras the original dedication to
the 8-year old Louis XIV is deleted as no longer applicable to a now middle-aged king.)
[24] *Le theatre moral de la vie humaine, representee en plus de cent tableaux divers, tirez du
poëte Horace, par le Sieur Otho Venius; et expliquez en autant de discours moraux par le Sieur
de Gomberville, avec le Tableau du philosophe Cebes*, Brussels, F. Foppens, 1672, folio; *ibid.*,
1678 and 1702. In this new title Foppens reinstates the names of both Horace and Vaenius,
while at the same time retaining that of Gomberville. The fact of publishing Gomberville's
purely French version of the work did not deter Foppens from also publishing in 1682 (and
again in 1683) a polyglot edition in Dutch, French and Italian of Vaenius's original work under
its original title: *Quinti Horatii Flacci emblemata, imaginibus in aes incisis, notisque
illustrata, studio Othonis Vaeni Batavo-Lugdunensis. Editio nova correctior, & SS patrum,
Senecae atque aliorum philosophorum & poëtarum sententiis, novisque versibus aucta*,
Brussels, F. Foppens, 1682, folio; *ibid.*, 1683.
[25] *Theatro moral de la vida humana, en cien emblemas; con el enchiridion de Epicteto, &c. y
la tabla de Cebes, philosofo platonico*, Brussels, F. Foppens, 1669, folio; *ibid.*, 1672. *The
Doctrine of Morality; or a View of Human Life. According to the Stoick Philosophy.
Exemplified in One Hundred and Three Copper Plates, done by the Celebrated Monsieur Daret*,

In both of the French titles given to Gomberville's version of Vaenius's Horatian emblems, as also in its various translations into other vernaculars, it is above all the moralising dimension of the work which is stressed, in a way that was not the case in Vaenius's own original title, which was more intent on highlighting the fact that all the emblems contained in it were derived from one single source, Horace. This strong preoccupation with moralising is further emphasised in the prose commentary which accompanies the emblems in Gomberville's version. In the preliminaries to the 1646 Paris edition, dedicated to the eight-year old Louis XIV, this moralising dimension is given a firmly French context. In his *épître* to the Queen Mother, Anne d'Autriche, Gomberville stresses the particular moral value that the work will hold for the young king to whom it is dedicated, describing it as 'une chose dont il se peut utillement servir en l'acquisition de la Vertu' (f.[4]r), while in an equivalent *épître* to Mazarin he tacitly alludes to Horace's maxim of *utile dulci* as he explains how - particularly for young readers - instruction must be presented in an agreeable manner, and stresses how important it is that reading matter for such a young person as Louis should be carefully selected in order to cultivate in him an enduring taste for books, in contrast to his father who - according to Gomberville - was put off books for life by being subjected to an inappropriate diet in his youth:

> Mais pour ce que son âge ne luy permet pas de s'appliquer à des operations toutes intellectuelles, je me suis advisé de luy toucher l'esprit en luy charmant les yeux; & luy proposant des divertissements qui luy plaisent, luy donner des instructions qui luy soient profitables...Il n'y a peut estre chose plus importante en la nourriture des Princes, que de sçavoir bien choisir les premiers livres qu'on leur met entre les mains. Il ne faut presque rien pour les exciter à l'amour des belles lettres. Il ne faut presque rien pour leur en donner le dégoust. Vous sçavez, MONSEIGNEUR, que le feu Roy avoit des inclinations fort hautes & fort spirituelles. Cependant pour n'avoir pas esté conduit par le chemin que son esprit vouloit prendre; & pour avoir espuisé sa patience dans la lecture utile, mais desagreable, des Antiquitez de Fauchet, il en conçeut une aversion pour toutes sortes de livres, si generale & si longue qu'elle n'a peu estre bornée que par la fin de sa vie.
>
> (Gomberville, *Doctrine des moeurs*, a1r-v)

Louis himself is also graced with a dedicatory poem running to several verses inciting him to follow the path of virtue, accompanied by an engraving of an appropriately small boy armed with helmet, lance and shield bearing the *fleurs de lis* of France,

---

Engraver to the Late French King, With an Explanation of each Plate: Written Originally in French by Monsieur De Gomberville, for the Use of the said Prince. Translated into English by T.M.Gibbs, late of Hart-Hall, Oxon., London, for E. Bell, J. Darby, A. Bettesworth, F. Fayram, J. Pemberton, J. Hooke, C. Rivington, F. Clay, J. Batley and E. Simon, 1721, folio. A further version, under the variant title *Moral Virtue Delineated*, was also produced by the same publishers in 1726. Versions in Dutch, German and Italian were also published, and the work continued to be published in its various linguistic forms throughout the eighteenth century. For further details see Praz, pp.523-4, and Landwehr, *Romanic Emblem Books*, nos 732-43.

accompanied by two female figures of Virtue, both pointing him towards the lofty heights:

> Prince ma gloire et ma deffance,
> Louis le miracle des Cieux;
> Montre qu'estant du sang des Dieux,
> Tu n'es point sujet à l'Enfance.
>
> Dans cette Peinture animée
> Voy mes graces et mes attraitz;
> Et sur la foy de mes pourtraiz
> Fais que ton Ame en soit charmée.
>
> Imite un autre jeune Alcide,
> Fuy bien loin de la Volupté;
> Et n'adorant que ma beauté
> Prend moy pour Maistresse et pour guide...
>   (Gomberville, *Doctrine des moeurs*, f.[3]r)

The cumulative effect of these preliminaries, all addressed by Gomberville to the French king, to his mother, the Regent, and to his minister, Mazarin, is to make this work look like a wholly French creation, and this impression is further reinforced by the absence of any reference to its original Dutch author.

In the earliest 1607 version of Vaenius's Horatian emblems each individual emblem occupied a double opening with the recto fully occupied by the detailed engraved figure, and with the facing verso containing the accompanying text. This text was made up of short quotations from the principal source, Horace, supported by further relevant quotations from other classics, and a very short passage of prose describing and commenting on the facing engraving, together with the two four-line verses in Dutch and in French.[26] In the later polyglot editions of this original version, where more space was needed to accommodate the various vernacular verses, the short prose commentary was simply excised to make way for these.[27] But in Gomberville's

---

[26]   In Verdussen's Latin-only edition of 1607, the same format was observed, but with the omission of the Dutch and French verses at the foot of each verso.

[27]   In, for example, the 1612 Lisaert edition a full page is still devoted to the engraved figure, while the top half of the recto is devoted to the Latin quotations, but the remainder of that verso is given over to the Spanish, Dutch, Italian and French verses, arranged in two columns for greater economy of space. (Interestingly in a copy in the Folger Shakespeare Library in Washington a further set of verses in yet another vernacular - English - have been added in manuscript.) In the 1682 Foppens folio edition which included verses in French, Dutch and Italian, a similar pattern is adopted, but the introduction of a second set of French verses, in addition to the original set means that while the majority of the text is accommodated on the verso, one set of French verses occupies part of the facing recto which hitherto had been reserved exclusively for the engraved figure. In the 1684 Wetstein edition, in which a German text was added for the first time, and where space is at an even greater premium since this edition is in the much smaller octavo format, the Dutch verse is added below the engraving,

version published in Paris in 1646 and designed specifically for a French readership there is a significant change in this pattern, with much greater weight being given to the passage of French prose commentary accompanying each emblem. In this substantial folio volume the emblems are generously laid out with a double opening devoted to each, and while the greater part of the recto is occupied by a large engraved figure, accompanied by a moralising French prose title, and followed by a four- to six-line explanatory French verse, in the general manner of the earlier quarto editions published in the Netherlands, the whole of the facing verso is devoted to a prose *explication du tableau*, which is quite unlike the very short prose commentary included by Vaenius to accompany each emblem. The structure adopted in this French version - and indeed also the approach adopted in the *explication du tableau* - seem (as Chatelain has pointed out[28]) to reflect the specifically French influence of Blaise de Vigenère's version of the *Images ou tableaux de platte peinture* by Philostratus, earlier published in Paris, with its emphasis on the ekphrastic approach. Thus, for example, in one of Vaenius's emblems in the opening series on nature versus nurture, the complex engraved figure depicts in the foreground women cleaning out jugs and bowls, while behind them are children drinking from equivalent jugs and bowls, and - depicted indirectly in the form of a picture on the wall in the background - is a classroom scene in which the virtuous pupils are shown applying themselves to their studies under the eye of their schoolmaster, whose rod is very visibly represented (see fig.13). The appearance of this figure (as of all those in the collection) remains unchanged from edition to edition, as new plates were simply created in imitation of those of earlier editions. In the earliest form of the work the French input to this emblem was no more than a short four-line verse, but in Gomberville's version this same verse is accompanied by a lengthy prose commentary leading the reader meticulously through every element represented in the engraving by the artist, and describing it as well as interpreting it:

> Le Peintre nous ayant fait voir un grand exemple de la puissance de l'education, & combien soigneusement il faut que dés l'enfance nous soyons retirez du commerce des vices, & netoyez de toutes les soüilleures, que nous apportons du ventre de nostre mere, nous represente cette excellente Institution, & les sollicitudes dont elle doit estre accompagnée par une comparaison qu'il emprunte du judicieux Horace. Il compare nos esprits aux vases, qui retiennent presque tousjours l'odeur, soit bonne, soit mauvaise des premieres liqueurs dont ils ont esté remplis. Mais d'autant qu'il a dessein de rendre nos yeux, les premiers juges de ses pensées, il nous figure une menagerie, dans laquelle plusieurs femmes sont occupées à nettoyer les vaisseaux dont elles se servent pour conserver leurs plus cheres liqueurs. Regardez cette jeune fille, qui verse de l'eau dans une vaisselle de terre, encore qu'elle n'ayt jamais servy. Elle vous enseigne que c'est ainsi qu'il faut

---

while the German and French (only one verse) occupy the facing verso, togther with the Latin quotations.
[28]   Chatelain, p.142.

LA NOVRRITVRE PEVT TOVT.

Succe auec le laict ce noble sentiment,
Que l'amour des vertus donne aux Ames bien nées,
Nos cœurs sont des vaisseaux qui gardent constamment
Les premieres odeurs que l'on leur a données.

Figure 13: Gomberville, *La doctrine des moeurs*, Paris, 1646, B2r.

nettoyer nos ames du mauvais goust qu'elles peuvent avoir receu, ou de la
corruption du sang ou de celle de la nourriture. Le Peintre fait luy mesme
l'explication de sa figure, par un tableau qu'il a industrieusement placé
contre la muraille de cette mesme menagerie. Nous y voyons plusieurs
enfans, qui sous la conduitte & la verge d'un maistre sage & sçavant,
reçoivent peu à peu, comme une terre toute neûve, les gouttes de cette rosée
spirituelle & feconde, qui fait germer dans les esprits, les semences des vertus
& des sçiences.

> Succe avec le laict ce noble sentiment,
> Que l'amour des vertus donne aux Ames bien nées,
> Nos coeurs sont des vaisseaux qui gardent constamment
> Les premieres odeurs que l'on leur a données.
>   (Gomberville, *Doctrine des moeurs*, B1v-2r)

The similarity between Gomberville's approach here, in this French adaptation of
Vaenius, and that of the similarly native French Vigenère's 'emblems' in his earlier
adaptation of Philostratus' *Images ou tableaux de platte peinture*, published from
1614, is very apparent. In Vigenère's *Les Marescages* a large engraving, which is
both highly ornate and highly complex, and which depicts the scene visually with
assorted birds, trees and animals in the shallow waters, and with a number of swans
being ridden by little cupids in the foreground (see fig. 14), is accompanied by a short
verse spelling out in very concise terms the allegorical meaning of two of the features
represented:

> Ces petits Cupidons nageans dessus les eaux,
> Montez sur des oyseaux,
> Enseignent que l'Amour est volage & flottant,
> Et tousjours inconstant.
> Que si les voluptez d'un lieu delicieux
> Font oublier les cieux:
> On vous apprend icy par tous ces hauts Cypres
> Que la mort suit de pres,
> Et que les vents mignards des douces voluptez
> Sont des mortalitez.
>   (Vigenère, *Images ou tableaux de platte peinture*, F4r)

Thereafter follows a lengthy and detailed verbal description of the scene, running to
several pages (followed by several more pages of annotated commentary), in which the
reader's attention is constantly directed to particular features. Vigenère's prose
description is too long to quote in its entirety, but the following extract clearly
demonstrates the similarity between his style and that later adopted by Gomberville in
his *Doctrine des moeurs*:

LES MARESCAGES.   67

Ces petits Cupidons nageans deſſus les eaux,   Font oublier les cieux :
Montez ſur des oyſeaux,   On vous apprend icy par tous ces hauts Cyprez
Enſeignent que l'Amour eſt volage & flottant,   Que la mort ſuit de pres ,
Et touſiours inconſtant.   Et que les vents mignards des douces voluptez
Que ſi les voluptez d'vn lieu delicieux   Sont des mortalitez.

Figure 14: Vigenère, *Les images ou tableaux de platte peinture*, Paris, 1615,
F4r.

Et ces Sapins là, que veulent ils dire autre chose, sinon l'aspreté du lieu, exposé aux tempestes & orages de l'air?...Quant aux fontaines, elles sourdent des croupppes que vous voyez; & de là se coulans en bas viennent à assembler leurs eaux, qui reduisent le vallon en un marez, non point autrement effondré ne bourbeux. Que si vous prenez garde aux ruisseaux, ils sont tout aussi bien menez de la main du peintre, que la nature propre sçauroit faire, quelque bonne & experte ouvriere qu'elle soit de toutes choses. Car ils poussent hors par endroits tout pleins de petits sourjons boüillonans, qui abondent en Persil aquatique, commode aux oyseaux qui nagent. De faict voyez un peu ces canars, comme ils se coulent, & connillent parmy; boursoufflans contremont de petits brins & filets d'eau. Que dirons nous apres de ce trouppeau d'oyes? lesquelles en ensuivant leur naturel, sont tres-naïfvement representées nageans sur la sur-face d'icelle? Mais ces oyseaux haut-montez sur de longues jambes, & si bien pourveus de bec, sont passagers (comme je croy) & fort agreables à voir; l'un d'une sorte de pennage, l'autre d'une autre: Et tous en differente assiette. En voila un sur cette pierre, planté tantost sur un pied, tantost sur l'autre. Cettui-cy se baigne & raffraichist l'aisle; Celuy-là espluche & provigne ses pennes: l'autre a pesché je ne sçay quoy; l'autre allonge le col vers la terre, pour en tirer quelque pasture. Or que les cygnes souffrent d'estre ainsi attellez par ces petits Amours, ce n'est pas de merveilles, car ce sont Dieux insolents: fort adroicts à follastrer & se donner du plaisir des oyseaux: Parquoy n'outre-passons point inutilement cette nouvelle façon de cochers; ne l'eau aussi où tous ces jeux se font. Cette eau du Marez de vray est tres-belle; une source la produisant de ce costé-là, qui se vient puis apres reduire en un vivier fort plaisant; dans le milieu duquel se hausse-baissent les passe-velours, qui de leurs beaux espics en lieu de fleur, battent l'eau: Et à l'entour ces Cupidons manient les sacrez Oyseaux, bridez d'un riche mors de fin or. Cettui-cy laschant les resnes du tout; l'autre les retirant à soy; l'autre se maniant de pied-quoy; l'autre se destournant doucement au bout de la carriere. Certes vous diriez que les cygnes oyent bien la voix de leurs conducteurs qui les hastent & sollicitent à grands criz, & se deffient là dessus entr'eux; Car cela se void aisement à leur mine...

(Vigenère, *Images ou tableaux de platte peinture*, F4v-5r)

For Vigenère, however, the skill with which the artist succeeds in achieving such a realistic representation as demonstrated in this description of the picture is not the most important skill. Even more important, as he explains, is the artist's ability to insert meaningful symbols into the picture, and the symbol which he singles out for particular praise in this picture is the familiar emblematic one of the palm trees bending towards each other in a gesture of affection:

Que si vous vouliez d'advanture loüer l'ouvrier, pour avoir sçeu si bien representer ces chievres saffres & simillantes: ou ces brebis qui marchent tout bellement, comme si c'estoient quelques fardeaux pesans: ou plustost s'amuser à considerer les flustes & les chalumeaux, ensemble ceux qui en joüent, de ce qu'ils serrent ainsi les levres en soufflant dedans: ce seroit extoller de loüanges la moins digne partie de cette peinture, en ce qu'elle tend à bien contrefaire & imiter les choses au plus prés de leur naturel, & lairrions en arriere l'industrie & occasion de l'ouvrage; qui sont les deux plus excellens & ingenieux poincts de l'art. Quel est doncques cet artifice? Le peintre a mis sur le bord du canal un couple de Palmiers, par une fort gentille & mignarde invention. Car n'estant pas ignorant de ce qui se dit de ces arbres; qu'il y a parmy eux masle & femelle: aye oüy parler quand & quand de leur mariage: & comme ils espousent leurs femmes, en les embrassans de leurs rameaux, & s'eslançans devers elles; il vous a portraict icy deux Palmiers, des deux sexes, chacun d'iceux sur chaque bord; dont cettui-cy est comme espris d'amour, & se soubaisse traversant la riviere. Sa femelle estant encores bien loing de luy, pource qu'elle ne peut atteindre à l'accoller, se couche & assubjectit à faire une planche sur l'eau, qui est fort seure pour les passans, à cause de sa rabotteuse escorce.

(Vigenère, *Images ou tableaux de platte peinture*, F5r-v)

Vaenius's second emblem book, the *Amorum emblemata*, published in 1608, only one year after his Horatian emblems, was - even more than his first work - tailored from the outset for a wide European audience. Where the Horatian emblems were initially available only as a purely Latin text or as a text with French and Dutch verses, the *Amorum emblemata* were from the outset published simultaneously in three variant polyglot forms, each offering a different combination of languages, with French figuring as one of the languages in two out of the three combinations, and Latin - predictably - in all three combinations: Latin, Italian and French; Latin, Dutch and French; Latin, Italian and English. This first edition was published in Antwerp by the author himself, but - as with the *Q Horatii Flacci emblemata*, which was initially published in Antwerp and then later by François Foppens in Brussels - the *Amorum emblemata* were similarly was taken over and published by Foppens in 1667, still with a trilingual text, of which French was only one component, but this time with a French title rather than a Latin one. (In order to distinguish this work from Vaenius's collection of emblems on divine love, the *Amoris divini emblemata*, which had appeared subsequent to the first edition of the *Amorum emblemata*, this later version of the *Amorum emblemata* introduces the word 'humain' into the new French title, *Les emblemes de l'amour humain.*[29])

But - as with Vaenius's Horatian emblems - his erotic emblems must also have been deemed to be particularly interesting to a specifically French reading public, since once again a wholly French version of the work was published in Paris, with no other language included. And once again, as was the case with Gomberville's version

[29] Brussels, F. Foppens, 1667, 4° obl. In this edition Foppens uses the original plates of the 1608 edition. Another edition had also earlier been published in Amsterdam by W. Janszon in 1618 under the title *Othonis Vaeni emblemata, aliquot selectiora amatoria,* with a new series of plates copied from those used in the original edition, and subsequently by Foppens. For details of other editions see Praz, pp.524-5, and Landwehr, *Romanic Emblem Books,* nos 744-54.

of Vaenius's Horatian emblems published in Paris, the Dutch origins of his erotic emblems are also suppressed in this French version published in Paris. Vaenius's name is not included in the title page of the *Emblemes d'amour illustrez d'une explication en prose fort facille pour entendre le sens moral de chaque embleme*, which were published anonymously,[30] and no indication of the original authorship is given in the text. Again, as with his Horatian emblems published in France under the title *Doctrine des moeurs*, these emblems also are further modified from the original polyglot versions published in the Netherlands, by the addition of passages of prose commentary. However these prose commentaries are much shorter than those included in the *Doctrine des moeurs*, and their function is much more modest. Here they simply provide a summary in French of the essence of the Latin motto and its identified classical source which preceded the Latin quatrain in the polyglot editions. But despite the addition of this new prose commentary, this French published collection of *Emblemes d'amour* is much shorter than the original version, since it includes only fifty of Vaenius's original full set of 124 emblems. The text is similar to that of the earlier French version in the polyglot editions, but it is in fact a new translation rather than a reissue of the earlier text. In, for example, the opening emblem of the *Emblemes d'amour*, depicting Cupid shooting his arrows at a globe, although the title, *Amour partout. Partout Amour. Tout par Amour. Par Amour tout*, is the same, the verse:

> Ce petit Dieu maintient, en ce grand Monde,
> L'ordre si beau, que nous recognoissons
> Aux jours, aux mois, aux ans & aux saisons:
> Car il regit le Ciel, la terre & l'onde.   (Vaenius, *Emblemes d'amour*, f.[2]r)

is different from that of the earlier French version (emblem 18 in the original version):

> Ce petit Dieu d'Amour le ciel, la terre, & l'onde,
> Transperce de ses dards, les joignants d'un accord:
> Sans l'Amour tout ne fut qu'un chaos de discord.
> Il nourrit & soustient le ciel, & ce bas monde.
> (Vaenius, *Amorum emblemata*, 1608, E1v)[31]

---

[30]   Paris, B. Loyson, n.d. (c.1620), 4°. Two copies of this edition are in the Library of Congress, Washington. Two variant editions of this wholly French text were also published n.p.n.d. under the same title. In one the engravings are encased in a decorative border, whereas in the other (which is wholly engraved) they are not, and the emblems are arranged in a different order. Copies of both versions are in Glasgow University Library, and copies of the wholly engraved version in the British Library and Bibliothèque Mazarine in Paris. In all these versions this wholly French text includes only half the number of Vaenius's original emblems.

[31]   Where the Latin verse in the polyglot editions cited the source of this emblem as Empedocles in its motto ('Empedocles. Conservat cuncta Cupido'), the brief prose commentary in the *Emblemes d'amour* similarly identify Empedocles as the source: 'Empedocles, d'où est tiré cet Embleme, a creu que toutes choses...'

As with Heinsius's collection of erotic love emblems, those of Vaenius are also unified by the recurrent appearance of Cupid (or often two Cupids) in each engraving, but again as in Heinsius's collection, when we look beyond the figure of Cupid we find many familiar emblematic themes, to which the figure of Cupid is simply attached. Alciato's emblem of the blind man and the lame man mutually helping each other, with the motto *Mutuum auxilium* finds a reworking in Vaenius's emblem 8 in which the French verse, which is rather crudely entitled *L'une main gratte l'autre*, initially follows closely the model of Alciato, with its reference to the 'boiteux' and the 'pauvre aveugle', only moving in the second couplet to focus the interpretation more narrowly on 'coeurs amoureux':

> Les jambes au boiteux le pauvre aveugle preste,
> L'Estropié luy rend la guide de ses yeux,
> Le secours mutuel fait aux coeurs amoureux
> Plus seurs passer la vie, à tout malheur subjette.
>   (Vaenius, *Amorum emblemata*, 1608, B3v)

In the Latin version of the text, however, the Alciato model is less faithfully followed since rather than referring to an unspecified blind man, as did Alciato, the text refers to blind Cupid (who is indeed depicted as such in the engraved figure):

> Caeci humeris gestatur Amor pede claudus utroque:
>   Mutuat hic oculos, commodat ille pedes.
> Candido amore nihil maius, nil dulcius, atque
>   Uberius, magis ac auxiliare nihil.
>   (Vaenius, *Amorum emblemata*, 1608, B3v)

Interestingly, despite the clear debt to Alciato, he is not cited as the source, but rather Aristotle:

> Arist: Duo simul viventes ad intelligendum et agendum plus valent quam unus. (Vaenius, *Amorum emblemata*, 1608, B3v)

Familiar also from many earlier emblem books including the earliest French emblem book, La Perrière's *Theatre des bons engins*, is the traditional theme of the mother bear licking her cub into shape, used by Vaenius with the French motto *Peu à peu*:

> Ceste masse de chair, que toute ourse façonne,
> En la leschant se forme, à son commencement.
> Par servir, par flatter, par complaire en aymant
> l'Amour rude à l'abord, à la fin se façonne.
>   (Vaenius, *Amorum emblemata*, 1608, G4v)

The engraving depicts the familiar scene, but with the usual addition of the figure of

Cupid kneeling down to look with childlike fascination at what is happening. As with Heinsius's collection, that of Vaenius includes as well as such familiar emblematic figures as these, other emblems clearly inspired from the equally familiar French source of Scève's *Délie*, such as Cupid fanning the flames beneath a cooking pot with the motto *Au dedans je me consume* (M4v) or Cupid watching moths fluttering around a candle with the motto *Pour un plaisir mille douleurs* (N3v).[32] But as with Alciato-derived emblem on the blind man and the lame man, in no emblem is Scève or any other French source acknowledged. In all cases it is classical sources who are cited, as for example in the case of *Au dedans je me consume* for which Virgil is cited rather than Scève:

> Virg: vulnus alit venis, et caeco carpitur igne.

> *Au dedans je me consume*
> La liqueur dans un pot bien fermé se consume,
> Or que le feu cuisant n'arde que par dehors:
> Les beaux yeux de la Dame outrepassans les corps
> Font fondre par dedans nos coeurs en amertume.
> (Vaenius, *Amorum emblemata*, 1608, M4v)

In both Heinsius's and Vaenius's collections of erotic emblems, it is clear that much of the material is derived from earlier sources although the form in which it is then recreated is quite different. Much more derivative, though, is another anonymous little collection of erotic emblems published in the Netherlands in the early seventeenth century, with engravings by Crispin de Passe, under the title *Thronus cupidinis*. The bulk of the emblems in this collection are actually taken straight from Vaenius and Heinsius, and the engravings are closely imitated from those of Vaenius's *Amorum emblemata* and from those of the 1616 *Nederduytsche poemata* in which Heinsius's emblems were accompanied by a new set of engravings (by De Passe).[33] This collection - which was clearly intended to take advantage of the current popularity of the emblems of Heinsius and Vaenius - was itself popular enough to run through three editions.[34] But interestingly it was clearly focused, initially at least, towards a French reading public. The dedicatee is a Frenchman, and the dedication and most of the preliminary material is in French,[35] and in the first edition the text was produced only in Latin and French, rather than in a polyglot version. Only in the

---

[32] See *Délie, Dedens je me consume* (*dixain* CCCXXXI) and *En ma joye douleur* (*dixain* CCLXXXVI).

[33] For discussion of the debt of this collection to Heinsius and Vaenius see Praz, p.117 *et seq.*

[34] The first edition was published without indication of place or date, and is identified only by the name of Crispin de Passe on the engraved title page: *Tronus cupidinis sive emblemata amatoria P.T.L. Excudit Crisp. Pass*, n.p.n.d., 16° obl. Thereafter it was published in two further editions under the title *P.T.L. thronus cupidinis. Editio altera*, and *P.T.L. thronus cupidinis. Editio tertia* in 1618 and 1620 by W. Janszon in Amsterdam. For details see Landwehr, *Dutch Emblem Books*, nos 666 and 662-3.

[35] 'A Tres Illustre Seigneur Messire Louys de Mongommery', 1618 ed., A3r.

second and third editions was a Dutch text added, thereby making it correspond more closely to the polyglot editions of Heinsius and Vaenius.

Reflecting the continuing interest in such love emblems even at the end of the seventeenth century, and also the extent to which the market for them continued to be an international one, is a further reworking of a selection of emblems from the *Thronus cupidinis*, together with others from Heinsius and Vaenius, which was published not in the Netherlands, but in London, in 1683. As its title suggests, Philip Ayres's *Emblemata amatoria. Emblems of love in four languages.* is another polyglot work produced in a range of languages to cover most European readers. Published under the imprint of five London printers, the work included text in Latin, French, English and Italian. In each of the 44 emblems in this collection the full-page engraving is accompanied on the facing page by a quatrain in each language. Reflecting interestingly the way in which material could be transported in both directions, this London-published emblem book, based on originally Dutch material, then found its way back to the Netherlands in the shape of an anonymous version of the same work published ostensibly 'A Londe chez L'Amoureux', but more probably in reality in Amsterdam. In this edition the range of languages is modified, with a Dutch text being introduced in place of the English text. A further migration of the work is seen in yet another polyglot version that was published in Augsburg in 1699, under a new title, *Triumphus amoris*.[36] Just as the Dutch published version replaced the English verses by Dutch verses, so also in this Augsburg edition a new set of German verses is substituted for the original English set, although the original Latin, French and Italian verses were retained, as they were likewise retained in the Dutch edition. Tracing the various migrations across Europe of the love emblems created in the Netherlands by Heinsius and Vaenius, in their various polyglot forms - emblems which, themselves, owed considerable debt to influences from other parts of Europe, shows clearly the extent to which the emblem had become a cross-European phenomenon, accessible to all reading publics either in a Latin text or in one or other of the various European vernaculars included in them.

When in 1615 Vaenius published his collection of emblems of divine love in deliberate contrast to his earlier collection of emblems erotic love, he did so once again in the form of a polyglot text of which French constituted one of the languages. But whereas his *Amorum emblemata* were published in a range of different polyglot combinations, this was not the case with his *Amoris divini emblemata* which were published in just one single combination of languages, with the verses in French, Dutch and Spanish, and the source material preceding the verses cited in Latin. Once again, as with his earlier collection of erotic emblems, despite the fact that a French version of the text of his emblems of divine love was included in the polyglot editions published first in 1615 and then again in 1660,[37] the work was clearly deemed to be

---

[36] The full title to the work is in fact bilingual: *Triumphus amoris, de cunctis universi huius incolis actus, emblematibus ac symbolis Latinis, Italicis, Gallicis, Germanicis oculis exhibitus. Oder: Die über den gantzen Erd-Kraiss triumphirende Liebe in nachdencklichen Sinn-Bildern neben sehr curiosen Lateinischen, Italianischen, Französischen und Teutschen Bey-Sprüchen, auch Kurtzweiligen Versen fürgestellet*, Augsburg, J. Friedrich, 1699, 8°.

[37] *Amoris divini emblemata, studio et aere Othonis Vaeni concinnata*, Antwerp, B. Moretus

of sufficient interest to a French reading public to warrant the publication within France of a purely French text, and the popularity of this version is reflected in the fact that it went through two editions. [38]

The links between Vaenius's collection of emblems of divine love and his earlier collection of emblems of human love are very apparent, despite the fact that in the emblems of divine love the formerly naked Cupid becomes clothed, gains a halo, and loses his impish facial expression in his new and more serious guise of *Amor divinus*, and that he is now accompanied by the female figure of *Anima*. Although some of the emblems of divine love are new creations, as for example *Sternit iter Deo*, in which *Amor divinus* is depicted leading *Anima* up the steep path to meet Christ waiting for her:

> Voicy la sente tant chantée,
> Par laquelle marchoyent les Dieux,
> C'est vrayement la voye lactée
> Par laquelle on s'esleve aux cieux.
> Aimez seulement, & nostre ame
> Pourra monter jusques à Christ;
> Aimez seulement, & luy mesme
> Descendra dans vostre esprit.   (Vaenius, *Amoris divini emblemata*, I4v)

in several cases they are created from an ingenious reworking of an equivalent earlier emblem of human love. In, for example, *Invia amanti nulla est via Anima* is depicted rowing towards *Amor divinus*, using her quiver as a raft and her bow as an oar, in precisely the same way that Cupid had earlier been shown rowing towards the lady in the similarly entitled erotic love emblem, *Via nulla est invia amori*. In the earlier *Amorum emblemata* the engraving was accompanied by the French quatrain:

> Voycy le Dieu d'Amour, qui hardy passer ose
> Les vagues de la mer, flottant sur son carquois,
> D'une rame luy sert son petit arc Turquois.
> L'amant pour voir sa Dame entreprend toute chose.
>   (Vaenius, *Amorum emblemata*, 1608, M2v)

(Officina Plantiniana), 1660, 4°.

[38] Of the two editions, both of which are undated, only one includes the full sixty emblems: *Emblemes de l'amour divin*, Paris, P. Landry, n.d. (c.1690), 8°. The other edition (*Emblemes de l'amour divin. Inventées par Otho Venus, avec l'explication de chacunes*, Paris, Le Blond, n.d. (c.1690), 4°) contains only 25 wholly engraved emblems. The Le Blond edition reproduces the text of the French 8-line verses of the polyglot edition, but in the Landry edition these 8-line verses are replaced by quatrains. In both editions of this French version, although the verse text is wholly in French, the mottoes remain in Latin. In this respect the treatment given here to Vaenius's emblems of divine love is different from that accorded to his erotic love emblems in the equivalent French published edition, in which all Latin elements as well as all other vernacular versions than French were excised.

while in the *Amoris divini emblemata* it is accompanied by a parallel verse, but one
which is appropriately differently angled:

> Les bois, le desert plus sauvage,
> Les torrens, & mesme la mer
> N'empescheront pas le passage
> A celui qui veut bien aymer:
> Ainsi voyez vous que ceste ame,
> Qui cherchant Dieu, traverse l'eau,
> Se sert de l'arcq d'amour pour rame,
> Et a son carquois pour vaisseau.   (Vaenius, *Amoris divini emblemata*, N3v)

Similarly in *Pia amoris lucta* the illustration of *Amor divinus* and *Anima* having a tug
of war over a palm frond is a reworking of the same scene between enacted by two
cupids in *Grata belli caussa* in the *Amorum emblemata*, and its accompanying French
verse:

> Quand deux s'ayment, chacun d'eux butte
> Sur l'autre estre victorieux,
> Et la fin de ceste dispute
> Est à qui aymera le mieux:
> Debatons en la mesme sorte,
> Et gaignons ainsi paradis;
> Comme Jacob d'une main forte
> A surmonté l'ange jadis.   (Vaenius, *Amoris divini emblemata*, D3v)

likewise reflects the change of emphasis from the earlier quatrain of the *Amorum
emblemata*, entitled *Guerre accroist l'amour*:

> L'amant vray sa partie attaque, sans se rendre,
> Chascun la palme veut de victoire emporter,
> Chascun son compaignon en bienfaits surmonter.
> Un combat mis à fin une autre guerre engendre.
>   (Vaenius, *Amorum emblemata*, 1608, B1v)[39]

   Although Mario Praz describes in striking terms the stark and dramatic contrast
which he perceives between Vaenius's emblems of human love and his emblems of
divine love:

---

[39]   See also *Superbiam odit* in which *Amor divinus* and *Anima* stand on the tail of a peacock
(P1r), echoing *Magni contemtor honoris*, translated as *Amour hayt l'orgueil* in the *Amorum
emblemata*, in which Cupid alone stands on the peacock's tail (Bb2r), or *Sit in amore
reciprocatio*, in which *Amor divinus* and *Anima* shoot arrows at each other (E1r), echoing
Optimum amoris poculum, ut ameris, ama, translated as *Combat heureux*, and depicting two
cupids shooting arrows at each other in the *Amorum emblemata* (B1r). Many other examples
could be cited.

The smiling Theocritean fields of the emblems of profane love, the wanton bowers, the formal gardens enlivened with the statue of Venus, the rustic nook of the beehives from which the little pilferer of honeycombs sneaked away wounded and tearful, seem a banished world. Now we find ourselves among the bare bones of hills crowned by grim monastery walls, by squat pyramids and cubes of stone, and by gaunt, austere churches, and if a grove here and there softens the valleys, there issues from it the warning spire of a solitary chapel, pointing towards the sky. The earth seems choked with grey heavy buildings, the sky is a pall of leaden clouds, sometimes shot through by livid flashes to remind sinful humanity of the omnipresent and vigilant eye of the Eternal Judge...Far, far away is the gay Renaissance palace haunted by the Cupid of the humanists and courtiers; here all is as mournful as in the Escorial. (Praz, p.134)

it is difficult to see quite such a strong contrast. In his introduction to his facsimile edition of the *Amorum emblemata*, Karel Porteman stresses the fact that despite the undoubted wit and humour of the collection, the work is not merely intended to amuse, but that it rather seeks at the same time to put across a clear educational message in favour of love, guided by reason, as a stabilising and beneficial force within society:

If love is an irresistible, universal force, it is also a manageable emotion, which must be subject to social control, civilized and adapted to the aristocratic way of life...Love may be a blind force of nature, which no-one can escape, but it is also the source of *virtù*; it changes people's nature for the better...Love and civilization go hand in hand.[40]

The fact that Vaenius creates so many parallels between his emblems of divine love and his earlier emblems of human love reflects the similarities perceived to exist between human and spiritual love. Certainly the *Amoris divini emblemata* operate on a higher spiritual level, but they do not represent a negation of the values of the earlier collection, but rather - as so often in the world of emblem literature - a manifestation of wit and ingenuity in giving a new interpretation to an old theme. The background scenery is indeed different in the later collection, but it is not as melancholic as Praz suggests. And while the mischievous figure of Cupid is replaced by the undoubtedly less picturesque figure of *Amor divinus*, the effect is to trace a calm, spiritual life culminating in the ultimate blessed unity of the final two emblems, *Finis amoris, ut duo unum fiant* and *Plenitudo legis est* (Q2v-3v), rather than the intensely anguished path of suffering suggested by Praz, in contrast to the insouciant picture of love of the *Amorum emblemata*.

Where Vaenius produced two separate collections of emblems on the subject of human love on the one hand and divine love on the other, another anonymous

---

[40] O. Vaenius, *Amorum emblemata*, ed. K. Porteman, Aldershot, 1996, p.14.

collection, published in Antwerp a few years after Vaenius's *Amoris divini emblemata*, brought the two kinds of love together in one single work. The *Amoris divini et humani effectus* was first published by Michael Snyders in 1626, and in this earliest edition the text was bilingual in Latin and French, but within three years he produced a polyglot version, in 1629, by the addition of text in Spanish and Dutch, *Amoris divini et humani antipathia*,[41] and this version was popular enough to run through two further editions in 1636 and 1648, and a further edition in 1655 (with a reissue in 1670), under the completely changed title *Theatrum amoris divini et humani*.[42] But the popularity of this work for a specifically French reading public is yet again apparent from the fact that although even the first edition published by Snyders in Antwerp included a French text, within two years an edition was published in Paris, by Guillaume Lenoir, also including - a year ahead of Snyders - a Spanish text (though not a Dutch one) as well as the original Latin and French.[43] But more significantly, further editions also continued to be published in Paris by a number of different printers which were clearly designed specifically for French readers since the text is almost exclusively French, the only Latin component being the biblical quotation accompanying the figure, and in some of these editions even the Latin title is abandoned, leaving a purely French title, *Les emblemes d'amour divin et humain ensemble*.[44]

Where Vaenius's two separate collections of emblems enabled him to celebrate the value of human love in the one as much as he then valued divine love in the other, in this collection where human and divine love are brought together, there is a clear lesson intended that divine love is preferable to human love. As so often, many of the emblems are derivative, taking their inspiration in particular from Cats's *Silenus*

---

[41]   *Amoris divini et humani effectus varii Sacrae Scripturae sanctorumque PP. sententiis ac Gallicis versibus   illustrati*, Antwerp, M. Snyders, 1626, 8°; *Amoris divini et humani antipathia. Sive effectus varii, e variis Sacrae Scripturae locis deprompti emblematis suis expressi SS. PP. authoritatibus nec non Gallicis, Hispanicis et Flandricis versibus illustrati. Editio II. aucta et recognita. Les effects divers de l'amour divin et humain richement exprimez par petits emblemes tirez des SS. Escritures et des SS. peres, et illustrez par vers François, Espagnols et Flamends*, Antwerp, G. Wolsschat for M. Snyders, 1629, 8°.
[42]   For details of the various Antwerp editions of this work under its different titles see *BFEB*, vol.1, nos 75 and 77.
[43]   *Amoris divini et humani antipathia e variis sacrae scripturae locis deprompta emblematis suis expressa. Et SS. PP. authoritatibus illustrata. Les effects divers de l'amour divin et humain, richement exprimez par petits emblemes tirés des SS. escritures et des SS. peres. Le tout mis en Latin et François*, Paris, G. Lenoir, 1628, 8°.
[44]   *Les emblemes d'amour divin et humain ensemble. Expliquez par des vers françois. Par un pere Capucin*, Paris, J. Messager, n.d. (after 1631), 8° (2 editions) ; *ibid.*, Paris, P. Mariette, n.d. (in or after 1637), 4°. Further editions of the *Amoris divini et humani antipathia* were published in Paris (P. Giffart, n.d., 4°, and J. Moncornet, n.d., 4°), and at the end of the century a further edition of the work was published in 1694 in Salzburg, in Latin, French and Spanish, by Johann Baptist Mayr under the variant title, *Antipathia amoris divini et humani duobus libris comprehensa, per themata et sententias, insuper et figuras aeneas. Adiectis versibus Gallicis et Hispanicis, illustrata*. For details of the various Paris editions see *BFEB*, vol.1, nos 76, 78-80 and 82-3.

Alcibiadis, but also from Heinsius and Vaenius.[45] Many of the emblems represent the trials and temptations of *Anima*, torn between Cupid and *Amor divinus*, as in *Negotiatio Amoris* in the 1629 Snyders edition, in which she is depicted standing between these two, with Cupid on one side displaying his panier of toys and masks and *Amor divinus* on the other, displaying his panier of wares including a crown of thorns and a scourge. Predictably she rejects the attractions offered by Cupid in favour of those of *Amor divinus* (see fig.15). The engraved figure includes a biblical quotation, 'Negotiamini dum venio. Luc.19' and a French couplet:

> Depuis que Dieu s'est fait marchand
> Cupidon n'a plus de chaland.

Negotiamini dum venio. *Luc. 19.*
Depuis que Dieu s'est fait marchand
Cupidon n'à plus de chaland.

Figure 15: *Amoris divini et humani antipathia*, Antwerp, 1629, between B1 and B2.

and this is accompanied on the following page by a six-line French verse making quite explicit the choice that all readers should make:

> *Traficq de l'Amour*
> L'Amour divin estale ses denrées
> L'humain aussy les siennes descriées;
> L'un vend le mal, l'autre donne le bien.
> Trousse pannier marchand de beatilles,
> Tu peus allieurs debiter tes coquilles,
> Car pour icy tu ne vendras plus rien.
> > (*Amoris divini et humani antipathia*, 1629, B2r)

---

[45]   See Praz, p.148.

followed by shorter verses in Spanish and Dutch. In addition a short prose gloss in Latin accompanies each emblem, including marginal references to sources in the Church Fathers.

In the subsequent Paris editions of the work the length of the French text is doubled, with the original 6-line verse being replaced by three 4-line stanzas. Thus, for example, in a reworking of emblem 4 of Hugo's *Pia desideria* in which *Amor divinus* whips on the unfortunate *Anima*, as she struggles to operate the mill stones to which she is harnessed, with the text from Psalm 24, 'Vide humilitatem meam, & laborem meum: & dimitte universa delicta mea', the same figure, accompanied by the same Latin quotation from Psalm 24, but with the addition of a French title, *Amour humiliant*, is accompanied by a 3-stanza verse passage:

> La bonté divine est contrainte
> De nous charger d'afflictions,
> Pour tirer nos affections
> Vers son amour par vive atteinte.
>
> Voy comme ce pecheur se lasse
> A tourner un moulin tousjours,
> Et de passer ainsi ses jours,
> Sans qu'aucun vray profit il fasse.
>
> Si ce n'est qu'il rentre en soy-mesme,
> Recognoissant son grand deffaut;
> Alors la lumiere d'en-haut
> Fait que les biens du Ciel il aime.
> (*Les emblemes d'amour divin et humain ensemble*, Paris, J. Messager, X1v-2r)

Even when, as here, the text is expanded, the emblems nevertheless still remain short, and this is true of all the various editions of the *Amoris divini et humani antipathia* and *Emblemes d'amour divin et humain ensemble*. It is true also of another similar collection of emblems in the same style as the *Amoris divini et humani antipathia*, produced by the class of Rhetoric of the Jesuit College in Antwerp in 1627, which was later, together with Hugo's *Pia desideria*, to provide the inspiration for Francis Quarles's *Emblemes* of 1635.[46] The *Typus mundi*, which is clearly inspired by the *Amoris divini et humani antipathia*, comprises 32 emblems in which the Latin verses, which run to around twenty lines each are accompanied by French and Dutch quatrains in the manner of Vaenius's polyglot emblems. Composed within a Jesuit institution, the emblems of the *Typus mundi* continue within the earlier tradition established by Vaenius, and continued in the *Amoris divini et humani antipathia*.

Yet predating both the *Amoris divini et humani antipathia* and the *Typus mundi*

---

[46]   Francis Quarles, *Emblemes*, London, G. Miller, 1635, 8°.

we find a very different manifestation of the Jesuit approach to emblematic writing. Within nine years of the appearance of Vaenius's *Amoris divini emblemata*, Herman Hugo's immensely influential *Pia desideria* was published, in 1624, also in Antwerp. Although the engraved figures of *Amor divinus* and *Anima* here bear a close resemblance to those of Vaenius, on which they are clearly based, this is the extent of the similarity between the two emblem books. That of Vaenius reflects on the effects of divine love in the same way in which his *Amorum emblemata* reflected on human love, with each engraving complemented by its accompanying short passage of verse. But Hugo's *Pia desideria* entirely changes the philosophy, the proportions, and also the structure, in accordance with the very different objective which he seeks to achieve. Designed as a Jesuit meditational work, the emblem book is divided into three distinct sections, each comprising fifteen emblems, corresponding to the three stages of the meditational process, the *via purgativa*, the *via illuminativa* and the *via unitiva*, and the penitent soul is expected to progress through the work in that order, from Book 1, entitled *Gemitus animae penitentis*, to Book 2, the *Desideria animae sanctae* and finally to Book 3, the *Suspiria animae amantis*, rather than dipping into the collection at will.[47] The textual part of the emblems is biblically inspired, in a way that was not the case with Vaenius's emblems, with a strong preference being shown for the Book of Psalms and the Song of Songs. Where in Vaenius's emblem book figure and verse could be seen together simultaneously, as two constituent parts of a single whole, in each of Hugo's emblems the engraved figures have a rather different function, serving as the initial visual trigger, after which the text takes over. After initial contemplation of the figure, in each emblem the reader is then led stage by stage through an essentially textual pilgrimage, which extends for several pages beyond the engraved figure. The figure is accompanied by a short scriptural passage in place of a motto, and thereafter follows first a lengthy meditational verse passage, also headed by the same scriptural passage, and then an equally lengthy passage of prose commentary also headed by the same scriptural passage, and accompanied by marginal annotations. As G. Richard Dimler remarks:

> Although the illustrations in Hugo and van Veen are similar, they stem from
> different traditions. Van Veen is within the Alciati tradition where there is an
> immediate connection between word and image, where the epigrams are
> shorter and the approach non-devotional. Hugo stands within the tradition of
> illustrated devotional literature where the picture is not so much an end in
> itself as it is a means to an end, the stirring of devotion in the reader.[48]

---

[47] In the French text these titles became *Gemissemens de l'ame penitente*; *Souhaits de l'ame saincte*; and *Souspirs de l'ame aymante*.

[48] 'Edmund Arwaker's translation of the *Pia desideria*: the reception of a continental Jesuit emblem book in seventeenth-century England', in P. Daly, ed., *The English Emblem and the Continental Tradition*, New York, 1988, pp.203-24. For discussion of the *Pia desideria* as a meditational emblem book, see also K-J. Höltgen, *Aspects of the Emblem*, p.49, and for discussion of the modifications made to the original Latin text for the benefit of a French reading public, see Lynette C. Black, '"Une doctrine sans étude": Herman Hugo's *Pia Desideria as Les Pieux Desirs*' in Marc van Vaeck and John Manning, eds, *The Jesuits and the*

Yet despite the strong biblical emphasis of the text of the emblems in the *Pia desideria,* the accompanying figures do not reflect this directly. Unlike biblical picture books in which figure and text relate the same scene, the connection between the engraved figure and the scriptural citation accompanying it is allegorical rather than direct, and many of the various charming representations of the domestic activities of *Amor divinus* and *Anima* accompanying the scriptural texts in the *Pia desideria* and representing them allegorically reflect their close kinship to those of Vaenius's *Amoris divini emblemata,* and indeed some of them can be traced back to much earlier emblematic ancestry in which there was no religious dimension. Among the more delightfully domestic scenes is that in emblem 18 of *Amor divinus* gently encouraging *Anima* to walk towards him, in the security of her baby-walker frame, with the text from Psalm 16 (17) *Perfice gressus meos in semitis tuis: ut non moveantur vestigia mea,* or rather differently delightful, the scene in emblem 17 of *Anima,* dressed as a pilgrim, confidently walking along the tops of the hedges of a maze, secure in the knowledge that she holds the end of a rope extended down to her by *Amor divinus* from the top of his lofty tower, accompanied by the text from another Psalm: *Utinam dirigantur viae meae ad custodiendas iustificationes tuas!* In both of these emblems in the *Pia desideria* the figures offer a striking and imaginative visual representation of the artist's interpretation of the scriptural citation, which serves as a vivid stimulus to meditation around the the text which follows, rather than an actual visual representation of what the text says. Reminiscent of Vaenius's figures is the engraving of emblem 3 depicting *Amor divinus* as the doctor, at the bedside of the sick *Anima,* accompanying here the text from Psalm 6, *Miserere mei Domine, quoniam infirmus sum: sana me Domine, quoniam conturbata sunt ossa mea.* A similar engraving appeared earlier in Vaenius's *Amorum emblemata,* but exploiting it to a quite different, purely secular purpose. In Vaenius's earlier version the engraving represents one Cupid figure as doctor at the bedside of the other sick Cupid, with the Latin motto *Amans amanti medicus,* and the accompanying French verse entitled *L'Un Amour guerist l'autre*:

> Qui un autre a blessé, le remede procure:
> Qui a donné le coup, paye au chirurgien,
> Qui a causé le mal, doit remettre le bien.
> L'Amour seul de l'Amour doibt guerir la blessure.
>   (Vaenius, *Amorum emblemata,* 1608, X4v)

In emblem 28 of the *Pia desideria Amor divinus* is shown carrying *Anima* on his back along a stormy seashore, while *Anima* herself also holds a large anchor. The textual accompaniment is once again from the Book of Psalms: *Mihi autem adherere Deo bonum est, ponere in Domino Deo spem meam.* Despite the anchor, and the stormy

---

Emblem Tradition, pp.233-47. For more general discussion of the meditational emblem see also J.-M. Chatelain, 'Lire pour croire: mises en texte de l'emblème et art de méditer au XVIIe siècle', *Bibliothèque de l'Ecole des Chartes,* 150, 1992, pp.321-51.

setting, the figure is similar to that of Alciato's *Mutuum auxilium* with the blind man carrying the lame man on his back, a figure which was also taken up by Vaenius in his *Amorum emblemata*.[49] In emblem 39 of the *Pia desideria*, *Anima* is depicted vainly striving to fly up to heaven from whence *Amor divinus* leans down encouragingly to her, but despite her wings, she is prevented from doing so by the heavy weight in the shape of a globe, attached to her ankle. The accompanying text for once is not taken from the Book of Psalms, but rather from Philippians: *Coarctor è duobus, desiderium habens dissolui, & esse cum CHRISTO*. Here again despite the fact that the burden holding *Anima* down to the earth is here a globe, the figure clearly echoes Alciato's *Paupertatem summis ingeniis obesse, ne prouehantur* in which the poor man is depicted striving to fly up to heaven, to which he stretches out his winged arm, representing his intellect, but is prevented from doing so by the weight of the rock to which his other hand is attached.[50] Hugo's exploitation of the figure is naturally quite different from that of Alciato, but nevertheless the original inspiration is clearly apparent.

Hugo's *Pia desideria* was as popular in the European market (and notably to the French reading public) as the works of Heinsius and Vaenius, but the way in which the book was produced to cater for this market was quite different, reflecting its different style and function. Where it was perfectly possible to put together a polyglot emblem book when all the individual verses were short, a work such as the *Pia desideria* in which the textual element was far more substantial did not lend itself so easily to this process, which would have resulted in a very cumbersome volume. Instead, after its initial appearance in Latin only (the language which would cater for the widest market), it was published thereafter in a series of different vernacular versions, as well as in further editions of the original Latin text, in some cases published in the Netherlands and in other cases elsewhere in Europe. As early as 1625 - within a year of the very first Latin edition published in Antwerp - a Latin edition was also published in Lyon, for sale in France, and further editions followed in Paris in 1654, 1661 and 1670, and again in Lyon in 1679.[51] Within three years of the publication of the original Latin text in Antwerp in 1624, the same publisher, Aertssens, produced a French translation of the work in 1627 in an edition shared with Jean Cnobbart and Cornille Woons, and some copies of this basically Netherlands published edition were also made available in Paris under the imprint of Sébastien Cramoisy.[52] In 1629 Aertssens also published a Dutch version of the text,[53]

---

[49]   *Emblemata*, 1550, L7r; *Amorum emblemata*, 1608, B3v.

[50]   *Emblemata*, 1550, I2v.

[51]   *Pia desideria elegiis et affectibus SS. patrum illustrata: auctore Hermanno Hugone Societatis Iesu*, Lyon, C. Larjot, 1625, 16°; *ibid.*,Paris, J. Henault, 1654, 1661 and 1670, 12°; Lyon, P. Guillimin, 1679. For details see *BFEB*, vol.1, nos 333, 336-8. Many other Latin editions of the work were published in the seventeenth and eighteenth centuries: for a full listing of these see De Backer and Sommervogel, *Bibliothèque de la Compagnie de Jésus*, vol.4, cols 513-20.

[52]   *Pieux desirs imités des Latins du R.P. Herman Hugo, par P.I. jurisc. Mis en lumiere par Boëce a Bolswert*, Antwerp, H. Aertssens, J. Cnobbart and C. Woons, 1627, 8°; *ibid.*, Paris, S. Cramoisy, 1627, 8°. Another edition was also published in 1627 in Paris, by Pierre Landry, but

but other European countries soon took over the successive publication of a range of further versions of this immensely popular work in a variety of different vernaculars, continuing well into the eighteenth century. An English version by Edmund Arwaker was published in London in 1686,[54] and Praz lists a German version published in Augsburg in 1627, a Spanish version published in Valladolid in 1633, a Polish version published in Cracow in 1673, and a Danish version published in Copenhagen in 1738.[55]

Reflecting the enduring interest in France of the *Pia desideria*, the work was still sufficiently popular in France to justify the publication in Paris in 1684 of a new French translation under a different title, in which for the first time the word 'emblem' is included: *Les justes sentimens de la pieté exposez sous des emblesmes familiers*, but in which paradoxically the name of the author, Herman Hugo, is suppressed.[56] In this latter version, published in France, the text is more wholly French than the earlier Antwerp version in which the Latin biblical texts which formed part of the engravings, were retained in that language, despite the rest of the work being in French, although a French translation of them was also included. But in the Paris printed French text, even these biblical quotations are translated into French, along with the rest of the text, and in addition a further short prose gloss in French accompanies each engraving, explaining what the scene depicts. Even more, therefore, than in the earlier versions - whether French or Latin - of the *Pia desideria*, the French published *Justes sentimens de la pieté* gives the reader every help in understanding the lesson which is to be derived from each of Hugo's meditational emblems. French interest in the work was still strong enough to give rise to yet another French translation/adaptation in the early eighteenth century, which was published originally in Cologne in 1717, but again right at the end of the century in France, in 1790. Under a new French title, *L'ame amante de son Dieu*, this work,

---

although this did include engravings, it did not include any text other than the scriptural quotations. (Copies of this rare edition are available in the British Library, the Folger Shakespeare Library, Washington, and Princeton University Library. For details of this edition see *BFEB*, vol.1, no. 335.

[53] *Goddelycke Wenschen verlicht met sinnebeelden, Ghedichten en vierighe uyt-spraecken der ovdvaders Naer-ghevolght de Latynsche vanden Eerw. P. Hermannus Hugo Priester der Societeyt Iesu door Iustus de Hardvyn P*, Antwerp, H. Aertssens, 1629, 8°.

[54] *Pia desideria: or Divine Addresses, in three books, illustrated with XLVII copper-plates. Written in Latine by Herm. Hugo; Englished by Edm. Arwaker*, London, H. Bonwicke, 1686, 8°. Francis Quarles's *Emblemes* was also heavily indebted to the *Pia desideria*. See K.J.Höltgen and J. Horden, eds, Francis Quarles, *Emblemes* (1635) Edward Benlowes Quarlëis and *Hieroglyphikes of the Life of Man* (1638), Hildesheim, Zurich, New York, 1993, introduction, p.11 *et seq.*

[55] Praz, pp.376-8.

[56] *Les justes sentimens de la pieté exposez sous des emblesmes familiers. Tirez de la Sainte Escriture, & divisez en trois livres. Le premier traite des larmes & des gemissemens de la penitence. Le second des desirs de l'ame juste. Le troisiéme des soupirs de l'ame convertie, & amante de son Dieu. Sur l'idée d'un livre Latin, qui a pour titre, Pia desideria. Traduit en François par un missionaire*, Paris, E. Couterot, 1684, 12°. For details of this rare edition see *BFEB*, vol.1, no.340.

produced by a woman, Mme de La Mothe-Guyon, included not just her French rendering of emblems from the *Pia desideria* but also of emblems from Vaenius's *Amoris divini emblemata*.[57]   Reflecting once again the trans-European interest of so many seventeenth-century emblem books originating in the Netherlands is the fact that this French version was itself thereafter translated into German within two years and published in Regensburg in 1719 and again in 1743,[58] but even more interesting as an indication of cultural migration is a copy of the original 1717, Cologne-published, edition of Mme de La Mothe-Guyon's French version, discovered by John Manning in the British Library, to which has been added in a more or less contemporary hand, a manuscript translation into English prose of her French rendering of the emblems of Hugo and Vaenius.[59]

The programmed meditational structure adopted by the Jesuit Hugo in the *Pia desideria* is similarly adopted a few years later by Benedict van Haeften in his two emblem books, the *Schola cordis* and *Regia via crucis* of 1629 and 1635 respectively, although Haeften was himself a Benedictine rather than a Jesuit. In both these works we find once again the figures of *Amor divinus* and *Anima*, but with the further refinement in that each of these two works is given a particular unifying theme, as reflected in their individual titles. The emblems of the *Schola cordis* all focus around the theme of the heart, while those of the *Regia via crucis* focus around the theme of the Cross. Very appropriately Haeften dedicated the *Regia via crucis* to St Teresa of Avila in honour of her strong desire to embrace the Cross, which he evokes in his dedication *Gloriosissimae Virgini S. Theresiae a Iesu Carmelitarum Exalceat. Fundatrici* (*6r). The charming little figures of the *Schola cordis*, busily active in a series of picturesque allegorical scenes accompanied always by the little heart, are very reminiscent of those of Hugo's *Pia desideria*, which is not surprising since the sets of engravings for both works were provided by the same artist, Boëtius à Bolswert. More dramatically emotional are the larger, full-page engravings of the *Regia via crucis* by Cornelis Galle, inspired possibly from Rubens. The major difference between these two works by Haeften and the *Pia desideria*, however, is that although the meditational passages following on from the figures in the *Pia desideria* were very substantial, they were nevertheless in verse, whereas in the equally substantial

---

[57]   Mme de La Mothe-Guyon, *L'ame amante de son Dieu, representée dans les emblémes de Hermannus Hugo sur ses Pieux desirs: & dans ceux d'Othon Vaenius sur l'Amour divin. Avec des figures nouvelles accompagnées de vers qui en font l'aplication aus dispositions les plus essentielles de la vie interieure*, Cologne, J. de la Pierre, 1717, 8°; *ibid.*, Paris, 'Chez les Libraires Associés', 1790, 8°.

[58]   *Die ihren Gott liebende Seele, vorgestellt in den Sinnbildern des Hermanni Hugonis uber seine Pia desideria, und des Ottonis Vaenii, uber die Liebe Gottes, mit neuen Kupffern und Versen, welche zielen auf das innere Christenthum, aus dem Frantzösischen ins Teutsche übersetzt*, Regensburg, E.F. Bader, 1719, 8°; *ibid.*, Regensburg, E.F. Bader, 1743, 8°. For further details see Praz, pp.378-9.

[59]   For a detailed description of this manuscript translation, and a transcription of the text see John Manning, 'An unedited and unpublished manuscript translation of Hermann Hugo's *Pia desideria*', *Emblematica*, 6,1, 1992, pp.147-79, and 'An unedited and unpublished manuscript translation of *Les emblemes d'Othon Vaenius*', *Emblematica*, 6,2, 1992, pp.325-55.

meditational passages which follow on from the engraved figures in his two works Haeften adopts the medium of prose. In the *Schola cordis* each half-page engraving is accompanied by a short title, a biblical citation backed up by two lines of Latin. Thereafter follow ten to twelve pages of directed meditation accompanied by marginal annotations, under the title *Lectio*. The same pattern is followed in the *Regia via crucis,* although here the engravings each occupy a full page, and the accompanying passages of directed meditation, here entitled *Caput,* although still substantial, are somewhat shorter, extending to only six or seven pages, rather than ten or twelve. Not only do we see, therefore, a departure from the more conventional emblematic process in that - other than the Latin couplet accompanying the engravings - the whole work in both cases is in prose, and any notion of brevity is wholly sacrificed in the interests of conveying the important meditational message. But furthermore in the *Regia via crucis,* at least, if not in the *Schola cordis,* we find another departure from more conventional emblematic patterns in that in several cases the engraved figure is not even always printed at the beginning of each section, but on occasion in the middle of the prose section, thus contributing further to the lack of symmetry of the work.

Reminiscent in style of the *Pia desideria* are two ingenious 'gardening' emblems in the *Schola cordis,* in the first of which *Amor divinus* is depicted carefully sowing seed in the heart, which is supported by *Anima* and in the second of which we see him equally carefully watering it. The first emblem (Book 3, *Lectio* V), entitled *Seminatio in cor,* is accompanied by the words 'Verbum seminatum est in corde' taken from the parable of the sower and the seed,[60] and the couplet:

> Semina iam terrae manda divine colone,
>   Ne nostri, sterilis, sit tibi, cordis ager.

after which the directed meditation leads the reader through the appropriate mental paths that he should follow after contemplation of this figure, beginning as always with the phrase 'Considera primo...':

> Considera primo quo fine creatus sis? quid agas? quò tendas? cur in hoc mundo positus... (Haeften, *Schola cordis,* Y8r)

The following emblem, *Cordis irrigatio,* is similarly accompanied by the words 'Rigabo hortum meum plantationum' from Ecclesiastes,[61] and the couplet:

> Telluri clausum, caelo patet: implue rorem,
>   Cordis ab hoc, vario flore virescet humus. (Haeften, *Schola cordis,* Z4v)

and by a lengthy meditational passage. But while there are occasional rare engravings in the *Regia via crucis* where there is still a whimsical element in the style of those of

---

[60] 'Omnis qui audit verbum regni, & non intelligit, venit Malus, & rapit quod seminatum est in corde eius: hic est qui secus viam seminatus est.' (Matthew 13, verse 19)
[61] 'Dixi, Rigabo hortum plantationum, & inebriabo partus mei fructum.' (Ecclesiasticus, 24, verse 42 (31))

the *Schola cordis*, as for example in the representation of *Anima* and *Amor divinus* in a sailing ship, in which *Anima* uses her cross as an oar while *Amor divinus* uses his as a rudder, with the title *Per multas tribulationes oportet nos intrare in regnum caelorum*,[62] and the accompanying couplet:

> Non timet Aeolios ratis haec, fera flamina fratres:
> CRUX malus, remus, CRUX cui clavus adest.
> > (Haeften, *Regia via crucis*, Aa1v, Book 3, *caput* 10)

more typical of the overall pattern of the work, with its characteristically emotional figures, is that of *Anima* sharing the Cross with Christ, in the form of *Amor divinus*, accompanied by the words *Christo confixus sum cruci*,[63] echoing St Teresa's desire to suffer with Christ. As with the *Schola cordis*, there is a Latin couplet:

> En meus est CRUCIFIXUS Amor! me figite clavi
> Et liceat Domino cum moriente mori.
> > (Haeften, *Regia via crucis*, S4v, Book 2, *caput* 20)

and a lengthy prose accompaniment, taking in part the form of a dialogue between *Anima*, or *Staurophila* (Cross-lover) as she is here named, and her divine mentor, as in the opening lines:

> Pergens porrò Staurophila, & coeptum continuans sermonem, ista subiunxit. Cum toto corde te desiderem, ô dilecte votorum meorum, & iugiter ad te suspirem...   (Haeften, *Regia via crucis*, S4r)

Both the *Schola cordis* and the *Regia via crucis* were first published in Antwerp, and both were - like the *Pia desideria* - initially composed wholly in Latin. But although not nearly so popular and influential as Hugo's *Pia desideria*, the *Regia via crucis* nevertheless followed the same pattern of being subsequently adapted to conform to the needs of vernacular readers in different countries and published elsewhere in Europe. Within a few years of the appearance of the first edition of the work in Latin, a French version was published in France for the benefit of a French reading public, under the title *Le chemin royal de la croix*, and this was clearly deemed to be a success, since the initial 1651 edition published in Paris was followed by further Paris editions in 1656, 1667, 1670, 1679 and 1685.[64] A version in Dutch

---

[62] The title includes a reference to the biblical source in Acts 14, verse 22: 'Confirmantes animas discipulorum, exhortantesque ut permanerent in fide, & quoniam per multas tribulationes oportet nos intrare in regnum Dei'.

[63] The title includes a reference to the biblical source in the epistle of Paul to the Galatians: 'Ego enim per legem, legi mortuus sum, ut Deo vivam: Christo confixus sum cruci.' (Galatians 2, verse 19).

[64] *Le chemin royal de la croix, composé par Dom Benoist Haeften d'Utrecht, Prieur du monastére réformé d'Afflighen, de l'Ordre de S. Benoist. Traduict de Latin en François, & dedié à Madame la Duchesse d'Orleans, par le R.P.Didac religieux de l'Observance de S.*

was also published in Bruges, a few years after the French version, while in the early eighteenth century a Spanish version was published in Spain,[65] but neither of these two vernacular versions enjoyed the popularity of the much republished French version.

Curiously Haeften's other emblem book, the *Schola cordis* did not enjoy anything like the same popularity in France, although it did elsewhere in Europe. Only one single edition of the *Schola cordis* was published in France, and it is interesting that it includes only the engraved plates. Thus all the text other than the small amount of Latin included in the engravings is deleted.[66] In England, in contrast, it inspired Christopher Harvey to produce an English reworking of the text, including in it a verse element in his 1647 *School of the Heart*.[67] It was also popular enough to lead to translations also into German in 1664 and Spanish in 1748.[68] Quite why it was less popular to a French readership than the *Regia via crucis* is something of a mystery, particularly in view of the fact that much of the remarkable popularity of Hugo's *Pia desideria* could be attributed to the charm of the illustrations of Boëtius à Bolswert, which were regularly imitated in successive editions, and it was this same artist who supplied the equally charming illustrations of the *Schola cordis*.

The creation of a series of allegorical figures focusing around the heart was not, of course, an original idea on the part of Haeften, but rather one which he took over and exploited as a source of inspiration for a devout meditational work, in much the same way that Hugo exploited the already existing pattern of emblems of divine and human love for his similarly meditational purposes. A little collection of engravings under the title *Cor Iesu amanti sacrum*, in which a large heart forms the backdrop against which the infant Jesus carries out a series of allegorical activities, such as sweeping out the heart, each accompanied by short verses in Latin, had already been produced in Antwerp at the end of the sixteenth century, by the Wierix family of engravers, and these engravings or reworkings and imitations of them were thereafter used as the basis for a series of emblem books produced in the Netherlands and elsewhere, in a

---

François son confesseur. Enrichy de quarante figures en taille-douce, Paris, N. Jacquard for J.Henault, 1651, 8°. The 1656 and 1667 editions were, like the first edition, published by N. Jacquard for J. Henault, while the 1670 edition came out under Henault's name alone. The 1679 edition was published by J. Villery, and the 1685 edition by Villery together with P. Aubouyn and J. Guignard. For details see *BFEB*, vol.1, nos 289-91.
[65] *De Heyr-Baene des Cruys Waer-langhs alle soorten van menschen worden ghewesen, ende sekerlijck gheleert, om de Cruycen van alderhande lijden oft teghenspoedt van dese bedroefde tijdelijcke wereldt ghemackelijck te gheraeken tot de eeuwighe vreught-saligheyt des Hemels...*, Bruges, L. vanden Kerchove, 1667, 4°; *Camino Real de la Cruz, que compuso en Latin el P.D. Benedicto Haefteno...*, Valladolid, J. Godinez, 1721, 4°.
[66] Paris, G. Lenoir, n.d., 4° obl. For details of this rare edition see *BFEB*, vol.1, no.294.
[67] *The School of the Heart, or the Heart of it selfe gone away from God, brought back againe to him, and instructed by him*, London, H. Blunden, 1647, 8°.
[68] *Hertzen Schuel. Oder des von Gott abgefüerten Herzens widerbringung zu Gott, und underweisung durch D. Benedictum Haeftenum...*, Augsburg, J. Weh, 1664, 8°; *Escuela del Corazon, que escribio en lengua latina el R.P.Don Benito Haeften de la Orden de S. Benito...*, Madrid, no publ., 1748, 8°.

range of different languages.[69] Among these are the *Coeur devot/Cor deo devotum* by the French Jesuit, Etienne Luzvic which was published in the 1620s in both French and Latin versions,[70] or Guillaume de Mello's rather later *Divines operations de Jesus, dans le coeur d'une ame fidelle. Par G.D.M*, published in Paris in 1673.[71]

All this demonstrates the danger of defining too closely what is and what is not a 'French' emblem book. While much of the emblem literature that was being read in France in the seventeenth century was indeed 'French' in the sense that it was composed in French, by a French national, and published in France, much of it was not 'French' in that sense. In the numerous polyglot editions produced in the Netherlands, many texts were made available to French readers in the same way that they were also made available to other European readers, and in this polyglot form their international character is retained. But as we have seen, many works originally published in the Netherlands were also thereafter actually published in a French text in France itself, for the benefit of French readers specifically, rather than for French readers among a number of other European vernacular readers, and in this form the fact that they were not originally indigenous French texts is by no means evident. A French reader of Gomberville's *Theatre de la vie humaine*, for example, could well be forgiven for assuming that he was reading a French work, although in reality what he would be seeing was a French translation of a work originally composed in Latin by a Dutchman, and published in the Netherlands.

By and large two distinct trends can be observed. The love emblems of Heinsius and Vaenius and their imitators tended to be published in polyglot editions rather than in single language-specific editions, and it was in this form that they were for the most part made available to a French reading public. This was likewise the case with the collections of short emblems of divine love initiated by Vaenius and taken up by a number of imitators. A different approach, however, was adopted in the meditational emblem books in which the proportion of text to figure is very different. In such works as Hugo's *Pia desideria* or Haeften's *Schola cordis* and *Regia via crucis* in which the text plays a vital role in leading the penitent through his meditation, a polyglot version would be too cumbersome, and consequently such works cater for the international market by being published either in a Latin version or in alternative versions in one or other vernacular. In many cases, as in the case of Haeften's *Pia desideria*, such vernacular versions were published not only in the Netherlands where they first

---

[69]   For discussion of the Wierix family of engravers in particular, and for 'heart' literature in general see Anne Sauvy, *Le Miroir du coeur. Quatre siècles d'images savantes et populaires*, p.55 *et seq*. Sauvy stresses the tremendous production of religious illustrations sent out from Antwerp across Europe and even to Latin America.

[70]   The earliest known edition of the French text was published in Antwerp by Aertssens in 1627, although Praz cites an earlier edition without illustrations as being published in Paris by S. Cramoisy, but gives no location for this. Originally composed in French the work was then translated into Latin by Charles Musart and published by Bellere in Douai, under the title *Cor Deo devotum, Iesu pacifici Salomonis thronus regius*. An edition was also published by Aertssens in Antwerp in 1628, a copy of which is to be found in the BnF.

[71]   Paris, J. Van-Merle, 1673, 12°. (Presumably Van-Merle originated in Antwerp, since his imprint is 'rue Saint Jacques, à la Ville d'Anvers').

originated, but also in the target country. Thus the *Pia desideria* was available in a French text published in Antwerp under the title *Pieux desirs* and also in a quite different French text published in Paris under the title *Justes desirs*. When we move in the next chapter to consideration of the religious emblem in France, we shall see again demonstrated the extent to which native French products and imported products coexisted, and interrelated.

CHAPTER VI

THE RELIGIOUS USES OF EMBLEMS IN FRANCE

We have already seen in the previous chapter the extent to which many of the religious emblem books circulating in France in the seventeenth century were not true native French products, but rather imports from the Netherlands, although this fact is by no means always evident from the outward appearance of the work. When, for example, editions of a French version of the anonymous *Amoris divini et humani antipathia* were published in France in the 1630s, within a decade of the earliest versions of the work being published in the Netherlands, there was nothing in these French-produced books to indicate that the text had originated anywhere other than in France. When Herman Hugo's immensely popular *Pia desideria* came to be published in Paris and also in Lyon, both in Latin and in French, again its non-French origins were no longer apparent. The enduring popularity in France of the devotional collections of emblems of the heart which originated in the Netherlands is reflected in the fact that as late as 1673 Guillaume de Mello's purely French *Divines operations de Jesus dans le coeur d'une ame fidele* was published in Paris in clear imitation of the earlier *Coeur devot throsne royal de Jesus pacifique Salomon* of the Jesuit Etienne Luzvic, published nearly fifty years earlier in Antwerp.

The Dutch influence on religious emblem literature in France in the seventeenth century is thus clearly very important. Yet as well as such works coming directly or indirectly from the Netherlands, there nevertheless also existed within France in the seventeenth century a substantial corpus of indigenous religious emblem literature which did not owe such a debt to the Netherlands, and this corpus embraces a number of different types of work, whose common thread is their religious intent, but all of which address this single intent in different ways.[1] It is striking to see once again in this domain as in so many others the extent to which there is a perceptible thread leading back to the sixteenth century. Several of the patterns which appear in the

---

[1]   Among the works in this corpus some actually use the word 'emblem' in the title, while others use emblematic techniques, but without actually using that word.

seventeenth-century French religious emblem book can be seen as natural developments from forms which were already present in France in the sixteenth century. We find, for example, a continuation of the fashion for biblical picture books which was a marked feature of the mid sixteenth century. We also find collections of emblems in which many of the individual images on which the emblems are based are traditional ones such as were seen in earlier collections, but the use to which they are put here is a specifically religious one. In such collections although a wide range of images is used, all are interpreted in one single way, and to one single purpose. Contrasting with these are other collections of religious emblems which are made up of a series of variations on one single unifying feature such as the heart or the Cross. Another variant form is provided by those collections of emblems in which the figures depict scenes from the Bible, and here we see a pattern developing which, unlike so many others, does not trace its ancestry back to the sixteenth-century French emblem book as such, although it does have clear affinities with the various biblical picture books which were published in the sixteenth century, and designed to look like emblem books. Among all these very diverse seventeenth-century religious emblem books, united only by their common religious motivation, some are designed for meditational purposes, and this is reflected in the particular structure they adopt, while others are not created with this particular function in mind. While many are the work of members of the Society of Jesus, several are composed by members of other religious orders, and some indeed are the work of writers and artists who do not claim membership of any particular order. In *Protestant Poetics and the Seventeenth-Century Religious Lyric*,[2] Barbara Lewalski suggests that religious emblems can be divided into five distinct categories which she identifies as: (i) 'discrete emblems on diverse subjects, which were given pervasive moral or Christian significance'; (ii) 'discrete emblems labelled sacred or Christian...often claiming that name from the use of biblical quotation or allusion in motto or inscription'; (iii) 'sacred emblem book using discrete plates ordered around a central theme' (such as a burning candle); (iv) the emblem book which 'transfers Eros and Anteros from the secular love emblems and presents them as characters in a series of exploits...rendering aspects of the spiritual life'; (v) 'schools of the heart, in which a heart figure is represented undergoing progressive purgation from sin and spiritual renovation'. This last category of heart emblems could, in fact, be merged with her third category of emblem books ordered around a single theme.

A number of biblical picture books were produced in the early seventeenth century which are very reminiscent of the picture-book versions of both the Old Testament and the New Testament, with verse text, which became so fashionable in France in the mid sixteenth century, and which were often produced by publishers specialising in emblem literature, like Janot in Paris or de Tournes in Lyon, and with the text also supplied in many cases by a writer of emblems. As early as 1539 Gilles Corrozet, one of the earliest French writers of an emblem book, produced a picture-book version of the first section of the Old Testament arranged like an emblem book, in a symmetrical

---

[2]   Princeton, 1979, pp.179-212.

pattern with each page containing a woodcut depiction of the biblical scene accompanied by a short summary of the scene in Latin, and a French quatrain paraphrasing this,[3] following this up a few years later with an equivalent version of the New Testament, in which the only differences from the earlier Old Testament work are that there is no Latin text, and the explanatory French verses are expanded to eight lines as opposed to four.[4] Conforming to this same pattern, the two main mid-century Lyon specialists in the production of illustrated literature also followed suit, each producing a similar picture-book version of both the Old Testament and the New Testament. Jean de Tournes published the *Quadrins historiques de la Bible* with verses by Claude Paradin and the *Figures du Nouveau Testament* with verses by Charles Fontaine in 1553 and 1554 respectively, while Guillaume Roville rather later similarly published a collection of *Figures de la Bible illustrée de huictains francoys pour l'interpretation et intelligence d'icelles* with verses by Guillaume Guéroult and an equivalent *Figures du Nouveau Testament illustrées de huictains francoys pour l'interpretation et intelligence d'icelles*, with verses by Claude de Pontoux in 1564 and 1570 respectively.[5] In all these biblical picture books, however, unlike conventional emblem books, the verses accompanying the woodcut images are narrative and/or descriptive rather than interpretative. Typical of their approach, for example, is Corrozet's quatrain accompanying the woodcut figure of Noah's Ark in his picture-book version of the Old Testament:

---

[3]   Although the main text is in the vernacular, the work is nevertheless given a Latin title, *Historiarum veteris testamenti icones ad vivum expressae. Unà cum brevi, sed quoad fieri potuit, dilucida earundem et Latina et Gallica expositione.* This Latin title follows, with only a slight change, that of an earlier version of the work published the previous year, which did not include Corrozet's French verses: *Historiarum veteris instrumenti icones, ad vivum expressae. Unà cum brevi sed quoad fieri potuit, dilucida earundem expositione* (Lyon, M and G Trechsel, 1538, 8°).

[4]   *Tapisserie de l'eglise chrestienne et catholique: en laquelle sont depainctes la nativité, vie, passion, mort, et resurrection de nostre Sauveur et Redempteur Jesus Christ. Avec un huictain soubz chacune hystoire, pour l'intelligence d'icelle.* Although this work was published by Etienne Groulleau rather than by Denis Janot, the fact that it is listed in the *Table des livres de Denys Janot, Imprimeur du Roy en langue françoyse* (Paris, D. Janot, n.d., 8°) indicates that Janot was in the process of publishing it when he died in 1544. After Janot's death uncompleted material like the *Tapisserie* passed into the hands of his successor, Etienne Groulleau.

[5]   For fuller discussion of these French sixteenth-century biblical picture books see Saunders, *Sixteenth-Century French Emblem Book,* pp.44-8. For discussion of the relative responsibility of writers and publishers in the production of such works see also Alison Saunders, 'The sixteenth-century French emblem book: writers and printers', *Studi francesi,* 92, 1987, pp.173-90. For a wide-ranging discussion of such works as produced in other parts of Europe as well as France see M. Engammare, 'Les Figures de la Bible. Le destin oublié d'un genre littéraire en image (XVIe-XVIIe s.)', *Mélanges de l'Ecole française de Rome. Italie et Méditerranée,* 106,2, 1994, pp.549-91.

Tous les humains par l'univers deluge
Furent peris, Noe le patriarche
(Du vueil de Dieu) pour se mectre à refuge
Avec les siens, entra dedans son arche.
                    (Corrozet, *Historiarum veteris testamenti icones*, B2r)

or similarly his *huitain* accompanying the woodcut depiction of the Crucifixion:

Luy estendu par ces gens inhumains,
Fut acomply ce que David escrit:
Ilz ont percé, & mes piedz, & mes mains
Nombré mes os, jusqu'à rendre l'esprit.
Pilate mit sur la croix un escrit,
Dequoy plusieurs furent depuys marriz:
Disans ainsi: Cestuy est Jesus Christ
De Nazaret, & le vray Roy des Juifz.
                    (Corrozet, *Tapisserie de l'eglise chrestienne*, M2r)

Superficially much the same pattern is still found at the very end of the sixteenth century in Paul Perrot de La Sale's *Tableaus sacrez...Qui sont toutes les histoires du Viel Testament representees & exposees selon leur sens en poesie françoise* of 1594, but with the significant difference that this much later work reveals a greater affinity with emblem books in that no longer are the verses accompanying the figures simply narrative or descriptive.[6] Instead they also include a clear moral lesson for the reader or onlooker to derive from the scene represented, such as was not present in the earlier sixteenth-century biblical picture books. This distinction is very apparent in, for example Perrot de La Sale's treatment of the Cain and Abel episode. The highly decorative woodcut figure gives a visual representation both of the sacrifice in the background and of Cain striking Abel in the foreground, and this is accompanied by the biblical reference to Genesis, and the brief Latin moral reflection 'Ab initio & deinceps inter bonos & malos perpetuum dissidium'. But unlike the earlier biblical picture books Perrot de La Sale's three-stanza French verse accompanying the figure and the French verse assumes awareness of the Cain and Abel story on the part of the reader, and rather than simply re-telling it concentrates instead on commenting on its implications for mankind:

L'Envie, & le desdain parents de la furie,
Sont cause qu'Abel est par Caïm massacré,
Dieu reprouve Caïm, & prend Abel à gré,
L'injustice demeure, & l'innocence crie.

---

[6]   Not every *tableau* in the collection includes an illustrative figure, but a large number do. Other than the brief Latin notes accompanying each *tableau* Perrot de La Sale's text is wholly in French. It is interesting that nevertheless the work was published in Frankfurt rather than in Perrot de La Sale's home town of Paris.

A ce commencement la justice opressee
  Marque les accidents de sa course advenir,
  Qu'elle a tousjours suivi, & suit pour parvenir
  Au triomphe d'honneur, dont on l'a desplacee.

Ne t'estonne donc point peuple esleu mais endure,
  Avec espoir & foy ces Caïms meurtriers,
  Leur reigne est ici bas, mais cil des droituriers
  S'assigne dans le ciel pour y faire demeure.
                 (Perrot de La Sale, *Tableaus sacrez*, pp.18-19)

The moral lesson expressed in this 'emblem' by Perrot de La Sale is intended to be of universal relevance, but this is not invariably the case. In, for example, his treatment of the Judgement of Solomon his approach is rather different. Here the moral lesson is more narrow directed towards the rulers of this world rather than towards the populace at large. The figure depicting Solomon with the child and the two claimant mothers is again accompanied by a brief Latin note 'Sola sapientia firmari & stabiliri imperium', and by a rather longer passage of verse narrating the story, but more importantly using it as a basis for comment on the particular responsibilities of kings, and their need to seek wisdom from God alone:

Celuy est roy vrayement
Lequel juge justement,
Et quoy qu'un throsne s'herite
Nul ce tiltre ne merite
S'il ne rend & ne maintient
Le droit à qu'il apartient,
Salomon en faict l'espreuve
Rendant chacun estonné
Pour son jugement donné
En tout sens l'arrest se treuve,
Egal, entier, & parfaict,
Sans qu'il mancque d'un seul traict.
L'enfant est rendu à celle
Qui est mere naturelle;
Veu l'affection qu'elle a
Au prix de cest'autre là.
Dessus la loy de prudence
Se fonde ceste sentence,
Et la prudence provient
De Dieu qui en faict largesse,
Et auquel seul il convient
O Roys de querir sagesse,
Et raison & jugement,
Qui veult regner justement.   (Perrot de La Sale, *Tableaus sacrez*, pp.148-9)

This verse is longer than that of the Cain and Abel *tableau*, and both are significantly longer than the very short verses typically found in the mid-sixteenth-century French biblical picture book, but nevertheless both are still relatively short and succinct in their treatment of the subject, and certainly no longer than many of the emblems of Aneau or Guéroult dating from earlier in the sixteenth century. Another aspect which distinguishes Perrot de La Sale's *Tableaus sacrez* from the earlier sixteenth-century biblical picture books is its lack of symmetry on the printed page. Not only are the individual verses of differing length and structure, but also instead of a full page or opening being devoted to each *tableau*, these are arranged in a continuous order without break from one to the next, and not every one is illustrated. This does not, however, invalidate it in any way as an emblem book, since many earlier emblem books - including those of Aneau and Guéroult - equally did not fulfil this criterion. Despite the fact that Perrot de La Sale describes his work as a collection of *tableaux sacrés* rather than a collection of *emblèmes sacrés*, and despite its purely biblical subject matter, the moralising interpretative element which he introduces brings the work much more closely into line with the emblematic tradition, than with that of earlier biblical picture books.

Within a few years of Perrot de La Sale's Frankfurt published *Tableaus sacrez* a similarly named collection of *Tableaux sacrez* was also published in Paris in 1601 by the prolific Jesuit, Louis Richeome. But whereas Perrot de La Sale simply describes himself as a priest on the title page of his work, with no further precision, Richeome states specifically that he is a member of the Society of Jesus, as was habitually the case in works produced by Jesuit writers,[7] and his particular allegiance is indeed very apparent in the work, which is quite different in motivation and approach from that of Perrot de La Sale. Whereas in the earlier work, despite the lack of symmetry there was a clearly emblematic approach with the succinct verse passages narrating briefly the biblical scene depicted prior to gloss its moral implications, Richeome's work is rather a meditational one, and the importance attached by the Jesuit philosophy to the close engagement of the contemplator with every detail of the subject of his meditation is very apparent in Richeome's much more discursive work. Richeome's text is in prose throughout, and in it he apostrophises the reader, pointing out to him as a spectator all the different features of the scene before proceeding to an exposition of its relationship to the holy sacrament. While it is true that Perrot de La Sale also apostrophised his reader, as for example in the last stanza of the Cain and Abel *tableau*, he did so rather differently, using the technique of direct address to the reader simply in order to convey to him authoritatively the message to be taken from the *tableau*. In contrast to this Richeome uses the technique in order to stimulate an emotional reaction on the part of the reader, as he is systematically led to contemplate one visual stimulus after another. The vivid ekphrastic descriptions which Richeome offers to his reader are in many ways reminiscent of those of Vigenère's translation of the *Images ou tableaux*

---

[7]   *Tableaux sacrez des figures mystiques du tres-auguste sacrifice et sacrement de l'Eucharistie...par Louis Richeome, Provençal de la Compagnie de Jesus.*

de platte peinture of Philostratus, of which the first (non-illustrated) edition had been published some twenty years before Richeome's *Tableaux sacrez*, in 1578.[8] Characteristic of Richeome's very different style from that of Perrot de la Sale is his evocation of the Garden of Eden, in which from the very beginning the spectator's emotional participation is engaged, as not just his sense of sight but also his other senses, including even that of smell, are stimulated:

> Chrestiens spectateurs, vous sçavez que cest admirable Chroniqueur & divin Cosmografe Moyse, dit en l'histoire de la creation que Dieu avoit planté au commencement un jardin de volupté vers l'Orient, auquel il mit l'homme qu'il avoit formé. C'est ceste belle & spacieuse region que le Peintre vous represente en ce tableau. Elle est haute d'assiete, riche de biens, rare en beauté, gracieuse en sejour, & abondante en toute sorte de delices. La terre y est en quelques endroicts applanie en platte campagne, en d'autres relevée en petits tertres & collines, chargees de plantes & d'arbres de rare bonté. Au lieu où elle est la plus haute, vous y remarquez une fontaine qui surgissant à gros boüillons, & se formant en riviere, serpente & arrouse tout le jardin, vers la fin duquel elle se divise en quatre chefs, & fait quatre grands fleuves coulans en divers endroicts de la terre. Le premier desquels appellé Phison jette au bord le sable d'or, & plusieurs belles pierres precieuses, mais personne ne les ramasse, parce qu'il n'y a encor qu'Adam & Eve au monde: leurs enfans les cueilliront apres. L'air y est tres-pur & tres-subtil: C'est pourquoy vous n'y voyez aucune marque de nuages ou broüillars, le Soleil luisant tousjours clair & brillant. Quant est du feu, qui est l'element le plus hautain, il se tient coy en son regne sur l'air, il contribue neantmoins sa lueur & chaleur d'une douce temperature, à guise de flambeaux du ciel. Ceste gaye verdure, dont la terre est tapissee par tout, & ces fleurs odoriferantes, qui vont diaprant de mille couleurs ceste verdure, & celles qui sont espanies aux arbres, monstrent le Printemps, avec lequel les autres saisons font leur quartier ensemble, & partant l'Esté à ja fait jaunir la moisson en ceste rase campagne, & meurir plusieurs fruicts de sa cueillette en ces prairies & vergers voisins. Comme aussi l'Automne monstre ses belles grappes de raisins meurs en ces collines-là, combien que la vigne ne soit encor plantee & cultivee par Noé...
> (Richeome, *Tableaux sacrez*, 1609, b3r-4r)[9]

At the point when Richeome first published his *Tableaux sacrez* in 1601, no

---

[8] See, for example, above, chapter 5, pp.177-80.

[9] See also Richeome's insistent apostrophe of the reader, urging him as onlooker to identify with, and dwell on every detail of the sleeping figure of Elijah beneath the juniper tree (1 Kings, 19, verse 5): 'N'avez vous pas compassion du bon Elie qui dort à l'ombre de ce genevre, plus semblable à un mort qu'à un homme dormant? Voyez-vous son visage blesme & desfaict, & baigné de sueur froide? Sa teste negligemment panchée vers la terre sur le costé, ses yeux entr'ouverts, ses bras jettez ça & là, nul signe de respiration en la bouche, & toute la posture du corps estendu, comme s'il venoit de rendre l'esprit...' (1609 ed., t5r).

illustrated edition of the *Images ou tableaux de platte peinture* of Philostratus had been published. Not until 1614 did the Veuve Abel l'Angelier publish the first of a series of illustrated editions of the work, and this would therefore have been much too late to influence Richeome. It is interesting, therefore, that Richeome does actually include some engraved figures in his *Tableaux sacrez*, providing thereby a visual trigger as well as a purely verbal one in the form of ekphrastic descriptions. Only a minority of the *Tableaux sacrez*, however, are illustrated, but given the vivid detail of his verbal descriptions, like those of Philostratus, the very beautiful, and highly ornate engraved figures which do accompany some of the *tableaux* (including notably that of the Garden of Eden) are not necessary for comprehension, although they undoubtedly add to the aesthetic appeal of the work.[10]

Although the works of both Perrot de La Sale and Richeome contain clear, albeit different, emblematic features, neither writer actually uses the word 'emblem', opting instead for the word 'tableaux', harking back, perhaps to their earlier ancestors, the sixteenth-century biblical picture books, and also - in the case of Richeome, at least - to the probable influence of Vigenère's *Images ou tableaux de platte peinture*. However, dating from a few years later than their two works we find another biblical picture book (in this case wholly in Latin) - by Bernard Sellius - in which the word 'emblem' *is* used in the title. Published in Amsterdam in 1613, his collection of *Emblemata sacra* comprises a series of full-page engravings of scenes from the Bible, each with a source reference, and each accompanied by a Latin title and a short four-line Latin verse.[11] Unlike the previous two works, symmetry of layout is once again observed here, in the manner of the earlier sixteenth-century biblical picture books, in

---

[10]   The Paris publisher Laurens Sonnius produced two editions of the work, one in 1601 and another in 1609. Both were illustrated, but curiously the earlier edition includes twice as many engravings as the later edition. Even more curious is the fact that in several of the *tableaux* which are illustrated in both editions, the publisher uses different engravings (though both depicting the same scene) in the two editions. Stressing Richeome's predilection for such literary painting, Terence Cave sees parallels between his use of the *peinture parlante* and that used by César de Nostredame in his poetry (*Devotional Poetry in France c.1570-1613*, Cambridge, 1969, pp.278-80).

[11]   *Emblemata sacra, è praecipuis utriusque Testamenti historiis concinnata a Bernardo Sellio Noviomago & a Petro vander Burgio figures aeneis elegantissimis illustrata*, Amsterdam, M. Colinius, 1613, folio obl. A copy of this edition is held in the Estampes of the BnF, as also a copy of a later edition dating from 1639. Praz, who states categorically that 'These are not emblems, but illustrations of the Bible', does not mention either of these editions, but cites only a later edition published in Amsterdam in 1654, from which the name of Sellius is excised. (Praz, p.324). The vast majority of Sellius's emblems are taken from Genesis, although a few are also taken from other parts of the Old Testament, and likewise a few from the Gospels. For an interesting discussion of the use of a series of 13 engraved figures from Hugo's *Pia desideria* to illustrate 'emblems' on the Song of Songs in a large Old Testament picture book (containing approximately 800 figures), the *Bibels tresoor* published in Amsterdam in 1646, see Max Engammare, 'Dans le Jardin du Bien-Aimé. Illustration et exégèse du *Cantique des Cantiques* au XVIIe siècle', *Graphè*, 8, *Le Cantique des Cantiques*, 1999, pp.123-62.

that one full page is devoted to each emblem, and the structure of the verses follows a regular pattern throughout, unlike the varied verse patterns and non-symmetrical layout of Perrot de La Sale, and the prose of Richeome. But, paradoxically, whereas Perrot de La Sale's verses offered a clear moral lesson for the reader to derive from the biblical scene depicted, thereby making his work more akin to an emblem book than a biblical picture book, the verse components of Sellius's emblems conform rather more to the pattern of the sixteenth-century biblical picture book in which the verse commonly simply describes the scene, rather than extrapolating from it a moral lesson.[12] As with Richeome's earlier work, the artistic quality of the engravings in Sellius's collection of sacred emblems is also very high, as for example in the representation in the opening emblem of the Garden of Eden, and the central scene of the creation of Adam, surrounded by beautifully engraved animals. This opening emblem is given the Latin heading *Ad umbrata humanitate divinitas*, and the engraved figure is accompanied by the quatrain:

> Nil non esse Dei magnum pote: si tamen ullum
> Fert palmam, palmam fabricae fert hominis.
> Vasta poli moles terraeque homo sed simul unus
> Effigiésque orbis, effigiésque Dei.
> > (Sellius, *Emblemata sacra*, 1613, emblem 1)

Although the text of Sellius's emblem book is wholly in Latin, a copy of the first edition of 1613 in the *Estampes* of the BnF is particularly interesting in that in it a French prose translation of both the title and the verse is added to each emblem in a neat seventeenth-century manuscript hand, thereby transforming it into a bilingual emblem work. The title to the opening emblem is thus rendered as *L'humanité esquisse de la Divinité*, and the verse as:

> Dieu ne peut rien faire que de grand, la creation de l'homme est son plus grand ouvrage. La grandeur enorme du ciel & de la Terre est admirable; mais l'Homme seul porte & la ressemblance de l'univers & la ressemblance de Dieu.   (Sellius, *Emblemata sacra*, 1613, emblem 1)

The phrase '*emblemata sacra*' as used here by Sellius denotes an emblem book based on figures derived from the Bible, but it does not necessarily have to carry this meaning. Several other collections of *emblemata sacra* were published across Europe in the late sixteenth century and early seventeenth century, many of which were either

---

[12] Daniel Russell argues that neither Perrot de La Sale's collection of *Tableaus sacrez* nor Sellius's *Emblemata sacra* can be deemed to be emblem books any more than could the earlier biblical picture books, since all are composed from extracts from one single source: 'While these works all bear some striking formal similarities to emblems, most of them are obviously not emblem books...Above all they differ from emblems in that they are constructed by fragmenting works that are coherent wholes existing as discrete literary works.' (*The Emblem and Device in France*, p.172).

bilingual or polyglot,[13] of which probably the best known is Daniel Cramer's *Emblemata sacra*, published in Frankfurt in a polyglot Latin, German, French and Italian text, in order to capture the widest market.[14] But in Cramer's collection, although biblical references are included, the engraved figures on which the emblems are based do not depict scenes from the Bible, as in Sellius's work. Instead they offer allegorical representations, for the most part showing the heart undergoing various activities, and it is only the textual gloss provided by Cramer in his accompanying verses which makes his emblems sacred, rather than - as in Sellius's work - both the text and the figures contributing to this same message. Among the more ingenious of Cramer's emblems is that depicting a winged heart perched on the back of a snail, and being transported thereby across a narrow bridge over a precipice, with the motto *Circumspecte*, accompanied by the text of Psalm 16 (17) verse 5 ('Hold up my goings in thy paths, that my footsteps slip not')[15] in Latin, French and German:

> Sustenta gressus meos in semitis tuis: & non moveantur vestigia mea.

> Erhalt meinen Gang auff deinen Fussstengen, dass meine Tritt nicht gleitten.

> Ayant affermi mes pas en tes sentiers, les plantes de mes pieds n'ont point chancelé.

by a Latin couplet:

> Repo, eo, serpo, volo, quocunque eo, semita falsa est,
> Ne à recto movear tramite, CHRISTUS agat.

and by quatrains in Latin and French:

---

[13]   Other collections of *emblemata sacra* cited by Praz include Augustus Callias's collection of *Emblemata sacra e libris Mosis excerpta*, published in Heidelberg in 1591, 8°; Bartholomew Hulsius's *Emblemata sacra, dat is, eenighe geestlicke sinnebeelden, met niewe ghedichten...ende bedenckinghen...door B.H*, n.p. (Amsterdam?), 1631, 4°; Hesius's *Gulielmi Hesii Antverpiensis è Societate Iesu emblemata sacra de fide, spe, charitate*, Antwerp, B. Moretus (Officina Plantiniana), 1636, 12°.

[14]   In the original version published by Lucas Jennis in 1622 the collection comprised only fifty emblems, but in 1624 it was doubled in size, and the original collection became Part 1 of a 2-part collection: *Emblemata sacra. Hoc est decades quinque emblematum ex Sacra Scriptura, de dulcissimo nomine & cruce Iesu Christi, figuris aeneis incisorum. Pars prior primò per Reverend. Dn. Danielem Cramerum, SS. Theologiae Doctorem collecta. Postea vero a Dn. Cunrado Bachmanno...epigrammatibus Latino-Germanicis illustrata, tandem opera M.C.R. versibus & rhythmis Gallo Italicis declarata, ornata & ad instar Philothecae Christianae sive albi amicorum exhibita*, Frankfurt, L. Jennis, 1624, 8°.

[15]   We saw earlier Hugo's equally ingenious emblem in the *Pia desideria* based on this same passage, depicting *Amor divinus* gently encouraging *Anima* to come towards him in her baby-walker. See above, chapter 5, p.192

Est via lubrica subqué via est profundus hiatus,
  Decipiens gressus lubricitate meos.
At tu, CHRISTE, pedes firma & mihi dirige passus
Ne cadam, & in casu funditus inteream.

Le sentier est estroict, lubrique & dangereux,
En ce monde incertain, & par tout trop scabreux:
Que donques je ne tombe & ne sois renversé
Seigneur guide mon pas, comme tu l'as dressé.
        (Cramer, *Emblemata sacra*, 1624, Book 1, emblem 49, N8v-O1r)

as well as in German and Italian.

The Carthusian Jean Martin uses the equivalent French phrase '*emblemes sacrez*' in the title of his *Paradis terrestre* of 1655, a work in which - as with Cramer's *Emblemata sacra* - the engraved figures are likewise not biblical in inspiration. Although the figures are inevitably intended to stimulate allegorical interpretation, they are more realistic in what they depict than Cramer's highly stylised heart figures. The full title of the work, *Le paradis terrestre, ou emblemes sacrez de la solitude, dediez au saint ordre des Chartreux. Avec un recueil des plus beaux vers Latins & François sur la solitude, la plus part non encore imprimez*,[16] explains clearly its particular orientation: this is an emblem book carrying a very particular message of special relevance to Martin's own order. Each emblem is interpreted as reflecting on one aspect or another of the virtue of solitude as practised by the Carthusians. Thus, although we find several traditional emblematic figures relating to the countryside in this work, they are all given a particular gloss relating to the theme of solitude. For example, the second emblem of the collection depicts the familiar figure of a beehive commonly used in many generalist emblem books (see fig.16), but the interpretation given here is not based on the obvious theme of the hardworking nature of the bees, but rather on the fact that they are all working hard in the isolation of their own individual little cells. Just like the bees the Carthusians strive in solitude to achieve a state of virtue. The engraved figure with its Latin motto, *Labor intus*, (A2v) is accompanied by a brief title 'Une Ruche de Mouches à Miel' and the Latin couplet:

Stipant, & dulci distendunt nectare cellas
  Sedulae apes, totus sed labor intus inest.
          (Martin, *Le paradis terrrestre*, A3r)

Again in emblem 19 the familiar image of the mighty oak tree being broken by the wind, while the humble reed which bends before the wind is spared is interpreted with particular reference to the Carthusian order. The engraving is accompanied by the motto *Cedens resisto* and French title 'Un Chesne déraciné par le vent, & un roseau debout proche du Chesne', and the Latin couplet:

---

[16] Paris, J. Henault, 1655, 8°.

Procumbit Quercus vulsa à radicibus imis,
  Cedendo intereà perstat arundo levis. (Martin, *Le paradis terrestre*, K1r)

Figure 16: Martin, *Le paradis terrestre*, Paris, 1655, A2v.

But as well as explaining the conventional lesson to be derived from this image,
Martin's French prose commentary also relates it to the solitary life of the Carthusian:

> Qu'avez-vous veu dans le desert, disoit Nostre Seigneur à ses Apostres, sinon
> un roseau agité du vent? Il entendoit parler de S. Jean Baptiste; dont la vie
> retirée est le veritable modele de nostre Solitaire. Les grands employs de la
> vie active sont exposez bien souvent à d'horribles tempestes, & la plus solide
> vertu se void quelque-fois contrainte de donner du nez en terre par la violence
> de l'orage. Mais le Solitaire est tapy contre terre, & ne donne aucune prise à
> son ennemy... (Martin, *Le paradis terrrestre*, K1r-v)

The importance that Martin attaches to ensuring that his message is clearly understood is evident in the fact that each of the twenty emblems of the collection is accompanied by some two pages of prose commentary in French, explaining in detail the particular significance to be derived from it.

Very different in approach, although not dissimilar in theme is another short bilingual Latin/French emblem book dating from ten years earlier than Martin's *Paradis terrestre*, and likewise devoted to praise of the virtues of the life of the cloister. The identity of the author of the *Lux claustri. La lumiere du cloistre. Representées par figures emblematiques*[17] is not known, but the engravings are by Jacques Callot, and the work is thus usually listed under his name, as is likewise another similarly structured emblem book on the theme of the Virgin Mary, also based on his engravings, the *Vita beatae Mariae virginis matris Dei. Emblematibus delineata. Vie de la bien-heureuse vierge Marie mere de Dieu. Representée par figures emblematiques.*[18] Unlike Martin's emblems, the twenty-seven emblems of the *Lux claustri* are not accompanied by any form of commentary. Instead, each short emblem stands alone, comprising no more than an engraved figure preceded by a bilingual motto or title, and followed by a Latin couplet and an equivalent French quatrain. But, as with Martin's collection of emblems, the engraved figures created by Callot as the basis for the *Lux claustri* again employ for the most part conventional emblematic themes onto which a particular interpretation is imposed in the accompanying verses. While there are occasional emblems in the collection in which the engraved figure itself depicts a sacred theme, such as St Teresa embracing the Cross in emblem 21,[19] these are the exception, and more commonly the practice in this emblem book, as in the *Paradis terrrestre* is to take familiar, non-religious emblematic figures, and subject these to a particular religious interpretation which they did not enjoy when used in earlier emblem books. Of such a kind are the caged bird of *Captiva, sed secura. Dans sa prison il est en seureté*:

---

[17] *Lux claustri. La lumiere du cloistre. Representées par figures emblematiques, dessignées & gravées par Jacques Callot*, Paris, F. Langlois, 1646, 4°.

[18] *Vita beatae Mariae virginis matris Dei. Emblematibus delineata. Vie de la bien-heureuse vierge Marie mere de Dieu. Representée par figures emblematiques, dessignées & gravées par Jacques Callot*, Paris, F. Langlois, 1646, 4°. In a chapter on Jacques Callot in *Emblèmes et pensée symbolique en Lorraine (1525-1633)* Paulette Choné suggests (pp.732-40) that the text of both books may be the work of François Rennel.

[19] The engraving of St Teresa and the Cross is accompanied by the title/motto *Haeret pede firmo. Elle demeure icy d'un pied ferme arrestée* and by a Latin couplet:
> Hanc indivulsus stringat complexibus aram,
>   Se qui mens dubio fluctuet acta metu.
and equivalent French quatrain:
> Qui se vouë à Jesus pour embrasser sa Croix,
> Taschant de l'imiter, doit se clouer sur elle;
> Et ne prendre autre voye, & n'entendre autre voix,
> Que celle du Pasteur, dont l'exemple l'appelle. (F1r, emblem 21)

Callidus incidias tendit, nec cantica laudat
  Felis: si caveam deseris, ungue cades.
Cet Oiseau prisonnier chante dans ce haut lieu,
Sans avoir peur du Chat, qui sans cesse l'éclaire;
Malgré tous les Demons, le Moine craignant Dieu,
Psalmodie, & benit sa Prison volontaire.
          (Callot, *Lux claustri*, C2r, emblem 10)

or the goldfinch feeding on thistles of *Nil aspera terrent. Rien de rude ne l'espouvante*:

Carduus horrenti non terret achantida spinâ!
  Tu Christi spinas mens malefida fugis.
Cet Oiseau patient, pour se nourrir le corps,
Sur les chardons piquans fait des douces rapines?
Et le Moine au Desert fait d'illustres efforts,
Pour suivre Jesus-Christ au milieu des Espines.
         (Callot, *Lux claustri*, D1r, emblem 13)[20]

Even the rather unlikely figure of Narcissus, who regularly appears in many emblem books from that of Alciato onwards, is included here to demonstrate that even the most devout monk can be subject to vanity, in *Se sedum deperit, perit. L'excez de l'Amour propre est cause de sa perte* (see fig.17):

Quid prosit placuisse sibi, tua facta fatentur
  Stulte puer: sapiens displicet ipse sibi.
Narcisse en se mirant au bord d'une fontaine,
Espris de sa beauté se laissa cheoir dans l'eau:
Ainsi, méme au Desert, quand une Ame est trop vaine,
Se perdant, elle perd ce qu'elle a de plus beau.
         (Callot, *Lux claustri*, F2r, emblem 22)[21]

In the other emblem book for which Callot also provided the engravings, the *Vita beatae Mariae virginis...Vie de la bien-heureuse vierge Marie*, exactly the same structure is followed in the edition of the work which was published in Paris by the same publisher and in the same year as the *Lux claustri*. The two works are clearly

---

[20] La Perrière used the caged bird singing in captivity in emblem 38 of his *Theatre des bons engins*, while Camerarius much later used the thistle-eating goldfinch in emblem 75 of his third book of emblems on the natural world, *Symbolorum et emblematum ex volatilibus et insectis desumtorum centuria tertia collecta* (Nuremberg, P. Kaufmann, 1596, 4°).
[21] Alciato, *Emblemata*, 1550, E7r, emblem 77, *Philautia*. For details of the use of Narcissus in other emblem books see A. Henkel and A. Schöne, *Emblemata. Handbild zur Sinnbildkunst des XVI. und XVII. Jahrhunderts*, Stuttgart, 1967, cols 1627-8. (Hereafter cited as 'Henkel and Schöne').

SE SE DVM DEPERIT, PERIT.[22]

L'excez de l'Amour propre est cause de sa perte.

Quid profit placuisse sibi , tua facta fatentur
Stulte puer : sapiens displicet ipse sibi.

NARCISSE en se mirant au bord d'vne fontaine,
Espris de sa beauté se laissa cheoir dans l'eau:
Ainsi ,méme au Desert, quand vne Ame est trop
vaine.
Se perdant, elle perd ce qu'elle a de plus beau.

F ij

Figure 17: Callot, *Lux claustri*, Paris, 1646, F2r.

intended as partner volumes, albeit on different themes. Although the overall subject
is the Virgin Mary, it is again only the verses which give this interpretation to
engraved figures which - as in the *Lux claustri* - do not themselves relate directly to
the Virgin, but instead depict once again familiar emblematic subjects such as, for
example, the vine and the elm, the two palm trees leaning together, and the pearl-
bearing oyster. In *Protegit, haud foecundat ulmus*, the engraved figure of the vine
receiving support from the elm, used in many emblem books from Alciato onwards,[22]
is here glossed as denoting the Virgin Mary receiving support from Joseph:

> Connûbii lex ista tui, castissime Joseph,
>   Non aliter coniux Virginis esse potés.
> La vigne a un ormeau fortement engagée,
> Suporte mieux le faix de son fruit meurissant:
> Et Marie a Joseph jointe d'un noeud puissant,
> Par ce ferme soutien est beaucoup soulagée.
>   (Callot, *Vita beatae Mariae virginis*, B2r, emblem 6)

while in *Vis secretior urget*, the two palm trees leaning tenderly together denote not
just living in harmony, as they did in Cats's *Vivite concordes*,[23] but more specifically
the harmonious affection between the Virgin Mary and Elizabeth, as also that between
their respective sons, Jesus and John the Baptist:

> Dulcia cognatae sunt Virginis oscula: nempe,
>   Illa quod impense quaerit, id ista gerit.
> La mere de St Jean, & la Vierge embrassées,
> Et Jesus caressant son saint Ambassadeur.
> Sont figurés icy par la puissante ardeur,
> Qui tient estroitement ces palmes enlacées.
>   (Callot, *Vita beatae Mariae virginis*, B4r, emblem 8)

and in *Obstetricante coelo*, the oyster conceiving its pearl from the heaven-given dew,
used earlier by both Camerarius and Covarrubias,[24] is interpreted as signifying the
Immaculate Conception:

---

[22]   Alciato, *Emblemata*, 1550, L6v, emblem 172, *Amicitia etiam post mortem durans*. For
details of the use of the vine and elm in other emblem books see Henkel and Schöne, cols 259-
60.
[23]   J. Cats, *Emblemata moralia et aeconomica*, in *Proteus ofte Minne-beelden verandert in
sinne-beelden*, Rotterdam, P. van Waesberge, 1627, 4°, Aaa1v.
[24]   Camerarius, *Symbolorum et emblematum ex aquatilibus et reptilibus desumtorum centuria
quarta*, Nuremberg, P. Kaufmann, 1604, 4°, emblem 59, *Clarescunt, aethere claro*; Sebastian
de Covarrubias Orozco, *Emblemas morales*, Madrid, L. Sanchez, 1610, 4°, *Centuria* II,
emblem 86. Among his little collection of twenty emblems, Jean Martin also included one on
the oyster in his *Paradis terrestre*, with the motto *Coelo plena salum respuo* (emblem 9).

Quis partum sacra Virgo tuum fando explicet? à quo,
  Et dolor omnis abest, & pudor omnis abest.
La Rosée a formé dans sa riche coquille,
Cette perle qui luit d'un éclat triomphant:
L'esprit sainct a produict ce Dieu qui est enfant,
Dans les pudicques flancs de cette chaste fille.
                    (Callot, *Vita beatae Mariae virginis*, C3r, emblem 11)

The publishing history of the *Vita beatae Mariae virginis..Vie de la bien-heureuse vierge Marie* is complex. Whereas only one edition of the *Lux claustri* was published - in Paris by François Langlois in 1646 - three undated editions of the *Vita beatae Mariae virginis...Vie de la bien-heureuse vierge Marie* were published in addition to that produced by Langlois in 1646 as a partner edition to the *Lux claustri*, and in all of these the text is different. A further variant version of the work, (including the engravings but no text) exists in the Getty Museum. In the 1646 edition (quoted here) each emblematic engraving is accompanied by a Latin motto, together with a Latin distich and a French quatrain. In one of the undated editions the mottoes are in French rather than in Latin, and there is a Latin distich, but no French quatrain,[25] while the other two follow the pattern of the *Lux claustri*, and include both Latin *and* French mottoes, together with a Latin distich and a French quatrain.[26] While the Latin mottoes remain the same in all editions that include them, the French mottoes in the undated Benoît Audran edition, in which they appear alone, are different from those which appear together with Latin mottoes in the other two undated editions.[27] Similarly, while the Latin distichs remain constant, there is considerable textual variation in the French quatrains from edition to edition. Thus, for example, the quatrain of emblem 11 on the pearl-bearing oyster appears in a variant form in the Benoît Audran edition, opening with a more traditional allusion to

---

[25] A copy of this edition, published in Paris under the title *Emblesmes. Sur la vie de la mere de Dieu. Vita beatae Mariae virginis matris Dei emblematibus delineata* (Paris, B. Audran, n.d., 8° obl.) is housed in Glasgow University Library. A facsimile of this copy is available, which includes in the preliminaries the text of the 1646 edition (*Emblesmes sur la vie de la Mere de Dieu (ca 1646)*, ed. C.N. Smith, Menston, 1974). No other copy of this edition is known.

[26] The unique copy of one edition, entitled *La vie de la mere de Dieu representee par divers emblesmes. Vita beatae Mariae virginis matris Dei emblematibus delineata* (n.p.n.d., 4°) is housed in Utrecht University Library, while copies of the other, with the slightly different title *Vie de la mere de Dieu representée par emblesmes. Vita beatae Mariae virginis matris Dei emblematibus delineata* (n.p.n.d., 4°) are housed *inter alia* in the Bibliothèque nationale de France, the Huntington Library and Harvard University Library. The unique copy in the Getty Museum which contains only the engraved figures without any text gives only the standard Latin title, without any French version. For details of all editions see *BFEB*, vol.1, nos 134-7.

[27] For example, the French motto accompanying emblem 6 on the vine and the elm in the undated Benoît Audran edition where it appears alone is *Ceste chaste union la met en seureté*, whereas in the undated editions which give no publisher's name the motto is *Cet arbre est ce qui la protege*.

the role played by the sun in the creation of the pearl, such as is not included in the other version quoted above which referred only to the dew, rather than to the dew *and* the sun:

> La Rosée a formé dans sa riche coquille
> Cette Perle qui luit aux rayons du Soleil
> Et dans les chastes flancs d'une divine Fille,
> L'Esprit sainct a produit cét Enfant sans pareil.[28]

Praz has rightly described the *Lux claustri* and *Vita beatae Mariae virginis matris Dei...Vie de la bien-heureuse vierge Marie* as 'two of the most attractive emblem books'[29] and in view of their undoubted great charm, and also of the distinguished engraver responsible for the illustrations, it is remarkable that the author of the text remains unknown and that the two works are so little discussed.[30]

When in 1667 Augustin Chesneau produced a French version of his *Orpheus eucharisticus*, which had originally been published in Latin ten years earlier in 1657, only two years after Martin's *Paradis terrestre*, like Martin he also incorporated the phrase '*emblemes sacrez*' into the vernacular title, *Emblemes sacrez sur le tres-saint et tres-adorable sacrement de l'Eucharistie*,[31] although he did not do use the word *sacra* in the much longer title of the original Latin version, *Orpheus eucharisticus*,[32]

---

[28] Similarly two variant forms of the quatrain accompanying the figure of the salamander in the opening emblem, *Chaldaeo praevalet una Deo*, are found:
> Sans me brusler jamais, je vis parmi la flâme,
> Et la Vierge au milieu du crime originel,
> Dans le brasier commun n'a point bruslé son Ame,
> Par l'absolu pouvoir de l'Arbitre Eternel. (Paris, F.Langlois, 1646)
and:
> Je vis sans me brûler au milieu de la flame:
> Et la Vierge au milieu du crime originel,
> Par labsolu pouvoir de l'Arbitre eternel,
> Dans le brasier commun n'a point brûlé son Ame.
> (*Vie de la mere de Dieu representée par emblesmes*, n.p.n.d.)
although in this case it is simply a case of the order of the lines being rearranged, rather than of any significant modification to the content.

[29] Praz, p.198.

[30] Daniel Russell does not mention them in either *The Emblem and Device in France* or *Emblematic Structures in Renaissance French Culture*. Similarly Jean-Marc Chatelain does not include them in his anthology, *Livres d'emblèmes et de devises, une anthologie*. Even studies devoted specifically to Callot's engravings habitually ignore them. Unusually they are discussed in some detail by Paulette Choné (see above, footnote 18), and by Anne-Elisabeth Spica, in *Symbolique humaniste et emblématique. L'évolution et les genres (1580-1700)*, pp. 348-50.

[31] Paris, F. Lambert, 1667, 8°.

[32] *Orpheus eucharisticus. Sive Deus absconditus humanitatis illecebris illustriores mundi partes ad se pertrahens, ultroneas arcanae maiestatis adoratrices. Opus novum. In varias historicorum emblematum aeneis tabulis incisorum centurias distinctum, quae strictâ,*

in which the emblems are simply described as emblems. Again, as with Martin's emblems, and indeed with those of Callot, Chesneau's sacred emblems are not based on representations of actual biblical scenes, but rather on a broad range of subject matter onto which Chesneau, a member of the Augustinian order, then imposes a specifically theological interpretation. Chesneau's work is, however, altogether a much larger and more grandiose creation than that of Martin, containing one hundred emblems as opposed to a mere twenty, and designed to embrace all aspects of God's creation, with the emblems systematically grouped according to subject matter: *humana sacra*; *humana profana*; *aves*; *quadrupedes*; *pisces*; *serpentes*; *insecta*; *zoophyta*; *arbores*; *flores*; *plantae*; *fructus*; *astra*; *meteora*; *montes*; *fontes fluvii*; *gemmae*; *aromata*.[33] As so often we find once again familiar emblematic figures being used by Chesneau, as for example the halcyon in the *Aves* section:

> Alcion nidulo clausa hyeme elementa tranquillans.
> *Ex latebris coelumque, solumque serenat*
> Dans ce petit nid qui l'enserre,
> Il calme le ciel, et la terre.
>
> (Chesneau, *Orpheus eucharisticus*, P2r, emblem 28)

or the remora in the *Pisces* section:

> Echeneis navem ventis impulsam sistens.
> *Potens exili in corpore fraenum*
> La vertu de mon petit corps
> Resiste aux plus rudes efforts.
>
> (Chesneau, *Orpheus eucharisticus*, Gg5v, emblem 68)

or the elm and vine in the *Arbores* section:

---

solutâque oratione explanantur, adiectis authorum fontibus ex quibus eruuntur...Authore P.Augustino Chesneau Victreensi communitatis Bituricensis Ordinis Eremitarum Sancti Augustini sacrae theologiae lectore Paris, F. Lambert, 1657, 8°. (The British Library copy of this edition is bound with the arms of Pope Alexander VII.)

[33]   As Chatelain has noted in his *Livres d'emblèmes et de devises, une anthologie* (p.153), there is a parallel between this classification adopted by Chesneau and that adopted rather earlier by the Jesuit Nicolas Caussin in his *Polyhistor symbolicus. Electorum symbolorum, & parabolarum historicarum stromata, XII. libris complectens. Auctore P. Nicolao Caussino Trecensi è Societate Iesu* (Paris, R. de Beauvais, 1618, 4°). This unillustrated collection of hieroglyphs, which forms a sequel to Caussin's compilation of Egyptian hieroglyphic material entitled *De symbolica Aegyptiorum sapientia* (*Electorum symbolorum et parabolarum historicarum syntagmata. Ex Horo, Clemente, Epiphanio & aliis cum notis & observationibus. Auctore P. Nicolao Caussino Trecensi è Societate Iesu*, Paris, R. de Beauvais, 1618, 4°) similarly groups them according to their different categories of existence - birds, animals, plants, stones etc.

Vitis ulmum collapsam amplexu fovens, et vis coronans.
Cadentis amicae perstat in amplexu
L'amour qui les lie est si fort,
Qu'il dure mesme apres la mort.
                    (Chesneau, *Orpheus eucharisticus*, Qq8r, emblem 89)[34]

Figure 18: Chesneau, *Emblemes sacrez*, Paris, 1667, M2v.

Not only does Chesneau's work contain a much larger number of emblems than

---

[34]   In the *Emblemes sacrez* these Latin titles are rendered as: 'L'Alcyon calmant avec son petit Nid les Elemens, au plus fort de l'Hyver' (D5v); 'L'Echeneis, arrétant un Navire fortement poussé par les vents' (T5v); and 'La Vigne, qui embrasse l'Orme abbatu & le couronne de ses raisins' (M2v).

that of Jean Martin, but - in the original Latin version at least - it also includes a much more substantial section of commentary accompanying each emblem. Each engraved emblem includes within the engraving a Latin motto and a French couplet, but thereafter follow two substantial passages of Latin verse, the first focusing on the content of the engraved figure and the second (entitled *Apodosis*) on the implications of the emblem from a theological point of view. Then follow two further passages of Latin prose, of which the first, entitled *Fons emblematis*, again focuses on the content of the emblem, while the second, the *Interpretatio*, focuses on its significance. Altogether this material runs to five or six pages per emblem in the Latin version. But in the French version, published ten years later, all this material is drastically cut, to the extent that each emblem (including its commentary) can be contained within the much shorter space of a double opening. In this heavily abridged vernacular version, the typographic verse passages are excised, and the prose sections are shortened to the extent that the *Source* (now occupying no more than a few lines) can be contained on the same page as the engraved figure, while the *Explication* occupies no more than the single facing recto. It is interesting that the element which is entirely sacrificed in the interests of concision is the verse. Where in the sixteenth century an emblem comprising figure and verse might well be accompanied by a prose commentary, an emblem comprising nothing but prose to accompany the figure would be very unusual. However, particularly within the domain of meditational emblem books in the seventeenth century, we do find such a pattern emerging, primarily though not exclusively in the hands of the Jesuits, in which the verse element comprises no more than at best a couplet, often incorporated into the engraved figure, while all the main printed text is in prose. We see an early manifestation of this phenomenon in the 1601 *Veridicus christianus* and 1607 *Paradisus sponsi et sponsae* by the Jesuit Jan David, or again somewhat later in the 1629 *Schola cordis* and 1635 *Regia via crucis* of the Benedictine Benedict van Haeften. The explanation of this difference between Latin and vernacular versions of a work must be that the vernacular French reading audience was perceived to have less interest in, or perhaps less tolerance of a substantial gloss to the emblems than the better educated and more sophisticated Latin readership.

In, for example, emblem 89, on the theme of the elm and the vine, the engraved figure with its brief Latin and French text included within the engraving is accompanied in the original Latin version by a four-line Latin verse:

> Claviculis aetate gravem pro viribus ulmum
> Fulcit, & amplexu vitis amica fovet.
> Palmitibus stringit moribundam, uvisque coronat,
> Mortis in extremâ sorte fidelis amans.
> (Chesneau, *Orpheus eucharisticus*, Qq8r)

and a much more substantial verse *apodosis*:

> Talis adest efflanti animam servator amico,
> Labentemque humeris tollit ad aestra suis.

Semianimem calicis generoso roborat haustu,
  Suppositoque pium corpore gestat onus.
Inviolata fides, & amor post fata superstes
  Exhibet aeternae pignus amicitiae
Ecquid amicitiam mundi miserabilis ambis,
  Qui tibi in extremis ferre recuset opem?
Deserit ille suos in mortis agone clientes,
  Quò fulcro fragili deficiente cadant.
Proiice te in Christum, non sese fidus amicus
  Subtrahet, ibit ovans desuper astra comes.
Labenti innixum labi non stare necesse est:
  Innixus mundo labili in ima rues.
Christus at in mediâ labentem morte tenebit:
  Stans etenim stantes, quos tenet, ille facit.
      (Chesneau, *Orpheus eucharisticus*, Qq8v)

Then follows, after a short prose *fons emblematis*, a very substantial passage of *interpretatio* running to six pages of detailed analysis and commentary in the course of which numerous authorities are cited. In striking contrast to the verbosity of this original Latin version, the later French version is much simplified. The descriptive Latin title is rendered in French: *La Vigne, qui embrasse l'Orme abbatu & le couronne de ses raisins* (*Emblemes sacrez*, M2v). The French couplet which forms part of the engraving naturally remains unchanged (see fig.18), but the lengthy verse *apodosis* is not replicated in French, and no other verse is included either. The even more lengthy Latin prose *interpretatio* is replaced by a much shorter and much simplified French *explication* from which all the authoritative references other than the first two are excised:

Source de l'embleme.

On a de coustume dans l'Italie, de faire monter les ceps de la Vigne sur les Ormeaux, qu'elle semble apres mesme qu'ils sont tombez & presque morts, vouloir soûtenir, embrasser & comme caresser de ses branches, les mettre à couvert sous l'ombre de ses feüilles, & enfin les couroner en quelque façon de ses pampres & de ses grappes. *S. Ambroise l.3. de son Hexameron c.12.*

Explication.

La Vigne sousteneuë de sa treille, ou liée à l'échalas, dans la pensée de S. Bernard, nous represente Jesus-Christ attaché au bois de la Croix, qui dit luy mesme qu'il est la veritable vigne, dont le fruit pressé au pressoir du Calvaire, fait couler dans nos poictrines, le vin qui germe les Vierges. Cette Vigne mystique ne desire rien tant que de s'allier au devot Chrestien, d'un lien qui ne se puisse rompre dans toute l'eternité. D'où vient que l'ayant pendant sa vie tousjours tenu sous l'ombre de sa protection, comme la vigne ombrage l'orme qui la soûtient, à mesme temps qu'elle le voit ébranlé, &

quasi porté par terre par le tourbillon d'une maladie mortelle, elle se panche
& s'encline pour l'embrasser, & soustenir dans son agonie, & luy donner
toutes les marques d'une amitié inviolable. C'est dans ce moment d'où
depend l'Eternité, que Jesus comme un fidele amy le vient visiter en son lit,
le fortifie du sacre Viatique de son Corps, & le rend invincible aux attaques
& derniers efforts du demon, ausquels ce pauvre moribond, effrayé des
approches de la mort, troublé par la crainte des Jugements de Dieu, & des
peines eternelles succomberoit aizement, sans le secours extraordinaire de cét
incomparable amy fidelle jusqu'à la mort, & mesme aprés la mort; puis qu'il
retire son ame des flammes du Purgatoire, dont il amortit les cuisantes
ardeurs par l'effusion de son Sang au Sacrifice de la sainte Messe.
(Chesneau, *Emblemes sacrez*, M2v-3r)

Dating from much the same time as Chesneau's *Orpheus eucharisticus/Emblemes
sacrez sur le tres-saint et tres-adorable sacrement de l'Eucharistie*, and following a
similar pattern, although with a rather more narrow range of reference, is Adrien
Gambart's purely French emblem book focusing on the life of St François de Sales, in
which the full title spells out clearly the meditational and morally improving aim of
the work:

*La vie symbolique du bienheureux François de Sales, evesque et prince de
Geneve. Comprise sous le voile de 52. emblemes, qui marquent le caractere
de ses principales vertus, avec autant de meditations, ou reflexions pieuses,
pour exciter les ames chrestiennes & religieuses, à l'amour & à la pratique
des mesmes vertus. Par M. Adrien Gambart, prestre.*

This work was privately printed in 1664 (as we are told on the title page), specifically
for the use of the nuns of the Order of the Visitation, founded forty years earlier by St
François de Sales.[35] As with Callot's *Vita beatae Mariae virginis...Vie de la bien-
heureuse vierge Marie* in which the engraved figures did not themselves relate
directly to the life of the Virgin, but were interpreted in the text as symbolising aspects
of her life, so also the engraved figures of Gambart's *Vie symbolique du bienheureux
François de Sales* cover a range of conventional emblematic figures, themselves
unconnected with the saint, but interpreted allegorically as relating to his life in the
accompanying text. Unlike Callot's work, with its very short verses and absence of any
further textual commentary, that of Gambart follows rather the pattern of Chesneau's
Orpheus eucharisticus or Martin's *Paradis terrestre* in which the textual component
of the emblem heavily overshadows the engraved figure. Again the text is
predominantly in prose: one page is occupied by the engraved figure incorporating
within it a Latin motto, accompanied by a French title and followed by a short French

---

[35] 'Paris. Aux frais de l'auteur pour l'usage des Religieuses de la Visitation, & à la
disposition de celles du Fauxbourg Saint Jacques', 1664, 12°. The Order of the Visitation was
founded in Annecy in 1610.

couplet which is the sole verse element within the emblem. The facing page and subsequent pages are devoted first to an *Eclaircissement* interpreting the association between what is depicted in the engraved figure and the virtuous life of St François de Sales, and then to a more general set of injunctions to good behaviour under the heading *Fruits et pratiques*. In emblem 9 we find the familiar emblematic figure of the swan, but Gambart exploits it in a new way. Under the motto *Tangor non tingor abunda* the swan is depicted swimming on a lake, with the accompanying French couplet developing the theme of its ability to preserve its purity despite its dirty surroundings (see fig.19):

> Bien que je sois plongé dans l'eau de ces marais,
> Ma blanche pureté ne s'y soüille jamais.
>   (Gambart, *Vie symbolique du bienheureux François de Sales*, C4v)

while the accompanying French title, *Son innocence & son integrité dans le monde*, introduces an allegorical interpretation of the scene which is then developed at length, and its specific reference to the life of St François, who managed to retain his own spiritual purity despite living in a world of impurity, spelt out in the following page of *Eclaircissement*:

> L'on ne peut gueres donner une plus naïfve expression de la candeur, de l'innocence & de l'integrité de vie d'un homme qui est engagé dans le commerce & dans la conversation du monde, que le Cygne, qui ne perd jamais rien de sa blancheur & de la netteté de son plumage, quoy qu'il soit toûjours dans les eaux fangeuses des Estangs & des marais. Il est rare de voir des hommes qui conservent cette integrité & cette pureté dans les intrigues de la Cour, & dans le commerce des Grands: c'est pourquoy tous ceux qui ont esté jaloux de leur innocence & leur integrité ont fuy la Cour & le monde, estant difficile, au dire de Saint Leon, d'y vivre sans y contracter quelques legeres soüilleures, mesme aux plus severes, & aux plus parfaits: *Necesse est de mundano pulvere etiam Religiosa corda sordescere.*
> C'est quasi la gloire unique de nostre Bienheureux, lequel quoy qu'obligé, & par sa naissance, & par sa dignité & ses fonctions de vivre dans le monde, parmy les Grands, & quelquefois mesme à la Cour des Roys; jamais toutefois il n'y a receu la moindre impression contraire à la pureté de sa conscience, ny à l'integrité de ses moeurs...
>   (Gambart, *Vie symbolique du bienheureux François de Sales*, C5r)[36]

---

[36] The swan image was exploited in a number of ways by emblem writers. For Alciato in *Insignia poëtarum* the swan, sacred to Apollo, symbolises the poet (Alciato, *Emblemata*, 1550, N3r), while for Coustau in *Cycnus. Honor alit artes* its refusal to sing unless the wind blows reflects the poet's need for praise and encouragement (*Pegma*, 1555, p.329). Camerarius uses the most familiar image of the swan singing to presage its own death in *Sibi canit et orbi* (*Symbolorum et emblematum ex volatilibus et insectis desumtorum centuria tertia collecta*, emblem 23). For other emblematic uses of the swan, see Henkel and Schöne, cols 814-18.

EMBLEME IX.

Son innocence & son integrité dans le monde.

Bien que je sois plongé dans l'eau de ces marais,
Ma blanche pureté ne s'y souille jamais.

Figure 19: Gambart, *La vie symbolique du bienheureux François de Sales*, Paris, 1664, C4v.

after which the final section of the emblem, *Fruits et pratiques*, extends the application of the emblem beyond St François himself to the reader, devoting a further two pages to a series of injunctions to the aspirant to virtue to seek solitude and in so far as possible to shun the world and worldly ideas.

In Gambart's emblem book, unlike many other meditational emblem books, there is no specific section entitled *Meditation* attached to each emblem. However, this important element is not omitted, but Gambart structures his emblem book in such a way that the *Meditations* are all grouped together as a discrete item. The work is divided into two parts so that the fifty-two core emblems are all contained together in Part 1, while Part 2 contains all the *Meditations*, with its own explanatory title page:

> *Seconde partie de la vie symbolique du B. François de Sales, contenant quelques meditations, où se voyent les paralelles & convenances de ses vertus, avec celles de nostre seigneur Jesus-Christ, prototype & original de toute sainteté.*

In all these works by Jean Martin, Callot, Chesneau and Gambart, despite considerable variations of structure and indeed of theme, there is nevertheless an important common pattern of intent. All are unambiguously religious emblem books, but in none of them is the material used in itself religious. As with the traditional generalist emblem book, the material used in these works is rich and varied. It is derived from a many different contexts, and frequently includes traditional emblematic symbols familiar from earlier works. What transforms these otherwise open symbols into specifically religious symbols is in all cases the textual interpretation which is imposed upon them, and in this respect, we can see these works as following in a tradition established back in the sixteenth century by Georgette de Montenay. But in other religious emblem books not only the textual component but also the engraved figure itself indicates the particular orientation of the work. Here again - though not in France, or in French - we find examples of works dating from the late sixteenth century, paving the way for those of the seventeenth century. In 1571 the Plantin Press in Antwerp published the first of several editions of a lavishly illustrated catholic work by Benito Arias Montano, almoner of Philip II of Spain, in which, although the word 'emblem' is not specifically used, we nevertheless see a clearly emblematic pattern of construction.[37] In his wholly Latin *Humanae salutis monumenta* Arias Montano offers a series of 71 two-page biblical emblems in which the recto contains a large ornate engraving of the biblical scene surrounded by a decorative frame of animals, fruits, flowers and plants in the style of the earlier sixteenth-century French emblem books produced in Paris by Janot and in Lyon by de Tournes or the Roville/Bonhomme partnership, accompanied by a Latin motto and distich, while on the facing verso is a longer passage of verse in the form of a Latin ode, taking its inspiration from the visual trigger provided by the engraved figure to which it refers, and explaining the significance of the scene depicted. The message of

---

[37] *Humanae salutis monumenta B. Ariae Montani studio constructa et decantata*, Antwerp, C. Plantin, 1571, 8°. Plantin produced a further edition in 1581 using the same set of copper plates, but without the decorative borders. Two years later in 1583 when he produced yet another edition, he used for this a new set of larger engravings which he also used that same year for his Latin folio edition of the Bible. For this new edition also he did not include decorative borders. For details of the publication history of this work see Voet, *The Plantin Press (1555-1589)*, vol.1, pp.182-7. Copies of the 1571 and 1583 editions are to be found in the British Library, and a copy of the 1581 edition in the British Museum, Department of Prints and Drawings.

each individual emblem is further reinforced by the inclusion of explanatory notes and biblical references in prose, although unusually these do not accompany the actual 'emblem' but - like Gambart's *Meditations* - they are all grouped together at the end. The collection begins with Moses holding the tables of the law, followed by Adam and Eve, and ends appropriately with the Last Judgement. A particularly ornate 'emblem' is that of Noah making sacrifice, surrounded by a variety of delightfully depicted animals. Together with the motto *Misericordiae prospectrici* and the distich:

> Fraude hominum Deus offensus cùm concipit iras,
> Consilii clemens est memor usque sui.
> > (Arias Montano, *Humanae salutis monumenta*, A8r)

it is accompanied on the facing verso by a shorter than usual Latin *ode sapphica* entitled *In tabulam Noë sacrificantis*:

> Sol ubi caelo faciem sereno
> Purus ostendit, decus atque rebus
> Redditum est, quales variata formas
> > Terra tenebat:
> (Nuper heu noxis hominum per omnes
> Ambitus Lunae, penitus negata his
> Usibus vitae & pelago innatanti
> > Cedere iussa.)
> Tunc senex, auctor sobolis futurae,
> Cespite instratas pia thura ad aras
> Admovet, iungens precibus probanda
> > Dona superstes.
> Annuit votis Deus, ac benigna
> Voce, sint, dixit, renovata certis
> Cursibus, iustos habitura mundi
> > Tempora fines.
> Iam semel vastis periisse in undis
> Secla brutorum sobolemque Adami,
> Sit satis, posthac potiora tecum
> > Foedera iungam.   (Arias Montano, *Humanae salutis monumenta*, A8v)

A few years after the *Humanae salutis monumenta*, Arias Montano produced another similarly emblematic work, also published in Antwerp by the Plantin Press, in 1575, focusing, like Callot's life of the Virgin or Gambart's life of St François de Sales, on the life of David,[38] but unlike Callot or Gambart, doing so, as in his earlier

---

[38] *David, hoc est virtutis exercitatissimae probatum Deo spectaculum, ex David pastoris, militis ducis exulis ac prophetae exemplis: Bened. Aria meditante, Philippo Gallaeo instruente, ad pietatis cultum propositis*, Antwerp, C. Plantin, 1575, 4° obl.

Humanae salutis monumenta, by means of a series of forty-eight engraved figures depicting appropriate scenes from the Bible. As with his earlier work, his *David* is also wholly in Latin, but in this later work each emblem is much more concisely expressed, occupying only one single page as opposed to two. In the first edition published by Plantin in 1575 the textual component is minimal. The work comprises no more than a series of engraved figures including within each engraving a brief Latin motto above the representation of a scene from the life of David, and a four-line Latin verse below it. When, sixty years later, the work was again published in the Netherlands, but in Amsterdam rather than Antwerp, this same simple structure was retained.[39]   But in the interim between these two editions published in the Netherlands, a quite different, expanded version was also published in Frankfurt, in which the engraved figures are smaller, but the textual component is much enlarged.[40] In this edition each 'emblem' now contains - in addition to the original Latin motto and quatrain - a biblical reference and a short prose description of the scene, accompanying the engraved figure on one page. But as well as this, on the facing page and continuing thereafter is a further prose *explicatio* and in most cases a lengthy passage of Latin verse entitled *specimen carminis eiusdem argumenti a M. Bergio discipulis propositum*. Thus, for example, in *Fidei victoria*, the 1575 and 1637 editions simply offer a splendidly energetic engraving of the youthful David casting a stone from his sling against the warrior-like figure of Goliath, with the accompanying quatrain:

> Male gravi et subito casu magnis ruit ausis
>   Vis expers sensus consiliisque pii.
> Hanc victrix pietas sternitque trahitque triumpho,
>   Non iactare minas docta, sed efficere.
>   (Arias Montano, *David*, 1575, emblem 6)

but the much more verbose Frankfurt edition includes a quite different engraving of the scene with the youthful David simultaneously striking off the head of Goliath with a sword, and also carrying it away (with the sword still in his hand, and curiously without any visible sling). This engraving is accompanied by a reference to 1 Kings 17, and a brief prose description: 'Goliath impius Deique contemtor monomachia victus a Davide trucidatur' with a lengthy prose *explicatio* on the facing page:

> Artibus vitae variis variisque hominum adinventionibus est ubi vita humana
>   opus habet, & uti potest sine impietate (quam prudentiam vocamus, excellens

[39]   *David, hoc est virtutis exercitatissimae probatum Deo spectaculum, ex David pastoris, militis, regis, exulis, ac prophetae exemplis*, Amsterdam, N.J. Visscher, 1637, 4°.
[40]   *David, virtutis exercitatissimae probatum Deo spectaculum, ex Davidis, pastoris, militis, ducis, exsulis ac prophetae exemplis, Benedicto Aria Montano meditante ad pietatis cultum propositis. Aeneis laminis ornatum a Ioanne Theodoro & Ioanne Israele de Bry, fratribus civib. Francofurtensibus. Quid huic nova editioni a Conrado Rittershusio ex biblioth. M. Bergii procurata accesserit, praefatio docebit*, Frankfurt, Z. Palthenius, 1597, 4°.

Dei donum). Est etiam ubi his nihil sit loci relictum, vel certe ubi non nisi summa cautione ac religione eas adhiberi oporteat. Vitae huius cultum dumtaxat spectantia resque mundanas arte & prudentia regi atque institui rectum est. At vero ubi gloria Dei & salus aeterna agitur, & eae res, in quibus haec versatur, hic non valebit, calliditas vel ars humana: sed fides verbo Dei nitens & huic obsequens, dux erit & viam muniet ac sternet. Etenim duplex homini concessa facultas est, geminumque in quo recte laboret iter datum. Unum commune ipsi cum ignobilioribus naturis, animantium scilicet & rerum terrenarum. Hic ratio dux est: hac efficit homo aliis animantibus inimitabilia: adeoque quisquis homine se dignum gerit, sedulo hanc partem excolit. Altera pars & sors hominis est, ut cum Deo coniungatur, cum in hac vita incipiendo, tum in altera consummate. In hac parte Dei ductum sequi oportet, ut recte ambuletur, nec quicquam sapientia humana suscipi praeter aut contra illius sententiam. In hoc itinere cum mille monstra obiicit Sathan, quae a recto itinere seducant, fidei armis utendum & occurrendum est: quae sunt confessio syncera, oratio ardens, patientia & spes Deo confisa, & quae praeterea schola Dei ad haec praelia subministrat.

Sic tibi vincitur Goliath, ô David pastor. Deiecto postea Dei armis Goliatho praeciditur caput suo ipsius ense. Ita nimirum humanae artes & inventa, quando impietatis arx & fundamenta Dei manu & armis eversa sunt, suum etiam locum habent, & in conficiendis reliquiis adhiberi possunt.

(Arias Montano, *David*, 1597, B2v)

Twenty years later, still in Antwerp, another highly decorative work was published by the Plantin Press, once again based on a series of engravings from the Bible. As with the works of Arias Montano, the Jesuit Geronimo Nadal's complementary *Adnotationes et meditationes* and *Evangelicae historiae imagines* of 1595/1593[41] are once again wholly in Latin, and although this work was never itself

---

[41] *Adnotationes et meditationes in Evangelia quae in sacrosancto Missae sacrificio toto anno leguntur. Cum Evangeliorum concordantia historiae integritati sufficienti. Accessit & index historiam ipsam Evangelicam in ordinem temporis vitae Christi distribuens. Secunda editio. Auctore Hieronymo Natali Societatis Iesu theologo,* Antwerp, M. Nutius, 1595, folio; *Evangelicae historiae imagines ex ordine Evangeliorum, quae toto anno in missae sacrificio recitantur, in ordinem temporis vitae Christi digestae. Auctore Hieronymo Natali Societatis Iesu theologo,* Antwerp, no publ., 1593, folio. A further edition of the *Adnotationes et meditationes* was published in 1607: *Adnotationes et meditationes in Evangelia...Editio ultima: in qua sacer textus ad emendationem Bibliorum Sixti V. et Clementis VIII restitutus* (Antwerp, J. Moretus (Officina Plantiniana), 1607, folio) which in BL 689.i.9 is bound with an edition of the *Evangelicae historiae imagines* dated 1596 (Antwerp, no publ., folio). De Backer and Sommervogel cite an edition published by Nutius dated 1594 on the title page, with colophon dated 1595, in which the text of the *Adnotationes* is followed by the 153 plates of the *Evangelicae historiae imagines*, but gives no location (*Bibliothèque de la Compagnie de Jesus*, vol.5, col.1518). A much later edition, dating from 1647, is cited in a Hartung and Hartung catalogue (catalogue 74, Munich, 1993, no.1213): *Adnotationes et meditationes in Evangelia quae in sacrosancto Missae sacrificio toto anno leguntur. Cum eorundem Evangeliorum*

translated into French, it did serve - in structure at least - as a model for similar works by another Jesuit priest, Jan David, also published at the Plantin Press in Antwerp, in the early years of the seventeenth century, in which part of the text was in French. Nadal's work is arranged in the same manner as Gambart's *Vie symbolique du bienheureux François de Sales*, where all the meditational material relating to the various engraved emblems is grouped together and printed at the end of the volume. In the case of Nadal's work, however, the material is actually physically divided into two separate folio volumes, the first of which, the *Evangelicae historiae imagines* contains the full-page engraved plates, and the second, the *Adnotationes et meditationes*, contains all the accompanying prose material. In accordance with the pattern often found in later Jesuit meditational emblem books, Nadal's engraved figures are each annotated with letters of the alphabet pinpointing significant features of the scene depicted, which are then identified in the brief prose notes incorporated into the lower part of the engraving, as in the opening 'emblem' depicting the Annunciation:

> A.   Conventus Angelorum, ubi declarat Deus Incarnationem Christi, & designatur Gabriel legatus.
> B.   Veniens Nazareth Gabriel, sibi ex aëre corpus accommodat.
> C.   Nubes è caelo, unde radii ad Mariam Virginem pertinent.
> D.   Cubiculum, quod visitur Laureti in agro Piceno, ubi est Maria.
> E.   Ingreditur Angelus ad Mariam Virginem; eam salutat; assentitur Maria: fit Deus homo, & ipsa mater Dei.
> F.   Creatio hominis, quo die Deus factus est homo.
> G.   Eadem die Christus moritur, ut homo perditus recreetur.
> H.   Pie credi potest Angelum missum in Limbum, ad Christi incarnationem Patribus nunciandam.   (Nadal, *Evangelicae historiae imagines*, plate 1)

In the companion volume of *Adnotationes et meditationes* each 'emblem' is first subjected to several pages of textual commentary and gloss, beginning with a repetition of the alphabetical annotations already included in the volume of engraved *Imagines*. Thereafter follow a lengthy quotation from the scriptural text on which the engraving is based,[42] and a two-page *adnotatio*, again structured around the points

---

concordantia, Antwerp, J. Galle, 1647, folio, while the enduring interest of the work is further attested by a copy in a private collection dating from the early 18th century: *R.P. Hieronymi Natalis Societatis Iesu theologi annotationes et meditationes in Evangelia quae in sacrosancto Missae sacrificio toto anno leguntur. Cum venustissimis Evangelicae historiae aeneis imaginibus ex ordine Evangeliorum in ordinem temporis vitae Christi digestis, cum eorundem Evangeliorum concordantia. Editio ultima in qua sacer textus ad emendationem Bibliorum Sixti V. et Clementis VIII. restitutus*, Antwerp, H. and C. Verdussen, 1707, folio.

[42]   In the case of the Annunciation 'emblem', this is taken from Luke 1: 'In mense autem sexto missus est Angelus Gabriel à Deo in civitatem Galilaeae cui nomen Nazareth, ad Virginem desponsatam viro cui nomen erat Joseph, de domo David, & nomen Virginis Maria. Et ingressus Angelus ad eam, dixit: ave gratia plena, Dominus tecum, benedicta tu in

identified in the engraving by the letters of the alphabet, after which the reader is finally led through the all-important four-page *meditatio*.[43]

It is this same formula which is used slightly later by the Jesuit Jan David in a series of devotional works all of which were published at the Plantin Press in the first decade of the seventeenth century. In two of these, the *Occasio arrepta* of 1605 and the *Duodecim specula* of 1610,[44] (in which latter work the soul is led through a spiritual pilgrimage, working through a series of twelve 'reflections' progressing upwards from the *Speculum suae vilitatis* (E2v) to the *Speculum visionis beatificae* (K7v), in each of which the starting point is an annotated engraved figure like those of Nadal) the text is, like Nadal's *Evangelicae historiae imagines* and *Adnotationes et meditationes*, wholly in Latin. But in two other - much more substantial - works although the prose sections are all in Latin, French and Dutch verses are also included, as well as Latin verses. These two works are his *Veridicus christianus* of 1601 and *Paradisus sponsi et sponsae* of 1607.[45]

The material on which David's emblems are based in the *Veridicus christianus* is very varied. Some use themes from the Bible, as for example the opening emblem, *Initium sapientiae timor Domini* in which the annotated engraved figure depicts Moses on Mount Sinai with the tables of the law, while others are based on allegorical figures, such as *Si malum pro malo reddis; tibi plus noces*, offering a reworking of the old Alciato theme of Cupid the honey-thief (see fig.20).[46] The first emblem, *Initium sapientiae timor Domini* is accompanied by a Latin couplet and a French verse:

> Quod sibi principium posuit Sapientia vera?
> Numinis, infixum summisso in corde, Timorem.
> Divine Sagesse, Donne moy addresse, Pour aller à vous?
> Commenc' à refraindre, Ton coeur, et à craindre, De Dieu le courroux.
>   (David, *Veridicus christianus*, facing A1r)

as well as a Dutch couplet, while emblem 59, *Si malum pro malo reddis; tibi plus*

---

mulieribus...' (*Adnotationes et meditationes*, p.405).

[43] *Adnotationes et meditationes*, pp.405-6; pp.406-10.

[44] *Occasio arrepta, neglecta, huius commoda: illius incommoda. Auctore R.P. Ioanne David, Societatis Iesu sacerdote*, Antwerp, J. Moretus (Officina Plantiniana), 1605, 4°; *Duodecim specula Deum aliquando videre desideranti concinnata. Auctore P. Ioanne David, Societatis Iesu sacerdote*, Antwerp, J. Moretus (Officina Plantiniana), 1610, 8°.

[45] The *Occasio arrepta* and *duodecim specula* both contain only twelve 'emblems', but the *Veridicus christianus* contains one hundred 'emblems', and the *Paradisus sponsi et sponsae* contains fifty for the first part on the Passion of Christ (entitled *Messis myrrhae et aromatum, ex instrumentis ac mysteriis Passionis Christi colligenda*), and a further fifty for the second part on the life of the Virgin (entitled *Pancarpium Marianum, septemplici titulorum serie distinctum: ut in B. Virginis odorem curramus et Christus formetur in nobis*).

[46] See *Emblemata*, 1550 ed., H5v, *Ferè simile ex Theocrito*. Whereas in Alciato's emblem it was Cupid who was stung by the bees while trying to steal their honey, in David's emblem the engraving depicts instead a human being who is attacked by the bees which swarm around his head as he strikes the beehive with a stick.

noces, is similarly accompanied by trilingual verses all developing the moral lesson of the title, as in the French version:

> Comment se revange/ Qui remet le change/ Au mal qu'on luy fait?
> Cruel à soy mesme/ Par le couroux blesme/ Son Ame il defait.
>   (David, *Veridicus christianus*, facing b2v)

Figure 20: David, *Veridicus christianus*, Antwerp, 1601, facing b2v.

These verses, as also the titles to the emblems, are all incorporated into the engravings themselves, and thereafter follows for each emblem a substantial Latin prose commentary on the scene depicted in the engraving, systematically drawing the onlooker's attention to the various flagged elements and explaining the particular significance of each, and finally a short *oratio*.

The same pattern is also followed in the *Paradisus sponsi et sponsae*, although here the material is more consistently biblical, with the first part offering a series of complex engravings on the Passion of Christ, and the second part a parallel series on the life of the Virgin. In, for example, emblem 7 of the first part, entitled *Osculum Iudae* (facing B5v), Judas's betrayal of Christ in the Garden of Gethsemane occupies the foreground of the engraved figure, while in the background are several subsidiary Old Testament scenes, all of which are again annotated alphabetically and identified in the accompanying text in the manner of Nadal's earlier work.[47] As in the *Veridicus christianus* the accompanying Latin, Dutch and French couplets are again here incorporated into the actual engraving.[48] The engravings of the second part of the *Paradisus sponsi et sponsae* are similarly complex. Although all have as their central unifying theme the Virgin Mary, they also include together with her a range of both realistically depicted figures and allegorical figures, as for example in emblem 49 in which she is depicted sitting in an open heart, supported by two angels, and surrounded by subsidiary scenes. Structurally the work follows the same pattern as that of the earlier *Veridicus christianus*, with the engraving complemented by a lengthy passage of commentary on the various aspects of the engraving, and thereafter by an *oratio*.

In these emblematic works of Jan David as in many of those discussed earlier we see clearly the influence of post-tridentine Catholic pedagogy as practised above all by the Society of Jesus. The approach followed here by Jan David is very akin to that embodied in the meditational structures laid down by Ignatius Loyola in his *Spiritual Exercises*, designed to aid the spiritual director charged with leading the penitent soul through its spiritual pilgrimage to salvation. In the course of this pilgrimage the soul moves from contemplation of sin to contemplation of the life of Christ and his Passion, and ultimately to contemplation of the Resurrection and Ascension, progressing from an initial state of spiritual desolation and contrition (stimulated by visions of hell and damnation) to an ultimate state of spiritual ecstacy stimulated by the contemplation of paradise, and the prospect of union with Christ. In this process as elaborated by Loyola, emotion and the imagination play an important role, with the penitent being required at each stage to react to a real or imagined visual stimulus: the 'compositio loci', in which the eyes are used to imagine a given scene, prior to

---

[47] These are identified in alphabetical order as: A) the daughters of Jerusalem lamenting, from Jeremiah 9:'Assumite super hoc facinus lamentum, filiae Jerusalem...'; B) Christ and Judas :'Iudas nefarius ille proditor hoc fecit...'; C) the harlot seducing a youth, from Proverbs 7:'Obscoenitas sit primum: quale quod impudens mulier iuveni in plateis arrepto fixisti, in domum tuam mira suâda pelliciens ac seducens...'; D) Absalom smiting all comers at the city gates, from 2 Kings 15:'Tale tu Absalom ambitiose, stans in porta civitatis omnem venientem apprehendens, osculabaris...'; and E) Joab and Amasam from 2 Kings 20:'Hoc fuco, simulans pacem crudelis Joab, sic affatus es Amasam...' (B5v-6v).

[48] The Latin and French verses are: 'Basiolo dum prodis herum, pietatis adulter,/Impia scorpiaco vipera more feris.' and 'Tu mords donc en baisant, comme fait la vipere?/ Tu es, en ce faisant, des traitres le vray pere.'

meditating upon the implications of that scene is the starting point for each exercise. As Loyola explains in the first prelude to the *Primum exercitium*:

> Primum Praeludium est, ratio quaedam componendi loci. Pro quâ Notandum est, quòd in quavis meditatione, sive contemplatione de re corporeâ, ut puta de Christo, effigendus erit nobis, secundùm visionem quandam imaginariam, locus corporeus, id quod contemplamur, repraesentans, veluti templum, aut mons; in quo reperiamus Christum Iesum vel Mariam Virginem, & caetera, quae spectant ad contemplationis nostrae argumentum. Sin autem speculationi subest res incorporea, ut est consideratio peccatorum nunc oblata; poterit loci constructio talis esse, ut si per imaginationem cernamus animam nostram in corpore isto corruptibili, velut in carcere constrictam: hominem quoque ipsum, in hac miseriae valle, inter animalia bruta exulantem.   (Loyola, *Exercitia spiritualia*, Antwerp, 1689, pp.81-2)

Not only the sense of sight, but all the other senses are to be deployed in imagining the scene, as is made clear in the fifth exercise, *De inferno*, where the penitent is urged not just to contemplate the horrors of hell and the suffering of those souls in hell, but also to imagine the smell of sulphur, the sound of the wailing, the taste of the tears and the feel of the flames of hell:

> Prius praeludium hîc habet compositionem loci, subiectâ oculis imaginationis inferni longitudine, latitudine, ac profunditate. Posterius verò, consistit in poscendâ intimâ poenarum, quas damnati luunt, apprehensione, ut si quando me ceperit divini amoris oblivio; saltem à peccatis supplicii timor coërceat.
>
> Punctum primum est, spectare per imaginationem vasta inferorum incendia, & animas igneis quibusdam corporibus, velut ergastulis, inclusas.
>
> Secundum, audire imaginariè, planctus, eiulatus, vociferationes, atque blasphemias in Christum, & Sanctos eius, illinc erumpentes.
>
> Tertium, imaginario etiam olfactu fumum, sulphur, & sentinae cuiusdam, seu faecis, atque putredinis graveolentiam persentire.
>
> Quartum, gustare similiter res amarissimas, ut lacrymas, rancorem, conscientiaeque vermem.
>
> Quintum, tangere quodammodò ignes illos, quorum tactu animae ipsae amburuntur.
>
> (Loyola, *Exercitia spiritualia*, Antwerp, 1689, pp.105-6)

From emotional contemplation of the scene the penitent then proceeds to a guided colloquy between himself and Christ structured around the scene. In the case of the fifth exercise on the vision of hell, he is urged to recall to memory those who are in hell, either because they did not believe in Christ, or because they broke his commandments, dividing these into three categories (those who were lost before the coming of Christ; those who were lost during his lifetime; and those who were lost thereafter), prior to giving thanks to God for thus far showing him mercy.

Colloquendo interim cum Christo, in memoriam adducendae erunt illorum animae, qui ad inferni poenas damnati sunt, vel quia credere noluerunt adventum Christi; vel licet crederent, non tamen conformem praeceptis eius vitam exegerunt: idque vel ante adventum Christi, vel eodem tempore, quo vixit Christus in hoc mundo, vel post illud deinceps. Gratiae postremò agendae sunt eidem Christo quàm maximae, quòd in tale quod piam exitium non permiserit me corruere, sed potiùs ad hunc usque diem summa pietate, & misericordiâ me prosecutus sit. Finis imponetur dicto, *Pater noster*.

(Loyola, *Exercitia spiritualia*, Antwerp, 1689, p.106)

Although Loyola stresses the use of the imagination in visualising scenes for meditation, many editions of the *Spiritual Exercises* included full-page engravings of the appropriate scenes to accompany and add further emotional stimulus to that of the verbal guidelines for meditation on each theme.[49] Thus not only in their philosophy do Jesuit meditational emblem books such as we have seen closely reflect the approach laid down by Loyola in his *Spiritual Exercises*, but also in many cases in their actual physical layout, with an engraved, often annotated, emblematic figure opening the way to guided meditation. In Antoine Sucquet's wholly Latin *Via vitae aeternae iconibus illustrata* of 1620[50] we find a classic example of this. Here a series of full-page engraved figures, with key points alphabetically annotated, as in David's *Veridicus christianus* and other works, are accompanied by a prose text in which the onlooker is urged not just to imagine a particular scene, but also to contemplate it as laid out before his eyes in visual engraved form. His gaze is then directed specifically to the key elements of the scene, and he is instructed, as in the *Spiritual Exercises*, as to the appropriate theme on which he should meditate, as inspired by the visual scene. Again as with the *Spiritual Exercises* Sucquet's meditational exercise also includes both a preparatory prayer and a concluding prayer. In Sucquet's important opening emblem, for example, the spiritual pilgrimage of man is rendered visually as the winding path of life in the engraving, with hell at the bottom and heaven at the top, and man at the base of the path (see fig.21). The *Annotatio* (headed 'Considera, ô homo, finem tuum & vias tuas' and *Caput primum, Consideratio de fine hominis* (A1r-2r) are followed by an *Oratio praeparatoria* (A2v), a *Meditatio* 'De fine ob quem homo creatus est' (A3r), a further *Oratio* (A5r) and a series of spiritual exercises. In 'Popular devotional emblematics: a comparison of Sucquet's *Le chemin de la vie eternele* and Hugo's *Les pieux desirs*' Lynette Black notes how 'Sucquet's images...provide strict guidelines for the imagination of the meditant.

---

[49]   Among these is the 17th-century Antwerp published edition quoted here: *Exercitia spiritualia S.P. Ignatii Loyolae, Fundatoris Ordinis Societatis Iesu. Cum Bullis Pontificum, tum approbationis Exercitiorum; tum Indulgentiae plenariae, pro omnibus, qui octiduò illis vacant in domibus eiusdem Societatis. Brevi insuper Instructione meditandi quae omnia & dilucidantur & illustrantur pluribus ex aere impressis imaginibus* (Antwerp, M. Cnobbart, 1689, 8°).

[50]   Sucquet's original wholly Latin version was also published three years later in a French translation by another Jesuit, Pierre Morin, under the title *Le chemin de la vie eternele*.

Figure 21: Sucquet, *Le chemin de la vie eternele*, Antwerp, 1623, facing p.2.

The imagination is not to be allowed free rein', whereas in the very different *Pieux desirs* Hugo appeals much more directly to the emotions of the meditant. (pp.14-15). She demonstrates how, unlike Hugo who engages the sympathy of the meditant by showing him 'his own human condition appealingly portrayed, his conflicts and emotions mirrored before him' in the charming little woodcut figures of *Anima* and *Amor divinus*, the spiritual pilgrim as depicted in Sucquet's full-page engravings with

14   LES DIVINES OPERATIONS
Scopabo eam in scopa terrens. Isaye 14.

O beatam cordis ædem!   Animose puer verre,
Te cui cælum dedit fedem   Monstra tuo vultu terre,
Purgat fuis manibus.   Tere tuis pedibus.
Anton. Wierx fecit et excud.

Mon cœur vous eftes glorieux,
Puifque mefme le Roy des Cieux
De fes propres mains vous nettoye
Cherchez de l'un à l'autre bout,
Nettoyez, exterminez tout
Doux JESUS autheur de ma joye.

Figure 22: Mello, *Les divines operations*, Paris, 1673, B1v.

his 'unchangingly austere visage' is intended to stimulate a very different, and more purely intellectual response.[51] It is interesting to see that, unlike the French translation of Chesneau's *Orpheus eucharisticus* which offered the vernacular reader a much shorter and simplified text than the Latin original, the French translation of Sucquet's meditational emblem book replicates almost exactly in each of the individual sections the pattern of the Latin original, in terms of both length and content.

---

[51]   *Emblematica*, 9,1, 1995, pp.1-20.

Among the various exploitations of the Wierix engravings of the heart, that by the Jesuit, Etienne Luzvic likewise follows both the structure and the terminology of Loyola's *Spiritual Exercises.* Originally composed in French under the title *Le coeur devot throsne royal de Jesus pacifique Salomon*, it was subsequently translated into Latin by Luzvic's fellow Jesuit, Charles Musart, and published under the title, *Cor deo devotum Iesu pacifici Salomonis thronus regius.*[52] In this Latin version the familiar engravings of the heart, together with their engraved Latin verses, appear on the verso while on the facing recto the accompanying guided prose meditation is divided into the *Imaginis expositio*, the *Praeambulum ad meditationem*, the *Meditatio* itself, beginning with its *Oratio praeparatoria*, and thereafter subdivided, as in the *Spiritual Exercises*, into a series of *puncta*, and concluding with a *Colloquium.* Although it follows the model of the *Spiritual Exercises*, the guided meditation in the *Cor deum devotum* is much lengthier than that of Loyola, running typically to some ten pages per engraved figure, and it is interesting to see that when much later in the century, in 1673, Guillaume de Mello again produced a French emblem book based on the same Wierix engravings, under the title *Les divines operations de Jesus dans le coeur d'une ame fidelle par G.D.M.*, his accompanying text is much shorter, running to no more than two to three pages. In Mello's version each engraving, with its short Latin verse included within it, is accompanied by a six-line French verse, paraphrasing the Latin, and by two and a half pages of prose meditation, also in French. Although Mello's approach is still clearly meditational, the formal structure and intellectual progression is less fully and less explicitly spelt out. Instead the stress is laid heavily on provoking a purely emotional reaction. To this end the reader is apostrophised, and his attention insistently drawn to key elements of the engraved figure, so that he can then be questioned as to his understanding of the relationship of these elements to himself, but above all Mello seeks to engage the emotions of the reader, by forcing him to identify wholly with the scene depicted in the engraved figure. In his introduction he insists on the great value of visual representations as emotional triggers which will stimulate the reader (or viewer) to progress to spiritual union with Christ:

On espere de la pieté des Fidelles qui verront ces Figures, & qui liront les

---

[52]   Praz cites an unillustrated edition of the original French version published in Paris in 1626 by Sebastian Cramoisy under the title *Le coeur devot, trone royal de Jesus pacifique Salomon*, and also an illustrated edition published in Douai in 1627 by Balthasar Bellere under the title *Le coeur devot, throsne royal de Jesus pacifique Salomon, par le R.P. Estienne Luzvic, de la C. de I, auquel sont premises les sainctes faveurs du petit Jesus au coeur qu'il ayme et qui l'ayme, par le R.P. Binet de la mesme Compagnie*, but gives no location for either of these. (Praz, pp.407-8). Landwehr likewise refers to these editions, but gives no locations. (Landwehr, *Dutch Emblem Books*, nos 423-4; *Romanic Emblem Books*, nos 494-5). The only known copy of the original French version is to be found in the Newberry Library, Chicago, and this copy is from an edition published under the same title in Antwerp in 1627 by H. Aertssens. Charles Musart's Latin translation of the work under the title *Cor deo devotum, Jesu Pacifici Salomonis thronus regius*, was published in Douai by Balthasar Bellere in 1627, and this was followed by an equivalent edition in 1628 by Aertssens in Antwerp.

paroles qui les accompagnent, & qui en sont comme autant d'instructions, qu'ils ne concevront rien qui soit indigne de la grandeur & de la Majesté de JESUS-CHRIST, qu'ils auront une estime toute particuliere pour les Divines Operations de ses graces, & qu'ils exciteront toutes les puissances de leurs ames pour augmenter leur devotion, pour émouvoir leurs tendresses, & pour embrazer leurs coeurs de l'amour du DIVIN JESUS, qui est la fin qu'on s'est proposée en donnant ce petit Ouvrage au Public.

(Mello, *Divines operations*, ĩ 1v- ĩ 2r)

and this preoccupation with emotional stimulus and involvement is clearly demonstrated in the work itself. Typical of is approach is the treatment he accords to the Wierix engraving of Jesus standing within a stylised heart, and sweeping out from it devils and snakes, watched by surrounding angels (see fig.22). The engraved figure is accompanied by a quotation from Isaiah 14, which gave the inspiration for the image, 'Scopabo eam in scopa terrens', and by a Latin verse:

> O beatam cordis aedem!
> Te cui caelum dedit sedem
> Purgat suis manibus.
> Animose puer verre
> Monstra tuo vultu terre,
> Tere tuis pedibus.

together with an equivalent French verse:

> Mon coeur vous estes glorieux,
> Puisque mesme le Roy des Cieux
> De ses propres mains vous nettoye.
> Cherchez de l'un à l'autre bout,
> Nettoyez, exterminez tout
> Doux JESUS autheur de ma joye.   (Mello, *Divines operations*, B1v)

But facing this is the meditational prose commentary on the scene, entitled *Jesus baliant le coeur d'une Ame fidelle, afin de le nettoyer de ses ordures* and in this section the repeated questions posed to the reader force his involvement and concentration on the implications of the scene before his eyes:

> Je ne sçay pas ce que le divin Jesus trouve de si charmant dans nostre coeur pour prendre tant de peine à le rendre le digne objet de son amour & de sa complaisance. Mais il est aisé de remarquer en le voiant dans cette posture qui tient les Anges mesme dans l'admiration, & dans l'étonnement, qu'il n'épargne ny ses peines ny ses soins pour en oster toutes les ordures & toutes les impuretez qui sont capables de la soüiller & d'empescher qu'il n'y puisse demeurer en asseurance. N'est ce point parce que le coeur est le centre de tous les desirs & qu'il est si jaloux qu'il n'en ait point d'autres que pour luy

seul, qu'il n'y veut rien souffrir de tout ce qui le pouroit partager par quelque attache criminelle? N'est-ce point qu'estant le principe de tous nos mouvemens, il ne veut pas qu'il en ait d'autres que pour luy. N'est-ce point enfin qu'estant un Vaisseau capable d'une souveraine plenitude, il veut qu'il ne soit remply que de luy seul? Mais disons plustost & asseurons que ce sont toutes ces qualitez ensemble qui l'obligent de prendre la peine & les soins de le purifier, pour le choisir pour sa demeure. Qu'heureux est donc ce coeur fidelle, dans lequel il veut habiter comme dans sa propre maison, pour y regler tous ses desirs, pour se rendre le maistre de tous ses mouvemens, & pour le remplir de la plenitude de ses graces! Et qu'heureux enfin est le coeur qui peut dire qu'il ne desire que JESUS, qu'il ne veut avoir de mouvement que pour JESUS, n'estre remply que de JESUS! Mais pour posseder ce bonheur si parfait, il faut necessairement qu'il soit vuide de toutes les affections aux creatures, qu'il soit purifié de toutes sortes d'impuretez, & qu'il n'ait en effet d'autres desirs durant sa vie que de posseder son divin JESUS, dans le temps & dans l'éternité. Comme c'est le seul JESUS qui nous peut accorder ces faveurs, mettons-nous en devoir de les luy demander avec humilité. Si nous luy sommes aussi fidelles que ce coeur qui par sa fidelité a merité de luy cette grace, nous en pouvons esperer une semblable.

(Mello, *Divines operations*, B2r-3r)

Thus, nearly fifty years after they were first exploited by Wierix in the Netherlands as a basis for meditational emblems following the classic structure as laid down by Loyola, we find the same engravings still being used in Paris by Mello, for the same essential purpose, but focusing more strongly on stimulating a highly charged emotional reaction.

The meditational structure as epitomised in the *Spiritual Exercises* thus clearly formed an important element in Jesuit emblem books in the seventeenth century, but it also played an important role in other associated illustrated works which were also published as part of the propaganda campaign of the Counter-Reformation, and which - while not strictly emblem books, nevertheless have many emblematic characteristics. We see, for example, the same heavily emotional approach of Mello used even more emphatically in another Jesuit meditational work which has strong emblematic features although it does not actually use the word in its title. In the *Meditations affectueuses sur la vie de la tressainte Vierge mere de Dieu* by Etienne Binet,[53] a series of full-page engravings of scenes from the life of the Virgin, each including a short Latin verse within the engraving, are accompanied on the facing recto by a French prose meditation in which the reader is led through a highly charged emotional gloss of the various aspects of the scene laid out before his eyes, as in the third meditation on the childhood of the Virgin. The engraving, entitled 'Maria ab Anna lactantur' depicts Anne nursing her baby daughter, with Joachim sitting beside

---

[53] *Meditations affectueuses sur la vie de la tressainte Vierge mere de Dieu. Par le R.P. Estienne Binet de la Compagnie de Jesus*, Antwerp, M. Nutius for Th. Galle, 1632, 8°.

her, with Gabriel and other angels in the background, and the accompanying meditation, entitled 'L'enfance de Nostre Dame' reflects on the joy and happiness of the idyllic scene, as in the opening two paragraphs:

> Qui vit jamais l'innocence, & la beauté du ciel, il conoistra fort aisement cette petite fille qui est dans le giron de S. Anne, & que S. Joachim tient par la petite main: je ne sçay comme le coeur n'esclatte de joye & à l'un, & à l'autre, voiant cette douceur, & cette beauté enfantine, le diamant du monde.
>
> Que les Anges sont aises voiant joüer cette tendre fillette dans le sein de sa fortunee mere, & sur les genoux du bon Joachim! Ilz ont fendu le ciel pour la mirer à leur aise, ilz joüent une chanson du ciel, & chantent des airs du paradis pour resjoüir cette petite fille, qui doit un jour manier le sceptre des monarchies du ciel... (Binet, *Meditations affectueuses*, A5r)

Again, in Jeremias Drexel's very different illustrated treatise on death, the *Avantcoureur de l'eternité*, which is remarkably reminiscent of the much earlier *Dances of Death* which were so popular in the fifteenth and early sixteenth centuries, we find a series of alphabetically annotated engravings of the skeletal figure of Death carrying out a range of activities, each of which is accompanied by a lengthy set of *Considerations* reflecting on the implications for humanity of the scene. As with the many other works of this prolific Jesuit writer, the *Avantcoureur de l'eternité* was originally composed in Latin and published in Munich in 1628, then in Douai and Cologne in 1629, and thereafter in a series of editions in Cologne. But it also obviously had lasting popularity to a French audience, as is clear from the fact that the first edition of the French version published in Paris in 1662 was followed by three further editions published in Rouen over the next quarter of a century. Furthermore, a second French translation, published under the variant title *La voye qui conduit au ciel*, which was first published in Paris in 1684, again ran through two more Paris editions in the course of the 1680s.[54]

But although it was so very successfully exploited by the Society of Jesus, this meditational technique did not remain its exclusive property, but was also exploited by

---

[54] *L'avantcoureur de l'eternité. Composé en Latin par le R. Pere Drexellius de la Compagnie de Jesus. Traduit de nouveau en François par Monsieur L.G.*, Paris, G. Marcher, 1662, 12°; *ibid.*, Rouen, J. Gruel, 1670, 12°; *ibid.*, Rouen, J. Oursel, 1683, 12°; *ibid.*, Rouen, J.B.Besongne, 1689, 12°; *La voye qui conduit au ciel, ou l'avant-coureur de l'eternité*, Paris, A. Auroy, 1684, 12°; *ibid.*,1687 and 1688. Drexel's work was also translated into German, Italian and English. (For details see Praz, pp.319-20). It was originally published in Latin in Munich in 1628 (*Aeternitatis prodromus, mortis nuntius quem sanis, aegrotatis, moribundis sistit Hieremias Drexelius è Societate Iesu*, Munich, C. Leysser, 1628, 12°), and thereafter in Douai in 1629, and in a series of editions in Cologne (Douai, B. Bellere, 1629, 12° ; Cologne, P. Henning, 1629, 12° ; Cologne, C. ab Egmond, 1630, 12°; *ibid.*, 1633 and 1645). For details see Landwehr, *German Emblem Books*, nos 243-7, and Praz, pp.319-20.

Figure 23: Berthod, *Emblemes sacrez*, Paris, 1665, p.204.

members of other orders, intent likewise on furthering the cause of the Counter-Reformation. The Observant Franciscan François Berthod indicates specifically in the full title of his collection of *Emblemes sacrez tirez de l'escriture saincte & des peres* of 1657 that each of his emblems is accompanied by a meditation 'pour servir à la conduite de la vie chrestienne'.[55] In the classic manner of the *Spiritual Exercises*, the work traces the spiritual progression of the soul to final salvation from a starting point

---

[55] *Emblemes sacrez tirez de l'Escriture Saincte & des Peres. Inventees et expliquees en vers François, avec une brieve meditation sur le mesme sujet. Pour servir à la conduite de la vie chrestienne. Par le P.F. Berthod religieux cordelier.* In the later edition of the work published in an expanded form by Loyson in 1665, Berthod is describes as 'religieux de l'Observance de S. François'.

of contemplation of hell and damnation, with each meditation divided into a series of itemised points. As Chesneau did in his *Emblemes sacrez*, Berthod also draws his symbols from a wide range of non-religious sources, and several are reworkings of traditional emblematic themes, but in each case, Berthod interprets them specifically in a religious context, as in his treatment of the figure of the crane in emblem 28. The engraving depicts the crane in its traditional pose, holding a stone in its claw (see fig.23), but Berthod's accompanying short passage of French verse explains that this denotes not just vigilance in general, as is normally the case, but rather specifically Christian vigilance:

> Par cette grue on voit quil faut toujours veiller
> Dessus sa conscience, et jamais sommeiller
> De peur de se laisser prendre par la paresse.
> Car qui veut des vertus acquerir les tresors
> Qui font dans le Chretien la plus grande richesse,
> Il y faut travailler et d'esprit et de corps.   (Berthod, *Emblemes sacrez*, I6v)

and this message is further emphasised in the prose commentary on the facing page:

> Cette grue qui porte une pierre dans son pied, qu'elle tient en l'air pour s'empescher de dormir, afin de n'estre point surprise, nous monstre la diligence que l'homme doit apporter aux choses de son salut; qu'il ne doit jamais se laisser surprendre par la paresse, & qu'incessamment il doit veiller pour la conservation de son ame & pour l'acquisition des vertus.
> (Berthod, *Emblemes sacrez*, K1r)

after which follows the directed passage of meditation, with its overall title, *De la diligence que nous devons apporter au travail de nostre salut*, and biblical reference to 2 Chronicles: 'Faites toutes choses avec diligence. 2. Par. 19. v.7', in which each successive argument (numbered, as in the *Spiritual Exercises*, *premier point; second point; troisieme point*) is introduced by an apostrophe to the reader, urging him to reflect on the scene, beginning with the exhortation 'Considerez que...'.

Similarly we saw earlier how Adrien Gambart (who describes himself simply as 'prestre') produced in 1664 a collection of meditational emblems in honour of St François de Sales for the nuns of the Order of the Visitation, in which once again the word 'meditation' is used specifically in the title:

> *La vie symbolique du bienheureux François de Sales, evesque et prince de Geneve. Comprise sous le voile de 52 emblemes, qui marquent le caractere de ses principales vertus, avec autant de meditations ou reflexions pieuses, pour exciter les ames chrestiennes & religieuses à l'amour & à la pratique des mesmes vertus. Par M. Adrien Gambart prestre.*[56]

---

[56]   See above, pp.224 *et seq.*

Here, although Gambart's debt to the Jesuit technique is clear, he does depart somewhat from the pattern of the *Spiritual Exercises* to the extent that - unlike Loyola - he groups his meditational passages together at the end of the work rather than having each passage of meditation follow immediately after the emblem to which it relates. In this respect, he follows rather the manner adopted in Nadal's much earlier *Evangelicae historiae imagines* and *Adnotationes et meditationes*, in which the engravings were similarly all grouped together, and the annotations and meditations similarly grouped together as as separate entity.

Discussion in this chapter has focused wholly on Catholic emblem books, as might be expected since France was so strongly a Catholic country, and for the minority of Huguenots in France, distrust of the use of pictorial images also lessened the attraction of this particular literary form. In Protestant England, however, the situation was much more flexible, as is demonstrated by the fact that Francis Quarles produced in 1625 a very successful collection of English emblems acceptable to a Protestant readership, which were actually derived from *Anima/Amor divinus* emblems from two Jesuit works, Hugo's *Pia desideria* and the *Typus mundi*, produced as a collective enterprise by the boys of the Jesuit College in Antwerp. As Höltgen remarks in his introduction to Quarles's *Emblemes*, 'Quarles' *Emblemes* brought to England - in a suitable guise - the emotional ardours and religious ecstacies of the Catholic Counter-Reformation, depicted on the title-page by the heart, burning with divine love, and rising above the world'.[57] Two decades later, in 1647, Christopher Harvey also produced a Protestant reworking in English of Haeften's *Schola cordis*, under the title *The School of the Heart*. However the situation in France, a Catholic country, as likewise in Catholic Antwerp where so much of the religious emblem literature that we have been discussing was published, was very different from that of England, and we do not find this same pattern of Protestant reworkings being published in either France or Antwerp. The French Protestant emblem book achieved its moment of glory with Georgette de Montenay in the later sixteenth century, but this glory was not thereafter sustained by further Protestant French emblem books in the seventeenth century.[58] Whether it actually originated in France or was - like many of the works

---

[57]   See Introduction to Francis Quarles, *Emblemes* (1635). Edward Benlowes Quarleïs and *Hieroglyphikes of the Life of Man* (1638), p.11*. For discussion of the adaptation of Jesuit emblems for the use of Protestant readers in England see also Barbara Lewalski, *Protestant Poetics and the Seventeenth-Century Religious Lyric*, pp.192-5; Karl-Josef Höltgen, 'The devotional quality of Quarles's *Emblemes*' in his *Aspects of the Emblem*, pp.31-65; and Karl-Josef Höltgen, 'Catholic pictures versus Protestant words? The adaptation of the Jesuit sources in Quarles' *Emblemes*', *Emblematica*, 9,1, 1995, pp.221-38. See also G.Richard Dimler, 'Edmund Arwaker's translation of the *Pia desideria*: the reception of a continental Jesuit emblem book in seventeenth-century England'. For discussion of the reception in Protestant England of other continental Catholic emblem books see also G. Richard Dimler, 'The Jesuit emblem book in seventeenth-century Protestant England', *Archivum Historicum Societatis Iesu*, 75, 1984, pp.357-69.

[58]   While Montenay's emblem book was republished several times, the various subsequent editions were published in Zurich, Heidelburg and Frankfurt rather than in France itself. Only

discussed in the previous chapter - an import from the Netherlands, the religious emblem book as it manifested itself so strongly in France in the seventeenth century, was invariably a Catholic (and very often a Jesuit) production. Although it could take a number of different approaches and different structural forms, as we have seen, it was composed almost invariably not solely to please or to divert, or even to educate, but by means of one or other of its various approaches, to strengthen piety and commitment to the faith, serving thereby one of the fundamental purposes of its creators, the advancement of the Counter-Reformation.[59]

the last edition in 1620 (which is in fact a re-issue of the 1571 edition) was published in France - and it is significant that it was produced in the Protestant stronghold of La Rochelle.
[59] For detailed discussion of the role of art in general, and of emblematic art in particular, in the Counter-Reformation see J.B.Knipping, *Iconography of the Counter-Reformation in the Netherlands. Heaven on Earth*. As well as painting and sculpture, Knipping examines also the work of the major specialist engravers such as Wierix, De Passe and Boëtius à Bolswert. For a detailed bibliography of Jesuit emblem books see Peter Daly and G. Richard Dimler, *The Jesuit Series* (Corpus Librorum Emblematum), Part 1 (A-D), Montreal, 1997. For a short-title list of Jesuit emblem books see G. Richard Dimler, 'Short title listing of Jesuit emblem books', *Emblematica*, 2,1, 1987, pp. 139-87.

CHAPTER VII

ROYAL GLORIFICATION AND CELEBRATIONS THROUGH THE MEDIUM OF EMBLEMS AND DEVICES

This chapter covers a number of different types of emblematic manifestations, all of which are united by their common objective of glorifying the monarch as both leader and figurehead of his country. As well as figuring in conventional printed texts and collections of engravings, emblems and devices also played a very important role in royal festivities and celebrations, including triumphal entries in which allegorical ephemeral architecture were a significant feature, and manifested themselves also in other, more permanent forms of the plastic arts in the shape of wall and ceiling paintings and tapestries, all likewise designed to make a public statement about the greatness of the royal owner. In several of the works discussed earlier in chapter 4, such as Ménestrier's metallic *Histoire du Roy Louis le Grand* or the anonymous *Explication en vers des tableaux de la galerie de Versailles*, for example, the role which they played was not solely an educational one, conveying information in a pleasing and palatable form. They also had an important role to play in disseminating to as wide a public as possible an awareness of the greatness of the reigning monarch, and the information which they conveyed in this manner was not simply educational, but was rather carefully selected and packaged as an important source of royal propaganda.

The strategies adopted in the seventeenth century for royal glorification and celebration, and in particular the exploitation of emblems and devices, do not spring newly into existence, but rather - as we have seen so often in the course of this study - represent a natural progression from patterns already well developed in the sixteenth century. Yet although the phenomenon was not new, the consistent and systematic glorification of kingship during the reign of Louis XIV reached a greater height than ever before, thanks in large part to the highly professional approach of Colbert who, as soon as he came to power in 1661, after the death of Mazarin, set out to create a sophisticated publicity machine to enhance the reputation of the young monarch which, once established, continued to operate throughout Louis's lengthy reign. In 1663, for example, Colbert initiated the *Petite Académie*, subsequently renamed the

Académie des inscriptions et belles lettres, with the remit of providing historiography
of the early exploits of the young king, together with circumstantial verses and devices
for notable occasions, and appropriate inscriptions for celebratory medals. Among the
most active members of the *Petite Académie* in this domain was its most famous
member, Charles Perrault, secretary of the organisation. It is not coincidental that
Louis XIV is still today habitually referred to as often by the epithet 'le Roi Soleil' or
the 'Sun King' as he is by his official title, alluding thereby to the device which was
given to him at birth, and which he continued to exploit throughout his life as a
forceful symbol of his supposedly unique greatness, reflected furthermore in the self-
aggrandising motto which often accompanied the image, *Nec pluribus impar*. While
many of the personal devices of earlier French monarchs are still familiar today, in no
case are they so familiar that they can be used as a substitute title for the king.[1]

Particularly within the domain of triumphal entries and court celebrations and
spectacle which were to become such an important feature of seventeenth-century
political and social life, the pattern of using emblematic materials for the expression of
particular iconographic messages was already well established in the sixteenth
century, and indeed even in the early decades of the century before the 'emblem' as
such had even been officially introduced, allegorical figures which are emblematic in
all but name were already being used. The earliest printed edition of Alciato's
collection of emblems bears the date 'die 28. Februarii, Anno M.D.XXXI' on the
colophon. That same February Eleanor of Austria, the new wife of François 1er, made
a triumphal entry into Rouen, together with the young *Dauphin*, recently returned to
France in 1530 after four years in prison in Spain, and the printed account of the
celebration describes a number of allegorical figures which were used emblematically
to convey the iconographic message of the occasion, with text accompanying the
visual representations.[2] The static allegorical figures of Justice and Peace, for
example, were accompanied by written Latin and French verses, and - more
ingeniously - an image of a phoenix was actually burned on its funeral pyre at the
appropriate moment in the procession, and from the ashes arose not just another
phoenix but also a salamander, in deference to François, accompanied once again by
written Latin and French verses:

> Dum sese renovat phenix comburitur igne
> Se tactis illesa manet salamandra favillis.
>
> Ardant amour au feu de charité
> Le phenix brusle. Et de lui pareil vient.

---

[1]   As, for example, Louis XII's porcupine, or Anne de Bretagne's ermine, or François 1er's
salamander, or Henri II's crescent moons. Elsewhere in Europe the Pillars of Hercules used by
the Emperor Charles V or the portcullis used by Henry VIII of England are equally familiar,
but likewise do not act as a substitute for the actual name of their royal owner.

[2]   See *Les entrées de la reyne et de monseigneur daulphin, lieutenant general du roy et
gouverneur en ce pays de Normandie. Faictes à Rouen en l'an mil cinq cents trente et ung*,
Lyon, R. Gaultier, n.d. (1531), 4°, ed. A. Pottier, Rouen, 1866.

> La salemandre en son integrité
> Dedens le feu son essence retient.
>
> *(Les entrées de la reyne et de monseigneur daulphin*, c4r)

But at an earlier stage in the procession the royal visitors had been confronted by another emblematic figure exploiting both figure and verse, but in this case a 'living emblem' in which the textual element was not inscribed, but rather spoken aloud by the figure of Pallas, bearing among her various attributes her habitual owl denoting wisdom, and it is this latter attribute which forms the basis of the French verse which she declaims to the royal visitors:

> Tous les tresors de sçavoir, sont ouvers
> En moy Pallas, par le vouloir des dieux:
> Dont je vous fais present en ces bas lieux
> Affin que en vous soient tousjours recouvers.
>
> *(Les entrées de la reyne et de monseigneur daulphin*, b4v)

Among the more splendidly ornate and iconographically complex of such sixteenth-century triumphal entries was that of Henri II and Catherine de Medici into Lyon in 1548, and perhaps not insignificantly the group responsible for designing and organising this event included such emblematic specialists as Maurice Scève, Barthélemy Aneau and the artist Bernard Salomon.[3] Similarly splendid were the separate triumphal entries of the same couple into Paris the following year, in which several of the iconographic themes were probably derived from Alciato's emblems,[4] but perhaps the most grandiose and complex royal entry of the sixteenth century was the 1571 entry into Paris of Charles IX and Elisabeth of Austria, daughter of the Emperor Maximilian, of which Simon Bouquet, who was responsible for orchestrating the celebration, produced a subsequent published account.[5] The overall message of

---

[3]   *La magnificence de la superbe et triumphante entrée de la noble et antique cité de Lyon faicte au treschrestien Roy de France Henry deuxiesme de ce nom, et à la Royne Catherine son espouse le XXIII. de Septembre M.D.XLVIII*, Lyon, G. Roville, 1549, 4°. Again it is significant that the publisher of this account was Guillaume Roville, one of the major emblematic specialists in Lyon at the time. For a critical facsimile edition of this work see R.Cooper, ed., *The Entry of Henri II into Lyon, September 1548*. Cooper also describes briefly earlier royal entries into Lyon from as early as 1507

[4]   *C'est l'ordre qui a esté tenu à la nouvelle et joyeuse entrée, que treshault, tresexcellent, trespuissant prince le Roy treschrestien Henry deuzieme de ce nom a faicte en sa bonne ville et cité de Paris, capitale de son royaume, le sezieme jour de Juin M.D.XLIX* and *C'est l'ordre et forme qui a esté tenu au sacre et couronnement de treshaulte et tresillustre dame Madame Catherine de Medicis, Royne de France, faicte en l'Eglise Monseigneur sainct Denys en France, le X. jour de Juin. M.D.XLIX*. For discussion of the influence of Alciato's emblems on this event see I.D.McFarlane's facsimile edition, *The Entry of Henri II into Paris 16 June 1549*.

[5]   Simon Bouquet, *Bref et sommaire recueil de ce qui a esté faict et de l'ordre tenuë à la joyeuse et triumphante entrée de tres-puissant tres-magnanime et tres-chrestien Prince Charles IX...avec le couronnement de tres-haute, tres-illustre et tres-excellente princesse Madame*

the entry was a political one, celebrating not only the coronation of Charles IX's new queen, but also the cessation of hostilities consequent upon the Peace of Saint Germain of the previous year, and so the iconographic themes of the event were victory, peace and marriage. In Bouquet's description and explanation of one of the set pieces at the Fontaine des Innocents celebrating allegorically the marriage of the youthful Charles and Elisabeth we see familiar emblematic figures appearing, including, for example, the turtledove and crow accompanying the figure of *Hymen*, possibly inspired from Barthélemy Aneau's *Figure de mariage* in his *Imagination poétique*:

> En l'honneur duquel mariage estoit devant la fontaine de sainct Innocent un autre grand colosse...C'estoit la figure du Dieu Hymenée en forme d'un jeune homme, embelli d'une petite barbe follette, crespelüe, et longs cheveux....
>
> A l'un de ses costez estoit une Jeunesse, sur laquelle il s'appuioit, signifiant qu'il fault entrer en nopces durant la verdeure de l'aage sans attendre si tard: afin de pouvoir voir ses enfans grandz...
>
> Sous les piedz de ce petit Amour estoit une sphere, representant le monde, pour monstrer que rien ne vit en ce monde qui ne soit subject à l'amour, affin de faire renaistre d'espece en espece son semblable pour l'entretenement, de l'immortelle mortalité, suivant ce que dit Platon.
>
> Autour de ceste sphere estoient force pommes d'orenges et guirlandes faictes de rozes et de liz, qui denotoient que la jeunesse s'amuse plus volontiers aux choses de plaisir qu'à son profit. Quant aux pommes d'orenges, qui signifient l'or, chacun sçait combien l'or est desiré en l'amour: tesmoing Athalante, qui en fut surprinse, et vaincue, et aussi que les pommes comme ayant formes rondes, sont tousjours dediées à Cupido. Philostrate en ses images en donne ample cognoissance. Sous les piedz de cest Hymenée estoit un chevreau animal lascif, pour signifier l'ardeur amoureuze de jeunesse...Et tout aupres estoit une corneille, denotant la fermeté inviolable qu'on doibt s'entregarder en mariage, pour ce que tel oyseau, comme la tourterelle, ne se racouple jamais apres qu'elle a perdu son premier party. (Bouquet, *Bref et sommaire recueil*, f.29r-v)[6]

Marguerite Elizabet d'Austriche son espouse...et entrée de ladicte dame en icelle ville le jeudi xxix dudict mois de mars M.D.LXXI. For an analysis of the importance of the iconography of this event see V. Graham and W. McAllister-Johnson, *The Paris Entries of Charles IX and Elisabeth of Austria 1571, with an Analysis of Simon Bouquet's Bref et sommaire recueil.* See also Frances Yates, 'Poètes et artistes dans les entrées de Charles IX et de sa reine à Paris en 1571', in J. Jacquot, ed., *Les fêtes de la Renaissance*, Paris, 1956, pp.61-84.

[6]   See the same allegorical birds incorporated, together with many other symbols of marriage into Aneau's highly complex emblem:

> Puys est aupres un arbre fruyct portant,
> Et maint oyseau sur ces rameaux montant,
>   Comme Colombz, qui l'un à l'autre plaisent,
> Tant par amour, que bec à bec se baisent.
> Et une paire aussi de Tourtourelles,

Reflecting the particular importance of this occasion, the most eminent poets were engaged to provide the necessary verses. Jean Dorat was charged with composing the Latin verses and Ronsard the French verses, including a patriotic sonnet to accompany the allegorical figure of *Hymen*:

> Heureux le siecle, heureuse la journée
> Où des Germains le sang tres-ancien
> S'est remeslé avec le sang Troien
> Par le bien-faict d'un heureux Hymenée
>   Telle race est derechef retournée
> Qui vint jadis du filz Hectorien,
> Que Pharamond prince Franconien
> Feit regermer sous bonne destinée.
>   O bon Hymen, bon pere des humains
> Qui tiens l'estat de ce monde en tes mains
> Bien favorable à ce sainct mariage,
>   Qu'un bon accord ne face qu'un de deux
> Et que les filz des filz qui viendront d'eux
> Tiennent la France eternel heritage.
>   (Bouquet, *Bref et sommaire recueil*, f.29v)

In the court festivities which became increasingly elaborate in the latter half of the sixteenth century, under the influence of Catherine de Medici, emblematic materials also played their part in conveying an appropriate iconographic message. Among the more detailed accounts of such events is the *Recueil des choses notables, qui ont esté faites à Bayonne, à l'entreveuë du Roy treschrestien Charles neufieme de ce nom, et la Royne sa treshonorée mere avec la Royne Catholique sa soeur*, recording the allegorical complexities of the lavish series of festivities which surrounded the meeting in 1565 of Charles IX and his mother with his sister Elisabeth, then married to Philip II of Spain, a politically highly important meeting, marking the culmination of a gruelling 27-month grand tour of his country by the young king, during which he undertook more than one hundred triumphal entries into the various towns on his itinerary.[7] Among the various stylised chivalric performances which punctuated this event one of the particular features was the ritualistic presentation of meaningful

---

> Qui ont assez de leur pair au tour d'elles...
> ...Là sont aussi Corneilles qui se suyvent:
> Et qui ensemble en grand concorde vivent...
> ...L'arbre fruyctier en fleurs, & fruictz plaisant,
> Mariage est, beaux enfans produysans. (Aneau, *Imagination poetique*, B2v)

[7]   For discussion of the political background to the Bayonne meeting see Frances Yates, *The Valois Tapestries*. For details of the lengthy tour of the country preceding the meeting at Bayonne and of the various entries into the different towns see V. Graham and W. McAllister-Johnson, *The Royal Tour of France by Charles IX and Catherine de Medici. Festivals and Entries 1564-66*, and J. Boutier, A. Dewerpe and D. Nordman, *Un tour de France royal. Le voyage de Charles IX 1564-1566*, Paris, 1984.

medallions. At one point, for example, individual medallions were distributed by the Muses to the various ladies on behalf of the various gentlemen, as described in the *Recueil des choses notables*, together with a note of their inscriptions and significance:

> Le premier present fut celuy du ROY, comme le Parrain & Chef de la trouppe des Chevaliers de la grand' Bretagne: lequel fut presenté à la Royne d'Espagne de la part du Roy, par une desdites Muses.
>
> Ledit present estoit une grande Medaille d'or, pendue à une chaine d'or. En ladite Medaille estoit la devise du Roy telle, qu'elle est pourtraite cy dessoubs.
>
> Le second present fut presenté de la part de ANDRON DE NIQUEE, qui estoit Monsieur de sainct Remy, à Madamoiselle la Guyonniere.
>
> Ledit present estoit semblable au susdit, en la Medaille duquel estoit la devise du Chevalier, telle que cy dessoubs.
>
> *(Recueil des choses notables, f.35r-v)*

The ceremonial exchange of such medallions by members of the court was also used again, as was also the technique of living emblems, fifteen years later, in 1581, in another particularly grandiose court festivity marking the marriage of one of Henri III's favourites, the Duc de Joyeuse. The ceremony at which this occurred was the culmination of a fortnight of celebrations of the marriage, and as usual a full published account of it was produced within a year by Balthasar de Beaujoyeulx,[8] in which he describes the exchange of symbolic medallions, all in this case relating to the single overall theme of water, in keeping with the ladies' attire as naiads and dryads:

> Ce Balet parachevé, les Naiades & Dryades feirent une grande reverence à sa majesté: et de ce pas la Royne approchant du Roy son seigneur, le print par la main, & luy feit present d'une grande medaille d'or, où il y avoit dedans un Daulphin qui nageoit en la mer: lors chacun print pour augure asseuré de celuy que Dieu leur donnera pour le bon-heur de ce royaume. A l'exemple de la Royne toutes les autres Princesses, dames, & damoyselles, furent aussi chacune selon leur rang & degré prendre les Princes, Seigneurs, & Gentils-hommes que bon leur sembla: à chacun desquels elles feirent leur present d'or, avec leurs devises, toutes choses de mer: d'autant qu'elles representoyent les nymphes des eaux, ainsi que vous verrez cy apres.
>
> Madame la princesse de Lorraine donna à Monsieur de Mercur la Sereine.

---

[8]   *Balet comique de la Royne, faict aux nopces de monsieur le Duc de Joyeuse et madamoyselle de Vaudemont sa soeur, par Baltasar de Beaujoyeulx, valet de chambre du Roy, et de la Royne sa mere.* For a full analysis of the event and of the exploitation of devices and emblematic materials see the facsimile edition by Margaret McGowan. See also her *L'art du ballet de cour en France 1581-1643*.

> Madame de Mercur à monsieur de Lorraine, le Neptune.
> Madame de Nevers à monsieur de Guise, le Cheval marin.
> Madame de Guise à monsieur de Genevois, l'Arion.
> Madame d'Aumalle au Marquis de Chaussim, la Baleine...
> (Beaujoyeulx, *Balet comique de la Royne*, f.63v)

Not only does Balthasar de Beaujoyeulx describe the devices on the medallions, together with their Latin mottoes, but he also includes in his account a set of engravings, depicting the familiar figures. The Princess of Lorraine's siren is shown clasping her traditional mirror, with the motto *Siren Virtute haud blandior ulla est*, while Madame de Guise's figure of Arion is shown in his habitual emblematic pose, triumphantly astride the dolphin, harp in hand, accompanied by the motto *Populi superat prudentia fluctus*.[9]

In these various ceremonial festivities dating from the sixteenth century we find patterns which continue to feature in equivalent events staged in the seventeenth century.[10] The pattern of celebratory royal entries both to Paris and to many provincial towns continues in the seventeenth century - occurring particularly on the occasion of the accession of a new king, or the arrival of a new queen - but in addition to these we also see a significant trend developing, particularly during the reign of Louis XIV, towards greater emphasis on more purely aristocratic, court-based, festivity, following the pattern begun in the latter half of the sixteenth century under the influence of Catherine de Medici. Sometimes - like the 1565 Bayonne festivities or those of the Joyeuse marriage in 1581 -these were organised to celebrate a particular event such as a military victory, a peace treaty, a royal marriage or a royal birth, and sometimes simply to provide a joyous occasion. But in both cases the underlying object of the event - to provide an important visual demonstration of royal presence, authority, and magnificence - remained the same, although the targeted audience differed according to where the event was staged. In the case of festivities mounted in Paris the demonstration of royal splendour would be visible not only to the participating and onlooking aristocratic audience, but also to the greater audience of the onlooking populace of the town, as was the case with the traditional triumphal entry, whereas in the case of celebrations held at Versailles - as was increasingly the case during the reign of Louis XIV - that message would be conveyed only to the participating and invited aristocratic audience (including also foreign ambassadors and other distinguished visitors from abroad who would also be a targeted audience) rather than to the more disparate wider audience who would have access to festivities held in the capital city itself. The audience for such court festivities held in the 1670s at Versailles as the *Plaisirs de l'Isle enchantée*, the *Relation de la feste de Versailles*, or the *Divertissemens de Versailles* would be restricted to invited participants only, but

---

[9] Although the illustration of Alciato's Arion emblem (*In avaros, vel quibus melior conditio ab extraneis offertur*) takes a number of different forms in the various editions of his *Emblemata*, the one element which never changes is the figure of Arion himself astride his dolphin, harp in hand, as in the medallion reproduced here.

[10] For discussion of the use of emblems and devices in sixteenth-century triumphant entries and court events see Saunders, *Sixteenth-Century French Emblem Book*, pp.279-92.

firework displays mounted in Paris, such as those organised by the municipality to celebrate the return of the eleven-year old Louis XIV to his capital city in 1649, whence he had fled for a period of several months with his mother from the first *Fronde*[11] or - some forty years later - to celebrate the birth of Louis's grandsons, Louis, Duc de Bourgogne in 1682 and his younger brother, the Duc de Berry, in 1686 would have been visible to a much broader audience.[12] Likewise although the participants in such chivalric tournaments as that staged in 1612 to celebrate the double marriage alliance of Louis XIII and Anne d'Autriche, and of his sister, Elisabeth, to the future Philip IV of Spain were aristocratic, the fact that the tournaments were staged in a public place like the Place Royale ensured that they would be visible also to a wider, non-aristocratic audience.[13]

The accession of Henri IV in 1589, after the assassination of Henri III, was fraught with conflict, and the early strife-ridden years of his reign were not characterised by large numbers of triumphal entries. However his marriage to Marie de Medici in 1600 did provide the opportunity for Avignon to open its gates to the new queen, and the elaborate arrangements made to welcome her are described in detail, with lavish illustration, in André Valladier's acccount of the event. The intention had been to welcome both king and queen to Avignon, but in the event Henri was engaged in war with the Duke of Savoy, and Marie de Medici entered the city alone. Nevertheless the complex iconography of the entry, focusing on the Labours of Hercules, and designed to relate to the king, rather than to Marie, carried too important a political message for it to be changed simply because he himself was not present. As reflected in the title of Valladier's account, *Labyrinthe royal de l'Hercule*

---

[11]   For a printed account of this event see Jean Valdor's *Explication du magnifique dessein du feu de joye, faict par ordre de messieurs les Prevost des Marchands, Echevins de la ville de Paris, pour le jour de la naissance de Louys 14. Roy de France & de Navarre, & en resjouïssance de son heureux retour dans sa bonne ville de Paris. Composé par le Sieur Valdor. Par commandement de Messieurs les Prevost des Marchands & Eschevins de la ville de Paris*, Paris, L. Ninain, 1649, 4°. See also N. Rozard's account of the celebration by the people of Paris on the safe return of the king to Paris: *Le triomphe royal, et la réjouïssance des bons François sur le retour du roy, de la reine et des princes...avec la harangue qui leur a esté faite à leur entrée à Paris, le 18 de ce mois...Dedié à Madamoiselle*, Paris, Veuve J. Rémy, 1649, 4°.
[12]   For a description of these two events see *Explication du feu d'artifice dressé devant l'hostel de ville par les ordres de messieurs les Prevost des Marchands & Echevins, pour la naissance du prince que nous vient de donner Madame la Dauphine*, n.p. (Paris), Veuve G. Adam, 1682, 4°; and *Explication du feu d'artifice dressé devant l'hostel de ville par l'ordre de messieurs les Prevost des Marchands & Eschevins de la ville de Paris. A la naissance de Monseigneur le Duc de Berry*, Paris, T. Guillain, n.d. (1686), 4°.
[13]   See Vulson's account of this event, entitled *Le magnifique et admirable carrosel qui fut fait à Paris dans la Place Royale, le cinq, le six, & le septiesme jour d'avril, l'an mil six cens & douze, pour les resjouissances de la publication de la double alliance, par les mariages du Roy Louis XIII, & de Madame sa soeur avec l'Infante & le Prince d'Espagne; & la description des machines, des habits, des armes, des livrées, des cartels, & des devises des chevaliers qui y parurent. Ensemble les courses qui s'y firent à la quintaine & à la bague &c*, included in his *Vray theatre d'honneur et de chevalerie* of 1648.

gaulois triomphant,[14] the whole city centre was transformed into a vast labyrinth around seven triumphal arches, each of which took as its unifying theme one of the Labours of Hercules, and using emblematic materials to build up a forceful cumulative allegorical message paralleling the strength and power of Henri IV with that of Hercules. In his discussion of the iconographic programme of this entry, Denis Crouzet suggests that the particular aim of identifying the French king with Hercules was to stress thereby his immortality, which would enable France to return to political stability after years of civil unrest.[15]

The overall association with Hercules, indicated already in the title to Valladier's account is further spelt out in the dedication of the work to the king by the 'Ville d'Avignon', equating each of Hercules's individual Labours with an equivalent triumph on the part of the French king:

> Conformément à cet horoscope les maistres traicts, & pourfils commencerent à se descouvrir en vostre bas aage, où vous avez eschappé, & estoufé mille embusches, & dangiers comme serpenteaux rampans sur le berceau de vostre adolescence. En laquelle desja, Sire, Roy seulement de Navarre, vous presentastes le duel en champ clos, à un lyon à Nerac, & le mittes par terre, & deslors esbauchates par divers succez, & victoires signalees tout le project de ses lineamens Herculins, lesquels vostre Majesté du depuis à coulourez, & reduicts à leur entiere, & inimitable perfection. Hercules desfit l'Hydre; vostre Majesté, par ces memorables journees d'Arques, d'Ivry, d'Amiens, & autres presque sans nombre a abbatu plus d'armees, que l'Hydre n'avoit de goziers; broyant à la moulette de vostre coutelas tranchant le plus beau vermillon de vostre peinture, Hercules chargea le ciel sur ses espaules, & vous endossates, le jour de vostre sacre, ce monde de France...
>
> (Valladier, *Labyrinthe royal*, †2r)

Similarly the more detailed individual associations between the large numbers of emblems depicted on the various triumphal arches of the labyrinth and specific military victories achieved by Henri are also pointed out in the *Table* at the beginning of the work, which lists all the arches and their iconography, prior to these being reproduced in large engravings and further described and explained later, as in, for

---

[14] *Labyrinthe royal de l'Hercule gaulois triomphant. Sur le suject des fortunes, batailles, victoires, trophées, triomphes, mariage, & autres faicts heroiques, & memorables de tres-auguste & tres-chrestien prince Henry IIII. Roy de France, & de Navarre. Representé à l'Entrée triomphante de la Royne en la cité d'Avignon. Le 19. novembre, l'an M.DC. Où sont contenuës les magnificences et triomphes dressez à cet effect par ladicte ville*, Avignon, J. Bramereau, 1601, folio.

[15] 'The king embodies life, and the principle of life, Reason. God, or half-god, he cannot die. Any questioning of the immortality of the king would signify the sweeping return of human passion and the forces of destruction', D. Crouzet, 'Henri IV king of reason?', in K. Cameron, ed., *From Valois to Bourbon. Dynasty, State and Society in Early Modern France*, Exeter, 1989, pp.73-106 (p.94). See also *Une entrée royale: Marie de Medicis à Avignon, 19 novembre 1600*, Avignon, 1985.

example, the description of the first arch (see fig.24):

Figure 24: Valladier, *Labyrinthe royal*, Avignon, 1601, p.51.

> Les cinq emblemes. Le 1. du labyrinthe de Dedale pour tout le suject. pag. 63. Le 2. du foudre pour la journee d'Yvry. pag. 63. Le 3. du Salus pour la journee d'Arques. p.65. Le 4. des stymphalides pour Fontaine Françoise. p.66. Le 5. de Troye, & de la roüe de fortune pour Amiens. pag.68...
> (Valladier, *Labyrinthe royal*, ††3v)

It is interesting to note among the emblems depicted on the sixth arch two on the subject of the sun triumphing over cloud, anticipating the better known later use of this image by Henri's grandson, Louis XIV:

> *L'Arc sixiesme du labyrinthe...*
> Le premier Embleme d'un Cerf beuvant à la pure fontaine...
> Le 2. du Soleil dissipant les nuees...
> Le 3. du Pegase se guindant au ciel, & frapant le roch des pieds de derriere...
> Le quatriesme du Soleil sortant plus brillant de la nuee...
> (Valladier, *Labyrinthe royal*, †††1v-2r)

As is often the case, in the printed account of this entry, no distinction is made between the word 'emblem' and the word 'device'. In, for example, his description of the representation of Hercules and the Hydra on one of the arches, Valladier uses both words in the same sentence:

> Les Devises ou Emblemes estoient cinq, un qui respondoit à l'Hydre, au frontispice de la seconde face: & quatre pour les quatre coins des frontispices des deux faces. Le premier estoit un labyrinthe, & une massüe d'Hercules au milieu, touchant du bout les nuees, quasi comme elle est dans la devise des gardes Escossoises: mais plantee toute droicte au centre dudict labyrinthe & accompagnee de cet hemistique
> HIC CAESTUS ARTEMQUE REPONO
> Je pose icy & mon Arc, & mon Art.
> (Valladier, *Labyrinthe royal*, G4r)

In contrast to his father, the young Louis XIII, who came to the throne in 1610, at the age of nine, after the assassination of Henri IV, embarked on a series of entries over the next few years, accompanied in the early days, at least, by his mother, Marie de Medici, as Regent during his minority, and thereafter by his own queen, Anne d'Autriche. The importance of such entries as face-showing propaganda for a new young monarch is made clear in a passing comment in an account of his ceremonial re-entry into Paris, after a tour of a number of French towns, published in 1614:

> Et desirant se faire voir en son jeune aage par ses subjects & les asseurer en l'effroy qu'ils avoient en ses troubles: Il part de sa ville de Paris va visiter ses

villes d'Orleans, Blois, Tours, Poictiers, Angers, Nantes, Le Mans & autres:
Qui joyeuses de la veue de leur prince le reçoivent avec triomphes.[16]

The published accounts of the entries of Louis XIII vary greatly both in the amount of
detailed information they give and in the lavishness or otherwise with which they are
produced. Some accounts comprise no more than a modest single-gathering octavo
plaquette with no illustrations, and with a text which sometimes does not even fill all
the pages. Others, in contrast, offer much lengthier and detailed accounts published in
luxurious quarto or folio editions, generously illustrated by numerous woodcut figures
of the showpieces of the entry in question. Typical of the more basic accounts is an
anonymous one produced on the occasion of the visit of Louis and his mother to
Poitiers in 1614, four years after his accession. The *Resjouissance de Poictiers sur
l'arrivée du Roy & de la Royne Regente, mere du Roy*[17] consists of little more than a
12-page general panegyric of Louis XIII and Marie de Medici, and gives no details at
all of the form taken by the celebrations organised in their honour. Similarly lacking
in such information is a rather later account of the entry of Louis and his wife, Anne
d'Autriche into Chartres in 1619. Although the reference in the title of the work to
'les magnificences & ceremonies qui s'y sont observées' might lead the reader to
expect such details, they are in fact no more forthcoming than in the account of the
earlier Poitiers entry. The anonymous author describes rather touchingly what a
daunting task the municipality had felt the whole operation to be, and how - not being
sure of what was expected of them - they sought advice from on high:

> Pendant cecy, ladite ville députe quelques-uns de leurs Eschevins pour aller
> trouver le Roy & la Royne son espouse, pour sçavoir de leurs Majestez quelles
> estoient leurs volontez, & comme elles désiroient leur entrée, en partie à
> cause que ladite ville n'avoit encore jusqu'à présent esté honorée de la
> personne de la Royne son espouse. Leurs Majestez, ne désirans souffrir que
> ladite ville & les habitans d'icelle fissent, au subject de leur entrée en ladite
> ville, aucuns fraiz, ny despends, défendirent absolument ausdits Eschevins de
> ne se mettre en aucun fraiz, & ne faire pour elles aucune dépense à ce
> subject.[18]

The bulk of the ten-page account of the Chartres entry concentrates on the
practicalities involved in preparing for the event - like the need to bring in extra
painters from outside, and generally tidy up the town - rather than on describing the

[16] *L'ordre, entree et ceremonies observees par la ville de Paris. A l'heureux retour de Louys
treiziesme, Roy de France & de Navarre. Avec la montre generalle faite au pré aux Clercs: Et
la reception des Sieurs Prevost des Marchans & Eschevins de ladicte ville. Faicte à Sa Majesté
le 16. de Septembre. Par Maistre C. Jourdan, huissier des comptes, Parisien,* Paris, J. Brunet,
1614, 8°, A4v.
[17] Poitiers, J. Thoreau, n.d., 8°.
[18] *La royalle entree du Roy et de la Royne en la ville de Chartres. Avec les magnificences &
ceremonies qui s'y sont observées le Jeudy 26. Septembre,* Paris, pour J. Chemin, 1619, 12°,
republ. Chartres, 1864, pp.6-7.

iconography of the showpieces that the painters actually produced.[19]

Rather more iconographic detail, but still no illustration, is given in the similarly short *plaquette* of 1614 describing the Paris entry. Here as so often in Paris celebrations one of the obvious images to be used was that of the ship, which was the badge of Paris, but in this case the symbolic value of the image of the ship, as depicted at the Porte St Jacques, was given a further level of meaning, since it was combined with a representation of the young king as pilot of his ship, ably assisted by his mother, the Regent, thereby conveying to the onlookers a clear and reassuring visual political message about royal authority. This message that despite political and social unrest the young king has firm control over his country is carefully explained in the account with its sustained image of the ship on a stormy sea:

> Arrivé qu'il fut à la porte S. Jacques une des portes Royalles de ladite ville, il contempla un tableau qui estoit attaché sur icelle, ou estoit peint un navirre, estant sur la marine, qui sont les armes de ladite ville, à un des bouts d'icelle estoit peinct sa Majesté, qui tenant un Sceptre en main, se rendoit maistre d'un vent contraire, qui s'efforçoit à perir le vaisseau; à l'autre bout estoit peinct la Royne Regente, tellement que l'un & l'autre ballançoient le vaisseau & guidoient iceluy malgré ce vent tempestueux. Certainement à Paris tu ne pouvois trouver au monde de meilleurs pilotes, pour guider un vaisseau au port de salut que ce Prince & ceste princesse qui malgré les flots & les vagues escumeuses & les vents furieux traverseront par tout, d'autant que Neptune les conduit & deffend. Au bas de ce tableau estoient escripts ces mots latins.
>
> D.O.M.
> SACRUM.
> Ludovico XIII. Regi pacifiquo & iustissimo.
> Mariae quae Regine matri pacis bellique moderatori.
>
> | Motes prestat | Regina quid |
> | Componere fluctus | optes. |
>
> (*L'ordre, entree et ceremonies, observees par la ville de Paris*, B2v-3r)[20]

---

[19] 'L'on donne ordre à faire venir des peintres des villes d'alentour, pour expédier les tableaux & devises qu'ils désiroient représenter en ladite entrée. L'on fait pareillement orner la porte des Espars...de charpenterie pour y poser lesdits tableaux.' (*La royalle entree*, p.5)

[20] Among other such very brief non-illustrated *plaquettes* describing various entries of Louis XIII in the first few years of his reign (copies of all of which are in the BnF) might be cited Reims (*Les ceremonies du sacre et couronnement du tres-chrestien roy de France & de Navarre, Louis XIII, plus son entree dans la ville de Reims, & son retour à Paris*, Paris, J. Richer, 1610, 8°); Orléans (*Entrée magnifique du roy faicte en sa ville d'Orleans, le mardy huictiesme juillet 1614, avec l'ordre et ceremonies observées en icelle*, Paris, M. Mondiere, 1614, 8°); Angoulême (*L'arrivée du Roy en sa ville d'Angoulesme, le dimanche 13. decembre. Avec le nombre des chefs & gens de guerre qui conduisent Sa Majesté*, Paris, A. du Brueil, 1615, 8°); Bordeaux (*Les magnificences faites en la ville de Bourdeaux à l'entrée du roy, le mercredi 7 de ce mois*, Paris, A. du Brueil, 1615, 8°). Dating from the 1620s are Saint Jean d'Angely (*Entrée royale faite au Roy en la ville de Sainct Jean d'Angely, le onziesme septembre mil six cent vingt; ensemble quels ont esté les portiques, amphitheatre, tableaux, devises et emblêmes en icelle ceremonie, et generallement tout ce qui s'est passé de plus*

Even in very basic unillustrated accounts of the various entries of Louis XIII such as these, the importance of the role played by emblematic material is apparent, but more interesting than these, which usually give only very brief descriptions of the iconography of the entry, are the much longer, and much more ornately illustrated accounts which not only describe in detail, but also depict visually, the iconographic images which were used. Notable among these are three particularly decorative accounts of Louis's entry into Arles, Avignon and Lyon in October, November and December 1622 respectively, and similarly detailed, although not illustrated is the Sieur de Morilhon's earlier account of the 1615 wedding celebrations and entry into Bordeaux, entitled *Le Persée françois*.[21] In all four works, as in the earlier sixteenth-century entries, we find familiar emblematic iconography being used. In *Le Persée françois* Morilhon describes, for example, the richly ornate boat in which the king rode, with statues of Neptune and a dolphin on board, and decorated with emblems with both Latin and French verses, once again emphasising the royal power and authority:

> Aussi ses divises sont si ingenieuses, sa structure si magnifique, & son ornement si relevé, qu'il faut croire, que tous les Arts se sont unis pour bastir un si superbe palais...c'estoit un grand Navire couvert d'un pavillon, dont le toit enrichi descailles peintes d'Azur, ou les quatre vertus portraittes avec leurs ordinaires outils serroyent au milieu...Or il estoit ceint d'une galerie...où l'on voyoit à chasque coin un Cupidon tenant un pied en l'air, tiré en peinture de relief...à la faveur de deux petits degrés...l'on pouvoit aller à la Proüe, contempler...Neptune...monté sur son Char, traisné par deux Ippopothames ou chevaux marins, le gouvernail à la main, ou bien au bec de ce navire un Daufin...faisant l'office de guide & de nocher en signe de rejouissance. Au dedans de ceste galerie l'on voyoit une grande sale, ouverte par quatre grandes portes, & vitrée par tout, avec un bon nombre de portraits, emblesmes & escriteaux.
>
> Le premier logé au coin droit sur le devant du batteau representoit un Cupidon sortant du Ciel, l'arc & le foudre à la main: auquel Neptune, en posture de suppliant, sembloit rendre hommage, ayant pour cest effet jetté son Trident en terre, avec ceste inscription au dessoubs.

---

particulier tant en ladite ville que depuis le depart de Sa Majesté de la ville de Poictiers jusques à son arrivée en icelle, Paris, I. Mesnier, 1620, 8°); Le Mans (*Arrivée du Roy en la ville du Mans, le 28. juillet 1620. Ensemble la harangue faicte à Sa Majesté au non des habitans de ladicte ville. Et generallement tout ce qui s'est passé és lieux circonvoysins, avant l'arrivée de Sadicte Majesté*, Paris, I. Mesnier, 1620, 8°); Niort (*Entrée du Roy en la ville et chasteau de Niort, le dimanche 23 mai 1621; ensemble tout ce qui s'est passé en icelle par ceux de la religion pretendue reformée*, Paris, N. Alexandre, 1621, 8°); Bergerac (*L'entrée royale et magnifique du Roy en sa ville de Bergerac. Ensemble l'humble remontrance des deputés de l'assemblée et bourgeois de La Rochelle à Sa Majesté*, Paris, E. de l'Oreille, 1621, 8°). Many other such *plaquettes* (also in the BnF) could also be cited.

[21] *Le Persée françois. Au Roy. Par le Sieur de Morilhon. Avec les mariages & entrée royale à Bourdeaus*, Bordeaux, G. Vernoy, 1612, 12°.

Sol calet igne meo flagrat Neptunus in undis,
Quamvis liber erat feci servire tonantem,
Quamvis liber erat martem, sive marte subegi.

Le Soleil lumineux s'embrase à ma chaleur,
Et Neptune ressent l'amoureuse douleur,
Ne pouvant esviter ma flame dans l'onde:
Je peux du vaillant Mars les fougues amortir,
Et la douce franchise en prison convertir,
A celuy dont la main tient le sceptre du monde.
(Morilhon, *Le Persée françois*, pp.238-42)

But Morilhon also describes the decorations on other ephemeral architecture, such as a pyramid on which are depicted the familiar emblematic figures of a camel stirring the water before drinking it with the inscription:

Maudit qui comme le chameau,
Ne peut boire sans troubler l'eau

and a sunflower with the inscription:

Je ne puis autre part tourner
Et me faut icy sejourner.   (Morilhon, *Le Persée françois*, p.341)

and once again the symbol of the sun, already seen being used earlier by Henri IV, but more commonly associated with Louis XIV rather than Henri IV or Louis XIII:

l'on voyoit à la base ou piedestal faict en triangle...deux Soleils descochans mille beaux rayons, avec ces vers Latins par le dessus.
Quid tantum eous, quid & hesperus emicat uno,
Sol geminus geminas iungit in orbe faces.

D'où vient que l'oeil de l'Orient,
Et du Couchant doux & riant,
De si vives flames desserre:
C'est qu'un Soleil double & besson,
Lie dans un mesme lasson,
Ces deux flambeaux dessus la terre.
(Morilhon, *Le Persée françois*, pp.340-41)

Elsewhere he describes other familiar figures such as Janus, Bacchus, Ceres or the four cardinal virtues, with their traditional attributes, but it is particularly interesting to see how Morilhon explains here that the function of such figures is *not* to make a political statement about the greatness and authority of the king for the benefit of the onlooking crowd, or even a moral statement for their benefit, but that they simply fulfil a decorative purpose, occupying an otherwise empty space with something which is visually pleasing and which will appeal to the king as he passes:

> Voilà tout ce qui paroissoit de curieux, & capable d'arrester l'oeil & l'esprit de leurs Majestez. Ce n'est pas qu'il n'y eust d'autres rencontres & inventions, que le Peintre avoit heureusement tirées, au naturel, afin de ne laisser en un ouvrage si celebre, rien de defectueux. Au dedans de ceste porte, par ce que le mur est fort espais, l'on advisa d'y portraire quelque gentillesse, & à ces fins les quatre Vertus furent peintes avec les mesmes outils que leur donna l'antiquité, à sçavoir la Justice avec la balance à la main, la Force tenant par le poil une hure de Lion, la Prudence secoüant un serpent qui s'allongeoit sur son visage, & la Temperance faisant couler d'un beau vase certaine liqueur.   (Morilhon, *Le Persée françois*, pp.335-6)

Again in his description of the Porte du Chapon Rouge, Morilhon explains how emblems were used to enhance the visual appearance of this gateway, since it was directly on the royal route:

> L'on sçait bien que ceste porte est belle de soy mesme: & son abord extremement agreable...Neantmoins puis que c'estoit le passage de l'entrée Royale, l'on l'embellist de tous les Emblesmes & portraicts que la despence publique & l'invention des beaux esprits peut rencontrer.
> (Morilhon, *Le Persée françois*, pp.328-9)

Although Morilhon's title suggests a clear association between Perseus rescuing Andromeda and then marrying her, and Louis XIII's marriage with Anne d'Autriche, the Perseus image did not in fact form a single *leitmotif* for the Bordeaux celebration. However, when seven years later Louis entered Arles in October 1622 it was this same Perseus and Andromeda theme which *did* provide the overall iconographic linking all the principal decorations which were created to celebrate the occasion, although many other familiar emblematic figures were also used incidentally, including once again that of the sun. The anonymous author of the beautifully produced folio account of the event[22] explains early in the work the political message to be taken from the association drawn between Louis XIII and Perseus:

---

[22] *Entree de Loys XIII. Roy de France et de Navarre. Dans sa ville d'Arles, le vingt-neufiesme Octobre mil six cens vingt-deux. Estans consuls et gouverneurs de ladicte ville Pierre de Boches, & Nicolas Dycard de l'Estat des Nobles, & Gauchier Peint, & Claude Janim de celuy des Bourgeois,* Avignon, J. Bramereau, 1623, folio. Among the decorative emblems described as figuring around the base of the statue of Boso, King of Arles in 877 (whose son and heir was named Louis) we find: 'Le second qui paroissoit à costé droit, estoit une parelie suivant son soleil, avec ce mot, SOLEM SOLA SEQUOR. La Parelie est une nuée retressie, & ramassee en sa partie plus esloignée du soleil: mais en celle qui en est plus voisine, diaphane & transparente, & recevant facilement à guise de miroir l'image & la ressemblance du corps qui luy est opposé; aussi elle a tousjours le portrait du soleil, & ne s'en esloigne jamais, ains le suit pas à pas comme amoureuse d'une lueur si esclattante.' (p.47)

> La France est l'Andromede que la Justice du Ciel a attachée pour ses pechez
> & le monstre qui la veut ruiner, est la rebellion: Le Roy en est le Persée, vray
> fils de Jupiter. *(Entree de Loys XIII...dans sa ville d'Arles,* p.3)

This same image had also been used thirty years earlier in 1594 for Louis's father,
Henri IV, in an emblematic broadsheet published by Jean Le Clerc in Paris, and
included in Pierre de l'Estoile's *Belles figures et drolleries de la Ligue.* Here also
Andromeda represented France, and Henri IV her saviour sent from heaven. In this
earlier broadsheet, however, the moral lesson that the French people should support
their king wholeheartedly, is forcefully and unambiguously expressed in the sonnet
accompanying the engraved figure of Perseus (visibly resembling Henri IV) coming to
the rescue of Andromeda:

> FRANCE, comme Andromede mort fut offerte,
> Mal voulue des siens, & d'un peuple estranger,
> Son pays fut son mal, sa guerre, & son danger,
> Où son bien devoit estre, y demeuroit sa perte:
>   Le ciel fasché de veoir une injustice aperte,
> Un Persée envoya à fin de la venger,
> Un Persée François qui la vint desgaiger
> Des vagues de la mort, qui l'avoient ja couverte:
>   Le monstre qui gardoit entre ses dens sa mort,
> Sentit combien le bras de Persée estoit fort:
> Comme feit l'Espagnol de HENRY quatriesme.
>   FRANCE, sois luy fidelle, & ne te laisse plus
> Attacher de doublons, & ne croy aux abus
> De ceux qui ont rongné l'or de ton Diadéme. [23]

In keeping with his central role in the iconography, Perseus was given the place of
honour at the top of a triumphal arch, but other emblematic figures also appeared on
the arch, all carrying their individual messages of royal authority. The base was
decorated with lions, which, as the account explains, were particularly appropriate
since they form part of the arms of the town, but which also carried the further
connotation of kingship reflected in the motto attached to the first of the lions on the
base of the column:

> Les bases estoient de lyons en diverses postures, parce que la Ville porte le
> lyon en ses armes...En la premiere base il y avoit un lyon dormant, avec ce
> mot.
> ### MAIESTATE SECURUS.
> Le lyon dort hors de son giste, ce que les autres animaux n'osent faire. Les

---

[23] For discussion of this broadsheet (BnF Rés g.Fol La^{25} 6, f.31r) see Daniel Russell,
Emblematic Structures in Renaissance French Culture, pp.198-201.

> Naturalistes disent qu'il recognoist en soy les marques de la royauté qu'il a
> par dessus le reste des animaux, & que cela luy donne l'asseurance de dormir
> en pleine campagne; ou bien parce qu'il dort les yeux ouverts & que les
> autres animaux croyans qu'il veille n'osent l'aborder. La Ville d'Arles tire
> son asseurance, & par le soin & diligence qu'elle apporte à sa conservation,
> & par les anciennes marques de sa royauté, qui la font encor respecter de ses
> voisins. (*Entree de Loys XIII...dans sa ville d'Arles*, pp.58-9)

Similarly reflecting the greatness of the king was the emblem of a high flying eagle
also depicted on this Perseus triumphal arch, at an appropriately higher level, above
the lions:

> En l'autre embleme, on descouvroit un aigle poussant à tire-d'aisle vers les
> espaces imaginaires: l'aigle est le roy des oyseaux, & le Roy est le Roy des
> hommes, la gloire à laquelle il aspire est hors de toute cognoissance, & se
> porte par la sublimité de son coeur au delà des espaces imaginaires, & n'a
> point d'arrest qu'au point de la parfaite gloire, le mot,
>   ALTIUS AUDET.
>   (*Entree de Loys XIII...dans sa ville d'Arles*, p.58)

Here as so often the author of this account regularly uses the word 'embleme' to
denote what might otherwise be deemed rather devices, comprising no more than
figure and motto. As in the earlier Bordeaux celebration, in which the decorations on
the boat were designed to reflect the glory of the king, here again the richly
ornamented boat is similarly adorned with allegorical scenes and figures serving the
same purpose, including, for example, Neptune and Jupiter to reflect Louis's victories
over his enemies:

> Ce bateau estoit en forme de maison avec ses fenestrages, peint en tous ses
> endroits, & enrichy de plusieurs beaux couronnemens, autour de la
> charpenterie y regnoit une frize, embellie de grotesques & autres phantasies
> tres-gentilles en façon de ceinture...On avoit fait dessein d'y peindre un
> Jupiter foulant un globe terrestre, & un Neptune qui auroit maistrisé l'Ocean:
> car la terre, & l'onde, sont les tesmoins irreprochables des victoires que le
> Roy a r'emportées par dessus ses ennemis. Ces vers y estoient pour animer
> ceste peinture.
>   JUPITER IN TERRIS, LIQUIDIS NEPTUNUS IN UNDIS
>   DICERIS, ET SEMPER VINCIS, UBIQUE DEUS.
>   (*Entree de Loys XIII...dans sa ville d'Arles*, p.5)

In the accounts of the entries of Louis XIII into Avignon and Lyon in 1622, the
titles to both works reflect the main iconographic theme of the occasion, and both also
draw on cosmic associations to underline further the grandeur of the monarch. The
Lyon entry, as was so often the case, took the lion, symbol of the city, as one of its
themes, but in this case it was not an ordinary lion, but rather the constellation, Leo,

that was selected to represent the city, while the king was represented by a second symbol, that of the sun, as is explained both in the title:

> Le Soleil au signe du Lyon. D'où quelques paralleles sont tirez, avec le tres-chrestien, tres-juste, & tres-victorieux monarque Louys XIII. Roy de France & de Navarre, en son entree triomphante dans sa ville de Lyon. Ensemble un sommaire recit de tout ce qui s'est passé de remarquable en ladite entree de sa Majesté, & de la plus illustre princesse de la terre Anne d'Austriche, Royne de France & de Navarre, dans ladite ville de Lyon le 11. Decembre 1622[24]

and in the prefatory comments by the anonymous author of the account:.

> Tous nos Portiques, Pyramides, Colomne, Temple, Fontaine, & autres ornemens, qui ont esté veus dans l'enceinte des murailles de la Ville, n'ont eu autre objet...que de representer par le Soleil au Signe de son Lyon celeste, nostre Roy, lequel parcourant les villes de son Royaume, comme le Roy des Planettes, les Signes du Zodiaque, est enfin arrivé dans celle, laquelle tant pour les autres rapports, que pour la semblance du mesme nom, merite justement d'estre appellee en terre le signe du Lyon.
> (*Le Soleil au signe du Lyon*, p.4)

Although the sun image is more commonly associated with Louis XIV rather than with his father, Louis XIII, it recurs in emblem after emblem throughout this account. Notably anticipatory of Louis XIV's use of the symbol is its appearance on the triumphal arch at the Pont de la Saone with the familiar motto *Ut vidit vicit*:

> Description de l'Arc des victoires, & Trophees de sa Majesté, à l'entree du Pont de la Saosne. Le Soleil dans le Signe du Lyon, victorieux des broüillars, & des nuees, lesquelles à guise de superbes Geants, s'eslevent contre le Ciel, pour en offusquer la lumiere...
>
> Soubs iceluy [the inscription] dans une grande ovale estoit une multitude de peuple de diverse stature, & posture, exposee aux rayons d'un Soleil ardant, comme mesme le tesmoignoit l'action de chascun d'iceux; car quelques uns commenceans à s'eschauffer quittoient leurs manteaux, les autres leurs pourpoints, & d'autres encor se despoüilloient entierement, & ostoient leurs chemises, ne pouvans supporter la force d'une si violente chaleur. Les paroles de l'embleme estoient;
> > *Ut vidit, vicit.*
> C'est une chose incroyable de la vistesse du Soleil, Roy de la Nature, en la visite generale de son empire: car ny le vol d'un oyseau, ny la violence d'un d'ard, ny le foudre du canon...ny chose aucune peut approcher de cette

---

[24] Lyon, J. Jullieron, 1623, folio.

> promptitude inimaginable.   (*Le Soleil au signe du Lyon*, pp.75-6)

which is a prefiguration of the same device with the motto *Ut vidi, vici*, to be used forty years later by Louis XIV in a *carrousel* held in Paris in 1662 to celebrate the birth of the *Dauphin*.[25]

But as well as the sun, other emblematic images were also used during this Lyon entry to denote royal virtues, as described in an accompanying work to the *Soleil au signe du Lyon* (which is equally lavishly illustrated), the *Reception de tres-chrestien, tres-juste, et tres-victorieux monarque Louys XIII. Roy de France & de Navarre, premier Comte & Chanoine de l'Eglise de Lyon; et de tres-chrestienne, tres-auguste, & tres-vertueuse royne Anne d'Austriche; Par Messieurs les Doyen, Chanoines, & Comtes de Lyon en leur cloistre & eglise, le XI. Decembre, M.DC.XXII.* A triumphal arch was liberally adorned with devices relating to the overall theme of the Age of Gold, but in particular the figure of *Abondance* was associated with the arms of the king, while *Paix* was associated with those of his queen, Anne d'Autriche.[26] Later we are given a description of yet another boat again adorned with emblems and devices, and again conveying a strong message of royal power and authority:

> Par le dehors dudit dome, & en la place qui s'estoit treuvee vuide entre lesdits pilastres, l'on avoit logé trois emblemes, le milieu duquel avoit un Sceptre François couronné, & aux deux costez des Lyons terrestres & marins, qui flechissoient, & faisoient hommage devant ledit Sceptre, au dessus duquel se lisoit:
>
> *Terrae iura dat, atque mari.*
>
> A costé droit dudit embleme, & entre deux pilastres, une espee Royalle, couppoit les superfluitez d'un olivier; ces parolles mises au dessus en rendoient la raison:
>
> *Pinguem pacis purgavit olivam.*
>
> A l'opposite & de l'autre costé une main de Justice, telle que la portent nos Roys, estoit logee toute droitte au milieu d'une mer orageuse, & pleine de quantité de personnes, qui recouroient tous à elle, comme à l'asyle & refuge asseuré contre leur malheur, ainsi que le denotoit cete fin de vers:
>
> *Afflictis portus, & aura viris.*
>
> (*Reception...de Louys XIII*, p.33)

---

[25] Perrault describes this in his *Courses de testes et de bague faites par le Roy et par les princes et seigneurs de sa cour en l'année M.DC.LXII*: 'Devises des chefs et des chevaliers des quadrilles. Devise de la premiere quadrille. Premiere devise. Du Roy. Un Soleil. Ut vidi, vici. Aussi-tôt que j'ay veu j'ay vaincu.' (f.28r).

[26] Lyon, J. Roussin, 1623, folio. 'A la dextre, au dessus des armes du Roy, estoit l'ABONDANCE, qui empoignoit en sa main droicte quelques espics de bled, & un sep chargé de raisons, pendillant au dessous du poing: Et le long de sa jambe, jusques sur le genoil, s'eslevoit une corne d'abondance...A la senestre, sur les armoiries de la Royne, estoit dressée la statue de la PAIX, ayant à ses pieds des armes renversées: & à la main gauche deux branches, l'une d'olivier & l'autre de laurier, entortillees ensemble, & un lis passant à travers, pointant la teste sur les autres: & au dessus estoit escript: PAX.' (pp.12-13).

As so often, a firework display formed part of the ceremony, with two set pieces, each embodying one of the two core images of the overall celebration, the lion and the sun (see fig.25).[27]

A cosmic note echoing that of the Lyon entry is likewise reflected in the title to the account of the Avignon entry which had taken place a month earlier, *La Voye de laict ou le chemin des heros au Palais de la gloire*.[28] This event was also designed and orchestrated, as the author tells us in the introduction, by priests from the local Jesuit college.[29] Here the central theme is the king's *gloire* as reflected in the *palais de la gloire* which marked the culmination of the progression through a series of allegorical arches, portals and theatres, all of which focus on one or other of the king's virtues, which all come together ultimately in the *Palais de la gloire*.[30] Even more than in the Lyon entry we find here, in addition to the central allegorical images of the king's virtues and overall *gloire*, innumerable individual contributory emblems, of which some are simply noted without explanation, as for example the familiar emblematic serpent torn apart by her young with the motto *Crueldad pagado* in one of the niches around the equestrian statue of the king (p.135), or the 'Elephant droict sur ses pieds' with the motto *Non flectitur* (p.168) and halcyons with the motto *In aequitate foecunditas* on the *Fontaine de justice*,[31] while others are explained more fully, as in a figure of the sun in the *Theatre de la force et de la pieté* denoting the king's piety:

---

[27] 'Les deux figures desdits feux...ont un Soleil couronné, & entouré d'estoilles, & un Lyon portant trois fleurs de Lys, comprenant en ces trois chefs la comparaison du Roy avec le Soleil, par la figure de ce mesme Soleil couronné; celle de la Royne avec l'Aurore, par les estoilles, compagnes ordinaires de cette Deesse matiniere qui ne pouvoit en cest endroit estre autrement representée & la Ville de Lyon que par cet animal duquel elle porte le nom...'

[28] *La Voye de laict ou le chemin des heros au Palais de la gloire. Ouvert à l'entrée triomphante de Louys XIII. Roy de France & de Navarre en la cité d'Avignon le 16. de Novembre 1622. Estans consuls illustres & magnifiques seigneurs Thom. de Berton, Escuyer de Crillon, gentilhomme ordinaire de la chambre du Roy, Charles Hugonenc, & Pier. Bayol, & magnifique Mr Pier. Jos. de Salvador Docteur es droicts, Assesseur de ladicte ville*, Avignon, J. Bramereau, 1623, 4°.

[29] 'Pour ce subject apres avoir deliberé en son Conseil ordinaire & extraordinaire de faire les apprests & fournir aux despens pour la magnificence d'un triomphe Royal à la venuë, qu'elle se promettoit de sa Majesté victorieuse, elle requit le R.P. Recteur du College de la Compagnie de Jesus de commettre la conduitte generale & direction à quelqu'un de ses Religieux pour le dessein & invention d'une entree Royale, telle qu'il jugeroit honorable à la ville & à la loüange immortelle d'un si grand Roy.' (pp.8-9).

[30] 'On y voit dedans une grande clarté la Noblesse, la Puissance, l'Authorité, l'Excellence, la Majesté, la Loüange, l'Honneur...' (p.233). Included in the architectural constructs leading up to the *Palais de la gloire* are a *Portal de felicité*; a *Trophée de sagesse*; a *Fontaine de justice* and a *Theatre de la force et de la pieté*.

[31] 'Des Alcyons dans leurs nids avec-que leurs couvées sur une mer tranquille & ces paroles qui font l'esprit de la peinture
IN AEQUITATE FOECUNDITAS.' (pp.178-9)

Figure 25: *Reception...de Louis XIII*, Lyon, 1623, between p.38 and p.39.

En ces autres on remarquoit exprimée la pieté des Roys de France & nommément de Louys le Juste. Un beau Soleil dardant ses rayons amoureusement sur des lis qui s'ouvrent à la douceur de sa lumiere un rouleau volant qui en porte l'explication.

LOS ABRE Y LOS DORA. *(La Voye de laict*, p.196)

and a second use of the figure of the halcyon on the *Trophee de sagesse* to denote Louis's capacity for calm amid storm and strife:

La troisiesme devise estoit un Alcyon dans son nid au milieu des ondes de la mer, avec ces mots.

SIEMPRE CALMA POR YO

C'est la sagesse qui a affermy le coeur de ce grand Roy, & luy a fait trouver le calme au milieu des tempestes. *(La Voye de laict*, p.146)

As in earlier sixteenth-century triumphant entries 'living emblems' were also used in this Avignon entry, with allegorical figures at various points along the route of the procession coming to life to recite their verses out loud as the king passed by. In the case of two such key figures the printed account reveals the identity of the individuals carrying out this function. The king was presented with the keys to the city by a 'nymphe avignonnoise' accompanied by a small cupid, denoting the love felt for the king by the city of Avignon, represented by its nymph. These roles were played by the young daughter and young son of two local dignitaries, both of whose names appear in the list of current consuls of the city, included on the title page of the work:

Ce fut là que Madamoiselle Margot de Berton, fille de Mr François de Berton, seigneur de Beauvais cy-dessus nommé, presenta les clefs de la Ville dorées & enlassées d'un gros cordon de soye à grosses houppes pendantes. Elle estoit revestuë d'une robbe de satin bleu couverte de large clinquant d'or, sa coiffure ressembloit à celle d'une Nymphe, enrichie de divers brillants & enseignes de grand prix. Un petit Cupidon aupres d'elle representant l'amour respectueux de ceste Nymphe Avignonnoise envers S.M.portoit un hoqueton de tafetas rouge orné de fleurs de lis & de clefs d'or joinctes par des las d'amour; sur le bas de saye pendoient de bandes faictes à ondes, enrichies de campanes d'argent, les hauts des manches couppez en fueillage de chesne & terminés de poirettes d'argent, le tout de la liberalité de la Ville, selon sa coustume en semblables solemnitez. La Nymphe parla au Roy d'une grace & asseurance qui surpassoit son aage, en ce petit sixain.

Grand Roy la merveille des Cieux
Qui faictes briller à nos yeux
Mille esclats de vostre Victoire,
Avignon ce divin sejour
Vous ouvre le Ciel de la Gloire,
Et donne les clefs de l'Amour.

Et alors elle les prit des mains du petit Cupidon, Jean François de Salvador fils de Mr l'Assesseur qui d'une belle hardiesse l'accompagna comme elle les presentoit à S.M. de ces deux petits vers.

       Ces clefs vous rendront ouverts
       Tous les coeurs de l'univers.

Il n'y a rien de si aperitif, ny de si inventif que l'Amour, c'est pourquoy les anciens luy ont mis en main les clefs de tout le monde, & nommement du Ciel qu'il a ouvert à tant de grands Heros. (*La Voye de laict*, pp.111-13)

The town of Aix was also graced by a visit from Louis on this same 1622 tour, and the account of this entry was similarly published in a richly illustrated folio volume,[32] but in this case, unlike the accounts of the 1622 entries into Avignon and Lyon which were anonymous, the author of the account is identified as Jean Galaup de Chasteuil, who was also the person responsible for the design and organisation of the event, and his insider view gives a rather different perspective of the occasion, since he is in a position to describe not just what actually happened, but also what had been intended to happen. In a manner reminiscent of Etienne Jodelle in the sixteenth century,[33] Galaup de Chasteuil grumbles about the problems of setting up an elaborate display at short notice, since the king's arrival in the town occurred earlier than expected. In his preliminary *épître* to the king he explains that 'Nos inventions n'eurent que sept jours pour leur conception & pour leur naissance' (ẽ 1r-v) while later in the account we find a description and illustration of a grandiose theatre which was designed to be occupied by an elaborately and allegorically attired troubadour, surrounded with musical instruments and with flames spurting from his feet, who would address the king. Unfortunately, although this was planned, none of it actually happened, due to lack of time: 'La venuë inopinée de sa MAJESTE ne me donna pas le temps d'étaler mon invention, ny au TROUBADOUR de le saluër en son langage.' (C3v).

As in the other triumphal entries we find here once again speaking statues, as in that representing the town of Aix who addresses the king in what Galaup de Chasteuil explains are verses borrowed from Malherbe:

      Grand fis du grand Henry, grand chef-d'oeuvre des Cieux
      Grand aise, & grand amour des ames & des yeux,

---

[32] Galaup de Chasteuil, *Discours sur les arcs triomphaux dressés en la ville d'Aix à l'heureuse arrivée de tres-chrestien, tres-grand & tres-juste monarque Louys XIII. Roy de France & de Navarre.*

[33] Jodelle was charged with organising at just three days notice an entertainment to be held in Paris in the presence of the king, Henri II, to celebrate the recapture of Calais from the English in 1558. His account of the innumerable problems he encountered is given in *Le recueil des inscriptions, figures, devises, et masquarades, ordonnées en l'hostel de ville à Paris, le Jeudi 17. de Fevrier. 1558. Autres inscriptions en vers heroïques latins, pour les images des princes de la Chrestienté. Par Estienne Jodelle Parisien*, Paris, A. Wechel, 1558, 4°. See V.E.Graham and W.McAllister Johnson, eds, E. Jodelle, *Le recueil des inscriptions 1558. A Literary and Iconographical Exegesis*, Toronto, 1972, p. 117.

> LOUYS dont ce beau jour la presence m'ottroye,
> Delices des sujects à ta garde commis,
> Le pourtraict de Pallas fut la force de Troye,
> Le tien sera la peur de tous mes ennemis.
>> (Galaup de Chasteuil, *Discours sur les arcs triomphaux*, B2r)

and message-bearing emblematic figures and verses adorning the seven triumphal arches which were erected to mark the occasion, as for example a pair of palm trees representing the king's victories:

> Deux palmes sont l'object premier que je presente aux yeux de sa Majesté.
> On sacre ces arbres à la Victoire, pource que leur bois, méme surchargé, porte plus haultement sa teste dans la nuë, & semble dépiter la violence.
> J'élevoy sur ces deux Palmes les trophées de mon Roy.
>> (Galaup de Chasteuil, *Discours sur les arcs triomphaux*, A1r)

Particularly interesting in this event is the series of emblems described by Chasteuil as *tableaux enigmatiques* which were displayed in a special gallery along the route, all of which depict allegorically Louis's great virtues and achievements. Some of these comprise no more than figure and motto, but others include a Latin verse (and in one case a French verse), and unusually the name of the individual author is noted. Thus one by Antonius Merindolus, depicts Louis receiving a globe which is handed down to him from heaven, with the motto *Iusto* and Latin verse:

> Teucris ut infestam perniciem machinans,
> Formosiori proposuit pomum Deae
> Discordia. Sic ocia seculis parans,
> Iusto Dea Regi Orbem defert concordia.
>> (Galaup de Chasteuil, *Discours sur les arcs triomphaux*, Q2r)

while another, also by Merindolus, depicts him slaying the chimera, with the motto *Furentes paro* (Q2r). Others, under the general heading *De l'Histoire Grecque rapportée à l'Histoire de France*, depict a lion overpowered by an eagle with the motto *Hunc inter scopulos aquila est enixa leonem* (R1r) and Louis riding triumphant on the back of an eagle, in a manner reminiscent of the woodcut illustrations of Alciato's Ganymede emblem, with the motto *Urit et irrigat* (R1r). The sole emblem with a French verse (signed 'Nostradame') depicts an earless and spotted camel-like animal with the motto *Cornua captans perdidit aures*, accompanied by the explanatory verse:

> Pour ne te contenir en ta forme, & tes bornes,
> Et vouloir des hydeuses cornes,
> LOUYS (que ta folie a cherché d'occuper)
> T'a faict les oreilles couper.
>> (Galaup de Chasteuil, *Discours sur les arcs triomphaux*, Q1r)

The importance of emblematic material as a vehicle for conveying a political message relating to the greatness of the king, his prowess, his wisdom and the overall authority of his reign in such triumphal entries as these is evident. But emblems and devices also played a similarly important, though different role in more purely courtly ceremonial occasions under Louis XIII, as they did earlier, in the sixteenth century under the influence of Catherine de Medici, and indeed also subsequently, during the reign of Louis XIV. A particularly important court festivity which went on for three days was mounted in 1612 to celebrate the double marriage alliance of the youthful Louis with Anne d'Autriche, and of his sister, Elisabeth, with the future Philip IV of Spain. Marc de Vulson gives a detailed (though non-illustrated) account of the *carrousel* which was held in the Place Royale in Paris, including a description not just of the participants, their attire and their meaningful devices, but also of the physical setting in which the display was enacted, in which - as in the town-organised triumphal entries - ephemeral architecture played a significant role, decorated likewise with allegorical figures and meaningful inscriptions, as described in the title to this section of his 1648 *Vray theatre d'honneur et de chevalerie*:

> *Le magnifique et admirable carrosel qui fut fait à Paris dans la Place Royalle, le cinq, le six, & le septiesme jour d'Avril, l'an mil six cens & douze, pour les resjouissances de la publication de la double alliance, par les mariages du Roy Louis XIII. & de Madame sa soeur avec l'Infante & le Prince d'Espagne; & la description des machines, des habits, des armes, des livrées, des cartels, & des devises des chevaliers qui y parurent; ensemble les courses qui s'y firent à la quintaine, & à la bague, &c.*

The *Palais de la felicité*, for example, which was erected in the Place Royale, was decorated with allegorical statues, including one of *Gloire* in the shape of a winged woman wearing a crown and bearing a palm and a trumpet in each hand, accompanied by Latin verse, and the lofty entry to the palace was adorned with the motto *Hilaritati publicae.*(p.365) Even more visibly striking than the architecture, however, would have been the active participants in the *carrousel*, all splendidly attired in specially designed costumes, and each bearing his own particular device. The knights were grouped in squadrons, and within each squadron the individual devices of the participants conformed to the overall theme. Thus the first squadron - that of the king, but which in view of the king's youth was under the leadership of the Prince de Conti - were the *chevaliers du Soleil*, and consequently all their individual devices related to the overall theme of the sun - reflecting by implication, as always, the greatness of the monarch:

> Monsieur de Sezy, *Aquilante*, un Soleil, vers lequel voloit un Aigle, avec cette ame, *Miratur & audet.*
> Monsieur le Baron de Fontaines Chalandray, *Lucidamor*, un seul Soleil, *Splendet & ardet.* (M. de Vulson, *Le vray theatre d'honneur*, p.376)

In such a festivity as this the impact of emblems and devices was a dual one. Certainly the political propaganda element *is* still apparent, as in the triumphal entries, in that the overall aim of the event was to make a public manifestation of the glory of the monarch, and the sheer magnificence of the event and of the dashing chivalric performance must have contributed significantly towards this aim. But in addition, the devices worn by the individual participants and chosen by themselves also served to fulfil a more traditional, chivalric role, such as we saw also in the sixteenth-century court festivities, offering an intellectual challenge not so much to the attendant public at large in the Place Royale for whom the intended message was of overall royal magnificence and dominance, but certainly to the smaller and more elitist aristocratic society who also participated in the event as spectators, who would be in more of a position to see such smaller details, than the larger crowd looking on from a distance.

Under Louis XIV we find a continuation of these established modes of glorifying monarchy by such public displays, exploiting allegorical, emblematic material in order to make indirectly a statement about the magnificence of the reigning monarch. Like his father before him, as a twelve-year old, Louis undertook in 1650 a series of visits to various parts of his troubled kingdom, which continued over the next two years, in order to show the royal presence, and as usual accounts of his triumphal entry into the various provincial towns were published in the wake of these.[34] But it was above all the peace treaty with Spain, and the royal marriage of 1660, and subsequent entry into Paris of the 22-year old king together with his new wife, Maria Theresa, which inspired a series of published accounts, describing and interpreting the significance of the iconography of the event, ranging from very basic 8-leaf *plaquettes* such as the *Relation de toutes les particularitez qui se sont faites et passees dans la celebre entrée du Roy et de la Reyne, avec l'ordre de la marche du clergé & des cours souveraines. Ensemble la magnifique pompe des seigneurs, & de toute leur suitte: Et toutes les ceremonies du Te Deum*[35] (which despite the grandiose claims of its title does little more than describe the procession and what everybody wore, but makes no mention of the decorations along the route) to the much more luxurious illustrated folio account published two years later under the title *L'entree triomphante de Leurs Majestez Louis XIV. Roy de France et de Navarre, et Marie Therese d'Austriche son espouse, dans la ville de Paris capitale de leurs royaumes, au retour de la signature de la paix generalle et de leur heureux mariage. Enrichie de plusieurs figures, des harangues & de diverses pieces considerables pour l'histoire. Le tout exactement recueilly par l'ordre de Messieurs de ville. Et imprimee l'an M.DC.LXII.*[36] As so

---

[34] See, for example the accounts of the entries into Auxerre and Bordeaux in the *Recit veritable de tout ce qui s'est fait et passé à l'entrée du roy en la ville d'Auxerre; avec les harangues faites à Leurs Majestés par Messieurs du clergé de ladite ville* (Paris, N. Bessin, 1650, 4°) and *Journal de ce qui s'est fait et passé tant durant la guerre et siége de Bordeaux que dans le traité de paix; avec les harangues faites lors de la magnifique entrée du roy dans ladite ville, et ce qui s'est observé à sa sortie*, n.p., 1650, 4°.
[35] Paris, J.-B. Loyson, 1660, 4°.
[36] Paris, P. le Petit, T. Joly and L. Bilaine, 1662, folio. Among the various other published accounts see *La glorieuse et triomphante entrée de la serenissime Princesse Marie Thereze*

often with Paris events, a boat was constructed for the occasion, in deference to the town's symbol,[37] but as well as a sun mounted on the mast around which the initials of Louis and Maria Theresa were entwined, reflecting the glory of the king and his new wife, the sides of the boat - which was moored on the Seine opposite the Louvre - were also adorned with devices reflecting the new peace which the royal couple had brought with them (see fig. 26):

> *Nobis haec otia fecit*
> THERESE en s'approchant de ces aimables lieux
> Y remit le repos & nous rendit heureux.

> *Divino foedere tuta*
> De THERESE & LOUYS la divine alliance
> Me fera désormais voguer en asseurance.

> *Contemnit tuta procellas*
> Sous les Astres benins de THERESE & LOUYS
> Ce Vaisseau ne craint plus les flots enorgueillis.
> (*L'entree triomphante de Leurs Majestez, Feu d'artifice*, p.5)

This boat formed the focal point of the dramatic firework display which marked the culmination of the celebration, ending with the whole boat disappearing in clouds of smoke with the sole exception of the sun on the top of the mast, which continued to shine brightly, as described eloquently in the account:

---

d'Austriche, infante d'Espagne, au retour de son tres-auguste mariage avec nostre invincible monarque Louis de Bourbon, Paris, L. Barbote, 1660, 4°; La royale maison du trone de la triomphante entrée de Leurs Majestez en la ville de Paris, n.p., 1660, 4°; La montre generale de Messieurs les bourgeois de la ville de Paris, qui sont choisis pour paroistre à la magnifique entrée du roy et et de la reine dans sa ville capitale, Paris, A. Lesselin, 1660, 4°; L'explication des figures et peintures qui sont representees pour l'entrée du roy et de la reine, Paris, J. Promé, 1660 4°; La veritable explication en prose et en vers des figures ovales, termes et portraits de tous les rois de France qui sont dessus le pont Nostre-Dame à Paris; ensemble quelques remarques curieuses et particulieres pour les amateurs de l'histoire; avec la description des arcs de triomphe elevés dans les places publiques pour l'entrée du roy et de la reine, Paris, J.-B. Loyson, 1660, 4°; Le feu royal et magnifique qui s'est tiré sur la riviere de Seine, vis-à-vis du Louvre, en presence de Leurs Majestés, par ordre de Messieurs de ville pour la resjouissance de l'entrée du roy et de la reine, le 29 aoust 1660, Paris, J.-B. Loyson, 1660, 4°. (All these works are in the BnF.)

[37] 'Sur cette pensée l'Ingenieur feit fabriquer un vaisseau de soixante & douze pieds de long equipé de ses mats, de ses voiles, & de ses cordages, comme ceux que l'on voit voguer sur les mers; Et qui bien que basty à l'antique, pourroit fort bien passer pour celuy qui sert de Hieroglyfique à la Ville de Paris, & qui remplit si heureusement l'Escusson de ses armes.' (*L'entree triomphante de Leurs Majestez, Feu d'artifice*, p.4)

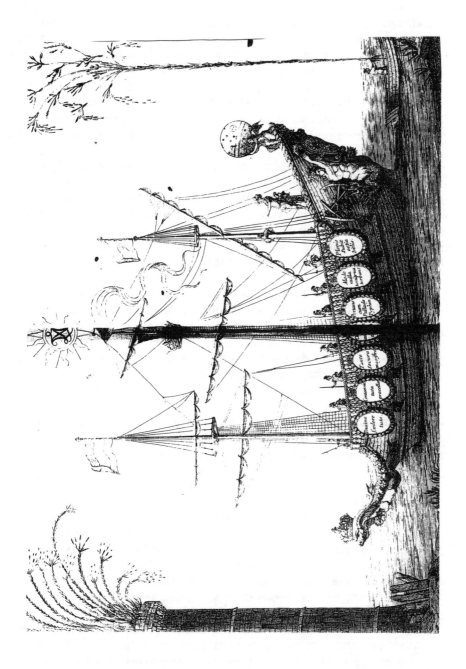

Figure 26: *L'entree triomphante de Leurs Majestez, Feu d'Artifice*, Paris, 1662, between p.4 and p.5.

Enfin un dernier partement de Fusées volantes, ayant fait un fracas effroyable, & remply l'air d'un feu surprenant, le Vaisseau demeura offusqué d'une si espaisse fumée qu'on l'eût perdu de veüe, si une nouvelle constellation n'eût paru au plus haut de son maistre Mats, pour dissiper tous ces nüages: ce qu'elle fit en un instant, & au lieu de ces bruits, de ces tonneres, & de ces obscuritez, on ne vit plus qu'un Soleil tres-lumineux & serain, au centre duquel s'estoit faite cette heureuse conjonction de LOUYS & MARIE THERESE, dont les noms formez par deux cent cinquante Estoilles, furent veus quelque temps, & benis pour l'Eternité par des millions de voeux tres-sinceres.

(*L'entree triomphante de Leurs Majestez, Feu d'artifice*, pp.7-8)

Elsewhere in Paris various triumphal arches and other constructs similarly focused attention on the particular virtues of the royal couple. At the Porte St Antoine, Maria Theresa was represented as Minerva, while Louis was depicted in the guise of Gallic Hercules clad in his traditional lion skin and leaning on his club. The account carefully explains the allegorical significance to be read into this:

...pour nous apprendre & à ceux qui viendront aprés nous, que nostre Monarque invincible, le veritable Hercule Gaulois, est venu prendre son repos dans cette Ville, aprés l'avoir procuré à toute la terre par la force de son bras, & c'est ce que veut dire cette inscription Latine qui se lit en lettres d'or sur le marbre noir entaillé dans le pied détail, PACAVIT ROBORE TERRAS, qui semble avoir esté tiré d'un passage d'Ovide.

(*L'entree triomphante de Leurs Majestez, Preparatifs*, p.5)

A triumphal arch at the Faubourg St Antoine equated the Queen with piety, innocence and fidelity, while the representation of Louis himself was surrounded by imagery of military victory and consequent well-being for the country:

...les deux autres portiques...laissoient une espace de trois pieds...que l'on reserva pour deux bas-reliefs; celuy de main droite fut consacré au triomphe du Roy, celuy de main gauche à celuy de la Reine.

Dans le premier on voyoit ce jeune Prince assis sur le derriere d'un char à l'antique tiré par quatre chevaux attelez de front, au lieu de sceptre il tenoit dans sa main une branche d'olive; une Victoire volante apres luy mettoit sur sa teste une couronne de Mirthe, feüillages qu'il prefere en cette rencontre comme les symboles de la paix & de l'amour qui le font triompher si glorieusement.

A la queüe de son char estoient liées les Divinitez que les autres victorieux avoient mesme respecté dans leurs triomphes: Mars & Bellonne servant de principalle matiere à celuy-cy, estoient contraints nonobstant leur fierté, d'y paroistre à la chaîne, les furies qui ne les abandonnent jamais les accompagnoient en leur desastre.

Diverses autres figures paroissoient autour du Roy faire la principale

> partie de sa pompe; les plus reconnoissables estoient, la Paix, l'Abondance, la
> Magnificence; qui par la gayeté de leur port & de leur marcher tesmoignoient
> la joye qu'elles recevoient de leur restablissement dans le plus florissant Estat
> de l'Europe.   (*L'entree triomphante de Leurs Majestez*, *Preparatifs*, p.2)

The decorations on the triumphal arch in the Place Dauphine focused on the well-being of France brought about by the royal marriage, with the four elements being represented in the guise of female figures. Earth was represented by Cybele with fruits, flowers, and agricultural instruments, while the nameless young woman representing Air was accompanied by wind instruments and a cage of birds, while the attributes of the other two figures representing Water and Fire related more directly to the peace treaty associated with the royal marriage:

> Les deux figures qui representent l'Eau & le Feu, soustiennent une Table, où
> il y a pour devise deux Canons, dont l'un est couvert de fleurs de Lys, &
> l'autre est orné des armes d'Espagne: l'ame de cette devise sont ces paroles
> COMMUNIA FATA DUORUM que l'on a traduit en nostre langue,
>> Le sort sera commun entre ces deux Puissances.
> (*L'entree triomphante de Leurs Majestez*, *Preparatifs*, p.25)

The motto accompanying this representation of the triumph of the young king further emphasised verbally his perceived dominance in Europe:

>> *Postquam terribili vicit rex omnia Marte*
>> *Vincere quem possit Mars super unus erat.*
> lequel peut estre ainsi traduit en nostre langue vulgaire,
>> Apres que ce Grand Roy s'est soûmis l'Univers,
>> Mars seul restoit à vaincre, il le tient en ses fers.
> (*L'entree triomphante de Leurs Majestez*, *Preparatifs*, p.2)

The decoration of the pedestals of this arch used further emblematic imagery to indicate the complexity of the peace process leading up to the royal marriage, with Cupid triumphing over the intricacies of a labyrinth on one side and unscrambling chaos on the other:

> Dans les deux pieds-d'estaux qui sont aux deux costez de l'Arc & qui
> soustienent les Termes, on a feint deux bas reliefs relevez d'or, où il y a un
> Amour representé en deux manieres differentes: Dans l'un ce Dieu tient un
> filet sur un Labyrinthe, au dessus duquel est escrit SOLUS. INVENIT.
> VIAM. pour signifier que luy seul pouvoit trouver le moyen d'accorder par la
> Paix & par le Mariage tant de choses contraires, & tirer les peuples de ce
> fameux Labyrinthe de divisions, & de desordres où ils estoient embarassez
> depuis si long-temps: & dans l'autre bas relief avec un mesme sens on a aussi
> representé l'amour, débroüillant le Chaos & rangeant chaque chose en sa
> place, comme les Philosophes anciens disent qu'il se fit en la naissance du

monde, & ces paroles sont escrittes au dessus. DISSOCIATI. LOCIS. CONCORDI. PACE. LIGAVIT.

(L'entree triomphante de Leurs Majestez, Preparatifs, p.25)

Many other individual emblematic figures were also included on this triumphal arch, some of which conveyed a message which extended the overall theme of praise of monarchy beyond the immediate royal couple themselves. One such image - a particularly complex one - demonstrating the triumph of piety over impiety, is explained in the published account as relating to the particular piety of the Queen Mother, Anne d'Autriche, since the pelican which featured in the image as symbol of piety was her own device:

> Au dessus de l'Arc est une Attique couronnée de deux Frontons, aux deux costez desquels sont deux figures peintes au naturel. Celle qui est au costé droit, est vestüe d'un grand manteau de pourpre relevé d'or, d'une main elle tient un Coeur enflammé, & de l'autre elle embrasse un Pelican qui s'ouvre l'estomac pour nourrir ses petits qui sont posez sur un Autel à l'antique, & sous les pieds paroist un loup renversé. Toutes ces marques font assez connoistre que cette figure est la Pieté qui renverse l'impieté representée d'ordinaire par un Loup, à cause de la fable de Lycaon. Mais il faut aller encore plus loing pour entendre tout le dessein du Peintre, & s'imaginer que par la Pieté il a voulu ainsi figurer la Reyne-Mere parce que la Pieté est une des plus hautes vertus de cette grande Princesse, & il a adjoûté en particulier le Pelican qui est sa devise, & qui marque si bien la tendresse qu'elle a toûjours euë pour les Enfans que le Ciel luy a donné.

(L'entree triomphante de Leurs Majestez, Preparatifs, pp.25-6)

Quite how apparent this particular association with the Queen Mother would have been to the general onlooker is difficult to judge, but certainly the overall theme of piety triumphing over impiety as represented by such emblematic figures as the pelican and the wolf would have been easily understandable, given the familiarity of these two symbols.

Not only did Louis XIV continue the traditional pattern of triumphal entries, in which the various messages relating to the virtue, the greatness and the authority of the reigning monarch were visibly and forcibly conveyed by such emblematic means to the onlooking populace, but he also continued to exploit the more chivalric kinds of court celebration in the form of *carrousels*. Two particularly notable *carrousels* were held in Paris in the earlier part of the reign of Louis XIV, the first in 1656 and the second - which was a much more grandiose event - six years later, in 1662, to celebrate the birth of the *Dauphin*. The magnificence of this latter spectacle, which extended over two days, echoed that of the 3-day *carrousel* mounted in the Place Royale fifty years earlier, in 1612, to mark the marriage alliance of Louis's parents, Louis XIII and Anne d'Autriche. After these two *carrousels*, however, although Louis continued to participate in such brilliant displays (taking an active role until 1676, and thereafter a more passive role as spectator), the events were no longer staged in Paris, but rather in his much preferred location of Versailles, with a consequent modification in both their style and their function, reflecting the henceforth rather different - exclusively aristocratic - audience, compared with the more popular audience who could share such spectacles when they were mounted more publicly in the capital city itself.[38]

Although the demonstration of equestrian skills was an important feature of such *carrousels*, more important was the opportunity they also offered for a dazzling visual display of splendour in the form of the richly ornate and exotic costumes adopted by the participants. But these costumes were not merely splendid. They also had a meaningful role to fulfil as conveyers of a specific message, as did also the devices chosen by the participants to adorn their costumes. The fact that both in 1656 as an 18-year old, and again in 1662 as a mature 24-year old monarch, father of a new son and heir to the throne, Louis took the guise of a Roman emperor at the head of his squadron offered a clear statement about his royal authority, a statement further underlined in both cases by the self-aggrandising devices which he also wore. In 1656, as we are told in Gissey's account of the costumes and devices worn by the participants in the Palais Cardinal *carrousel*, Louis wore two devices, both of which were based on the image of the sun, and the second of which made a clear statement of his unequalled personal status, comparable with that of the sun:

> NE PIU NE PARI
> Point de superieur ny d'égal.
> Figuré par un Soleil le premier & le plus beau de tous les Astres. A quoy l'on compare justement nostre grand Monarque, qui n'a rien au dessus de luy, & qui n'a pas son pareil en excellence.[39]

Similarly in the 1662 *carrousel*, which gave its name to the Place du Carrousel where it was held, Louis once again made his appearance in the guise of a Roman emperor, and once again he wore an equally self-aggrandising sun device as part of his costume, but this time with a motto, *Ut vidi, vici*, which was clearly intended to call up echoes of that other great Roman emperor, Julius Caesar, as Charles Perrault notes in his richly illustrated account of the event, published subsequently by the *Imprimerie royale*:

> Il seroit mal-aisé de trouver un Corps de Devise qui convint mieux au Roy que celuy du Soleil, veu le nombre presque infiny de convenances illustres qui se rencontrent entre ce Grand Prince, & ce bel Astre; Mais sans doute qu'une des plus remarquables, & qui est touchée par cette Devise, est que comme le Soleil n'a qu'à se faire voir pour dissiper les tenebres, ainsi ce Grand Monarque n'a besoin que de sa presence pour vaincre ses ennemis. Ce

---

[38] For discussion of the various *carrousels* which were held during the reign of Louis XIV see Marie-Christine Moine, *Les fêtes à la cour du Roi Soleil 1653-1715*, Paris, 1984, pp.21-32.
[39] H. de Gissey, *Les emblesmes et devises du Roy, des princes et seigneurs qui l'accompagnerent en la Calvacate Royale, et course de bague que Sa Majesté fit au Palais Cardinal 1656*, p.5.

qui est heureusement exprimé par ces mots, UT VIDI, VICI, qui font allusion à ce mot de Jules Cesar, *Veni, vidi, vici.*[40]

Not only the king's own device, but also those of the other members of his squadron also were designed to reflect and complement that of their leader, as for example the Conte de Saint-Aignan's laurel and the Conte de Noailles's eagle, both turning towards the sun (see fig. 27):

> III. Devise du Conte de Saint-Agnan. Un Laurier exposé au Soleil. SOLI. A luy seul....
> IV. Devise du Conte de Novailles. Une Aigle regardant le Soleil. PROBASTI. Vous m'avez éprouvé...
> (Perrault, *Courses de testes et de bague*, 1670, f.28r)

As well as reflecting greatness by being the supposed apparel of a Roman emperor, Louis's costume for this occasion was also designed to contribute to the important statement of royal magnificence by the very richness of the materials from which it was fashioned, as is evident from Perrault's detailed description:

> Le Roy étoit vétu à la Romaine, d'un corps de brocart d'argent rebrodé d'or, dont les épaules & le bas du Busq étoient terminez par des écailles de brocart d'or rebrodé d'argent, avec de gros Diamans enchassez dans la broderie, & bordez encore d'un rang de Diamans. Aux extremitez de la gorgerette de même parure que le corps & composée de quarante quatre roses de Diamans, se joignoient par des agraffes de Diamans, les épaulettes de même étoffe & broderie que le corps, & au bout de chacune desquelles pendoit une campane de Diamans remplie de pendeloques de même. Au milieu de l'estomac pendoit une grosse camane de mesme sorte...
> (Perrault, *Courses de testes et de bague*, 1670, f.25v)

All the members of his squadron were attired in complementary costume to that of their leader, as were similarly the members of the other four squadrons: that of Persians led by Louis's brother, Philippe d'Orléans; of Turks led by the Prince de Condé; of Indians led by the Duc d'Enghien; and of Americans led by the Duc de Guise. The large engravings by Silvestre in Perrault's description of the festivity show clearly how spectacular the event must have been to all the onlookers.

This 1662 *carrousel* was, however, the last great Paris display of royal magnificence by Louis XIV. Thereafter, although *carrousels* were a continuing feature of the reign, they were staged in the very different physical and social environment of Versailles, and in a quite different context. Rather than being organised as discrete celebrations in their own right, they came to be incorporated as just one single element, sharing the stage with plays, ballets, operas, firework displays, in the

---

[40] *Courses de testes et de bague, faites par le Roy*, f.28r.

Figure 27: Perrault, *Courses de testes et de bague*, Paris, 1670, facing p.28.

increasingly complex and essentially aristocratic festivities which were mounted at Versailles, as for example the week-long *Plaisirs de l'Isle enchantée* which took place in 1664, whose title in André Félibien's detailed account of the occasion (again with illustrations by Silvestre) indicates the rich variety of entertainment provided:

> *Les plaisirs de l'Isle enchantée. Course de bague; collation ornée de machines; comedie, meslée de danse et de musique; ballet du Palais d'Alcine; feu d'artifice; et autres festes galantes et magnifiques, faites par le Roy à Versailles, le VII may M.DC.LXIV. et continuées plusieurs autres jours.*

Here the overall theme of the festivity was inspired from Ariosto's *Orlando furioso*, and in accordance with this unifying theme, in the *carrousel* which was held on the first day, Louis led his equestrian squadron in the guise of Roger, rather than in the guise of a Roman emperor, as in the two previous events. Once again the emphasis was on richly exotic attire, but in this case since it was for a purely aristocratic participatory audience at Versailles, rather than for the citizenry of Paris, the message was more of royal magnificence and splendour rather than of royal authority.[41] Here again each individual member of the king's squadron bore his own device, and these are, as usual, described and explained in the text, but also incorporated into the foreground of one of the large engravings by Silvestre of different aspects of the festivities (see fig.28).

Emblematic iconography played an important role in many of the rich and complex spectacles which formed part of such festivities mounted at Versailles, but it is perhaps in the dramatic firework displays which were a regular feature in these festivities, and which frequently carried an allegorical message, that their contribution is most evident. A good example is found in the firework display which formed one of the high spots of the prolonged series of festivities that took place in the summer of 1674 to mark Louis's conquest of the Franche Comté. This display was particularly rich in emblematic material, as is clear from André Félibien's account (which was once again published, like Perrault's earlier *Courses de testes et de bague*, and like the *Plaisirs de l'Isle enchantée* and the *Relation de la feste de Versailles* in a richly illustrated folio volume by the *Imprimerie royale*). In the *Divertissemens de Versailles donnez par le Roy à toute sa cour au retour de la conqueste de la Franche Comté en l'annee M.DC.LXXIV* Félibien describes the various events which happened in the course of this extended celebration which began on 4 July, and went on until the very

---

[41] The first day of the festivity (7 May) was devoted to the *carrousel* together with a *collation*; Day 2 (8 May) saw a performance of the ballet-comedy, *La princesse d'Elide* by Molière and Lully; Day 3 (9 May) saw a ballet (the *Palais d'Alcine*) and firework display; Day 4 (12 May) saw a performance of Molière's *Tartuffe*. For a description of subsequent *carrousels* in court festivities at Versailles in 1667, 1676, 1682 and 1685 see Marie-Christine Moine, *Les fêtes à la cour du Roi Soleil*, pp.31-2.

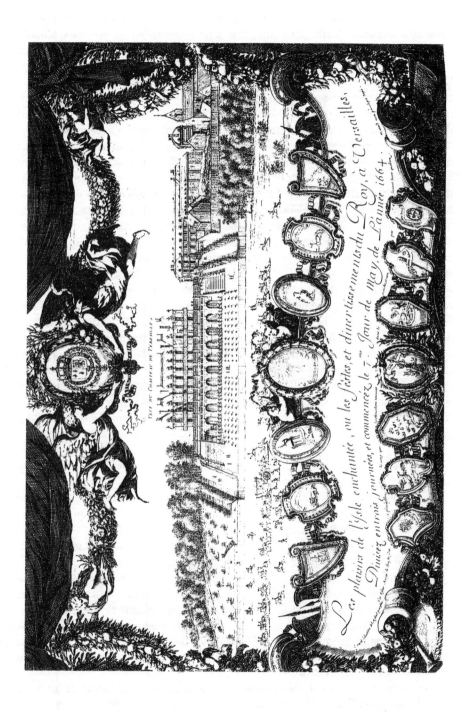

Figure 28: Félibien, *Les plaisirs de l'Isle enchantée*, Paris, 1673, p.27.

end of August, with different events being staged on each of six separate days spaced out across this period. Day 1 (4 July) saw a performance of *Alceste* by Quinault and Lully; Day 2 (11 July) a concert by Lully; Day 3 (19 July) a performance of Molière's *Malade imaginaire*; Day 4 (28 July) a performance of Lully's *Eglogue de Versailles*; Day 5 (18 August) a performance of Racine's *Iphigénie* and a firework display. Only on Day 6 (31 August) was there no formal performance of a play, opera or concert, but instead an elaborate night-time *son et lumière* display with musical accompaniment as the court all took their places in gondolas on the Grand Canal. On each of the six days ornate and complex collations also formed part of the celebrations. Félibien's account of the event (*Les divertissemens de Versailles*) includes large, double-page engravings by Le Paultre of the key events in the festivities.[42] The firework display, which was mounted on the fifth day of the celebration, made clear reference to the event which had triggered the whole celebration - the conquest of the Franche Comté, but in addition it included a whole range of meaningful imagery reflecting on the greatness of the king in general terms in addition to his specific success in this military campaign. The focal scene of the firework display over the Grand Canal was a rocky island on which was mounted a large obelisk at the foot of which was a bas relief representing Louis at the head of his army crossing the Rhine, but this direct political reference to his military success was accompanied also by a series of indirect references in the shape of emblematic figures also included in the display. In his very detailed account, which includes among the engravings a particularly magnificent one by Le Paultre of the climax of the firework display, Félibien describes the spectacle and also carefully explains the iconographic significance to be derived from it. The obelisk was surmounted by a flaming sun, while beneath the obelisk were to be seen a dragon, a lion and an eagle. Hercules and Pallas were also both represented in their traditional emblematic guise, together with a couple of figures of *Renommée* and some *putti*:

> Dans le milieu du piedestal estoit un grand bas relief d'or sur un fond de lapis, où le Roy estoit representé à la teste d'une armée, traversant un large Fleuve. Les Divinitez de ce fleuve paroissoient couchées sur le devant, & appuyées sur leurs urnes. Ce bas relief estoit environné d'un quadre doré avec les armes du Roy au dessus.
>
> Du bas du piedestal sortoient de part & d'autre deux grands rouleaux en forme de console, qui s'étendoient sur toute la face du rocher. Ces rouleaux estoient enrichis d'or & de pierreries: & estant joints l'un à l'autre au dessous du bas relief par une maniére de frise, formoient une espece d'ornement, qui avoit la figure d'un jonc. Au dessous estoient, d'un costé un Aigle, & de l'autre un Lion. Le Lion sembloit abbatu sous le joug; & l'Aigle qui estoit soûmis de mesme, paroissoit tout étonné, & dans une action de vouloir encore se défendre. Sur ces rouleaux & proche de l'Obélisque estoient

---

[42]   For discussion of this and other festivities at Versailles see Orest Ranum, 'Islands and the self in a Ludovician fête', in David L. Rubin, ed., *Sun King. The Ascendancy of French Culture during the Reign of Louis XIV*, Washington, 1992, pp.17-34, and Marie-Christine Moine, *Les fêtes à la cour du Roi Soleil*.

deux grandes Figures. Celle du costé droit representoit Hercule assis, & comme se reposant, appuyé d'une main sur des armes, & de l'autre tenant sa massuë.[43] A ses pieds estoient deux Captifs attachez contre un trophée d'armes.

L'autre Figure qui estoit du costé gauche representoit une Femme richement vestuë d'un corselet à l'antique & d'un grand manteau de pourpre tel qu'on peint Pallas. Elle avoit un casque en teste, & tenoit un baston de commandement à la main. Elle estoit aussi assise sur un monceau d'armes & à ses pieds on voyoit un autre Captif contre un trophée d'armes.

Il y avoit parmi ces Figures plusieurs petits Enfans. Les uns mettoient des couronnes de laurier et des fleurs sur la teste d'Hercule et de Pallas; les autres sembloient vouloir arracher des mains de ces Divinitez le baston et la massuë qu'elles tenoient. D'autres environnoient ceste mesme massuë de festons; & d'autres encore s'occupoient à lier les Captifs de semblables festons, au lieu de chaînes...Ceste machine estoit précedée de deux grandes figures en l'air qui, tenant une trompette à la bouche, representoit deux Renommées.

(Félibien, *Les divertissemens de Versailles*, F1v-2r)

The political message contained in all these allegorical elements is carefully explained by Félibien. The sun over the obelisk predictably reflects the overall 'gloire du Roy', but each of the other elements carries its own individual contributory message. The vanquished lion and eagle, and the captives represent Louis's success in crushing his enemies; Hercules and Pallas reflect his invincible power and his valiant and prudent conduct respectively; while the *putti* reflect the love of his people, and the dragon the vain envy of his rivals :

Toute cette décoration avoit un sens symbolique & mystérieux. Par l'Obélisque & le Soleil on prétendoit marquer la Gloire du Roy toute éclatante de lumiére & solidement affermie au dessus de ses ennemis, & malgré l'Envie representée par le Dragon. Les Figures d'Hercule & de Pallas marquoient l'une la puissance invincible & la grandeur des actions de Sa Majesté; l'autre sa valeur & sa prudente conduite dans toutes ses entreprises, dont le Lion & l'Aigle ressentent les effets. Les Enfans signifient l'amour des peuples qui couronnent tant de genereux exploits.

(Félibien, *Les divertissemens de Versailles*, F2r-v)

But although the use of emblematic and other allegorical material is particularly apparent in this and similar firework displays, it also played an important part in other elements in such royal festivities, such as the ballets which also formed a regular part, and in which - in the early days of his reign, at least - Louis himself took an active

---

[43] This representation of Louis as Gallic Hercules leaning on his club, and resting after his military successes is very similar to that on the triumphal arch at the Porte St Antoine for the entry of Louis and Maria Theresa in 1660. See above, p. 276.

part, enacting roles which reflected and augmented allegorically the magnificence of his royal personage. At a court ballet as early as 1653 he danced in the role of Apollo in the *Ballet royal de la nuict* wearing a richly decorated allegorical costume made of cloth of gold encrusted with rubies and diamonds. His head was adorned by a large sunburst, and he similarly wore a sun on his chest and sunbursts on his ankles, knees and cuffs. He again danced in the role of the sun in further ballets in 1661, 1662 and 1669.[44] In 1662 Louis danced the role of Hercules in a ballet on the theme of Hercules in love, in which Maria Theresa also participated. (The performance had originally been scheduled for 1660 to mark the royal wedding which took place that year, but this was prevented by a fire in the Tuileries where the event was due to be staged.)[45] The *ballet de cour* was not, of course, a new invention in the seventeenth century, but rather had a long history going back into the sixteenth century, and was notably favoured by Catherine de Medici, but undoubtedly in the reign of Louis XIV it became more heavily used for conveying a political message than had hitherto been the case, as Marie-Claude Canova-Green has argued. Discussing court ballets of the 1650s and 1660s she suggests that the underlying message of these ballets was invariably the same: that Louis, as king of France, was the authoritative restorer of order, being victorious over civil disorder within his country in the shape of the *Fronde*, and similarly victorious over his enemies elsewhere in Europe:

> En tant qu'incarnation d'un ordre politique restauré, le roi Louis XIV paraît alors surtout sous les traits d'Apollon ou de Phaëton...Ailleurs il est le Soleil chassant la Nuict ou les nuages, ou encore le Printemps dissipant les brouillards de l'Hiver...mais derrière l'apparente diversité de ces images et de leur champ lexical, c'est la signification unique d'une victoire de l'ordre sur le désordre, du bien sur le mal, compris à la fois comme atteinte à l'absolutisme monarchique et comme menace pour la sécurité nationale qu'il faut lire.[46]

The function of almost all the different aspects of such grandiose festivities which were held at Versailles was to make a clear statement of the magnificence of the personage of Louis XIV, of his power, his virtues and - above all - of his authority. Perhaps the only exception to this general principle was in the plays of Molière and

---

[44] This 1669 performance (in the *Ballet de Flore*) was his last. For discussion of Louis's performance in court ballets see Régine Astier, 'Louis XIV, "Premier Danseur"', in David L. Rubin, *Sun King. The Ascendancy of French Culture during the Reign of Louis XIV*, pp.73-102.

[45] See Marie-Christine Moine, *Les fêtes à la cour du Roi Soleil*, pp.36-7.

[46] See 'Représentations de l'ordre et du désordre dans le ballet de cour' in R. Duchêne and P. Ronzeaud, eds, *Ordre et contestation au temps des classiques: Actes du 21e Colloque du Centre Méridional de Rencontre sur le XVIIe Siècle jointe avec le 23e Colloque de la North American Society for Seventeenth-Century French Literature, Marseille 19-23 juin 1991*, Paris, 1992, pp.309-19, p.314. For full discussion of the *ballet de cour* and its sixteenth-century history see also M. McGowan, *L'art du ballet de cour en France 1581-1643*, and for a facsimile edition and discussion of a particularly important *ballet de cour* see M. McGowan, ed., Balthasar de Beaujoyeulx, *Le Balet comique de la Royne*.

Racine which were performed as part of the festivities: *La princesse d'Elide* on 8 May 1664; *Tartuffe* on 12 May 1664; *Georges Dandin* on 18 July 1668; *Le malade imaginaire* on 19 July 1674; and Racine's *Iphigénie* on 18 August 1674. Of these all but *Le malade imaginaire* were given their first performance before a court audience at Versailles. While plays like *Tartuffe* or *Le malade imaginaire* did, of course, carry a message, it was not a political one of relevance to the courtly audience, for whom the function of such plays was pure entertainment. Court festivities had from a much earlier date already formed part of the cultural life of the Valois monarchs, and been exploited by them for political ends,[47] but in the extent to which he adopted a policy of consistent self aggrandisement throughout his long reign, Louis XIV far outstrips his predecessors, as he does also in his exploitation of emblematic material for that purpose. Certainly we find him following in the familiar paths already trodden by his ancestors, in such events as triumphal entries, but we also find important new developments and a new range of strategies being introduced during the reign of Louis XIV, in which allegorical, and often emblematic, iconography is again used to promote and glorify the image of the king not just within France, but also throughout Europe.

When Louis came to the throne as a five-year old child in 1643 he inherited a country which had for many decades been suffering not only as a result of external wars, but also from internal strife both on the political and the religious front. One of his early experiences as a young king was being obliged to flee from his capital city for a period of seven months in 1649, under threat from the first *Fronde*. A high priority was to restore public confidence in the power and strength of the monarchy in order to unite the country in solidarity and fidelity to its one central and wholly authoritative ruler. The means by which this goal was to be achieved was by the establishment of a highly professional publicity machine whose function was to exploit every possible medium to create a strongly positive public image of Louis XIV as a godlike and authoritative figurehead, uniting and dominating his own country, but also - in the wider context - establishing himself (and France) as the dominant force in Europe. From the early 1660s we see the full impact of this systematic publicity campaign that was launched around the figure of Louis XIV, coinciding with the coming to power of Colbert at this same date. Prior to this, under the authority of Mazarin, propaganda for the young king had followed in the traditional patterns established for earlier monarchs, but after the death of Mazarin in 1661 Colbert instigated a new and more systematic approach to the glorification of the monarch, exploiting the varied skills of practitioners of all the different art forms.

---

[47] As Roy Strong has argued in *Art and Power: Renaissance Festivities 1450-1650* (Berkeley, California, 1984, p.28), in which a large section is devoted to Valois pageantry under Catherine de Medici, 'Festivals offer one aspect of a phenomenon that is central to both the sixteenth and the seventeenth centuries, the allegorical tableau whereby ideas were conveyed by a combination of more or less naturalistic pictorial representations on the one hand, with, on the other, some kind of organisation in space which is not naturalistic but artificial, schematic or diagrammatic. Festivals were aggregates of symbolic images held together by words, spoken or written, which were an essential part of the visual statement and without which it became virtually meaningless.'

One of Colbert's earliest initiatives in this domain was the launching of the Gobelins tapestry manufacture, in 1662, bringing together in that part of Paris (where it still is today) the various other workshops which already existed in Paris, together with that at Maincy, near Fontainebleau, which had until then been working for the now disgraced Fouquet. The tapestries produced at the Gobelins were exclusively for royal use, serving on the one hand to adorn the various royal palaces, and on the other hand to be used as royal gifts. But the key feature of all the tapestries produced at the Gobelins was the fact that all were designed to publicise, by the representation either of realistic or of allegorical scenes, the greatness of the young king. The aesthetic quality of the designs of the tapestries to be produced was ensured by the appointment in 1663 of Charles Le Brun (*Premier peintre du Roy* from 1664) to the post of Director of the Gobelins. That same year, 1663, the *Petite Académie* was set up with the remit of providing the inscriptions which would be needed for the medals and devices which would glorify the king, together with appropriate circumstantial and eulogistic verse for all notable occasions. The first secretary of the *Petite Académie* (which was renamed *Académie des Inscriptions et Belles Lettres* in 1696) was Charles Perrault, best known today for his fairy tales, but more relevantly here, also the author of the *Courses de testes et de bague* of 1670, and of numerous allegorical circumstantial verses in honour of Louis XIV.[48] The *Académie Royale de Peinture et de Sculpture* had already been in existence for thirteen years when Colbert came to power in 1661, but it was reorganised within two years of his arrival, and placed under the Chancellorship of Le Brun. Under the revised structure all new members were expected to provide an artwork relating to the life of the king, and an annual prize was also introduced for the best such work representing the greatness of the king. A few years later in 1671 the *Académie Française* also instigated an annual prize for the best panegyric of the king.[49] As *Surintendant et ordonnateur général des bâtiments, arts, tapisseries et manufactures de France* Colbert created the new post of *Historiographe des bâtiments du Roy* to which André Félibien was appointed, with responsibility for producing descriptions of the various royal buildings and their contents, and - importantly - of providing at the same time an explanation of the iconographic significance of the various paintings, sculptures, tapestries and other representations which adorned the royal buildings, all designed to represent allegorically the greatness of the monarch.

In his preface to one such account, his description of one of the earliest sets of tapestries produced by the Gobelins, the tapestries of the Four Seasons and the Four Elements, Félibien explains the way in which allegorical works such as these are

---

[48] Laurence Grove suggests that Perrault was also the author of the anonymous *Discours sur l'art des devises* which forms part of Arsenal Ms. 3328. See '*Discours sur l'Art des Devises*: an edition of a previously unidentified and unpublished text by Perrault', *Emblematica*, 7,1, 1993, pp.99-144.

[49] For details of these and other *académies* see François Bluche, *Louis XIV*, transl. Mark Greengrass, Oxford, 1990, pp.163-8, and Peter Burke, *The Fabrication of Louis XIV*, Yale, 1992, pp.50-51. Many other *académies* were also founded under royal patronage at this period, as for example the *Académie de Danse* (1661); the *Académie des Sciences* (1666); the *Académie Royale de Musique* (1672) (originally the *Académie d'Opéra*).

created in order to convey by indirect visual means a message about the king's glory:

> C'est par ces Peintures ingénieuses qu'on veut apprendre la grandeur de son Nom à ceux qui viendront aprés nous, & leur faire connoistre par ces Images allégoriques ce que des paroles n'exprimeroient pas avec assez de force.
>
> En effet, de quelle maniére pourroit-on assez bien écrire tout ce que S. M. a fait depuis qu'Elle est montée sur le Trône, & comment pourroit-on assez dignement representer les avantages arrivez à l'Etat, depuis qu'Elle en a pris la conduite? Cependant, toutes ces merveilles sont si misterieusement dépeintes dans les quatre Tableaux que je veux décrire, que l'oeil les découvre d'abord avec plaisir, & l'entendement les connoist avec admiration.[50]

In this last sentence Félibien echoes similar comments made over a century earlier by one of the earliest French emblem writers, Gilles Corrozet, about the way in which art forms could be pleasing to the eye, and also convey a meaningful message. In the preface to his *Hecatomgraphie* Corrozet remarked:

> Pour le plaisir qu'on y pourra comprendre
> Et pour le bien qu'on y pourra apprendre,
> Et pour autant que l'esprit s'esjouit
> Quand avecq luy de son bien l'oeil jouit
> Chascune hystoire est d'ymage illustrée
> Affin que soit plus clairement monstrée
> L'invention... (Corrozet, *Hecatomgraphie*, A2v)

and again in his slightly earlier biblical picture book, the *Historiarum veteris testamenti icones* he made a similar point, about the persuasive nature of such works, albeit within a devotional context, even using the tapestry image to do so:

> En regardant ceste tapisserie
> L'oeil corporel, qui se tourne & varie,
> Y peult avoir ung singulier plaisir,
> Lequel engendre au cueur ung grand desir
> D'aymer son Dieu, qui a faict tant de choses
> Dedans la letre & saincte Bible encloses...
> (Corrozet, *Historiarum veteris testamenti icones*, A3r-v)

A similar point is also made by the 16th-century Lyon publisher specialising in emblem books and similar illustrated didactic literature, Jean de Tournes, in his preface to his edition of another biblical picture book, Charles Fontaine's *Figures du Nouveau Testament*:

---

[50] Félibien, *Tapisseries du Roi, où sont representez les quatre elemens et les quatre saisons*, 1670, A1r.

Les choses d'instruccion qui sont representees à la vuë, & par icelle ont
entree en l'apprehension, & de là en avant en l'entendement, & puis en la
memoire, esmeuvent & incitent davantage, & demeurent plus fermes &
stables, que celles qui ont leur seule entree par l'oreille.

(Fontaine, *Figures du Nouveau Testament*, A2r)

Félibien explains likewise that Louis XIV's deliberate policy is to exploit all art forms
to contribute to his own glory and - by extension - to the glory of his country.
Furthermore, the publicity of this glory is intended to spread beyond the confines of
France across Europe, and also down to posterity:

Aussi comme il n'y a rien dans tous les Arts que le Roy ne fasse servir à
l'utilité de ses Peuples, & à la gloire de son Regne, il ne se contente pas
d'élever de magnifiques Edifices, d'orner ses Palais de Peintures, & de
Statuës inimitables, de les parer de Vases & de Meubles précieux, de faire
travailler à toutes sortes de riches Tapisseries, & d'employer une infinité de
personnes à tous les Ouvrages qui peuvent embellir son Royaume: il veut
encore que les Peuples éloignez en jouissent en quelque sorte, & que par les
Descriptions & les Figures de ses superbes Bastimens, & de ses Royales
entreprises, ils en connoissent l'excellence. C'est dans cette pensée que Sa
Majesté ayant jetté les yeux sur des Personnes capables d'exécuter ses
intentions, fait mettre au jour des Recueïls pareils à celuy-cy, où la beauté des
Caractéres, jointe à celle des Figures, ne laisse rien à desirer, afin qu'ils
soient un jour de précieux Monumens de tout ce qui se fait aujourd'hui & que
ceux qui viendront aprés nous soient en quelque sorte spectateurs des
merveilles dont nous sommes témoins.

(Félibien, *Tapisseries du Roi*, 1670, π2r)

The success of this policy of publicising the greatness of the French monarch across
Europe is attested by the number of copies of accounts of splendid happenings in
France which were standardly published in large-format luxury editions by the
Imprimerie royale, which having been presented as royal gifts to other European
princes, were then placed in the royal library, and are now housed in the big national
libraries of Europe, often still bearing their original French royal binding.[51] Indicative
also of the interest that a work like Félibien's *Tapisseries du Roy* attracted elsewhere
in Europe, as well as in France, is the fact that as well as going through several
editions in French, three editions of a bilingual French/German version were also
published in Germany, as well as an edition of a bilingual French/Dutch version in the
Netherlands.[52]

---

[51]   See, for example, a copy of the 1679 edition of Félibien's own *Tapisseries du Roy* in the
Österreichische National Bibliothek in Vienna, or a copy of the 1670 edition of Perrault's
Courses de testes et de bague in the Bayerische Staatsbibliothek in Munich.
[52]   *Tapisseries du Roy, où sont representez les quatre elemens et les quatre saisons. Avec les
devises qui les accompagnent & leur explication. Königliche FranzösischeTapezereijen. Oder*

The royal tapestries which Félibien describes in this work offer a particularly good example of emblems in applied art being used for royal propaganda and aggrandisement.[53] Shortly after his appointment as director of the Gobelins, Le Brun produced in 1664 designs for a set of four large allegorical tapestries representing the four elements, and later that same year, for a further companion set representing the four seasons. Several sets of each series of tapestries were produced, the earliest of which were completed by 1669. While the ostensible subject of the tapestries was the four elements and the four seasons, their underlying allegorical message was the greatness of Louis XIV. They thus complement the other great series of realistic tapestries depicting the early achievements of the king, the fourteen-piece *Histoire du Roy*, on which the Gobelins manufacture began work in 1665, the year after they embarked on the Seasons and Elements tapestries. Most of the sets of both the Seasons and the Elements series were produced in *basse lisse* (low warp), but some were produced in the more prestigious *haute lisse* (high warp), and it is these which are particularly interesting, since in addition to the central representation of the season or the element, these *haute lisse* tapestries also include in their decorative borders a series of emblematic figures which make a very significant further contribution to the iconographic programme already embodied in the main body of the tapestry.[54] The underlying theme of all the eight tapestries making up the Seasons and the Elements is praise of Louis XIV for his achievements in general since he came to the throne, but in particular for his role in bringing glorious peace to his country, but the emblems around the borders take this message one stage further, by representing the four key virtues of the young monarch which have allowed him to achieve this - his piety,

---

überaus schöne Sinn-Bilder, in welchen die vier Element, samt den vier Jahr-Zeiten...vorgestellet werden, Augsburg, J. Koppmayer for J.U. Krauss, 1687, folio (also another edition in 1690, and an undated edition published by Krauss alone); *Tapisseries du Roy, où sont representez les quatre elements, avec les devises, qui les accompagnent & leur explication. Tapyten van den Konink van Vrankryk verbeeldende de Vier Elementen, Beneffens haar wonderlyke Zinnebeelden, en uytlegging op dezelve* and *Suite des tapisseries du Roy de France, où sont representées les quatre saisons [avec les devises] qui les accompagnent & leurs explications. Tapyten van den Koning van Vrankryk, verbeeldende de Vier Jaargetyden, benevens haar verwonderlyke Zinnebeelden en Uytleggingen op dezelve*, Amsterdam, P. van den Berge, n.d. (c.1700), 4°. For details of all editions see *BFEB*, vol.1, nos 240-52.
[53] For discussion of these tapestries and of the way in which they exploit emblematic material for royal propaganda see Alison Saunders, 'Emblems to tapestries and tapestries to emblems: contrasting practice in England and France'.
[54] Of the seven sets which were made of the Four Seasons tapestries, only one (made for the king himself) was done in *haute lisse*, and thus contains the emblematic borders. This set (minus Summer) is now housed in the *Mobilier National* in Paris. A set of *basse lisse* Seasons (minus Spring) without the emblematic borders is housed in the *Antichambre de l'Impératrice* at Fontainebleau. Eight sets of the Four Elements series were made, four in *haute lisse*, and three in *basse lisse*, while the last set was done in *haute lisse* for Earth, Fire and Water, but *basse lisse* for Air. A set of *haute lisse* tapestries of the Four Elements is hung in the *Salle du Conseil* in the *Ecole de Médecine* in Paris. For a detailed description of all the different sets of tapestries and their history see Maurice Fénaille, *Etat général des tapisseries de la manufacture des Gobelins depuis son origine jusqu'à nos jours*, Paris, 1903, pp.50-83.

magnanimity, *bonté* and *valeur*, and linking each of these virtues to the particular theme of each of the eight tapestries which make up the two series. In addition, the Four Seasons tapestries also include within these decorative borders further emblems relating to the king's favourite seasonal pastimes (see figs 29 and 30), while the Four Elements similarly include further emblems which draw associations between the particular element and particular military achievements by Louis.

Thus the Spring tapestry carries a far greater message than just a simple representation of that season. The central scene depicts Mars, Venus and Cupid, since spring is the season for love, with a clear allegorical subtext that the young king, in the spring of his life, is tempted away from bellicose pursuits by the power of love. (The royal marriage forming part of the peace settlement with Spain had occurred in 1660). But the message, as Félibien explains in his account of the tapestries, goes further than this. The love that is represented here is not just Louis's love for his new wife, Maria Theresa, but also more generally his love of his people, inciting him to bring about a peace settlement in the interests of the well-being of his country and his people. Within the central scene is also included, as well as Mars, Venus and Cupid, a representation of Versailles, since that was Louis's favourite palace for that season, and this particular section of the tapestry also includes a further level of meaning in that Louis can be seen preparing for his favourite springtime activity, which was jousting.[55] The emblems around the borders contribute further to the complex message. In one a swallow is depicted, with the motto *Et tempora laeta reducit*. At one level this simply represents the appearance of the bird heralding the happy season of spring after the rigours of winter, but at a further level it also represents Louis heralding a happy period of peace after the rigours of war. Another emblem represents a lance with the motto *Ludo pugnaeque* reflecting the dual function in Louis's life of such a weapon, serving for serious purposes in time of war, but equally for the pleasurable pursuit of jousting in peacetime, thereby echoing the preparations for jousting at Versailles depicted within the central part of the tapestry.

Similarly in the Earth tapestry the central scene represents Cybele and Ceres bringing well-being to the country with the motto *Ubertas maior ab illo*, but a clear association is made with Louis also bringing well-being to his country by representations in the borders of his military triumph in winning back Dunkirk from the English in 1662, and of his distribution of corn to the people of Paris during a period of famine, and this is further backed up by a series of familiar emblematic figures representing his four key virtues, also incorporated into the decorative borders around the central theme. A pine with the motto *Recta se tollit* denotes his magnanimity; a marigold with the motto *Coelestes sequitur motus* denotes his piety; a lion with the motto *Quis hunc impunè lacessit* denotes his valeur and (less familiar) a shepherd's crook with the motto *Et regit et servat* denotes his *bonté*. While these tapestries were clearly designed to make a public statement about the glory of the French king, the audience to which this message could be directed in this form was

---

[55] Louis's other favoured seasonal residences are similarly depicted in each of the other three Seasons tapestries: Fontainebleau in the Summer tapestry; Saint Germain in the Autumn tapestry; and Paris in the Winter tapestry.

Figure 29: 'Autumn' tapestry from the Gobelins tapestries of the Four Seasons.

Figure 30: Detail from the border of the Gobelins 'Autumn' tapestry, showing the emblem *Et fulminis ocyor alis.*

only a relatively small one, restricted solely to those privileged people with access to the rooms in which the tapestries were displayed. But such a message could become accessible to a much wider audience once it was made available in printed form, in the manner outlined by Félibien, and in the case of these tapestries this happened very quickly. As early as 1668, the year before the earliest sets of the actual tapestries themselves were completed, Jacques Bailly, *peintre ordinaire des bâtiments*, produced for the royal library a manuscript set of miniatures of the devices incorporated into the borders of the eight tapestries. (Curiously he did not at this stage include in his manuscript illustrations of the central scenes of the tapestries. These were not added to the manuscript until four years later.) But the particularly interesting feature of Bailly's manuscript is that as well as his painted reproductions of each of the emblematic figures, together with the mottoes which had from the outset been designed to accompany them in the tapestries, he included also a significant new textual element to accompany each emblematic figure. A series of madrigals, newly composed for the purpose, for the most part by Charles Perrault, but occasionally by other members of the *Petite Académie*, accompany the emblems, together with a few lines of prose, adding a further gloss, spelling out more clearly the intended allegorical meaning of each emblem which in the original tapestries was conveyed solely by the combination of figure and motto.[56] Thus the emblem of the swallow with the motto *Et tempora laeta reducit* in the Spring tapestry is in Bailly's manuscript version accompanied by an additional verse by Perrault:

> Quand par l'ordre des temps une fascheuse guerre
> De biens & de plaisirs a depouillé la terre,
> Et fait languir ses habitans;
> Je viens leur rendre l'esperance,
> Je viens aporter l'abondance,
> Et rameine avec moy la joye & le beau temps.

and by an explanatory prose gloss:

> Pour le Printemps. Dans la piece de la saison du Printemps. Une Irondelle, avec ce mot *Et tempora laeta reducit*. Comme cét Oyseau est estimé chasser l'Hyver & ramener le Printemps avec luy, On peut dire de mesme que le Roy a ramené le beau-temps & la Paix apres une longue & ennuyeuse guerre.
> (Bailly ms., ed. Grivel and Fumaroli, p.69)

making it clear that the underlying function of the emblem is to represent allegorically the king's success in bringing victorious peace and consequent well-being to his country.

More clearly formulated though the message was in this new form, in comparison to its original textless tapestry form, the readership which it could reach via the medium of one single manuscript copy housed in the royal library was still very restricted.[57] But even before Bailly produced his manuscript, and again well before

[56] Bailly's manuscript is housed in the Bibliothèque nationale de France (Ms.fr. 7819). A facsimile edition exists, ed. M. Grivel and M. Fumaroli, *Devises pour les tapisseries du Roi*, Paris, 1988.
[57] In 'Le Cabinet du Roy et les projets encyclopédiques de Colbert' in *L'art du livre à*

even the first set of tapestries was completed, Félibien, as *Historiographe des bâtiments du Roy*, published in 1665 a non-illustrated description of the emblems of the Four Elements tapestries, following this two years later, in 1667, by a fuller, but still non-illustrated version, including the verses supplied by Perrault and other members of the *Petite Académie*, together with an equivalent text for the Four Seasons tapestries.[58] But - more significantly - in 1668 appeared the first of a series of large, illustrated folio editions of Félibien's work, in which Elements and Seasons were brought together, with engravings supplied by Sébastien Le Clerc. This first edition was published in Paris by Claude Blageart,[59] but subsequent editions of the work were published (like Valdor's earlier *Triomphes de Louis le Juste XIII. du nom*, similarly glorifying Louis's predecessor) by the *Imprimerie royale* in 1670, and again in 1679 (see fig.31).[60] It is thus essentially via the medium of the printed book that this emblematic message of glorification of Louis XIV, originally transmitted in tapestry form, and thereafter in manuscript form, came ultimately to be addressed to a much greater audience both within France itself and beyond.

The case of the Gobelins tapestries of the Four Seasons and the Four Elements is thus a particularly interesting one, demonstrating not only the way in which emblematic iconography could be exploited as a medium for glorification of the king within the actual tapestries themselves, hung for public display to those who were privileged to see them and absorb their message, but also the way in which that

---

l'Imprimerie Nationale (Paris, 1973, pp.102-27), Anne Sauvy refers to the existence of one or two copies of a supposedly early printed edition of Bailly's manuscript dating from 1667, but gives no indication of location of these. It is possible that one copy she is referring to is a volume in the British Library (Harleian Ms. 4377). This undated folio volume, entitled *Devises pour les tapisseries du Roy*, in a French royal binding, comprises a series of hand-coloured engravings of the emblems to which the verses have been added in manuscript.

[58] *Les quatre elements peints par Mr Le Brun et mis en tapisseries pour Sa Majesté*, Paris, P. Le Petit, 1665, 4°; *ibid.*, Paris, P. Le Petit, 1667, 4°; *Les quatre saisons peintes par Mr Le Brun et mises en tapisseries pour Sa Majesté*, Paris, P. Le Petit, 1667, 4°.

[59] *Devises pour les tapisseries du Roy, où sont representez les quatre elemens et les quatre saisons de l'année, peintes en mignature par I. Bailly, peintre du Roy en son Academie Royale de Peinture & Sculpture. Et gravées par S. Le Clerc*, Paris, C. Blageart, 1668, folio. Copies of this rare edition are found in the Getty Museum in California, in the Victoria and Albert Museum in London, and in the Bibliothèque Mazarine in Paris. For details see *BFEB*, vol.1, no. 243.

[60] As well as being widely disseminated in these illustrated editions, a further non-illustrated version of Félibien's explanation of the allegorical significance of the tapestries was also included in his 1671 *Descriptions de divers ouvrages de peinture faits pour le Roy* (Paris, S. Mabre-Cramoisy, 1671, 12°) which was popular enough to be republished in 1689 in an expanded version (*Recueil de descriptions de peintures et d'autres ouvrages faits pour le Roy*, Paris, Veuve S. Mabre-Cramoisy, 1689, 12°; and Paris, F. and P. Delaulne, 1689, 12°) and again in 1696 (*Description du chateau de Versailles, de ses peintures, et d'autres ouvrages faits pour le Roy. Par Monsieur Felibien de l'Académie Royalle des Sciences*, Paris, F. and P. Delaulne, 1696, 12°). In addition, a selection of the madrigals composed to accompany the emblems were also included in La Fontaine's *Recueil de poésies chrêtiennes et diverses*, Paris, J. Couterot, 1679, 12°, 3 vols, vol.2, pp.371-3.

DIVERTISSEMENT
DANS LA PIECE
DE LA SAISON DE L'AUTOMNE.

Un Faucon fondant fur fa Proye, & ce Mot, ET FULMINIS OCYOR
ALIS. Cét Oifeau eft le plus vifte & le plus vigoureux de tous ; en forte
qu'il reprefente parfaitement cette diligence & cette vigueur incroyable avec
laquelle Sa Majefté exécute tous fes deffeins.

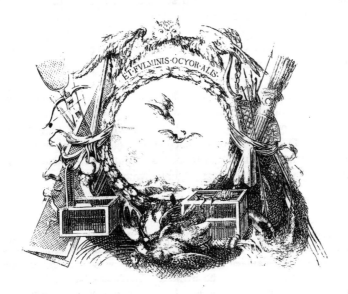

Lors que le Combat m'eft permis .
Et qu'à perdre mes Ennemis .
Leur mauvais fort m'a fait refoudre :
Je fonds fur eux d'un mouvement
Aufsi terrible que la Foudre ,
Et plus rapide que le Vent.

CHARPENTIER.

Figure 31: Félibien, *Tapisseries du Roi*, Paris, 1670, f.35, showing the engraved
version of the 'Autumn' tapestry emblem *Et fulminis ocyor alis.*

message of royal propaganda could also be extended to reach a far wider audience via the medium of the printed book. But although it affords a striking example of this process, it is not by any means unique. Part of Félibien's remit as *Historiographe des bâtiments du Roy* was precisely to provide such printed descriptions of the numerous allegorical paintings, sculptures and other art forms which adorned the various royal palaces, and to accompany these with an explanation of the iconographic significance of the various items described, and his description of these Gobelins tapestries is only one among several such descriptions which he produced. His *Descriptions de divers ouvrages de peinture faits pour le Roy* includes, as well as his description of the tapestries, a description of *Les Reines de Perse aux pieds d'Alexandre, peinture du Cabinet du Roy* and *Le Portrait du Roy*, both by Le Brun, while his 1674 *Description sommaire du Chasteau de Versailles* gives an interim description of the still unfinished palace.[61] In the course of this description he stresses the care which has been taken in all parts of the palace to use the themes depicted in the grandiose decor to convey symbolically the magnificence of the personage of the king, as for example in his description of the *Petit Cabinet*, in which the relevance to the king of each individual element is carefully itemised:

> Les plafonds doivent estre enrichis de peintures par les meilleurs Peintres de l'Academie Royale. Et comme le Soleil est la devise du Roy, l'on a pris les sept Planettes pour servir de sujet aux Tableaux des sept pieces de cét appartement. De sorte que dans chacune on y doit representer les actions des Heros de l'antiquité, qui auront rapport à chacune des Planetes & aux actions de Sa Majesté. On en voit des Figures symboliques dans les ornemens de

---

[61] Paris, G. des Prez and C. Savreux, 1674, 12°. Louis XIV's transformation of the existing hunting lodge at Versailles into a splendid palace began in 1661, but it was a major project which was to extend for some fifty years. When Félibien produced this account, the work was far from completed. In 1696 Félibien produced an updated version of this account, taking account of the modifications effected by the architect J. Hardouin-Mansart. It is interesting to see from Félibien's description of the exterior of the building that one section was adorned with allegorical representations of the Four Elements using exactly the same iconographic elements as in the tapestries: 'Ceux qui ont la conduite de ces grands Ouvrages ont fait representer les quatre Elemens sur le haut des portiques de ces deux aisles, puis qu'à l'envy l'un de l'autre, ils fournissent ces offices de tout ce qu'ils ont de plus exquis pour la nourriture des hommes. Car la Terre donne liberalement ses animaux, ses fruits, ses fleurs & ses liqueurs. L'Eau fournit les Poissons; l'Air les Oiseaux; Et le Feu le moyen d'apprester la pluspart de ces alimens. Et parce qu'il y a douze Figures sur chaque balcon, chaque Element a trois figures qui le representent.

La Terre est figurée par Ceres, Pomone & Flore. Ces trois figures sont sur le balcon à gauche en entrant.

L'Eau est representée par Neptune, Thetis & Galathée qui sont ensuite sur le mesme balcon.

L'Air est representé par Junon, Iris & le Zephire. Ces figures sont sur le balcon à main droite.

Le Feu par Vulcain & deux Cyclopes Sterops & Bronte, qui sont ensuite sur le mesme balcon.' (Félibien, *Description sommaire du Chasteau de Versailles*, pp.12-14)

> sculpture qu'on a faits aux corniches, & dans les plafonds.
>
> (Félibien, *Description sommaire du Chasteau de Versailles*, pp.33-4)

In this passage Félibien makes a passing reference to Louis's sun device inspiring the theme of the decor, but in an earlier passage in the work he points to the extent to which Louis's sun device has been used as a recurrent iconographic leitmotif in the decor throughout the palace, forcing a mental association to be drawn by the onlooker between Louis, the Sun King and Apollo, the Sun God:

> Il est bon de remarquer d'abord que comme le Soleil est la Devise du Roy, & que les Poëtes confondent le Soleil & Apolon, Il n'y a rien dans cette superbe Maison qui n'ait raport à cette divinité; Aussi toutes les figures & les ornemens qu'on y voit n'estant point placez au hazard, ils ont relation, ou au Soleil, ou aux lieux particuliers où ils sont mis.
>
> (Félibien, *Description sommaire du Chasteau de Versailles*, pp.11-12)

While Félibien was officially charged with supplying such accounts as these, passing on in printed form to the wider public the message of royal magnificence which only the privileged could see in its original painted form in royal palaces such as Versailles, he did not have exclusive rights to such material. As seen in an earlier chapter, a similar, but anonymous, *Explication en vers des tableaux de la galerie de Versailles* dating from 1691 also provides a detailed description of the set of allegorical paintings by Le Brun on the ceiling of the *Grande Galerie* representing key events in the life of the king from the point when he took over control of the country in 1661 ('Le Roy prend luy-mesme la conduite de ses Etats, & se donne tout aux Affaires') to his triumphant conclusion to the Wars with the Netherlands in 1678, with the Treaty of Nijmegen. Although this work is dedicated specifically to Louis's nine-year old grandson, the Duc de Bourgogne, who would naturally have had access to the original paintings, for which the work serves as a commentary, it also serves, in the same way as did Félibien's various accounts, to spread to a much wider audience in printed verbal form the allegorical message of royal grandeur which was originally expressed in purely visual form to the small privileged minority who enjoyed the right to pass through the *Grande Galerie* at Versailles, and cast their eyes upwards to contemplate the meaningful message of its gloriously painted ceiling.[62]

These various examples demonstrate the way in which emblems and devices originally designed for use in triumphal entries, court celebrations or interior (or exterior) decoration of royal palaces to convey a message of royal magnificence, could be reproduced thereafter in printed form as a published account of the particular celebration, or the particular set of paintings or tapestries, in order that the message be more accessible to a wider audience, and also - in the case of emblems used in ephemeral architecture - that their otherwise short-lived message might be preserved for posterity in the more enduring form of the printed book. But emblems and devices which had not necessarily all served together in one particular festivity could also be

---

[62] See above, chapter 4, p.134 *et seq.*

brought together for posterity in printed collections whose object was also to glorify the reigning monarch. The prolific Ménestrier was a particularly enthusiastic producer of such works, but his fellow Jesuit, Pierre Le Moyne was also a also very active in this domain. In Ménestrier's *Devise du Roy justifiée* one single section whose subtitle, *Le monde entier consacré à la gloire du Roy*, gives a clear indication of the tenor of the collection, contains 132 sun devices in honour of Louis XIV (P2r-T2v), while a further group of 435 sun devices in his 1682 *Philosophie des images* includes in the section *Le Ciel et les Astres en Devises* (part 2, A1r-V3v) several which relate to Louis XIV, as in the following examples:

> Le Soleil qui se couche dans l'Océan.
> ME SUBIECTIS EXCIPIT UNDIS.
> L'Océan me reçoit & me soûmet ses eaux.
> Le mot est du mesme livre des Metamorphoses, & rien n'exprime plus heureusement le grand pouvoir que le Roy a presentement sur la mer.
>
> Un Soleil levant qui dissipe des nuages.
> ME CRESCENTE CADENT.
> Ils s'abaisseront quand je m'éleveray.
> Pour les troubles des Guerres Civiles dissipez par le Roy en sa Majorité.
> (Ménestrier, *La philosophie des images*, part 2, C4v-D1r)

Le Moyne also includes in his 1666 *De l'art des devises* a little collection of *Devises royales*, likewise on the theme of the sun (pp.425-56). These are more fully worked out emblems than those of Ménestrier, with a verse and lengthier prose gloss, but once again they focus on the virtues and achievements of the king, expressed allegorically through his device of the sun, as in:

> Le Soleil aime à paroistre seul, & à faire seul tout ce qu'il fait. Aussi-tost qu'il se découvre toute autre lumiere se retire: & tous les autres Astres ne sont plus Astres qu'en son absence. Aussi agit-il absolument & sans leur participation. Il est le Principe independant, & la cause universelle de tout ce qui se fait au dessous de luy: & ce n'est qu'à luy qu'on s'adresse, quand on a besoin de calme, de serenité & d'abondance. Autant de mots, autant de traits de l'Authorité du Prince. Comme le Soleil, il ne peut avoir de compagnon ny d'égal: il ne doit recevoir personne à la participation de ses pouvoirs: & s'il preste par fois quelques rayons de sa Couronne, il ne doit jamais se dessaisir du Cercle d'où ces rayons partent.
>
> L'AUTHORITE ROYALE
> *Le Soleil en son Midy*
> Lucet agit-que unus
>
> Par tout où s'étend mon Empire,
> Je suis connu tout seul, & tout seul reclamé:

Tout autre quoy que grand, & quoy que renommé,
Quand je parois ou tombe, ou se retire.
Rien n'agit que dependamment,
De la force & du mouvement,
Que ma presence inspire, & que ma vertu donne:
Et quoy que l'on ait dit de certains faux Soleils,
Je preste mes rayons, sans prester ma Couronne,
Et ne souffre jamais ny seconds ny pareils.
(Le Moyne, De l'art des devises, pp.440-41)

Often the devices which appear in such collections may have been used originally on one particular occasion, but unlike the printed accounts which were published subsequently to perpetuate the memory of the whole event, the purpose of these collections of emblems and devices is not to commemorate any one single event, but rather to bring together in printed form a series of groups of emblems and devices originally displayed for public view on a variety of different occasions. These various occasions are usually simply noted in passing by the author, since the prime interest is in bringing together the emblems and devices so that cumulatively they convey a particular message, rather than as a testimony to the particular occasion for which they were devised, as was the case in the works we have discussed hitherto in this chapter. Thus Ménestrier's *Science et l'art des devises* of 1686 includes among many other groups of devices designed by himself for various occasions, listed under such subheadings as *La vie du Roy en devises* (p.79); *Devises sur divers evenemens de ce regne* (covering the period from 1684 onwards) (p.167); *Divers evenemens de ce regne en devises* (covering the earlier period from 1666) (p.195); and *Pour les grands ouvrages du Roy* (p.220).

But in other cases collections of devices are put together from scratch, designed from the outset with the sole purpose of providing a eulogy of the king in purely printed form. Of such a kind is the little collection of ten Latin emblems on the sun published in 1715 by yet another Jesuit, Gabriel-François Le Jay, to mark the death of Louis XIV, under the title *Ludovici Magni vita symbolis heroicis designata*,[63] of which the opening emblem offers a typical example:

---

[63] *Ludovici Magni vita symbolis designata. Auctore Gabriele Francisco Le Jay, Societatis Iesu*, Paris, L. Sevestre, 1715, 4°. Although this particular collection is exclusively in Latin, Le Jay later produced in 1723 another short collection of eight emblems for Louis XV which were wholly in French other than the motto, perhaps taking into account the fact that Louis was only thirteen at the time (*Les vertus royales mises en devises et presentées au Roy à sa majorité*, Paris, S. Langlois, 1723, 4°). For discussion of these two works see Alison Saunders, 'What happened to the native French tradition? The decline of the vernacular emblem in the seventeenth century'. Several decades before Le Jay's panegyric emblems on the death of Louis XIV, Leonard de Chaumelz had similarly produced in 1667 a collection of panegyric emblems to mark the death of Louis's mother, Anne d'Autriche in 1666: *Devises panegyriques pour Anne d'Austriche, Reine de France, dediees à Monsieur le Marquis de Saint-Luc...Par le Sieur de Chaumelz, Conseiller du Roy en ses Conseils & en sa Cour des Aydes de Guyenne*, Bordeaux, J. Mongiron Millanges, 1667, 4°.

I SYMBOLUM
ORTUS
Sol Exoriens
Mirabil' subito che pare

Conspicuos nondum vultus Solaureus orbi
  Extulit, aut medio totus ab axe micat.
Sed quanta attonitis retegit miracula terris!
  Vel primo in cursûs limine quantus adest!
Cùm tua te primo, LODOICE, excepit in ortu
  Gallia, & auditas gestiit esse preces;
Nondum MAGNUS eras, sed rerum laeta tuarum
  Iam dederas populis omnia multa tuis.
          (Le Jay, *Ludovici Magni vita*, p. [3])

Another particularly ingenious collection of eulogistic sun devices composed in honour of Louis XIV is the *Ludovici Magni Galliarum Regis elucubratrio anagrammatica-historica* produced by the Minim, Gaspard Laugier in 1679.[64] Here each engraved device depicting an aspect of Louis's sun is accompanied by one or other version of Louis's name and title (or on occasion that of a close member of his family), which is then rearranged into an anagram forming an appropriate motto for the device, as in that for Maria Theresa, in which the name, anagram and verse:

MARIA, TERESIA, AUSTRIACA
SIC RARA, ITA VISA, TE AMARE.
Modum nesciens ac terminum
pura dilectio
in Te, ô Rex
effusa, tota profusa:
Heliotropio,
augustior, foeliciorque.
Solem
Secuta, & assecuta.   (Laugier, *Ludovici Magni...elucubratio*, C1r)

are accompanied by an engraved device of the sunflower with the motto *Assecuta quiescat.*

More conventional and less ingenious is a little group of five sun emblems by the Jesuit Charles de la Rue included in his *Idyllia* of 1669 under the title *Emblemata heroica*, three of which relate to Louis himself, while the remaining two are addressed to the *Dauphin* and to Colbert. Here the three relating to Louis himself depict a sun shining on a cloud with the motto *Satis est vidisse*; the sun shining through rain with the motto *Par si durasset*; five eagles flying up to the sun with the motto *Crescunt*

---

[64] *Ludovici Magni Galliarum Regis elucubratio anagrammatica-historica. A P.F. Gasparo Laugier, sacri Ordinis Minimorum alumno*, Aix en Provence, C. Marchy, 1679, 4°.

vires animique videndo, while those to the *Dauphin* and Colbert depict respectively another sun shining on a cloud with the motto *Caelestis facit unda parem*, and an eagle with two young with the motto *Iovi educat*.[65] Similarly extending praise of Louis himself to embrace also his family and minister is a much earlier collection of ten bilingual Latin/French emblems by Charles Patin published in 1660.[66] Here the collection includes Mazarin, Anne d'Autriche, Maria Theresa, and the newly born *Dauphin*, as well as Louis's brother Philippe, the Prince de Condé, the Duc d'Enghien and the Prince de Conti. Anne d'Autriche is praised in particular for her role in bringing about the peace settlement with Spain. The engraved figure depicting Minerva holding an olive tree with the motto *Oleaque Minerva inventrix* is accompanied by the Latin title and couplet:

> In Piam Annam Austriacam, reginam Christ. Ludovici XIV Franc. & Navar. Regis Matrem.
>> Aurea Pax, opus, ANNA, tuum est Oleaque Minerva
>> Inventrix, sacras hâc tibi cinge comas.

and equivalent - but fuller - French version:

> Pour l'Auguste Princesse Anne d'Austriche, Reine Mere du Roy. Voila la Minerve qui a surmonté toutes les difficultez, & qui a heureusement trouvé les moyens de conclure la Paix.
>> Cette Reine par son adresse,
>> Par son esprit & sa sagesse,
>> A fait ce qui se peut pour ne mourir jamais,
>> S'estant par tout ouvert le Temple de Memoire:
>> Car lors qu'elle a trouvé le secret de la Paix,
>> Elle a trouvé celuy d'une immortelle gloire.
>> (Patin, *In stirpem regiam epigrammata*, p.10)[67]

---

[65] *Caroli de la Rue è Societate Iesu Idyllia*, Rouen, R. Lallemant, 1669, 12°, pp.41-57. Three of the five (*Satis est vidisse*; *Crescunt vires animique videndo*; and *Caelestis facit unda parem*) had been included in La Rue's *Emblemata regia. Auctore C.D.L.R. è Soc.Iesu*, published in Paris the previous year by the royal printer, Sébastien Mabre-Cramoisy, and all five were published subsequently in an expanded collection of 27 *Symbola heroica* accompanied by a collection of inscriptions in praise of Louis XIV's exploits in Book 3 of La Rue's 4-volume collection of *Carmina* (*Caroli Ruaei è Societate Iesu carminum libri quatuor ad celsissimum principem Ferdinandum Episcopum monasteriensem et Paderbornensem*, Paris, S. Benard, 1680, folio).

[66] *In stirpem regiam epigrammata. Authore M. Carolo Patin, doctore medico Parisiensi, & scholarum professore. Devises et emblemes de la Maison Royale. Par M. Charles Patin, docteur regent de la Faculté de Medecine de Paris*, Paris, no publ., 1660, 4°. It is interesting that only in the French title to the work does Patin use the phrase 'Devises et emblemes', whereas in the Latin title he simply uses the more all-embracing word 'epigrammata'.

[67] For discussion of a series of little *plaquettes* by Oronce Finé de Brianville, similarly containing emblems and devices in honour of Louis, Maria Theresa, Colbert and the Prince of Orange (*Devise pour le Roy, sur les preparatifs de la campagne de l'an 1672. Expliquée par un*

In all these different manifestations we see how the emblem and device (terms which are by now often inextricably confused in usage) played a major role in the seventeenth century in propagating a message of royal glorification by a remarkably diverse range of approaches. In durable visual form, incorporated into painted ceilings, sculptures, tapestries, pictures, carvings, they adorned the public rooms of royal palaces with pleasing but at the same time, and more importantly, meaningful messages. In less durable but no less visible form they played an important role in the ephemeral architecture of triumphal entries and court festivities where similarly they made a meaningful, albeit indirect, statement about the magnificence of the monarch and the particular achievement that was being celebrated. Yet as always the printed form was of major importance. Even as emblematic iconography was thus heavily exploited in the plastic arts, so also traditional printed collections of emblems and devices continued to be published serving to glorify the monarch and his entourage, while at the same time other printed volumes began to appear, whose function was not only to perpetuate ephemeral emblematic material which would otherwise be ephemeral, but also to disseminate in printed form to a wider audience the meaningful messages of the original plastic art form, since the audience enjoying access to the original artefacts was necessarily much more limited than the audience who could be reached by means of the printed book. While the basic patterns of exploitation of emblematic materials in triumphal entries and court festivities were already becoming well established in the later sixteenth century, their use in such events in the seventeenth century became ever more significant, particularly under Louis XIV. Even more markedly, however, was the reign of Louis XIV characterised by a systematic programme of glorification of the monarch, and it is above all in this process, which manifested itself in so many different domains, that emblematic materials had such a major role to play.

---

sonnet traduit en plusieurs langues; ensemble une fable Latine traduite en François, sur le mesme sujet, Paris, C. de Sercy, 1672, 4°; *Devise heroique pour les tettons de la reine en Janvier 1668*, n.p.n.d., 4°; *Coluber gentilitius illustrissimi viri Ioan. Bapt. Colberti regi a sanctioribus consiliis, aedificiis regiis et aerario praefecti, quaestoris regiorum ordinum, regni administri, symbolis heroicis expressus*, Paris, S. Mabre-Cramoisy, 1666, folio; *Devises heroiques sur les armes de Monseigneur Colbert*, Paris, S. Mabre-Cramoisy, 1667, 4°; *Pour Monseigneur le Prince d'Orange, devise*, n.p.n.d., 4°) and also of Pierre L'Abbé's *Trois devises sur les armes de Monseigneur l'eminentissime Cardinal Mazarin* (n.p.n.d., folio), see Alison Saunders, 'What happened to the native French tradition? The decline of the vernacular emblem in the seventeenth century'.

CHAPTER VIII

THEORY AND PRACTICE OF EMBLEMS AND DEVICES.

In the complex domain of emblem theory a striking change took place between the sixteenth and the seventeenth century. In the sixteenth century, although a number of emblem books were produced in France by several different writers, very little was written on the theory underlying these. While interest in the theory of devices gained ground in the sixteenth century to the extent that a French translation of Giovio's *Dialogo dell imprese militari et amorose* was published in France as early as 1561, within six years of its original publication in Rome in an Italian text, no full treatises were published in France on the subject of emblem theory, either by the practitioners themselves or by any interested outside observer of the developing genre. From the earliest exponents of the emblem the most that we find is brief comment in the preliminaries confined by and large to statements about the antiquity of the genre, about its didactic function, and about the particular efficacy of the combination of the verbal and the visual stimulus to exercise that function, and also about the usefulness of emblems as sources of material for artists and craftsmen.

Alciato himself says little on the subject in the dedication of his pioneering work to Conrad Peutinger, other than referring to his emblems as meaningful badges which can be attached to garments:

> Dum pueros iuglans, iuvenes dum tessera fallit,
>   Detinet & segnes chartula picta viros:
> Haec nos festivis Emblemata cudimus horis,
>   Artificum illustri signaque facta manu:
> Vestibus ut torulos, petasis ut figere parmas,
>   Et valeat tacitis scribere quisque notis.   (Alciato, *Emblemata*, 1550, A3v)

though elsewhere he also makes comments - albeit equally brief ones - on the nature of his emblems. In his often quoted letter to Francesco Calvi of 1522, he describes them as a particular kind of meaningful epigram and refers to the way in which they can be exploited by craftsmen:

His Saturnalibus...libellum composui epigrammaton, cui titulum feci *Emblemata*; singulis enim epigrammatibus aliquid describo, quod ex historia vel ex rebus naturalibus aliquid elegans significet, unde pictores, aurifices, fusores id genus conficere possint, quae scuta appellamus et petasis figimus, vel pro insignibus gestamus, qualis anchora Aldi, columba Frobenii, et Calvi elephas tam diu parturiens, nihil pariens.[1]

while in his *De verborum significatione* he draws a parallel between his emblems and Egyptian hieroglyphs, describing both as 'things' which have the power to convey meaning such as is more conventionally conveyed by words:

Verba significant, res significantur. Tametsi et res quandoque etiam significant, ut Hieroglyphica apud Horum et Chaeremonem, cuius argumenti et nos carmine libellum composuimus, cui titulus est Emblemata.[2]

These brief points made by Alciato to explain what he understands by the word *emblema* in this context are taken up and further developed by his subsequent French translators and commentators. Jean le Fevre, the first French translator, picks up the 'meaningful badge' theme, and points to the utility of an emblem book such as that created by Alciato, given the contemporary fashion for wearing devices:

Plusieurs gentilz hommes de la court se delectent non seullement à faire paindre: ains à faire effigier de orfavrerie diversitez de ymages, qu'ilz nomment devises, y adjoustans quelques sentences propres et consonantes. A quoy m'a semblé ce present livret estre tresconforme.
(Alciato, *Livret des emblemes*, 1536, A3v)

while the second translator, Barthélemy Aneau, reiterates the same point, but at greater length, and with more emphasis on the range of practical applications:

...encore tel est l'usaige, et utilité: que toutes et quantesfoys que aulcun vouldra attribuer, ou pour le moins par fiction applicquer aux choses vuydes accomplissement, aux nues aornement, aux muetes parolle, aux brutes raison, il aura en ce petit livre (comme en un cabinet tresbien garny) tout ce qu'il pourra, et vouldra inscripre, ou pindre aux murailles de la maison, aux verrieres, aux tapis, couvertures, tableaux, vaisseaulx, images, aneaulx, signetz, vestemens, tables, lictz, armes, brief à toute piece et utensile, et en tous lieux: affin que l'essence des choses appartenantes au commun usage

---

[1]   This letter is quoted in James Hutton, *The Greek Anthology in Italy to the Year 1800*, New York, 1935, pp.201-2.

[2]   *Dn. Andreae Alciati iureconsulti clarissimi de verborum significatione, libri quatuor. Eiusdem in tractatum eius argumenti veterum iureconsultorum, commentaria. Ex ultima autoris recognitione*, Lyon, V. de Portonariis, 1536, 8°, A3r. (Alciato's various statements on the subject of his emblems can all be consulted together in Holger Homann, *Studien zur Emblematik des 16. Jahrhunderts*, Utrecht, 1971, pp.125-7.)

> soit en tout, et par tout quasi vivement parlante, et au regard plaisante.
> (Alciato, *Emblemes d'Alciat*, 1549, A3v-4r)

Aneau also refers back, in his preface, to the etymological Greek sense of the word *emblema*, implied but not explicitly stated by Alciato:

> Car Emblemes (comme bien ha interpreté le tresdocte Francoys Monsieur Budaeé) sont ouvraiges bigarrez de petites pieces de marcqueterie. Ce que aussi donne à entendre l'origine Graecque du mot. Quiconque doncq vouldra enrichir ses besoignes de la divise d'une briefve sentence, et grace d'une plaisante image: il pourra abondamment trouver, et prendre en ce livre, ce que bon luy semblera, pour estre approprié à une chascune chose, et ce tres-promptement et tresfacilement. (Alciato, *Emblemes d'Alciat*, 1549, A4r-v).

while in his dedication of his translation to the Count of Arran, he focuses also on the didactic role of the emblem, spelling out the way in which verbal and visual triggers complement each other to contribute to this end, using the pleasing to lead to the useful:

> Avec images, et histoires figurées convenantes à la lettre. Esquelles regarder pourra vostre oeil juvenil autant prendre de plaisir, comme de profict à la parolle et au sens desdictz Emblemes. Premierement pour vous delecter, et passer temps à la plaisante contemplation des belles pinctures non vaines. Apres pour vous instruire de bonnes sentences, et vertueux exemples. Et finalement pour vous exercer à la langue Françoise par vous aimée, et desirée. L'une des choses donnant facile voye à l'aultre. C'est à savoir la lettre donnant à entendre la figure: et l'image declarant le sens de la parolle à veuë d'oeil, et representant vive action de la lettre morte.
> (Alciato, *Emblemes d'Alciat*, 1549, A2v)

Mignault, the third translator, writing much later than his two predecessors, makes significantly fuller comments on the nature of the emblem than either of them in the preliminaries to his translation. Not only does he trace its etymological Greek origins as a piece of decoration to be attached to something else, but he also introduces a further dimension to this function by noting also the subsequent use of the word in Latin to denote a piece of rhetorical ornamentation. He points to the association with the Egyptian hieroglyphic tradition, but takes this further by referring to the perceived hermetic dimension of that tradition, and he also stresses the importance of the element of ingenuity in the composition of emblems. In addition he traces different types of emblem, identifying these as historical, physical and ethical, anticipating here similar subsequent efforts to classify emblems according to kind:[3]

---

[3]   Aneau had earlier classified some of the emblems according to their rhetorical structure, subtitling them, for example, *dialogismus*; *prosopopeia*; *apologesis*, but Mignault's classification relates to theme rather than structure.

Embleme est un mot Grec, qui vient du verbe *emballesthai*, qui signifie entrelasser, ou mettre dedans. Car en premier sens il est prins pour quelque enrichissement qui se peust oster ou mettre à plaisir aux vases d'argent, d'or et autres: comme sont les seaux, et pourtraits des choses et fleurs ingenieusement fabriquez ou depeints: ce que nous enseigne Ciceron, et les livres des jurisconsultes. Ainsi donq' tout ce qui est entrelassé, ou attaché à quelque chose pour ornement, et non seullement aux vases, mais aux dressoirs ou buffets, parois, pavez, vestemens, brief à toutes autres choses quelconques, se peut appeller Embleme...Toutesfois par translation, ce nom se prent pour une maniere d'oraison ornée et revestue de quelques couleurs, et comme peintures de sentences. Mais icy, Emblemes ne sont autre chose que quelques peintures ingenieusement inventées par hommes d'esprit, representées, et semblables aux lettres Hieroglyphiques des Egyptiens, qui contenoient les secrets de la sagesse de ces anciens là, par le moyen de certaines devises, et comme pourtraits sacrez: de laquelle doctrine ils ne permettoient que les mysteres fussent communiquez sinon à ceux qui en estoient capables, et qui d'ailleurs estoient bien entendus: et non sans bonne raison en excluoient le vulgaire profane. Car nostre auteur, à l'imitation d'iceux...de plusieurs endroits des meilleurs ouvriers il a en partie choisy quelques devises pleines de bon sens et invention; et en partie aussi en a basti d'autres à sa fantasie, qu'il a revestu de nouvelle parure: toutes lesquelles...il a illustrées et enrichies d'explication bien elegante, et docte, là ou chasque peincture a son Epigramme pour esclarcissement, par mots purs et choisis autant que ce peust. Or bien qu'il y ait de diverses sortes d'Emblemes, ils peuvent ce neantmoins estre reduits à trois genres, tellement que les uns soient historiques, comme est celuy de la statue de la Lionne d'airain, eslevée en la citadelle d'Athenes: le triomphe de Marc Antoine sur Ciceron, occis: la description du Hun Scythic. Il y en a qui sont Physiques: comme les simulacres de Bacchus et Pallas: la pieté de la Cicongne: qui toutesfois peuvent tous estre rapportez aux moeurs.

(Alciato, *Emblemata...Les emblemes Latin-François*, 1584, ã7v-8r)[4]

The various sixteenth-century native French writers of emblems are almost as succinct as Alciato himself on what they understand to be the nature of the emblem. They make much the same points as Alciato and his translators, referring to the antiquity of the form, and to its association with the hieroglyphic tradition, as in La Perrière's dedication of his *Theatre* to Marguerite de Navarre:

---

[4]   In this French version Mignault notes only two out of his three categories, but in his Latin *Syntagma de symbolis* all three types are noted: 'Ceterum ne hoc quidem praetermissum velim, symbola & Emblemata, de quibus hoc agitur libro, multiplicia esse & varia: quorum tamen rationem multiplicem ad quosdam quasi cancellos revocare possumus. Quaedam enim historica sunt, alia physica, alia ethica, & certè allegorica, quibus aliquid petitum à fabulis aut rerum natura, ingeniosè ad mores ut plurimùm traducitur' (*Omnia Andreae Alciati v.c. emblemata*, Antwerp, 1581, A5v).

> Au surplus (Madame) ce n'est pas seulement de nostre temps que les
> Emblemes sont en bruict, pris & singuliere veneration, ains c'est de toute
> ancienneté & presque des le commencement du monde: Car les Egiptiens qui
> se reputent estre les premiers hommes du monde, avant l'usage des lettres,
> escripvoient par figures & ymages tant d'hommes, bestes & oyseaulx,
> poissons, que serpentz, par icelles exprimant leurs intentions, comme recitent
> tresanciens autheurs Chaeremon, Orus Apollo, & leurs semblables qui ont
> diligemment & curieusement travaillé à exposer & donner l'intelligence
> desdictes figures hierogliphicques. (La Perrière, *Theatre*, A4v-5r)

although they tend to give much greater emphasis than Alciato to the didactic function
underpinning their emblems, as in Corrozet's preliminary comments in his
Hecatomgraphie, in which his equivalent reference to the hieroglyphic tradition is
immediately followed by a couplet stressing the moralising aim of his emblems:

> Chascune hystoire est d'ymage illustrée
> Affin que soit plus clairement monstrée
> L'invention, & la rendre autenticque
> Qu'on peult nommer lettre hierogliphicque
> Comme jadis faisoient les anciens
> Et entre tous les vieulx Egyptiens
> Qui denotoient vice ou vertu honneste
> Par ung oyseau, ung poison, une beste.
> Ainsi ay faict affin que l'oeil choisisse
> Vertu tant belle & delaisse le vice. (Corrozet, *Hecatomgraphie*, A3v)

It is very striking how often Egyptian hieroglyphs are cited among the earliest writers
as a key source of inspiration for the emblem form - by Alciato himself, by his
translator and commentator, Mignault, by La Perrière, and by Corrozet - whereas no
mention is made of the *Greek Anthology*, which was actually the direct source of a
significant proportion of Alciato's emblems. This emphasis on the influence of the
hieroglyphic tradition continues to be made by seventeenth-century theorists as much
as by sixteenth-century writers. In the preface to his second emblem book, the
Morosophie, La Perrière introduces a quite different note from that of his *Theatre*,
insisting, like Mignault, on the importance of ingenuity as a key element of his
emblems, associated in this case with brevity:

> en chacun de noz Cent Emblemes Moraux du present oeuvre j'ay encloz aux
> deux premiers vers Latins la description du pourtrait figuré, & aux deux vers
> suyvantz, le sens Allegoricque & Moral dudit pourtrait: & yceux quatre vers
> Latins...j'ay reduit en quatre vers Françoys, ce que n'a pas esté sans vexation
> de mon esperit. Mais je l'ay fait, à fin qu'en petit lieu, l'artifice fust trouvé
> plus grand, & plus ingenieux, d'autant qu'il est comprins en un Tetrastique
> ou quatrain, estant memoratif que la Iliade d'Homere ha esté en tout temps
> admirable, mais fut estimé estre chose miraculeuse & surpassant engin

humain, de l'enclorre & faire contenir au creux d'une noix: comme recitent
plusieurs bons auteurs, & entre autres Pline & Solin. A ceste brefveté m'a
induit Valere disant, que clorre grand sens en peu de parolles, n'est pas petit
artifice. (La Perrière, *Morosophie*, A8r-v)

while in his dedication 'aux bons espritz & amateurs des lettres' Corrozet also makes
another important point concerning the efficacity of the combination of the visual and
the verbal stimulus as a didactic tool, combining the agreeable and the profitable, and
serving to *plaire* and *instruire*:

> Pour le plaisir qu'on y pourra comprendre
> Et pour le bien qu'on y pourra apprendre,
> Et pour autant que l'esprit s'esjouit
> Quand avecq luy de son bien l'oeil jouit
> Chascune hystoire est d'ymage illustrée...   (Corrozet, *Hecatomgraphie*, A3v)

a point which he also makes on other occasions, as in his preface to the illustrated
Biblical picture book, the *Historiarum veteris testamenti icones*:

> En regardant ceste tapisserie
> L'oeil corporel, qui se tourne & varie,
> Y peult avoir ung singulier plaisir,
> Lequel engendre au cueur ung grand desir
> D'aymer son Dieu, qui a faict tant de choses
> Dedans la letre & saincte Bible encloses.
>   Ces beaulx pourtraictz serviront d'exemplaire
> Comme il fault au Seigneur Dieu complaire:
> Exciteront de luy faire service,
> Retireront de tout peché & vice
> Quand ilz seront insculpez en l'esprit
> Comme ilz sont painctz, & couchez par escript.
>   (Corrozet, *Historiarum veteris testamenti icones*, A3r-v)

This point, which is so central to emblems, is made in the sixteenth century not
just by writers of emblem books like Corrozet, but also by the publishers of emblem
books and other cognate forms. Thus, for example, Jean de Tournes explains briefly in
his preface to his 1554 New Testament picture book, the *Figures du Nouveau
Testament* - but in terms which clearly anticipate the much more fully elaborated ideas
of the seventeenth-century emblem theorists such as Ménestrier - how information
passes through a series of internal senses of which the visual is just the first stage, but
that it is retained more effectively by the memory if it is presented in this visual form,
rather than just verbally:

> Les choses d'instruccion qui sont representees à la vuë & par icelle ont entree
> en l'apprehension, & de là en avant en l'entendement, & puis en la memoire,

esmeuvent & incitent davantage, & demeurent plus fermes & stables, que
celles qui ont leur seule entree par l'oreille.

(Fontaine, *Figures du Nouveau Testament*, A2r)[5]

Again in his equivalent Old Testament picture book, the *Quadrins historiques de la
Bible*, published the previous year, he points to the power of the visual stimulus as an
aid to memory:

J'ay tasché de te plaire en cestui labeur, qui est la representation de la sainte
Bible, à celle fin, que si tu n'as le loisir de lire & jouir de la lettre comme tu
desirerois, tu puisses pour le moins tapisser les chambres de ta memoire des
figures d'icelle. (Paradin, *Quadrins historiques*, A5v)

Georgette de Montenay also echoes this same theme in her dedication to Jeanne
d'Albret of her *Emblemes, ou devises chrestiennes* in which yet again she describes
her emblems as visual aids to memorising morally edifying passages of scripture,
particularly fitting for women:

Pensant aussi qu'il sera bien propice
A mainte honneste et dame et damoiselle
Touchées au coeur d'amour saint et de zele,
Qui le voyans voudront faire de mesmes,
Ou quelqu'autre oeuvre à leur gré plus qu'Emblémes:
Que toutesfois pourront accommoder
A leurs maisons, aux meubles s'en aider,
Rememorans tousjours quelque passage
Du saint escrit bien propre à leur usage,
Dont le Seigneur sera glorifié,
Et cependant quelcun edifié.

(Montenay, *Emblemes, ou devises chrestiennes*, a4r)

---

[5] In *L'art des emblemes où s'enseigne la morale*, Ménestrier spells out Horace's theory of
the *utile dulci* in the context of emblems, with their 'peinture pour le plaisir des yeux' and
'sens mystique pour l'instruction' and concludes with the same point as made by Jean de
Tournes: 'Tout Emblême de quelque nature qu'il puisse estre, a essentiellement deux parties;
l'une pour les yeux, & l'autre pour l'esprit: c'est à dire, une peinture pour le plaisir des yeux,
& un sens mystique pour l'instruction. C'est ce doux meslé à l'utile qu'Horace appelle la
perfection des ouvrages de l'esprit.
Omne tulit punctum qui miscuit utile dulci.
Et c'est ce caractère de la juste Poësie, qui cherche également à plaire et à instruire.
Et prodesse volunt & delectare Poëtae.
Ainsi tout l'artifice des Emblêmes consiste à sçavoir bien trouver ce doux & cet utile, ce
plaisir des yeux, & cette instruction de l'esprit; parce qu'il y a tant de rapport de l'un à l'autre,
que nous apprenons plus aisément & plus agreablement ce que nous apprenons par les yeux,
que ce que nous apprenons par les oreilles.' (p.207)

These, then, are the key theoretical points concerning the nature of the emblem which are made by Alciato, his translators, and those sixteenth-century writers of emblems who do actually discuss the subject. Some sixteenth-century writers of emblems - as for example Pierre Coustau - do not see the need to include any element of theoretical comment at all, and in the case of those who do, their treatment of the subject is invariably very brief. Only Mignault, writing rather later in the century than most, makes a contribution which is at all substantial in length.

It is Alciato himself whose understanding of the term *emblema* has subsequently attracted the greatest interest among critics attempting in the latter part of the twentieth century to formulate a theoretical framework for the evolving genre. Over the last forty or so years a number of modern critics have discussed in detail the thought processes behind Alciato's choice of the word *emblema*, and their implications for the form of the poetic emblem as it thereafter developed into a fully fledged genre, often focusing on the relative importance of the various constituent elements of the emblem and the relationship between them, and moving on from the theories of the supposedly normative tripartite structure of picture, verse and motto, as elaborated by William Heckscher and August Wirth in the 1950s, and the somewhat later theories of the *res picta/res significans* elaborated by Albrecht Schöne.[6] Among the most ground-breaking of the earlier articles on Alciato is Hessel Miedema's 1968 article, 'The term *Emblema* in Alciati' in which he traces in detail the etymological development of the word prior to analysing its particular sense as used by Alciato,[7] while important also are Claudie Balavoine's rather later 'Archéologie de l'emblème littéraire: la dédicace à Conrad Peutinger des *Emblemata* d'André Alciat' of 1981,[8] and 'Les *Emblemes* d'Alciat: sens et contresens' of the following year.[9] Less critical attention has been focused on the apparent understanding of the term by Alciato's subsequent French followers, since this is in fact fairly fluid, with the word 'embleme' being used variously to refer to the figure, the verse, or to the overall combination.[10]

---

[6]   William Heckscher and Karl-August Wirth, 'Emblem, Emblembuch', in *Reallexikon zur Deutschen Kunstgeschichte*, Stuttgart, 1959, vol.5, cols 85-228; Albrecht Schöne, *Emblematik und Drama im Zeitalter des Barock*, Munich, 1964. For an account of the writings of modern German theorists on the emblem, see Peter Daly, *Emblem Theory. Recent German Contributions to the Characterisation of the Emblem Genre*, Neudeln, 1979.

[7]   *Journal of the Warburg and Courtauld Institutes*, 31, 1968, pp.234-50.

[8]   In M.-T. Jones-Davies, ed., *Emblèmes et devises au temps de la Renaissance*, Paris, 1981, pp.9-22.

[9]   In Y. Giraud, ed., *L'emblème à la Renaissance. Actes de la journée d'études du 10 mai 1980*, Paris, 1982, pp.49-59. See also Bernard Scholz, '"Libellum composui epigrammaton, cui titulum feci Emblemata": Alciatus's use of the expression *emblema* once again', *Emblematica*, 1,2, 1986, pp.213-26. For a survey of other research in this area see Bernard Scholz, 'The 1531 Augsburg edition of Alciato's *Emblemata*: a survey of research', *Emblematica*, 5,2, 1991, pp.213-54.

[10]   La Perrière uses the word to denote the figures alone in both the preliminaries to the *Theatre*, in which he describes the work as containing 'cent Emblemes moraulx, accompaignez de cent dixains uniformes declaratifz, & illustratifz d'iceulx' (A3v-4r), and in the title to the *Morosophie*, in which he uses the phrase 'cent Emblemes moraux, illustrez de Cent Tetrastiques Latins, reduitz en autant de Quatrains Françoys', whereas in contrast in the

However Daniel Russell has analysed sixteenth-century French usage of the word in 'The term 'Emblème' in sixteenth-century France' and also in *The Emblem and Device in France*,[11] while rather earlier R.J. Clements also studied the subject in his *Picta poesis. Literary and Humanistic Theory in Renaissance Emblem Books.*[12] But given the range of different forms which the emblem took in the sixteenth century, critical discussion has concentrated more on actual structural patterns and forms of emblems than on theoretical understanding of the term, as in Russell's later, broad-reaching study, *Emblematic Structures in Renaissance French Culture* or in my own articles, 'The long and the short of it: structure and form in the early French emblem book'; '*Picta poesis*: the relationship between figure and text in the sixteenth-century French emblem book'; and 'Word, image and illustration in sixteenth- and seventeenth-century emblems in France'.[13]

In contrast to the very sparse picture in the sixteenth century, where although important points were made about the nature of emblems, they were not elaborated at substantial length in full-scale treatises devoted to the subject, the seventeenth century saw a major awakening of interest in the domain of emblem theory. A number of treatises on the subject were produced throughout the century, although it is interesting to note that, even as late as the mid seventeenth century, still perpetuating the earlier sixteenth-century pattern, much greater emphasis continued to be given to discussion of devices rather than emblems, and commonly such seventeenth-century treatises are given titles which give priority to the word 'devise', so that when the word 'embleme' is included in the title it figures only as a subsidiary element.[14]

---

preliminaries to the *Hecatomgraphie* Corrozet uses the word 'embleme' together with the words 'Authoritez, Sentences, Appophthegmes':

> C'est ce livret qui contient cent emblemes,
>
> Authoritez, Sentences, Appophthegmes
>
> Des bien lettrez comme Plutarque & autres. (A3v)

clearly meaning thereby the textual element, rather than the visual figure. In several of the longer verse commentaries accompanying each emblem in the *Hecatomgraphie* Corrozet uses the word 'embleme' rather differently again, to refer to the full combination of figure and short verse and (presumably) motto, printed all together on the facing page, as in 'On void souvent c'est embleme & enigme/Verifié...' (C8r), or 'Cest embleme nous faict scavoir' (D6r).

[11] 'The term 'Emblème' in sixteenth-century France', *Neophilologus*, 59, 1975, pp.337-51; *The Emblem and Device in France*, chapter 2, pp.76-89.

[12] Rome, 1960, 4°.

[13] *Emblematic Structures in Renaissance French Culture*, chapter 7, pp.151-88; 'The long and the short of it: structure and form in the early French emblem book', in Bernard Scholz, Michael Bath and David Weston, eds, *The European Emblem. Selected Papers from the Glasgow Conference 11-14 August, 1987*, Leiden, 1990, pp.55-83; '*Picta poesis*: the relationship between figure and text in the sixteenth-century French emblem book', *Bibliothèque d'Humanisme et Renaissance*, 48, 1986, pp.621-52; 'Word, image and illustration in sixteenth- and seventeenth-century emblems in France', in Gyorgy Szonyi, ed., *European Iconography East and West. Selected Papers of the Szeged International Conference June 9-12, 1993*, Leiden, 1996, pp.175-89.

[14] See, for example, Adrian d'Amboise's *Discours ou traicté des devises. Où est mise la raison et différence des emblemes, enigmes, sentences & autres. Pris & compilé des cahiers de*

Discussion of the nature of the emblem is often conducted within a framework of its differences from and similarities to the device, rather than in its own right, as, for example, in Ménestrier's 1662 *Art des emblemes* (which is the earliest treatise to give such priority to the word 'embleme'), in which his attempts at defining the genre in the opening sections of the work are based on the extent to which they do or do not conform to Giovio's set of rules for the device. Ménestrier stresses here the similarity of the two forms, explaining that of the five rules elaborated by Giovio for the device, only two are not applicable also to the emblem:

> Paul Jove, que l'on considere comme le Pere des devises, pour ce qu'il est le premier, qui a pris soin de les recueillir & de reduire en Art ce qui n'avoit eu jusqu'à luy d'autre regle que la fantaisie, demande cinq conditions dans la devise dont trois luy sont communes avec l'embleme & deux seulement l'en distinguent.[15]

Likewise, in the section on recommended emblem books which every gentleman's library should contain, in his earlier manuscript treatise on the education of the *honnête homme*, Ménestrier further remarks on the dearth of independent emblem theory, compared to that relating to devices, commenting that: 'Nous n'avons presque personne qui ait ecrit des regles des emblemes que ceux qui ont escrit celles des devises'.[16]

This strong association between emblem and device in the minds of the seventeenth-century theorists colours their approach to the subject. Although we have seen in the course of this study how effectively - and indeed how frequently - the emblematic form was exploited for devotional and meditational purposes, this important function of the emblem is little touched on by the theorists, despite the fact that two of the most important among them, Pierre Le Moyne and Ménestrier, were members of the Jesuit order. In his 1684 *Art des emblemes où s'enseigne la morale* in which he cites a large number of varied types of emblem writers, including even Maurice Scève, Ménestrier does refer briefly to Hugo's *Pia desideria* as an example of sacred emblems being used for a particular kind of *enseignement* (p.69) and to Haeften's *Schola cordis*, and Hesius's *Emblemata sacra* in the section devoted to emblems as allegorical theology (p.266), but this is unusual. More commonly the theorists concentrate on discussion of broader issues relating to the origins of the genre, the symbolic nature of the emblem and device, and the kinship between these

---

feu Messire François d'Amboise...Par Adrian d'Amboise son fils (Paris, R. Boutonne, 1620, 8°), or Henry Estienne's 1645 *L'art de faire les devises, où il est traicté des hieroglyphiques, symboles, emblemes, aenygmes, sentences, parabolles, revers de medailles, armes, blasons, cimiers, chiffres & rebus. Avec un traicté des rencontres ou mots plaisans.*
[15] *L'art des emblemes par le P. C-François Menestrier de la Compagnie de Jesus*, Lyon, B. Coral, 1662, 8°, p.22.
[16] Bibliothèque Municipale de Lyon, Ms 1514, f.10r (cit. Loach). For discussion of this important unpublished manuscript treatise by Ménestrier see Judi Loach, 'Ménestrier's emblem theory', p.320, and for discussion of Ménestrier's theory of images more generally, see Anne-Elisabeth Spica, *Symbolique humaniste et emblématique*, pp.293-304 and 396-401.

and other cognate forms such as the enigma, fable or hieroglyph, and, of course, the similarities and differences between emblem and device. Although they cover much the same ground, and the points which they make are often the same, there are nevertheless significant differences in the writings of the various theorists. In some cases the difference is one of structure rather than content, in the sense that some treatises, such as Henry Estienne's *Art de faire les devises*, are purely theoretical, whereas others, like Le Moyne's *De l'art des devises* or Ménestrier's 1682 *Philosophie des images*, combine theory and examples of practice within the one treatise, and yet others, like Jean Baudoin's *Recueil d'emblemes divers* or Florent Chovayne's *Divertissements*, take the form of a theoretical treatise serving as no more than a preface to a collection of emblems or devices. Different again is Dominique Bouhours's remarkably popular *Entretiens d'Ariste et d'Eugene*, first published in 1671, in which he departs from the more conventional pattern and adopts the dialogue form in order to present his material to the reader in a more animated manner than that of the normal treatise.[17] But in other cases the difference lies not in structure, but rather in the individual writer's approach to his subject, since some of the seventeenth-century theorists consider the various rules that they elaborate to be absolute and allow of no room for compromise, while others are less dogmatic and more flexible in their judgements of right and wrong. Notable among the absolutists is Pierre Le Moyne, whereas his fellow Jesuit, Ménestrier is far more tolerant and pragmatic in his approach. Typical of Le Moyne's approach is the brusque conclusion to his exposition of the distinctions between the emblem and the device, which admits of no areas of overlap or ambiguity and states this in no uncertain terms:

> Toutes ces choses si essentielles & si necessaires à la Devise, n'ont rien à faire dans l'Embleme: où elles n'y entrent point, où elles y entrent par surerogation, & y sont comme estrangeres.
> Il n'y a donc rien de commun entre la Devise & l'Embleme: & il faut avoir la veuë de l'esprit bien courte, pour ne les pas distinguer.
> (Le Moyne, *De l'art des devises*, p.223)

In contrast Ménestrier remarks more tolerantly in his 1684 *Art des emblemes où*

---

[17] Dominique Bouhours, *Les entretiens d'Ariste et d'Eugene*, Paris, S. Mabre-Cramoisy, 1671, 4°. Mabre-Cramoisy published a number of editions in Paris, after this first edition, several of them dated 1671, but also 1673, 1678, 1682, 1683 and 1691; an edition was published in Amsterdam by Jacques Le Jeune in 1682, followed by another in 1691; and one edition was also published in Lyon in 1682, by Jean Bruyset. The work continued to be popular well into the eighteenth century, with several further editions being published up to 1768. For details of seventeenth-century editions see *BFEB*, vol.1, nos 118-29, and for these and later editions see also Peter Daly and G. Richard Dimler, *The Jesuit Series*, Part 1, nos 56-80. Bouhours's work contains six *entretiens*, each dedicated to a particular topic, the last of which is *Les devises*. (The others in this remarkably eclectic compilation are *La mer*; *La langue francoise*; *Le secret*; *Le bel esprit*; and *Le je ne scay quoy*.) Unusually no indication of the fact that Bouhours was yet another Jesuit priest is given on the title page of any of the editions of the *Entretiens d'Ariste et d'Eugene*.

s'enseigne la morale that there is considerable potential for overlap between the two forms, and that:

> ...la plûpart des Devises peuvent devenir Emblêmes, lors qu'au lieu d'en faire l'image d'un dessein particulier, nous en faisons un enseignement general.
> (Ménestrier, *L'art des emblemes où s'enseigne la morale*, p.17)

echoing here a similar comment which he made twenty-two years earlier in his 1662 *Art des emblemes*, in the context of Ruscelli's analysis of the similarities and differences between the two forms:

> Ruscelli ajoute quelques autres rapports, & quelques differences de l'Embleme & de la devise...Il semble qu'on ayt maintenant confondu l'un & l'autre, car nous voyons des devises morales qui sont des instructions; & des Emblemes Heroïques, qui expliquent les actions genereuses des grands hommes.   (Ménestrier, *L'art des emblemes*, pp.22-3)

Elsewhere in this same later treatise he states categorically that the two forms are now totally confused:

> On a tellement confondu jusqu'icy les Emblêmes, les Devises, les Symboles, les Hieroglifiques, & les autres Images sçavantes, qui sont de differentes especes, qu'il n'est aucune d'elles à qui on ne donne encore tous les jours le nom d'Emblêmes.
> (Ménestrier, *L'art des emblemes où s'enseigne la morale*, p.3)

and goes on to explain the historical reasons which he considers must probably lie behind this confusion, with Valeriano running everything together under the heading of hieroglyph and Alciato running everything together under the heading of emblem:

> Cela vient sans doute de ce que ces Images ne furent jamais distinguées par les Anciens, qui n'eurent ny l'usage des Devises, ny celuy des Armoiries, du moins de la maniere dont nous les avons aujourd'huy; & comme leur Theologie estoit ou naturelle ou Poëtique, les Images naturelles, & les Images fabuleuses passerent pour Hieroglyphiques, aussi bien que pour Emblémes parmy eux. C'est ce qui a fait que Pierius a confondu toutes ces Images sous le nom de Hieroglyphiques, & Alciat sous celuy d'Emblêmes.
> (Ménestrier, *L'art des emblemes où s'enseigne la morale*, pp.3-4)[18]

---

[18]   By 'Pierius' Ménestrier means Valeriano (Giovanni Pierio Valeriano Bolzani) whose highly influential *Hieroglyphica sive de sacris Aegyptiorum aliarumque gentium...commentarii* had first become available in its original Latin version in 1556, and in a French version from 1576 - the title of which reflects the affinity it was seen to enjoy with other symbolic forms (*Commentaires hieroglyphiques ou images des choses de Jan Pierius Valerian, esquels comme en un vif tableau est ingenieusement depeinct & representé l'estat de plusieurs choses antiques: comme de monnoyes, medales, armes, inscriptions & devises, obelisques, pyramides & autres*

Valeriano's treatise referred to here by Ménestrier follows the same sort of pattern as that of the various editions of Horapollo, with individual prose descriptions and interpretations of each hieroglyphic figure accompanied by small woodcuts depicting the image in question, though the text is much more fully developed and explained, and is accompanied by marginal classical references confirming the sense of the hieroglyphs. Although it was a very influential source of iconographic material, despite the mention in the title of other cognate forms, it does not include any general theorising about the nature of symbols, and about possible relationships between hieroglyphs and other cognate forms. However, within a few years of the appearance of the first French version of the work, Pierre L'Anglois published in 1583 a treatise in which - although his main concern is still undoubtedly hieroglyphics - he does already broach some of the more comparative theoretical questions beloved of his seventeenth-century successors, and in particular the affinities between emblems, devices, enigmas and hieroglyphs, as suggested in the title: *Discours des hieroglyphes aegyptiens, emblemes, devises et armoiries. Ensemble LIIII. tableaux hieroglyphiques pour exprimer toutes conceptions, à la façon des Aegyptiens, par figures, & images des choses, au lieu de lettres. Avecques plusieurs interpretations des songes & prodiges. Le tout par Pierre L'Anglois, Escuyer, Sieur de Bel-Estat.* In his opening section he traces a clear progression in the emblem form, originating with the Egyptian hieroglyph, but modified and enriched thereafter via Greek and Latin culture, spelling out yet again the etymological sense of the word, as earlier explained by Aneau and Mignault:

> Car les Grecs, eveillez de plus gentil esprit, sans doute, & puis les Romains l'ont enrichy par plusieurs autres inventions gentiles, de proverbes, symboles, sentences, aenigmes, devises, et sur tout a gaigné le prix l'industrieuse façon de l'Embleme dont les Grecs, comme on voit aux Epigrammes, ont tant fourny d'argumens, qu'à luy, en grace, nul autre des dessusdits à bon droit s'accompare. Or est il qu'Embleme, est un mot Grec (à fin que celuy qui ne le sçait l'entende) qui signifie premierement tout ouvrage fait de marqueterie à ornemens & enrichissemens, attachez à de petites vis, ou autrement à vaisselles d'or, d'argent, ou autre besongne d'orfevrie, lesquelles s'ostoient de la piece, & se remetoient quand on vouloit, comme pourroit estre antiquitez, images, fleurettes, & choses semblables. Et par metaphore, on appelle Embleme, les Epigrammes qui interpretent ces gentilles & industrieuses peintures.   (L'Anglois, *Discours des hieroglyphes*, B1r)

He goes on to explain that although they all derive from the hieroglyph and have affinities in that ingenuity and ornament are important to all of them, the essential difference between emblem on the one hand and enigma and device on the other lies in the fact that the one explains, whereas the other two hide meaning:

---

monumens: outre une infinité de diverses & profitables histoires, proverbes & lieux communs: avec la parfaicte interpretation des mysteres d'Aegypte...). Ménestrier's use of the phrase 'sans doute' here reflects his more open-minded attitude, compared with that of Le Moyne.

Il y a difference entr'eux tous, comme du general au special. Ce n'est pas premierement comme de l'Enigme (combien qu'il y ait en leur façon quelque chose qui se raporte). Car en l'Enigme on cache bien obscurément ce qu'on veut dire, tout y est ambigu, & qui le plus souvent se peut prendre en deux sens: où en l'Embleme, on se decouvre plus ouvertement, on y voit à jour, & à travers le corps ainsi industrieusement imagé par le subtil & ingenieux ouvrier, qui nous represente par sa peinture quasi la chose qu'il nous veut dire, garny apres de devises & epigrammes, comme de beaux ornemens, & enrichissemens attachez à tel ouvrage. Et quelquefois il n'y a que la seule peinture, sans autre escrit, si bien significative neantmoins, qu'on peut recognoistre ce que l'homme ingenieux avoit voulu dire par telle marque symbolique...Mais ce que nous appellons aujourd'huy Devise, doit tenir un peu plus de l'Aegyptien. Si diray-je bien aussi, que la façon de l'un & de l'autre est toute Aegyptienne, puis que, comme par marques hieroglyphiques, on declare à couvert ce qu'on veut exprimer de sa principale intention, de son courage, de ses desseins, & resolution.

(L'Anglois, *Discours des hieroglyphes*, B1v-2r)

Adrian d'Amboise's treatise - the earliest of the seventeenth-century treatises, published in 1620 but actually dating in composition from earlier than this[19] - attributes such great importance to the distinction to be drawn between these various cognate forms that this question is even incorporated into the title of the work: *Discours ou traicté des devises. Où est mise la raison et difference des emblemes, enigmes, sentences & autres.* Thus although the work is primarily concerned with devices, and owes an evident debt to Giovio, its author nevertheless attempts to define the various other forms of symbol, and stresses the importance of distinguishing between them all.[20] As L'Anglois did before him, Adrian d'Amboise also stresses the importance of ingenuity, but he makes a clearer distinction than L'Anglois between emblem and device by emphasising the fact that emblems should make a general point, whether moral, political or philosophical, whereas devices, which are more personal, should reflect 'une signification de nostre esprit'. He defines an emblem as 'la peinture d'une histoire, ou fable, ou d'autre chose ingenieusement inventee, afin

---

[19]   As the full title indicates, this work is '*Pris & compilé des cahiers de feu Messire François d'Amboise*'. In his preface Adrian d'Amboise explains that his father, François d'Amboise, originally composed the treatise in the year in which the two greatest kings made an alliance. In the course of the consequent celebrations there was much wearing of devices, and confusion as to what was and was not acceptable in this domain, and for this reason the work was composed by François d'Amboise in order to clarify the situation, but - through diffidence - he never in the event presented it to the king as he had originally intended. The alliance to which Adrian d'Amboise refers is presumably the Treaty of Vervins, signed in 1598 between Henri IV and Philip II of Spain, bringing to an end hostilities between France and Spain.
[20]   'Et pour ce dés le commencement se faut tenir averty de ne point confondre les diverses especes des symboles: dont les unes sont Emblemes, les autres Enigmes, les autres Anagrammes, autres Epigrammes, autres sentences ou proverbes, autres apofthegmes, autres devises.' (pp.7-8) Interestingly 'emblemes' appear at the head of his list, and 'devises' come only at the end.

d'en tirer quelques avis moraux, politiques ou filosofiques' (p.8) whereas the object of devices is 'd'exprimer par une peinture de chose visible, & par une brefve sentence, comme parlante quelque gentile conception ou apprehension, que l'on veut tenir partie ouverte, partie cachee' (p.18). He follows this up with a formal definition of the device in which its essentially personal nature is clearly stated:

> C'est pourquoy on a dit que devise se peut definir en cette sorte: une signification de nostre esprit & pensee, soubz un noeud de paroles & de choses, sans que les devises soient attachees à certaines peintures, ny à certain subject, autre que de la franche volonté, & du choix, qu'il a pleu en faire au porteur. (A. d'Amboise, *Discours ou traicté des devises*, pp.18-19)

For Adrian d'Amboise, the rules and conventions governing the device are important, and he discusses these in some detail, accompanying his comments with examples of good and bad practice. But in contrast to the strict rules which he sees governing the device, he describes the much greater freedom of form enjoyed by the emblem, citing once again in the passing Horapollo and the hieroglyphic tradition:

> Vous pouvez y representer tout ce qui vous vient à gré, tout ce qu'Orus Apollon & ceux de sa suitte ont rapporté de leurs hieroglyphiques: mesmes y peindre des hommes en Emblemes voire des armees entieres, pour de là en tirer quelque gentil sens: ce qui n'est permis en matiere de devises, esquelles peu ou point ne se doit voir de faces humaines.
> (A. d'Amboise, *Discours ou traicté des devises*, p.9)

Interestingly, where L'Anglois saw similarities between the enigma and the device, but not between the enigma and the emblem, Adrian d'Amboise suggests that the enigma can be appropriately used in either emblem or device:

> Il peut bien avenir quelque-fois qu'un Enigme se trouvera bon, ores pour Embleme, ores pour devise; selon l'usage où il sera appliqué.
> (A. d'Amboise, *Discours ou traicté des devises*, p.10)

The treatise produced twenty-five years later by Henry Estienne, Sieur des Fossez is very much a work of compilation, synthesising and commenting on the opinions of earlier writers, including notably those of the Italian theorists Giovio, Bargagli and Ruscelli. Although the opening phrase of the title *'L'art de faire les devises'* accurately reflects the main preoccupation of the treatise, the title goes on to cite a long list of all the other allied forms also to be discussed - *'hieroglyphiques, symboles, emblemes, aenygmes, sentences, paraboles, revers de medailles, armes, blasons, cimiers, chiffres & rebus'*. Estienne, who describes how he spent much time as a youth composing devices, and how addictive an occupation this could be, is non-dogmatic in the views he puts forward, discussing with an open mind the merits and demerits of the various theories he propounds. It is curious that although this work did not run to more than one edition in France, it was translated into English by Thomas Blount within a year of the original French version being published, and Blount's English version ran through four editions over the next ten years. This is the only one of the various seventeenth-century French treatises on emblems and devices which was translated into English, and it may perhaps be because of its more open-minded approach, in contrast to the much more dogmatic approach of Pierre Le Moyne, for example, that it was so popular across the Channel. As part of his general synthesis of other people's theories Estienne gives a brief synopsis Giovio's often cited set of rules and conditions for devices:

> Paul Jove propose cinq regles requises aux devises parfaictes.
> 1. Premierement une juste proportion ou rapport de l'ame & du corps.
>
> 2. Qu'elle ne soit pas si obscure qu'elle ayt besoin de la Sybille pour estre entenduë, ny si claire que le menu peuple la puisse comprendre.
>
> 3. Que sur tout elle ayt belle apparence...toutesfois il me semble que les figures colorées ne sont pas recevables dans le corps des devises.
>
> 4. Qu'elle ne reçoive pas une figure humaine.
>
> 5. Et que le mot, qui est l'ame de la devise, soit d'une langue estrangere.
>
> De plus il requiert cinq conditions à la devise, dont la premiere est.
> 1. Que le mot soit bref ou court sans estre pourtant douteux...
>
> 2. Il faut prendre garde que l'ame & le corps estans fort beaux, ne produisent une pensée trop superbe, de peur que l'on n'accuse de vanité & de presomption, celuy pour lequel elle est faicte.
>
> 3. La devise doit avoir quelque chose de magnanime, de genereux, & de subtil.
>
> 4. Il faut qu'elle satisfasse la veuë par le corps, & qu'elle contente l'esprit par l'ame.
>
> 5. Les devises qui n'ont qu'une seule parole, ou bien une syllabe, sont estimées grossieres par cét Autheur.
>   (Estienne, *L'art de faire les devises*, pp.71-2)[21]

---

[21] Giovio's original version of this reads as follows: 'Sachez donques, mon amy M. Louis, que l'invention, ou devise, si elle doit avoir quelque chose de bon, faut qu'elle ait cinq conditions. La premiere, juste proportion d'ame & de corps. La deuxiéme, qu'elle ne soit obscure de sorte, qu'il soit mestier d'avoir la Sybille pour truchement, à la vouloir entendre: ne tant clere, que toute basse personne l'entende. La troisiéme, que sur tout elle ait belle prospective: laquelle se presente moult allaigre, si on y entremesle Estoiles, Soleils, Lunes, Feu, Eau, arbres verdoyans, instrumens mecaniques, animaux bizarres, et oiseaux fantastiques.

and likewise quotes Bargagli's well known definition of the device which has been so often wrongly interpreted as a definition of the emblem:

> La devise est un assemblage de figures, & de parolles si estroitement liées ensemble, qu'estans considerées à part, elles ne se puissent expliquer distinctement l'une sans l'autre. (Estienne, *L'art de faire les devises*, p.32)

Again quoting Bargagli, Estienne points to the important element of 'similitude ou comparaison' between figure and text in the device:

> La devise n'est autre chose que l'expression d'une particuliere & rare conception d'esprit, qui se faict par le moyen d'une similitude ou comparaison, ayant pour cét effect la figure d'une chose ou naturelle (pourveu qu'elle ne soit pas humaine) ou artificielle accompagnée necessairement de parolles courtes, aigues & subtiles.
> (Estienne, *L'art de faire les devises*, pp.37-8)

but he departs from Bargagli on the question of the hieroglyphic origins of devices. Stressing the antiquity of the genre, Estienne states that 'Ceux qui recherchent de plus haut l'origine des Devises la derivent de Dieu mesme' (p.53), citing the building of the Tabernacle, and God's instructions to Moses on its symbolic decoration in the Old Testament, and in the New Testament the symbols of the four Evangelists, or the Holy Spirit as dove, but going on to remark that even if the divine ancestry of devices is not accepted, at least their Egyptian hieroglyphic ancestry must be accepted:

> Que si l'on ne veut pas tirer la source des devises d'une si noble & ancienne Origine, au moins la tirera-t'on des Hieroglyphiques des Aegyptiens, qui par des formes & des figures de divers animaux, de differens instrumens, de fleurs, d'herbes, d'arbres, & choses semblables accouplées & composées ensemble, declaroient au lieu de lettres leurs pensées & conceptions.
> (Estienne, *L'art de faire les devises*, p.55)

Here, however, he explains that on this point he disagrees with Bargagli, who according to Estienne rejects the association between devices and hieroglyphs, since the latter were purely to do with religion.[22]

La quatriéme ne recherche aucune forme humaine. La cinquiéme requiert le mot qui est l'ame du corps: & veut estre communement d'une autre langue diverse au parler de celuy, qui fait la devise, à fin que le sentiment en soit quelque peu plus couvert: veut encores le mot estre brief; mais non pas tant qu'il se rende doubteux, de sorte qu'estant de deux ou trois parolles il est tresconvenable, excepté s'il estoit en forme de vers, ou entier, ou rompu. Et pour declarer ces conditions, nous dirons que la susdicte ame & le corps aussi s'entendent par le mot, ou par le subjet: & l'on estime que defaillant ou le subjet à l'ame, ou l'ame au subjet, la devise n'en revient point entiere.' (Giovio, *Dialogue des devises d'armes et d'amours*, b1r-v)

[22]   As well as such ancient sources, Estienne is happy to include more recent influences, citing the reverses of medals (and noting that these are somewhat incorrect since they do not include

On the subject of emblems Estienne makes the familiar point that the emblem has a moral point to make, but in so doing he identifies it as a particular kind of 'Symbole doux & moral',[23] thus tying emblems in with his earlier definition of the 'symbole' as something hidden and mysterious, tracing this back to the Greeks:

> Et comme les Grecs se sont servis de Symboles pour les villes, & les loix, aussi s'en sont-ils servis pour des sentences cachées & des choses mystiques...En fin le propre des Symboles est d'estre caché & envelopé dans des labyrinthes de sentences obscures.
>
> (Estienne, *L'art de faire les devises*, pp.12-13)

Thus although in his definition of the emblem he acknowledges its essentially didactic function, he considers that it should also contain a certain element of mystery, with both elements, visual and verbal, coming together to contribute to the meaning, but indirectly by analogy, rather than directly. He identifies the various types of didactic emblem and goes on to explain the way in which the two elements should work together wittily and subtly to convey meaning:

> Les Emblesmes sont reduits en trois principaux genres: des moeurs, de la nature, de l'Histoire, ou de la fable. Le principal but de l'Emblesme est d'enseigner en touchant notre veuë par les figures, & en frappant nostre esprit par leurs sens: il faut donc quelles soyent un peu couvertes, subtiles, joyeuses, & significatives. Que si les Peintures en sont trop communes, il faut quelles monstrent un sens caché, si elles sont un peu obscures il faut qu'elles enseignent plus clairement par les parolles, pourveu quelles soyent Analogiques ou correspondantes.
>
> (Estienne, *L'art de faire les devises*, pp.20-21)

Later he returns to the question of the verbal component stressing that although emblems may or may not contain words, if they do then they *must* have universal moral application, whereas such a universal application is not acceptable in a device:

> Les Devises et les Emblemes ont cela de commun & de ressemblance entre elles, qu'elles peuvent estre indifferemment avec paroles, ou sans paroles. Et leur difference se prend de ce que les paroles de l'Embleme peuvent démonstrer des choses universelles, & tenir lieu de preceptes moraux, qui serviront aussi bien à tout le monde, qu'au propre Autheur de l'Embleme. Ceste application generale du mot est un grand vice dans la devise, qui doit estre si particuliere, & dont les paroles ne doivent estre propres ny convenables, qu'à la personne en faveur de laquelle la devise est inventée.
>
> (Estienne, *L'art de faire les devises*, pp.86-7)

---

text), and also the devices adopted by mediaeval French kings:'Renard de Montauban portoit un Lion barré; Ogier le Danois un eschalier; Salomon de Bretagne un Eschiquier...' (p.66)
[23] 'L'Emblesme est proprement un Symbole doux & moral, qui consiste en la peinture & aux parolles par lequel on declare quelque grave sentence.' (p.20)

It is interesting that this is one point on which Estienne is quite firm, whereas other theorists like Ménestrier are more flexible about the overlap in some cases between the two forms.

While Pierre Le Moyne, writing some twenty years later in 1666, covers much of the same ground in his *De l'art des devises*, his approach is markedly more dogmatic than that of Estienne, and he adopts a more aggressively patriotic tone, stressing that Giovio did not himself invent the device, but that it was rather a French invention, taken over only subsequently by the Italians, who coined the word *imprese* from the French word *emprise*, and drew up the rules, after the French had already been long practising the genre.[24] The reason he gives for composing this treatise ties in also with his sense of patriotism: as he explains in his preface, he feels that his fellow countrymen are so ignorant and ill-versed in the rules of composition for devices that they are exposing themselves to ridicule across Europe because of the barbarity and inadequacy of the devices used for public display in France, but that being the case they should not be obliged to look to the Italians for a rule book, in the absence of a suitable French manual (õ1r-v). It is interesting that for this purpose he obviously chooses to ignore the existence of the earlier treatises of Adrian d'Amboise and Henry Estienne, Sieur des Fossez.

Le Moyne goes into considerable detail in his analysis of the nature of devices and of the rules for their composition, although in the early part of the treatise he does make rather more general and familiar points concerning the antiquity of the form, yet again tracing back to the Egyptians and to the Old Testament what he describes as a form of silent rhetoric:

> De tout temps on a parlé par Figures & par Symboles: On a fait des metaphores, avant que le nom de metaphore fust fait. Les Egyptiens ont commencé; les Hebreux les ont suivis: & cette Rethorique muette qui s'explique par les choses, sans le secours des paroles, a esté longtemps en usage parmy les Peuples de l'Orient.
>
> A prendre les choses en ce sens, les Lys, les Grenades, les Cherubins qui estoient dans l'Arche, se peuvent nommer des Devises. Il faut dire le mesme de la Baguette de Moïse, du Serpent d'Airain...Toutes ces choses estoient des Symboles; leur signification estoit figurée & metaphorique: & il falloit regarder par dessus elles, & passer de la peinture à l'intention pour les entendre.   (Le Moyne, *De l'art des devises*, p.17)

Later in the treatise he returns to the question of the exploitation of symbols in

---

[24] *De l'art des devises*, pp.22-9. For discussion of the ideas of the Italian theorists see D. Drysdall, 'The emblem according to the Italian *impresa* theorists', in Alison Adams and Anthony Harper, eds, *The Emblem in Renaissance and Baroque Europe. Tradition and Variety*, Leiden, Brill, 1992, pp.22-32. See also André Stegman, 'Les théories de l'emblème et de la devise en France et en Italie (1520-1620)', in Y. Giraud, ed., *L'embleme à la Renaissance*, pp.61-77. For a more broad-ranging study of the theory of emblems and devices, including a survey of modern critical thought on the subject, see Michael Bath, *Speaking Pictures. English Emblem Books and Renaissance Culture*, London, 1994.

devices, and offers his own broad definition of the device as 'une expression metaphorique, par maniere de similitude tacite, composée de figures & de paroles, pour declarer quelque grand dessein, quelque belle passion, ou quelque noble sentiment' (p.38). But thereafter he follows this broad definition with a very detailed analysis of how devices should be created, considering first the sort of figure that should or should not be used in devices, and then - in equally great detail - the sort of language that should be used in the *mot*. The figure should not be whimsical or non-serious, nor yet should it be monstrous or fantastic (p.84). It should rather be noble and dignified in concept, reflecting the nobility of the form itself. It should depict a real subject (although, as he admits, phoenixes, salamanders, sirens and harpies are commonly to be found (p.101). Similarly real animals endowed with extra attributes such as the Duc de Bourbon's winged stag are deplored as ill-conceived symbols in a device. As Le Moyne remarks rather testily on the subject of this animal, 'La Nature ne luy avoit-elle donné d'assez bonnes jambes, sans qu'on ajoustast des aisles à ses jambes pour le faire aller plus viste?' (p.109). On the subject of undignified and fantastic animals, Le Moyne casts blame on early astrologers for the invention of representations of the planets and constellations in the form of inappropriate and monstrous animals:

> J'ay opinion que cét abus a commencé par les Astrologues, qui ont esté les Autheurs du plus ancien & du plus scandaleux déguisement que le Monde ait jamais veu. Et que pensoient-ils faire, quand ils ont donné aux Constellations des noms si bizarres & si barbares, des figures si extravagantes & si monstreuses...mais qu'y ont affaire les Scorpions & les Serpens, les Centaures & les Lapithes... (Le Moyne, *De l'art des devises*, p.109)

But while real animals are appropriate for use in devices, real human figures are not acceptable since the device is based on comparison between two things, and one thing cannot be a metaphor of the same thing:

> La Devise est similitude de son essence; & sa propre fonction est de representer une chose dans une autre, par voye de comparaison, mais couverte & dissimulée. Or la similitude...n'est pas des Corps ny des Substances; elle est des qualitez inherantes à ces Corps, & attachées à ces substances: & par consequent, la comparaison qui se feroit d'un homme à un homme, n'estant pas fondée en similitude, mais en identité...ne seroit pas de celles que demande la Devise. (Le Moyne, *De l'art des devises*, p.135)

Interestingly Le Moyne also rejects hieroglyphic images as being inappropriate in devices (although again he concedes that they are used as such), since hieroglyphic symbolism is arbitrary, whereas the symbol in a device should be derived from reality, if it is to be used as the basis for a comparison, and this, he remarks proudly, is a new point that he is making:

> La signification Ieroglifique est celle qui est purement arbitraire; qui n'a

point de fondement en la nature de la chose; qui ne se prend ny de ses proprietez, ny de ses effets; qui ne vient que de la seule phantaisie, & du bon plaisir des hommes.

L'observation est nouvelle.   (Le Moyne, *De l'art des devises*, pp.95-6)

Descending to more practical considerations, reflecting the fact that Le Moyne was not just a pure theorist, but also an active practitioner of the art of creating devices, he points to the importance of not making the figure so small that it cannot easily be seen by the crowd when worn in a tournament, and likewise to the desirability of avoiding the use of colour, since this cannot subsequently be replicated in engraved form (pp.113-16).

On the subject of the *mot* Le Moyne goes into equally great detail. The language used should be elevated. Ideally Latin should be used, but Spanish or Italian would be acceptable. The use of unnecessarily obscure languages is an affectation to be avoided. While there is nothing intrinsically wrong with using French, it is preferable not to do so in France, since the use of a foreign language conveys a certain distancing effect which is desirable (p.187). Since this is essentially a gentlemanly form, any vulgarity of expression should be avoided. Indeed Le Moyne devotes a full chapter to this subject, under the title 'Que les Locutions basses ne doivent point estre receuës dans le Mot de la Devise' (p.181). Amusingly he cites in this chapter the thistle used as a printer's mark by Denis Janot as an example of an ingenious device which is quite ruined by the vulgarity of the motto, *Nul ne s'y frotte*.[25] Brevity in the *mot* is desirable, with one to four words being the ideal length, and if a rhyme can be worked in, like 'eminus et cominus', then this again is desirable. Similarly the fact that the *mot* has an identifiable source is desirable but not essential, but in no case should the meaning of the phrase in its original context be altered (pp.193-9). The *mot* should not be specifically moralising (p.178), nor yet should it spell out the meaning too clearly, but rather should afford the reader or onlooker the intellectual pleasure of working the sense out for himself (p.184). Again reflecting its elitist character, the device does not need to be understandable to everybody, as explained in a chapter entitled 'Que la Devise doit estre Enigmatique pour quelques-uns; & ingenieuse pour tout le Monde' (p.217).

In his discussion of the *mot* Le Moyne explains the way in which the two elements of the device interact to form a meaningful metaphor, with the *mot* being necessary to 'fix' the meaning to be derived from the figure, which otherwise would be vague and unspecified:

...encore que la Figure qui se voit dans la Devise, soit specifique & particuliere quand à l'estre; elle est pourtant generique & universelle, quand à la qualité de Signe, & capable par consequent de significations differentes,

---

[25]   He describes this device (which, not surprisingly, he does not identify as Janot's mark, but rather suggests for it a more elevated possessor) as 'une ancienne Devise, où se voit un grand chardon avec le Mot NUL NE SI FROTE. La pensée en est belle; & le sentiment des Princes qui l'ont portée estoit noble. Mais & la beauté de la pensée, & la noblesse du sentiment sont gastées par la bassesse de l'expression.' (p.182)

> selon les differentes veuës de ses diverses proprietez. Avec cette capacité
> neantmoins, elle est incapable de descendre de soy-mesme à une de ces
> significations plutost qu'à une autre: Et partant il luy faut un Adjoint, qui
> develope cette capacité de signifier vague & confuse, & la tourne vers
> quelque chose de specifique & de precis. L'Esprit qui demeureroit incertain,
> & indeterminé sans cela, & ne sçauroit à quoy se prendre, se determine par la
> jonction du Mot, qui fixe le Signe & la veuë du Signe à une signification
> particuliere, qu'il demesle de la masse des autres, & qu'il presente
> separément à la pensée. (Le Moyne, *De l'art des devises*, p.144)

and he similarly explains the relationship of the *mot* to the person figured, as also as
to the figure itself:

> La Devise veut donc qu'il y ait une juste convenance, entre le Comme &
> l'Ainsi, entre la comparaison & l'application, entre la Figure & la Personne
> figurée. Elle veut que la jointure y soit si propre, & les pieces si bien unies,
> qu'il n'y ait rien qui se démante. Ainsi la Similitude estant complète, la
> Devise le sera aussi: & le Mot ne sera point dementy, soit qu'il se die de la
> Figure ou de la Personne figurée.   (Le Moyne, *De l'art des devises*, p.157)

For Le Moyne the device is an elevated form, far removed from the vulgarity of
everyday life.[26] In times of war, he explains, the device belongs on the field of battle,
but in times of peace it belongs essentially to the court, forming an essential ingredient
in festivities, in contrast to the emblem whose natural home, he explains, is in the
schools, stressing clearly thereby its didactic character:

> En temps de Paix, elle est toute de la Cour: elle entre en toutes les Parties,
> elle est de tous les spectacles, & de tous les divertissemens de la Cour.
> L'Embleme est bien esloigné de là & a bien d'autres usages. Il est tout de
> l'Escole, & toutes ses fonctions, toutes ses paroles, toutes ses pensées sont
> scolastiques: & par consequent autant qu'il y a de difference entre la Cour &
> l'Ecole, entre la Lice & la Chaire, autant y en a-t-il entre la Devise &
> l'Embleme. (Le Moyne, *De l'art des devises*, p.223)

Much earlier in his treatise Le Moyne also describes the appropriateness of the device
to the court, as opposed to the schools, but looking at it from a rather different, and
somewhat disillusioned perspective, as he points to the lack of interest at court in
anything requiring more than the smallest degree of sustained intellectual
concentration. For courtiers with such a limited span the combination of brevity and
wit make the device an ideal form which can easily be assimilated without need for

---

[26] In terminology reminiscent of that used to describe seventeenth-century tragedy he defines
its elevated nature: 'Il est certain, que le propre Sujet de la Devise, doit estre, ou quelque
dessein qui tienne du grand & de l'Heroïque: ou quelque Passion où il entre de l'honneur & de
la gloire: ou quelque sentiment elevé, genereux, purifié des ordures de l'Interest, & de la crasse
des Esprits vulgaires.' (p.47)

sustained application. But what is particularly interesting about this early passage in Le Moyne's treatise is the fact that he is not here describing the device as easily assimilable entertainment for courtiers, as might be expected, but rather as easily assimilable *instruction* for courtiers, and the words 'instruire' and 'enseigner' which he uses are terms which we might expect him to use in the context of the emblem rather than of the device:

> ...on ne se pouvoit aviser d'un moyen d'instruire, plus court & plus efficace que celuy-là...par la voye des Devises, on arrive en un moment & d'une veuë, avec plaisir mesme & comme en joüant, où l'on n'iroit pas en six journées de travail & de chagrin, par les chemins de l'Ecole.
>
> Voilà justement la Philosophie qu'il faut à la Cour, qui est Antipode du College. Voila les Livres qui sont à l'usage des Grands, qu'une Requeste de quatre lignes effraye: à qui deux feüilles de papier paroissent une Montagne. Et si l'on a pû trouver le moyen de leur enseigner l'Histoire par les Medailles, pourquoy ne leur enseignera-ton pas aussi bien la Politique & la Morale par les Devises? (Le Moyne, *De l'art des devises*, pp.61-2)[27]

Although Le Moyne refers here to the instructional application of devices at court, this is in striking contrast to the clear distinction he draws in the passage quoted above between devices for *divertissement* at court and emblems for education in the schools. It is curious that in this categorical distinction that he draws between the two forms, Jesuit priest though he is, Le Moyne takes no note of the extent to which devices played a significant role in Jesuit pedagogy, with the composition of devices actually forming part of the curriculum in Jesuit colleges.

In the section of the treatise entitled 'Comparaison de la Devise & de l'Embleme, & leurs differences' Le Moyne analyses a number of differences between the two forms, embracing subject matter, form, and function, all of which differences he sees as being so fundamental that he is led to the conclusion that the two forms have in fact virtually nothing in common.[28] Some of the contrasts he makes are familiar ones, such as the fact that the emblem offers a moral lesson which is universally applicable, and which is put across in a readily accessible visual form, whereas the device is person-specific and wittily challenging, rather than moralistic:

> Davantage, le sujet...est tout autre dans la Devise que dans l'Embleme. La Devise recherche le particulier & le personnel. Elle ayme à s'esloigner du commun, & à se reserrer dans les singularitez. Ce qui s'approche de

---

[27]   It is interesting that Le Moyne's comment about teaching history through the medium of medals predates Ménestrier's *Histoire du Roy Louis le Grand par les medailles* by 23 years, and by even longer the official metallic history of the reign, which took so long to produce that Ménestrier got in ahead of it, the *Medailles sur les principaux evenemens du regne de Louis le Grand avec des explications historiques, par l'Academie royale des medailles et des inscriptions* (Paris, *Imprimerie royale*, 1702, folio).

[28]   'Il n'y a rien qui leur soit commun, ny en la matiere, ny en la forme, ny en la fin mesme...' (p.220)

l'Axiome, ce qui tient de l'Aphorisme n'y est point receu. Elle laisse tout cela
à l'Embleme, qui se tient aux notions generales...Non seulement l'Embleme
tient de la These & de l'Axiome, par l'universalité de son sujet; il en tient
encore par la moralité, qui y doit entrer, comme partie essentielle à sa
composition. Tous ses desseins sont des leçons de vertu, & des regles de bien
vivre: mais des leçons & des regles déguisées en Symboles & en Images. Sa
fin principale est d'instruire & de dogmatiser par la veuë de ces Images, qui
étourdissent moins la teste, & persuadent mieux l'esprit, que les
Syllogismes...Il n'y a rien dans les sujets de la Devise, rien dans ses desseins
qui approche de cela.   (Le Moyne, *De l'art des devises*, pp.220-21)[29]

and the freedom from constraints enjoyed by the emblem form compared with the
numerous rules and conventions governing the device:

La Devise...n'y veut rien de capricieux ny de bizarre; rien qui offense la veuë,
ou qui blesse l'imagination...elle ne souffre quoy que ce soit, qui puisse
laisser dans l'esprit une image ou mal-honneste ou funeste. L'Embleme n'est
pas si delicat ny si scrupuleux: toutes figures luy sont propres: Il ne distingue
point les naturelles des imaginaires, ny les regulieres des bizarres...
                    (Le Moyne, *De l'art des devises*, p.221)

But Le Moyne draws a further, less familiar, distinction between the two forms,
suggesting that although both emblem and device use the combination of the visual
and the verbal they do so differently. The emblem he describes as a 'these proposée en
peinture' (p.221) where the message is clearly and directly conveyed to its recipient,
whereas the intellectual process of reading a device -described earlier in the treatise as
'une expression metaphorique, par similitude tacite, composée de figures & de
paroles' (p.38) - is more complex, involving the deciphering of simile and metaphor:

A toutes ces differences, ajoutez la Similitude, qui est la propre forme de la
Devise: ajoutez-y encore la Metafore, par laquelle les proprietez du sujet
representé à la veuë, sont transportez à un autre sujet que l'esprit se
represente. Ajoutez-y enfin le Mot...Toutes ces choses si essentielles & si
necessaires à la Devise, n'ont rien à faire dans l'Embleme: où elles n'y
entrent point, où elles y entrent par surerogation, & y sont comme
estrangeres.   (Le Moyne, *De l'art des devises*, pp.222-3)

Le Moyne thus provides a very full description of the rules and conventions
governing the device, as well as of the philosophy and the theory of the symbol
underpinning these, and he goes into considerable detail also on the nature of the

---

[29]   Le Moyne cites here the *Tabula* of Cebes as an early example of the technique he describes
of conveying a moral lesson by visual means, and suggests that it may well have inspired
Alciato and his early imitators: 'Le tableau de Cebez...est une leçon de cette forme: & il y a
grande apparence, que ç'a esté sur ce tableau, qu'Alciate & les Eleves d'Alciate, Peintres de
Moralitez comme luy, ont dessiné les Peintures Morales qu'ils nous ont laissées.' (p.222)

emblem, but this he sees clearly as an inferior form to the device, both socially and intellectually, and throughout his treatise he strives to emphasise the absence of common ground between the two forms, rather than any similarities and overlap between them.

Quite different is the approach of his fellow Jesuit, the prolific Claude-François Ménestrier. Where most theorists on the subject of emblems and devices confined themselves to one single treatise, this is not the case with Ménestrier who, in the course of a long lifetime devoted both to the practical application of emblems and devices and to the theory behind them, published not only a large portfolio of accounts of celebratory and commemorative events at all levels and of all types, designed and orchestrated by himself, and of devices created by himself for particular occasions, but also a very substantial number of theoretical treatises on emblems, devices and other cognate forms such as heraldic *blasons*, and of practical treatises on the application of these in different types of circumstance.[30] One of Ménestrier's earliest works, *L'autel de Lyon consacré à Louys Auguste, & placé dans le temple de la gloire. Ballet dedié à Sa Majesté en son entrée à Lyon*, published in 1658 when he was only 25 years old, describes the allegorical ballet designed by him and performed under his aegis by the pupils of the Jesuit Collège de la Trinité in Lyon in honour of the royal entry into the city of Louis XIV, while his *Description de l'appareil dressé pour la ceremonie de l'octave de S. François de Sales. A l'occasion de la solemnité de sa canonisation, celebree dans l'Eglise du premier Monastere de la Visitation Sainte Marie de Grenoble, qui est le quatriéme de l'Institut: Depuis les premieres Vespres du 8 Septembre, jusques apres les dernieres du 17. du mesme mois* describes the triumphal arch and all the other meaningful decoration designed by himself to mark an important Church celebration.[31] Different again is his *Resjoüissances de la paix, avec un recueil de diverses pieces sur ce sujet* of 1660, describing the ephemeral architecture erected in Lyon to celebrate the peace treaty between France and Spain, but including also an account of the firework and other displays organised as part of the celebration, and a treatise on how to design appropriate firework displays. Turning his attention from celebration to mourning, Ménestrier was also adept at organising appropriate ceremonial displays for important funerals, as described in *Les devoirs funebres rendus à la memoire de Madame Royale chrestienne de France, duchesse de Savoye, reine de Chypre, &c, espouse de Victor Amé, le 19 mars 1664 et de Madame la duchesse royale Françoise de Valois, espouse de S.A.R. Charles Emanuel II, le 21.*

---

[30] Mario Praz paints a splendid imagined picture of this redoubtable Jesuit polymath practitioner going about his emblematic business: 'We see his tall, black figure move to and fro among canvas wings, theatrical costumes, scaffoldings, ladders, and lapidary inscriptions, giving orders to troops of engineers, carpenters and painters, like a general on the battle-field; or beating time at the rehearsal of a ballet in costume, in which the pagan genii dance with the theological virtues, Christ and the Virgin go hand in hand with Jupiter and Juno, and Hercules, Orpheus and Argus lay club, lyre and rod at the feet of a cardinal.' (Praz, p.194)

[31] Grenoble, R. Philippes, 1666, 4°. See also his similar account, *Les transfigurations sacrées de S. Francois de Sales ou le Thabor de sa gloire. Dessein de l'appareil de la solemnité de sa canonisation, faite dans le second Monastere de la Visitation Sainte Marie de Grenoble: avec le Journal des Ceremonies depuis le 19. may jusques au 27*, n.p. (Grenoble), n.d. (1666?), 4°.

du mesme mois. Par le souverain Senat, et la souveraine Chambre des comptes de Savoye, à Chambery.[32] His practical experience in all these various aspects of applied emblematics led him to produce, in addition to these accounts of actual events, a series of treatises on applied emblematics, each dealing with a different aspect, beginning in 1669 with a treatise on tournaments and ending in 1683 with a treatise on funeral decoration. In the opening pages of *Des decorations funebres. Où il est amplement traité des tentures, des lumieres, des mausolées, catafalques, inscriptions & autres ornemens funebres. Avec tout ce qui s'est fait de plus considerable depuis plus d'un siécle, pour les papes, empereurs, rois, reines, cardinaux, princes, prelats, sçavans & personnes illustres en naissance, vertu & dignité. Par le P.C.F. Menestrier de la Compagnie de Jesus* he describes this work as the logical sequel to his earlier treatises on tourneys, *carrousels*, music, ballet and fireworks.[33]

As well as these practical manuals on applied emblematics, Ménestrier also produced a large number of more general and theoretical treatises on emblems and devices and other similar forms such as heraldic *blasons*. Among these his very early treatise on heraldry, the *Veritable art du blason*, which was published anonymously in 1659 is interesting in that it gives an early indication of Ménestrier's characteristically combative and critical nature.[34] It is the attacks directed by Ménestrier in this work against what he considers to be ill-judged and faulty statements in an earlier work on the same subject by Claude Le Laboureur[35] which led to a two-year long literary quarrel between Ménestrier, the young and ambitious Jesuit priest, and his much older rival who was also a priest. This was a particularly strong quarrel, but it was not the only such in the course of Ménestrier's long writing career. Several of his works contain characteristically aggressive attacks on what he considers to be shortcomings or failings on the part of his emblematic rivals, as for example his *Des decorations funebres* in which he criticises the decorative arrangements which were made for the funeral in Notre Dame of the Queen, Maria Theresa, in 1683, and suggests how he

---

[32] n.p.n.d., 4°. These are just a few examples from among many such works by Ménestrier.

[33] Paris, R.J.B. de la Caille and R. Pepie, 1683, 8°, p.7. See also his *Traité des tournois, joustes, carrousels et autres spectacles publics* (Lyon, J.Muguet, 1669, 4°); *Des representations en musique anciennes et modernes* (Paris, R. Guignard, 1681, 12°); and *Des ballets anciens et modernes selon les regles du theatre* (Paris, R. Guignard, 1682, 12°). In the opening section of *Des decorations funebres* Ménestrier includes what is in effect a bibliography, extending to several pages, of all the various works which he has written on the subject of such celebrations. (p.9 *et seq.*) For a fuller list of Ménestrier's many accounts of ceremonial occasions organised by himself, and of his treatises on how they should be organised, see Judi Loach, 'Ménestrier's emblem theory', pp.330-31.

[34] His liking for criticising the efforts of his rivals is even reflected in the full title, in which he refers to the faults of others: *Le veritable art du blason, où les regles des armoiries sont traitées d'une nouvelle methode, plus aisée que les precedentes; les origines expliquées, & establies par de solides raisons, & de fortes authoritez; les erreurs de plusieurs autheurs corrigées, la pratique de chaque nation examinée; & les causes de leur diversité fidellement raportées*, Lyon, B Coral, 1659, 12°.

[35] Claude Le Laboureur, *Discours sur l'origine des armes receüs et usitez pour l'explication de la science heraldique...enrichy des blasons des roys, princes et autres maisons illustres de la chrestienté*, Lyon, G. Barbier, 1658, 8°.

himself would have better approached the challenge. He had hoped to be invited to organise these arrangements himself, and his consequent disappointment at having been passed over undoubtedly led to his criticism of what was done. Although he was entrusted with the decorations for the subsequent ceremony at St Denis, this did not compensate for not being asked to do Notre Dame.[36] The original *Veritable art du blason* was followed up by two further studies on heraldry, both published two years later in 1661, the *Methode abbregée des principes heraldiques ou la maniere d'apprendre le blason. Par le Pere Claude François Menestrier de la Compagnie de Jesus* and *L'art du blason justifié par le Pere Claude François Menestrier de la Compagnie de Jesus*,[37] neither of which, however, have anything to add to the chapter on devices and the use of heraldic colours in devices contained in the earlier work. More important for the ideas they contain on the art and theory of emblems specifically are his early *Art des emblemes* of 1662, and the much longer and more developed version of the work which he produced twenty-two years later in 1684 under the fuller and more explanatory title, *L'art des emblemes où s'enseigne la morale par les figures de la fable, de l'histoire, & de la nature. Ouvrage rempli de pres de cinq cent figures*. On the subject of devices his main treatise, *La science et l'art des devises* of 1686, is also - like the *Art des emblemes* and *Art des emblemes où s'enseigne la morale* - illustrated by large numbers of actual devices demonstrating what he considers to be good and bad practice, and also - importantly - demonstrating his own ingenuity and virtuosity as a composer of devices.[38]   Finally among Ménestrier's various theoretical writings the last which must be mentioned is a work whose all-embracing short title, *La philosophie des images*, suggests that this will be an ambitious theoretical work, bringing together his ideas on all aspects of visual imagery, but in reality this is not the case. In fact it is a work of synthesis which, as the full title explains, brings together not so much Ménestrier's own ideas as those of other people: *La philosophie des images. Composée d'un ample recueil de devises, & du jugement de tous les ouvrages qui ont été faits sur cette matiere. Par le P.C.F. Menestrier de la Compagnie de Jesus*. In this work Ménestrier lists in the first part the various treatises on devices written by other authors, and summarises their main arguments, and includes also various collections of devices, as well as published accounts of court celebrations exploiting devices, while the second part comprises a collection of devices of the great and good of Europe, as explained in its subtitle: *Devises des princes, cavaliers, dames, sçavans, et autres personnages illustres de l'Europe, ou la philosophie des images. Tome second*. The first part of the work in

---

[36]   For details of this affair and Ménestrier's consequent quarrel with his rivals from the *Petite Académie* see Judi Loach, 'Ménestrier's emblem theory', pp.327-8. For description of his quarrel with Le Laboureur, see Paul Allut, *Recherches sur la vie et sur les oeuvres du P. Claude-François Ménestrier de la Compagnie de Jesus*. See also Praz, pp.180-85.

[37]   Lyon, B. Coral and A. du Perier, 1661, 12°; Lyon, B. Coral, 1661, 12°.

[38]   The full title to the work includes careful reference to the collections of devices by Ménestrier contained in the treatise: *La science et l'art des devises dressez sur de nouvelles regles, avec six cens devises sur les principaux evenemens de la vie du Roy. Et quatre cens devises sacrées, dont tous les mots sont tirés de l'Ecriture Sainte. Composées par le P. Menestrier de la Compagnie de Jesus.*

particular offers an excellent bibliographical tool, but overall it is less interesting as a synthesis of Ménestrier's own ideas and theories on the philosophy of images than its short-title might suggest, and these are found best expressed in his other theoretical works.

It is with Ménestrier that the emblem comes into its own as a form worthy of its own full treatise, whereas in earlier theoretical writings, as we have seen, it was discussed in the broader context of devices, and the main interest of the writers of these treatises lay in establishing the differences between emblem and device. In particular in the later *Art des emblemes où s'enseigne la morale* he gives a very detailed exposition of his understanding of the emblem, and its function as a didactic tool, developing much more fully the ideas already outlined over twenty years earlier in his original *Art des emblemes* of 1662.[39] In the earlier work Ménestrier begins by contextualising the emblem among other forms of what he describes as *peintures sçavantes*, including hieroglyphs, enigmas, *chiffres*, *blasons*, devices and *empreintes des medailles*, prior to going on to analyse the emblem itself, but in the later version this opening section on other forms is omitted, since by 1684 he had already discussed these more fully elsewhere, and the treatise concentrates more narrowly on the emblem alone.

Above all Ménestrier insists on the didactic nature of emblems, reiterating this key feature many times in the opening pages of the work. In his dedication of the work to 'Monseigneur Nicolai, Premier President en la Chambre des Comptes', he describes the way in which their pleasing combination of word and image is exploited towards a moralising end:

> L'Art des Emblemes que je vous presente est l'artifice dont se sert la Poësie pour gagner l'Esprit par les yeux, employant les secours de la Peinture pour persuader les veritez qui sont propres à regler les moeurs, & les maximes importantes pour la conduite des hommes... C'est...cette partie de la Philosophie des Images, qui met sous les yeux la Morale & la Politique, en tirant de l'Histoire, de la Nature, & de la Fable des instructions salutaires. C'est par ce doux artifice que l'on ôte aux enseignemens cét air de dureté qui les fait paroître severes...C'est de ces Images que l'Eloquence & la Poesie se servent avec tant de succés que rien n'est si efficace pour la persuasion que ce qui entre de cette maniere dans les coeurs & dans les esprits.
>
> (Ménestrier, *L'art des emblemes où s'enseigne la morale*, pp.[5]-7)

while in the first part of the main text he continues to stress this aspect, which he sees as differentiating the emblem from other forms of *peinture sçavante*, repeatedly using such words as *enseigner*, *enseignement* or *instruction* to emphasise the point:

> L'Art des Emblêmes n'est plus à present que l'Art de peindre les moeurs, &

---

[39]   For a detailed analysis of the differences between the 1662 *Art des emblemes* and the 1684 *Art des emblemes où s'enseigne la morale*, see Judi Loach, 'Ménestrier's emblem theory', pp.323-8.

de mettre en images les operations de la nature pour l'instruction des
hommes...C'est le propre des Emblêmes de rendre intelligibles les choses les
plus difficiles, parce que c'est le propre des Emblêmes d'enseigner. Il n'en
est pas de même des Devises, des Hieroglyfiques, & des Symboles, qui ont
presque toûjours quelque chose de mysterieux & de caché, que tout le monde
ne penetre pas.

Tout Emblême est donc aujourd'huy une espece d'enseignement mis en
image, pour regler la conduite des hommes.

(Ménestrier, *L'art des emblemes ou s'enseigne la morale*, p.3 and p.15)

While acknowledging Alciato's pioneering role as creator of the emblem in its
modern form,[40] Ménestrier insists on the great antiquity of the genre when he uses the
word emblem in its broadest sense of an image through which a further truth may be
perceived, as in his opening chapter entitled 'De l'origine des Emblemes' which
begins with the forthright statement that 'Les Emblêmes sont aussi anciennes que le
monde, puisque le monde est pour ainsi dire, une Emblême de la Divinité'. This
statement he substantiates by citing the authority of St Paul:

C'est du moins la pensée de S. Paul, qui nous apprend que les choses que
nous voyons, sont à l'homme autant d'images & de figures sensibles qui luy
representent la sagesse aussi bien que la puissance de celuy qui les a faites.

(Ménestrier, *L'art des emblemes où s'enseigne la morale*, p.5)

and follows it with references to other ancient manifestations of the emblem as used by
the Chaldeans, by Pythagoras, Socrates, Plato, Cebes and Philostratus, introducing
here also an association with the veil of allegory of the enigma:

Les Chaldéens furent les premiers qui mirent le Ciel en Emblêmes, en
donnant des noms & des figures aux constellations...Pythagore sur cet
exemple des Emblêmes des Chaldéens, mit toute la Philosophie en paraboles
enigmatiques faisant des Emblêmes obscurs d'une chose qui d'elle-même
n'est déja que trop obscure. Il crut rendre plus venerable cette science divine
& humaine, en la cachant aux esprits mediocres sous les voiles de ces
Enigmes, qui representent d'abord un sens où tout paroist intelligible,
trompent les ignorans, en instruisant ceux qui penetrent sous l'écorce de ces
figures les mysteres de ces Enigmes.

Socrate fut plus heureux dans les Emblêmes qu'il fit de la Morale, puis
qu'il la rendit si aisée & si intelligible, que l'on dit qu'il avoit fait descendre

---

[40] Describing inscriptions on statues, bas-reliefs and paintings as another source of emblems,
Ménestrier remarks with a rather imprecise grasp of dates: 'Ce fut-là l'origine des Emblêmes
que l'ignorance de cinq ou six siecles avoit comme ensevelis, lors qu'Alciat en releva & le
souvenir & la gloire, par le recueil qu'il publia sur la fin du quinziéme siecle.' (pp.11-12)
Earlier he had already cited Alciato as the first to exploit decorative images as a means of
instruction: '...cet Autheur semble avoir esté le premier qui ait tiré de ces ornemens anciens,
les Images qui servent à nous instruire pour l'étude & pour les moeurs.' (pp.2-3)

des Cieux la Sagesse & la Philosophie, que Pythagore & les Arabes sembloient y avoir guindée. C'est sur ces Emblêmes que Platon forma le plan de ses idées, & le monde par son moyen commença à se remplir de ces Images ingenieuses, qui donnerent lieu à tant de Fables, & à tant d'inventions Poëtiques. Le fameux tableau de Cebes tira de là son origine, & les tableaux de Philostrate.

> (Ménestrier, *L'art des emblemes où s'enseigne la morale*, pp.8-10)

Later in the work, still using the word in its general sense of image, he describes as emblems the Old Testament prefigurations of the New Testament,[41] and likewise Christ's teaching by parables as another form of emblematic approach,[42] prefacing this with the comment that:

la Religion des Juifs fut à proprement parler une Religion d'Emblêmes, comme à dit S. Paul: *Omnia in figura contingebant illis*: comme dit le même Apostre. Ces figures qui furent pour eux des Mysteres & des Enigmes où ils n'entendoient rien, sont des Emblêmes pour nous.

> (Ménestrier, *L'art des emblemes où s'enseigne la morale*, p.208)

In the section devoted to *emblemes sacrez* Ménestrier stresses the importance of the Old Testament as a source of emblematic material, unequalled by anything produced by 'la Philosophie Payenne', remarking further that many of the best elements in the work of the Ancients are taken from the Old Testament, and citing Plato taking his ideas from Moses, and Ovid basing his *Metamorphoses* on Genesis as notable examples of this.[43]

But emblems can be derived from many other ancient sources as well as the Bible. Ovid's *Metamorphoses* are cited as a useful source of emblematic material, as are likewise Aesop's *Fables*, which Ménestrier describes as ready-made emblems:

Les Apologues d'Esope sont aussi d'eux-mêmes des Emblêmes, parce que ces Apologues ou les Autheurs font parler les plantes, les animaux, & les autres choses naturelles ou artificielles ont toûjours leur instruction morale jointe

---

[41] 'Toutes les figures de l'ancien Testament sont des Emblêmes des Mysteres du nouveau. Le Sacrifice d'Abraham est l'Image ou l'Emblême de la mort du Fils de Dieu, comme figure du Sacrifice de Justice qu'il a souffert pour nous sur la Croix.' (pp.61-2)

[42] 'C'est pour cela que le Fils de Dieu parloit des plus grands Mysteres de nostre Religion sous les voiles des Paraboles, pour en faire autant d'Emblêmes.' (p.208)

[43] 'L'Ecriture sainte est l'original de ces Emblêmes, & quelque ingenieuse qu'ait paru la Philosophie Payenne en ses inventions, elle n'a jamais rien eu qui approchât des Symboles mysterieux de nostre Theologie. Si Platon a merité parmi les Anciens le nom de *Divin*, à cause des idées sous lesquelles il a representé sa Philosophie, c'est des livres de Moyse qu'il a tiré ses plus belles connoissances. Et Clement d'Alexandrie a fort sagement remarqué que tous les anciens Philosophes ont pris dans les Livres sacrez ce qu'ils ont eu de plus ingenieux; comme il semble que le Poëme des Metamorphoses d'Ovide n'est qu'une imitation grossiere du livre de la Genese.' (p.64)

aux discours & aux actions de ces animaux.
(Ménestrier, *L'art des emblemes où s'enseigne la morale*, p.27)

Alluding to modern potentially emblematic re-workings of both these texts, he cites La Fontaine's *Fables*, and Benserade's 226 *rondeaux* based on the *Metamorphoses*,[44] which could easily have been made into emblems if he had incorporated moral lessons into the verses.[45] Similarly *sententiae* and proverbs should be considered an appropriate source of emblematic material, since they reflect on aspects of the human condition.[46] But emblematic material need not be sought only in ancient literary sources. It can be found in nature, in art, or in any form which leads to some manner of edification.

Ménestrier divides the figures, which he considers to be the starting point for the emblematic process, into three categories, described as *naturelles*, *symboliques* and

---

[44] Benserade, *Metamorphoses d'Ovide en rondeaux imprimez et enrichis de figures par ordre de sa Majesté, et dediez à Monseigneur le Dauphin*, Amsterdam, A. Wolfgang, 1689, 12°.

[45] 'Monsieur de Benserade qui a fait deux cens vingt-six Rondeaux sur les Metamorphoses d'Ovide, en auroit pû faire autant d'Emblêmes, s'il avoit pris soin de choisir dans Ovide des bouts de Vers propres à expliquer d'une maniere morale les sujets de ses figures. Quelques-uns de ces Rondeaux font des applications morales ou politiques de ces Metamorphoses, & en font des Emblêmes.' (p.22) Ménestrier's reservations about the lack of moral focus of Benserade's emblematic *rondeaux* is curious, since most in fact (rather than just some, as he suggests) do contain a moral lesson, as for example his emblematic reworking of the Lycaon tale. On one page the engraved figure depicting the scene of Lycaon transformed into a wolf is accompanied by a brief prose explanation: 'Lycaon fut un Tyran qui fit tant de méchancetez, & commit tant de meurtres, que Jupiter le changea en Loup, aprés avoir foudroyé sa maison, & détruit son Royaume' together with a Latin note at the foot of the page 'notus feritate Lycaon'. On the facing page is the *rondeau* with its title *Lycaon en Loup*:
> Pour estre grand comme estoit Lycaön
> Il ne faut rien que l'odieux renom
> D'estre ennemi des choses legitimes,
> Empoisonné de méchantes maximes,
> Et d'estre moins un homme qu'un Démon.
>
> Il prit d'un Loup la figure, & le ton,
> Et sans jamais esperer de pardon
> N'en fut pas moins abaissé par ses crimes.
> Pour estre grand.
>
> Il vid perir son Regne, & sa Maison,
> L'éclat de foudre alla jusqu'à son Nom,
> Luy qui des Monts frapant les hautes cimes
> N'épargne point les criminels sublimes.
> Il faut qu'un Roy soit juste, sage, & bon.
> Pour estre grand. (Benserade, *Metamorphoses d'Ovide en rondeaux*, pp.14-15)

[46] 'Les Sentences Morales des Histoires sont aussi une autre source d'Emblêmes, aussi bien que les Proverbes; parce que ces Sentences sont ou des reflexions sur les évenemens des choses, sur les usages des peuples, ou sur les actions des hommes.' (p.32)

poëtiques. Under the heading *naturelles* belong the animal world and other natural phenomena, while *symboliques* covers hieroglyphic or otherwise symbolic figures such as the caduceus or the cornucopia, and *poëtiques* covers allegorical figures such as Time, Fortune or Death. But since it is above all the overall didactic value of emblems which Ménestrier considers to be their most important feature, when he classifies emblems as a whole into different types, he does so according to the different form of instructive message which they impart. Dividing them up therefore 'selon les enseignemens qu'ils donnent', he defines them as falling into six categories: *sacrez*, *moraux, doctrinaux, politiques, heroiques* and *satyriques* (p.61), and for each category as well as describing its particular character, he also cites what he considers to be good examples of that particular kind of emblem. These are the six categories which he lists at the beginning of the chapter entitled 'Des diverses especes des Emblêmes, à les considerer selon leur fin', but in fact he also includes two further categories in the course of the chapter: *chimiques* (by which he means alchemical) and *passionnez*. On the subject of the use of hermetic imagery in alchemy, Ménestrier is strongly disapproving:

> ...ceux qui ont affecté de chercher dans la nature le secret de faire l'or, & les transformations metalliques qu'ils appellent le grand Oeuvre, la Pierre Philosophale, le Magistere, & l'Art occulte, se sont aussi servis d'images pour rendre plus mysterieuses ces sombres rêveries de leur imagination, par lesquelles ils promettent tout & ne donnent qu'un peu de fumée à ceux qui s'engagent à les suivre. Outre les noms, les figures & les chiffres des Planettes qu'ils ont donnez aux metaux, il n'y a ny songes, ny visions, ny symboles, ny chimeres, qu'ils n'ayent peintes & figurées, pour parler en Prophetes des secrets de ce grand oeuvre recherché depuis si long-temps, & si vainement tenté par des gens de tout pays.
>
> (Ménestrier, *L'art des emblemes où s'enseigne la morale*, p.122)

The reason why the extra category subtitled 'Des emblemes passionnez' does not figure in the list at the beginning of the chapter is presumably because - as Ménestrier accepts - these emblems are not really instructive. Several of his examples in this category are taken from Scève's *Délie*, and rightly Ménestrier describes these as 'plûtost des expressions des passions & des affections de l'ame, que des enseignemens.' (p.159)

His discussion of sacred emblems is interesting, since although Ménestrier was a Jesuit priest, he was also a teacher of rhetoric[47] and a professional designer and organiser of ceremonial for festivities of all kinds, and the emblems and devices with which he was primarily concerned for both these purposes were not commonly sacred,

---

[47]   In his early days in the 1650s he taught variously at the Jesuit colleges of Chambéry and Vienne, and at his own old school, the Collège de la Trinité in Lyon, where he subsequently became librarian in 1667, prior to leaving Lyon in 1669 to spend a year travelling in Italy and Germany, returning thereafter to base himself in Paris in 1670. For biographical details see Paul Allut, *Recherches sur la vie et sur les oeuvres du P. Claude-François Ménestrier*, and Judi Loach, 'Ménestrier's emblem theory'.

and his discussion of emblems and devices in his various theoretical works, as also that of the other theoretical writers discussed in this chapter more commonly does not extend to cover sacred material of this kind. His criteria for defining sacred emblems are broad:

> *Les Sacrez* sont ceux qui expriment des maximes Chrétiennes de Religion, ou nos Mysteres mêmes, de quelque nature que soient les figures, Naturelles ou Symboliques, Historiques, Poëtiques, &c.
> (Ménestrier, *L'art des emblemes où s'enseigne la morale*, p.61)

The figure does not need to be taken from Scripture, so long as the motto is taken either from Scripture or from the writings of the Holy Fathers, or indeed so long as the emblem overall relates to sacred matters, although - relating his theories, as so often, to the practical applications of emblems - he makes the proviso that profane subjects should not be represented in the figure if the emblem is to be used in a holy place.[48] It is interesting to see the particular works which he singles out as examples from among the many possible collections of sacred emblems. Reflecting the strong seventeenth-century emblematic input from the Netherlands, all the works which he cites in this section originated in Antwerp. As a Jesuit, it might be expected that he would give priority to Jesuit emblem books, but this is not altogether the case. Certainly the first example which he gives is Hugo's *Pia desideria*, and indeed he spells out how the emblems in the collection are ordered to show the Jesuit progression from *via purgativa* to *via illustrativa* and ultimately to *via unitiva* (pp.75-6), and he also describes a series of heart emblems painted on the *Grand escalier* of the Jesuit noviciate in Paris, whose object was to convey ingeniously 'la vocation de la Vie Religieuse, ses epreuves & sa perfection' (p.76). But as well as these he also cites Vaenius's *Amoris divini emblemata* and the *Amoris divini et humani antipathia* (pp.82-4), neither of which are Jesuit. Other emblematic works by Jesuit writers like, for example, Richeome's *Tableaux sacrez* or Jan David's *Veridicus christianus* are not mentioned.

When discussing *emblêmes moraux*, which he describes as 'de tous les Emblêmes les plus naturels, parce que les Emblêmes ne sont faits que pour l'instruction des moeurs' (p.86), once again Ménestrier cites a work which originated in the Netherlands rather than a native French product, although it is a French version of it that he mentions - Gomberville's *Doctrine des moeurs*, based on Vaenius's Horatian emblems, which were again originally published in Antwerp. He also cites the variant French version of the work published subsequently in Brussels under the new, but still moralising, title *Theatre moral de la vie humaine*. Under *emblêmes politiques* Ménestrier does at last offer a genuinely native French example:

---

[48] 'Il n'est pas necessaire pour faire des Emblêmes sacrez, que les figures soient tirées de l'Histoire sainte, il suffit que les mots soient de l'Ecriture ou des Peres, & même que l'application de l'Emblême se fasse des matieres saintes...Les Figures de l'Histoire prophane & de la Fable même, peuvent servir à faire des Emblêmes sacrez, mais il ne s'en faut pas servir dans les lieux saints.' (pp.68-9)

> Les Emblêmes Politiques sont ceux qui expriment les maximes du
> gouvernement & de la conduite des Etats, comme sont plusieurs de ceux que
> Monsieur Baudoin a recueillies en deux Volumes, & expliquez par d'élegans
> discours.
>
> (Ménestrier, *L'art des emblemes où s'enseigne la morale*, p.97)

although his European outlook comes to the fore yet again when he offers as an
example of such political emblems being used practically in architectural decoration a
ducal castle in Munich, rather than a French model.[49]

Under the heading *Des Emblemes Doctrinaux*, which he then subdivides into
doctrinaux and *academiques*, Ménestrier includes the most specifically educational
types of emblems, defined as:

> ...ceux où les mysteres des Sciences & des Arts sont representez par des
> figures qui nous découvrent ces mysteres, & qui nous les font entendre non
> pas par ces figures Geometriques de Lignes, de Points, & de Lettres, qui sont
> propres des demonstrations Mathematiques, mais par des figures Naturelles,
> Historiques, Poëtiques, & Symboliques, de la nature de celles qui entrent dans
> les Emblêmes.
>
> (Ménestrier, *L'art des emblemes où s'enseigne la morale*, p.111)

Here it is interesting that although once again he cites Gomberville's *Doctrine des
moeurs* as providing examples of *emblêmes academiques*, defined as 'ceux qui sont
des enseignemens generaux pour les études' (p.112), for *emblêmes doctrinaux*, which
he defines as 'des expressions des Arts & des Sciences, & des Regles mises en figures
pour pratiquer les Arts & les Sciences' (p.116), he cites not only a French example,
but a sixteenth-century French example, in the shape of Aneau's *Picta poesis*,
although his second example is Alciato, whose emblem book must count as a
European emblem book rather than a French one, despite the fact that so many more
editions were published in France than anywhere else in Europe.

In the little section on *emblêmes passionnez* which is tagged on at the end of this
section, although this category is not included in the list at the beginning of the
section, Ménestrier cites the example of another sixteenth-century French writer,
Maurice Scève, but in none of the other three remaining sections - *emblêmes
chimiques*, *heroïques* and *satyriques* - does he offer any named writer as an example,
whether French or otherwise. Although he gives a number of illustrated examples of
alchemical emblems, he does not cite a particular author, while in both the section on
satirical emblems and that on heroic emblems his examples are mainly derived from
the domain of applied emblematics rather than from published collections of emblems.
In particular *emblêmes heroïques* are described as having a major role to play in the
various applied arts, serving to convey visually the greatness of the person whom they
represent:

---

[49] 'Il y a plusieurs de ces Emblêmes peints au Palais du Duc de Baviere à Munick, dans
l'appartement que l'on nomme de l'Empereur.' (p.97)

> J'appelle Emblêmes Heroïques ceux par qui les belles actions des grands
> hommes sont exprimées, & qui sont si frequens aux entrées des Princes sur
> les arcs de triomphe qu'on leur dresse, dans les galeries où l'on represente les
> plus beaux évenemens de leur vie, sur les revers de leurs Medailles, & aux
> decorations qui se font à leurs funerailles.
>
> (Ménestrier, *L'art des emblemes où s'enseigne la morale*, p.133)

but *emblêmes satyriques*, whose function is the reverse, are similarly described as
visual, painted artefacts,[50] and in both cases Ménestrier cites actual paintings rather
than printed emblem books, as for example a series of twelve in 'l'Alcove de la feu
Reine' in the Louvre (p.134), and others depicting the magnificence of François 1er in
the Galerie François 1er at Fontainebleau, identified by Ménestrier as the work of
Rosso (p.145).[51]

Several interesting points emerge from Ménestrier's discussion of the various
categories of emblem. Given that he was a French writer who was operating very
much within a French domain[52] it is striking to see how few are the French
emblematic models which he cites, relative to those originating elsewhere - most
commonly in the Netherlands. It is likewise striking to see that among the small
number of French examples which he does cite, the majority date from the sixteenth
century rather than from his own century. Particularly interesting in that it reflects
Ménestrier's strong commitment to applied emblematics as much as to emblems in a
more purely literary form is the fact that a large number of the examples which he
cites - particularly in the sections on heroic and satirical devices, but elsewhere in the
treatise also - refer to emblems which had already been used in practical ways, in
architectural decoration, festivities, *revers de médailles* funerals etcetera, rather than
to emblems as published in printed books. Finally it is interesting to note how
relatively little he privileges Jesuit emblematics, in view of his own status as a Jesuit
priest.

Ménestrier's flexible and tolerant approach to rules and conventions governing
the emblem is apparent again when he broaches the subject of the constituent parts
which it ought to include, with the comment that usually it has three parts, but some
people prefer four:

> On donne ordinairement trois parties aux Emblêmes, la Peinture, le Mot, &
> les Vers... Quelques-uns donnent quatre parties aux Emblêmes, la Peinture, le

---

[50] 'Si les Emblêmes Heroïques sont des eloges en tableaux & en peintures, qui font
connoistre les belles actions & les vertus des grands hommes, les Emblêmes Satyriques sont
des peintures injurieuses à la reputation des personnes contre lesquelles ils sont faits.' (p.150)

[51] The emblematic paintings in the Galerie François 1er as also those in the Grande Galerie
were earlier described by Pierre Dan also in his *Tresor des merveilles de la maison royale de
Fontainebleau* (pp.87-8 and 119-20).

[52] Other than the short period he spent travelling in Italy and Germany, he was based in
France, first in the Jesuit province of Lyonnais, and subsequently in Paris, and the festive
occasions with which he was himself involved took place in one or other of these parts of
France.

Titre, le Mot & les Vers.
(Ménestrier, *L'art des emblemes où s'enseigne la morale*, p.168)

A few pages later he remarks furthermore that even these two norms are not sacrosanct, and that some emblems may contain no more than one single element - the figure - while others may contain two, three or four, and all can still be perfectly acceptable as emblems.[53]   Later, however, in a chapter entitled 'Des deux parties essentielles des Emblêmes' he suggests that both figure and text are essential, 'l'une pour les yeux, & l'autre pour l'esprit' (p.207), developing this with the further remark with its Horatian echo:

Combien d'enseignemens des Poëtes deviennent agreables par de semblables images, qui unissent ces deux soeurs, la Peinture & la Poësie; la Peinture pour les yeux, & la Poësie pour l'esprit.
(Ménestrier, *L'art des emblemes où s'enseigne la morale*, p.212)

and later still in 'Du Mot de l'Emblême' he suggests that - despite his earlier remarks about the acceptability of emblems comprising only one single element - the *mot* generally is a necessary element, with the possible exception only of allegorical emblems (p.309). In common with other theorists he agrees that the *mot* in the emblem is less constrained by conventions than that of the device. It can take one of several different forms:

Ces mots peuvent estre ou de simples titres, ou des enseignemens, ou des sentences, ou des mots semblables à ceux des Devises qui ne font qu'un avec tout le corps.
(Ménestrier, *L'art des emblemes où s'enseigne la morale*, p.309)

and it can be either in Latin or in one or other vernacular language, and - reflecting the way in which the emblem is designed for clarity rather than for hermeticism - the *mot* can name the figure directly in a way that is not permissible in the device, where it can allude only indirectly.[54]

While the accompanying text which serves to clarify the message of the figure can be in prose or verse, Ménestrier's strong preference is for verse, since not only are picture and poetry closely associated as sister arts, and the two elements work well together to convey the lesson effectively:

---

[53] 'Quoy que l'on assigne aux Emblêmes ces quatre parties, ils ne les demandent pas necessairement. Quelques-uns n'ont que la Peinture seule, & sont complets avec cette seule partie; d'autres en demandent deux, quelques-uns en demandent trois, & tous en peuvent recevoir quatre, quand on veut les leur donner.' (p.182)
[54] 'La difference qu'il y a entre ce mot et celuy de la Devise, est que celuy de l'Emblême, peut nommer les figures, ce que celuy de la Devise ne doit jamais faire...On peut faire ces sentences en langue vulgaire, ou en langue Latine, ou quelque langue étrangere, particulièrement en Italien ou en Espagnol.' (pp.315-7)

> Si la Peinture est une Poësie muette, & la Poësie une Peinture parlante,
> l'Emblême qui a les beautez de l'un & de l'autre, merite aussi les deux noms.
> Il est une Peinture d'instruction, & les vers qui luy servent de truchement,
> contribuent beaucoup à rendre ses enseignemens efficaces.
>
> (Ménestrier, *L'art des emblemes où s'enseigne la morale*, p.321)

but also poetry brings to the emblem its own aesthetic qualities, such as would not be
present in a prose exposition.[55] Nevertheless, since its essential function is to convey a
message, the verse should above all be clear and simple to understand, and it should
also be short, preferably not exceeding the length of a conventional epigram.
Reflecting his period, Ménestrier suggests the madrigal or the sonnet as appropriate
verse forms for the emblem, as well as the epigram. But other than this suggestion,
what he has to say on the subject of short, clear verse passages is a remarkably faithful
echo of what the sixteenth-century practitioners had to say on the subject nearly one
hundred and fifty years earlier, and indeed it is Alciato himself whom Ménestrier cites
as a good example of a composer of clear and succinct emblems:

> Ces vers doivent estre extremement nets & faciles, puis qu'ils ne servent qu'à
> expliquer les enseignemens moraux, qui sont cachez sous les figures de
> l'Emblême. Ceux d'Alciat ont cette netteté...Il faut aussi tâcher de renfermer
> cette explication en peu de vers, & de ne pas exceder le nombre de ceux
> qu'on assigne à l'epigramme.
>
> (Ménestrier, *L'art des emblemes ou s'enseigne la morale*, pp.322-3)

Throughout this work, as in his other treatises, Ménestrier makes repeated
reference to the practical applications of emblems, but at the end of the work, once he
has discussed all the theoretical aspects of emblems, he devotes a substantial section,
entitled 'De l'usage des Emblêmes', specifically to the many ways in which emblems
can be used in the applied arts, drawing a contrast between the way in which the
Ancients originally used them purely decoratively, and the way in which they
thereafter came to be used which was no less decorative, but meaningfully decorative.
He describes how they are used in architecture, citing once again the rich example of
Fontainebleau, and singling out for mention here the series of 58 paintings
representing the 'travaux d'Ulysse' (pp.340-41), and likewise their use in triumphal
entries and other festivities, and in funerals. Appropriateness is a feature which
Ménestrier values highly, and here as in other treatises he insists that themes for
emblems in the applied arts should be chosen with reference to the setting in which
they were to be used. Thus Semele being burnt up by Jupiter's thunderbolt or the Fire
of Troy are appropriate emblematic themes to be represented on a fireplace, (pp.385-6)
whereas Thisbe losing her veil in a fountain or Arion on his dolphin would be
appropriate themes for a fountain (p.387).

---

[55] 'Enfin la Poësie a je ne sçay quoy qui plaist & qui attire, & une grace particuliere qui lui a
fait meriter le titre de divine chez tous les peuples.

Il ne faut pas donc s'étonner si pour animer les peintures sçavantes, on a fait plûtost choix de
la Poësie que de la Prose.' (p.321)

This particular treatise by Ménestrier is particularly interesting from two points of view. Firstly it emerges much more evidently than the offerings of other seventeenth-century theorists as the work of a practising expert in the field, and secondly - and perhaps because of Ménestrier's practical experience in applied emblematics - it emerges as a much more tolerant treatise than many others. Certainly Ménestrier insists on the fundamental didactic role of emblems, and thus on clarity as being a key element, though even so he does not reject ingenuity, since this can contribute to the pleasure with which the message is received,[56] but thereafter he is more interested in discussing the range of different types of emblem that can be created, and the range of different ways in which these can be exploited, offering a wealth of illustrated examples to demonstrate these, rather than in analysing the extent to which certain emblems are or are not acceptable in terms of hard and fast rules and conventions. The contrast between Ménestrier's approach and that of his fellow Jesuit theorist Le Moyne is striking indeed.

Writers like Henry Estienne, Pierre Le Moyne and Claude-François Ménestrier are the major theorists on emblematics, and for this reason we have concentrated primarily on the various treatises by these core contributors. But it must not be forgotten that there was also considerable interest being expressed in seventeenth-century polite society and court society in emblems and devices generally, as reflected in the discussions of the subject by Ariste and the naive Eugene in Bouhours's *Entretiens d'Ariste et d'Eugene*, and as Ménestrier explains in Part 1 of his *Philosophie des images*, much of this interest among polite and court society was stimulated by the work of several individuals who never actually published this work. Among the seven or eight influential figures he cites are Louis Habert de Montmor, several of whose devices were subsequently published by Le Moyne in his *De l'art des devises*,[57] Monsieur Clément, and various members of the Académie Françoise appointed by Mazarin, with a specific remit to oversee royal devices, including notably Chapelain, Charpentier and Perrault:

> Les Devises doivent leur progrez en ce Royaume à sept ou huit personnes, qui pour n'avoir publié aucun ouvrage sur cette matiere n'ont pas laissé de la rendre illustre par un grand nombre de Devises qu'ils ont faites. L'un est Messire Henry Loüis Habert de Montmor...Il cultivoit l'amitié des sçavans & des personnes d'esprit...Il inspira cet amour des Devises à plusieurs personnes de qualité qui essayerent d'en faire, & les Dames les plus spirituelles en remplirent leurs cabinets.
>
> Si les Devises doivent à Monsieur de Montmor leur rétablissement en France, elles doivent leur progrez & leur éclat à Monsieur Clement Conseiller de la Cour des Aides. Jamais homme n'a eu tant de commerce avec les graces & avec les belles Lettres...Il sçavoit parfaitement l'Art & la Nature des Spectacles; les Ballets qui sont de sa façon & de son invention

---

[56] 'La signification de l'Embleme doit toûjours estre ingenieuse, pour avoir l'agrement, & enseigner avec plaisir.' (p.337)

[57] They appear under the subtitle 'Devises adoptées' (p.457).

sont admirables. Il avoit une Bibliothèque choisie de toutes les Festes & de tous les divertissemens qui se font dans les Cours les plus spirituelles & les plus galantes de l'Europe. Les Princes & les Dames aimoient à l'entendre parler de ces sortes de choses, & luy en confioient la conduite. Il avoit sur tout un talent merveilleux pour les Devises....

Ce sage Ministre [Mazarin] qui s'applique avec tant de soin à tout ce qui peut contribuer à la gloire du Roy, & au bonheur de son Royaume, pour rectifier les Devises, & les revers de Medailles qui se font tous les ans pour conserver la memoire des belles actions du Roy, fit choix de Monsieur l'Abbé de Bourzeys, de M. Chappelain, de M. Charpentier & de Monsieur Perraut de l'Academie Françoise...

(Ménestrier, *La philosophie des images,* Book 1, pp.105-8)

Of these individuals cited by Ménestrier it is interesting that two did produce manuscript treatises on the art of devices. Daniel Russell has identified that of M. Clément in one of the *Recueil Conrart* manuscripts in the Bibliothèque de l'Arsenal, entitled *Regles pour la connoissance des devises*, while Laurence Grove has similarly identified that of Perrault in another manuscript in the Arsenal.[58] Clément's treatise is, as its title suggests, almost exclusively concerned with devices for which it elaborates the usual set of rules and conventions, and it has little to say on the subject of the emblem other than concluding the treatise with the remark that the aim of the emblem is to convey a moral lesson and for this purpose it requires less finesse than the more subtle device.[59] As so often in printed treatises the little treatise which appeared in the 1678 *Mercure Galant*, which Russell reproduces together with the Clément treatise, considers first the device, and then the emblem in contrast to the device, covering much the same ground that we have already seen covered by other theorists, but it makes an interesting comment at the end of the section on the emblem, describing a very different interpretation of the function of the emblem from its usual didactic role, but further pointing out that this is a minority view held by only one man in opposition to the views of all others:

Un sçavant Homme a estimé que l'instruction & la moralité n'estoient pas le

---

[58]   In 'Two seventeenth-century French treatises on the art of the device' (*Emblematica*, 1,1, 1986, pp.79-106) Daniel Russell discusses and reproduces the text of *Regles pour la connoissance des devises, par M...*, *Conseiller en la Cour des Aydes* in Arsenal Ms. 5420, part 1, pp.513-20. Although Russell does not mention this, the treatise also appears in BnF Ms.fr. 11911 (ff.327-30). In this article Russell also reproduces and discusses a *Discours sur les devises, emblesmes, et revers de medailles* published in the 1678 *Mercure Galant, extraordinaire d'octobre* (pp.214-68). In '*Discours sur l'art des devises*: an edition of a previously unidentified and unpublished text by Charles Perrault' (*Emblematica*, 7,1, 1993, pp.99-144) Laurence Grove similarly discusses and reproduces the text of this treatise in Arsenal Ms. 3328, ff.1-46.
[59]   According to Clément the emblem was invented 'pour donner, comme il a esté dit, des préceptes, & des enseignemens de moralité, qui, pour ne rien dissimuler, ne requiérent pas une délicatesse pareille à celle des Devises' (Arsenal Ms. 5420, p.519; art.cit., p.91).

propre de l'Embléme, & qu'il ne diféroit de la Devise que parce que celle-cy a une pensée particuliere pour estre aussi appliquée particulierement à quelque Personne, & que l'Embléme a pour l'ordinaire une pensée universelle & indépendante d'individus déterminez. C'est ainsi qu'il s'explique; mais ce Sçavant est, comme je croy, le seul de cette opinion. Il a tous les autres contre luy, aussi bien que l'usage, suivant lequel ils veulent tous que la moralité soit le propre de l'Embléme, & que par conséquent les plus clairs & qui s'entendent le mieux d'abord, sont toûjours les meilleurs.

> (*Mercure Galant, extraordinaire d'octobre*, 1678, pp.255-6; art.cit, p.103)

This novel interpretation of the emblem as not necessarily having a didactic function is itself interesting, but the further comment about different views about the nature of emblems and devices being exchanged among - in this case learned - society tying in with Ménestrier's comments in the *Philosophie des images* about the interest in emblems and devices both at the level of the *Académie Française* and at the level of court and polite society reflects how widespread this practice of discussing the nature of emblems and devices actually was. Perrault's autobiographical comments at the beginning of his manuscript treatise similarly bear this out, describing differences of opinion being expressed, again in the *Académie Française*, concerning the nature of these fashionable but difficult forms and the rules governing them:

> Lorsque le Roi eut donné la Charge d'Admiral à Monsieur le Comte de Vermandois, je fis pour ce jeune Prince une devise, dont le corps étoit un Alcion naissant, voguant dans son nid sur la mer, avec ce mot, *Et nascens temperat aequor*. Cette devise fut gravée sur les jetons qui se firent pour lui, au commencement de l'année 166 . (sic) et fut trouvée ne convenir pas mal à un Admiral fils du Roi, n'ayant que cinq ans. Cependant un des plus sçavans hommes du siècle, qui avoit fait une étude particulière de l'Art des devises, et qui se vantoit d'avoir lû tous les livres qui en ont traité, y trouva fort à redire, et fit une longue dissertation pour prouver qu'elle péchoit contre les règles principales de ce bel Art. Il lut la dissertation à l'Académie Françoise à la réception d'un Académicien, où il se trouva un grand nombre de sçavans hommes, outre ceux qui la composent. La dissertation, quoique bien écrite, et pleine d'un nombre infini d'eruditions très-curieuses, ne persuada personne, et la devise fut approuvée de toute la compagnie. La première fois que je me rencontrai avec ce sçavant homme que j'honorois extrémement, je ne pus m'empêcher de lui dire avec la liberté académique dont nous usons ensemble: Mr. l'Abbé, la lettre tue, et l'esprit vivifie. Il entendit ce que je voulois lui dire; et il me repondit, Cela est vrai; mais vous avez peché, et contre la lettre, et contre l'esprit de la devise...

> (Arsenal Ms. 3328, ff.1r-2r; art. cit., pp.105-6)

Grove suggests that the unnamed 'sçavant homme' who criticised Perrault's device could have been Ménestrier himself, but was more probably the Abbé de Bourséis, who was among the influential figures named by Ménestrier in his *Philosophie des images*. Certainly, as Judi Loach has pointed out, Ménestrier was in a position of rivalry with his colleagues in the *Académie*, and he disapproved both of what he considered to be their professional incompetence in designing funeral decorations in particular, and of their 'willful lack of respect for antique precedent',[60] whereas Perrault, in contrast, was a leading modernist in the *Querelle des anciens et des modernes*, as is borne out in his strong advocacy in the manuscript *Discours* of the use of vernacular languages (including French) for the mottoes of devices and categorical rejection of the suggestion that Latin is preferable:

> Toutes les Langues bien connuès, comme l'Italienne et l'Espagnole, y sont bonnes, et la Françoise autant que pas une autre, mais la difficulté y est beaucoup plus grande. La devise d'une hirondelle, avec ce mot, *Le froid me chasse*, est aussi agréable et plus galante que toutes celles qui ont jamais été faites en Latin. Il est vrai que les sçavans soutiennent qu'elles sont plus belles en cette Langue; mais j'ose dire qu'ils se trompent.
>
> (Arsenal Ms. 3328, ff.9v-10r; art. cit., p.110)

Not only among the writers of the major theoretical treatises, but also at the level of mauscript treatises such as these, therefore, we see differences of opinion as to what precisely constitutes a device and what constitutes an emblem, and concerning the rules and conventions governing their correct composition, while oral discussion of such questions at the level of both salon and *Académie* was also actively undertaken. Book 6 of Bouhours's *Entretiens d'Ariste et d'Eugene* which is a treatise on devices couched in dialogue form offers a stylised replica of salon discussion. Interest in theory as well as in practice was thus clearly very strong and very widespread, and perhaps the fact that no clear set of definitive rules and conventions, acceptable to everybody without exception, was ever produced to end the discussions is an indicator of the life and vigour of the form which enabled it to recreate and regenerate itself, constantly adapting to changing external constraints. Had a single universally acceptable form been arrived at, that form would surely have quickly died out as an essentially sterile, fixed form, limited in interest and appeal as a result of its own self-imposed rigidity.

Treatises such as we have considered so far, numerous though they are, have all been concerned with generalist emblems and devices. Although Le Moyne, Ménestrier and Bouhours were all Jesuits, they did not by and large discuss the theory behind the more specifically focused Jesuit meditational emblem books in their treatises. The most we find is brief mention of Hugo's *Pia desideria* in Ménestrier's *Art des emblemes où s'enseigne la morale* in the section on *Emblêmes sacrez*. Yet the Jesuit meditational emblem book, and the various other devotional works which were not strictly emblem books, but were emblematic in concept if not in name were important. For the theory behind these, however, it is not to treatises on emblematics that we must look, but rather to treatises on meditation, and above all to Loyola's own

---

[60] See 'Ménestrier's emblem theory', p.328.

Spiritual Exercises, for - as we saw in chapter 6 - it is in this work above all that
Loyola spells out the way in which the soul can make its spiritual pilgrimage via
contemplation, emotion and imagination, with the real or imagined visual stimulus
being in every case the starting point for each meditational exercise. Similarly we do
not find them discussing the theory behind the use of emblematics as a teaching device
in Jesuit colleges, since this also is a specialised area of interest. Such questions are
discussed, but not by and large in such generalist French treatises as those we have
been considering. It is to Jesuit treatises on rhetoric and to the *Ratio studiorum* that we
must look to see the theory behind specifically Jesuit emblematic works.

G. Richard Dimler has devoted several articles to the subject of Jesuit rhetoric,
focusing in particular on the writings of the German Jesuit, Jakob Masen who - like
Ménestrier - also spent some time as a teacher of rhetoric. In *'Imitatio, Innovatio* and
Jesuit emblem theory' he looks at a number of Jesuit textbooks on rhetoric, including
Masen's *Ars nova argutiarum*,[61] and also at the *Ratio studiorum* to show the
progressive movement towards greater emphasis on *inventio* and *elocutio* and to the
development of the *stylus argutus*, associated with brevity and ingenuity, into which
style the emblem clearly fits. In 'Jakob Masen's *Imago Figurata*: from theory to
practice'[62] he analyses Masen's general theories on symbolism and its use in rhetoric,
while in 'Jakob Masen's critique of the *Imago primi saeculi*'[63] he focuses more
narrowly on Masen's analysis in his own treatise on imagery, the 1650 *Speculum
imaginum*, of a series of emblems from the *Imago primi saeculi* which had been
published with great ceremony ten years earlier in 1640, to mark the centenary of the
foundation of the Jesuit order.[64]   In his discussion of the figurative image Masen
analyses the relationship between the *res significans* and the *res significata*, which, as
usual, he explains must be a relationship of similitude, and he uses a selection of
emblems from the self-aggrandising monument which is the *Imago primi saeculi
Societatis Iesu*, to demonstrate the various possible patterns that this relationship can
take, ranging from clear similarity to indirect allusion to direct opposition, and to
what Masen calls *alienatio* in which 'there are not merely opposite qualities in the
signifier and significant but they come from ontologically diverse areas where the
viewer can discover no natural relationship'.[65]   As Dimler remarks in 'Jakob Masen's

---

[61]   In Gyorgy Szonyi, ed., *European Iconography East and West*, pp.209-22. J. Masen, *Ars
nova eruditae et honestae recreationis, in duas partes divisa. Prima est epigrammatum, altera
inscriptionum argutarum, autore R.P. Jacobo Masenio...editio secunda*, Cologne, J.A.
Kinchius, 1660, 12°.

[62]   *Emblematica*, 6,2, 1992, pp.283-306.

[63]   In Marc van Vaeck and John Manning, eds, *The Jesuits and the Emblem Tradition*, pp.279-
95.

[64]   *Imago primi saeculi Societatis Iesu a Provincia Flandro-Belgica eiusdem Societatis
repraesentata*, Antwerp, B. Moretus (Officina Plantiniana), 1640, folio; J. Masen, *Speculum
imaginum veritatis occultae, exhibens symbola, emblemata, hieroglyphica, aenigmata, omni,
tam materiae, quam formae varietate, exemplis simul, ac praeceptis illustratum. Anno 1650.
Quo Romanus orbis Iubilabat. Authore R.P.Iacobo Masen, è Soc. Iesu*, Cologne, J.A. Kinchius,
1664, 8°.

[65]   'Jakob Masen's critique of the *Imago primi saeculi*', p.282.

Imago figurata: from theory to practice' it is interesting and surprising that Masen consistently seeks his examples in the *Imago primi saeculi* and 'takes little notice of the profound use of Jesuit spirituality and theology in the emblem books produced by his fellow Jesuits Hugo, Drexel and Sucquet'.[66] While he does discuss other Jesuit meditational works based on biblical or devotional pictures, such as Nadal's *Adnotationes et meditationes* or Sucquet's *Via vitae aeternae* or Jan David's *Duodecim specula*, Masen considers these to be unsatisfactory since their meaning is too obvious and fully worked, and they lack the appeal of the esoteric or ingenious. Only a more conventionally structured emblem book like the *Imago primi saeculi* with its short verses and absence of substantial prose gloss fulfils his criteria of ingenuity and brevity.

In her article on the use of emblematics and other symbolic imagery in the Jesuit school curriculum,[67] as well as analysing the extent to which emblematics was actually taught within the main curriculum, as opposed to featuring in less formal out-of-hours teaching, Judi Loach also examines the rationale for incorporating emblematics into the teaching of rhetoric. The basic academic curriculum which was to be followed in all Jesuit colleges was laid down in the *Ratio studiorum* which was originally drafted in the 1580s,[68] at the instigation of Aquaviva, then General of the Society, and produced in a definitive version in 1599. The *Ratio studiorum* set out the subjects to be studied at each stage of the three-cycle educational programme with, as Judi Loach remarks, the stress in the first cycle being laid on 'developing skills in *imagination* and *mémoire*, whereas the second cycle was preoccupied with similarly developing skills in *jugement* and *entendement*' in preparation for the study of theology in the third and final cycle.[69] It is in the first cycle that rhetoric takes its place, as the art of persuasion, and the images or ornaments of rhetoric which are to be used to render the argument pleasing and thus persuasive, are commonly the images and symbols of emblematics.

We come back here, in a sense, to the theoretical treatises on emblematics and the philosophy of images generally that we considered earlier, since although Ménestrier does not relate his theories directly to the teaching of rhetoric in the schools, any more than does Jakob Masen, the connection is clearly there, and it is not insignificant that both Masen and Ménestrier were at one time teachers of rhetoric. But having returned to the theoretical treatises on emblematics it is now time to compare these with reality, to see the extent to which the actual practitioners of emblems and devices actually conform to the rules as laid down by the theorists. To an extent we know already that

---

[66] 'Jakob Masen's *Imago figurata* from theory to practice', p.288.

[67] 'The teaching of emblematics and other symbolic imagery by Jesuits within town colleges in seventeenth- and eighteenth-century France'.

[68] *Ratio atque institutio studiorum, per sex patres ad id iussu R.P. Praepositi Generalis deputatos conscripta*, Rome, 'In collegio Societatis Iesu', 1586, 8°.

[69] 'The teaching of emblematics...', p.170. Judi Loach further comments on the parallel between the mental progression outlined here and the similar mental progression of the Jesuit meditant: 'It seems more than merely coincidental that the three stages devised by these Jesuit educators parallel Ignatius' three levels of meditation, or contemplation: imagining, remembering and understanding.' (art.cit., p.170)

it would not be possible for them to do so totally, since we have seen that the theorists themselves were frequently not in agreement over what is and is not acceptable. Indicative of this lack of agreement and of the heat of feeling which it provoked is the fact that Ménestrier was inspired to compose a treatise running to over two hundred pages, under the title *La devise du Roy justifiée*, to prove that Louis XIV's sun device, *Nec pluribus impar*, did not in his view break any of the rules. He identifies twelve key rules which he solemnly elaborates in order to demonstrate that none of them are being contravened by this device. Similarly Perrault's manuscript *Discours sur l'art des devises* opens with a description of the disproportionate disapproval which he incurred over the device which he designed for Louis XIV's natural son, Louis de Bourbon, Duc de Vermandois.[70] One of the core points discussed repeatedly by the theorists is the distinction between emblem and device. On the face of it the distinction between the two forms should be evident, since the theorists insist that although both forms use the combination of word and image, their object in so doing is quite different. Devices are person-specific, whereas emblems are universal in their application; emblems seek to teach a lesson, whereas devices do not; in order to teach that lesson effectively emblems aim for clarity, whereas devices seek to offer an intellectual challenge or puzzle.[71] Thus although we may well find the same visual image being used in both an emblem and a device, we should expect the accompanying text itself to be rather different in the two forms, and likewise the relationship between figure and text to be different in the two forms. Since the emblem aims for clarity its text should be easily understandable, and thus may well be in the vernacular for ease of comprehension. Although it should ideally be short, it should be not so short as to pose a challenge to understanding, whereas Giovio's rules make it clear that in the interests of offering an intellectual challenge the text of the device should comprise no more than two or three words, and furthermore these should not be in the familiar native language.[72]

   With such basic criteria for emblem and device, there should be little room for ambiguity between the two forms, and by and large in the sixteenth century this was in fact the case.[73] Alciato's emblems were always thus entitled both in the original Latin

---

[70] See Laurence Grove, '*Discours sur l'art des devises*: an edition of a previously unidentified and unpublished text by Charles Perrault' pp.105-7.

[71] To quote Ménestrier again: 'La devise n'est que l'image des desseins & des entreprises que nous formons'; 'Tout Emblême est donc aujourd'huy une espece d'enseignement mis en image, pour regler la conduite des hommes'; 'C'est le propre des Emblêmes de rendre intelligibles les choses les plus difficiles, parce que c'est le propre des Emblêmes d'enseigner. Il n'en est pas de même des Devises, des Hieroglyfiques, & des Symboles, qui ont presque toûjours quelque chose de mysterieux & de caché, que tout le monde ne penetre pas.' (*L'art des emblemes ou s'enseigne la morale*, pp.3 and 15).

[72] As Giovio explains, the *mot* 'veut estre communement d'une autre langue diverse au parler de celuy qui fait la devise, à fin que le sentiment en soit quelque peu plus couvert...veut encores le mot estre brief...de sorte qu'estant de deux ou trois parolles il est tresconvenable.' (*Dialogue des devises d'armes et d'amours*, b1v).

[73] I am grateful to the editors of *Emblematica* for permission to use in the following pages some material already published in my article 'When is it a device and when is it an emblem: theory and practice (but mainly the latter) in 16th- and 17th-century France' (*Emblematica*,

and in the various French translations, while native French writers of emblems like La Perrière, Corrozet, Aneau, Guéroult, Coustau or Bèze similarly used the term in their preliminaries and in their main text if not always on their title page. As for devices, Paradin compiled a straightforward collection of these in 1551, and when he produced a revised version in 1557, with short prose glosses added to each device, these additional glosses did not change the nature of the actual devices themselves. When three years later the publisher Guillaume Roville produced a version of Giovio's and Simeoni's devices in which each individual device was accompanied by a short verse in French, making them look structurally indistinguishable from emblems, he nevertheless did not call them emblems, but rather avoided the issue by using the neutral phrase '*Tetrastiques faictz sur les devises*'.[74] Only with the first edition of Georgette de Montenay's Christian emblem book do we find for the first time ambiguity of terminology, in that she uses both words together in her title, *Emblemes, ou devises chrestiennes*. There is no obvious reason why she does this, and indeed it is only in the title to the first edition that the word *devise* is included. In her dedication of the work to Jeanne d'Albret, Montenay uses the word 'embleme' throughout, and not the word 'devise', and in all subsequent editions of the work the word 'devise' is dropped from the title.[75] Montenay's collection of Christian emblems is firmly moralising in intent, and although highly decorative visually, it is not (and does not attempt to be) an intellectually challenging work. The term 'embleme' is a much more appropriate term than 'devise' to describe Montenay's creation. The writer herself gives no indication as to why she used the word 'devise', but a possible suggestion might be that she does so because for the first time in an emblem book her mottoes, encased in decorative scrolls, are actually incorporated into the copper engraved figures, in a manner similar to that of collections of devices published in Lyon a few years earlier by Guillaume Roville. The effect of incorporating the motto into the actual engraved figure, rather than having it printed typographically above the woodcut figure as in other, earlier, emblem books, is to underline the essential inseparability of the two elements of figure and *mot*, both produced by one single process of copperplate engraving and impossible to reproduce the one without the other since they form part of the same copperplate. In contrast, the verse passage *is* separable from the other two elements, since it is printed typographically, and thus independently of the engraved figure and *mot*. Thus it is possible that Montenay used the phrase '*Emblemes, ou devises chrestiennes*' to denote the dual nature of the work - a collection of emblems if the combination of engraved figure (including *mot*) and typographically printed verse is seen as a single item, but a collection of devices if only the copperplate engraved figure and *mot* are regarded.

Other than with Montenay, however, the position in the sixteenth century is not on the whole a complicated one. But in the seventeenth century, in contrast, the situation becomes more complex, as on the one hand much more theoretical writing is

---

7,2, 1993, pp.239-57).

[74] *Tetrastiques faictz sur les devises du Seigneur Paulo Jovio, et de Messire Gabriel Simeon, pour servir en verrieres, chassis, galeries et tableaux, ainsi qu'il plaira au lecteur de les accommoder.*

[75] It *does* appear in the 1620 La Rochelle edition, but this is a reissue of the 1571 edition.

produced than in the previous century on the nature of emblems and devices, and on
the other hand both emblems and devices become, as we have seen, increasingly
popular, making their influence felt in many different domains, including notably
chivalry, political propaganda, religious devotion and education. In the domain of
chivalry, perhaps not surprisingly, devices in general continue to be described as such.
In Vulson's *Vray theatre d'honneur et de chevalerie ou le miroir heroique de la
noblesse*, described in the full title as containing '*les triomphes, les tournois, les
joustes, les pas, les emprises ou entreprises, les armes, les combats à la barriere, les
carrosels, les courses de bague & de la quintaine, les machines, les chariots de
triomphe, les cartels, les devises...*' he gives an account of the *carrousel* held in the
Place Royale in 1612 to celebrate the double marriage alliance of Louis XIII with
Anne d'Autriche and his sister Elisabeth with the future Philip IV of Spain, including
in this a description of the devices worn by the various participants. Similarly Perrault
describes a *carrousel* staged fifty years later by Louis XIV, in his *Courses de testes et
de bague, faites par le Roy et par les princes et seigneurs de sa cour, en l'année
M.DC.LXII*, including in it a detailed description of the *Devises des chefs et des
chevalliers des quadrilles*. In the same style also is Gissey's *Emblesmes et devises du
Roy, des princes et seigneurs qui l'accompagnerent en la Calvacate Royale, et course
de bague que Sa Majesté fit au Palais Cardinal 1656*, giving an account of an earlier
carrousel staged by the then eighteen-year old Louis XIV, and describing the devices
worn by the participants. But here we do encounter a problem, since - like Montenay
nearly a century earlier - Gissey uses both the words 'embleme' and 'devise' in his
title, although unlike Montenay Gissey does offer an explanation of why he uses the
two terms, making a distinction between the two which is a perfectly valid one, albeit
not one which is made elsewhere:

> Au reste, quoy que vous trouviez en ce Discours le nom d'Emblême ou de
> Devise, ne croyez pas que j'en use indifferemment. Car par le mot
> d'Emblême j'entens la Peinture qui en compose le corps, & par la Devise qui
> en est l'ame, je ne pretens proprement parler que de l'inscription.
> (Gissey, *Les emblesmes ou devises du Roy*, A2r-v)

In such accounts as these, while the devices which are described may well be
accompanied by further explanatory material in prose, this material is clearly distinct
from the actual device itself, in the same way that the prose glosses which Paradin
added to his devices in the mid sixteenth century were also clearly distinct from the
devices themselves, with their classic combination of figure and *mot*. In the more
lavishly produced seventeenth-century accounts of such chivalric celebrations, the full
device is reproduced, while in others only the motto appears. But this distinction is a
function of resource, rather than of philosophy, since it is obviously cheaper to
produce a purely descriptive text without illustration than it is to produce an edition
including a large number of engraved figures. On the whole, therefore, within the area
of chivalry devices remain what they always had been. But in other fields than that of
chivalry the picture is less clearcut, as devices become ever more complex structures,
accompanied often not just by prose glosses and commentaries, but also increasingly

by explanatory commentaries in verse also, and in such cases the distinction between device and emblem becomes very blurred, particularly when these verses include a moralising or otherwise didactic element.

A particularly interesting case of the blurring of frontiers is afforded by the history of the set of devices designed to adorn the borders of the royal tapestries of the Four Seasons and the Four Elements. As originally conceived, these were classic devices comprising figure and Latin motto, each encased in its own frame, and each relating to whichever season or element was the central theme of the particular tapestry it adorned, which in turn also related to the central theme of all the tapestries, which was, of course, the glory of Louis XIV. Yet, as we saw in chapter 7, when these were reproduced subsequently, first in manuscript form, and thereafter in various printed versions, the devices were each accompanied not just by a prose commentary, but also by a madrigal composed by Perrault and other members of the *Petite Académie*, and in this expanded form they take on a quite different character. As devices around the borders of the tapestry they conveyed their message of royal greatness indirectly, via allusion and similitude. Thus in the Water tapestry an ocean represented Louis's piety, a fountain his magnanimity, a dolphin his *valeur* and a river his *bonté*. The river was accompanied by the motto *Facit omnia laeta*. In theory this device could refer to anyone, but the fact that it forms part of the large tapestry in which all elements relate to Louis XIV, gives it a much more specific focus. Its context makes clear that it alludes indirectly to the king. Yet when the device is taken away from its physical context of the overall tapestry, and set in a manuscript collection accompanied by Perrault's madrigal, its royal association is no longer so apparent, and it is susceptible of being read as an emblem with a universally applicable moral lesson:

> Loin de moy tout perit, tout languit de foiblesse,
> Et seiche de tristesse
> Faute de mon secours
> Prés de moy tout fleurit, tout profite & s'avance,
> Et l'on me voit porter la joye & l'abondance
> Par tout où je porte mon cours.   (Bailly ms., ed. Grivel and Fumaroli, p.52)

It is only the accompanying prose commentary which makes clear that this is not intended as a generally moralising emblem but that the beneficent river must be seen quite specifically as representing the equivalent beneficence of Louis XIV:

> Pour la Bonté dans la piece de l'element de l'eau. Un Grand Fleuve, avec ce mot *Facit omnia laeta*. Les grands Fleuves portent l'abondance & la fertilité partout où ils passent; De mesme les bons Princes tels que sa Majesté, font le bonheur & la richesse des peuples qui leur obeïssent.
> (Bailly ms., ed. Grivel and Fumaroli, p.51)

Similarly the device of the halcyon building its nest in the middle of the sea with the motto *Miratur natura silens* in the borders of the Summer tapestry is related indirectly by means of its physical context to Louis XIV. In this tapestry it is used to represent Louis's favourite summer preoccupation which was his ambitious building programme. But like the river device, when it appears in the manuscript collected anthology of devices from the two sets of tapestries, and again thereafter in printed editions, the accompanying madrigal (again by Perrault) similarly confers on it a more universal emblematic application, rather than the person-specific interpretation which it carried in its original tapestry form:

> Lorsque de l'Edifice où je dois habiter,
> Et que le temps doit respecter
> J'entreprens la structure à nulle autre pareille
> La Nature s'impose une profonde Paix
> Pour mieux considerer l'incroyable merveille
> Du Bastiment que je me fais.   (Bailly ms., ed. Grivel and Fumaroli, p.86)

and the person-specific interpretation relating it to Louis XIV is only re-established by the prose commentary which at the same time explains the background to the halcyon symbol:

> Pour les Bastimens, divertissement. Dans la piece de la saison de l'Esté. Un Alcion bastissant son nid sur la Mer qui se tient calme pour ne pas troubler un bastiment si merveilleux, avec ce mot *Miratur natura silens*. Pour exprimer la beauté des Bastimens du Roy qui est telle qu'il semble que toute l'Europe ne se soit tenue en Paix lorsque sa Majesté a recommencé d'y faire travailler, que pour en admirer mieux la structure surprenante & incomparable.   (Bailly ms., ed. Grivel and Fumaroli, p.85)

In Bailly's manuscript, as in all the printed editions of this collection of devices from the tapestries of the Four Seasons and the Four Elements, the word 'devise' is nevertheless retained in the title, despite the fact that the addition of universally applicable moralising verses makes the original devices much more akin to emblems. We see here a good example of the increasing ambiguity between the two forms, as described by Ménestrier in particular.[76]

   In the domain of chivalry and royal propaganda, therefore, we find that the word 'devise' is commonly retained, even in cases where the structure and form of the device and the function to which it is put make it more akin to an emblem. In the domain of religion, however, we find a rather different pattern. In the field of religious devotion it is the word 'embleme' which is most commonly used, presumably because of the didactic character of the devotional emblem. In some cases, such as the emblematic works of Richeome or Perrot de la Sale, the issue of terminology is

---

[76] As late as 1723 we find in Le Jay's *Vertus royales mises en devises et presentées au Roy à sa majorité* dedicated to Louis XV, another example of the intellectually challenging element being removed from a series of devices aimed at glorifying the monarch by the inclusion of a series of explanatory French verses (and also by the inclusion of a French translation of the Latin mottoes, thereby further simplifying the text).

avoided by the use of the neutral phrase 'tableaux sacrez', but both Berthod and Chesneau, for example, use the phrase 'emblemes sacrez', while Callot similarly describes both his bilingual *Lux claustri* and *Vita beatae Mariae virginis* as 'representée(s) par figures emblematiques'. Berthod's emblems are wholly conventional emblems, often based on familiar emblematic symbols, and comprising figure, motto and explanatory, moralising verse, onto which further meditational apparatus is grafted, and it is not at all surprising to see them thus entitled. Callot's *Vita beatae Mariae virginis* is slightly more problematic in that, as we saw in chapter 6, not all the various editions of this work included French verses. In the editions which, like the *Lux claustri*, do include a short explanatory French verse, to accompany the figure, motto and Latin distich, the emblematic character of the work is apparent, like that of Berthod. But in versions where the figure is accompanied only by the Latin motto, or by the Latin motto and distich, not only do the emblems look visually much more like devices, but the absence of French verses offering a universally applicable gloss also leaves them with a stronger person-specific orientation, more akin to that of the device than the emblem.

In the field of religious education, in contrast, it is on the whole the word 'devise' which is more commonly used, rather than 'embleme', regardless of whether or not the basic combination of figure and motto are accompanied by a passage of explanatory verse, although here again there is ambiguity of practice. As we saw in chapter 4, the composition of emblems and devices formed part of the educational training offered in Jesuit schools as a means of developing mental agility, creativity and ingenuity in the witty exploitation of the wisdom of the best authors. Such emblems and devices could be created either for public display on open days as in the case of the Brussels *affixiones*, or for presentation to a visiting dignitary, as in the case of the *Devises presentees à Monseigneur de Mascon* in 1682, or to commemorate a particularly notable event such as the royal wedding of the *Dauphin* with Marie-Anne Christine of Bavaria in 1680 celebrated by the pupils of the Jesuit college in Paris, or the peace treaty of 1659 celebrated by the pupils of the Collège de la Trinité in Lyon. In the case of the celebration of the royal wedding of 1680 the boys produced a series of unillustrated Latin emblems, which included substantial verses, but in this collection the question of terminology is neatly sidestepped by the use of the all-embracing word 'symbolum' rather than either 'embleme' or 'devise'. In Ménestrier's account of the contribution to the peace celebrations by the Collège de la Trinité pupils in his *Resjoüissances de la paix* he describes the combination of device plus explanatory verse that the pupils composed as 'emblemes',[77] but conversely his fellow Jesuit Gabriel-François Le Jay uses the word 'devise' to describe the same combination of device plus explanatory verse in his 1686 *Triomphe de la religion sous Louis le Grand*. In this work he gives an account of ceremony for the opening of the new school year at the Collège de Louis le Grand in Paris, for which the overall theme was Louis's successful suppression of heresy. As part of this ceremony devices

---

[77]   'Le sujet des Emblemes de Rhetorique est la gloire des Sciences restablie par la Paix...Le Sujet des Humanistes est l'utilité des Arts dans la Paix representée par onze Emblemes...Les Troisiemes ont pour sujet les Vertus tributaires à la Paix, qui les a restituées.' (pp.14-18)

comprising figure and Latin motto were affixed around the walls of the hall representing the king's achievement, but when these were reproduced in printed form in Le Jay's account, they were acompanied by Latin and French verses, and by a French prose gloss, all of which enhance their universally applicable didactic character, and yet nevertheless Le Jay still calls them 'devises'.

As Ménestrier rightly stated, the distinction in actual practice between emblem and device is quite often unclear in the seventeenth century, despite the emphatically expressed views of many of the theorists concerning the rules and conventions governing the two forms, and their ostensibly different aims and philosophy. In some areas such as chivalry, which is, of course, the area in which devices first came into being, the original sense of the word is retained. In the domain of chivalry devices remain by and large what they always were: a striking combination of figure and pithy saying designed to communicate in a witty and allusive way the personal hopes, aspirations or intentions of the bearer of that device. This remains broadly true also when devices are used in the ephemeral architecture of triumphal entries, or in more permanent architectural form when carved onto bridges, columns, facades of buildings, or painted onto ceilings or walls, since in such cases the physical context does not allow for additional verbiage. When such devices are also reproduced subsequently in printed or manuscript form, often as part of a published account of the triumphal entry or of a description of the architecture of a particular building, in many cases the original basic device is accompanied by supporting explanatory or descriptive material which may be in prose, in verse, or in both, but since such supporting material is no more than an adjunct to the essential device which itself remains coherent and self contained, it is not surprising to see the word 'devise' retained. But where devices become used increasingly in didacticising or moralising contexts which are ostensibly the domain of the emblem rather than the device, then the temptation to add explanatory verses to the device is evidently very strong. When, furthermore, these verses move away - as they often do - from an expression of the person-specific implications of the device to a more general, universal application, then such devices do indeed become much more akin to emblems, and are frequently thus entitled.

The seventeenth century was a century which took great interest in elaborating literary rules and conventions which could then form the basis for much discussion and indeed heated argument among the theorists and critics as to the extent to which particular works did or did not conform to the established norms. The strong views expressed by the various seventeenth-century theorists on the nature of the emblem and the device, and their occasional expressions of outrage when a particular work, or a particular device, or a particular emblem appears not to conform to the rules and conventions which they hold so dear, should not therefore surprise us, any more than we should be surprised by the relative looseness with which the various key terms are used in reality, in contrast to the tautly formulated definitions elaborated by the theorists. It is important to look, as we have done in this chapter, at the various theories adduced about the nature of emblems and devices, but it would be naive to expect that theory and practice would dovetail neatly together, as indeed this chapter has shown not to be the case. It has been with this awareness that in the course of the earlier chapters we have not sought to establish too clearcut definitions which could only have led to artificial distinctions and exclusions, but have rather opted to use the terms 'emblem' and 'device' in the relatively loose way that the practitioners, if not the theorists themselves, used them.

CONCLUSION

In the course of this study we have traced a number of different trends in the development and diversification of the emblem in France as it evolves from the sixteenth century into the seventeenth century. France was effectively the birthplace of the emblem, and for the earliest decades of its existence the phrase 'emblem book' and the phrase 'French emblem book' can be seen as virtually synonymous. Only in the latter decades of the sixteenth century did France lose its early virtual monopoly of the emblem, but nevertheless by this stage a strong French tradition had grown up, and it is not surprising to see significant elements of that earlier French tradition continuing to manifest themselves in the emblems produced in France in the seventeenth century. But at the same time with the increasing development of the emblematic form in other parts of Europe, additional influences began to affect the development of the French emblem, so that it is no longer so much the purely national phenomenon that it had been in the sixteenth century. With the increasing internationalisation of the emblem form we see the popularity in France not just of indigenous French emblem books, but also of works originating elsewhere in Europe. From Spain, for example, came Saavedra's immensely influential *Prince chrestien et politique* while from Germany came Friedrich's *Emblemes nouveaux*, but the most marked impact in France came from the Netherlands, and it is for this reason that an entire chapter has been devoted to this subject. But as well as being affected by increasing influence from elsewhere in Europe, the evolution of the French emblem in the seventeenth century was also affected considerably by changing social, cultural and political circumstances within France itself.

What we have seen in the course of this study is no sudden dramatic change as the sixteenth century gives way to the seventeenth, but rather a gradual change of focus both in structure and in content, in the course of which some important features nevertheless remain unchanged. As we saw in chapters 2 and 3, certain emblematic traditions whose roots lie clearly in the sixteenth century continue to flourish in the seventeenth century. Visually the copperplate engravings of the seventeenth century emblem book look very different from the woodcut figures which graced most sixteenth-century emblem books, and structurally the increasing use of (often substantial) prose commentaries likewise change the physical appearance of many emblem books, as also, and more importantly, the chemistry of their effect upon the reader. Yet the strong moral and didactic aims which lay at the heart of the emblem in the sixteenth century remain unchanged in the seventeenth century, as indeed do many of the themes exploited in the seventeenth-century emblem to achieve these aims. In the case of the device, we see a similar continuation of many traditional themes, but an even greater diversity of structure and above all of purpose to which these traditional themes are applied.

Where the sixteenth-century French emblem book was for the most part generalist in its purpose, we see a significant difference emerging in the seventeenth century with the increasing exploitation of the emblem book for more narrowly defined or specific purposes. Where we see the biggest differences between seventeenth-century emblem and device and sixteenth-century emblem and device is in three domains in particular, all of which are clearly inspired by changing social and political trends within France. These are the domains of religion, education and political propaganda. Emblems were already being used for religious purposes in the sixteenth century, notably by two Protestant writers Georgette de Montenay and Théodore de Bèze, but as we have seen in chapter 6 the emblem came to be exploited to a far greater extent in the seventeenth century by the other side, as a powerful tool of the Counter-Reformation. To this end it was used by a number of different orders, but particularly heavily by the Jesuits, and we have seen how important Ignatius of Loyola considered such visual stimuli to the imagination as an initial stage in the meditational process. But the emblem was not used only for devotional purposes by the Jesuits. As we have seen in chapter 4, together with its sister form, the device, it was also exploited quite differently for educational purposes, being used not simply to teach a moral lesson, but rather to teach rhetorical skills to the pupils in Jesuit colleges. The third domain in which emblems and devices came to play such a major role in France - that of political propaganda and royal glorification - was not a new phenomenon in the seventeenth century, but the extent of its use and the increasing complexity and lavishness of its use in the seventeenth century, particularly under Louis XIV, is particularly striking. Notable also is the way in which increasingly in the seventeenth century the *Imprimerie royale* was charged with producing grandiose folio accounts of particular festivities demonstrating the glory of the French king which were then themselves used as further political propaganda both within France and elsewhere in Europe.

Associated with the increasing complexity and sophistication in the applied use of emblems and devices is the significant trend towards producing treatises which are not just theoretical but also practical, on the correct or appropriate use of emblematic material for particular architectural purposes, whether permanent or ephemeral. Certainly the proliferation in the seventeenth century of theoretical treatises on the art of emblems and devices reflects a wider cultural interest in the rules and conventions governing other literary forms than these alone, but a writer like Ménestrier is particularly interesting in that his expertise covers not just the theory but also the applied practice.

Although emblems and devices play an important part in the cultural life of France in the seventeenth century as they did also in the sixteenth century, we do not find, by and large, in the seventeenth century, any more than we did in the sixteenth that major writers become directly involved to any large extent in their production.

Although they are undoubtedly a literary form with a highly respectable classical ancestry, as both sixteenth- and seventeenth-century writers and theorists insist, emblems are not perceived as high literature in the seventeenth century any more than they were in the sixteenth. Just as in the sixteenth century we did not find emblems composed by notable writers such as Clément Marot in the first half or Ronsard or Du Bellay in the second half, so also we do not find writers of the calibre of Racine or Molière composing emblems or devices in the seventeenth century, even though the device at least does become a form approved by the *Académie*. Nevertheless, by and large the only seventeenth-century writer of distinction who practised the art is Charles Perrault, whose lasting distinction undoubtedly owes more to his fairy tales than to his contribution to emblematics.

The large market for emblem books in the seventeenth century and the remarkably enduring popularity of certain works in particular is very striking (and it is in order to demonstrate this that the Bibliography does not cite just one edition of any particular work, but gives a list of other editions, as well as the one actually used). Certainly no other work enjoyed anything like the extraordinarily enduring popularity of Alciato's original emblem book, which continued to run through edition after edition in both Latin and French a century after it first appeared. But many works - often on the face of it somewhat unlikely ones, like Albert Flamen's *Devises et emblesmes d'amour moralisez*, as well as more obviously attractive one like Vaenius's Horatian emblems - were popular enough to run through several editions, sometimes extending over several decades, reflecting the extent to which their universally applicable subject matter did not quickly become old-fashioned. But above all the seventeenth-century market for emblem books and generalist collections of devices was to a large extent an international market, with the significant development of the trend towards the polyglot book, a trend already started in the late sixteenth century by the publishers of Montenay's emblem book, but developed to a far higher degree in the seventeenth century. Not only did the proliferation of polyglot editions of emblems and devices open up a much wider European market, but so also did the move towards international publication, as increasingly we find emblematic works in French being published not just in France, but also in Brussels, in Antwerp or in Frankfurt.

As increasing levels of literacy led to greater demand, so we find a much greater diversity of emblem books being produced in the seventeenth century than in the preceding century. Not only are many more of them published, covering a wider range of material and taking a wider range of different forms, but also catering for a wider range of different types of reading public, with likewise different spending powers. Tantalisingly we still know far too little about actual readership, but nevertheless the evidence of what was printed gives clear indication of a great diversity of readership being targeted, ranging from luxury large-format editions at one end of the scale, published by the *Imprimerie royale* and lavishly embellished by numerous full-page engravings by the best artists of the time, and frequently bound in French royal bindings, to much more modest little manuals or pattern books for craftsmen like Nicolas Verrien's *Livre curieux et utile pour les sçavans, et artistes* at the other end of the scale, with many other levels in between.

In the title of my earlier study of the sixteenth-century French emblem book I described the form as 'a decorative and useful genre'. While that description could still be applied to the seventeenth-century French emblem, it would not do justice to the much increased number of roles that the form came to play, nor yet to the much greater extent to which it was exploited in these various roles. Emblems and devices came to be used in the seventeenth century in court celebrations and joyous entries, in ephemeral architecture as in permanent architecture, and in other forms of applied plastic arts on a far larger scale than had been the case in the sixteenth century. In addition the increasingly important role which they came to play in the domains of education, religion and political propaganda makes their contribution to seventeenth-century French society much more significant than the modest phrase 'decorative and useful' might suggest. The French emblem in the seventeenth century was above all a richly diverse form with a wide range of practical applications, enabling it not only to make a significant contribution to its own national culture, but also to play its part in an increasingly cross-European culture.

BIBLIOGRAPHY

Locations are not given here except in the case of rare works which are available in neither the Bibliothèque nationale de France nor the British Library. In the case of such works no more than, at most, three locations are given. (See note at the end of this Bibliography for a key to locations.) For a full list of known locations of sixteenth and seventeenth-century emblem books see *BFEB*. Full titles are normally given in this Bibliography, except in the case of well-known works which are listed in Volume 1 of *BFEB*, for some of which a shortened title is given here. In the case of rare works which are available in neither the BnF nor the BL a full title is given. *BFEB* references are given for all works included in Volume 1.

I PRINTED WORKS FROM THE FIFTEENTH, SIXTEENTH, SEVENTEENTH AND EIGHTEENTH CENTURIES

i) AUTHORS

Aesop: *Les fables d'Esope phrygien, mises en ryme francoise, avec la vie dudit Esope extraite de plusieurs autheurs par M. Anthoine du Moulin Masconnois*, Lyon, J. de Tournes and G. Gazeau, 1547, 16°.

— *Ibid.*, Lyon. J. de Tournes and G. Gazeau, 1549, 16°.

— *Ibid.*, Lyon, J. de Tournes and G. Gazeau, 1551, 16°.

— *Ibid.*, Lyon, Jean II de Tournes, 1583, 16°.

— See Audin, Prieur de Thermes.

— See Baudoin, Jean.

— See Corrozet, Gilles.

— See Du Fresne, Raphael.

Alciato, Andrea: *Dn. Andreae Alciati iureconsulti clarissimi de verborum significatione, libri quatuor. Eiusdem in tractatum eius argumenti veterum iureconsultorum, commentaria. Ex ultima autoris recognitione*, Lyon, V. de

Portonariis, 1536, 8°.

— *Viri clarissimi D. Andree Alciati iurisconsultiss. Mediol. ad D. Chonradum Peutingerum Augustanum, iurisconsultum emblematum liber*, Augsburg, H. Steyner, 1531, 8°.

— *Andreae Alciati emblematum libellus*, Paris, C. Wechel, 1534, 8°. (*BFEB*, F.001)

— *Livret des emblemes de maistre Andre Alciat, mis en rime francoyse, et presente à mon seigneur ladmiral de France*, Paris, C. Wechel, 1536, 8°. (*BFEB*, F.005)

— *Andreae Alciati emblematum libellus, nuper in lucem editus*, Venice, Aldus, 1546, 8°.

— *Les emblemes de M. Andre Alciat, traduits en ryme Françoise par Jean le Fevre*, Lyon, J. de Tournes, 1548, 16°. (Huntington; Wolfenbüttel). (*BFEB*, F.022)

— *Emblemata Andreae Alciati iurisconsulti clarissimi*, Lyon, M. Bonhomme and G. Roville, 1548, 8°. (*BFEB*, F.020)

— *Emblemata Andreae Alciati iurisconsulti clarissimi. Locorum communium ordine, ac indice, novisque posteriorum eiconibus aucta*, Lyon, M. Bonhomme and G. Roville, 1548, 16°. (Glasgow UL; New York). (*BFEB*, F.021)

— *Emblemes d'Alciat, de nouveau translatez en François vers pour vers jouxte les Latins. Ordonnez en lieux communs, avec briefves expositions, et figures nouvelles appropriées aux derniers emblemes*, Lyon, M. Bonhomme and G. Roville, 1549, 8°. (*BFEB*, F.026)

— *Emblemata D.A. Alciati, denuo ab ipso autore recognita, ac quae desiderabantur, imaginibus locupletata. Accesserunt nova aliquot ab autore emblemata, suis quoque eiconibus insignita*, Lyon, M. Bonhomme and G. Roville, 1550, 8°. (*BFEB*, F.030)

— *Clarissimi viri D. And. Alciati, emblematum lib. II. Nuper adiectis Seb. Stockhameri Germ. in primum librum succinctis commentariolis*, Lyon, J. de Tournes and G. Gazeau, 1556, 16°. (*BFEB*, F.037)

— *Omnia D. And. Alciati emblemata ad quae singula, praeter concinnas acutasque inscriptiones, lepidas & expressas imagines, ac caetera omnia quae prioribus nostris editionibus cum ad eorum distinctionem, tum ad ornatum & correctionem adhibita continebantur. Nunc primùm perelegentia persubtiliaque adiecta sunt epimythia, quibus emblematum amplitudo, & quaecunque in iis dubia sunt aut obscura tanquam perspicuis illustrantur*, Lyon, M. Bonhomme and G. Roville, 1557, 16°. (Berlin; Wroclaw UL). (*BFEB*, F.038)

— *Toutes les emblemes de M. Andre Alciat, de nouveau translatez en Françoys vers pour vers, jouxte la diction Latine. Et ordonnez en lieux communs, avec sommaires inscriptions, schemes, & briefves expositions epimythiques, selon l'allegorie naturelle, moralle, et historialle. Avec figures nouvelles appropriées aux derniers emblemes envoyées par l'autheur, peu avant son decez, cy devant non imprimées*, Lyon, M. Bonhomme and G. Roville, 1558, 16°. (Arsenal; Glasgow UL). (*BFEB*, F.039)

— *Emblematum clarissimi viri D. Andreae Alciati libri II. In eadem succincta commentariola, nunc multo quàm antea, castigatiora et longe locupletiora, Sebastiano Stockhamero Germano, auctore*, Antwerp, C. Plantin, 1565, 16°.

— *Omnia And. Alciati v.c. emblemata cum luculenta et facili ennaratione, qua cuiusque emblematis origo, mensque autoris explicatur: & obscura vel dubia illustrantur. Per Claudium Minoem Divionensem. Excerpta omnia ex integris eiusdem in eadem emblemata commentariis*, Paris, D. du Pré, 1571, 4°. (*BFEB*, F.049)

— *Omnia Andreae Alciati v.c. emblemata. Adiectis commentariis et scholiis, in quibus emblematum fermè omnium aperta origine, mens auctoris explicatur, et obscura omnia, dubiaque illustrantur. Per Claudium Minoem Divionensem*, Antwerp, C. Plantin, 1573, 16°.

— *Omnia Andreae Alciati v.c. emblemata: cum commentariis quibus emblematum omnium aperta origine, mens auctoris explicatur, et obscura omnia dubiaque illustrantur. Per Claudium Minoem Divionensem. Editio tertia aliis multo locupletior*, Antwerp, C. Plantin, 1581, 8°.

— *Emblemata Andreae Alciati I.C. clariss. Postremo ab autore recognita, vivisque imaginibus artificiosissime illustrata. Adiuncta sunt epimythia quibus, quae obscuriora videbantur sunt declarata*, Frankfurt, N. Bassee, 1583, 8°.

— *Emblemata Andreae Alciati I.C. clariss. Latinogallica, unà cum succinctis argumentis, quibus emblematis cuiusque sententia explicatur. Ad calcem Alciati vita. Les emblemes Latin-François du Seigneur Andre Alciat excellent jurisconsulte. Avec argumens succincts pour entendre le sens de chasque embleme. En fin est la vie d'Alciat. La version Françoise non encore veuë cy devant*, Paris, J. Richer, 1584, 12°. (*BFEB*, F.058)

— *Ibid.*, Paris, J. Richer, 1587, 12°. (Arsenal; Glasgow UL). (*BFEB*, F.059)

— *Omnia Andreae Alciati v.c. emblemata, cum commentariis, quibus emblematum aperta origine mens auctoris explicatur, & obscura omnia, dubiaque illustrantur. Adiectae ad calcem notae posteriores. Per Claud. Minoem, Iurisc.*, Paris, J. Richer, F. Gueffier and E.Vallet, 1589, 8°. (*BFEB*, F.061)

— *Andreae Alciati. v.c. emblemata. Cum Claudii Minois ad eadem commentariis & notis posterioribus. Quibus emblematum omnium aperta origine, mens auctoris explicatur, & obscura omnia dubiaque illustrantur*, Lyon, Heirs of G. Roville, 1600, 8°. (*BFEB*, F.063)

— *Andreae Alciati I. v.c. emblemata. Elucidata doctissimis Claudii Minois commentariis: Quibus additae sunt eiusdem auctoris notae posteriores...Postrema hac editione à mendis quamplurimis, quibus superiores scatebant, omnia repurgata, atque in nitidiorem sensum reducta*, Lyon, Heirs of G. Roville, 1614, 8°. (*BFEB*, F.067)

— *Clariss. viri Dn. Andreae Alciati emblematum libri duo. Aucti & restituti & perelegantibus figuris illustrati. Cum succinctis commentariolis. Additus est index locupletissimus*, Cologny/Geneva, Jean II de Tournes, 1614, 16°. (*BFEB*,

F.066)

— *Ibid.*, Geneva, Jean III de Tournes, 1628, 16°. (Huntington; Wiesbaden). (*BFEB*, F.066)

— *Ibid.*, Geneva, Jean III de Tournes, 1639, 16°. (Glasgow UL; Wiesbaden). (*BFEB*, F.072)

— *Les emblemes de M. André Alciat, traduits en rime Françoise, enrichis de belles figures, & esclarcis par petits commentaires, lesquels expliquent les fables & histoires qui y sont contenues*, Cologny, Jean II de Tournes, 1615, 16°. (Arsenal; Glasgow UL). (*BFEB*, F.068)

— *Ibid.*, Geneva, Jean III de Tournes, 1628, 16°. (Minnesota UL). (*BFEB*, F.068)

— *And. Alciati emblemata, ad quae singula, praeter concinnas inscriptiones, imagines, ac caetera, quae ad ornatum & correctionem adhibita continebantur. Nunc recens adiecta sunt epimythia, quibus emblematum amplitudo & qua in iis dubia sunt, aut obscura, illustrantur*, Lyon, Heirs of G. Roville, 1616, 16°. (Vatican). (*BFEB*, F.069)

— *Ibid.*, Lyon, Heirs of G. Roville, 1626, 16°. (Folger). (*BFEB*, F.071)

— *Omnia Andreae Alciati v.c. emblemata, cum commentariis, quibus emblematum detecta origine dubia omnia, et obscura illustrantur. Per Claud. Minoem I.C. Accesserunt huic editioni Fed. Morelli Profess. Reg. decani corollaria et monita* Paris, J. Richer for F. Gueffier, 1618, 8°. (*BFEB*, F.070)

— *Andreae Alciati emblemata cum commentariis Claudii Minois I.C. Francisci Sanctii Brocensis, et notis Laurentii Pignorii Patavini novissima. Hac editione in continuam unius commentarii seriem congestis, in certas quasdam quasi classes dispositis, et plusquam dimidia parte auctis. Opera et vigiliis Ioannis Thuilii Mariaemontani Tirol. Phil. et Med. D. atque olim in Archiduc Friburg. Brisgoiae Universitate human. liter. professoris ordinarii. Opus copiosa sententiarum, apophthegmatum, adagiorum, fabularum, mythologiarum, hieroglyphicorum, nummorum picturarum et linguarum varietate instructum et exornatum: proinde omnibus antiquitatis et bonarum litterarum studiosis cum primis viris. Accesserunt in fine Federici Morelli professoris regii corollaria et monita, ad eadem emblemata. Cum indice triplici*, Padua, P. Tozzi, 1621, 4°.

— *Ibid.*, Padua, P. Frambotti, 1661, 4°.

— *Emblemata v.c. Andreae Alciati Mediolanensis Iurisconsulti. Cum facili & compendiosa explicatione, qua obscura illustrantur, dubiaque omnia solvuntur, per Claudium Minoem Divionensem. Eiusdem Alciati vita. Editio novissima a mendis expurgata, priorique integritati restituta*, Madrid, O. de Mercede, 1749, 8°.

— *Ibid.*, Madrid, P. Aznar, 1781, 8°.

— *Les emblemes de Maistre Andre Alciat, mis en rime Francoyse*, n.p.n.d. (Lyon, D. de Harsy), 8°. (*BFEB*, F.010)

Amboise, Adrian d': *Discours ou traicté des devises. Où est mise la raison et difference des emblemes, enigmes, sentences & autres. Pris & compilé des cahiers de feu Messire François d'Amboise...par Adrian d'Amboise son fils*, Paris, R. Boutonne, 1620, 8°. (*BFEB*, F.074)

— *Devises royales par Adrian d'Amboise. Au Roy*, Paris, R. Boutonne, 1621, 8°. (*BFEB*, F.073)

Amboise, François d': See Paradin, Claude.

Aneau, Barthélemy: *Imagination poetique, traduicte en vers François, des Latins, & Grecz, par l'auteur mesme d'iceux. Horace en l'art. La poësie est comme la pincture*, Lyon, M. Bonhomme, 1552, 8°. (*BFEB*, F.084)

— *Ibid.*, Lyon, M. Bonhomme, 1556, 16°. (Arsenal). (*BFEB*, F.086)

— *Picta poesis. Ut pictura poesis erit*, Lyon, M. Bonhomme, 1552, 8°. (*BFEB*, F.085)

— *Picta poesis. Ab authore denuò recognita. Ut pictura poesis erit*, Lyon, M. Bonhomme, 1556, 16°. (*BFEB*, F.087)

— *Ibid.*, Lyon, L. and C. Pesnot, 1563/64, 16°. (*BFEB*, F.088)

Arias Montano, Benito: *Humanae salutis monumenta B. Ariae Montani studio constructa et decantata*, Antwerp, C. Plantin, 1571, 8°.

— *Ibid.*, Antwerp, C. Plantin, 1581, 8°.

— *Ibid.*, Antwerp, C. Plantin, 1583, 4°.

— *David, hoc est virtutis exercitatissimae probatum Deo spectaculum, ex David pastoris, militis ducis exulis ac prophetae exemplis: Bened. Aria meditante, Philippo Gallaeo instruente, ad pietatis cultum propositis*, Antwerp, C. Plantin, 1575, 4° obl.

— *David, virtutis exercitatissimae probatum Deo spectaculum, ex Davidis, pastoris, militis, ducis, exsulis ac prophetae exemplis, Benedicto Aria Montano meditante ad pietatis cultum propositis. Aeneis laminis ornatum a Ioanne Theodoro & Ioanne Israele de Bry, fratribus civib. Francofurtensibus. Quid huic nova editioni a Conrado Rittershusio ex biblioth. M. Bergii procurata accesserit, praefatio docebit*, Frankfurt, Z. Palthenius, 1597, 4°.

— *David, hoc est virtutis exercitatissimae probatum Deo spectaculum, ex David pastoris, militis, regis, exulis, ac prophetae exemplis*, Amsterdam, N.J. Visscher, 1637, 4°.

Audin, Prieur de Thermes: *Histoire de France representée par tableaux, commencant au regne de Hugues Capet, chef des roys de la troisiéme branche. Avec des discours & reflexions politiques. Par le Sieur Audin, prieur de Termes & de la Fage*, Paris, T. Quinet, 1647, 4°, 2 vols.

— *Fables heroïques, comprenans les veritables maximes de la politique chrestienne, et de la morale. Enrichies de plusieurs figures en taille-douce. Avec des discours enrichis de plusieurs histoires tant anciennes que modernes, sur le sujet de chaque fable. Le tout de l'invention du Sieur Audin, Prieur de Termes, & de la*

Fage, Paris, J. Guignard and J.-B. Loyson, 1648, 8°. (Mazarine (vol.2 only); Princeton UL (vol.1 only)). (*BFEB*, F.089)

— *Ibid.*, Paris, J. Guignard and E. Loyson, 1660, 8°. (*BFEB*, F.090)

— *Ibid.*, n.p., 1664, 8°. (*BFEB*, F.091)

— *Les fables heroiques, imitées de celles d'Esope, avec des moralitez historiques, pour l'explication de chaque fable. Comprenans les veritables maximes de la politique, & de la morale. Enrichies de figures en taille douce*, Paris, R. Guignard and E. Loyson, 1669, 12°. (*BFEB*, F.092)

Ayres, Philip: *Emblemata amatoria. Emblems of Love. Embleme d'amore. Emblemes d'amour. In Four Languages. Dedicated to the Ladies, by Ph. Ayres Esq.*, London, R. Bently and S. Tidmarch, J. Osborn, H. Overton, J. Wren, 1683, 8°. (*BFEB*, F.093)

— See *Emblemata amatoria. Emblemes d'amour en quatre langues.*

— See *Triumphus amoris.*

Bailly, Jacques: See Grivel, M. and Fumaroli M.

Baudoin, Jean: *Iconologie, ou explication nouvelle de plusieurs images, emblemes, et autres figures hyeroglyphiques des vertus, des vices, des arts, des sciences, des causes naturelles, des humeurs differentes, & des passions humaines. Oeuvre necessaire à toute sorte d'esprits, et particulierement à ceux qui aspirent à estre, ou qui sont orateurs, poetes, sculpteurs, peintres, ingenieurs, autheurs de medailles, de devises, de ballets, & de poëmes dramatiques. Tirée des recherches & des figures de Cesar Ripa, desseignées & gravées par Jacques de Brie, et moralisées par J. Baudoin*, Paris, 'chez l'autheur', 1636, folio.

— *Ibid.*, Paris, J. Villery, 1637, folio.

— *Ibid.*, Paris, M. Guillemot, 1644, folio.

— *Ibid.*, Paris, L. Billaine, 1677, 4°.

— *Ibid.*, Paris, L. d'Houry, 1681, 4°.

— *Iconologie ou la science des emblemes*, Amsterdam, A. Braakman, 1698, 12°.

— *Recueil d'emblemes divers. Avec des discours moraux, philosophiques, et politiques, tirez de divers autheurs, anciens & modernes. Par J. Baudoin*, Paris, J. Villery, 1638/39, 8°, 2 vols. (*BFEB*, F.095)

— *Ibid.*, Paris, J. Villery, 1646/47, 8°, 2 vols. (Glasgow UL; Mazarine). (*BFEB*, F.096)

— *Ibid.*, Paris, J.B. Loyson, 1659/60, 8°, 2 vols. (Mazarine; Wolfenbüttel). (*BFEB*, F.097)

— *Ibid.*, Paris, J. Cochart, 1685, 8°, 3 vols. (*BFEB*, F.099)

— *Ibid.*, Paris, J. Cochart, 1698, 8°, 3 vols. (Princeton UL). (*BFEB*, F.099)

— *Tableaux des sciences et des vertus morales. Contenant tout ce qu'il y a de plus beau & de plus curieux, à sçavoir de la peinture, de l'histoire, de l'embleme, de la fable, de la morale, & de la politique. Enrichies de figures. Par M. B. de l'Academie Françoise*, Paris, J.B. Loyson, 1679, 12°. (*BFEB*, F.098)

— *Les fables d'Esope Phrygien. Illustrées de discours moraux, philosophiques & politiques. Nouvelle edition. Augmentée de beaucoup en divers endroits. Où sont adjoutées les fables de Philelphe. Avecque des reflexions morales, par J. Baudoin*, Paris, A. Courbé, 1649, 8°, 2 vols.

— *Ibid.*, Paris, A. Courbé, 1659, 8°.

— *Ibid.*, Rouen, J. and D. Berthelin, 1660, 8°.

— *Ibid.*, Brussels, F. Foppens, 1669, 8°.

— *Ibid.*, Rouen, J. and D. Berthelin, 1670, 8°.

— *Ibid.*, Brussels, F. Foppens, n.d. (1680), 8°.

— *Ibid.*, Paris, C. Osmont, 1683, 8°.

Beaujoyeulx, Balthasar de: *Balet comique de la Royne, faict aux nopces de monsieur le Duc de Joyeuse et madamoyselle de Vaudemont sa soeur, par Baltasar de Beaujoyeulx, valet de chambre du Roy, et de la Royne sa mere*, Paris, A. le Roy, R. Ballard and M. Patisson, 1582, 4°.

— See McGowan, Margaret.

Benserade, Isaac: *Fables d'Esope en quatrains, dont il y en a une partie au labyrinthe de Versailles*, Paris, S. Mabre-Cramoisy, 1678, 12°.

— *Metamorphoses d'Ovide en rondeaux imprimez et enrichis de figures par ordre de sa Majesté. et dediez à Monseigneur le Dauphin*, Amsterdam, A. Wolfgang, 1689, 12°.

Berthod, François: *Emblemes sacrez tirez de l'Escriture Saincte & des Peres. Inventees et expliquees en vers François, avec une brieve meditation sur le mesme sujet. Pour servir à la conduite de la vie chrestienne. Par le P.F. Berthod religieux cordelier*, Paris, E. Loyson, 1657, 12°. (*BFEB*, F.100)

— *Emblemes sacrez...Augmentez d'exemples tirez des histoires de la Sainte Bible...Par le R.P. François Berthod, religieux de l'Observance de S. François*, Paris, E. Loyson, 1665, 12°. (*BFEB*, F.101)

Bèze, Théodore de: *Icones, id est verae imagines virorum doctrina simul et pietate illustrium, quorum praecipuè ministerio partim bonarum literarum studia sunt restituta, partim vera religio in variis orbis Christiani regionibus, nostra patrúmque memoria fuit instaurata: additis eorundem vitae & operae descriptionibus, quibus adiectae sunt nonnullae picturae quas emblemata vocant. Theodoro Beza auctore*, Geneva, J. de Laon, 1580, 4°. (*BFEB*, F.104)

— *Les vrais pourtraits des hommes illustres en pieté et doctrine, du travail desquels Dieu s'est servi en ces derniers temps, pour remettre sus la vraye religion en divers pays de la Chrestienté, avec les descriptions de leur vie & de leurs faits plus memorables. Plus, quarante quatre emblemes chrestiens. Traduicts du Latin de Theodore de Besze*, Geneva, J. de Laon, 1581, 4°. (*BFEB*, F.105)

— *Theodori Bezae poëmata varia. Sylvae. Elegiae. Epitaphia. Epigrammata. Icones. Emblemata. Cato Censorius. Omnia ab ipso auctore in unum nunc corpus collecta & recognita*, Geneva, J. Stoer, 1597/98, 4°. (*BFEB*, F.106)

— *Ibid.*, Geneva, J. Stoer, 1599, 4°. (*BFEB*, F.107)

— *Ibid.*, Geneva, J. Stoer, 1614, 4°. (*BFEB*, F.108)

Binet, Etienne: *Meditations affectueuses sur la vie de la tressainte Vierge mere de Dieu. Par le R.P. Estienne Binet de la Compagnie de Jesus*, Antwerp, M. Nutius for Th. Galle, 1632, 8°. (*BFEB*, F.110)

— See Luzvic, Etienne.

— See Hawkins, Henry.

Boissard, Jean-Jacques: *Iani Iacobi Boissardi Vesuntini emblemata cum tetrastichis latinis*, Metz, J. Aubry, n.d. (1584), 4° obl. (Arsenal; Huntington). (*BFEB*, F.111)

— *Iani Iacobi Boissardi Vesuntini emblematum liber. Emblemes Latins de I.I. Boissard, avec l'interpretation Françoise du I. Pierre Joly Messin*, Metz, J. Aubry and A. Faber, 1588, 4°. (*BFEB*, F.113)

— *Tetrasticha in emblemata Iani Iacobi Boissardi Vesuntini*, Metz, A. Faber, 1587, 8°. (*BFEB*, F.112)

— *Iani Iacobi Boissardi Vesuntini emblematum liber. Ipsa emblemata ab auctore delineata: a Theodoro de Bry sculpta, & nunc recens in lucem edita*, Frankfurt, Th. de Bry, 1593, 8°.

— *Emblemes de I.I. Boissard nouvellement mis de Latin en François par Pierre Joly Cons. du Roy, & son proc. general aux gouvernemens Messin & Verdunois. Le tout taillé en cuivre & mis en lumiere par Theodore de Bry*, Metz, A. Faber, 1595, 4°. (Folger; Mazarine). (*BFEB*, F.114)

Boissière, Monsieur de: *Les devises de Monsieur de Boissiere. Avec un traitté des reigles de la devise, par le mesme autheur*, Paris, A. Courbé, 1654/57, 8°. (Sainte Geneviève). (*BFEB*, F.116)

Bouhours, Dominique: *Les entretiens d'Ariste et d'Eugene*, Paris, S. Mabre-Cramoisy, 1671, 4°. (*BFEB*, F.118)

— *Ibid.*, Paris, S. Mabre-Cramoisy, 1673, 1678, 1682, 1683 and 1691, 4°. (*BFEB*, F.124-F.128)

— *Ibid.*, Amsterdam, J. Le Jeune, 1682 and 1691, 4°. (*BFEB*, F.127 and F.129)

— *Ibid.*, Lyon, J. Bruyset, 1682, 4°. (*BFEB*, F.126)

Bouquet, Simon: *Bref et sommaire recueil de ce qui a esté faict et de l'ordre tenuë à la joyeuse et triumphante entrée de tres-puissant tres-magnanime et tres-chrestien Prince Charles IX...avec le couronnement de tres-haute, tresillustre et tres-excellente Princesse Madame Marguerite Elizabet d'Austriche son espouse...et entrée de la dicte dame en icelle ville le jeudi xxix dudict mois de mars M.D.LXXI*, Paris, D. du Pré for O. Codoré, 1572, 4°.

— See Graham, V. and McAllister-Johnson, W.

— See Yates, Frances.

Brianville, Oronce Finé de: See Finé de Brianville, Oronce.

Bruck-Angermundt, Jacob à: *Iacobi à Bruck Angermundt cogn. sil. emblemata moralia & bellica. Nunc recens in lucem edita/Les emblemes moraulx et militaires du sieur Jacob de Bruck Angermundt. Nouvellement mis en lumiere,* Strasbourg, J. van der Heyden, 1615. (*BFEB*, F.130)

Callias, Augustus: *Emblemata sacra e libris Mosis excerpta,* Heidelburg, no publ., 1591, 8°.

Callot, Jacques: *Lux claustri. La lumiere du cloistre. Representées par figures emblematiques, dessignées & gravées par Jacques Callot,* Paris, F. Langlois, 1646, 4°. (*BFEB*, F.133)

— *Vita beatae Mariae virginis, matris Dei emblematibus delineata. Vie de la bienheureuse vierge Marie mere de Dieu. Représentée par figures emblematiques, dessignées & gravées par Jacques Callot,* Paris, F. Langlois, dit Chartres, 1646, 4°. (*BFEB*, F.134)

— *Emblesmes. Sur la vie de la mere de Dieu. Vita beatae Mariae virginis matris Dei emblematibus delineata,* Paris, B. Audran, n.d., 8° obl. (Glasgow UL). (*BFEB*, F.135)

— See Smith, C.N.

— *La vie de la mere de Dieu representee par divers emblesmes. Vita beatae Mariae virginis matris Dei emblematibus delineata,* n.p.n.d., 4°. (Utrecht UL). (*BFEB*, F.136)

— *Vie de la mere de Dieu représentée par emblesmes. Vita beatae Mariae virginis matris Dei emblematibus delineata,* n.p.n.d., 4°. (*BFEB*, F.137)

— *Vita beatae Mariae virginis matris Dei emblematibus delineata,* n.p.n.d., 4°. (engravings only). (Getty). (*BFEB*, F.137)

Camerarius, Joachim: *Symbolorum et emblematum ex animalibus quadrupedibus desumtorum centuria altera collecta,* Nuremberg, P. Kaufmann, 1595, 4°.

— *Symbolorum et emblematum ex volatilibus et insectis desumtorum centuria tertia collecta,* Nuremberg, P. Kaufmann, 1596, 4°.

— *Symbolorum et emblematum ex aquatilibus et reptilibus desumtorum centuria quarta,* Nuremberg, P. Kaufmann, 1604, 4°.

Caseneuve, Louis de: *Ioannis Pierii Valeriani Bellunensis hieroglyphica, seu de sacris Aegyptiorum, aliarúmque gentium literis commentarii, libri quinquaginta octo digesti: quibus additi sunt duo hieroglyphicorum libri, Caelii Augustini Curionis: Eiusdem Pierii pro sacerdotum barbis declamatio, & poëmata varia, cum diversis hieroglyphicis collectaneis, in sex libros ordine alphabetico dispositis, & nunc diligenter expurgatis. Accesserunt in hac postrema editione Hori Apollonis hieroglyphicorum libri duo...Authore Ludovico a Casanova,* Lyon,

P. Frellon, 1626, folio.

Cats, Jacob: *Silenus Alcibiadis sive Proteus, vitae humanae ideam, emblemate trifariàm variato, oculis subiiciens. Deus nobis haec otia fecit*, Middelburg, J. van der Hellen, 1618, 4°. (*BFEB*, F.147)

— *Proteus ofte minne-beelden verandert in sinne-beelden*, Rotterdam, P. van Waesberge, 1627, 4°. (*BFEB*, F.154)

— *Sinne- en minnebeelden; Studie-uitgave met inleidung en commentaar* (ed. H. Luijten, The Hague, 1996).

Caussin, Nicolas: *Electorum symbolorum et parabolarum historicarum syntagmata. Ex Horo, Clemente, Epiphanio & aliis cum notis & observationibus. Auctore P. Nicolao Caussino Trecensi, è Societate Iesu*, Paris, R. de Beauvais, 1618, 4°. (*BFEB*, F.172)

— *Symbolica Aegyptiorum sapientia, Authore P. Nicolao Caussino è Societate Iesu. Olim ab eo scripta, nunc post varias editiones denuò edita*, Paris, J. Jost and A. Tapinart, 1633 and 1634, 8°. (*BFEB*, F.173)

— *Ibid.*, Paris, S. Piget, 1647, 4°. (*BFEB*, F.174)

— *Polyhistor symbolicus, Electorum symbolorum, & parabolarum historicarum stromata, XII. libris complectens. Auctore P. Nicolao Caussino Trecensi è Societate Iesu*, Paris, R. de Beauvais, 1618, 4°. (*BFEB*, F.172)

— *Ibid.*, Paris, J. Jost and A. Tapinart, 1633 and 1634, 4°. (*BFEB*, F.173)

— *Ibid.*, Paris, S. Piget, 1647, 4°. (*BFEB*, F.174)

Chappuys, Gabriel: See Valeriano Bolzani, Giovanni Pierio.

Charonier, Gabriel: *Devises sur les armes de Monseigneur Le Tellier, secretaire d'estat. Presentées à Monsieur l'Abbé Le Tellier, revenant d'Italie*, Lyon, A. Jullieron, 1668, 4°. (*BFEB*, F.177)

— *Devises sur le nom, les armes, et la charge de Messire François du Gué...Recitées au mesme Seigneur par les rhetoriciens du Collège de la tres-sainte Trinité, de la Compagnie de Jesus, le huitiesme Janvier 1667, jour auquel il leur fit l'honneur d'assister à une de leurs Déclamations*, Lyon, P. Guillimin, 1667, 4°. (*BFEB*, F.176)

— See *Egapathe martyr de Lyon*.

Chasteuil, Jean Galaup de: See Galaup de Chasteuil, Jean.

Chaumelz, Leonard de: *Devises panegyriques pour Anne d'Austriche, Reine de France, dediees à Monsieur le Marquis de Saint-Luc...Par le Sieur de Chaumelz, Conseiller du Roy en ses Conseils & en sa Cour des Aydes de Guyenne*, Bordeaux, J. Mongiron Millanges, 1667, 4°. (*BFEB*, F.178)

Chesneau, Augustin: *Orpheus eucharisticus. Sive Deus absconditus humanitatis illecebris illustriores mundi partes ad se pertrahens, ultroneas arcanae maiestatis adoratrices. Opus novum. In varias historicorum emblematum aeneis tabulis incisorum centurias distinctum, quae strictâ, solutâque oratione explanantur, adiectis authorum fontibus ex quibus eruuntur...Authore P. Augustino Chesneau Victreensi communitatis Bituricensis Ordinis Eremitarum Sancti Augustini sacrae theologiae lectore*, Paris, F. Lambert, 1657, 8°. (*BFEB*, F.181)

— *Emblemes sacrez sur le tres-saint et tres-adorable sacrement de l'Eucharistie*, Paris, F. Lambert, 1667, 8°. (*BFEB*, F.182)

Chevalier, Nicolas: *Histoire de Guillaume III, Roy d'Angleterre, d'Ecosse, de France, et d'Irlande, Prince d'Orange &c. Contenant ses actions les plus memorables, depuis sa naissance jusques à son elevation sur le trône, & ce qui s'est passé depuis jusques à l'entiere reduction du royaume d'Irlande. Par medailles, inscriptions, arcs de triomphe, & autres monumens publics. Recueillis par N. Chevalier*, Amsterdam, no publ., 1692, folio. (*BFEB*, F.183)

Chovayne, Florent: *Les divertissements de Florent Chovayne Chartrain. Contenans un recueil de diverses devises & emblesmes, la plus grande partie de son invention, divisé en vingt-cinq centuries*, Chartres, M. Georges, 1645, 8°. (*BFEB*, F.184)

Combe, Thomas: *The Theater of Fine Devices, containing an hundred morall emblemes: first penned in French by Guillaume de la Perriere, and translated into English by Thomas Combe*, London, R. Field, 1593 (?), 16°. (Glasgow UL).

— *Ibid.*, London, R. Field, 1614, 16°. (Huntington).

Corrozet, Gilles: *Historiarum veteris testamenti icones ad vivum expressae. Unà cum brevi, sed quoad fieri potuit, dilucida earundem et Latina et Gallica expositione*, Lyon, M. and G. Trechsel, 1539, 4°.

— *Hecatomgraphie. C'est à dire les descriptions de cent figures et hystoires contenantes plusieurs appophtegmes, proverbes, sentences et dictz tant des anciens que des modernes*, Paris, D. Janot, 1540, 8°. (*BFEB*, F.189)

— *Ibid.*, Paris, D. Janot, 1541, 8°. (Arsenal). (*BFEB*, F.191)

— *Hecatomgraphie...Le tout reveu par son autheur*, Paris, D. Janot, 1543, 8°. (*BFEB*, F.193)

— *Hecatongraphie...Le tout reveu par son autheur*, Paris, D. Janot, 1543 (=1544?), 8°. (*BFEB*, F.195)

— See Adams, Alison.

— *Ibid.*, Paris, E. Groulleau, 1548, 16°. (Congress; Getty; Institut). (*BFEB*, F.196)

— *Ibid.*, n.p.n.d. (Lyon, D. de Harsy), 8°. (BL; BnF). (*BFEB*, F.190)

— *La fleur des sentences certaines, apophthegmes, et stratagemes, tant des anciens, que des modernes, enrichy de figures, & sommaires Françoys & Italiens, propres à chascune sentence*, Lyon, C. de la Ville, 1548, 16°. (Arsenal). (*BFEB*, F.197)

— *Ibid.*, Valence, P. Rollet and B. Frain for C. de la Ville, 1549, 16°. (Versailles). (*BFEB*, F.197)

— *La fleur des sentences moralles, extraictes tant des anciens que des modernes*, Lyon, B. Arnoullet, 1551, 16°. (Mazarine). (*BFEB*, F.198)

— *Les fables du tresancien Esope phrigien premierement escriptes en Graec, et depuis mises en rithme Françoise*, Paris, D. Janot, 1542, 8°.

— *Le tableau de Cebes de Thebes, ancien philosophe, et disciple de Socrates: auquel est paincte de ses couleurs la vraye image de la vie humaine, et quelle voye l'homme doit elire, pour pervenir à vertu et perfaicte science. Premierement escript en Grec, & maintenant exposé en ryme francoyse*, Paris, G. Corrozet, 1543, 8°. (*BFEB*, F.192)

— See Adams, Alison.

— *Tapisserie de l'eglise chrestienne et catholique: en laquelle sont depainctes la nativité, vie, passion, mort, et resurrection de nostre Sauveur et Redempteur Jesus Christ. Avec un huictain soubz chacune hystoire, pour l'intelligence d'icelle*, Paris, E. Groulleau, n.d., 16°.

— *Emblemes ou preceptes moraulx. Tirez des escrits de feu Gilles Corrozet non encore imprimez. A Monseigneur le Dauphin*, Paris, J. Corrozet, 1641, 8°. (Arsenal; Mazarine). (*BFEB*, F.199)

Coustau, Pierre: *Petri Costalii pegma, cum narrationibus philosophicis*, Lyon, M. Bonhomme, 1555, 8°. (*BFEB*, F.200)

— *Le pegme de Pierre Coustau, mis en Francoys par Lanteaume de Romieu gentilhomme d'Arles*, Lyon, M. Bonhomme, 1555, 8°. (*BFEB*, F.201)

— *Le pegme de Pierre Coustau, avec les narrations philosophiques, mis de Latin en François par Lanteaume de Romieu gentilhomme d'Arles*, Lyon, M. Bonhomme for Michel Bonhomme and B. Molin, 1560, 8°. (*BFEB*, F.202)

Covarrubias Orozco, Sebastian de: *Emblemas morales de Don Sebastian de Covarrubias Orozco, Capellan del Rey N.S. Maestrescuela, y Canonigo de Cuenca, Consultor del santo Oficio*, Madrid, L. Sanchez, 1610, 4°.

Cramer, Daniel: *Emblemata sacra, Hoc est decades quinque emblematum ex Sacra Scriptura, de dulcissimo nomine & cruce Iesu Christi, figuris aeneis incisa. Primò opera ac studio, Rever. DN. Danielis Crameri SS. Theologiae Doctoris. Nunc vero in hac secundo editione non solum una decade ab ipso aucta, sed etiam rhythmis sive versibus Latinis, Germanicis, Gallicis & Italicis ab aliis ornata, & ad Philothecam Christianam seu album amicorum utilia*, Frankfurt, L. Jennis, 1622, 8°. (*BFEB*, F.203)

— *Ibid.*, with variant title page: *Emblemes sacrez, c'est à dire recueil de cinquante figures en taille doulce, tirez de l'Escriture saincte, traictans du doulx & amiable nom et croix de Jesu Christ*, Frankfurt, L. Jennis, 1622, 8°. (Congress). (*BFEB*, F.203)

— *Emblemata sacra, Hoc est decades quinque emblematum ex Sacra Scriptura, de dulcissimo nomine & cruce Iesu Christi, figuris aeneis incisorum. Pars prior primò per Reverend. Dn. Danielem Cramerum, SS. Theologiae Doctorem collecta. Postea vero a Dn. Cunrado Bachmanno...epigrammatibus Latino-Germanicis illustrata, tandem opera M.C.R. versibus & rhythmis Gallo Italicis declarata, ornata & ad instar Philothecae Christianae sive albi amicorum exhibita* [plus *Pars secunda*], Frankfurt, L. Jennis, 1624, 8°. (*BFEB*, F.203)

— *Emblemata moralia nova, Das ist: Achtzig sinnreiche nachdenckliche figuren auss heyliger Schrifft in Kupfferstücken fürgestellet, worinnen schöne Anweisungen zu wahrer Gottesforcht begrieffen*, Frankfurt, L. Jennis, 1630, 8°. (*BFEB*, F.204)

Dan, Pierre: *Le tresor des merveilles de la maison royale de Fontainebleau, contenant la description de son antiquité, de sa fondation, de ses bastimens, de ses rares peintures, tableaux, emblemes, et devises; de ses jardins, de ses fontaines, et autres singularitez qui s'y voyent. Ensemble les traictez de paix, les assemblées, les conferences, les entrées royales, les naissances, et ceremonies de baptesme de quelques enfans de France; les mariages, les tournoys, et autres magnificences, qui s'y sont faictes jusques à present. par le R.P.F. Pierre Dan...*, Paris, S. Cramoisy, 1642, folio. (*BFEB*, F.205)

David, Jan: *Veridicus christianus: auctore P. Ioanne David, sacerdote Societatis Iesu*, Antwerp, J. Moretus (Officina Plantiniana), 1601, 4°. (*BFEB*, F.206)

— *Occasio arrepta, neglecta, huius commoda: illius incommoda. Auctore R.P. Ioanne David, Societatis Iesu sacerdote*, Antwerp, J. Moretus (Officina Plantiniana), 1605, 4°.

— *Paradisus sponsi et sponsae: in quo messis myrrhae et aromatum, ex instrumentis ac mysteriis passionis Christi colligenda, ut ei commoriamur. Et Pancarpium Marianum, septemplici titulorum serie distinctum: ut in B. Virginis odorem curramus, et Christus formetur in nobis. Auctore P. Ioanne David, Societatis Iesu sacerdote*, Antwerp, J. Moretus (Officina Plantiniana), 1607, 8°. (*BFEB*, F.209)

— *Duodecim specula Deum aliquando videre desideranti concinnata. Auctore P. Ioanne David, Societatis Iesu sacerdote*, Antwerp, J. Moretus (Officina Plantiniana), 1610, 8°.

Dene, Edewaerd de: *De warachtighe fabulen der dieren*, Bruges, P. de Clerck, 1567, 4°.

Desprez, Philippe: *Le theatre des animaux, auquel sous plusieurs diverses fables & histoires est representé la pluspart des actions de la vie humaine. Enrichy de belles sentences tirées de l'Escriture saincte, et orné de figures pour ceux qui ayment la peinture*, Paris, J. Le Clerc, 1620, 4°.

Domenichi, Lodovico: See Giovio, Paulo.

Drexel, Jeremias: *Aeternitatis prodromus, mortis nuntius quem sanis, aegrotatis, moribundis sistit Hieremias Drexelius è Societate Iesu*, Munich, C. Leysser, 1628, 12°.

— *Ibid.*, Douai, B. Bellere, 1629, 12°.

— *Ibid.*, Cologne, P. Henning, 1629, 12°.

— *Ibid.*, Cologne, C. ab Egmond, 1630, 1633 and 1645, 12°.

— *L'avantcoureur de l'eternité. Composé en Latin par le R. Pere Drexellius de la Compagnie de Jesus. Traduit de nouveau en François par Monsieur L.G.*, Paris, G. Marcher, 1662, 12°.

— *Ibid.*, Rouen, J. Gruel, 1670, 12°.

— *Ibid.*, Rouen, J. Oursel, 1683, 12°.

— *Ibid.*, Rouen, J.B. Besongne, 1689, 12°.

— *La voye qui conduit au ciel, ou l'avant-coureur de l'eternité*, Paris, A. Auroy, 1684, 12°.

— *Ibid.*, Paris, A. Auroy, 1687 and 1688, 12°.

Du Fresne, Raphael: *Figures diverses tirées des fables d'Esope et d'autres et expliquées par R.D.F.*, Paris, C. Cramoisy for F. Léonard, 1659, 4°.

Du Moulin, Antoine: See Aesop.

Estienne, Henry, Sieur des Fossez: *L'art de faire les devises, où il est traicté des hieroglyphiques, symboles, emblemes, aenygmes, sentences, parabolles, revers de medailles, armes, blasons, cimiers, chiffres & rebus. Avec un traicté des rencontres ou mots plaisans*, Lyon, J. Paslé, 1645, 8°.

— (trans. Thomas Blount) *The art of Making Devises: treating Hieroglyphicks, Symboles, Emblemes, Aenigmas, Sentences, Parables, Reverses of Medalls, Armes, Blazons, Cimiers, Cyphres & Rebus. First written in French by Henry Estienne Lord of Fossez and translated into English by Tho. Blount*, London, W.E. and J.G., 1646, 4°.

— *Ibid.*, London, R. Royston, 1648, 4°.

— *Ibid.*, London, J. Holden, 1650, 4°.

— *Ibid.*, London, for H. Herringman, 1655, 4°.

— See Valdor, Jean.

Félibien, André: *Les quatre elements peints par Mr Le Brun et mis en tapisseries pour Sa Majesté*, Paris, P. Le Petit, 1665, 4°. (*BFEB*, F.240)

— *Ibid.*, Paris, P. Le Petit, 1667, 4°. (*BFEB*, F.241)

— *Les quatre saisons peintes par Mr Le Brun et mises en tapisseries pour Sa Majesté*, Paris, P. Le Petit, 1667, 4°. (*BFEB*, F.242)

— *Devises pour les tapisseries du Roy, où sont representez les quatre elemens et les quatre saisons de l'année, peintes en mignature par I. Bailly, peintre du Roy en son Academie Royale de Peinture & Sculpture. Et gravées par S. Le Clerc*, Paris C. Blageart, 1668, folio. (Getty; Mazarine; Victoria and Albert). (*BFEB*, F.243)

— *Tapisseries du Roi où sont representez les quatre elemens et les quatre saisons*, Paris, S. Mabre-Cramoisy for the *Imprimerie royale*, 1670, folio. (*BFEB*, F.244)

— *Ibid.*, Paris, S. Mabre-Cramoisy for the *Imprimerie royale*, 1679, folio. (*BFEB*, F.246)

— *Tapisseries du Roy, où sont representez les quatre elemens et les quatre saisons avec les devises qui les accompagnent & leur explication. Königliche Französische Tapezereijen. Oder überaus schöne Sinn-Bilder, in welchen die vier Element, samt den vier Jahr-Zeiten, neben den Dencksprüchen und ihren Außlegungen, vorgestellet werden...*, Augsburg, J. Koppmayer for J.U. Krauss, 1687, folio. (Congress; Glasgow UL; Wolfenbüttel). (*BFEB*, F.247)

— *Ibid.*, Augsburg, J. Koppmayer for J.U. Krauss, 1690, folio. (Glasgow UL). (*BFEB*, F.250)

— *Ibid.*, Augsburg, J.U. Krauss, n.d., folio. (Congress; Utrecht UL). (*BFEB*, F.251)

— *Tapisseries du Roy, où sont representez les quatre elements, avec les devises, qui les accompagnent & leur explication. Tapyten van den Konink van Vrankryk verbeeldende de Vier Elementen, Beneffens haar wonderlyke Zinnebeelden, en uytlegging op dezelve*; and *Suite des tapisseries du Roy de France, ou sont representées les quatre saisons qui les accompagnent & leurs explications. Tapyten van den Koning van Vrankryk, verrbeeldende de Vier Jaargetyden, benevens haar verwonderlyke Zinnebeelden en Uytleggingen op dezelve*, Amsterdam, P. van den Berge, n.d. (c.1700), 4°. (Amsterdam UL; Glasgow UL). (*BFEB*, F.252)

— See Bailly, Jacques.

— *Descriptions de divers ouvrages de peinture faits pour le Roy*, Paris, S. Mabre-Cramoisy, 1671, 12°. (*BFEB*, F.245)

— *Les plaisirs de l'Isle enchantée. Course de bague; collation ornée de machines; comedie, meslée de danse et de musique; ballet du Palais d'Alcine; feu d'artifice; et autres festes galantes et magnifiques, faites par le Roy à Versailles le VII may M.DC.LXIV et continuées plusieurs autres jours*, Paris, S. Mabre-Cramoisy for the *Imprimerie royale*, 1673, folio.

— *Description sommaire du Chasteau de Versailles*, Paris, G. des Prez and C. Savreux, 1674, 12°.

— *Les divertissemens de Versailles donnez par le Roy à toute sa cour au retour de la conqueste de la Franche Comté en l'année M.DC.LXXIV*, Paris, S. Mabre-Cramoisy for the *Imprimerie royale*, 1676, folio.

— *Relation de la feste de Versailles. Du 18 Juillet mil six cens soixante-huit*, Paris, S. Mabre-Cramoisy for the *Imprimerie royale*, 1679, folio.

— See Meade, Martin.

— *Recueil de descriptions de peintures et d'autres ouvrages faits pour le Roy*, Paris, Veuve S. Mabre-Cramoisy, 1689, 12°. (*BFEB*, F.248)

— *Ibid.*, Paris, F. and P. Delaulne, 1689, 12°. (*BFEB*, F.248)

— *Description du chateau de Versailles, de ses peintures, et d'autres ouvrages faits pour le Roy. Par Monsieur Felibien de l'Academie Royalle des Sciences*, Paris, F. and P. Delaulne, 1696, 12°. (*BFEB*, F.248)

Finé de Brianville, Oronce: *Coluber gentilitius illustrissimi viri Ioan. Bapt. Colberti regi a sanctioribus consiliis, aedificiis regiis et aerario praefecti, quaestoris regiorum ordinum, regni administri, symbolis heroicis expressus*, Paris, S. Mabre-Cramoisy, 1666, folio. (*BFEB*, F.254)

— *Devises heroiques sur les armes de Monseigneur Colbert*, Paris, S. Mabre-Cramoisy, 1667, 4°. (*BFEB*, F.255)

— *Devise pour le Roy, sur les preparatifs de la campagne de l'an 1672. Expliquée par un sonnet traduit en plusieurs langues; ensemble une fable Latine traduite en François, sur le mesme sujet*, Paris, C. de Sercy, 1672, 4°.

— *Devise heroique pour les tettons de la Reine en janvier 1668*, n.p.n.d., 4°.

— *Pour Monseigneur le Prince d'Orange, devise*, n.p.n.d., 4°.

Flamen, Albert: *Devises et emblesmes d'amour moralisez. Gravez par Albert Flamen, peintre demeurant au Faux bourg S. Germain, rüe des Fossoyeurs*, Paris, Veuve J. Rémy, 1648, 8°. (*BFEB*, F.258)

— *Ibid.*, Paris, S. Margat, 1650, 8°. (*BFEB*, F.258)

— *Ibid.*, Paris, O. de Varennes, 1653, 8°. (*BFEB*, F.259)

— *Ibid.*, Paris, O. de Varennes, 1658, 8°. (*BFEB*, F.260)

— *Ibid.*, Paris, G. Clouzier, 1666, 8°. (Mazarine; Sainte Geneviève). (*BFEB*, F.260)

— *Ibid.*, Paris, E. Loyson, 1672, 8°. (*BFEB*, F.261)

Fontaine, Charles: *Figures du Nouveau Testament*, Lyon, J. de Tournes, 1554, 8°.

Friedrich, Andreas: *Emblemata nova, das ist New Bilderbuch: darinnen durch sonderliche Figuren der jetzigen Welt Lauff und Wesen verdeckter Weise abgemahlet und mit zugehörigen Reymen erkläret wird ...durch Andreas Friedrichen*, Frankfurt, J. de Zetter, 1617, 4°.

— *Emblemes nouveaux: esquels le cours de ce monde est depeint et representé par certaines figures, desquelles le sens est expliqué par rimes: dressés pour plus grande incitation au (sic) gens de bien & honorables, d'ensuivre la pieté & vertu, & pour sincere instruction & advertissement aux meschans & dissolus de fuïr le vice. Premierement en Allemand par André Frideric, & maintenant en François, pour le bien de la jeunesse, & du simple peuple. Mis en lumiere par Jaques de Zettre*, Frankfurt, L. Jennis, 1617, 4°. (*BFEB*, F.262)

— *Ibid.*, 'Imprimé à Francfort. Et se vendent à Paris chez Abraham Pacard...1617', 4°. (BnF). (*BFEB*, F.262)

— *Ibid.*, 'Se vendent chez B. Vincent. A Lyon 1608', 4°. (BnF). (*BFEB*, F.262)

— *Ibid.*, 'Francofurti apud Jacobum de Zetter. Anno 1644', 4°. (Wolfenbüttel). (*BFEB*, F.262)

Galaup de Chasteuil, Jean: *Discours sur les arcs triomphaux dressés en la ville d'Aix à l'heureuse arrivée de tres-chrestien tres-grand & tres-juste monarque Louis XIII. Roy de France & de Navarre*, Aix, J. Tholosan, 1624, folio. (*BFEB*, F.263)

Gambart, Adrien: *La vie symbolique du bienheureux François de Sales, evesque et prince de Geneve. Comprise sous le voile de 52. emblemes, qui marquent le caractere de ses principales vertus, avec autant de meditations, ou reflexions pieuses, pour exciter les ames chrestiennes & religieuses, à l'amour & à la pratique des mesmes vertus. Par M. Adrien Gambart prestre*, Paris, 'Aux frais de l'auteur', 1664, 12°. (*BFEB*, F.264)

Giovio, Paulo: *Dialogo dell'imprese militari et amorose di Monsignor Paulo Giovio Vescovo di Nocera*, Rome, A. Barre, 1555, 8°.

— *Dialogo dell'imprese militari et amorose di Monsignor Giovio Vescovo di Nocera; et del S. Gabriel Symeoni Fiorentino. Con un ragionamento di M. Lodovico Domenichi, nel medesimo soggetto. Con la tavola*, Lyon, G. Roville, 1574, 8°. (*BFEB*, F.270)

— *Dialogue des devises d'armes et d'amours du S. Paulo Jovio, avec un discours de M. Loys Dominique sur le mesme subjet. Traduit de l'Italien par le S. Vasquin Philieul. Auquel avons adjousté les Devises heroiques et morales du Seigneur Gabriel Symeon*, Lyon, G. Roville, 1561, 4°. (*BFEB*, F.268)

— *Le sententiose imprese di Monsignor Paulo Giovio, et del Signor Gabriel Symeoni ridotte in rima per il detto Symeoni al sereniss. Duca di Savoia*, Lyon, G. Roville, 1561, 4°. (*BFEB*, F.266)

Tetrastiques faictz sur les devises du Seigneur Paulo Jovio, et de Messire Gabriel Simeon, pour servir en verrieres, chassis, galeries et tableaux, ainsi qu'il plaira au lecteur de les accommoder, Lyon, G. Roville, 1560, 4°. (Arsenal). (*BFEB*, F.267)

Gissey, Henri de: *Les emblesmes et devises du Roy, des princes et seigneurs qui l'accompagnerent en la Calvacate Royale, et course de bague que Sa Majesté fit au Palais Cardinal 1656. Recueillies & dediees à son Altesse de Guise, par Gissey*, Paris, A. de Sommaville, 1657, 4°. (*BFEB*, F.271)

Gomberville, Le Roy Marin, Sieur de: See Le Roy, Sieur de Gomberville, Marin.

Grévin, Jacques (trans.): See Junius, Hadrianus.

Guéroult, Guillaume: *Le premier livre des emblemes*, Lyon, B. Arnoullet, 1550, 8°. (*BFEB*, F.280)

— *Figures de la Bible illustrées de huictains francoys pour l'interpretation et intelligence d'icelles*, Lyon, G. Roville, 1564, 8°.

Guyon, Madame: See La Mothe-Guyon, Madame de.

Haeften, Benedict van: *Schola cordis sive aversi à Deo cordis ad eundem reductio, et instructio. Auctore D. Benedicto Haefteno Ultraiectino, reformati monast. Affligeniensis, Ordinis S. Benedicti praeposito*, Antwerp, J. Verdussen, 1629, 8°.

— *Ibid.*, Paris, G. Lenoir, n.d., 4° obl. (engraved leaves only). (*BFEB*, F.294)

— *Hertzen Schuel. Oder des von Gott abgefüerten Herzens widerbringung zu Gott, und underweisung durch D. Benedictum Haeftenum...*, Augsburg, J. Weh, 1664,

8°

— *Escuela del Corazon, que escribio en lengua latina el R..P. Don Benito Haeften de la Orden de S. Benito...*, Madrid, no publ., 1748, 8°.

— See Harvey, Christopher.

— *Regia via crucis auctore D. Benedicto Haefteno Ultraiectino reformati monasterii Affligeniensis ordinis S. Benedicti praeposito*, Antwerp, B. Moretus (Officina Plantiniana), 1635, 8°.

— *Le chemin royal de la croix, composé par Dom Benoist Haeften d'Utrecht, Prieur du monastére réformé d'Afflighen, de l'Ordre de S. Benoist. Traduict de Latin en François, & dedié à Madame la Duchesse d'Orleans, par le R.P. Didac religieux de l'Observance de S. François son confesseur. Enrichy de quarante figures en taille-douce*, Paris, N. Jacquard for J. Henault, 1651, 8°. (*BFEB*, F.289)

— *Ibid.*, Paris, N. Jacquard for J. Henault, 1656, 8°. (*BFEB*, F.289)

— *Ibid.*, Paris, N. Jacquard for J. Henault, 1667, 8°. (*BFEB*, F.290)

— *Ibid.*, Paris, J. Henault, 1670, 8°. (*BFEB*, F.291)

— *Ibid.*, Paris, J. Villery, 1679, 8°. (*BFEB*, F.292)

— *Ibid.*, Paris, J. Villery, P. Aubouyn and J. Guignard, 1685, 8°. (*BFEB*, F.293)

— *De heyr-Baene des Cruys Waer-langhs alle soorten van menschen worden ghewesen, ende sekerlijck gheleert, om de Cruycen van alderhande lijden oft teghenspoedt van dese bedroefde tijdelijcke wereldt ghemackelijck te gheraeken tot de eeuwighe vreught-saligheyt des Hemels...*, Bruges, L. vanden Kerchove, 1667, 4°.

— *Camino Real de la Cruz, que compuso en Latin el P.D. Benedicto Haefteno...*, Valladolid, J. Godinez, 1721, 4°.

Harvey, Christopher: *The School of the Heart, or the Heart of it selfe gone away from God, brought back againe to him, and instructed by him*, London, H. Blunden, 1647, 8°.

Hawkins, Henry: *The Devout Hart or Royal Throne of the Pacifical Salomon. Composed by F. St. Luzvic S.I. Translated out of Latin into English. Enlarged with Incentives by F. St. Binet of the same S. and now enriched with Hymnes by a new hand*, Rouen, J. Cousturier, 1634, 12°.

Heinsius, Daniel: *Quaeris quid sit amor*, n.p.n.d. (Amsterdam, H. de Buck for J. Matthijsz, 1601), 4° obl. (*BFEB*, F.296)

— *Emblemata amatoria; iam demum emendata*, Amsterdam, D. Pietersz, 1608, 4° obl. (Getty; Glasgow UL). (*BFEB*, F.302)

— *Emblemata amatoria nova; in quibus vis & natura Amoris graphicè depingitur; auctore Theocrito à Ganda*, Leiden, J. Marcusz, 1613, 4°. (Glasgow UL; Harvard). (*BFEB*, F.305)

— *Dan. Heinsii Nederduytsche poemata; By een vergadert en uytgegeven door P.S.*,

Amsterdam, W. Jansz Blaeu, 1618, 4°. (*BFEB*, F.310)

Hesius, Wilhelm: *Gulielmi Hesii Antverpiensis è Societate Iesu emblemata sacra de fide, spe, charite*, Antwerp, B. Moretus (Officina Plantiniana), 1636, 12°.

Heyns, Pierre: See *Esbatement moral des animaux*.

Hooft, Pieter Corneliszoon: *Emblemata amatoria. Afbeeldinghen van minne. Emblemes d'amour*, Amsterdam, W. Jansz Blaeu, 1611, 4° obl. (*BFEB*, F.320)

Horapollo: *Habentur hoc volumine haec, videlicet: vita et fabellae Aesopi...Ori Apollonis Niliaci hieroglyphica*, Venice, Aldus, 1505, folio.

— *Ori Apollinis hieroglyphica*, Paris, P. Vidoue, 1521, 8°. (*BFEB*, F.325)

— *Orus Apollo de Aegypte de la signification des notes hieroglyphiques des Aegyptiens, c'est à dire des figures par les quelles ilz escripvoient leurs mysteres secretz & les choses sainctes & divines. Nouvellement traduict de grec en francoys & imprimé avec les figures à chascun chapitre*, Paris, J. Kerver, 1543, 8°. (*BFEB*, F.328)

— See Caseneuve, Louis de.

Hugo, Herman: *Pia desideria emblematis elegiis & affectibus SS. patrum illustrata. Authore Hermanno Hugone Societatis Iesu...Vulgavit Boetius a Bolswert*, Antwerp, H. Aertssens, 1624, 8°.

— *Pia desideria elegiis et affectibus SS. patrum illustrata: auctore Hermanno Hugone Societatis Iesu*, Lyon, C. Larjot, 1625, 16°. (Sainte Geneviève). (*BFEB*, F.333)

— *Ibid.*, Paris, J. Henault, 1654, 12°. (*BFEB*, F.336)

— *Ibid.*, Paris, J. Henault, 1661, 12°. (Glasgow UL). (*BFEB*, F.337)

— *Ibid.*, Paris, J. Henault, 1670, 12°. (*BFEB*, F.338)

— *Ibid.*, Lyon, P. Guillimin, 1679, 12°. (Getty; Glasgow UL). (*BFEB*, F.339)

— *Pieux desirs imités des Latins du R.P. Herman Hugo de la Compagnie de Jesus, par P.I. jurisc. Mis en lumiere par Boëce a Bolswert*, Antwerp, H. Aertssens, J. Cnobbart and C. Woons; and Paris, S. Cramoisy, 1627, 8°. (*BFEB*, F.334)

— *Pieux desirs imités des latins du R.P. Herman Hugo de la Compagnie de Jesus, par P.I. jurisc. Mis en lumiere par Boëce a Bolswert*, Paris, P. Landry, 1627, 8°. (engraved leaves only). (*BFEB*, F.335)

— *Les justes sentimens de la pieté exposez sous des emblesmes familiers. Tirez de la Sainte Escriture, & divisez en trois livres. Le premier traite des larmes & des gemissemens de la penitence. Le second des desirs de l'ame juste. Le troisiéme, des soupirs de l'ame convertie, & amante de son Dieu. Sur l'idée d'un livre Latin, qui a pour titre, Pia desideria. Traduit en François par un missionaire*, Paris, E. Couterot, 1684, 12°. (*BFEB*, F.340)

— *Goddelycke Wenschen verlicht met sinnebeelden. Ghedichten en vierighe uyt-spraecken der ovdvaders Naer-ghevolght de Latynsche vanden Eerw. P.*

Hermannus Hugo Priester der Societeyt Iesu door Iustus de Hardvyn P, Antwerp, H. Aertssens, 1629, 8°.

— *Pia desideria: or Divine Addresses, in three books, illustrated with XLVII copper-plates. Written in Latine by Herm. Hugo; Englished by Edm. Arwaker*, London, H. Bonwicke, 1686, 8°.

— See La Mothe-Guyon, Madame de.

Hulsius, Bartholomew: *Emblemata sacra, dat is, eenighe geestlicke sinnebeelden, met niewe ghedichten...ende bedenckinghen...door B.H*, n.p. (Amsterdam?), 1631, 4°.

Ignatius of Loyola, Saint: *Exercitia spiritualia. Auctore S. Ignatio de Loyola. Andreas Frusius Latine vertit. Praemittuntur annotationes quaedam aliquid adferentes intelligentiae ad Exercitia spiritualia*, Rome, A. Bladus, 1548, 8°.

— *Exercitia spiritualia S.P. Ignatii Loyolae, Fundatoris Ordinis Societatis Iesu. Cum Bullis Pontificum, tum approbationis Exercitiorum; tum Indulgentiae plenariae, pro omnibus, qui octiduò illis vacant in domibus eiusdem Societatis. Brevi insuper Instructione meditandi quae omnia & dilucidantur & illustrantur pluribus ex aere impressis imaginibus*, Antwerp, M. Cnobbart, 1689, 8°.

Janot, Denis: *Table des livres de Denys Janot, Imprimeur du Roy en langue françoyse*, Paris, D. Janot, n.d., 8°.

Jaugeon, Le Sieur: *Le jeu du monde ou l'intelligence des plus curieuses choses qui se trouvent dans tous les estats, les terres, & les mers du monde. Ouvrage enrichy des devises des plus grands princes de l'Europe. Dedié au Roy. Par le Sieur Jaugeon*, Paris, A. Auroy, 1684, 12°. (*BFEB*, F.351)

Jodelle, Etienne: *Le recueil des inscriptions, figures, devises, et masquarades, ordonnées en l'hostel de ville à Paris, le Jeudi 17. de Fevrier. 1558. Par Estienne Jodelle Parisien*, Paris, A. Wechel, 1558, 4°.

— See Graham, V.E. and McAllister Johnson, W.

Jourdan, C.: *L'ordre, entree et ceremonies observees par la ville de Paris. A l'heureux retour de Louys treiziesme, Roy de France & de Navarre. Avec la montre generalle faite au pré aux Clercs: Et la reception des Sieurs Prevost des Marchans & Eschevins de ladicte ville. Faicte à Sa Majesté le 16. de Septembre. Par Maistre C. Jourdan, huissier des comptes, Parisien*, Paris, J. Brunet, 1614, 8°.

Junius, Hadrianus: *Hadriani Iunii medici emblemata, ad D. Arnoldum Cobelium. Eiusdem aenigmatum libellus, ad D. Arnoldum Rosenbergum*, Antwerp, C. Plantin, 1565, 16°.

— *Ibid.*, Antwerp, C. Plantin, 1566, 16°.

— *Ibid.* Antwerp, C. Plantin, 1569, 16°.

— *Ibid.*, Antwerp, C. Plantin, 1575, 16°.

— *Ibid.*, Antwerp, C. Plantin, 1585, 16°.

— *Ibid.*, Leiden, Officina Plantiniana, 1585, 16°.

— *Ibid.*, Leiden, Officina Plantiniana, 1595, 16°.

— *Ibid.*, Leiden, Officina Plantiniana, 1596, 16°.

— *Les emblesmes du S. Hadrian le Jeune medecin et historien des Estats de Hollande. Au S. Arnold Cobel*, Antwerp, C. Plantin, 1567, 16°. (Glasgow UL; Huntington). (*BFEB*, F.352)

— *Ibid.*, Antwerp, C. Plantin, 1570, 16°.

— *Ibid.*, Antwerp, C. Plantin, 1575, 16°.

— *Emblemata Adriani Iunii medici, overgheset in Nederlantsche tale deur M.A.G.*, Antwerp, C. Plantin, 1567, 16°.

— *Ibid.*, Antwerp, C. Plantin, 1575, 16°.

L'Abbé, Pierre: *Trois devises sur les armes de Monseigneur l'eminentissime Cardinal Mazarin*, n.p.n.d., folio.

La Faye, Antoine: *Emblemata et epigrammata miscellanea selecta ex stromatis peripateticis Antonii Fayi*, Geneva, P. and J. Chouet, 1610, 8°.

La Feuille, Daniel de: *Livre nouveau et utile pour toutes sortes d'artistes. Et particulierement pour les orfevres, les orlogeurs, les peintres, les graveurs, les brodeurs &. Contenant quatre alphabets de chiffres fleuronnez au premier trait avec quantité de devises, d'emblemes et de noeuds d'amour. Avec une table exacte pour trouver en général tous les noms et surnoms entrelassez. Le tout exactement recherché, dessiné et gravé. Par Daniel de La Feuille*, Amsterdam, D. de La Feuille, 1690, 8° obl.

— *Ibid.*, Amsterdam, D. de La Feuille, 1691, 8° obl.

— *Devises et emblemes anciennes et modernes, tirées des plus celebres auteurs. Avec plusieurs autres nouvellement inventées et mises en Latin, en François, en Espagnol, en Italien, en Anglois, en Flamand et en Allemand par les soins de Daniel de La Feuille*, Amsterdam, D. de La Feuille, 1691, 4°.

— *Ibid.*, with date on title page altered in manuscript to read 1693, 1697 or 1712.

— *Emblematische Gemüths-Vergnügung bey Betrachtung der curieusten und ergözlichsten Sinnbildern mit ihren zuständigen Deutsch-Lateinisch-Frantzösisch und Italienischen Beyschrifften*, Augsburg, L. Kroniger and C. Göbels, 1693, 4°.

— *Ibid.*, Augsburg, L. Kroniger and C. Göbels, 1695, 4°.

— *Ibid.*, Augsburg, L. Kroniger and C. Göbels, 1697, 4°.

— *Ibid.*, Augsburg, L. Kroniger and C. Göbels, 1699, 4°.

— *Ibid.*, Augsburg, L. Kroniger and C. Göbels, 1702, 4°.

— *Ibid.*, Augsburg, L. Kroniger and C. Göbels, 1703, 4°.

— *Methode nouvelle pour apprendre l'art du blason, ou la science des nobles par dialogues. Avec un discours sur les devises, supports, cimiers, lambrequins, &*

tombeaux. Enrichis des pavillons & des enseignes que chaque nation porte en mer, & des figures necessaires pour leurs explications, Amsterdam, D. de La Feuille, 1695, 4°.

— *Devises & emblemes d'amour, anciens & modernes moralisez & expliquez en sept sortes de langue par M. Pallavicini, professeur des langues etrangeres*, Amsterdam, D. de La Feuille, 1696, 4°.

— *Ibid.*, Amsterdam, 1697, 4°.

— *Essay d'un dictionnaire contenant la connoissance du monde, des sciences universelles, et particulierement celle des medailles, des passions, des moeurs, des vertus, et des vices &c. Representé par des figures hyerogliphiques, expliquées en prose & en vers*, Amsterdam, D. de La Feuille; D. de La Feuille and N. Chevallier; and Wesel, J. van Wesel, 1700, 4°.

La Fontaine, Jean de: *Fables choisies mises en vers par M. de la Fontaine*, Paris, C. Barbin, 1668, 4°.

— *Recueil de poésies chrêtiennes et diverses*, Paris, J. Couterot, 1679, 12°, 3 vols.

La Mothe-Guyon, Madame de: *L'ame amante de son Dieu, representée dans les emblémes de Hermannus Hugo sur ses Pieux desirs: & dans ceux d'Othon Vaenius sur l'Amour divin. Avec des figures nouvelles accompagnées de vers qui en font l'aplication aus dispositions les plus essentielles de la vie interieure*, Cologne, J. de la Pierre, 1717, 8°.

— *L'ame amante de son Dieu, representée dans les emblemes de Hermannus Hugo, et dans ceux d'Othon Vaenius sur l'Amour divin...Par Madame J.M.B. de La Mothe-Guyon*, Paris, 'Chez les Libraires Associés', 1790, 8°.

— *Die ihren Gott liebende Seele, vorgestellt in den Sinnbildern des Hermanni Hugonis uber seine Pia desideria, und des Ottonis Vaenii, uber die Liebe Gottes, mit neuen Kupffern und Versen, welche zielen auf das innere Christenthum, aus dem Frantzösischen ins Teutsche übersetzt*, Regensburg, E.F. Bader, 1719, 8°.

— *Ibid.*, Regensburg, E.F. Bader, 1743, 8°. (Glasgow UL; Harvard UL).

L'Anglois, Pierre: *Discours des hieroglyphes aegyptiens, emblemes, devises et armoiries, ensemble LIIII tableaux hieroglyphiques pour exprimer toutes conceptions, à la façon des Aegyptiens, par figures, et images des choses, au lieu de lettres. Avecques plusieurs interpretations des songes et prodiges. Le tout par Pierre l'Anglois, escuyer, Sieur de Bel-Estat*, Paris, pour A. l'Angelier, 1583, 4°.

La Perrière, Guillaume de: *Le theatre des bons engins, auquel sont contenuz cent emblemes*, Paris, D. Janot, n.d. (1540), 8°. (Edition 1). (BL; BnF).

— *Ibid.*, Paris, D. Janot, n.d. (1540), 8°. (Edition 2). (Versailles).

— *Ibid.*, Paris, D. Janot, n.d. (after 1542?), 8°. (Edition 3). (BL; BnF).

— *Ibid.*, Paris, D. Janot, n.d. (1544?), 8°. (Edition 4). (Beaux Arts; Glasgow UL).

— *Ibid.*, Paris, E. Groulleau, 1548, 16°. (Congress).

— *Ibid.*, Paris, E. Groulleau, 1551, 16°. (Wolfenbüttel).

— *Ibid.*, Lyon, J. de Tournes, 1545, 16°. (BnF).

— *Ibid.*, Lyon, J. de Tournes, 1546, 16°. (Congress; Munich).

— *Ibid.*, Lyon, J. de Tournes, 1549, 16°. (Harvard UL).

— *Ibid.*, Lyon, J. de Tournes, 1553, 16°. (Princeton UL).

— *Ibid.*, Lyon, Jean II de Tournes, 1583, 16°. (Illinois UL; Virginia UL).

— *Ibid.*, n.p.n.d. (Lyon, D. de Harsy), 8°. (BL; BnF).

— *Tpalays der gheleerder ingienen oft der constiger gheesten; inhoudende hondert morale figueren*, Antwerp, Widow J. van Liesfeldt, 1554, 8°.

— *Ibid.*, Antwerp, Widow J. van Liesfeldt, 1556, 8°.

— *Ibid.*, Antwerp, H. van Liesfeldt, 1564, 8°.

— See Combe, Thomas.

— *La morosophie de Guillaume de la Perriere tolosain, contenant cent emblemes moraux illustrez de cent tetrastiques latins, reduitz en autant de quatrains françoys*, Lyon, M. Bonhomme; Toulouse, J. Mounier, 1553, 8° . (Edition 1) (Arsenal; BL; Glasgow UL).

— *Ibid.*, Lyon, M. Bonhomme; Toulouse, J. Mounier, 1553, 8°. (edition 2) (BL; BnF).

La Rue, Charles de: *Emblemata regia. Auctore C.D.L.R. è Societate Iesu*, Paris, S. Mabre-Cramoisy, 1668, 4°.

— *Caroli de la Rue è Societate Iesu Idyllia*, Rouen, R. Lallemant, 1669, 12°.

— *Caroli Ruaei è Societate Iesu carminum libri quatuor ad celsissimum principem Ferdinandum Episcopum monasteriensem et Paderbornensem*, Paris, S. Benard, 1680, folio.

Laugier, Gaspard: *Ludovici Magni Galliarum Regis elucubratio anagrammatica-historica. A P.F.Gasparo Laugier, sacri Ordinis Minimorum alumno*, Aix en Provence, C. Marchy, 1679, 4°.

Le Jay, Gabriel-François: *Le triomphe de la religion sous Louis le Grand représenté par des inscriptions & des devises, avec une explication en vers Latins & François*, Paris, G. Martin, 1687, 12° .

— *Ludovici Magni vita symbolis heroicis designata. Auctore Gabriele Francisco Le Jay, Societatis Iesu*, Paris, L. Sevestre, 1715, 4°.

— *Les vertus royales mises en devises et presentées au Roy à sa majorité*, Paris, S. Langlois, 1723, 4°.

Le Laboureur, Claude: *Discours sur l'origine des armes receüs et usitez pour l'explication de la science heraldique...enrichy des blasons des roys, princes et autres maisons illustres de la chrestienté*, Lyon, G. Barbier, 1658, 8° .

Le Moyne, Pierre: *Devises heroiques et morales du P. Pierre Le Moine de la Compagnie de Jesus*, Paris, A. Courbé, 1649, 4°.

— *De l'art de regner. Au Roy. Par le Pere Le Moyne de la Compagnie de Jesus*, Paris, S. Cramoisy and S. Mabre-Cramoisy, 1665, folio.

— *De l'art des devises. Par le P. le Moyne de la Compagnie de Jesus. Avec divers recueils de devises du mesme autheur*, Paris, S. Cramoisy and S. Mabre-Cramoisy, 1666, 4°.

Le Roy, Sieur de Gomberville, Marin: *La doctrine des moeurs. Tiree de la philosophie des Stoiques: representee en cent tableaux. Et expliquee en cent discours pour l'instruction de la jeunesse. Au Roy*, Paris, L. Sevestre for P. Daret, 1646, folio.

— *Ibid.*, Paris, A. Soubron, 1681, 12°·

— *Ibid.*, Paris, A. Soubron, 1682, 12°.

— *Ibid.*, Paris, A. Soubron, 1683, 12°.

— *Ibid.*, Paris, A. Soubron, 1684, 12°. (Wolfenbüttel).

— *Ibid.*, Paris, A. Soubron and J. Le Gras, 1685, 12°. (Folger).

— *Ibid.*, Paris, J. Le Gras, 1682, 12°. (Getty).

— *Ibid.*, Paris, J. Le Gras, 1688, 12°.

— *Le theatre moral de la vie humaine, representee en plus de cent tableaux divers, tirez du poëte Horace, par le Sieur Otho Venius; et expliquez en autant de discours moraux par le Sieur de Gomberville, avec le Tableau du philosophe Cebes*, Brussels, F. Foppens, 1672, folio.

— *Ibid.*, Brussels, F. Foppens, 1678, folio.

— *Ibid.*, Brussels, F. Foppens, 1702, folio.

— *Theatro moral de la vida humana, en cien emblemas; con el enchiridion de Epicteto, &c. y la tabla de Cebes, philosofo platonico*, Brussels, F. Foppens, 1669, folio.

— *Ibid.*, Brussels, F. Foppens, 1672, folio.

— *The Doctrine of Morality; or a View of Human Life. According to the Stoick Philosophy. Exemplified in One Hundred and Three Copper Plates, done by the Celebrated Monsieur Daret, Engraver to the Late French King, With an Explanation of each Plate: Written Originally in French by Monsieur De Gomberville, for the Use of the said Prince. Translated into English by T.M. Gibbs, late of Hart-Hall, Oxon.*, London, for E. Bell, J. Darby, A. Bettesworth, F. Fayram, J. Pemberton, J. Hooke, C. Rivington, F. Clay, J. Batley and E. Simon, 1721, folio.

— *Moral Virtue Delineated in One Hundred and Three Short Lectures, both in French and English, on the Most Important Points of Morality*, London, for E. Bell, J. Darby, A. Bettesworth, F. Fayram, J. Pemberton, J. Hooke, C. Rivington, F. Clay, J. Batley and E. Simon, 1726, folio.

— See Vaenius, Otto.

L'Estoile, Pierre de: *Les belles figures et drolleries de la Ligue*, in *Mémoires-Journaux de P. de l'Estoile*, ed. G. Brunet, Paris, 1875-96, 12 vols, vol.4.

Le Vasseur, Jacques: *Les devises des empereurs romains, tant italiens que grecs & allemans, depuis Jules Caesar jusques à Rodolphe II à present regnant. Avecques les expositions d'icelles par quatrains. Par Jaques Le Vasseur Archidiac. de Noyon. A Monseigneur le Daulphin*, Paris, F. Bourriquant, 1608, 8°.

— *Les devises des roys de France latines et françoises. Tirées de divers autheurs, anciens & modernes. Avec une briefve exposition d'icelles, en vers françois. Par I.L.V.R.D.L.D.P. Et la paraphrase en vers latins par Michel Grenet de Chartres. Le tout enrichi des figures de tous les rois de France, jusques à Henry IIII. à present regnant. A Monseigneur le Dauphin*, Paris, F. Bourriquant, 1609, 8°.

Loyola, Saint Ignatius of: See Ignatius of Loyola, Saint.

Luzvic, Etienne: *Le coeur devot throsne royal de Jesus pacifique Salomon. Par le P. Estienne Luzvic de la Compagnie de* Jesus, Antwerp, H. Aertssens, 1627, 12°. (Chicago).

— *Cor Deo devotum Iesu pacifici Salomonis thronus regius è gallico P Stephani Luzvic, cui adiunctae ex P. Binet imaginum expositiunculae Latinitati dedit, & ad calcem auxit P. Carolus Musart eiusdem cum prioribus Societatis Iesu*, Douai, B. Bellere, 1627, 12°. (Folger; Vienna; Wolfenbüttel).

— *Ibid*, Antwerp, H. Aertssens, 1628, 12°.

— See Hawkins, Henry.

Malingre, Claude: *Entrée magnifique du Roy, faicte en sa ville d'Orleans, le mardy huictiesme juillet 1614, avec l'ordre et ceremonies observées en icelle. Par Claude Malingre*, Paris, M. Mondiere, 1614, 8°.

Marolles, Michel de: *Tableaux du temple des Muses; tirez du cabinet de feu M. Favereau, conseiller du Roy en sa Cour des aydes, & gravez en tailles douces par les meilleurs maistres de son temps, pour representer les vertus & les vices, sur les plus illustres fables de l'antiquité. Avec les descriptions, remarques & annotations. Composées par Mre Michel de Marolles, Abbé de Villeloin*, Paris, A. de Sommaville, 1655, folio.

Martin, Jean: *Le paradis terrestre, ou emblemes sacrez de la solitude, dediez au saint ordre des chartreux. Avec un recueil des plus beaux vers Latins & François sur la solitude, la plus part non encore imprimez*, Paris, J. Henault, 1655, 8°.

Martinet, Le Sieur: *Emblesmes royales à Louis le Grand, par le Sr Martinet, Aide des ceremonies de France*, Paris, C. Barbin, 1673, 12°.

Masen, Jakob: *Ars nova eruditae et honestae recreationis, in duas partes divisa. Prima est epigrammatum, altera inscriptionum argutarum, autore R.P.Jacobo Masenio...editio secunda*, Cologne, J.A. Kinchius, 1660, 12°.

— *Speculum imaginum veritatis occultae, exhibens symbola, emblemata, hieroglyphica, aenigmata, omni, tam materiae, quam formae varietate, exemplis simul, ac praeceptis illustratum. Anno 1650. Quo Romanus orbis Iubilabat.*

Authore R.P.Iacobo Masen, è Soc. Iesu, Cologne, J.A. Kinchius, 1664, 8°.

Mello, Guillaume de: *Les divines operations de Jesus, dans le coeur d'une ame fidelle. Par G.D.M*, Paris, J. Van-Merle, 1673, 12°.

Mendo, Andrés: *Principe perfecto, y ministros ajustados, documentos politicos, y morales. En emblemas. Por el R.P. Andrés Mendo, de la Compaña de Jesus, Calificador del Consejo de la Inquisicion Suprema, Lecto de Theologia, y de Sagrada Escritura en Salamanca*, Lyon, H. Boissat and G. Remeus, 1661, 4°. (Glasgow UL).

— *Ibid.*, Lyon, H. Boissat and G. Remeus, 1662, 4°.

Ménestrier, Claude-François: *L'autel de Lyon consacré à Louys Auguste, & placé dans le temple de la gloire. Ballet dedié à Sa Majesté en son entrée à Lyon*, Lyon, J. Molin, 1658, 4°.

— *Les devises, emblemes, et anagrammes, à Monseigneur le Chancelier par C.F.M. de la Compagnie de Jesus*, Lyon, G. Barbier, 1659, 4°.

— *Estreines de la cour*, Lyon, G. Barbier, 1659, 4°.

— *Les genereux exercices de la Majesté, ou la montre paisible de la valeur representée en devises & en emblesmes*, Lyon, G. Barbier, 1659, 4°.

— *Le veritable art du blason, où les regles des armoiries sont traitées d'une nouvelle methode, plus aisée que les precedentes; les origines expliquées, & establies par de solides raisons, & de fortes authoritez; les erreurs de plusieurs autheurs corrigées, la pratique de chaque nation examinée; & les causes de leur diversité fidellement raportées*, Lyon, B. Coral, 1659, 12°.

— *Les resjoüissances de la paix, avec un recueil de diverses pieces sur ce sujet: dedié à Messieurs les prevost des marchands & eschevins de la ville de Lyon. Par le P.C.F.M. de la Compagnie de Jesus*, Lyon, B. Coral, 1660, 8°.

— *L'art du blason justifié par le Pere Claude François Menestrier de la Compagnie de Jesus*, Lyon, B. Coral, 1661, 12°.

— *Methode abbregée des principes heraldiques ou la maniere d'apprendre le blason. Par le Pere Claude François Menestrier de la Compagnie de Jesus*, Lyon, B. Coral and A. du Perier, 1661, 12°.

— *L'art des emblemes par le P. C-François Menestrier de la Compagnie de Jesus*, Lyon, B. Coral, 1662, 8°.

— *Description de l'appareil dressé pour la ceremonie de l'octave de S. François de Sales. A l'occasion de la solemnité de sa canonisation, celebree dans l'Eglise du premier Monastere de la Visitation Sainte Marie de Grenoble, qui est le quatriéme de l'Institut: Depuis les premieres Vespres du 8 Septembre, jusques apres les dernieres du 17. du mesme mois*, Grenoble, R. Philippes, 1666, 4°.

— *Les transfigurations sacrées de S. François de Sales ou le Thabor de sa gloire. Dessein de l'appareil de la solemnité de sa canonisation, faite dans le second Monastere de la Visitation Sainte Marie de Grenoble: avec le Journal des*

Ceremonies depuis le 19. may jusques au 27, n.p. (Grenoble), n.d. (1666?), 4°.

— *Traité des tournois, joustes, carrousels et autres spectacles publics*, Lyon, J. Muguet, 1669, 4°.

— *La devise du Roy justifiée. Par le P. Menestrier de la Compagnie de Jesus. Avec un recueil de cinq cens devises faites pour S.M. & toute la maison royale*, Paris, E. Michalet, 1679, 4°.

— *Des representations en musique anciennes et modernes. Par le P.C.-F. Menestrier de la Compagnie de Jesus*, Paris, R. Guignard, 1681, 12°.

— *Des ballets anciens et modernes selon les regles du theatre. Par le P.C.-F. Menestrier de la Compagnie de Jesus*, Paris, R. Guignard, 1682, 12°.

— *La philosophie des images. Composée d'un ample recueil de devises, & du jugement de tous les ouvrages qui ont été faits sur cette matiere. Par le P.C.F. Menestrier de la Compagnie de Jesus*, Paris, R.J.B. de la Caille, 1682, 8°.

— *Des decorations funebres. Où il est amplement traité des tentures, des lumieres, des mausolées, catafalques, inscriptions & autres ornemens funebres. Avec tout ce qui s'est fait de plus considerable depuis plus d'un siécle, pour les papes, empereurs, rois, reines, cardinaux, princes, prelates, sçavans & personnes illustres en naissance, vertu & dignité. Par le P.C.F. Menestrier de la Compagnie de Jesus*, Paris, R.J.B. de la Caille and R. Pepie, 1683, 8°.

— *L'art des emblemes où s'enseigne la morale par les figures de la fable, de l'histoire, & de la nature. Ouvrage rempli de pres de cinq cent figures. Par le P.C.F. Menestrier de la Compagnie de Jesus*, Paris, R.J.B. de la Caille, 1684, 8°.

— *La science et l'art des devises dressez sur de nouvelles regles, avec six cens devises sur les principaux evenemens de la vie du Roy. Et quatre cens devises sacrées, dont tous les mots sont tirés de l'Ecriture Sainte. Composées par le P. Menestrier de la Compagnie de Jesus*, Paris, R.J.B. de la Caille, 1686, 8°.

— *Histoire du Roy Louis le Grand par les medailles, emblêmes, devises, jettons, inscriptions, armoiries, et autres monumens publics, recueillis, et expliquez par le Pere Claude François Menestrier de la Compagnie de Jesus*, Paris, J.B. Nolin, 1689, folio.

— *Histoire du Roy Louis le Grand par les medailles, emblêmes, devises, jettons, inscriptions, armoiries, et autres monumens publics. Recuëillis, et expliquéz par le Pere Claude François Menestrier de la Compagnie de Jesus. N. E. Augmentée de 5. planches*, Paris, I.B. Nolin (Amsterdam), 1691, 4°.

— *Histoire du Roy Louis le Grand par les medailles, emblêmes, devises, jettons, inscriptions, armoiries, et autres monumens publics, recuëillis, et expliquéz par le Pere Claude François Menestrier de la Compagnie de Jesus. Seconde edition. Augmentée de plusieurs figures et corrigée*, Paris, I.B.Nolin, R. Pepié and J. Le Fevre, 1693, folio.

— *Ibid.*, under variant title, *Histoire du regne de Louis le Grand par les medailles, emblemes, devises, jettons, inscriptions, armoiries, & autres monumens publics.*

Recueillis & expliquez par le Pere Claude François Menestrier de la Compagnie de Jesus. Edition nouvelle. Corrigée & augmentée d'un discours sur la vie du Roy, & de plusieurs médailles & figures, Paris, I.B. Nolin and R. Pepié, 1693, folio. (Princeton UL).

— *Ibid.*, Paris, I.B.Nolin and R. Pepié, 1699, folio. (Vienna).

— *Ibid.*, Paris, I.B.Nolin and R. Pepié, 1700, folio. (Mazarine).

— *La philosophie des images enigmatiques, où il est traité des enigmes, hieroglyphiques, oracles, propheties, sorts, divinations, loteries, talismans, songes, centuries de Nostradamus, de la braguette. Par le P. Cl. Menestrier de la Compagnie de Jesus*, Lyon, H. Baritel, 1694, 8°.

— *Les devoirs funebres rendus à la memoire de Madame Royale chrestienne de France, duchesse de Savoye, reine de Chypre, &c, espouse de S.A.R. Charles Emanuel II, le 21. du mesme mois. Par le souverain Senat, et la souveraine Chambre des comptes de Savoye, à Chambery*, n.p.n.d., 4°.

— (attrib.) *Les vertus chrestiennes et les vertus militaires en deüil. Dessein de l'appareil funebre dressé par l'ordre du roy dans l'eglise de Nostre Dame de Paris le neuviéme septembre 1675 pour la ceremonie des obseques de tres-haut et tres-puissant prince Monseigneur Henry de la Tour d'Auvergne, vicomte de Turenne*, Paris, E. Michallet, 1675, 4°.

— (attrib.) *Explication du feu d'artifice dressé devant l'hostel de ville par les ordres de messieurs les Prevost des Marchands & Echevins, pour la naissance du prince que nous vient de donner Madame la Dauphine*, n.p. (Paris), Veuve G. Adam, 1682, 4°.

— (attrib.) *Les illuminations de la galerie du Louvre pour les rejouissances de la naissance de Monseigneur le Duc de Bourgogne*, Paris, R.J.B. de la Caille, 1682, folio.

Mercier, Jean: *Io. Mercerii I.C. emblemata*, Bourges, no publ., 1592, 4°.

Montenay, Georgette de: *Emblemes, ou devises chrestiennes, composées par Damoiselle Georgette de Montenay*, Lyon, J. Marcorelle, 1567, 4°. (Copenhagen).

— *Ibid.*, Lyon, J. Marcorelle, 1571, 4°.

— *Georgiae Montaneae nobilis gallae emblematum christianorum centuria. Cum eorundem latina interpretatione. Cent emblemes chrestiens de Damoiselle Georgette de Montenay*, Zurich, C. Froschover, 1584, 4°.

— *Ibid.*, Heidelburg, J. Lancelot and A. Cambieri, 1602, 4°.

— *Livre d'armoiries en signe de fraternité, contenant cent comparaisons de vertus et emblemes chrestiens*, Frankfurt, J.C. Unckels, 1619, 4°. (This polyglot edition was produced with variant title pages for the different languages included).

— *Emblemes, ou devises chrestiennes, composées par Damoiselle Georgette de Montenay*, La Rochelle, J. Dinet, 1620, 4°.

Montlyart, J. de: See Valeriano Bolzani, Giovanni Pierio.

Morilhon, Le Sieur de: *Le Persée françois. Au Roy. Par le Sieur de Morilhon. Avec les mariages & entrée royale à Bourdeaus*, Bordeaux, G. Vernoy, 1612, 12°.

Musart, Charles: *Adolescens academicus sub institutione Salomonis. Authore R.P. Carolo Musart Belga, è Soc. Iesu Doct. Theol. et in Viennensi Austriae Academia Sacr. literarum interprete*, Douai, B. Bellere, 1633, 8°.

— See Luzvic, Etienne.

Nadal, Geronimo: *Evangelicae historiae imagines ex ordine Evangeliorum, quae toto anno in missae sacrificio recitantur, in ordinem temporis vitae Christi digestae. Auctore Hieronymo Natali Societatis Iesu theologo*, Antwerp, no publ., 1593, folio.

— *Ibid.*, Antwerp, no publ., 1596, folio.

— *Adnotationes et meditationes in Evangelia quae in sacrosancto Missae sacrificio tot anno leguntur. Cum Evangeliorum concordantia historiae integritati sufficienti. Accessit & index historiam ipsam Evangelicam in ordinem temporis vitae Christi distribuens. Secunda editio. Auctore Hieronymo Natali Societatis Iesu theologo*, Antwerp, M. Nutius, 1595, folio.

— *Adnotationes et meditationes in Evangelia...Editio ultima: in qua sacer textus ad emendationem Bibliorum Sixti V. et Clementis VIII. restitutus*, Antwerp, J. Moretus (Officina Plantiniana), 1607, folio.

— *Adnotationes et meditationes in Evangelia quae in sacrosancto Missae sacrificio toto anno leguntur. Cum eorundem Evangeliorum concordantia*, Antwerp, J. Galle, 1647, folio. (Hartnung and Hartnung catalogue 74, Munich, 1993, no.1213).

— *R.P. Hieronymi Natalis Societatis Iesu theologi annotationes et meditationes in Evangelia quae in sacrosancto Missae sacrificio toto anno leguntur. Cum venustissimis Evangelicae historiae aeneis imaginibus ex ordine Evangeliorum in ordinem temporis vitae Christi digestis, cum eorundem Evangeliorum concordantia. Editio ultima in qua sacer textus ad emendationem Bibliorum Sixti V. et Clementis VIII. restitutus*, Antwerp, H. and C. Verdussen, 1707, folio. (Private collection).

Offelen, Henri: *Devises et emblemes anciennes et modernes*: See La Feuille, Daniel de.

Pallavicini, Monsieur: See La Feuille, Daniel de.

Paradin, Claude: *Devises heroiques par M. Claude Paradin, Chanoyne de Beaujeu*, Lyon, J. de Tournes and G. Gazeau, 1551, 8°.

— *Ibid.*, Lyon, J. de Tournes and G. Gazeau, 1557, 8°.

— *Les devises heroiques de M. Claude Paradin, Chanoine de Beaujeu, du Seigneur Symeon et autres aucteurs*, Antwerp, C. Plantin, 1561, 8°.

— *Ibid.*, Antwerp, C. Plantin, 1562, 8°.

— *Ibid.*, Antwerp, Veuve J. Stelsius, 1563, 8°.

— *Ibid.*, Antwerp, C. Plantin, 1567.

— *Devises heroiques et emblemes. De M. Claude Paradin. Reveues et augmentées de moytié*, Paris, J. Millot, 1614, 8°.

— *Devises heroiques et emblemes de M. Claude Paradin. Reveuës et augmentées de moytié par Messire François d'Amboise. Et dedié à Monseigneur le premier President*, Paris, R. Boutonne, 1621/22, 8°.

— *Heroica M. Claudii Paradini Belliiocensis Canonici, & D. Gabrielis Symeonis, symbola: Iam recens ex idiomate Gallico in Lat...a Iohan Gubernatore*, Antwerp, C. Plantin, 1562, 16°.

— *Ibid.*, Antwerp, Veuve J. Stelsius, 1563, 16°.

— *Ibid.*, Antwerp, C. Plantin, 1567, 16°.

— *Ibid.*, Antwerp, C. Plantin, 1583, 16°.

— *Ibid.*, Leiden, F. Raphelengius (Officina Plantiniana), 1600, 16°.

— *Princelijcke devijsen ofte wapenen van M. Claude Paradyn Canonick van Beaujeu. Ende van den Heere Gabriel Simeon, ende meer ander Auteurs*, Antwerp, W. Silvius, 1563, 16°.

— *Ibid.*, Leiden, F. Raphelengius (Officina Plantiniana), 1615, 12°.

— *The Heroicall Devises of M. Claudius Paradin Canon of Beaujeu. Whereunto are added the Lord Gabriel Symeon's and others. Translated out of Latin by P.S.*, London, W. Kierney, 1591, 12°.

— *Quadrins historiques de la Bible*, Lyon, J. de Tournes, 1553, 8°.

Patin, Charles: *In stirpem regiam epigrammata. Authore M. Carolo Patin, doctore medico Parisiensi, & scholarum professore. Devises et emblemes de la Maison Royale. Par M. Charles Patin, docteur regent de la Faculté de Medecine de Paris*, Paris, no publ., 1660, 4°.

Perrault, Charles: *Courses de testes et de bague, faites par le Roy et par les princes et seigneurs de sa cour, en l'année M.DC.LXII*, Paris, S. Mabre-Cramoisy for the *Imprimerie royale*, 1670, folio.

— *Le labyrinthe de Versailles*, Paris, S. Mabre-Cramoisy for the *Imprimerie royale*, 1677, 8°.

— *Cabinet des Beaux Arts ou recueil d'estampes gravés d'apres les tableaux d'un plafond ou les beaux arts sont representés. Avec l'explication de ces mêmes tableaux*, Paris, G. Edelinck and A.C. Boulle, 1690, 4° obl.

Perret, Etienne: *XXV. fables des animaux. Vray miroir exemplaire, par lequel toute personne raisonnable pourra voir & comprendre, avec plaisir & contentement d'esprit, la conformité & vraye similitude de la personne ignorante (vivante selon les sensualitez charnelles) aux animaux & bestes brutes: composé et mis en lumiere par Estienne Perret, citoyen d'Anvers*, Antwerp, C. Plantin, 1578, folio.

— *Ibid.*, Delft, A. Gerards, 1618, folio.

— *Ibid.*, Delft, A. Gerards, 1621, folio.

Perrot de La Sale, Paul: *Tableaus sacrez de Paul Perrot Sieur de La Sale. P. Qui sont toutes les histoires du Viel Testament representees & exposees selon leur sens en poesie françoise*, Frankfurt, J. Feyrabendt, 'aux despends de Theodore de Bry', 1594, 8°.

Philieul, Vasquin: See Giovio, Paulo.

Philostratus: See Vigenère, Blaise de.

Pontoux, Claude de: *Figures du Nouveau Testament illustrées de huictains francoys pour l'interpretation et intelligence d'icelles*, Lyon, G. Roville, 1570, 8°.

Quarles, Francis: *Emblemes*, London, G. Miller, 1635, 8°.

— See Höltgen, Karl-Josef and Horden, John.

Reusner, Nicolas: *Emblemata Nicolai Reusneri IC partim ethica, et physica: partim verò historica & hieroglyphica, sed ad virtutis, morumque doctrinam omnia ingeniosè traducta: & in quatuor libros digesta, cum symbolis & inscriptionibus illustrium & clarorum virorum*, Frankfurt, S. Feyerabendt, 1581, 4°.

— *Nicolai Reusneri Aureolum emblematum liber singularis. Thobiae Stimmeri iconibus affabre effictis exornatus*, Strasbourg, B. Iobinus, 1591, 8°.

Richeome, Louis: *Tableaux sacrez des figures mystiques du tres-auguste sacrifice et sacrement de l'Eucharistie. Dediez à la tres chrestienne Royne de France et de Navarre Marie de Medicis par Louis Richeome, Provençal de la Compagnie de Jesus*, Paris L. Sonnius, 1601, 8°.

— *Ibid.*, Paris, L. Sonnius, 1609, 8°.

Ripa, Cesare: *Iconologia overo descrittione dell'imagini universali cavate dall'antichità et da altri luoghi da Cesare Ripa Perugino. Opera non meno utile, che necessaria à poeti, pittori, & scultori, per rappresentare le virtù, vitii, affetti & passioni humane*, Rome, Heirs of G. Gigliotti, 1593, 4°.

— *Iconologia...Di nuovo revista, & dal medesimo ampliata di 400 & più imagini et di figure ad intaglio adornata. Opera non meno utile che necessaria a poeti, pittori, scultori, & altri...*, Rome, L. Faci, 1603, 4°.

— See Baudoin, Jean.

Rollenhagen, Gabriel: *Nucleus emblematum selectissimorum, quae Itali vulgo impresas vocant privata industria studio singulari, undique conquisitus, non paucis venustis inventionibus auctus, additis carminibus illustratus. A Gabriele Rollenhagio Magdeburgense/Les emblemes de maistre Gabriel Rollenhague, mis en vers françois par un professeur de la langue françoise a Colongne*, Cologne, S. Erffens and Arnhem, J. Jansson, 1611, 4°.

— *Gabrielis Rollenhagii selectorum emblematum centuria secunda (La seconde centurie des emblemes du Sr Gabriel Rollenhague Magdeburgeois, paraphrastiquement mise en ryme francoyse. Par T.D.L.S.D.O.)*, Utrecht, C. de

Passe and Arnhem, J. Jansson, 1613, 4°.

— *Emblemata vollsinnighe uytbeelsels by Gabrielem Rollenhagius uyt andere versamelt en vermeerdert met syn eygene sinrijcke vindingen gestelt in Nederduytsche rijme door Zacharias Heyns*, Arnhem, J. Jansson, 1615/1617, 4°.

Romieu, Lanteaume de: See Guéroult, Guillaume.

Rozard, N.: *Le triomphe royal, et la réjouïssance des bons François sur le retour du roy, de la reine et des princes... avec la harangue qui leur a esté faite à leur entrée à Paris, le 18 de ce mois... Dedié à Madamoiselle*, Paris, Veuve J. Rémy, 1649, 4°.

Saavedra Fajardo, Diego de: *Idea de un principe politico christiano representada en cien empresas Dedicada al Principe de las Españas nuestro Señor por D. Diego Saavedra Fajardo del Consejo de su Magestad en el Supremo de las Indias, i su embajador extraordinario en Mantua I Esguizaros I residente en Alemania*, Munich, N. Heinrich, 1640, 4°.

— *Idea principis christiano-politico, centum symbolis expressa A Didaco Saavedra Faxardo, Equite &c*, Brussels, J. Mommartius and F. Vivien, 1649, folio.

— *Le prince chrestien et politique, traduit de l'Espagnol de D. Diegue Savedra a Faxardo, et dedié à Mr le Dauphin, par I. Rou, Advocat au Parlement*, Paris, Compagnie des marchands libraires du Palais, 1668, 12°, 2 vols.

— *Ibid.*, Amsterdam, J. Schipper, 1670, 12°.

— *The Royal Politician represented in One Hundred Emblems Written in Spanish by Don Diego Saavedra Faxardo, Knight...*, London, for M. Gilliflower and L. Meredith, 1700, 8°.

Sambucus, Johannes: *Emblemata, cum aliquot nummis antiqui operis, Ioannis Sambuci Tirnaviensis Pannonii*, Antwerp, C. Plantin, 1564, 8°.

— *Ibid.*, Antwerp, C. Plantin, 1566, 8°.

— *Ibid.*, Antwerp, C. Plantin, 1569, 8°.

— *Ibid.*, Antwerp, C. Plantin, 1576, 8°.

— *Ibid.*, Leiden, Officina Plantiniana, 1584, 8°.

— *Ibid.*, Leiden, Officina Plantiniana, 1599, 8°.

— *Emblemata I. Sambuci. In Nederlantsche tale ghetrouwelick overgheset*, Antwerp, C. Plantin, 1566, 8°.

— *Les emblemes du Signeur Jehan Sambucus, traduits de Latin en François*, Antwerp, C. Plantin, 1567, 8°.

Scève, Maurice: *Delie. Object de plus haulte vertu*, Lyon, S. Sabon for A. Constantin, 1544, 8°.

Sellius, Bernard: *Emblemata sacra, è praecipuis utriusque testamenti historiis concinnata a Bernardo Sellio Noviomago & a Petro van der Burgio figuris aeneis elegantissimis illustrata*, Amsterdam, M. Colinius, 1613, folio obl.

— *Ibid.*, Amsterdam, M. Colinius, 1639, folio obl.

Simeoni, Gabriele: See Giovio, Paulo.

— See Paradin, Claude.

Sucquet, Antoine: *Antoni Sucquet è Societate Iesu via vitae aeternae iconibus illustrata per Boëtium a Bolswert*, Antwerp, M. Nutius, 1620, 4°.

— *Den Wech des eeuwich levens beschreven int Latijn door p. Antonius Sucquet, over-geset door p. Gerardus Zoes, beyde priesters de Societeyt Iesu...*, Antwerp, H. Aertssens, 1622, 4°.

— *Le chemin de la vie eternele composé en Latin par le R.P. Antoine Sucquet de la Compagnie de Jesus. Translaté par le R.P. Pierre Morin, Parisien, de la mesme Compagnie. Declaré par images de Boëte a Bolswert*, Antwerp, H. Aertssens, 1623, 4°.

— *Weg zum Ewigen Leben, durch R.P.F. Carolum Stengelium verteutscht*, Augsburg, M. Langenwalder, 1627, 4°.

Typotius, Jacobus: *Symbola divina & humana pontificum imperatorum regum. Accessit brevis & facilis Isagoge Iac. Typotii*, Prague, no publ., 1601-3, folio, 3 vols.

Vaenius, Otto: *Q. Horatii Flacci emblemata. Imaginibus in aes incisis notisque illustrata, studio Othonis Vaeni Batavolugdunensis*, Antwerp, J. Verdussen, 1607, 4°.

— *Ibid.*, Antwerp, P. Lisaert, 1612, 4°.

— *Quinti Horatii Flacci emblemata...Editio nova correctior, & SS. patrum, Senecae atque aliorum philosophorum & poëtarum sententiis, novisque versibus aucta*, Brussels, F. Foppens, 1682, folio.

— *Ibid.*, Brussels, F. Foppens, 1683, folio.

— *Othonis Vaeni emblemata horatiana, imaginibus in aes incisis atque Latino Germanico Gallico et Belgico carmine illustrata*, Amsterdam, H. Wetstein, 1684, 8°.

— *Amorum emblemata, figuris aeneis incisa studio Othonis Vaeni Batavo-Lugdunensis*, Antwerp, 'Venalia apud auctorem', 1608, 4° obl.

— See Porteman, Karel.

— *Othonis Vaeni emblemata, aliquot selectiora amatoria*, Amsterdam, W. Janszon, 1618.

— *Emblemes d'amour illustrez d'une explication en prose fort facille pour entendre le sens moral de chaque embleme*, Paris, B. Loyson, n.d., 4°. (Congress).

— *Ibid.*, n.p.n.d., 4°. (Glasgow UL; Mazarine).

— *Ibid.*, n.p.n.d., 4°. (variant) (Glasgow UL).

— *Les emblemes de l'amour humain*, Brussels, F. Foppens, 1667, 4° obl.

— *Amoris divini emblemata studio et aere Othonis Vaeni concinnata*, Antwerp, M. Nutius and J. Meursius, 1615, 4°.

— *Ibid.*, Antwerp, B. Moretus (Officina Plantiniana), 1660, 4°.

— *Emblemes de l'amour divin*, Paris, P. Landry, n.d. (c.1690), 8°.

— *Emblemes de l'amour divin. Inventées par Otho Venus, avec l'explication de chacunes*, Paris, Le Blond, n.d. (c.1690), 4°. (Folger; Getty).

— See Le Roy, Sieur de Gomberville, Marin.

— See La Mothe-Guyon, Madame de.

Valdor, Jean: *Explication du magnifique dessein du feu de joye, faict par ordre de messieurs les Prevost des Marchands, Echevins de la ville de Paris, pour le jour de la naissance de Louys 14. Roy de France & de Navarre, & en resjouïssance de son heureux retour dans sa bonne ville de Paris. Composé par le Sieur Valdor. Par commandement de Messieurs les Prevost des Marchands & Eschevins de la ville de Paris*, Paris, L. Ninain, 1649, 4°.

— *Les triomphes de Louis le Juste XIII. du nom, Roy de France et de Navarre. Contenans les plus grandes actions ou Sa Majesté s'est trouvée en personne, representées en figures aenigmatiques exposées par un poëme heroïque de Charles Beys, & accompagnées de vers François sous chaque figure, composez par P. de Corneille. Avec les portraits des rois, princes et generaux d'armees, qui ont assisté ou servy ce belliqueux Louis le Juste combattant; et leurs devises & expositions en forme d'eloges, par Henry Estienne escuyer, Sieur des Fossez, poete et interprete du Roy és langues Grecque & Latine. Ensemble le plan des villes, sieges et batailles, avec un abregé de la vie de ce grand Monarque, par René Barry, Conseiller du Roy & historiographe de Sa Majesté. Le tout traduit en Latin par le R.P. Nicolai, Docteur en Sorbonne de la Faculté de Paris, & premier regent du grand Convent des Jacobins. Ouvrage entrepris & fini par Jean Valdor, Liegeois, Calcographe du Roy. Le tout par commandement de leurs Majestez*, Paris, A. Estienne for the *Imprimerie royale*, 1649, folio.

Valeriano Bolzani, Giovanni Pierio: *Hieroglyphica sive de sacris Aegyptiorum aliarumque gentium literis, commentarii Ioannis Valeriani Bolzani Bellunensis*, Basle, M. Isengrin, 1556, folio.

— *Ibid.*, Lyon, B. Honorat, 1579, folio.

— *Ibid.*, Lyon, B. Honorat, 1586, folio.

— *Ibid.*, Lyon, T. Soubron, 1595, folio.

— *Ibid.*, Lyon, P. Frellon, 1602, folio.

— *Ibid.*, Lyon, P. Frellon, 1610, folio.

— *Commentaires hieroglyphiques ou images des choses de Jan Pierius Valerian, esquels comme en un vif tableau est ingenieusement depeinct & representé l'estat de plusieurs choses antiques: comme de monnoyes, medales, armes, inscriptions & devises, obelisques, pyramides & autres monumens: outre une infinité de diverses & profitables histoires, proverbes & lieux communs: avec la parfaicte interpretation des mysteres d'Aegypte, & de plusieurs passages de l'escriture saincte conformes à iceux, plus deux livres de Coelius Curio, touchant ce qui est signifié par les diverses images & pourtraits des dieux & des hommes, mis en François par Gabriel Chappuys Tourangeau,* Lyon, B. Honorat, 1576, folio.

— *Les hieroglyphiques de Jan-Pierre Valerian vulgairement nommé Pierius. Autrement commentaires des lettres et figures sacrées des Aegyptiens & autres nations. Oeuvre reduicte en cinquante huict livres, ausquels sont adjoincts deux autres de Coelius Curio, touchant ce qui est signifié par les diverses effigies, et pourtraicts des dieux, et des hommes, nouvellement donnez aux François par J. de Montlyart,* Lyon, P. Frellon, 1615, folio.

— See Caseneuve, Louis de.

Valladier, André: *Labyrinthe royal de l'Hercule gaulois triomphant. Sur le suject des fortunes, batailles, victoires, trophées, triomphes, mariage, & autres faicts heroiques, & memorables de tres-auguste & tres-chrestien prince Henri IIII. Roy de France, & de Navarre. Représenté à l'entrée triomphante de la royne en la cité d'Avignon. Le 19. novembre, l'an M.DC. Ou sont contenuës les magnificences et triomphes dressez à cet effect par ladicte ville,* Avignon, J. Bramereau, 1601, 4°.

— See (anon.):*Une entrée royale: Marie de Medicis à Avignon.*

Veneroni, Le Sieur de: *Fables choisies traduites en Italien, avec le François à côté. Par le Sieur de Veneroni, maître des langues Italienne & Françoyse, à Paris. Le tout enrichi de figures en taille douce à chaque fable,* Amsterdam, G. Gallet, 1700, 8°.

Verrien, Nicolas: *Livre curieux et utile pour les sçavans, et artistes. Composé de trois alphabets de chiffres simples, doubles & triples, fleuronnez et au premier trait. Accompagné d'un tres grand nombre de devises, emblêmes, médailles et autres figures hieroglyfiques. Ensemble de plusieurs supports et cimiers pour les ornemens des armes. Avec une table tres ample par le moyen de laquelle on trouvera facilement tous les noms imaginables. Le tout inventé, dessiné et gravé par Nicolas Verrien maistre graveur,* Paris, N. Verrien, 1685, 8°.

— *Recueil d'emblêmes, devises, medailles et figures hieroglyphiques, au nombre de douze cent, avec leurs explications,* Paris, J. Jombert, 1696, 8°.

— *Ibid.,* Paris, J. Jombert, 1724, 8°.

Vigenère, Blaise de: *Les images ou tableaux de platte-peinture de Philostrate Lemnien sophiste Grec. Mis en François par Blaise de Vigenere. Avec des argumens & annotations sur chacun d'iceux,* Paris, N. Chesneau, 1578, 4°.

— *Les images ou tableaux de platte peinture des deux Philostrates sophistes grecs et les statues de Callistrate. Mis en Francois par Blaise de Vigenere Bourbonnois. Enrichis d'arguments et annotations. Reveus et corrigez sur l'original par un docte personnage de ce temps en la langue Grecque. Et representez en taille douce en cette nouvelle edition. Avec des epigrammes sur chacun d'iceux par*

Artus Thomas Sieur d'Embry, Paris, Veuve A. l'Angelier, 1614, folio.

Ibid., Paris, Veuve A. l'Angelier, 1615, folio.

Ibid., Paris, Veuve A. l'Angelier, 1629, folio.

Ibid., Paris, Veuve A. l'Angelier, 1630, folio.

Ibid., Paris, Veuve A. l'Angelier, 1637, folio.

Vulson, Marc de: *La science heroique, traitant de la noblesse, de l'origine des armes, de leurs blasons, & symboles, des tymbres, bourlets, couronnes, cimiers, lambrequins, supports, & tenans, & autres ornemens de l'escu, de la devise, & du cry de guerre, de l'escu pendant & des pas & emprises des anciens chevaliers, des formes differentes de leurs tombeaux, et des marques exterieures de l'escu de nos roys, des reynes, & enfans de France, & des officiers de la couronne, & de la maison du Roy. Avec la genealogie succincte de la maison de Rosmadec en Bretagne. Le tout embelly d'un grand nombre de figures en taille douce, sur toutes les matieres. Par Marc de Vulson, Sieur de la Colombiere, Chevalier de l'Ordre de S. Michel, & gentilhomme ordinaire de la maison du Roy*, Paris, S. Cramoisy and G. Cramoisy, 1644, folio.

— *Le vray theatre d'honneur et de chevalerie ou le miroir heroique de la noblesse, contenant les combats ou jeux sacrez des Grecs & des Romains, les triomphes, les tournois, les joustes, les pas, les emprises ou entreprises, les armes, les combats à la barriere, les carrosels, les courses de bague & de la quintaine, les machines, les chariots de triomphe, les cartels, les devises, les prix, les voeux, les sermons, les ceremonies, les statuts, les ordres, & autres magnificences & exercices des anciens nobles devant la paix. Avec le formulaire d'un tournoy tel qu'on le pourroit faire à present avec les armes dont les gentils-hommes se servent à la guerre. Le tout enrichy de figures en taille-douce sur les principales matieres. Dedié à Monseigneur le Cardinal Mazarin. Par Marc de Vulson, Sieur de la Colombiere*, Paris, A. Courbé, 1648, 2 vols, folio.

— *Les portraits des hommes illustres françois qui sont peints dans la gallerie du Palais Cardinal de Richelieu: avec leurs principales actions, armes, devises, & eloges latins; desseignez & gravez par les Sieurs Heince & Bignon, peintres & graveurs ordinaires du Roy. Dediez a Monseigneur Seguier Chancelier de France, Comte de Gyen, &c. Ensemble les abregez historiques de leurs vies, composez par M. de Vulson, Sieur de la Colombiere, gentil-homme ordinaire de la chambre du Roy, &c*, Paris, J. Paslé and C. de Sercy, 1650, folio.

— *Ibid.*, Paris, C. de Sercy, E. Pepingué and G. de Luynes, 1655, folio.

— *Ibid.*, Paris, C. de Sercy, G. de Luynes, J.B. Loyson, J. Guignard, E. Loyson and C. Barbin, 1664, folio.

— *Ibid.*, Paris, M. Bobin and N. Le Gras, 1667, 12°.

— *Ibid.*, Paris, F. Mauger and J. Cottin, 1668, 12°.

— *Ibid.*, Paris, J. Cottin, 1669, 12°.

Whitney, Geffrey: *A Choice of Emblemes and Other Devises, for the most parte gathered out of sundrie writers, Englished and Moralized. And divers newly devised, by Geffrey Whitney*, Leiden, F. Raphelengius for C. Plantin, 1586, 4°.

Zincgref, Julius Wilhelm: *Emblematum ethico-politicorum centuria Iulii Guillielmi Zincgrefi*, n.p. (Heidelburg), M. Merian, 1619, 4°.

ii) ANONYMOUS WORKS

Amoris divini et humani antipathia e variis sacrae scripturae locis deprompta emblematis suis expressa. Et SS. PP. authoritatibus illustrata. Les effects divers de l'amour divin et humain, richement exprimez par petits emblemes tirés des SS. Escritures et des SS. peres. Le tout mis en Latin et François, Paris, G. Lenoir, 1628, 8°. (Wolfenbüttel). (*BFEB*, F.076)

— *Ibid.*, Paris, P. Giffart, n.d., 4°. (Glasgow UL). (*BFEB*, F.082)

— *Ibid.*, Paris, J. Moncornet, n.d., 4°. (Getty). (*BFEB*, F.083)

Amoris divini et humani antipathia. Sive effectus varii, e variis Sacrae Scripturae locis deprompti emblematis suis expressi SS. PP. authoritatibus nec non Gallicis, Hispanicis et Flandricis versibus illustrati. Editio II. aucta et recognita. Les effects divers de l'amour divin et humain richement exprimez par petits emblemes tirez des SS. Escritures et des SS. peres, et illustrez par vers François, Espagnols et Flamends, Antwerp, G. Wolsschat for M. Snyders, 1629, 8°. (*BFEB*, F.077)

— *Ibid.*, Antwerp, G. Wolsschat for M. Snyders, 1636, 8°. (Plantin-Moretus). (*BFEB*, F.077)

— *Ibid.*, Antwerp, G. Wolsschat for M. Snyders, 1648, 8°. (*BFEB*, F.077)

Amoris divini et humani effectus varii Sacrae Scripturae sanctorumque PP. sententiis ac Gallicis versibus illustrati, Antwerp, M. Snyders, 1626, 8°. (Glasgow UL; Mazarine). (*BFEB*, F.075)

Antipathia amoris divini et humani duobus libris comprehensa, per themata et sententias, insuper et figuras aeneas. Adiectis versibus Gallicis et Hispanicis, illustrata, Salzburg, J.B. Mayr, 1694, 8°. (Glasgow UL). (*BFEB*, F.081)

— See *Theatrum amoris divini et humani*.

— See *Les emblemes d'amour divin et humain ensemble. Expliquez par des vers françois. Par un pere Capucin.*

Arrivée du Roy en la ville du Mans, le 28. juillet 1620. Ensemble la harangue faicte à Sa Majesté au nom des habitans de ladicte ville. Et generallement tout ce qui s'est passé és lieux circonvoysins, avant l'arrivée de. Sadicte Majesté, Paris, I. Mesnier, 1620, 8°.

L'arrivée du Roy en sa ville d'Angoulesme, le dimanche 13. decembre. Avec le nombre des chefs & gens de guerre qui conduisent Sa Majesté, Paris, A. du Brueil, 1615, 8°.

Les ceremonies du sacre et couronnement du tres-chrestien roy de France & de

Navarre, Louis XIII, plus son entree dans la ville de Reims, & son retour à Paris, Paris, J. Richer, 1610, 8°.

C'est l'ordre et forme qui a esté tenu au sacre et couronnement de treshaulte et tresillustre dame Madame Catherine de Medicis, Royne de France, faicte en l'eglise Monseigneur sainct Denys en France, le X. jour de Juin. M.D.XLIX, Paris, J. Dallier, 1549, 8°.

— See McFarlane, I.D.

C'est l'ordre qui a esté tenu à la nouvelle et joyeuse entrée, que treshault, tresexcellent, trespuissant prince, le Roy treschrestien Henry deuxiesme de ce nom a faicte en sa bonne ville et cité de Paris, capitale de son royaume, le sezieme jour de Juin M.D.XLIX, Paris, J. Dallier, 1549, 8°.

— See McFarlane, I.D.

Collegii Parisiensis Societatis Iesu festi plausus ad nuptias Ludovici Galliarum Delphini et Mariae Annae Christianae Victoriae Bavarae, Paris, S. Benard, 1680, folio.

Le colloque des trois supposts du Seigneur de la Coquille: où le char triomfant de Monseigneur le Daufin est representé par plusieurs personnages, figures, emblemes & enigmes. A Monseigneur d'Halincourt, Lyon, 'Par les supposts de l'Imprimerie', 1610, 8°. (Arsenal).

Devises presentees à Monseigneur de Mascon par les escoliers du college de la Compagnie de Jesus. Le premier jour de l'annee 1682, n.p.n.d., 8°. (BFEB, F.221)

Discours sur les devises, emblesmes, et revers de medailles, in Mercure Galant, extraordinaire d'octobre, 1678, pp.214-68.

Egapathe martyr de Lyon, tragedie. Representée le 27 de May 1668, jour de la Tres-sainte Trinité par les Rhetoriciens du College de la Trinité de la Compagnie de Jesus, en la reception solenelle de Messieurs les Prevost des Marchands & Eschevins en qualité de fondateurs, Lyon, J. Canier, 1668, 4°.

— See Charonier, Gabriel.

Emblemata amatoria. Emblemes d'amour en quatre langues, 'A Londe, chez l'Amoureux', n.d., 8°.

— See Ayres, Philip.

— See Triumphus amoris.

Emblemata anniversaria Academiae Altorfinae studiorum iuventutis exercitandorum causa proposita et variorum orationibus exposita, Nuremberg, C. Lochner, 1597, 4°.

Emblemata anniversaria Academiae Noribergensis, quae est Altorfii: studiorum iuventutis exercitandorum caussa inde ab ann. Christi 1577 usque ad annum 1616 proposita...Editio II, Nuremberg, A. Wagenman, 1617, 4°.

Les emblemes d'amour divin et humain ensemble. Expliquez par des vers françois.

Par un pere Capucin, Paris, J. Messager, n.d. (after 1631), 8°. (Folger; Wolfenbüttel). (*BFEB*, F.078)

— *Ibid.*, Paris, P. Mariette, n.d. (in or after 1637), 8°. (Glasgow UL; New York). (*BFEB*, F.080)

— See *Amoris divini et humani antipathia*.

Entrée de Loys XIII. Roy de France et de Navarre. Dans sa ville d'Arles, le vingt-neufiesme Octobre mil six cens vingt-deux..., Avignon, J. Bramereau, 1623, folio.

Entrée du Roy en la ville et chasteau de Niort, le dimanche 23 mai 1621. Ensemble tout ce qui s'est passé en icelle par ceux de la religion pretendue reformée, Paris, N. Alexandre, 1621, 8°.

Entrée magnifique du roy faicte en sa ville d'Orleans, le mardy huictiesme juillet 1614, avec l'ordre et ceremonies observées en icelle, Paris, M. Mondiere, 1614, 8°.

L'entrée royale et magnifique du Roy en sa ville de Bergerac. Ensemble l'humble remonstrance des deputés de l'assemblée et bourgeois de La Rochelle à Sa Majesté, Paris, E. de l'Oreille, 1621, 8°.

Entrée royale faite au Roy en la ville de Sainct Jean d'Angely, le onziesme septembre mil six cent vingt; ensemble quels ont esté les portiques, amphitheatre, tableaux, devises et emblêmes en icelle ceremonie, et generallement tout ce qui s'est passé de plus particulier tant en ladite ville que depuis le depart de Sa Majesté de la ville de Poictiers jusques à son arrivée en icelle, Paris, I. Mesnier, 1620, 8°.

Les entrées de la reyne et de monseigneur daulphin, lieutenant general du roy et gouverneur en ce pays de Normandie. Faictes a Rouen en l'an mil cinq cents trente et ung, Lyon, R. Gaultier, n.d. (1531), 4°, ed. A. Pottier, Rouen, 1866.

L'entree triomphante de Leurs Majestez Louis XIV. Roy de France et de Navarre, et Marie Therese d'Austriche son espouse dans la ville de Paris capitale de leurs royaumes, au retour de la signature de la paix generalle et de leur heureux mariage. Enrichie de plusieurs figures, des harangues & de diverses pieces considerables pour l'histoire. Le tout exactement recueilly par l'ordre de Messieurs de ville. Et imprimee l'an M.DC.LXII, Paris, P. Le Petit, T. Joly and L. Bilaine, 1662, folio.

Esbatement moral des animaux, Antwerp, G. Smits for P. Galle, n.d. (1578), 4°. (*BFEB*, F.238)

L'explication des figures et peintures qui sont representees pour l'entrée du roy et de la reine, Paris, J. Promé, 1660, 4°.

Explication du feu d'artifice dressé devant l'hostel de ville par l'ordre de messieurs les Prevost des Marchands & Echevins à la naissance de Monseigneur le Duc de Berry, Paris, T. Guillain, n.d. (1686), 4°.

Explication en vers des tableaux de la galerie de Versailles. Dediée à Monseigneur le Duc de Bourgogne, Paris, M. Guerout and T. Girard, 1691, 4°.

Le feu royal et magnifique qui s'est tiré sur la riviere de Seine, vis-à-vis du Louvre, en presence de Leurs Majestés, par ordre de Messieurs de ville pour la resjouissance de l'entrée du roy et de la reine, le 29 aoust 1660, Paris, J.-B. Loyson, 1660, 4°.

La glorieuse et triomphante entrée de la serenissime Princesse Marie Thereze d'Austriche, infante d'Espagne, au retour de son tres-auguste mariage avec nostre invincible monarque Louis de Bourbon XIV. Roy de France et de Navarre, dans leur ville de Paris, Paris, L. Barbote, 1660, 4°.

Historiarum veteris instrumenti icones, ad vivum expressae. Unà cum brevi sed quoad fieri potuit, dilucida earundem expositione, Lyon, M. and G. Trechsel, 1538, 8°. (Arsenal).

Imago primi saeculi Societatis Iesu a Provincia Flandro-Belgica eiusdem Societatis repraesentata, Antwerp, B. Moretus (Officina Plantiniana), 1640, folio.

Le jardin d'honneur, contenant plusieurs apologies, proverbes, et ditz moraux, avec les histoires & figures. Aussi y sont ajoustez plusieurs ballades, rondeaux, dixains, huitains & trioletz fort joyeux. Reveu & corrigé outre les precedantes impressions, Paris, E. Groulleau, 1550, 16°. (*BFEB*, F.348)

— *Ibid.*, Paris, E. Groulleau, 1555, 16°. (Wolfenbüttel). (*BFEB*, F.349)

— *Ibid.*, Paris, E. Groulleau, 1559, 16°. (Vienna). (*BFEB*, F.350)

Journal de ce qui s'est fait et passé tant durant la guerre et siége de Bordeaux que dans le traité de paix; avec les harangues faites lors de la magnifique entrée du roy dans ladite ville, et ce qui s'est observé à sa sortie, n.p., 1650, 4°.

La magnificence de la superbe et triomphante entrée de la noble et antique cité de Lyon faicte au treschrestien Roy de France Henry deuxiesme de ce nom, et de la Royne Catherine son espouse le XXIII. de Septembre M.D.XLVIII, Lyon, G. Roville, 1549, 4°.

— See Cooper, Richard.

Les magnificences faites en la ville de Bourdeaux à l'entrée du roy, le mercredi 7 de ce mois, Paris, A. du Brueil, 1615, 8°.

Medailles sur les principaux evenemens du regne de Louis le Grand avec des explications historiques, par l'Academie royale des medailles et des inscriptions, Paris, Imprimerie royale, 1702, folio.

La montre generale de Messieurs les bourgeois de la ville de Paris, qui sont choisis pour paroistre à la magnifique entrée du roy et de la reine dans sa ville capitale, Paris, A. Lesselin, 1660, 4°.

L'ordre, entree et ceremonies observees par la ville de Paris. A l'heureux retour de Louys treiziesme, Roy de France & de Navarre. Avec la montre generalle faite au pré aux Clercs: et la reception des Sieurs Prevost des Marchans & Eschevins de ladicte ville. Faicte à Sa Majesté le 16. de Septembre. Par Maistre C. Jourdan, huissier des comptes, Parisien, Paris, J. Brunet, 1614, 8°.

Ratio atque institutio studiorum, per sex patres ad id iussu R.P. Praepositi Generalis deputatos conscripta, Rome, 'In collegio Societatis Iesu', 1686, 8°.

Reception de tres-chrestien, tres-juste, et tres-victorieux monarque Louys XIII. Roy de France & de Navarre, premier Comte & Chanoine de l'Eglise de Lyon; et de tres-chrestienne, tres-auguste, & tres-vertueuse royne Anne d'Austriche; Par Messieurs les Doyen, Chanoines, & Comtes de Lyon en leur cloistre & eglise, le XI. Decembre, M.DC.XXII, Lyon, J. Roussin, 1623, folio.

Recit veritable de tout ce qui s'est fait et passé à l'entrée du roy en la ville d'Auxerre; avec les harangues faites à Leurs Majestés par Messieurs du clergé de ladite ville, Paris, N. Bessin, 1650, 4°.

Recueil des choses notables, qui ont esté faites à Bayonne, à l'entreveuë du Roy treschrestien Charles neufieme de ce nom et la Royne sa treshonorée mere avec la Royne catholique sa soeur, Paris M. de Vascosan, 1566, 4°.

Recueil des plusieurs enigmes, airs, devises et medailles. Enrichis des figures, Amsterdam, J. de Waesberge, 1680, 12°.

— *Ibid.*, Amsterdam, J. de Waesberge, 1684, 12°.

Relation de toutes les particularitez qui se sont faites et passees dans la celebre entrée du Roy et de la Reyne, avec l'ordre de la marche du clergé & des cours souveraines. Ensemble la magnifique pompe des seigneurs, & de toute leur suitte: Et toutes les ceremonies du Te Deum, Paris, J.-B. Loyson, 1660, 4°.

La resjouissance de Poictiers sur l'arrivée du Roy & de la Royne Regente, mere du Roy, Poitiers, J. Thoreau, n.d., 8°.

La royale maison du trone de la triomphante entrée de Leurs Majestez en la ville de Paris, n.p., 1660, 4°.

La royalle entree du Roy et de la Royne en la ville de Chartres. Avec les magnificences & ceremonies qui s'y sont observées le Jeudy 26. Septembre, Paris, pour J. Chemin, 1619, 12°. (Republ. Chartres, 1864).

Le Soleil au signe du Lyon. D'où quelques paralleles sont tirez, avec le tres-chrestien, tres-juste, & tres-victorieux monarque Louys XIII. Roy de France & de Navarre, en son entrée triomphante dans sa ville de Lyon. Ensemble un sommaire recit de tout ce qui s'est passé de remarquable en ladite entrée de Sa Majesté, & de la plus illustre princesse de la Terre Anne d'Austriche, Royne de France & de Navarre, dans ladite ville de Lyon le 11. Decembre 1622, Lyon, J. Jullieron, 1623, folio.

Theatrum amoris divini et humani, emblematis tanquam scenis expressi, Latinis, Gallicis, Hispanicis & Flandricis versibus illustrati, Antwerp, M. Snyders, 1655, 8°. (Folger).

— *Ibid.*, Antwerp, J. Galle, 1670, 8°. (Glasgow UL).

— See *Amoris divini et humani antipathia*.

Timandre. Poesie pastorale à l'honneur de Philippe de France Duc d'Anjou, pour son heureux avenement à la couronne d'Espagne. Elle sera representée par les Rhetoriciens du College de Louis le Grand chez les Peres de la Compagnie de Jesus. Mercredy 22. Decembre de l'annee 1700 à 2. heures aprés midy, Paris, Veuve A. Lambin, 1700, 4°.

Triumphus amoris, de cunctis universi huius incolis actus, emblematibus ac symbolis Latinis, Italicis, Gallicis, Germanicis oculis exhibitus. Oder: Die über den gantzen Erd-Kraiss triumphirende Liebe in nachdencklichen Sinn-Bildern neben sehr curiosen Lateinischen, Italienischen, Französischen und Teutschen Bey-Sprüchen, auch Kurzweiligen Versen fürgestellet, Augsburg, J. Friedrich, 1699, 8°.

— See Ayres, Philip.

— See *Emblemata amatoria. Emblemes d'amour en quatre langues.*

P.T.L. thronus cupidinis. Editio altera; priori emendatior, & multo auctior, Amsterdam, W. Janszon, 1618, 16° obl.

P.T.L. thronus cupidinis. Editio tertia; prioribus emendatior, & multo auctior, Amsterdam, W. Janszon, 1620, 16° obl. (Glasgow UL; Wolfenbüttel).

Tronus cupidinis sive emblemata amatoria P.T.L. Excudit Crisp. Pass., n.p.n.d., 16° obl. (Amsterdam UL).

Typus mundi in quo eius calamitates et pericula nec non divini humanique amoris antipathia, emblematice proponuntur a R.R.C.S.I.A., Antwerp, J. Cnobbart, 1627, 12°.

La veritable explication en prose et en vers des figures ovales, termes et portraits de tous les rois de France qui sont dessus le pont Nostre-Dame à Paris; ensemble quelques remarques curieuses et particulieres pour les amateurs de l'histoire; avec la description des arcs de triomphe elevés dans les places publiques pour l'entrée du roy et de la reine, Paris, J.-B. Loyson, 1660, 4°.

La Voye de laict ou le chemin des heros au Palais de la gloire. Ouvert à l'entrée triomphante de Louys XIII. Roy de France & de Navarre en la cité d'Avignon le 16. de Novembre 1622..., Avignon, J. Bramereau, 1623, 4°.

II. MANUSCRIPTS AND ENGRAVINGS

i) NAMED WORKS

BnF Ms. fr. 7819: Bailly, Jacques: *Devises pour les tapisseries du Roy.*

— See Grivel, M. and Fumaroli, M.

— See Félibien, André.

BnF Ms. fr. 11911: Clément, Monsieur: *Regles pour la connoissance des devises* (pp.327-30).

BnF Ms. fr. 15257: *Devises royalles et heroiques*, 1626.

BnF Ms. Smith Lesouëf 98: *Devises sur differans sujets.*

Arsenal Ms. 3184: *Ces soixantes et douze devises sont des roys, princes et seigneurs dames et roynes de France.*

Arsenal Ms. 3328: Charles Perrault, *Discours sur l'art des devises* (ff.1-46).

Arsenal Ms. 5217 (rés): *Recueil de devises données à Marie de la Tour, Duchesse de la Tremoille.*

Arsenal Ms. 5420: Clément, Monsieur: *Regles pour la connoissance des devises, par M..., Conseiller en la Cour des Aydes*, (part 1, pp.513-20).

Bibl. de l'Institut Ms. 623: Boissard, Jean-Jacques: *Emblemata.*

Bibl. Municipale de Lyon Ms. 1514: Ménestrier, Claude-François: *L'idée de l'estude d'un honeste homme.*

BL Add. Ms. 61822: Sidney, Philip: *Astrophel and Stella* (containing *Pithie sentences and wise sayinges*).

BL Harleian Ms. 4377: Bailly, Jacques: *Devises pour les tapisseries du Roy.*

BL Sloane Ms. 3794: Palmer, Thomas: *Two hundred poosees devysed by Thomas Palmer.*

ii) OTHER COLLECTIONS

BnF Ms. lat. 10170

BnF Ms. lat. 10171

BnF Ms. lat. 13064

BnF Ms. fr. 894

BnF Ms. fr. 13426

BnF Ms. fr. 20159

BnF Ms. fr. 20244

BnF Ms. fr. 23045

BnF Ms. fr. 24447

BnF Ms. fr. 24713

BnF Ms. fr. nouv. acq. 11253

BnF Estampes Te 120

III. WORKS OF CRITICISM AND REFERENCE

Adams, Alison: 'The woodcuts of Alciato's Death emblems', *Emblematica*, 6,2, 1992 (1994), pp.391-7.

— '*Les Emblemes ou devises chrestiennes* de Georgette de Montenay: édition de 1567', *Bibliothèque d'Humanisme et Renaissance*, 62, 3, 2000 (forthcoming).

Adams, Alison (ed.): Gilles Corrozet, *L'Hecatongraphie (1544) & Les Emblemes du Tableau de Cebes (1543)*, Geneva, 1997.

Adams, Alison, and Harper, Anthony (eds): *The Emblem in Renaissance and Baroque Europe. Tradition and Variety*, Leiden, 1992.

Adams, Alison; Rawles, Stephen; and Saunders, Alison: *A Bibliography of French Emblem Books of the Sixteenth and Seventeenth Centuries*, vol.1, Geneva, 1999.

Allut, P.: *Recherches sur la vie et sur les oeuvres du P. Claude-François Ménestrier de la Compagnie de Jesus, suivies d'un Recueil de lettres inédites de ce Père à Guichenon, & de quelques autres lettres de divers savans de son temps, inédites aussi*, Lyon, 1856.

Astier, Régine: 'Louis XIV, "Premier Danseur"', in David L. Rubin, ed., *Sun King. The Ascendancy of French Culture during the Reign of Louis XIV*, Washington, 1992, pp.73-102.

Balavoine, Claudie: 'Archéologie de l'emblème littéraire: la dédicace à Conrad Peutinger des *Emblemata* d'André Alciat', in M.-T. Jones Davies, ed., *Emblèmes et devises au temps de la Renaissance*, Paris, 1981, pp.9-22.

— 'Les *Emblemes* d'Alciat: sens et contresens', in Y. Giraud, ed., *L'emblème à la Renaissance. Actes de la journée d'études du 10 mai 1980*, Paris, 1982, pp.49-59.

Bath, Michael: *Speaking Pictures. English Emblem Books and Renaissance Culture*, London, 1994.

Black, Lynette C.: 'Popular devotional emblematics: a comparison of Sucquet's *Le chemin de la vie eternele* and Hugo's *Les pieux desirs*', *Emblematica*, 9,1, 1995, pp.1-20.

— '"Une doctrine sans estude": Herman Hugo's *Pia Desideria* as *Les Pieux Desirs*', in Marc van Vaeck and John Manning, eds, *The Jesuits and the Emblem Tradition*, Turnhout, 1999, pp.233-47.

Bluche, François: *Louis XIV* (trans. Mark Greengrass), Oxford, 1990.

Bos, J., and Gruys, J.A.: *Cats Catalogus: de werken van Jacob Cats in de Short-Title Catalogue*, Netherlands, The Hague, 1996.

Boutier, J.; Dewerpe, A.; and Nordman, D.: *Un tour de France royal. Le voyage de Charles IX 1564-1566* , Paris, 1984.

Breugelmans, R.: '*Quaeris quid sit amor?* Ascription, date of publication and printer', *Quaerendo*, 3, 1973, pp.281-90.

Burke, Peter: *The Fabrication of Louis XIV*, Yale, 1992.

Cameron, Keith (ed.): *From Valois to Bourbon. Dynasty, State and Society in Early Modern France*, Exeter, 1989.

Campa, Pedro: *Emblemata Hispanica. An Annotated Bibliography of Spanish Emblem Literature to the Year 1700*, Durham, North Carolina, 1990.

Canova-Green, Marie-Claude: 'Représentations de l'ordre et du désordre dans le ballet de cour' in R. Duchêne and P. Ronzeaud, eds, *Ordre et contestation au temps des classiques: Actes du 21e Colloque du Centre Méridional de Rencontre sur le XVIIe Siècle jointe avec le 23e Colloque de la North American Society for Seventeenth-Century French Literature, Marseille 19-23 juin 1991*, Paris, 1992, pp.309-19.

Cartier, A.: *Bibliographie des éditions des De Tournes imprimeurs lyonnais*, Paris, 1937, 2 vols.

Cave, Terence: *Devotional Poetry in France c.1570-1613*, Cambridge, 1969.

Chastel, A.; McAllister-Johnson, W.; and Béguin, S.: 'VI. Le programme', *Revue de l'Art*, 16-17, 1972, pp.143-72. (Special issue devoted to the Galerie François 1er at Fontainebleau).

Chatelain, Jean-Marc: *Livres d'emblèmes et de devises, une anthologie (1531-1735)*, Paris, 1993.

— 'Lire pour croire: mises en texte de l'emblème et art de méditer au XVIIe siècle', *Bibliothèque de l'Ecole des Chartes*, 150, 1992, pp.321-51.

Chevalier, C.: 'La pédagogie des collèges jésuites', *Littérature*, 7, 1972, pp.120-28.

Choné, Paulette: *Emblèmes et pensée symbolique en Lorraine (1525-1633)*, Paris, 1991.

— '"*Domus optima*". Un manuscrit emblématique au collège des jésuites de Verdun (1585)', in Marc van Vaeck and John Manning, eds, *The Jesuits and the Emblem Tradition*, Turnhout, 1999, pp.35-68.

Clements, R.J.: *Picta poesis. Literary and Humanistic Theory in Renaissance Emblem Books*, Rome, 1960.

Compère, M.-M., and Julia, D.: *Les collèges français, 16e-18e siècles*, Paris, 1988.

Cooper, Richard (ed.): *The Entry of Henri II into Lyon, September 1548*, Tempe, Arizona, 1997.

Crouzet, D.: 'Henri IV king of reason?' in Keith Cameron, ed., *From Valois to Bourbon. Dynasty, State and Society in Early Modern France*, Exeter, 1989, pp. 73-106.

Dainville, F. de: *L'éducation des Jésuites XVIe-XVIIIe siècles*, Paris, 1978.

Daly, Peter: *Emblem Theory. Recent German Contributions to the Characterisation of the Emblem Genre*, Neudeln, 1979.

— (ed.) *Andreas Alciatus. I. The Latin Emblems. Indexes and Lists; II. Emblems in*

Translation, Toronto, 1985, 2 vols.

— (ed.) *The English Emblem and the Continental Tradition*, New York, 1988.

Daly, Peter, and Dimler, G. Richard: *The Jesuit Series* (Corpus Librorum Emblematum), Part 1 (A-D), Montreal, 1997.

De Backer, A. and A., and Sommervogel, C.: *Bibliothèque de la Compagnie de Jesus*, Brussels and Paris, 1890-1972, 11 vols.

Desgraves, L.: *Répertoire des programmes des pièces de théâtre jouées dans les collèges en France (1601-1700)*, Geneva, 1986.

Dimler, G. Richard: 'The Jesuit emblem book in seventeenth-century Protestant England', *Archivum Historicum Societatis Iesu*, 75, 1984, pp.357-69.

— 'Short-title listing of Jesuit emblem books', *Emblematica*, 2,1, 1987, pp.139-87.

— 'Edmund Arwaker's translation of the *Pia desideria*: the reception of a continental Jesuit emblem book in seventeenth-century England' in P. Daly, ed., *The English Emblem and the Continental Tradition*, New York, 1988, pp.203-24.

— 'Jakob Masen's *Imago Figurata*: from theory to practice', *Emblematica*, 6,2, 1992, pp.283-306.

— '*Imitatio, Innovatio* and Jesuit emblem theory', in Gyorgy Szonyi, ed., *European Iconography East and West*, Leiden, 1996, pp.209-22.

— 'Jakob Masen's critique of the *Imago primi saeculi*', in Marc van Vaeck and John Manning, eds, *The Jesuits and the Emblem Tradition*, Turnhout, 1999, pp.279-95.

Drysdall, Denis: 'The emblem according to the Italian *impresa* theorists', in Alison Adams, and Anthony Harper, eds, *The Emblem in Renaissance and Baroque Europe. Tradition and Variety*, Leiden, 1992, pp.22-32.

Dubois, E.: 'Some interpretations of the notion of *coeur* in seventeenth-century France', *Seventeenth-Century French Studies*, 9, 1987, pp.4-25.

Duchêne, R. and Ronzeaud, P. (eds): *Ordre et contestation au temps des classiques: Actes du 21e Colloque du Centre Méridional de Rencontre sur le XVIIe Siècle jointe avec le 23e Colloque de la North American Society for Seventeenth-Century French Literature, Marseille 19-23 juin 1991*, Paris, 1992.

Engammare, Max: 'Les Figures de la Bible, Le destin oublié d'un genre littéraire en image (XVIe-XVIIe s.)', *Mélanges de l'Ecole française de Rome. Italie et Méditerranée*, 106,2, 1994, pp. 549-91.

— 'Dans le Jardin du Bien-aimé. Illustration et exégèse du *Cantique des Cantiques* au XVIIe siècle', *Graphè*, 8, *Le Cantique des Cantiques*, 1999, pp.123-62.

Fénaille, Maurice: *Etat général des tapisseries de la manufacture des Gobelins depuis son origine jusquà nos jours*, Paris, 1903.

Ford, Philip, and Jondorf, Gillian (eds): *Intellectual Life in Renaissance Lyon*, Cambridge, 1993.

Fumaroli, Marc: *Aspects de l'humanisme jésuite au début du XVIIe siècle*, Paris,

Revue des Sciences Humaines, 40, 1975.

— *L'âge de l'éloquence. Rhétorique et 'res literaria' de la Renaissance au seuil de l'époque classique*, Paris, 1994.

Funck, M.: *Le livre belge à gravures*, Paris and Brussels, 1925.

Giraud, Yves (ed.): *L'emblème à la Renaissance, Actes de la journée d'études du 10 mai 1980*, Paris, 1982.

Graham, V., and McAllister-Johnson, W.: *The Paris Entries of Charles IX and Elisabeth of Austria 1571, with an Analysis of Simon Bouquet's Bref et sommaire recueil*, Toronto, 1974.

— *The Royal Tour of France by Charles IX and Catherine de Medici. Festivals and Entries, 1564-66*, Toronto, 1979.

— (eds) E. Jodelle, *Le recueil des inscriptions 1558. A Literary and Iconographical Exegesis*, Toronto, 1972.

Green, Henry: *Alciati and his Books of Emblems. A Biographical and Bibliographical Study*, London, 1872.

Griffin, Nigel: *Jesuit School Drama. A Checklist of Critical Literature*, London, 1976.

Grivel, M., and Fumaroli, M. (eds): Jacques Bailly, *Devises pour les tapisseries du Roi*, Paris, 1988.

— See BnF Ms. fr. 7819.

— See BL Harleian Ms. 4377.

— See Félibien, André.

Grove, Laurence: '*Discours sur l'Art des Devises*: an edition of a previously unidentified and unpublished text by Perrault', *Emblematica*, 7,1, 1993, pp.99-144.

— 'Jesuit emblematics at La Flèche (Sarthe) and their influence on René Descartes', in Marc van Vaeck and John Manning, eds, *The Jesuits and the Emblem Tradition*, Turnhout, 1999, pp.87-114.

Heckscher, William, and Wirth, Karl-August: 'Emblem, Emblembuch', in *Reallexikon zur Deutschen Kunstgeschichte*, Stuttgart, 1959, vol.5, cols 85-228.

Henkel, A., and Schöne, A.: *Emblemata. Handbuch zur Sinnbildkunst des XVI. und XVII. Jahrhunderts*, Stuttgart, 1967.

Höltgen, Karl-Josef: *Aspects of the Emblem. Studies in the English Emblem Tradition and the European Context*, Kassel, 1986.

— review of P. Daly (ed.), Andreas Alciatus, vol.1, *The Latin Emblems* and vol.2, *Emblems in Translation*, Toronto, 1985, in *Emblematica*, 1, 2, 1986, pp.361-7.

— 'Catholic pictures versus Protestant words? The adaptation of the Jesuit sources in Quarles' *Emblemes*', *Emblematica*, 9,1, 1995, pp.221-38.

Höltgen, Karl-Josef, and Horden, John (eds): Francis Quarles, *Emblemes* (1635) Edward Benlowes Quarlëis and *Hieroglyphikes of the Life of Man* (1638), Hildesheim, 1993.

Homann, Holger: *Studien zur Emblematik des 16. Jahrhunderts*, Utrecht, 1971.

Hughes, T.: *Loyola and the Educational System of the Jesuits*, New York, 1892.

Huppert, G.: *Public Schools in Renaissance France*, Urbana, 1984.

Hutton, James: *The Greek Anthology in Italy to the Year 1800*, New York, 1935.

Jacquot, J. (ed.): *Les fêtes de la Renaissance*, Paris, 1956.

Jones-Davies, M.-T. (ed.): *Emblèmes et devises au temps de la Renaissance*, Paris, 1981.

Knipping, J.B.: *Iconography of the Counter-Reformation in the Netherlands. Heaven on Earth*, Nieuwkoop and Leiden, 1974, 2 vols.

Lachèvre, Frédéric: *Bibliographie des recueils collectifs de poésies du XVIe siècle*, Paris, 1922.

Lacotte, J.: 'La notion de "jeu" dans la pédagogie des Jésuites au XVIIe siècle', in M. Fumaroli, ed., *Aspects de l'humanisme jésuite au début du XVIIe siècle*, Paris, *Revue des Sciences Humaines*, 40, 1975, pp.245-93.

Landwehr, John: *Emblem Books in the Low Countries 1554-1949. A Bibliography*, Utrecht, 1970.

— *German Emblem Books, 1531-1888. A Bibliography*, Utrecht, 1972.

— *French, Italian, Spanish, and Portuguese Books of Devices and Emblems, 1534-1827. A Bibliography*, Utrecht, 1976.

Ledré, C.: 'Théâtre et 'exercices' publics dans les collèges lyonnais du XVIIe et du XVIIIe siècles', *Bulletin de la Société Littéraire de Lyon*, 16, 1947, pp.1-29; *ibid.*, 17, 1950, pp.4-19.

Lewalski, Barbara: *Protestant Poetics and the Seventeenth-Century Religious Lyric*, Princeton, 1979.

Loach, Judi: 'Ménestrier's emblem theory', *Emblematica*, 2,2, 1987, pp.317-36.

— 'Jesuit emblematics and the opening of the school year at the Collège Louis le Grand', *Emblematica*, 9,1, 1995 (1997), pp.133-76.

— 'The teaching of emblematics and other symbolic imagery by Jesuits within town colleges in seventeenth- and eighteenth-century France', in Marc van Vaeck and John Manning, eds, *The Jesuits and the Emblem Tradition*, Turnhout, 1999, pp.161-86.

Lowe, R.: 'Les représentations en musique au Collège Louis-le-Grand 1650-1688', *Revue de la Société d'histoire du Théâtre*, 10, 1958, pp.21-34.

— 'Les représentations en musique au Collège Louis-le-Grand 1689-1762', *Revue de la Société d'Histoire du Théâtre*, 11, 1959, pp.205-12.

— 'Les représentations en musique dans les collèges de Paris et de province 1632-1757', *Revue de la Société d'Histoire du Théâtre*, 15, 1963, pp.119-26.

McFarlane, I.D. (ed): *The Entry of Henri II into Paris, 16 June 1549*, New York, 1982. (Facsimile edition).

McGowan, Margaret: *L'art du ballet de cour en France 1581-1643*, Paris, 1978.

— (ed.) Balthasar de Beaujoyeulx, *Le Balet comique de la Royne*, New York, 1982.

Manning, John: 'Continental emblem books in sixteenth-century England: the evidence of Sloane MS. 3749', *Emblematica*, 1,1, 1986, pp.1-11.

— 'An unedited and unpublished manuscript translation of Hermann Hugo's *Pia desideria*', *Emblematica*, 6,1, 1992, pp.147-79.

— 'An unedited and unpublished manuscript translation of *Les emblemes d'Othon Vaenius*', *Emblematica*, 6,2, 1992, pp.325-55.

— 'An unedited and unpublished sixteenth-century English translation of some Alciato emblems', *Emblematica*, 7,1, 1993, pp.181-88.

— '"*Tres potentiae animae*": the aims and methodology of Royal Library, Brussels MS 4040, in Marc van Vaeck and John Manning, eds, *The Jesuits and the Emblem Tradition*, Turnhout, 1999, pp.323-40.

Mauquoy-Hendrickz, M.: *Les estampes des Wierix conservées au Cabinet des Estampes de la Bibliothèque Royale Albert 1er. Catalogue raisonné enrichi de notes prises dans diverses autres collections*, Brussels, 1978-83, 4 vols.

Meade, Martin (ed.): A. Félibien, *Les fêtes de Versailles. Chroniques de 1668 et 1674*, Paris, 1994.

Miedema, Hessel: 'The term *Emblema* in Alciati', *Journal of the Warburg and Courtauld Institutes*, 31, 1968, pp.234-50.

Moine, Marie-Christine: *Les fêtes à la cour du Roi Soleil 1653-1715*, Paris, 1984.

Mortimer, Ruth: *Harvard College Library Department of Printing and Graphic Arts. Catalogue of Books and Manuscripts. Part 1. French Sixteenth-Century Books*, Cambridge, Mass., 1964, 2 vols.

Porteman, Karel (ed): *Emblematic Exhibitions (affixiones) at the Brussels Jesuit College (1630-1685). A Study of the Commemorative Manuscripts (Royal Library, Brussels)*, Brussels, 1996.

— (ed.) Otto Vaenius, *Amorum emblemata, figuris aeneis incisa studio Othonis Vaeni Batavo-Lugdunensis* (Antwerp, 'Venalia apud auctorem', 1608, 4° obl.), Aldershot, 1996.

Praz, Mario: *Studies in Seventeenth-Century Imagery*, 2nd ed., Rome, 1964.

Ranum, Orest: 'Islands and the self in a Ludovician fête', in David L. Rubin, ed., *Sun King. The Ascendancy of French Culture during the Reign of Louis XIV*, Washington, 1992, pp. 17-34.

Rawles, Stephen: 'Corrozet's *Hecatomgraphie*: where did the woodcuts come from and where did they go?', *Emblematica*, 3,1, 1988, pp.31-64.

Renard, J.: See Sommervogel, C.

Rubin, David L. (ed.): *Sun King. The Ascendancy of French Culture during the Reign of Louis XIV*, Washington, 1992.

Russell, Daniel: *The Emblem and Device in France*, Lexington, Kentucky, 1985.

— *Emblematic Structures in Renaissance French Culture*, Toronto, 1995.

— 'The term 'Emblème' in sixteenth-century France', *Neophilologus*, 59, 1975, pp.337-51.

— 'Two seventeenth-century French treatises on the art of the device', *Emblematica*, 1,1, 1986, pp.79-106.

Saunders, Alison: *The Sixteenth-Century French Emblem Book: a Decorative and Useful Genre*, Geneva, 1988.

— 'Emblem books for a popular audience? Gilles Corrozet's *Hecatomgraphie* and *Emblemes*', *Australian Journal of French Studies*, 17, 1980, pp.5-29.

— 'The sixteenth-century French emblem book: writers and printers', *Studi francesi*, 92, 1987, pp.173-90.

— '*Picta poesis*: the relationship between figure and text in the sixteenth-century French emblem book', *Bibliothèque d'Humanisme et Renaissance*, 48, 1986, pp.621-52.

— 'The long and the short of it: structure and form in the early French emblem book', in Bernard Scholz, Michael Bath, and David Weston, eds, *The European Emblem. Selected Papers from the Glasgow Conference 11-14 August, 1987*, Leiden, 1990, pp.55-83.

— 'When is it a device and when is it an emblem: theory and practice (but mainly the latter) in 16th- and 17th-century France', *Emblematica*, 7,2, 1993, pp.239-57.

— 'Paris to Lyon and back again: trends in emblem publishing in the mid sixteenth century in France', in Philip Ford and Gillian Jondorf, eds, *Intellectual Life in Renaissance Lyon*, Cambridge, 1993, pp.63-80.

— 'What happened to the native French tradition? The decline of the vernacular emblem in the seventeenth century', *Seventeenth-Century French Studies*, 17, 1995, pp.69-86.

— 'Word, image and illustration in sixteenth- and seventeenth-century emblems in France', in Gyorgy Szonyi, ed., *European Iconography East and West. Selected Papers of the Szeged International Conference June 9-12, 1993*, Leiden, 1996, pp.175-89.

— 'French emblem books or European emblem books: transnational publishing in the sixteenth and seventeenth centuries', *Bibliothèque d'Humanisme et Renaissance*, 61, 1999, pp.415-27.

— 'Make the pupils do it themselves: emblems, plays and public performance in

French Jesuit colleges in the seventeenth century', in Marc van Vaeck and John Manning, eds, *The Jesuits and the Emblem Tradition*, Turnhout, 1999, pp.187-206.

— 'Emblems to tapestries and tapestries to emblems: contrasting practice in England and France', *Seventeenth-Century French Studies*, 21, 1999, pp.243-55.

Sauvy, Anne: *Le miroir du coeur. Quatre siècles d'images savantes et populaires*, Paris, 1989.

— 'Le Cabinet du Roy et les projets encyclopédiques de Colbert', in *L'art du livre à l'Imprimerie Nationale*, Paris, 1973, pp.102-27.

Scaglione, A.D.: *The Liberal Arts and the Jesuit College System*, Amsterdam, 1986.

Scholz, Bernard: '"Libellum composui epigrammaton, cui titulum feci Emblemata": Alciatus's use of the expression *emblema* once again', *Emblematica*, 1,2, 1986, pp.213-26.

— 'The 1531 Augsburg edition of Alciato's *Emblemata*: a survey of research', *Emblematica*, 5,2, 1991, pp.213-54.

Scholz, Bernard; Bath, Michael; and Weston, David (eds): *The European Emblem. Selected Papers from the Glasgow Conference 11-14 August, 1987*, Leiden, 1990,

Schöne, Albrecht: *Emblematik und Drama im Zeitalter des Barock*, Munich, 1964.

Smith, C.N. (ed.): Jacques Callot, *Emblesmes. Sur la vie de la mere de Dieu.Vita beatae Mariae virginis matris Dei emblematibus delineata* (Paris, B. Audran, n.d., 8° obl.), Ilkley, 1974.

Smith, Paul: 'Les fables emblématiques d'Etienne Perret (1578)', *Emblematica*, 8,2, 1994, pp.221-42.

Sommervogel, C. (ed.): J. Renard, *Catalogue des oeuvres imprimées de Claude-François Ménestrier de la Compagnie de Jesus*, Lyon, 1883.

Spica, Anne-Elisabeth: *Symbolique humaniste et emblématique. L'évolution et les genres (1580-1700)*, Paris, 1996.

Stegman, André: 'Les théories de l'emblème et de la device en France et en Italie (1520-1620)', in Y. Giraud, ed., *L'emblème à la Renaissance. Actes de la Journée d'études du 10 mai 1980*, Paris, 1982, pp.61-77.

Stopp, F.J.: *The Emblems of the Altdorf Academy. Medals and Medal Orations 1577-1626*, London, 1974.

Strong, Roy: *Art and Power: Renaissance Festivities 1450-1650*, Berkeley, California, 1984.

Szonyi, Gyorgy (ed.): *European Iconography East and West. Selected Papers of the Szeged International Conference June 9-12, 1993*, Leiden, 1996.

Vaeck, Marc van: 'Sixteenth- and seventeenth-century Dutch 'emblematic' fable books from the Gheeraerts filiation', *Emblematica*, 7,1, 1993, pp.25-38.

Vaeck, Marc van and Manning, John (eds): *The Jesuits and the Emblem Tradition*.

Selected Papers of the Leuven International Emblem Conference 18-23 August, 1996, Turnhout, 1999.

Voet, L: *The Golden Compasses. A History and Evaluation of the Printing and Publishing Activities of the Officina Plantiniana*, Amsterdam, 1967-72, 2 vols.

— *The Plantin Press (1555-1589). A Bibliography of the Works Printed and Published by Christopher Plantin at Antwerp and Leyden*, Amsterdam, 1980-83, 6 vols.

Wischerman, H.: 'Ein Emblembuchmanuskript von Jean-Jacques Boissard', *Archiv für Geschichte des Buchwesens*, 14, 1974, pp.433-64.

Yates, Frances: *The Valois Tapestries*, London, 1959.

— (ed.) Simon Bouquet, *La joyeuse entrée de Charles IX roy de France en Paris 1572*, Amsterdam, 1974.

— 'Poètes et artistes dans les entrées de Charles IX et de sa reine à Paris en 1571', in J. Jacquot, ed., *Les fêtes de la Renaissance*, Paris, 1956, pp.61-84.

(anon.): *L'art du livre à l'Imprimerie Nationale*, Paris, 1973.

(anon.): *Une entrée royale: Marie de Medicis à Avignon, 19 novembre 1600*, Avignon, 1985.

— See Valladier, André.

KEY TO LIBRARY LOCATIONS:

Amsterdam UL: Universiteitsbibliotheek, Amsterdam, Netherlands

Arsenal: Bibliothèque de l'Arsenal, Paris, France

Beaux Arts: Ecole Nationale des Beaux Arts, Paris, France

Berlin: Staatsbibliothek, Berlin, Germany

Chicago: Newberry Library, Chicago, USA

Congress: Library of Congress, Washington, USA

Copenhagen: Det Kongelige Bibliotek, Copenhagen, Denmark

Folger: Folger Shakespeare Library, Washington, USA

Getty: J. Paul Getty Museum, Los Angeles, California, USA

Glasgow UL: Glasgow University Library, Glasgow, UK

Harvard UL: Harvard University Library, Cambridge, Massachusetts, USA

Huntington: Henry E. Huntington Library, San Marino, California, USA

Illinois UL: University of Illinois Library, Urbana, Illinois, USA

Institut: Bibliothèque de l'Institut, Paris, France

Mazarine: Bibliothèque Mazarine, Paris, France

Minnesota UL: University of Minnesota Library, Minneapolis, Minnesota, USA

Munich: Bayerische Staatsbibliothek, Munich, Germany

New York: New York Public Library, New York, USA

Plantin-Moretus: Plantin-Moretus Museum, Antwerp, Belgium

Princeton UL: Princeton University Library, New Jersey, USA

Sainte Geneviève: Bibliothèque Sainte Geneviève, Paris, France

Utrecht UL: Rijksuniversiteitsbibliotheek, Utrecht, Netherlands

Vatican: Biblioteca Apostolica Vaticana, Rome, Italy

Versailles: Bibliothèque Municipale, Versailles, France

Victoria and Albert: National Art Library, Victoria and Albert Museum, London, UK

Vienna: Österreichische Nationalbibliothek, Vienna, Austria

Virginia UL: University of Virginia Library, Charlottesville, Virginia, USA

Wiesbaden: Hessisches Landsbibliothek, Wiesbaden, Germany

Wolfenbüttel: Herzog August Bibliothek, Wolfenbüttel, Germany

Wroclaw UL: Universytecka Biblioteka, Wroclaw, Poland

LIST OF ILLUSTRATIONS:

Figure 1: Baudoin, *Contre la gourmandise, Recueil d'emblemes*, Paris, 1638, M6v. 42

Figure 2: Friedrich, *Emblemes nouveaux*, Frankfurt, 1617, I1v. 51

Figure 3: Martinet, *Emblesmes royales*, Paris, 1673, G5v. 54

Figure 4: Flamen, *Devises et emblemes d'amour moralisez*, Paris, 1648, F1r. 71

Figure 5: Verrien, *Livre curieux et utile*, Paris, 1685, A1v-2r. 87

Figure 6: La Feuille, *Abregé de l'histoire de France par les devises*, in *Essay d'un dictionnaire*, Amsterdam, 1700, between pp.136 and 137. 114

Figure 7: Valdor, *Les triomphes de Louis le Juste*, Paris, 1649, [2]A1v. 121

Figure 8: Ménestrier, *Emblémes et dévises sur ce que le Roy a fait pour la religion*, in *Histoire du Roy Louis le Grand*, Paris (Amsterdam), 1691, M4r. 125

Figure 9: Chevalier, *Histoire de Guillaume III*, Amsterdam, 1692, P4r. 129

Figure 10: Musart, *Adolescens academicus*, Douai, 1633, S4v. 145

Figure 11: Le Jay, *Le triomphe de la religion*, Paris, 1687, C4r. 153

Figure 12: Hooft, *Emblemata amatoria*, Amsterdam, 1611, I2r. 170

Figure 13: Gomberville, *La doctrine des moeurs*, Paris, 1646, B2r. 176

Figure 14: Vigenère, *Les images ou tableaux de platte peinture*, Paris, 1615, F4r. 178

Figure 15: *Amoris divini et humani antipathia*, Antwerp, 1629, between B1 and B2. 189

Figure 16: Martin, *Le paradis terrestre*, Paris, 1655, A2v. 212

Figure 17: Callot, *Lux claustri*, Paris, 1646, F2r. 215

Figure 18: Chesneau, *Emblemes sacrez*, Paris, 1667, M2v. 220

Figure 19: Gambart, *La vie symbolique du bienheureux François de Sales*, Paris, 1664, C4v. 225

Figure 20: David, *Veridicus christianus*, Antwerp, 1601, facing b2v. 232

Figure 21: Sucquet, *Le chemin de la vie eternele*, Antwerp, 1623, facing p.2. 236

Figure 22: Mello, *Les divines operations*, Paris, 1673, B1v. 237

Figure 23: Berthod, *Emblemes sacrez*, Paris, 1665, p.204. 242

Figure 24: Valladier, *Labyrinthe royal*, Avignon, 1601, p.51. 256

Figure 25: *Reception...de Louis XIII*, Lyon, 1623, between p.38 and p.39. 268

Figure 26: *L'entree triomphante de Leurs Majestez, Feu d'Artifice*, Paris, 1662, between p.4 and p.5 275

Figure 27: Perrault, *Courses de testes et de bague*, Paris, 1670, facing 275p.28. 281

Figure 28: Félibien, *Les plaisirs de l'Isle enchantée*, Paris, 1673, p.27. 283

Figure 29: 'Autumn' tapestry from the Gobelins tapestries of the Four Seasons. 293

Figure 30: Detail from the border of the Gobelins 'Autumn' tapestry, showing the emblem *Et fulminis ocyor alis*. 294

Figure 31: Félibien, *Tapisseries du Roi*, Paris, 1670, f.35, showing the engraved version of the 'Autumn' tapestry emblem *Et fulminis ocyor alis*. 297

Figures 29 and 30 are reproduced by kind permission of the *Administration Générale du Mobilier National* in Paris, and all other illustrations are reproduced by kind permission of the Librarian, Glasgow University Library.

GENERAL INDEX

Académie de Danse: 288

Académie des Sciences: 288

Académie Française: 288, 342-5

Académie Royale de Musique: 288

Académie Royale de Peinture et de Sculpture: 288

ADAMS, Alison: 2-3, 27

AESOP: 22-3, 56-63, 334-5

— See also AUDIN, Prieur de Thermes; BAUDOIN, Jean; CORROZET, Gilles; and DU FRESNE, Raphael.

ALCIATO, Andrea: 5-7, 23-30, 34-5, 37, 41-8, 55, 60, 64-5, 75, 82, 86, 91, 97-8, 162, 167-8, 182-3, 192-3, 213-16, 224, 231, 248-9, 253, 271, 305-10, 312, 316-17, 333, 338, 348, 359

ALVA, Duke of: 75-6

AMBOISE, Adrian d': 13, 22, 313-14, 318-19

AMBOISE, François d': 318

Amoris divini et humani antipathia: 188-90

Amoris divini et humani effectus: 187

ANEAU, Barthélemy: 5-6, 25-6, 28, 32, 34, 75, 93, 206, 249-51, 306-7, 338, 349

ANJOU, Philippe, Duc d': 84, 110, 126, 159

ANNE D'AUTRICHE: 17, 83, 97, 134, 175, 254, 257, 259, 262, 266, 278, 301, 303, 350

ANNE DE BRETAGNE: 248

ARIAS MONTANO, Benito: 226-9

ARRAN, James, Count of: 307

ARWAKER, Edmund: 191, 194

AUDIN, Prieur de Thermes: 62-4, 111, 116-17

AYRES, Philip: 3, 10, 184

BARGAGLI, Scipione: 319, 321

BAILLY, Jacques: 105, 295-6, 351-2

BATH, Michael: 323

BAUDOIN, Jean: 7, 12, 22, 63-4

— *Recueil d'emblemes divers*: 7, 22, 34-5, 41-7, 315

BAUFREMONT, Marie Claire de, Comtesse du Freix: 97

BEAUJOYEULX, Balthasar de: 252-3, 286

BEAUMONT, Comte de: 66

BENSERADE, Isaac: 59-61, 335

BERRY, Charles, Duc de: 17, 84, 110, 126, 254

BERTHOD, François: 242-3, 353

BEZE, Théodore de: 6-8, 32, 34, 349, 358

Bible: 203-10, 226-33, 334

— See also *Figures de la Bible*;
Figures du Nouveau Testament;
*Historiarum veteris testamenti
icones*; *Quadrins historiques de la
Bible*; *Tapisserie de l'eglise
chrestienne et catholique*; G.
NADAL: *Adnotationes et
meditationes* and *Evangelicae
historiae imagines*; P. PERROT
DE LA SALE: *Tableaus sacrez*;
L. RICHEOME: *Tableaux sacrez*;
B. SELLIUS: *Emblemata sacra*.
BINET, Etienne: 240
BLACK, Lynette: 191, 235
BLOUNT, Thomas: 120, 319-20
BOLSWERT, Boëtius à: 3, 198
BOISSARD, Jean-Jacques: 33-4, 36-8,
   41
BOISSIERE, Monsieur de: 66-71
BOUHOURS, Dominique: 315, 342,
   345
BOUQUET, Simon: 15, 249-51
BOURGOGNE, Louis, Duc de: 17, 84,
   110, 126, 134, 254, 299
BOURSEIS, Abbé de: 343-4
BRUCK-ANGERMUNDT, Jacob à:
   35-6
BRY, Théodore de: 8, 33, 228

CALLIAS, Augustin: 210
CALLOT, Jacques: 9, 213-19, 223,
   226-7, 353
CAMERARIUS, Joachim: 72, 214,
   216, 224
CASENEUVE, Louis de: 11
CATHERINE DE MEDICI: 15, 99,
   249, 251, 253, 286-7
CATS, Jacob: 19, 72, 90, 164-6, 168,
   216
CAUSSIN, Nicolas: 11, 219
CAVE, Terence: 208
CEBES: 328, 333
CHAPELAIN, Jean: 342-3
CHAPPUYS, Gabriel: 11
CHARLES V, Emperor: 113, 115, 248

CHARLES IX, King of France: 15,
   249-52
CHARONIER, Gabriel: 13, 155-157,
   159
CHARPENTIER, François: 105, 342-
   3
CHASTEUIL, Jean Galaup de: See
   GALAUP DE CHASTEUIL, Jean.
CHATELAIN, Jean-Marc: 1, 33, 45-6,
   175, 191, 219
CHAUMELZ, Leonard de: 301
CHESNEAU, Augustin: 218-23, 226,
   237, 243, 353
CHEVALIER, Nicolas: 110, 118, 126-
   30, 135
CHONE, Paulette: 151, 213, 218
CHOVAYNE, Florent: 13, 66-70, 315
CLEMENT, Monsieur: 342-3
COLBERT, Jean-Baptiste: 103-4, 249,
   287-8, 302-3
*Colloque des trois supposts du
   Seigneur de la Coquille*: 120
COMBE, Thomas: 30, 34
CONDE, Prince de: 280, 303
CONTI, Prince de: 303
Cor Iesu amanti sacrum:
CORROZET, Gilles: 7, 19, 34, 349
— *Fables d'Esope*: 22, 56-62
— *Hecatomgraphie*: 5, 10, 30-31,
   50, 56, 75, 78, 84, 119, 289, 309-
   10, 313
— *Historiarum veteris testamenti
   icones*: 8, 202-4, 289, 310
— *Tableau de Cebes de Thebes* and
   Emblemes: 5, 30, 34, 56, 117
— *Tapisserie de l'eglise chrestienne*:
   8, 202-4
CORROZET, Jean: 30
COURBE, Augustin: 70, 74-5, 78
COUSTAU, Pierre: 5-6, 32, 34, 39,
   48, 224, 312, 349
COVARRUBIAS OROZCO,
   Sebastian de: 35, 216
CRAMER, Daniel: 4, 10, 210-11

DAN, Pierre: 131-3, 339

Dauphin: 17, 82, 103, 138, 147, 157-8, 248, 266, 278, 302-3, 353

DAVID, Jan: 8, 221, 231-3, 235, 357

DE PASSE, Crispin: 183

DESPREZ, Philippe: 58-9

Devises sur le nom...de Messire François du Gué: See CHARONIER, Gabriel.

Devises sur les armes de Monseigneur Le Tellier: See CHARONIER, Gabriel.

DIANE DE VALOIS: 101

DIMLER, G. Richard: 191, 346-7

Discours sur l'art des devises: 104

Divers emblesmes & devises d'empereurs: See TYPOTIUS, Jacobus.

Divertissemens de Versailles: See FELIBIEN, André.

Doctrine des moeurs: See LE ROY, Sieur de Gomberville, Marin.

DORAT, Jean: 251

DREXEL, Jeremias: 241, 347

DU FRESNE, Raphael: 62

DU GUE, François: 155-7

Edict of Nantes, Revocation of: 152

Egapathe, martyr de Lyon: 159

ELEANOR OF AUSTRIA: 248

ELISABETH OF AUSTRIA: 15, 249-51

ELISABETH, Queen of Spain, wife of Philip II: 15, 251

ELISABETH, Queen of Spain, wife of Philip IV: 17, 254, 272, 350

Emblemes d'amour divin et humain ensemble: 188, 190

ENGAMMARE, Max: 208

ENGHIEN, Duc d': 280, 303

Entries:
— AIX: See GALAUP DE CHASTEUIL, Jean: *Discours sur les arcs triomphaux* (1624).
— ANGOULEME:
—*Arrivée du Roy en sa ville d'Angoulesme* (1615): 259
— ARLES:
—*Entree de Loys XIII...Dans sa ville d'Arles* (1622): 262-4
— AUXERRE:
—*Recit veritable de tout ce qui s'est fait...en la ville d'Auxerre* (1650): 273
— AVIGNON: See VALLADIER, André: *Labyrinthe royal de l'Hercule gaulois triomphant* (1601); and *La Voye de laict ou le chemin des heros au Palais de la gloire* (1622).
— BERGERAC:
—*Entrée royale et magnifique du Roy en sa ville de Bergerac* (1621): 260
— BORDEAUX:
—*Les magnificences faites en la ville de Bourdeaux à l'entrée du Roy* (1615): 259
—*Journal de ce qui s'est fait durant la guerre et siége de Bordeaux...avec les harangues faites lors de la magnifique entrée du roy* (1650): 273
—See also MORILHON, Le Sieur de: *Le Persée françois* (1612).
— CHARTRES:
—*La royalle entrée du Roy et de la Royne en la ville de Chartres* (1619): 258-9
— LE MANS:
—*Arrivée du Roy en la ville du Mans* (1620): 260
— LYON:
—*La magnificence de la superbe et triomphante entrée de la noble et antique cité de Lyon* (1549): 249
—*Reception...de Louis XIII* (1622): 266-8

—See also *Le Soleil au signe du
Lyon* (1623):
— NIORT:
　—*Entrée du Roy en la ville et
chasteau de Niort* (1621): 260
— ORLEANS:
　—*Entrée magnificque du roy
faicte en sa ville d'Orleans*
(1614): 259
— PARIS:
　—*C'est l'ordre qui a esté tenu a
la nouvelle et joyeuse entrée,
que...le Roy treschrestien Henry
deuxiesme de ce nom a faicte*
(1549): 249
　—*L'ordre, entrée et ceremonies
observees par la ville de Paris*
(1614): 258-9
　—*L'entree triomphante de Leurs
Majestez...dans la ville de Paris*
(1660): 273-8, 285
　—*L'explication des figures et
peintures qui sont representees
pour l'entrée du roy et de la
reine* (1660): 274
　—*Le feu royal et magnifique qui
s'est tiré sur la riviere de
Seine...pour la resjouissance de
l'entrée du roy et de la reine*
(1660): 274
　—*La glorieuse et triomphante
entrée de...Marie Thereze
d'Austriche...avec nostre
invincible monarque Louis de
Bourbon XIV dans leur ville de
Paris* (1660): 273
　—*La montre generale de
Messieurs les bourgeois de la
ville de Paris...à la magnifique
entrée du roy et de la reine*
(1660): 274
　—*Relation de toutes les
particularitez qui se sont
faites...dans la celebre entrée du
Roy & de la Reyne* (1660): 273

　—*La royale maison du trone de
la triomphante entrée de Leurs
Majestez en la ville de Paris*
(1660): 274
　—*La veritable explication en
prose et en vers des figures...qui
sont dessus le pont Nostre-Dame
à Paris...pour l'entrée du roy et
de la reine* (1660): 274
　See also BOUQUET, Simon: *Bref
et sommaire recueil* (1571); and
JODELLE, Etienne: *Recueil des
inscriptions* (1558).
— POITIERS:
　—*La resjouissance de Poictiers
sur l'arrivée du Roy & de la
Royne Regente, mere du Roy*
(1614): 258
— REIMS:
　—*Les ceremonies du sacre et
couronnement du tres-chrestien
roy...Louis XIII, plus son entree
dans la ville de Reims* (1610): 259
— ROUEN:
　—*Les entrées de la reyne et de
monseigneur daulphin...Faictes a
Rouen* (1531). 248-9
— SAINT JEAN d'ANGELY:
　—*Entrée royale faite au Roy en
la ville de Sainct Jean d'Angely*
(1620): 259
Esbatement moral des animaux: 58
ESTIENNE, Henry, Sieur des Fossez:
　120, 315, 319-23, 342
*Explication du feu d'artifice dressé
devant l'hostel de ville...à la
naissance de Monseigneur le Duc
de Berry*: 254
*Explication en vers des tableaux de la
galerie de Versailles*: 62, 110,
134-7, 247

FELIBIEN, André: 288-99
— *Divertissemens de Versailles*: 18,
　253, 282, 284-5

— *Plaisirs de l'Isle enchantée*: 18, 253, 281-2
— *Relation de la feste de Versailles*: 18, 253, 282
— *Tapisseries du Roi*: 105, 290-97
Figures de la Bible: See GUEROULT, Guillaume.
Figures du Nouveau Testament: See FONTAINE, Charles; and PONTOUX, Claude de.
FINE DE BRIANVILLE, Oronce: 303-4
FLAMEN, Albert: 22-3, 70-74, 359
La fleur des sentences certaines: 31
La fleur des sentences morales: 31
FONTAINE, Charles: 8, 203, 289-90, 310-11
Fontainebleau: 292, 341
— See also DAN, Pierre.
FONTENELLE, Bernard le Bovier, Sieur de: 152, 154
FRANÇOIS 1er, King of France: 111-12, 115, 131-3, 248, 339
FRANÇOIS II, King of France: 115
FRANÇOIS DE SALES, Saint: 223-6, 230, 243
FRIEDRICH, Andreas: 4, 7, 35, 49-52, 357

GALAUP DE CHASTEUIL, Jean: 16, 270-71
Galerie François 1er, Fontainebleau: 132, 339
GALLE, Cornelis: 195
GAMBART, Adrien: 223-7, 230, 243-4
GIOVIO, Paulo: 12-13, 21, 84, 305, 314, 318-21, 348-9
— *Tetrastiques faictz sur les devises*: 12, 84, 349
GISSEY, Henri de: 18, 279, 350
Gobelins: 104, 288, 291-9
GOMBERVILLE, Le Roy Marin, Sieur de: See LE ROY, Sieur de Gomberville, Marin.

GREEN, Henry: 5
GRENET, Michel: 111-12
GREVIN, Jacques: 162
GROULLEAU, Etienne: 30-31
GROVE, Laurence: 157, 288, 343-4
GUEROULT, Guillaume: 5, 8, 32-4, 39-40, 52, 56, 203, 206, 349
GUISE, Duc de: 280

HAEFTEN, Benedict van: 9, 19, 164, 195-9, 221, 244, 314
HARVEY, Christopher: 198
HAWKINS, Henry: 145
HECKSCHER, William: 312
HEINSIUS, Daniel: 10, 19, 90, 163, 166-9, 181-4, 188, 199
HENRI II, King of France: 15, 17, 115, 133, 249
HENRI III, King of France: 112-13, 252, 254
HENRI IV, King of France: 15-16, '101, 111, 133-4, 254-7, 261, 263
HENRY VIII, King of England: 248
HESIUS, Wilhelm: 210, 314
HEU, Catherine de: 36
HEYNS, Pierre: 58
Historiarum veteris testamenti icones: See CORROZET, Gilles.
HÖLTGEN, Karl-Josef: 1, 24, 191, 244
HOOFT, Pieter Corneliszoon: 163, 168-70
HORACE: 19, 81, 164, 171-7, 181, 337-8, 340, 359
HORAPOLLO: 10-11, 39, 317, 319
HUGUES CAPET: 111, 116
HUGO, Herman: 3, 19, 163, 190-99, 201, 210, 235-6, 244, 337, 345, 347
— See also LA MOTHE-GUYON, Madame de.
HULSIUS, Bartholomew: 210

IGNATIUS OF LOYOLA, Saint: 2, 163, 233-5, 238, 240, 345-7, 358

Imprimerie royale: 17-18, 60, 282, 290, 296, 358-9

JANOT, Denis: 30-31, 56, 202, 226, 325
Jardin d'honneur: 31
JAUGEON, Le Sieur: 145-7
JENNIS, Lucas: 35
Jesuits: 2, 233, 337, 345-7
— Jesuit colleges: XI, 14, 147-8, 347, 358
——Antwerp: 151, 190, 244
——Brussels: 148-51, 156, 353
——Compiègne: 158
——Courtrai: 151, 155
——La Flèche: 157
——Lyon (Collège de la Trinité): 148, 155-9, 353
——Paris (Collège de Clermont; thereafter Collège de Louis le Grand): 148, 152-5, 157-60, 353
— *Imago primi saeculi*: 346
— *Ratio studiorum*: 346-7
— See also IGNATIUS OF LOYOLA, Saint.
JODELLE, Etienne: 270
JOLY, Pierre: 33
JOYEUSE, Duc de: 15, 252-3
Joyous entries: See Entries.
JUNIUS, Hadrianus: 162

KERVER, Jacques: 10-11
KNIPPING, J.B.: 3, 245

L'ABBE, Pierre: 3
LA FAYE, Antoine: 34, 47-50
LA FEUILLE, Daniel de: 86, 96
— *Abregé de l'histoire de France*: 111, 114-16
— *Devises et emblemes anciennes et modernes*: 13, 88-9
— *Devises & emblemes d'amour, anciens & modernes*: 90-91
— *Essay d'un dictionnaire*: 91-5, 111, 114

LA FONTAINE, Jean de: 59, 296, 335
LA MOTHE-GUYON, Madame de: 194-5
L'ANGLOIS, Pierre: 11, 317-19
LA PERRIERE, Guillaume de: 7, 34
— *Morosophie*: 5-6, 31-2, 39, 43, 52, 309-10, 312
— *Theatre des bons engins*: 5, 10, 29-32, 34, 38, 41, 72, 182, 214, 308-9, 312
LA RUE, Charles de: 302
LA TREMOILLE, Marie de la Tour, Duchesse de: 97, 102, 111
LAUGIER, Gaspard: 302
LE BRUN, Charles: 134, 288, 296, 298-9
LE CLERC, Sébastien: 60, 296
LE FEVRE, Jean: 26-7, 29, 306
LE JAY, Gabriel-François: 301-2, 352
— *Triomphe de la Religion*: 152-5, 353-4
LE LABOUREUR, Claude: 330
LE MOYNE, Pierre: 21, 78, 314, 320, 342
— *De l'art des devises*: 66, 78-81, 300-301, 315, 323-8
— *Devises heroiques et morales*: 13, 66, 70, 74-8, 104
LE PAULTRE, Pierre: 61, 284
LE ROY, Sieur de Gomberville, Marin: 172-7, 181, 199, 337-8
L'ESTOILE, Pierre de: 263
LE VASSEUR, Jacques: 14, 111-16
LEWALSKI, Barbara: 202
LOACH, Judi: 67, 147, 155, 314, 330-32, 336, 345, 347
LORRAINE, Cardinal de: 167
LOUIS XII, King of France: 248
LOUIS XIII, King of France: 13-16, 69-70, 110-12, 118-22, 133-4, 254, 257-72, 350
LOUIS XIV, King of France: XI, 14-17, 22, 30, 52-5, 62, 70, 76-9, 95, 102-5, 110, 114, 116, 118, 122-7, 134-8, 147, 152, 155-6, 175, 247-

8, 253-4, 257, 261, 265, 273-304,
347, 350-52, 358
LOYOLA, Saint Ignatius of: See
IGNATIUS OF LOYOLA, Saint.
LULLY, Jean-Baptiste: 282, 284
LUZVIC, Etienne: 78, 144-5, 198-9,
201, 238

MCGOWAN, Margaret: 15, 252, 286
MACON, Monseigneur de: 156, 353
MALHERBE, François de: 270
MANNING, John: 23-4, 195
MARGUERITE DE NAVARRE: 10,
98
MARIA THERESA, Queen of France:
16, 273-7, 285, 302-3, 330
MARIE DE MEDICI: 254, 257-9
MARIE-ANNE CHRISTINE OF
BAVARIA: 157-8, 353
MAROLLES, Michel de: 47, 117
MARTIN, Jean: 211-13, 216, 218-9,
221, 223, 226
MARTINET, Le Sieur: 7, 52-6
MARY II, Queen of England: 93-4,
128
MASEN, Jakob: 346-7
MAZARIN, Cardinal: 17, 175, 247,
287
MELLO, Guillaume de: 199, 201,
237-40
MENDO, Andrès: 138, 142
MENESTRIER, Claude-François: 16,
19, 66, 69, 81, 85, 310, 314, 323,
329-48, 352, 354, 358
— L'art des emblemes: 314, 316,
331
— L'art des emblemes ou s'enseigne
la morale: 21, 57, 311, 314-17,
331-41, 345
— L'autel de Lyon: 67, 329
— La devise du Roy justifiee: 77, 82,
104, 300, 347
— Devises, emblemes, et
anagrammes, a Monseigneur le
Chancelier: 67

— Les estreines de la cour: 67
— Les genereux exercises: 22, 67
— Histoire du Roy Louis le Grand
par les medailles: 83, 110, 118,
122-7, 130, 135, 137, 247, 327
— La philosophie des images: 67,
82-3, 300, 315, 331
— Les resjoüissances de la paix: 67,
84, 157, 329, 353
— La philosophie des images
enigmatiques: 120
— La science et l'art des devises:
67, 81-4, 301, 331
— Les transfigurations sacrées de S.
François de Sales: 329
— Explication du feu
d'artifice...pour la naissance du
prince que nous vient de donner
Madame la Dauphine (attrib.):
254
MERCIER, Jean: 33-4, 36, 38-41
Mercure Galant: 343
MERINDOLUS, Antonius: 271
MIEDEMA, Hessel: 312
MIGNAULT, Claude: 24-9, 162, 307-
9, 312, 317
MOLIERE: 282, 284, 286-7, 359
MONTENAY, Georgette de: XI, 2, 6-
8, 10, 19, 22, 32, 34, 47, 50, 64,
95, 156, 162, 226, 244, 311, 349-
50, 358-9
MONTMOR, Louis Habert de: 78-81,
342
MOREL, Fédéric: 24
MORILHON, Le Sieur de: 260-62
MORIN, Pierre: 235
MUSART, Charles: 78, 143-5, 199,
238

NADAL, Geronimo: 229-30, 233, 244

OFFELEN, Henri: 86-90, 95
ORANGE, William III, Prince of:
See WILLIAM III, Prince of
Orange; later King of England.

OVID: 334-5

PALLAVICINI, Monsieur: 90-91, 96
PALMER, Thomas: 23
PARADIN, Claude: 8, 12-13, 19, 22,
    41, 65-6, 68, 72, 80, 93, 97, 113,
    161-2, 166-7, 203, 311, 349
PATIN, Charles: 303
PERRAULT, Charles: 17-18, 60-62,
    248, 266, 279-82, 288, 295, 342-
    4, 348, 350-51, 359
PERRET, Etienne: 57-8
PERROT DE LA SALE, Paul: 8, 204-
    9, 352
Petite Académie: 247-8, 288, 295, 351
PEUTINGER, Conrad: 305, 312
PHARAMOND, King of France: 111,
    115
PHILIP II, King of Spain: 226, 251
PHILIP IV, King of Spain: 17, 138,
    254, 272, 350
PHILIPPE 1er, King of France: 117
PHILIPPE D'ORLEANS: 280, 303
PHILOSTRATUS: 45-6, 175, 177-80,
    333
— See also VIGENERE, Blaise de.
Plaisirs de l'Isle enchantée: See
    FELIBIEN, André.
Plantin Press: XI, 2, 13, 28, 57, 65,
    144, 161-2, 226-30
PLATO: 43, 333-4
PONTOUX, Claude de: 8, 203
PORTEMAN, Karel: 148, 151, 187
PRAZ, Mario: 166, 186-7, 218, 329
PYTHAGORAS: 38, 333
Quadrins historiques de la Bible: See
    PARADIN, Claude.
Quaeris quid sit amor: See
    HEINSIUS, Daniel:

QUARLES, Francis: 190, 244
QUARTIER, Le Père: 152
QUINAULT, Philippe: 284

RACINE, Jean: 284, 287, 359

RAWLES, Stephen: 3, 32, 56
Recueil des choses notables, qui ont
    esté faites à Bayonne: 251-3
Relation de la feste de Versailles:
    See FELIBIEN, André.
REUSNER, Nicolas: 72, 98
RICHELIEU, Cardinal de: 102, 109,
    133-4
RICHEOME, Louis: 9, 206-9, 337,
    352
RIPA, Cesare: 11-12
ROLLENHAGEN, Gabriel: 35-6
RONSARD, Pierre de: 251, 359
ROVILLE, Guillaume, and heirs: XI,
    6, 24-9, 34, 39, 84, 203, 226, 349
ROZARD, N.: 254
RUSCELLI, Girolamo: 316, 319
RUSSELL, Daniel: 19, 209, 263, 313,
    343

SAAVEDRA FAJARDO, Diego de:
    137-44, 357
SALOMON, Bernard: 249
SAMBUCUS, Johannes: 162
SAUNDERS, Alison: 1, 3-4, 7, 13-15,
    26, 56, 105, 157, 203, 253, 301,
    304, 313
SAUVY, Anne: 3, 198
SCEVE, Maurice: 166, 183, 249, 314,
    338
SCHOLZ, Bernard: 312
SCHÖNE, Albrecht: 312
SEGUIER, Le Chancelier: 67, 96
SELLIUS, Bernard: 9, 208-10
SIDNEY, Philip: 23
SILVESTRE, Israel: 280-81
SIMEONI, Gabriele: 12-13, 21, 65,
    84, 162, 349
— See also GIOVIO, Paulo:
    Tetrastiques faictz sur les devises;
    and PARADIN, Claude: Devises
    heroiques.
Le Soleil au signe du Lyon: 264-6
SPICA, Anne-Elisabeth: 1, 33, 218,
    314

STOCKHAMER, Sebastian: 24, 26-7, 162
SUCQUET, Antoine: 8-9, 235-7, 347
SUGER, l'Abbé: 110, 134

Tableau de Cebes de Thebes: See CORROZET, Gilles.
Tapestries of the Four Seasons and the Four Elements: 288-98, 350
— See also BAILLY, Jacques; Gobelins; and FELIBIEN, André.
Tapisserie de l'eglise chrestienne: See CORROZET, Gilles:
TERESA OF AVILA, Saint: 195, 197, 213
Tetrastiques faictz sur les devises: See GIOVIO, Paulo.
Theatre moral de la vie humaine: See LE ROY, Sieur de Gomberville, Marin.

Theatrum amoris divini et humani: See *Amoris divini et humani antipathia*:
Thronus Cupidinis: 90, 183-4
Timandre: 159
TOURNES, Jean I de: 24-6, 56-7, 161-2, 202-3, 226, 289-90, 310-11
TOURNES, Jean II de and Jean III: 23-30, 34
Triumphant entries: See Entries.
Triumphus amoris: 184
TOZZI, Paulo: 24, 28-9
TURENNE, Viconte de: 17
TYPOTIUS, Jacobus: 111
Typus mundi: 190, 244

VAECK, Marc van: 58
VAENIUS, Otto van: 3, 19, 90
— *Amoris divini emblemata*: 3, 163, 180, 184-8, 190-92, 199, 337
— *Amorum emblemata*: 3, 10, 163-4, 171, 180, 182-8, 191-2, 199

— *Emblemes d'amour illustrez d'une explication en prose*: 180-81
— *Emblemes de l'amour divin*: 180
— *Les emblemes de l'amour humain*: 180
— *Q. Horatii Flacci emblemata*: 164, 171-5, 177, 180-81, 337, 359
VALDOR, Jean: 118-22, 126, 254, 296
VALERIANO BOLZANI, Giovanni Pierio: 11, 316-7
VALLADIER, André: 16, 254-7
Valois Tapestries: 17
VEEN, Otto van: See VAENIUS, Otto.
VENERONI, Le Sieur de: 62
VERRIEN, Nicolas: 84-9, 91-2, 95, 359
Versailles: 18, 60-62, 110, 134-7, 253, 280-7, 298-9
—See also BENSERADE, Isaac; FELIBIEN, André; and PERRAULT, Charles.
VIGENERE, Blaise de: 45-7, 117, 175, 177-80, 206
La Voye de laict ou le chemin des heros au Palais de la gloire: 264, 267-70
VULSON, Marc de: 17, 109-10, 133-4, 136-7, 254, 349

WHITNEY, Geffrey: 23
WIERIX, Antoine II, Jean and Jérôme: 198, 239
WILLIAM III, Prince of Orange; later King of England: 93, 110, 118, 126-30, 135
WIRTH, August: 312

YATES, Frances: 15, 250-1

ZETTER, Jacques de: 4, 35, 49
ZINCGREF, Julius Wilhelm: 88

INDEX OF SUBJECTS OF EMBLEMS
AND DEVICES

Abstinence: 144
Abundance: 99, 266, 276
Acteon: 42
Adolescence: 143-5, 150
Air: 277, 298
Alembic: 166
Amor divinus: 163, 185-96
Anchor: 38, 48, 52, 112, 192
Andromeda: 262-3
Angel: 97
Anger: 140
Anima: 163, 185-96
Annunciation: 230
Ant: 98
Argonauts: 70
Arion: 253, 341
Armed king: 132
Armed man: 85, 112
Arrow: 146, 150, 181
Autumn: 293-4, 297

Baby-walker: 192, 210
Bacchus: 93, 144, 261
Bat: 88
Bear: 182
Bee: 90, 97, 211
Beehive: 97, 140-41, 211
Beetle: 98
Bellona: 276
Bird (caged): 169-70, 213

Bird of Paradise: 81, 91, 101
Blind man: 182, 192
Blindfolded men and women: 132
Boiling pot: 166, 183

Caduceus: 336
Cain and Abel: 204-6
Camel: 261
Candle: 102
Captives: 285
Centaurs: 150
Ceres: 93, 261, 292, 298
Chameleon: 72-3, 140
Chariot: 43, 85
Chimera: 271
Clavichord: 100
Clock: 69, 140-42
Cloister: 213-6
Club: 120, 133
Cockerel: 61
Column: 68, 122
Compasses: 140-42, 144
Concord: 99, 150
Cornucopia: 336
Crab: 102
Crane: 243
Crescent moon: 133, 146
Cross: 195-8, 213
Crow: 93, 250
Crucifixion: 204

Cupid: 90, 92, 102, 166-7, 169, 171,
    181-5, 188-9, 192, 231, 260, 292
Cybele: 277, 292
Cyclops: 298
Cyprus: 68

David: 228-9
Dawn: 154-5
Death: 144, 241
Diamond: 61, 147, 336
Discord: 150
Divine love: 163, 184-99
Dog: 56
Dolphin: 38, 52, 112, 351
Dove: 128, 250
Dragon: 103, 285
Drunkenness: 144
Dunkirk (capture of): 123

Eagle: 82-3, 98, 103-5, 128, 155, 264,
    271-2, 280, 284-5, 302
Earth: 277, 292, 298
Echo: 54-5
Education: 143
Eels: 48
Elephant: 103, 267
Elm: 38, 167-8, 216-7, 219-22

Falcon: 75, 105
Fire: 38, 72, 277, 298
Fisherman: 98, 171
Flattery: 140
Flora: 298
Flowers: 79-80
Fortune: 37, 92-3, 257, 336
Fountain: 351
François de Sales (Saint): 224-6
Friendship: 37, 48, 150, 167-8
Frogs: 52

Galathea: 298
Ganymede: 271
Garden of Eden: 207-9
Globe: 271
Gluttony: 42-3

Goat: 85
Goldfinch: 214
Goliath: 228-9
Goodness: 292
Graces: 101
Grasshopper: 98

Halcyon: 42, 52, 219-20, 267, 269,
    344, 351
Hatchet: 146
Heart: 195-9, 201, 210, 238-40, 337
Hedgehog: 58-9
Hen and chicks: 156-7
Hercules: 16, 86, 121-2, 139-40, 255,
    257, 276, 285
Heresy (extirpation of): 124, 152
Honey thief: 90, 231
Hope: 85, 88-9
Horse: 43
Hydra: 125, 152-4, 257
Hymen: 250-51
Hypocrisy: 73

Idleness: 85, 151
Ingenuity: 93
Iris: 298
Ivy: 74-5, 166

Janus: 261
Judas: 233
Juno: 298
Jupiter: 341
Justice: 262, 266

Labyrinth: 192, 257, 277
Lamb: 60
Lame man: 182, 192
Landscape: 72
Lantern: 166
Laurel:101, 280
Lily: 146-7
Lion: 85, 105, 140, 170, 262-7, 271,
    284-5, 292
London: 128
Love: 163-71, 180-99

Magnanimity: 292
Marigold: 97-8, 292
Mars: 52, 276-7, 292
Minerva: 276
Monkey: 72, 165
Moon: 94-5
Moses: 227, 231

Narcissus: 44, 54-5, 85, 214
Neptune: 52, 99, 253, 260, 298
Noah: 203-4, 227

Oak: 52-3, 211
Observatory: 124
Ocean: 351
Old man: 85
Olive branch: 88, 128, 266, 276, 303
Owl: 50-52
Oyster: 94, 216

Pallas: 99, 249, 285
Palm tree: 72, 98, 216, 271
Parrot: 170
Patience: 127
Peace: 88, 99-100, 159, 266, 276, 295
Pearl: 94, 218
Pegasus: 257
Pelican: 91, 278
Peony: 83
Perseus: 260-63
Phaeton: 43
Phoenix: 38, 72-3, 77, 94, 101, 103-4, 248
Piety: 79, 276, 278, 292
Pine: 292
Pomona: 298
Prudence: 69, 104, 262

Raft: 185
Raptors: 48, 156-7, 170
Reed: 211
Remora: 219-20
River: 284, 351
Rose: 80, 94, 146

Salamander: 66, 111, 113, 115, 133, 218, 248
Satyr: 86
Scales: 149-50
Sceptre: 133
Seahorse: 253
Sedition: 50-51
Self-love: 85
Semele: 341
Serpent: 39-40, 58-9, 85, 89, 103-4
Shepherd's crook: 292
Ship: 48, 56, 85, 87-9, 196, 259-60, 264, 266, 274
Siamese twins: 55-6
Siren: 252
Snail: 210
Solitude: 211-2
Solomon: 205
Spring: 292, 295
Squirrel: 169
Stag: 257, 324
Stymphalides: 257
Summer: 351-2
Sun: 52-4, 73, 76-9, 82, 88, 94-5, 103-4, 123, 146, 218, 257, 261, 265-7, 272-4, 279-80, 285, 298-303
Sunflower: 72, 261, 302
Swallow: 292, 295
Swan: 224
Swine: 40-41
Sword: 38, 88, 133

Temerity: 43, 86
Temperance: 262
Teresa of Avila (Saint): 213
Thetis: 298
Thisbe: 341
Thistle: 325
Thorn: 94
Thunderbolt: 105, 124, 341
Time: 336
Tityus: 99
Tomb: 101
Trumpets: 68

Unicorn: 140-41

Valour: 292
Vanity: 214
Venus: 93, 292
Victory: 276
Vigilance: 140, 243
Vine: 167-8, 216-22
Viper: 39-40
Virgin Mary: 214-18, 233, 240-41
Virtue: 127, 139, 174
Virtues: 261-2
Voluptuousness: 37
Vulcan: 298

War: 88, 100
Water: 72, 277, 298, 351
Well: 150
Whale: 253
Winged woman: 272
Winter: 292
Wolf: 60
Woman: 85, 89
Work: 139, 150
World: 100
Worms: 48

Zephyr: 298

INDEX OF TITLES AND MOTTOES OF EMBLEMS
AND DEVICES

I) LATIN:

Abstinentia: 55
Accenditur. Extinguend: 102
Adolescentia vaga: 150
A domino venit pax et victoria laeta:
    128
Ad umbrata humanitate divinitas: 209
Aetas brevis aptáque Regno: 116
Afflictis portus, & aura viris: 266
Alis non armis venit liberator: 128
Altius audet: 264
Amans amanti medicus: 192
Amari nocet: 72
Amicitiae immortali: 38
Amicitia etiam post mortem durans:
    75, 167, 168, 216
Amicitia sit inter aequales: 150
Amor, formae condimentum: 165
Amor omnia vincit: 112
Anchora. Amicitia fida: 48
*Anguillae. Hospes non ingratus. Ex
    Plinio*: 48
Aqua vehementius ardet: 72
Armisque potens: 116
Aspice & abstine: 80
A tergo calva est: 37
Cadentis amicae perstat in amplexu:
    219
Caecus amor sobolis: 72

Caelestis facit unda parem: 302
Captiva sed secura: 213
Carcer voluntarius: 169
Cedens resisto: 211
Chaldaeo praevalet una Deo: 218
Coelestes sequitur motus: 292
Coelo plena salum respuo: 216
Coelo sola mihi requies: 103
Coelo tenus altum: 68
Coelum ferit ardua fama: 68
Communia fata duorum: 277
Contemnit tuta procellas: 274
Conveniunt si quando pares: 150
Cordis irrigatio: 196
Cornua captans perdidit aures: 271
Crescens in fulmina: 83
Crescunt vires animique videndo: 302
Curae lacerant in amore iacentem: 99
Cycnus. Honor alit artes: 224
Dedit convulsa ruinam: 124
Desidia: 85
Dissociati locis concordi pace ligavit:
    278
Divino foedere tuta: 274
Donec totum impleat orbem: 133
*Dunkerka liberata, providentia
    principis MDCLXII*: 123
Duo protegit unus: 133

Eadem cantilena: 169

Ebrietatis vesania: 144

Erit haec quoque cognita monstris: 133

Est aliquid quo dirigis arcum: 150

Et charites nectuntur in orbem: 101

Etcunque: 111

Et dum tenet otia terret: 105

Et fulminis ocyor alis: 294, 297

Etiam ferocissimos domari: 85

Et nascens temperat aequor: 344

Et regit et servat: 292

Et tempora laeta reducit: 292, 295

Ex latibris coelumque, solumque serenat: 219

Ex pace ubertas: 42

Expers fortunae est sapientia: 38

Facit omnia laeta: 351

Fames pietate principis sublevata. MDCLXI: 123

Fatis confisus avorum: 82

Ferè simile ex Theocrito: 231

Festina lente: 112

Fidei victoria: 228

Finis amoris, ut duo unum fiant: 187

Frustra inhiant praedae: 156

Funestos dissipat ignes: 154

Grata belli caussa: 186

Gratior est post bella quies: 99

Gula: 43

Haeresis extincta. Edictum Octobris MDCLXXXV: 124

Haeret pede firmo: 213

Hanc unam secula plura vident: 94

Hic caestus artemque repono: 257

Hic labor est fructusque laboris: 144

Hic sese atque arcas arcanaque continet arcus: 100

Hilaritati publicae: 272

Hinc labor et virtus: 139

Homo vermis. In contemptores aliorum: 48

Hunc inter scopulos aquila est enixa leonem: 271

Hydra recisis capitibus: 153

Idem exodem: 101

Illic plus micat: 95

Imperium sine fine dedit: 115

In aequitate foecunditas: 267

In avaros, vel quibus melior conditio ab extraneis offertur: 253

Industria, et constantia: 144

In eos qui supra vires quicquam audent: 86

Ingenii largitor: 93

In Hectora solus Achilles: 115

Initium sapientiae timor Domini: 231

In mortem praeproperam: 55

In receptatores sicariorum: 42

Insignia poëtarum: 224

In tabulam Noë sacrificantis: 227

In Temerarios: 43

Invia amanti nulla est via Anima: 185

In victoriam dolo partam: 55

Invidia: 85, 89

Invito funere vivet: 73

Invitum qui servat idem facit occidenti: 38

Iovi educat: 303

It clamor Coelo: 68

Iungit amor: 72

Iusta ultio: 98

Iuvat requies alterna laborem: 150

Labor alternus facilis: 150

Labore et constantia: 144

Labor intus: 211

Laetatur genuisse parem: 83, 104

Latet error: 171

Loca sola caveto: 72

Lucet agit-que unus: 300

Ludo pugnaeque: 292

Luxuria: 86

Magni contemtor honoris: 186

Maiestate securus: 263

Maledicentia: 55

Manet ultima coelo: 113

Maria ab Anna lactantur: 240

Me crescente cadent: 300

Meos ad sydera tollo: 101

Meruitque timeri nil metuens: 105

Me subiectis excipit undis: 300
Micat inter omnes: 94
Mihi non senuit: 74
Mihi vigor omnis ab illo: 104
Miratur & audet: 272
Miratur natura silens: 351, 352
Misericordiae prospectrici: 227
Mole tutus Amor: 102
Multa latent, propiora Deo: 101
Mutabile semper: 73
Mutuum auxilium: 182, 192
Nec lex est iustior ulla: 130
Nec me movent fulmina terrae: 112
Nec numen nec nomen erit: 117
Nec parcitur ostro: 83
Nec pluribus impar: 146
Nec temere nec segniter: 38
Negotiatio Amoris: 189
Nemo me impunè: 94
Neque suunt neque nent: 147
Nequeunt abscissa nocere: 153
*Nil addit honoris. Praestat sapientia
    formae*: 40
Nil aspera terrent: 214
Nil terrestre: 91
Nititur in pondus: 98
Nobis haec otia fecit: 274
Nocet empta dolore voluptas: 98
Non dormit qui custodit: 87
Non flectitur: 267
Non inferiora sequutus: 97
Non maiestate securus: 140
Non pulchrior ullo: 146
Non radium excutient: 76
Non sum terra tuus: 81
Non sustinet alter: 103
Nulla mihi terris requies:103
Nullas recipit victoria metas: 122
Nulli patet: 141
Nulli prestat velox Fortuna fidem: 37
Nutrisco et extinguo: 66, 111, 133
Obdurandum adversus urgentia: 98
Obstetricante coelo: 216
Oleaque Minerva inventrix: 303
*Optimum amoris poculum, ut ameris,
    ama*: 186
Ora impia lege repressi: 115
*Ordo et felicitas. Curas imperii
    capessente. MDCLXI*: 123
Otium adversis expellitur: 151
Pacavit robore terras: 276
Palma labori: 98
Palmam ferre: 98
Par pari: 90
Par si durasset: 302
Patientia & virtute: 127
Patre viam monstrante: 104
Patrios sequitur ausus: 83
*Paupertatem summis ingeniis obesse,
    ne provehantur*: 193
Pax: 266
Perit qui fata parabat: 98
*Per multas tribulationes oportet nos
    intrare in regnum caelorum*: 196
Philautia: 44, 85, 214
Pia amoris lucta: 186
Pinguem pacis purgavit olivam: 266
Plenitudo legis est: 186
Plus ultra: 113
Populi superat prudentia fluctus: 253
*Postquam terribili vicit rex omnia
    Marte/Vincere quem possit Mars
    super unus erat*: 277
Post requiem requies: 103
Potens exili in corpore fraenum: 219
Potiùs mori quam abstinere: 88
Prae oculis ira: 141
Probasti: 280
Pro grege: 91
Prostibuli elegantia: 41
Protegit, haud foecundat ulmus: 216
Prudens et sedula: 97
*Quae mundum claudunt tenuem
    clauduntur in orbem*: 100
Quae sonat haec agit: 70
Qualis apex ortus tanti?: 82
Qui a secretis ab omnibus: 142
Quis hunc impunè lacessit: 292
*Quod fecit patitur/Quod tibi non optes
    fieri, ne feceris ulli*: 39

Quoque post patrem: 77
Quo videt ire patrem: 155, 156
Raptores esurient: 48
Recta se tollit: 292
Regno nata: 94
Respicio ut perficiar: 79
Satis est vidisse: 302
Se sedum deperit, perit: 214
Seminatio in cor: 196
Se purius reget: 67
Serva sed secura: 170
*Servet ius dominae custodes servet et
     ipsos*: 100
Sibi canit et orbi: 224
Sibi damna parat: 85
*Sic itur ad astra. Turris siderum
     speculatoria. MDCLXVII*: 124
Signa fortium: 55
*Si malum pro malo reddis, tibi plus
     noces*: 231
Siren Virtute haud blandior ulla est:
     253
Sit in amore reciprocatio: 186
Sola per alta quiescam: 103
Sola vivit in illo: 101
Solem sola sequor: 262
Soli: 280
Solus invenit viam: 277
Spes proxima: 85, 88, 89
Splendet & ardet: 272
Sternit iter Deo: 185
Strenuorum immortale nomen: 55
Sub luce lues: 140

Superbiam odit: 186
Superius reget: 96, 97
Surge per te ius: 96
Tangor non tingor abunda: 224
Temeritas: 43, 86
Terrae iura dat, atque mari: 266
Terris nulla mihi requies: 103
Te stante virebo: 166
Timui nec infans: 120
*Tumulus Ioannis Galeacii Vicecomitis,
     prim. Ducis Mediol.*: 55
Tumulus meretricis: 55
Ubertas maior ab illo: 292
Una mihi coelo requies: 103
Undique collatis: 82
Uni redatur: 141
Unum nihil, duo plurimum posse: 85
Urit et irrigat: 271
*Uritur, nec sterilem sperando nutrit
     amorem*: 73
Usque sequar: 72
Ut incepit sic desinet in se: 101
Utroque clarescere pulcrum: 88
Ut vidit, vicit: 265
Ut vidi, vici: 279, 280
Via nulla est invia amori: 185
Vincula restant sola mihi: 75
Vires ultra sortemque iuventae: 127
Virtutis remis, velisque fortunae: 70
Vis secretior urget: 216
Vivite concordes: 72, 216
Vivit post funere virtus: 38
Vulnere uno cecidit: 125

II) FRENCH:

Abondance: 99
Accroissement d'yre est à eschever:
     38
A luy seul: 280
Amour hayt l'orgueil: 186
Amour domté: 92
Amour humiliant: 190

L'Amour les joint: 72
*Amour partout. Partout Amour. Tout
     par Amour. Par Amour tout*: 181
Amour propre: 85
*Aucun autre que luy ne m'ose
     regarder*: 103
Au dedans je me consume: 166, 183

Au dessus de ses forces & de son âge: 127

Aussi excellent en ma nature que rare en mon espece: 94

Aussi-tôt que j'ay veu j'ay vaincu: 266

Bonne Fortune: 92

Bonne pour la guerre & pour la paix: 88

Caresses nuisibles: 72

Celer ne le puis: 166

Celuy qui a le secret, a tout: 142

C'est ainsi qu'on va Jusqu'aux Cieux. L'Observatoire: 124

Ceste chaste union la met en seureté: 217

C'est la paresse: 85

C'est l'Envie: 85, 89

C'est parce qu'il se sert de ses ayeuls: 82

C'est une temerité que cette insulte: 86

Cet arbre est ce qui la protege: 217

Le Chesne: 52

Le ciel sera mon seul repos: 103

La colere au devant des yeux: 141

Combat heureux: 186

Concorde: 99

Contre la gourmandise: 43

Contre l'Amour de soy-mesme: 44, 64

Contre les temeraires: 43

Dans sa prison il est en seureté: 213

Dedens je me consume: 183

De mille endroits elles sont ramassées: 82

Des fruits de la paix: 42

Dés icy le Travail & la Vertu: 139

Dunkerque recouvrée par la Providence du Prince en 1661: 123

D'un seul coup abbatuë. Pour l'Edit d'Octobre 1685: 125

Elle demeure icy d'un pied ferme arrestée: 213

Elle sera pareillement connue aux monstres: 133

Elle travaille pour sa rüine: 85

En ma joye douleur: 183

Et moy encore apres mon Pere: 77

L'exces de l'Amour propre est cause de sa perte: 214

La faim soulagée par la Pieté du Roy, en 1661: 123

Faire sedition ce n'est pas grande science: 50

Guerre accroist l'amour: 186

L'Heresie éteinte. L'Edit d'Octobre 1685. 124

Le Herisson et le Serpent: 58

L'Homme sage peut dompter & venir à bout des plus emportez & des plus furieux: 85

L'humanité esquisse de la Divinité: 209

Il croît pour porter les foudres: 83

Il le rend plus ardent: 72

Il marche sur les traces de son Pere: 83

Il ne me reste que les liens: 75

Il n'est point vieux pour moy: 74

Il n'y eut jamais de Loy plus juste: 130

Il se rejoüit d'avoir fait son semblable: 83

Il vivra malgré la mort: 73

Il y a de quoy craindre: 171

Ils ne m'osteront pas un seul rayon: 76

Ils s'abaisseront quand je m'éleveray: 300

Ingratitude: 75

Ingratitude on doibt fuyr grandement: 30

Insuffisance: 56

Jamais laides amours, ny bele prison: 165

Je le suyvray jusques la: 72

Je ne le puis celer: 166

Je ne les ay pas crains dés mon enfance mesme: 120

Je nourry & étein: 66, 133

Je pose ici & mon Arc & mon Art: 257
J'inspire un amour respectueux: 94
Les Jumeaux de la Trape: 55
Jusques à ce que tout le monde soit remply: 133
Leur faux brillant trompoit, son éclat les dissipe: 154
Luxure: 86, 93
La majesté ne luy suffit pas: 140
Le malfaiteur retourne à son maistre. De la vipere et du serpent: 39
Ma prison est volontaire: 169
Mes pleurs mon feu decelent: 166
Mon éclat fait ombre à mille autres: 95
Mon mal est sans fin: 169
La mort sera mon seul repos: 103
Nécessité, Mere d'invention: 93
Nul ne si frote: 325
Nul n'y peut voir: 141
Nuysible copulation: 75
L'Océan me reçoit & me soûmet ses eaux: 300
L'Ordre & la Felicité, en gouvernant par luy même, en 1661: 123
Paix: 99
La Paix vient du Seigneur, & la Victoire agreable: 128
Par trop manger, plus meurent, que par glaive: 30
Patience & vertu: 127
Peril incongneu: 56
Peu à peu: 182
Plus oultre: 113
Plus seur que libre: 169
Plûtôt mourir, que s'abstenir: 88
Point de commerce avec la terre: 91
Point de supérieur ny d'égal: 279
Pour les miens: 91
Le pourpre ne met pas à couvert de la mort: 83
Pour sa Beauté: 94
Pour un plaisir mille douleurs: 183
Que la Curiosité est toujours nuisible: 42

Que l'honneste Amour, l'Honneur & Verité sont inseparables: 41
Que les choses douces deviennent souvent ameres: 41
Quel sera le midi d'un si bel Orient?: 82
Que ne vis-je en mes jours naistre un second Hector?: 115
Que par la Valeur & par la Prudence on vient à bout de la fourberie & des efforts les plus violents: 41
Qui cele le mesfaict, cerche amitié: 165
Qui est ingat sans raison: 30
Qui le gouverne, ne dort pas: 87
Qu'il ne faut point publier le secret des Princes: 41
Qu'il n'y a point de prosperité perdurable: 41
Le Renversement a causé la ruine: 124
Rien de constant: 73
Rien de rude ne l'espouvante: 214
Le Roy gouverne par luy-mesme: 123
Sans Ceres et Bacchus Venus est froide: 93
Sans luy je serois sans vigueur: 104
Sa victoire n'a point de bornes qui l'arrestent: 122
Separez-les du corps, leur venin ne peut nuire: 153, 154
Ses triomphans exploits ne souffrent point de bornes: 122
Le Soleil & les grenoüilles: 52
Son desir est sur le point d'estre accomply: 85, 88, 89
Son innocence & son integrité dans le monde: 224
Le sort sera commun entre deux Puissances: 277
Sous le miel le fiel: 140
Sur la perfection de toutes ses illustres qualitez: 94
Sur la vipere selon les hieroglyfiques des Aegyptiens: 39

Tel grain, tel pain. De mere piteuse, fille teigneuse: 165
Tous à un: 141
Traficq de l'Amour: 189
La troisiesme m'attend au Ciel: 113
Le trop manger conduit l'homme à la mort: 30
L'Un Amour guerist l'autre: 192
Un des deux ne peut rien faire seul, mais estans ensemble, ils peuvent tout: 85
Un en defend deux: 133
L'une main gratte l'autre: 182
La Vigne, qui embrasse l'Orme abbatu & le couronne de ses raisins: 220, 222
Vous m'avez éprouvé: 280

III) OTHER LANGUAGES:

A la pareja: 90
Aquesta es embidia: 89
Aquilante: 272
Assi mi mano como mi sonido: 70
Chi là custodisce non dorme: 87
Crueldad pagado: 267
Daer schuijlt: 171
Der es bewahrt schläfft nicht: 88
Die t'bewaart, en slaapt niet: 87
Elk zijn maal: 90
Es ist der neid: 89
For mine own: 91
Furentes paro: 271
Gleich mit gleichem: 90
He that governs it, does not sleep: 88
His wishes are to be accomplished: 89
I am for war and peace: 88
Ich bin für fried und krieg: 88
La sua speranza stà per essere compita: 89
Lieber sterben als aufhören: 88
Liever sterven, als onthouden: 88
Like with like: 90
Los abre y los dora: 269
Lucidamor: 272
Mas presto morir que abstener: 88
Mirabil' subito che pare: 302
Ne piu ne pari: 279
Nichts irdisch: 91
Niente de terrestre: 91
Niets aardisch: 91
Nothing terrestial: 91
Para la manada: 91
Per la greggia: 91
Più presto morire, che astenersi: 88
Quest' è l'Invidia: 89
Quien lo govierna no duerme: 87
Rather dye than hold up: 88
Seine wünsche werden erfüllet werden: 89
Siempre calma por yo: 269
Son per la pace, et per la guerra: 88
Soy por la guerra y la paz: 88
T'is de Nijd: 89
T'is Envy: 89
'Touwde deuntjen: 169
Voor de meine: 91
Voor vryheyt vaylicheyt: 170
Vor die meine: 91
Willighe vankhenis: 169
Zyn wensch staat vervult te worden: 89

Dans la même collection

1. SANCIER-CHÂTEAU, Anne, *Une esthétique nouvelle: Honoré d'Urfé correcteur de* L'Astrée *(1607-1625).* 1995
   ISBN: 2-600-00055-0

2. DE SMET, Ingrid A. R., *Menippean Satire and the Republic of Letters 1581-1655.* 1996
   ISBN: 2-600-00147-6

3. JUNIUS, Franscicus (Du Jon), *De pictura veterum libri tres (Roterodami, 1694). Livre I.* Edition critique par Colette Nativel. 1996
   ISBN: 2-600-00174-3

4. *Le Loisir lettré à l'âge classique.* Edité par Marc Fumaroli, Philippe-Joseph Salazar et Emmanuel Bury. 1996
   ISBN: 2-600-00175-1

5. CAYUELA, Anne, *Le paratexte au Siècle d'Or. Prose romanesque, livres et lecteurs en Espagne au XVIIe siècle.* 1996
   ISBN: 2-600-00124-7

6. BOLD, Stephen, GEOMETER, Pascal, *Discovery and Invention in Seventeenth-Century France.* 1996
   ISBN: 2-600-00155-7

7. ARMSTRONG, Brian G., *Bibliographia Molinaei. An Alphabetical, Chronological and Descriptive Bibliography of the Works of Pierre Du Moulin (1568-1658).* 1997
   ISBN: 2-600-00186-7

8. COTTEGNIES, Line, *L'Eclipse du Regard. La poésie anglaise du baroque au classicisme (1625-1660).* 1997
   ISBN: 2-600-00197-2

9. LOSADA GOYA, José Manuel, *Bibliographie critique de la Littérature espagnole en France au XVIIe siècle.* 1999
   ISBN: 2-600-00313-4

10. CRESCENZO, Richard, *Peintures d'instruction. La postérité littéraire des Images de Philostrate en France de Blaise de Vigenère à l'époque classique.* 1999
    ISBN: 2-600-00304-5

11. *Femmes savantes, savoirs de femmes. Du crépuscule de la Renaissance à l'aube des Lumières.* Actes du colloques de Chantilly (22-24 septembre 1995). Réunis par Colette Nativel. 1999
    ISBN: 2-600-00334-7

12. WORTH-STYLIANOU, Valérie, *Confidential Strategies. The Evolving Role of the Confident in French Tragic Drama (1635-1677).* 1999
    ISBN: 2-600-00339-8

13. HOPE, Quentin M., *Saint-Evremond and His Friends.* 1999
    ISBN: 2-600-00345-2

14. *La Lyre jésuite. Anthologie de poèmes latins (1620-1730).* Préface de Marc Fumaroli. Edités par Andrée Thill et Gilles Banderier. 1999
    ISBN: 2-600-00372-X

15. WINE, Kathleen, *Forgotten Virgo. Humanism and Absolutism in Honoré d'Urfe's* L'Astrée. 2000
    ISBN: 2-600-00393-2

16. MARTIN, Catherine, *Les Compagnies de la Propagation de la foi des origines à la Révocation (1632-1685).* 2000
    ISBN: 2-600-00425-4

17. VUILLERMOZ, Marc, *Le Système des objets dans le théâtre français des années 1625-1650. Corneille, Mairet, Rotrou, Scudéry.* 2000
    ISBN: 2-600-00443-2